ERRATA

Due to a temporary break in communications between author and printer certain corrections marked on the proofs were not implemented. The publishers wish to apologise for this omission.

Page	
72 (top)	. . . at the breech, the locks engraved . . .
98 (bottom	prickers
281 (third)	. . . Saxe-Weimar, Schloss Ettersburg
(bottom)	Hohenelbe
285 (top)	Fruwirth
290 (top)	Lisieux

TOWER OF LONDON ARMOURIES

The publishers wish to emphasise that any price ranges shown opposite photographs supplied by the Tower of London Armouries, in no way refer to specific items in the Tower of London Armouries, and further that the Master of the Armouries has no connection whatsoever with such prices.

The Price Guide to ANTIQUE GUNS & PISTOLS

Peter Hawkins

ANTIQUE COLLECTORS' CLUB

SBN 902028 11 1

Printed in England by
Baron Publishing, Woodbridge, Suffolk

Index To Makers.

ADAMS (Revolvers) 225
226
339
ADAMS, Joseph 76
Birmingham
ADAMS, Robert 209
76 King William Street, London
ADAMS, Walter 339
King William Street, London
AERTS, Jan 32
Maastricht
ALBAREZ, Diego 111
Madrid
ALDURDI, M. 27
ALLEN, C.B. 268
Springfield, Mass., U.S.A.
ALLEN & THURBER 248
Worcester, U.S.A. 249
ALLEN & WHEELOCK 263
Worcester, Mass., U.S.A.
AMES, N.P. 267
Springfield, Mass., U.S.A.
ANDERSON, R. 205
31 Cockspur Street, London
ASH, R. 351
U.S.A.
ASHMORE 351
U.S.A.
ASKEW & PAXSON 350
Philadelphia, U.S.A.
ASTON 364
Manchester
ASTON, H. 267
Middletown, Conn., U.S.A.
AUBRON jeune 307
Nantes
AVERAN, Guiseppe 375
AZZONI 42
Brescia

BAILEY, T. 156
Stamford
BAKER (revolver) 221
BAKER (rifle) 314
342
BALES, H. 122
Ipswich
BANISTER, T. 36
BARBAR, Lewis and James 45
London 47
52
74
187
191
196
BARBER 76
Newark
BARKER 96
London
BARNES, Frederick & Co. 220
109 Fenchurch Street, London
BARTH 105
Colmar
BARTON (Wogdon and Barton) 85
BASS 189
London 307
BATE 79
London 309
334
369
370
BEATTIE, J. 161
London
BEAUMONT-ADAMS 227
BECHER, Leopold 72
Carlsbad
BECKWITH 202
London
BEHR, J.J. 300
BELON 311
Dole
BENNETT 81
Royal Exchange, London
BENNETT AND LACY 130
BERETTA, Giovanni 17
Brescia
BERSELLI, Giacomo 337
Bologna
BIGONI, F. 69
Brescia
BISSELL, Isaac 98
Birmingham
BLAKE 93
London
BLANCH 124
London 157
BLEIBERG 36
London
BLETTERIE 66
Paris
BLISSETT, I. 156
69 Leadenhall Street, London
BLISSETT, John 223
322 High Holborn, London
BLISSETT, T. 333
Liverpool
BOND, E. & W. 127
Cornhill, London
BOND, W. 92
London
BONGARDE, Armand 39
Dusseldorf 309
BONOMINO, Domenico 43
Brescia
BOOWLES, R. 35
London(?)
BOUILLET 334
Paris
BOUTET 132
Versailles 133
134
138
139
140
142
277
BOUTET et Fils 141
BRANDER 362
London
BRANDER & POTTS 240
BRAZIER 53
London
BRENT, Moses (silversmith) 86
88
90
91
BRETGE, J. 310
Goslar
BREVETE (Mariette) 213
Liège 222
BROOKE, R. 236
London
BRUETON 362
London
BUDDING 214
Stroud
BUMFORD 50
London
BUNNEY 77
London 94
182
BURGESS, I. 55
Elgin
BURNAND 323
Newcastle-on-Tyne
BUSTINDUI 24
Madrid 27
305
BUTTERFIELD 264
Philadelphia, U.S.A.

CADDELL, Thomas 56
Doune 59
60
CALISHER & TERRY 333
CALVERT 149
Leeds
CAMPBELL, Alexander 59
Doune
CAMPBELL, John 56
Doune
CAMS 23
Ripoll or Barcelona 303
CARBO 22
Ripoll
CARLISLE, H. 351
U.S.A.
CARON, A. 168
Passage de l'Opéra, Paris
CATCHPOOL 190
Dover
CHARLET, J.S. 187
Lyons
CHASTEAU 306
Paris
CHRISTIE, Io 98
CHRISTY and MURDOCH 58
Doune
CLARK 176
Holborn, London
CLARKE & Son 113
62 Cheapside, London
CLARKSON 50
London
CLEMMES, Theophilus 91
London, successor to James Barbar
CLIVE 154
CLOETER family 36
Mannheim
COLLIER & Co. 224
54 Strand, London
COLLIER, E.H. 336
London
COLT, Samuel 250
Paterson address 251
353
354
New York City address 251
252
253
254
255
256
259
260
261
London address 253
254
257
Hartford address 256
258
261
354
COMINAZ, Lazar 28
Brescia 43
COMINAZZO, Lazarino 9
Brescia 28
44
288
294
297
CONSTABLE, R. 246
Philadelphia, U.S.A. 247
CONTRINER, Josef 370
Vienna

COON, L. 351
U.S.A.
COOPER, B. & J. 246
New York
COOPER, J.R. 215
Birmingham
COOPER & GOODWIN 364
CORNFORTH 33
COSENS, James 35
(Gunmaker in Ordinary to
Charles II)
CRAMON 306
Bordeaux
CRAUSE, C.P. 332
Hertzberg am Harz
CURRY, N. & Bros. 248
San Francisco
CUSSON et ROSSIGNOL BREVETE . . 173

DANNER, Peter 279
Nuremberg 280
DAVIDSON 129
London
DAVIER CADET 102
Lyons
DAW, George H. 228
57 Threadneedle Street, London
DAY'S PATENT 379
DE SAINTE 302
Versailles
DE SERET, Isaac 316
London
DE SOTO, Juan 295
Madrid
DE ZELAYA, Joachin 303
Madrid
DEANE, ADAMS & DEANE 225
30 King William Street, London
DEANE & SON 232
London Bridge
DELANY, Henry 317
London
DELCOMYN 313
Copenhagen
DEL MORO, Nicolo 296
DENNIS, James 305
London
DEOP, Joseph 25
Barcelona or Ripoll 70
303
DERINGER 247
Philadelphia, U.S.A. 248
267
DESACA 104
DES GRANGES 30
Paris
DEVILLERS 106
Liège 180
DEVISME 332
Paris
DICKSON, John & Son 326
63 Princes Street, Edinburgh
DOBSON, T. 129
35 Chiswell Street, London
DOUGALL, J.D. 201
Glasgow
DREW, I. 53
London

ECHEBERRIA, Artura 24
EDGE 236
London
EGG, Durs 118
London 119
182
239
240
308
315
318
363
EGG, Joseph 123
1 Piccadilly, London 181
183
207
ELGIN'S PATENT 268
U.S.A.
ELLS 264
U.S.A..
ENFIELD 244
346
(Snider-Enfield) 347
ESTEVA, Pedro 70
Barcelona 75
111
EVANS, J.R. 377
London
EVANS, W.L. 266
U.S.A.
FATOU 135
Paris 136
FERGUSON PATENT 319
FERNANDEZ, Geronimo 296
Salamanca
FLORKIN 174
Liège
FORGE, V. 266
U.S.A.
FORSYTH & Co. 145
London 146
147
320
337
FOWLER, Thomas 113
Dublin 114
FRANCI, Piero Inzi 11
Brescia(?)
FREEMAN, James 47
London 48
195
FREETH, Charles (silversmith) 80
94
182
191
369
FRENEL 65
Paris
FRUGONE, G. 37
FRUWIRTH, Joseph 285
Vienna

GAUVAIN 167
Paris
GERHARDT, A. 68
Stockholm
GESSLER, Georg 7
Dresden
GIBSON 75
London
GIRAND 100
Thonon
GIRANDONI 370
Vienna
GLAZE, Wm. & Co. 267
U.S.A.
GLEN, Robert 20
Edinburgh
GODSALL 93
Gloucester
GOFF, D. 184
London
GOLCHER, J. 351
U.S.A.
GOODWIN, G. & Co. 193
London
GOSSET 148
Paris
GRAY 19
Dundee
GRICE 271
London 340
GRIFFIN 50
London 51
73
77
179
180
305
GROS, Christoph Gottfried 309
Nimptsch
GRUCHE 40
Paris
GUERINO, Giovanni Battista 304
GUMPF, J. 350
Lancaster, Pa., U.S.A.

HADDOU 123
Newcastle
HALL, H. 355
U.S.A.
HALL & POWELL 336
HARDING, J. & Son 239
London
HARKOM, Joseph 203
Edinburgh 329
HARPERS FERRY 265
U.S.A. 268
355
HARVEY, Robert 48
London
HARVEY'S revolver 233
HAWKES MOSELY & Co. 122
London
HEATON & SMITH 125
London
HELLER, Hans (H.H.) 281
HENHAM'S Lock 318
HENRY, J. 265
Philadelphia, U.S.A.
HENSHAW 185
Strand, London
HENSHAW 189
Cambridge
HERMANN, Johann Andreas 72
Wiesenthal
HEWSON 128
London
HEYLIN 73
Cornhill, London 91
HOROLT, Lorenz 6
Nuremberg
HOSEY, John 54
London(?)
HUNT 319

INNES 128
Edinburgh 154
JACKSON 91
Maidstone
JACKSON, Thomas 217
London 338
JOHNSON, R. 266
Middletown, Conn., U.S.A.
JOHNSON, I.N. 267
U.S.A.
JOINER 80
London
JONES, John & Co. 186
JORDAN 237
London
JOSLYN, B.F. 263
U.S.A.
JOVER 200
London
JUNG, S. 170
Suhl

KALTHOFF 337
Copenhagen

KAPPEL, Heinrich 378
Copenhagen
KAVANAGH 208
Dublin
KERR (London Armoury) 227
KETLAND & Co. 90, 182, 185, 363
KING, Richard 317
London
KOLBE, Johann 370
London
KOSTERS, J. 40
Maastricht
KUCHENREITER, J. Adam 170
Regensburg
KUCHENREITER, Johann Christoph . 169
Regensburg
KUCHENREITER, Johann Jacob 109
Regensburg
KUCHENREUTER, Johann André ... 110, 300
Regensburg
KUNZ, J. 353
Philadelphia, U.S.A.
LA BROSSE 101
Paris
LACY (Bennett and Lacy) 130
LAMOTTE ainé 104
St. Etienne
LAMOTTE, Joseph 174
St. Etienne(?)
LANCASTER, Charles 338
151 New Bond Street, London
LANG, J. 211, 212, 218, 222, 323, 327, 380
7 Haymarket and 22 Cockspur Street, London
LAZARINO, Lazaro 28, 42
Brescia
LAZARI, Lazaro 42
Brescia
LEBEDA, A.V. 325
Prague
LEBLAN, Oger 68
Maastricht
LE BOURGEOYS, Pierre 290
Lisieux
LE CLERC (barrelsmith) 302, 306
Paris
LE MAIRE 46
London
LE MAT (Col. Le Mat Bté) 235
LE PAGE 133, 134, 144, 148, 164, 302
Paris
LESCONNE, A. 31
LES LAROCHE 102
aux Galleries du Louvre, Paris
LIGNITZ, I.H. 10
LONDON, E. 158, 372
London
LORENZONI, Michele 198, 337
Florence
LORENZONI (system) 196, 197
LOWE, James 50, 74
London
LUDWIG 281
Hohenelbe
McBURNIE 189
London
MAERCKL, T.A. 311
Carlsbad
MAIRET 194
Artiste aux Ponts (Ponts de Martel)
MANN, Michael 14
Nuremberg
MANTON, John 87, 88, 95, 121, 151, 306, 324
London
MANTON, Joseph 87, 120, 145, 185, 321
London
MARCELINO 322
Aragon
MARIETTE BREVETE 213, 222
Liège
MARR, Valentin 67
Copenhagen
MARSHALL & Sons 99
Edinburgh
MARSTON, W.P. 353
Toronto
MARTINONI, P. 365
MASSACHUSETTS ARMS Co. 263
MASSIN 63
Liège
MATHES FRERES 166
Paris
MATZENKOPF 72
MAUBEUGE, Manuf. Roy. de 241
MAYBURY, C. 339
Birmingham
MAYNARD (primer) 263, 268, 355
U.S.A.
MEIER, Felix 299, 300
Vienna
MICHARIUS, T. 178
Breda
MIGEON 65
Charleville
MILLS, W. 324
120 High Holborn, London
MISSILEUR 66
Paris
MONTAUBAN 103
Geneva
MONTMAIN, Paul 64
MOORE, Charles 150, 153
77 St. James's Street, London
MOORE, Daniel 77, 343
London
MOORE, William 314
London
MORTEMORE 75
London
MORTIMER 94, 161
MORTIMER, H.W. 82, 90, 116, 117, 197, 238, 362, 364
London
MORTIMER, T. 116, 161
London
MURDOCH, I. 57
Doune
MURDOCH, T. 97
Leith
MUTTI, Giesu 17
MUTTI, Gerolimo 16
Gardone
MUTTO, Geronimo 43
NEGRONI 16
Brento
NEWTON 50
Grantham
NICHOLES, J. 35, 49
Oxford
NICHOLSON 192
75 Cornhill, London
NICOLI, C. 68
NIQUET, Claude 62
Liège
NOCK, Henry 125, 239, 307, 319, 334, 343
London
NOCK, Samuel 159, 319
London
NOEL, A. 377
Paris
NORTH, E. 74
London
NORTH, H.S. 263
U.S.A.
NORTH, S. 265, 266
U.S.A.
OFFERMAN le jeune 335
Cologne
ORTNER, Bernard 310
Stettin
PARKER, W. 115, 371
Holborn, London
PATERSON, N.J. (COLT) 250, 251, 353, 354
PATRICK 118
Liverpool
PATTISON, T. 123
Dublin
PENTERMAN 38, 67
Utrecht
PERRY 190
London
PERRY, I. 107
PETHER 212
Oxford
PETITJEAN 106, 175
Liège
PETTENGILL 264
U.S.A.
PFEUFFER 320
Oberndorff
PICKFATT, Humphrey 34, 340
London
PIRAUBE 272
Paris
PIRMET 172
15 Allée D'Antin, Paris
POUS, Eudal 25
Barcelona
POWELL 340
London
PREVOTEAU 175
Paris
PROBIN, J. 193
London
PROSSER 190
Charing Cross, London
PUIFORCAT 302
Paris

PURDEY, J. 308
Princes Street, Leicester Square, London
314½ Oxford Street, London 152, 204, 206, 327, 328, 330, 331

RANSFORD 52
Dublin
RASMUSSEN 339
REBELLA, Antoine 103
Béziers
REEVE'S PATENT 234
REMINGTON & Sons 262
Ilion, New York, U.S.A.
RENETTE, Gastinne 165
Paris 167, 168
REYNOLDS 96
Leeds
RICHARDS 122
Birmingham
RICHARDS, J. 94
Strand, London
RICHARDS, T. 78
Birmingham
RICHARDS, Westley 161
London and Birmingham 210
(see also under Westley) 229, 244, 333, 366
RIGBY, W. & J. 153
Dublin 156, 207, 208, 216, 328, 338
RIZZI, Francisco 304
Piacenza
ROBBINS & LAWRENCE Co. 249
Windsor, U.S.A.
RONGE, A. 134
Liège
ROSS 306
Edinburgh
ROTHROCK, D. 351
U.S.A.
ROUMA, P. 137
ROVIRA, Antonio 23
Igualada
ROWLAND, R. 199
London 316
RUDOLPH, Johann Caspar 284
Crembs
RUGGLES, A. 248
Stafford, Conn., U.S.A.

SANDWELL 305
Minories, London
SANTOS, Juan 103
Madrid
SARTORIS PATENT 318
SAVAGE, R.F.A. Co. 263
Middletown, Conn., U.S.A.
SCHERTIGER 298
SCHIRMER 315
Bamberg
SCHULTZ, A. 350
U.S.A.
SEGALAS, Israel 106
London
SEGLAS 106, 175
SENEVAY 330
Fleurier
SHARP'S PATENT 355
U.S.A.
SHARPE 33
SHAW, I. 34
London
SHOREY, I. 53
SIBLEY, I. 236
SILKE, Robert 361
London
SIMMONDS 366
SINCKLER 45
London
SMITH 125
London 158, 186, 209, 224
SMITH, Samuel & Charles 207
Princes Street, Leicester 308
Square, London 331
SOIRON 299
Sedan
SOLER 13
Ripoll
SPANGENBERG, Wilhelm & Heinrich . 204
Suhl
SPANGENBURG, J.W. 179
Suhl
SPATZIRER, Wenzel 299
Vienna
SPENCER 371
Lynn
SPENCER, James 361
London
STANTON 54
London
STARR ARMS Co. 262
New York, U.S.A.
STAUDENMAYER 124
London 126, 313
STEINGASTINGER, A. 108
Prague
ST. ETIENNE (Manufactory) 241, 344
STEVENS 322
London
STIFFTER, Johann 283
Prague
STOCKING & Co. 248
Worcester, U.S.A.
STOCKMANN, Hans 6
Dresden
STOCKMAR family 300
Heidersbach
STUART, John 19
Aberdeen
STURMAN 112
Boro Market
SWINBURN & Son 348
Birmingham
SYKES 114
Oxford

TANNER 330
Hanover
TANNER & SCHULTZ 313
TATHAM 314
London
THOMSON, Alexander 323
Edinburgh
THOMSON, J. 98
Edinburgh
TIPPING & LAWDEN 216
London
TOMLINSON 123
Dublin
TOWER (of London) 242, 243, 334, 341, 342, 346, 348
TRANTER 230
London
TRULOCKE 316
TRYON 351
Philadelphia, U.S.A.
TULA (Manufactory) 71
TULLE, Manuf. Rle. 245
TURVEY 50
London
TWIGG 83
London 89, 177, 194

ULRICH, F. 138
Berne
UNWIN & ROGERS 380
Birmingham

VANDEBAIZE 373
London
VANNOD, J. 163
Lausanne
VELUT 106
Liège
VIGNIAT, H. 143
St. Etienne
VOISIN 345
Geneva

WALCH FIREARMS Co. 264
New York, U.S.A.
WATERS, A. 266
Milbury, Mass., U.S.A.
WATERS & Co. 92
WATERS, John 98
WEBLEY, James 230
Birmingham 232, 276
WESCHGIN, Melchior 36
Augsburg
WESTLEY RICHARDS 161
London and Birmingham 210, 229, 244
(see also under Richards) 333, 366
WHITWORTH 244
(and Manchester Ordnance 327
& Rifle Co.) 330
WILKINSON, James & Son 155
27 Pall Mall, London
WILLIAMS & POWELL 208
London
WILLMORE, James 49
London
WILSON 51
London 93
WILSON, Alexander 149
London
WIRGLER, Joseph 312
Bruschsal
WITTON 321
82 Old Broad Street, London
WOGDON, Robert 84
London 85, 86
WYNN, D. 45
London 46, 54

YBARRA, Joseph 26

ZELNER, Kaspar 285
Vienna

CONTENTS

Page

Wheel-Lock Pistols .. 1
Snaphaunce Pistols .. 16
Miquelet-Lock Pistols .. 21
Flintlock Pistols – 1650-1700 .. 29
English Flintlock Pistols – 1700-1750 .. 45
Scottish Flintlock Pistols – 1700-1750 .. 55
Continental Flintlock Pistols – 1700-1750 .. 61
English Flintlock Pistols – 1750-1800 .. 73
Scottish Flintlock Pistols – 1750-1830 .. 97
Continental Flintlock Pistols – 1750-1800 .. 100
English Flintlock Pistols – 1800-1830 .. 112
Continental Flintlock Pistols – 1800-1830 .. 132
Detonator Pistols .. 145
English Percussion Cap Pistols 1830-1860 .. 149
Scottish Percussion Cap Pistols 1830-1860 .. 161
Continental Percussion Cap Pistols .. 162
Double-Barrelled Flintlock Pistols .. 174
Flintlock, Multishot, Revolving, Repeating and Breech-Loading Pistols .. 189
Double-Barrelled Percussion Cap Pistols .. 201
Percussion Cap Patent Revolvers .. 224
Flintlock Service Pistols .. 236
Percussion Cap Service Pistols .. 242
American Pistols .. 246
Colt Revolvers .. 250
Various American Revolvers .. 262
American Martial Pistols .. 265
Eastern Pistols .. 269
Matchlock Long Guns .. 278
Wheel-Lock Long Guns .. 280
Snaphaunce, Miquelet-Lock and Baltic-Lock Guns .. 294
Flintlock Sporting Guns .. 299
Flintlock Sporting Rifles .. 310
Flintlock Breech-Loading Rifles .. 316
Detonator Guns .. 320
Percussion Cap Sporting Guns .. 322
Percussion Cap Sporting Rifles .. 327
Percussion Cap Breech-Loading Rifles .. 333
Multishot Guns and Rifles .. 334
Flintlock Military Long Guns .. 340
Percussion Cap Military Long Guns .. 346
American Long Guns .. 350
Eastern Long Guns .. 356
Blunderbusses .. 361
Air Weapons .. 367
Combination Pistols, Powder Testers and Curiosa .. 373

Introduction

CONTENTS

The thousand or so items illustrated in this Guide have been selected in an attempt to give an overall picture of the antique pistols and guns which are available to collectors today. The range covered is from matchlock to percussion cap ignition. The only cartridge weapons included are those which employ the wheel-lock and flintlock mechanisms. No firearm in the Guide requires a Firearms Certificate under the law as it stands at the time of writing.

Firearms which are readily available are covered in greater detail than those which are not, but a few outstanding pieces have been added in the interests of perspective. Many more pistols than guns have been included, for they have survived in greater numbers and are more popular today mainly because of their size. It is usually the pistols that command the higher price. They were nearly always made in pairs and a surprising number have so remained. This gives them a marked advantage over guns, and they are usually to be found in better condition. Whereas cased pairs of pistols of the late 18th and early 19th centuries are not uncommon, cased guns of the same period are extremely difficult to find. Many guns were broken up when they were no longer of use; pistols presumably demanded less storage space, so they were retained.

HOW TO USE THE GUIDE

Each item in the Guide is evaluated as an individual piece as illustrated. Each piece is given a quality and condition rating which applies to that particular specimen. Almost every piece has been sold at public auction within the last five years, in most cases within the last two. Where no suitable example could be found near the date of writing, the price it commanded when sold has been increased by a suitable amount. Public auction has been chosen as the source because it was felt to represent as fair and reliable a level of value as can be found. Where the auction price is thought to have been exceptionally high, the figure in the Guide has been fixed at a lower level. In all cases similar examples sold have been taken into consideration, as has the fluctuation in price to which auction sales are subject.

The price range of each item thus represents what a purchaser might expect to pay *at auction* for the piece illustrated (or for a similar piece making allowances for quality and condition). If the item is purchased from a dealer the price will clearly be higher, but none but the experienced collector should buy at auction without expert advice. The dealer will charge more, but the purchaser will have some guarantee of satisfaction, and the reputable dealer will probably save him money by virtue of his experience. Better a genuine piece at a high price than a fake at a moderate price.

To use the guide find the illustrated item most similar to the one you have in mind and compare quality and condition, taking into account any special features which may contribute to greater rarity. In this way you should be able to arrive at an approximate value.

INVESTMENT

It is hoped that the reader will not enter the field of antique firearm collecting purely for investment, but if investment forms part of his interest he will probably not be disappointed as long as he is discerning in his choice of acquisitions. The price of antique firearms is still low compared with that of other works of art, but the increase has been rapid in recent years.

FACTORS WHICH AFFECT VALUE

1. QUALITY

Any judgment of quality must be to some extent subjective, but experience of collecting and a knowledge of the art of gun-making as practised by the principal makers gives the collector an ability to make such an appraisal. In each school of gun-making quality manifests itself in a different way. The very best English work of the early 19th century is not as elaborate as that of the contemporary Continental makers, but the quality is in many cases better. It should be remembered that the presence of lavish decoration does not necessarily bear witness to good quality.

Each piece in the Guide is given a quality rating which enables the reader to place it approximately within its own group, and it is hoped that this will be acceptable to most collectors. Where the quality is standard, as in patent revolvers and service weapons, only a condition rating is given. When the quality of a particular part of the item illustrated is outstanding, mention is made of this in the description. Many of the finer pieces have silver mounts. This greatly increases their value, particularly when full silver hallmarks are present, allowing the weapon to be dated accurately. The earlier the hallmark, the greater the increase in value. A full set of marks prior to 1740 is very rare – 17th century examples exceedingly so. Finer still, however, are the best chiselled steel mounts. These, usually unsigned, can be identified in some cases as the work of a known master.

Literature on antique firearms is plentiful, and a study of decoration is beyond the scope of this Guide.

2. CONDITION.

For those firearms generally available, the range of price between a poor and an excellent example may be as much as 200%. Pristine condition gives a status which is hard to price, as the normal ceiling figure for a particular type will be exceeded, but it will rarely be found on anything but 19th century weapons. The finer the condition the steeper the rise in value, and as condition has become so important, each item in the Guide is given a rating which it is hoped will prove serviceable. The range is from exceptional to poor, the latter being the lowest grade which collectors are likely to consider acceptable except in cases of outstanding rarity or early date. Where original finish is present this is mentioned in the description.
The following factors lower value:

a. **Damage.** The commonest area of damage on flintlocks is the cock and this is often replaced or repaired. On a pair, look to see that they match. If a cock has been repaired you can often detect the join by removing it and examining the inner side. Look also at the stock, especially at the fore-end of pistols and the small of the butt both on pistols and guns. In the case of percussion fire-arms it is usually the hammer that suffers. The same observations apply.

b. **Restoration.** Repairs to the metal can be detected by careful examination under a magnifying glass, and replaced parts usually stand out in contrast to the overall wear on the weapon or differ in the colour of the metal. Re-stocking is usually betrayed by the poor fit of the mounts and the fresh look of the wood under the lock and side-plate. Re-finishing of metal parts can only be distinguished by practice, but the effect is more dull than the original, and the definition of the engraving is removed when the metal is struck off prior to re-colouring.

Collectors much prefer untouched state (even if it looks poor to the inexperienced eye) to restored or overcleaned condition. "Sleepers" always make a higher price than renovated pieces. Where work has been done one cannot be sure how many faults have been made good. Cleaning must be left to the experts – and they are few.

c. **Modernisation.** **Barrel lengths.** Many 17th century pistols were shorted during the 18th century, and many early 18th century guns were shortened in the second half of the century. Where this has been done the value is reduced by between 50% and 100%. Shortened barrels can be detected by the lack of a front sight, also of the small degree of flare which is usually found over the last inch or so of the muzzle. When they have been restored to full length in recent years they are no more desirable to collectors than those which have been left shortened. It is often difficult to see when this has been done from the outside, but a careful inspection of the inner walls of the barrel will show a join where the extra section has been added. The fact that the fore-end has been spliced is not necessarily evidence of barrel lengthening as many fore-stocks are repaired, the wood being weak at this point.

Stock Lengths. Most long guns from the 16th century up to the middle of the 18th century, and sometimes later, were stocked to the muzzle (the term "full stock" is used in the descriptions). When the fashion changed in the latter part of the 18th century (about 1780) many stocks were cut back, and a ramrod rib was braised to the underside of the barrel, or the pipe fitted to it direct. Those retaining their full stocks are now rare and worth considerably more than those which have been shortened. Do not, however, assume that a half-stocked gun of the early 18th century must have once been full-stocked, especially in the case of Continental weapons.

The fashion for half-stocks in pistols came in at about the same time, perhaps ten years later, and some duelling pistols are found which have been modernised in the early 19th century in the same way. Their value is likewise reduced.

Conversion to Percussion

Many flintlock guns and pistols were converted to the improved system of ignition by copper cap in about 1830. Only practice can enable the collector to spot the conversion, but a general rule is to see if the original flint mechanism can be visualised. The flintlock form of the lock is often plainly visible. In many cases the conversion entails letting in a small piece of metal where the pan was, and this can be seen both inside and outside the plate. Also the forward part of the lock-plate shows the positions of the screw and the pin which held the steel-spring in place. This part of the lock, the breech and the hammer are nearly always engraved in a later style than the rest of the mounts, and the metal is sometimes finished in a different colour. Conversions vary from shoddy to very good, and the price is reduced accordingly. Generally the value is reduced by half. The exception to this is when the conversion is to a rarer system (patch-lock, pellet-lock, etc. see pages 145 and 321).

In recent years many guns and pistols have been converted back to flintlock in an effort to increase their value. This is particularly common with Kentucky rifles and U.S. martial firearms. Where this has been done the working of the lock is usually poor and the pan-cover often fails to make a good joint with the pan. The shape of the cock, steel and steel-spring is usually poor, and the colour of the metal different. If a really skilled hand has been at work an examination of the interior of the lock will be necessary. The line where the new pan has been let in will normally be visible, if not an X-ray is the only means of definite proof.

Re-conversion back to flintlock does not raise the value unless it is flawlessly executed. Most collectors would rather have a converted piece than a re-converted one, and most serious students will not consider acquiring any re-conversion at all. However, it is surprising how many re-conversions have been sold for high prices.

3. RARITY

Singles, pairs, sets.

A pair of firearms is always worth more than the value of the two individual pieces added together. The increase in value is usually between 20% and 50%. The rarer the item the greater the increase.

A case with full accessories raises the value by between 50% and 100%. Again, the rarer the item the greater the increase. Where the case and accessories are not original, the increase in value falls steeply, in some cases as low as 5% or the value of the case as a separate item. Original trade labels add to the price, as does the engraving of the owner's name, crest or initials on the case as well as on the weapons. On later cased sets the serial number of the case will often match the serial number of the contents, particularly with Purdey items. Cases are rare before 1780, and early ones increase the value by a greater degree than late ones. Where the case is later, but original to the pistols, the value is not as high as for a contemporary casing. Where the casing is particularly elaborate the increase in value can be well over 100%. Cased flintlock long guns are now very rare, and the price increase is accordingly higher than for pistols.

In the best pistol cases each pistol will only fit in the position designed for it and the two cannot be interchanged. Most flintlocks are made to fit in at half-cock so that they can be carried loaded. If they do not, be suspicious. If they are loose in the case, it was probably not intended for them. Look to see if the partitions have been changed. The lining is usually of green baize, but velvets of different colours were used after about 1820. An experienced collector can recognise the famous makers by their cases, and can even date a set approximately without looking inside. The carrying handle is a good guide. Up to 1780 a Chippendale style handle is used, and this remains proud of the lid; by 1790 it becomes a ring handle which folds flush with the lid, normally forming half a circular plate. By 1820 the plate is usually of rectangular form. Accessories can also be attributed to individual makers and can also be dated accurately.

Sets of more than two can only be evaluated by considering the item in question, and two examples are given as a guide on pages 276 and 277.

Presentation pieces also form an entirely separate category and the value depends on the importance of the presentation as well as the quality of the piece. Various examples are given throughout the Guide. Presentation inscriptions should be treated with care and the engraving studied closely. A knowledge of the different styles of engraving through the centuries is a great help. The forger usually slips up on some small detail.

Extreme rarity can overcome rules imposed by condition. In some cases, the Whitneyville Walker Dragoon for instance, collectors are highly suspicious unless the condition *is* poor. Rarity itself is not, however, an ultimate criterion. The Colt Paterson rifles are rarer than the pistols, yet they are worth less. Some extremely rare items are of such poor quality, and of such unattractive appearance, that the price remains low. The highest value is achieved by a combination of quality, rarity and aesthetic appeal.

4. FAKES

Fakes are most likely to be found in the field of wheel-locks, duck's foot pistols, Forsyths and Colts. Only very few fakes are included in the Guide as they are felt to be of little interest to the serious collector. Many replicas are to be found on the market today, but most are unlikely to deceive. Some reproductions (see pages 15, 20, 60, 146 and 251) have a certain interest if they can be identified as the work of a particular hand.

However, collectors are likely to come across genuine firearms with false signatures. The name of a famous gunmaker is often found on an item which he would not have let out of his workshop. Each of the great gunsmiths had his own particular style, and also his signature which is hard to copy sufficiently well to deceive the expert.

Some signatures were copied by contemporary makers. The Liège school is an outstanding example of this practice (see pages 106-107, 175 and 192). In the 19th century both the Birmingham and Liège gun traders furnished large quantities of weapons for sale in London, and these often bear the signature of a London maker. In some cases they bear genuine Birmingham proof marks, in others spurious London marks. Although they do not conform to the style of the maker whose signature they bear they were probably retailed by him and should therefore not be regarded as forgeries in the strict sense of the term. The lesser quality of such pieces usually causes them to command a lower price than the genuine London product. The same applies to Paris signatures on pieces supplied by the Liège workmen; always look for Liège proof marks. They are often stamped under or on the side of the barrel near the breech.

We acknowledge the help of the Auctioneers who have been kind enough to supply the illustrations – Messrs. Christie's, Knight Frank & Rutley (who no longer hold gun sales), Sotheby's, Wallis & Wallis and Weller & Dufty. Thanks are also due to Major Noel Corry for giving permission to reproduce items from his collection, and to H.M. Stationery Office for the items from the Tower of London Armouries.

Wheel-Lock Pistols

Italian wheel-lock pistol with external lock mechanism, the barrel in three stages, the butt in the form of a wooden dagger handle. Extremely rare and probably one of the earliest wheel-locks known. First quarter of the 16th century. 12in. *Sotheby's*

Over £5,000

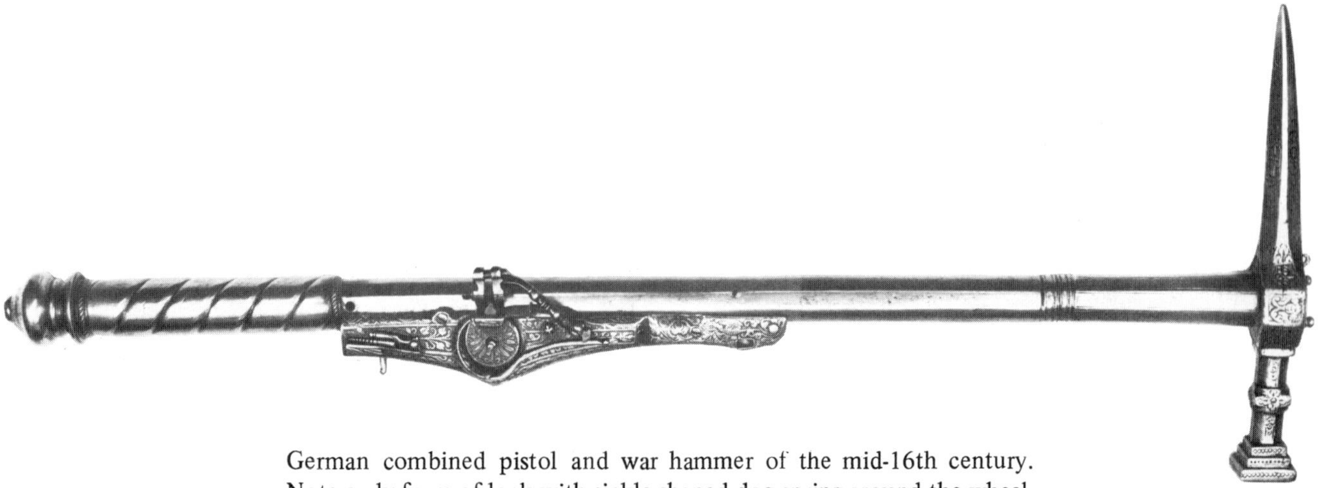

German combined pistol and war hammer of the mid-16th century. Note early form of lock with sickle-shaped dog-spring around the wheel, also early shape of dog nearly circular in section. 21½in. *Sotheby's*

Over £5,000 Extremely rare

German (probably Nuremberg) wheel-lock pistol of about 1570. Early features are the shape of the dog, as above, the internal dog-spring and the small flattened ball pommel. The stock is decorated with carved panels of horn at the lock etched and gilt. Fine quality, good condition. 25½in. *Sotheby's*

Over £8,000

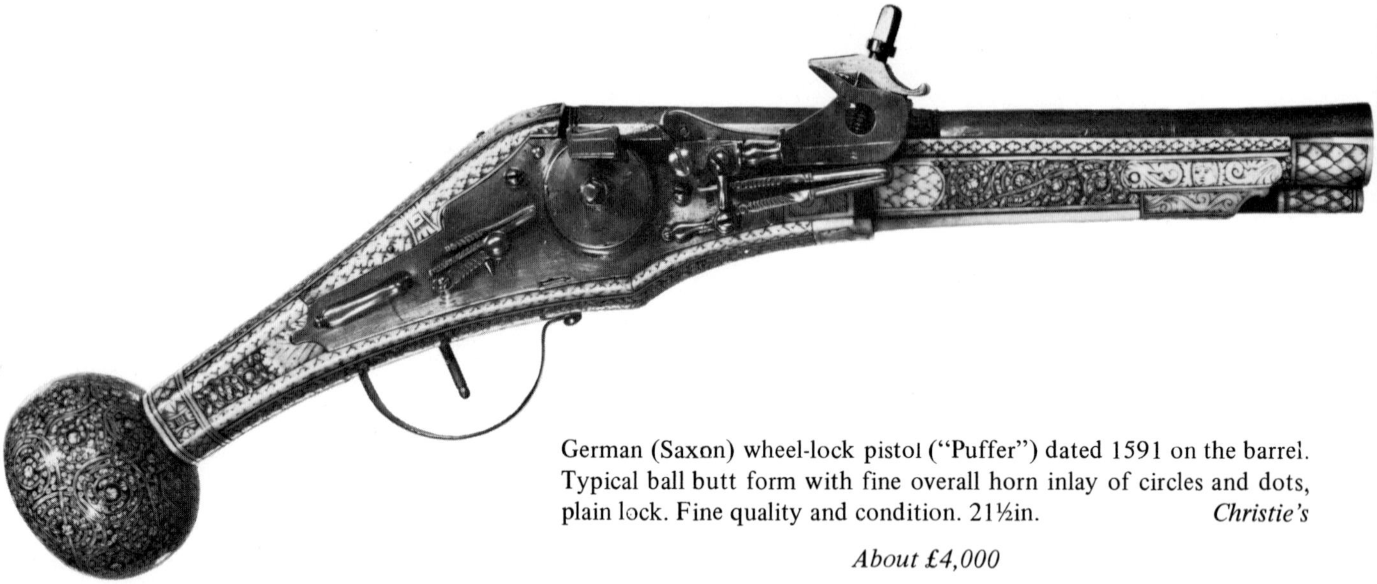

German (Saxon) wheel-lock pistol ("Puffer") dated 1591 on the barrel. Typical ball butt form with fine overall horn inlay of circles and dots, plain lock. Fine quality and condition. 21½in. *Christie's*

About £4,000

German long wheel-lock pistol, the barrel and lock-plate damascened over their whole surface with scrolling foliage in gold and silver, the lock of early type with enclosed wheel and internal dog-spring, walnut full stock profusely inlaid with engraved staghorn, with hunting scenes on each side of the forestock, the belt hook and trigger-guard damascened *en suite* with the barrel. Outstanding quality and condition. 36½in. Circa 1550/60. *Renwick Collection*

£15,000 – £20,000

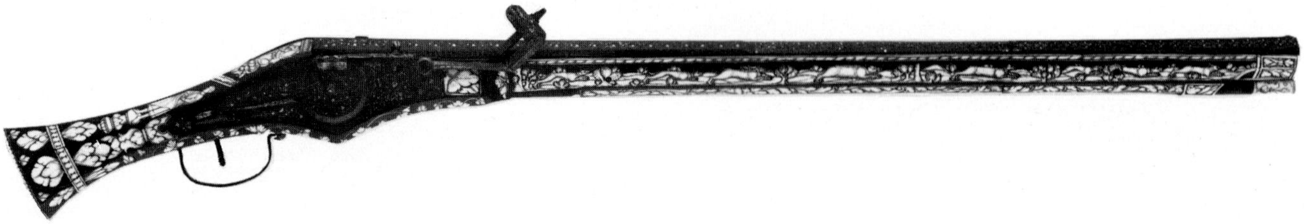

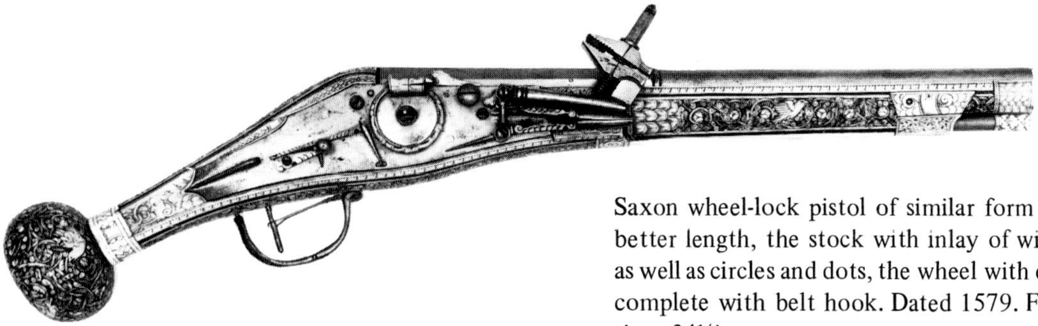

Saxon wheel-lock pistol of similar form to page 2 (top) but of better length, the stock with inlay of winged figures and birds as well as circles and dots, the wheel with engraved brass border, complete with belt hook. Dated 1579. Fine quality and condition. 24½in. *Sotheby's*

Over £4,000

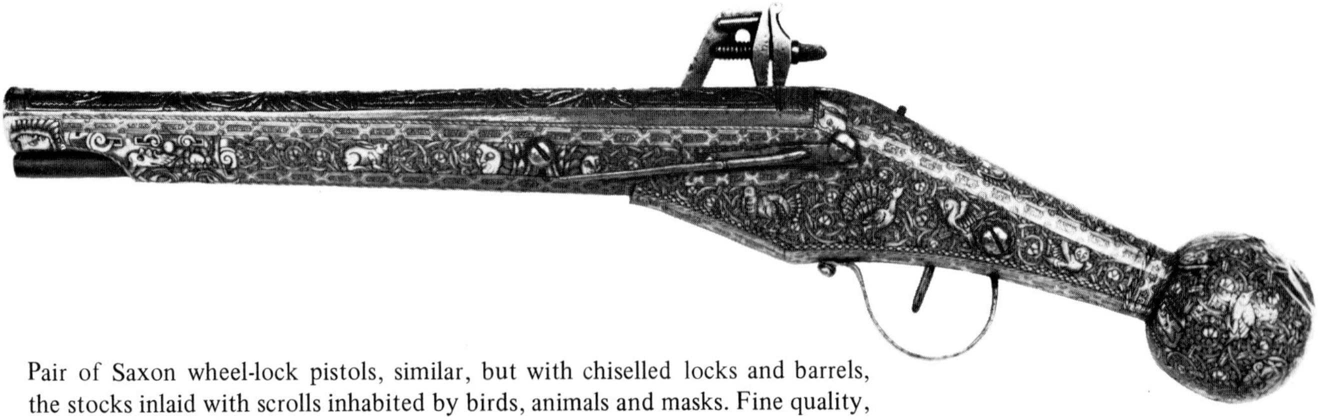

Pair of Saxon wheel-lock pistols, similar, but with chiselled locks and barrels, the stocks inlaid with scrolls inhabited by birds, animals and masks. Fine quality, good condition. Circa 1580. 23in. At one time in the Dresden Armouries. *Sotheby's*

Over £8,000 the pair

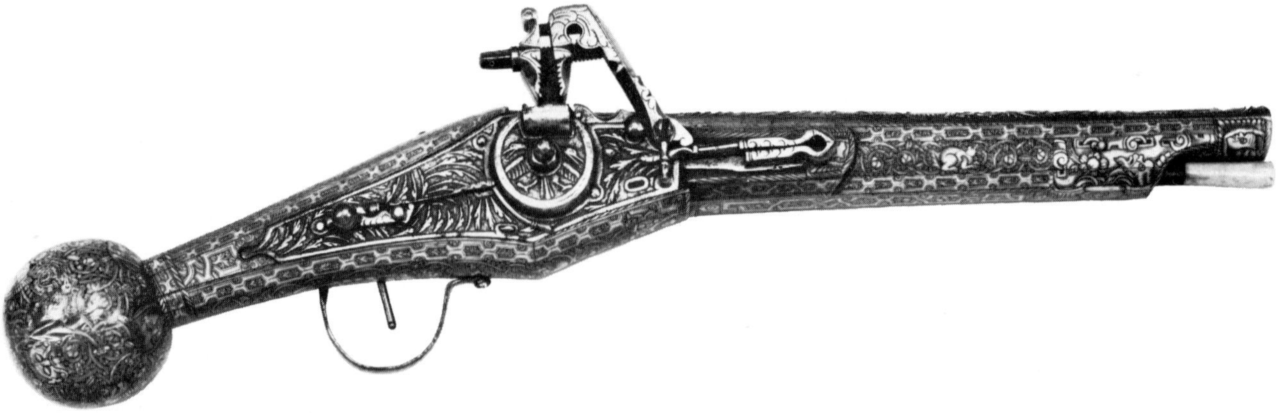

In the sale from the Dresden Armouries, Sotheby's, 1970, a single pistol of this type made *£4,800.* (Detail of top shown)

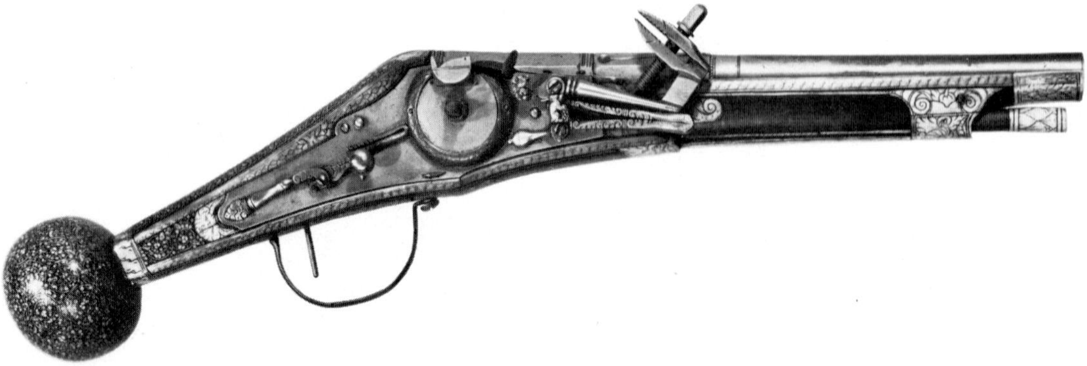

Pair of similar pistols with plain locks (except gilt mounts) and lightly ornamented barrels, the stocks half inlaid and half plain. Fine quality and condition. Circa 1580/1590. 22½in. At one time in the Dresden Armouries.

Over £6,000 the pair

With birds inhabiting the scrolls and retaining original finish on the metal parts, Over £7,000 *Christie's*

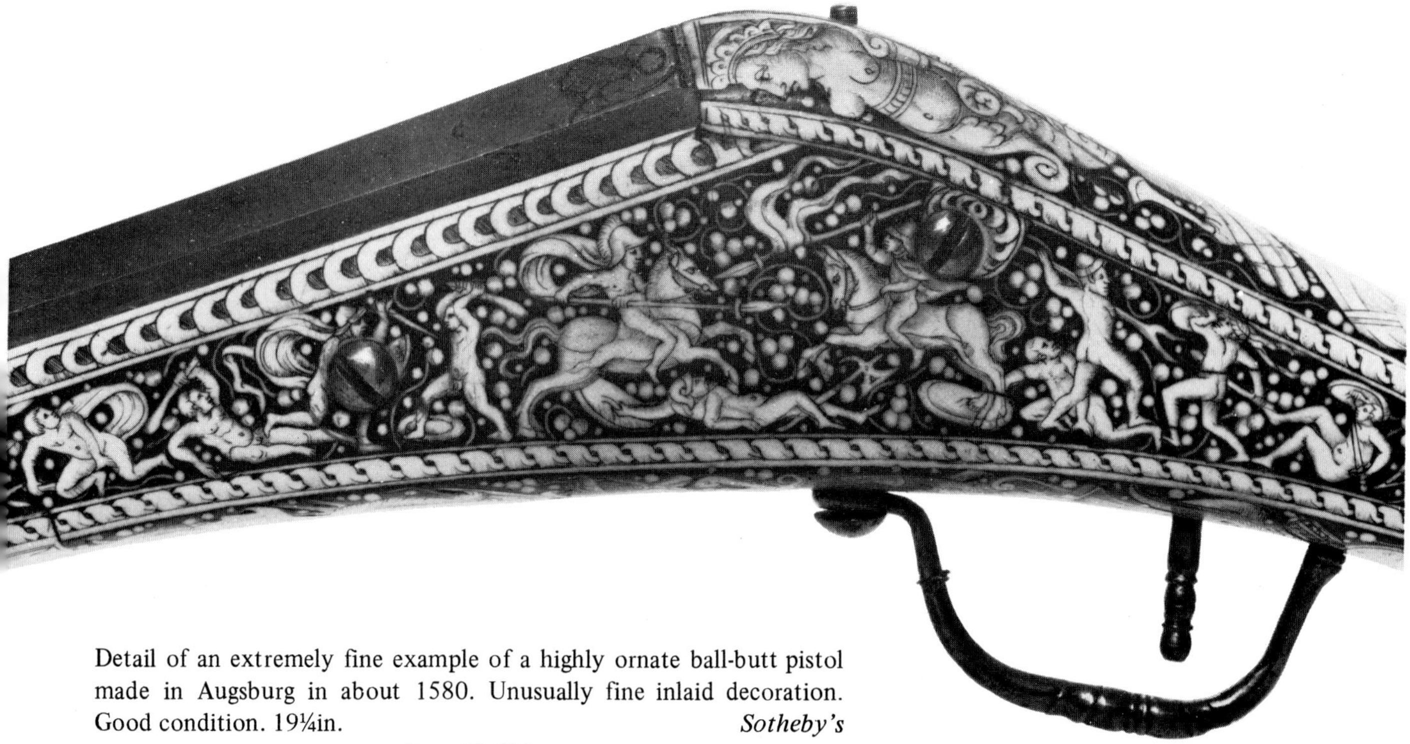

Detail of an extremely fine example of a highly ornate ball-butt pistol made in Augsburg in about 1580. Unusually fine inlaid decoration. Good condition. 19¼in. *Sotheby's*

Over £8,000

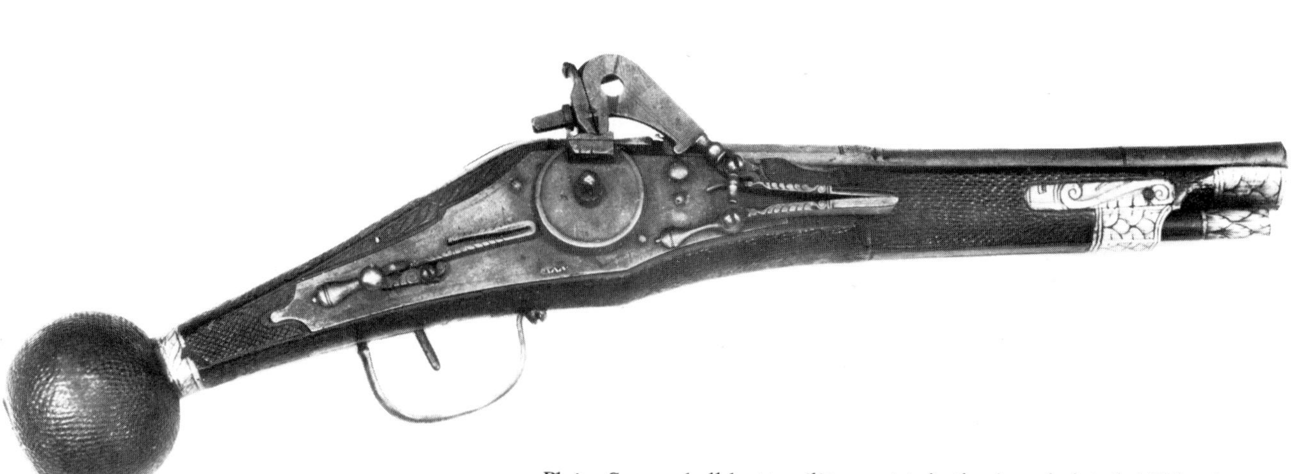

Plain Saxon ball-butt military pistol, the barrel dated 1591, the stock stamped to simulate staghorn and with slight horn inlays, the butt engraved with the Arms of Saxony. A large number of these pistols survive, having been sold from the Dresden Armouries in 1832, 1919, 1920, 1927 or 1970. Most are in fine condition with original blueing on the locks and barrels. The quality is always good. 22½in. *Christie's*

£1,000 – £1,300

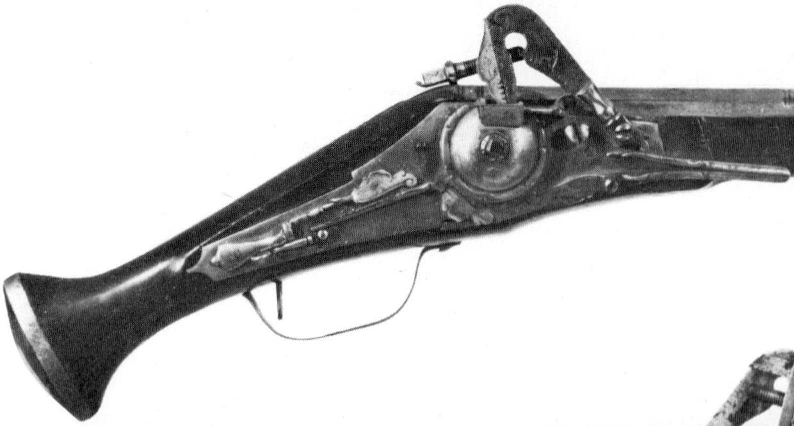

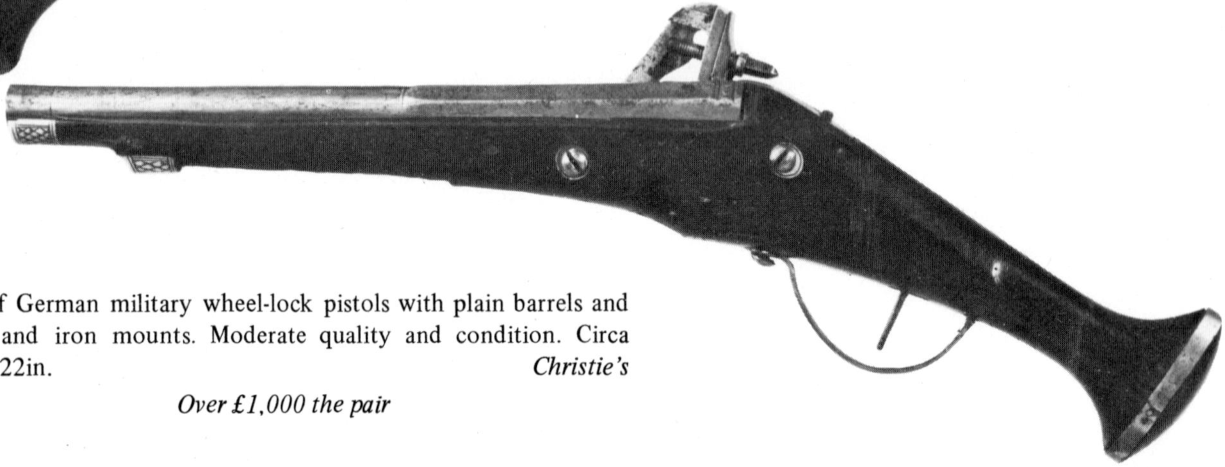

Pair of German military wheel-lock pistols with plain barrels and locks and iron mounts. Moderate quality and condition. Circa 1600. 22in. *Christie's*

Over £1,000 the pair

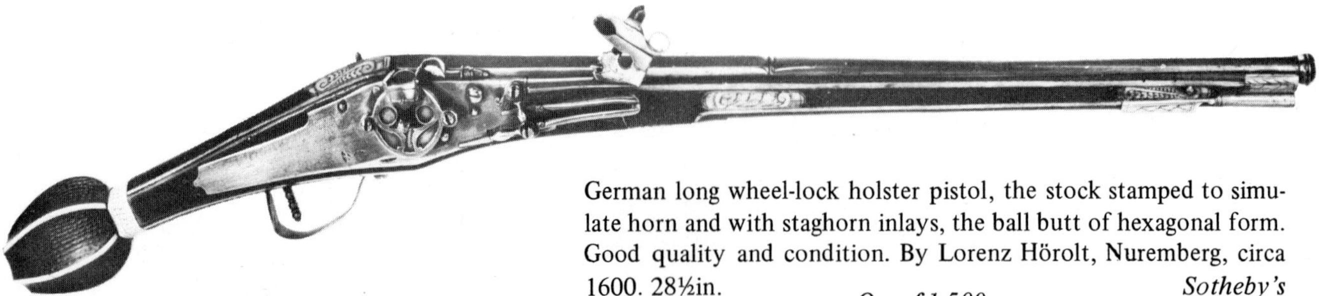

German long wheel-lock holster pistol, the stock stamped to simulate horn and with staghorn inlays, the ball butt of hexagonal form. Good quality and condition. By Lorenz Hörolt, Nuremberg, circa 1600. 28½in. *Sotheby's*

Over £1,500

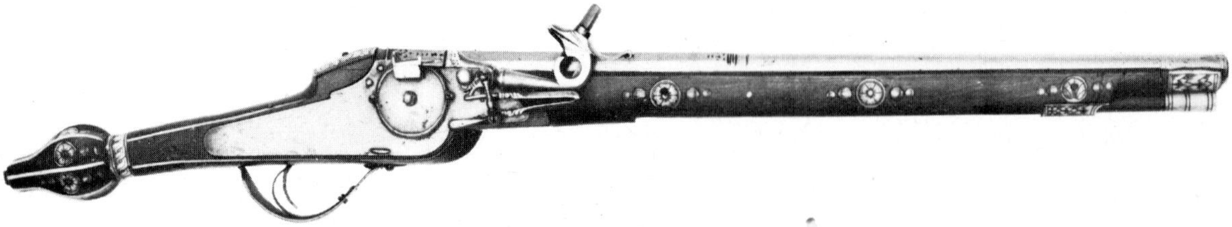

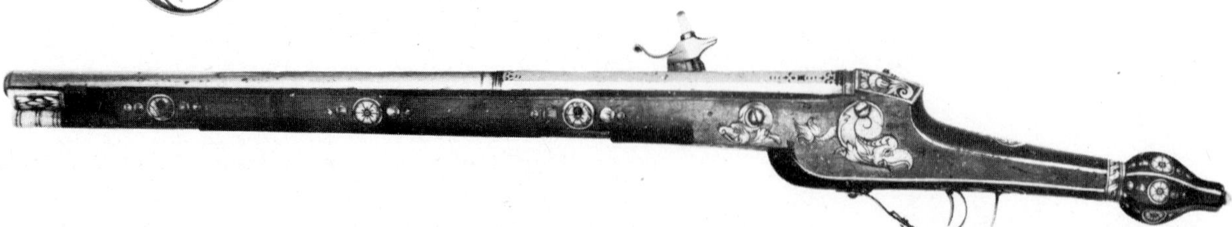

Pair of German wheel-lock pistols made by Hans Stockmann of Dresden, from the Saxon Armouries. The stocks are inlaid with bone and have small fluted pear-shaped pommels. Good quality and condition. Circa 1610. 30in. *Sotheby's*

Over £6,000 the pair

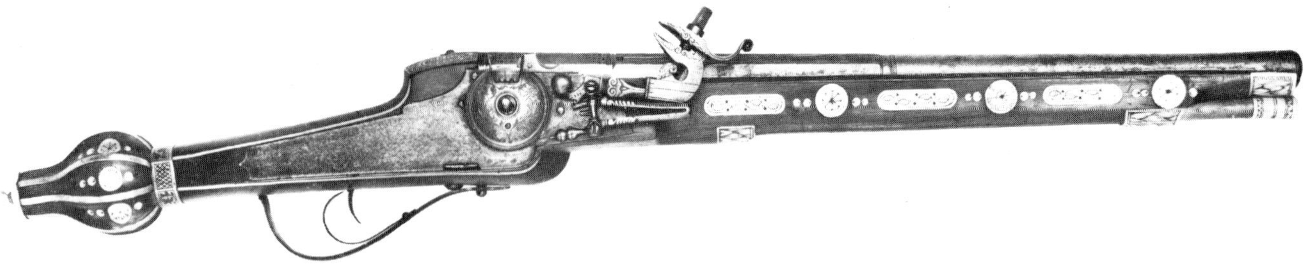

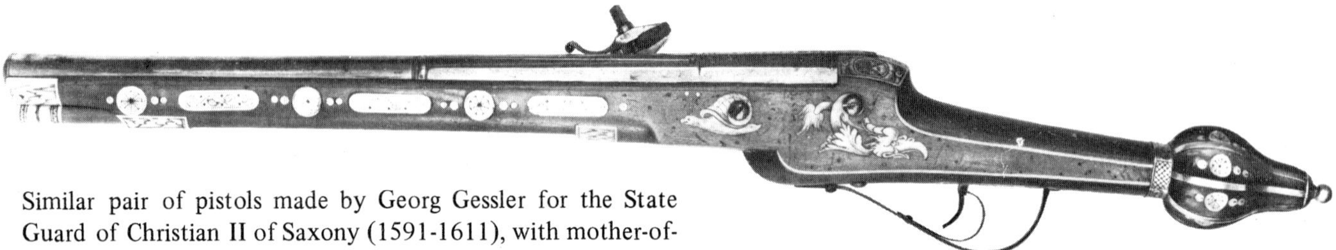

Similar pair of pistols made by Georg Gessler for the State Guard of Christian II of Saxony (1591-1611), with mother-of-pearl as well as staghorn inlays to the stocks and gilt bands and wheel-covers. Good quality and condition. 29in. *Sotheby's*

Over £8,000 the pair

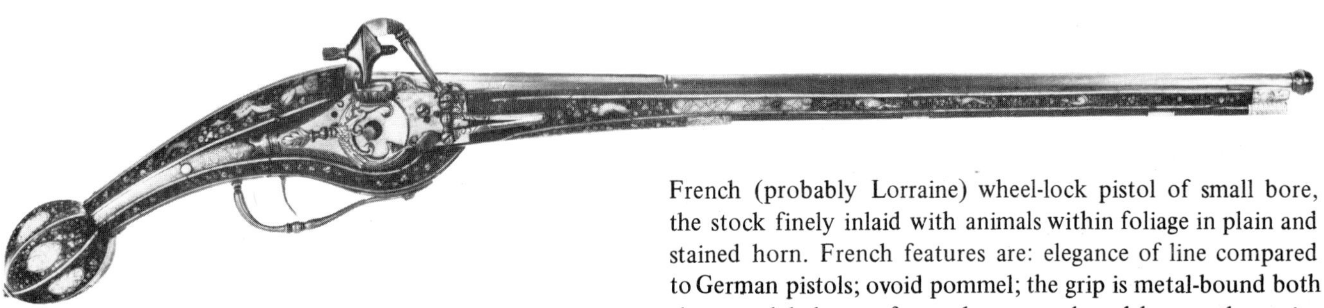

French (probably Lorraine) wheel-lock pistol of small bore, the stock finely inlaid with animals within foliage in plain and stained horn. French features are: elegance of line compared to German pistols; ovoid pommel; the grip is metal-bound both above and below as far as the pommel, and houses the main-spring of the lock; the V-shaped side-plate. Fine quality and condition. Early 17th century. 29½in. *Sotheby's*

Over £10,000

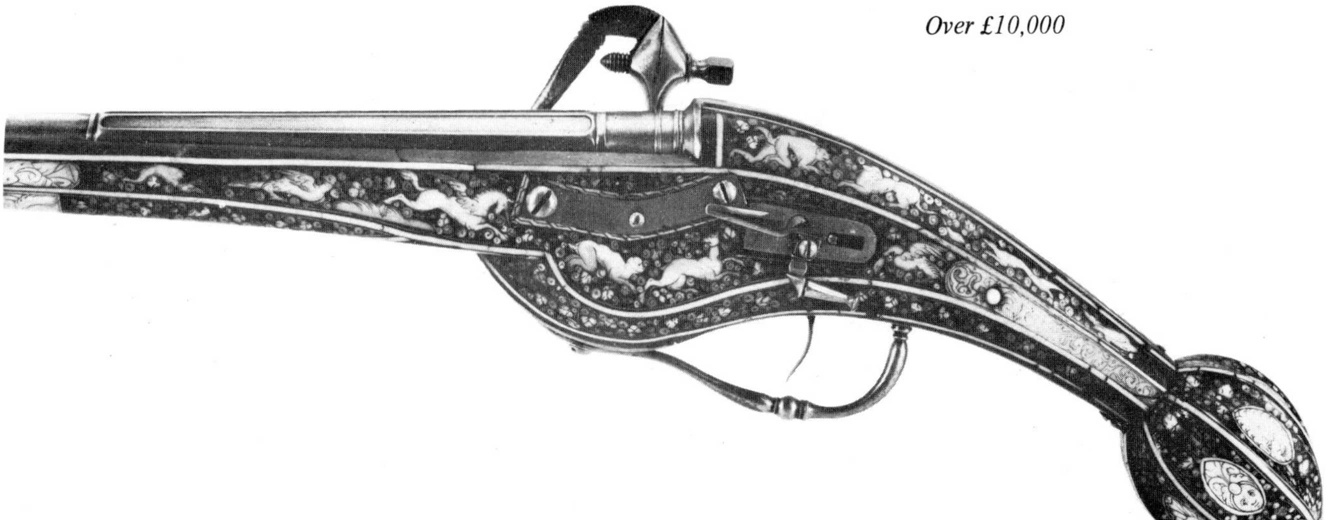

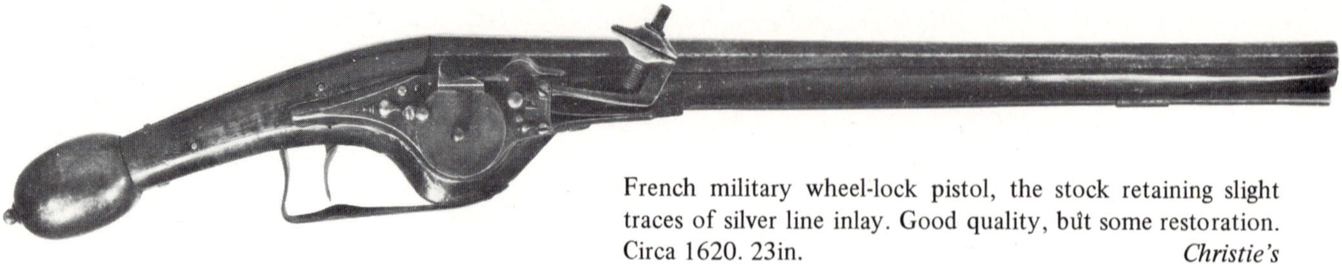

French military wheel-lock pistol, the stock retaining slight traces of silver line inlay. Good quality, but some restoration. Circa 1620. 23in. *Christie's*

£500 – £1,000. French wheel-lock pistols are rare.

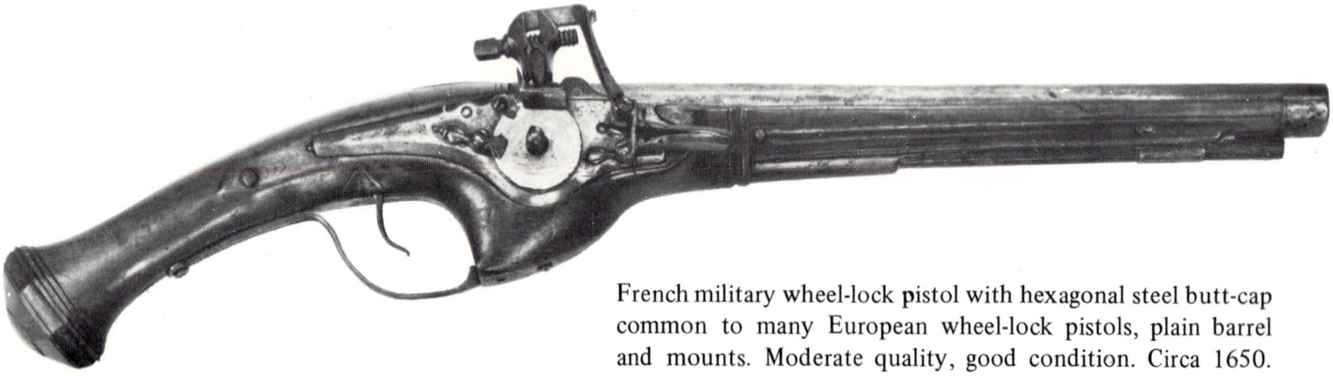

French military wheel-lock pistol with hexagonal steel butt-cap common to many European wheel-lock pistols, plain barrel and mounts. Moderate quality, good condition. Circa 1650. 21¼in. *Sotheby's*

£500 – £700

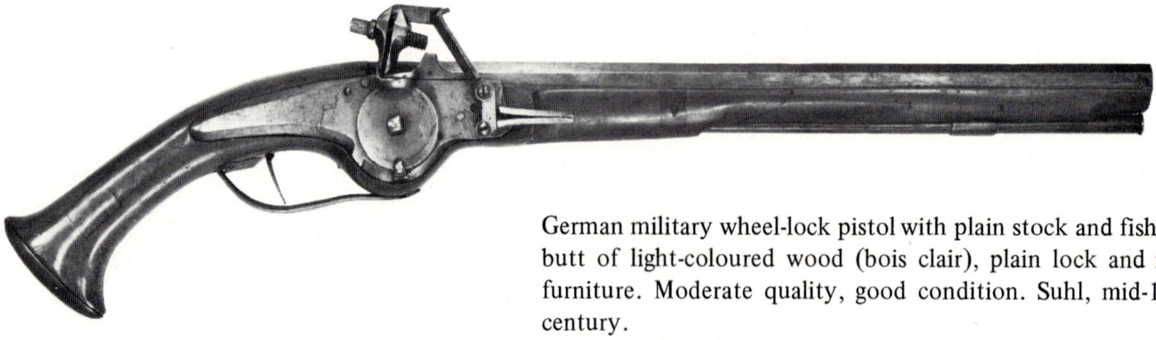

German military wheel-lock pistol with plain stock and fish-tail butt of light-coloured wood (bois clair), plain lock and iron furniture. Moderate quality, good condition. Suhl, mid-17th century.

Pistols of this type may equally well be Austrian, Dutch, Swedish or Swiss, as Suhl parts were widely exported, and a virtually standard form of military holster pistol was used in the Thirty Years War. Fair condition. 22½in. *Sotheby's*

£400 – £500

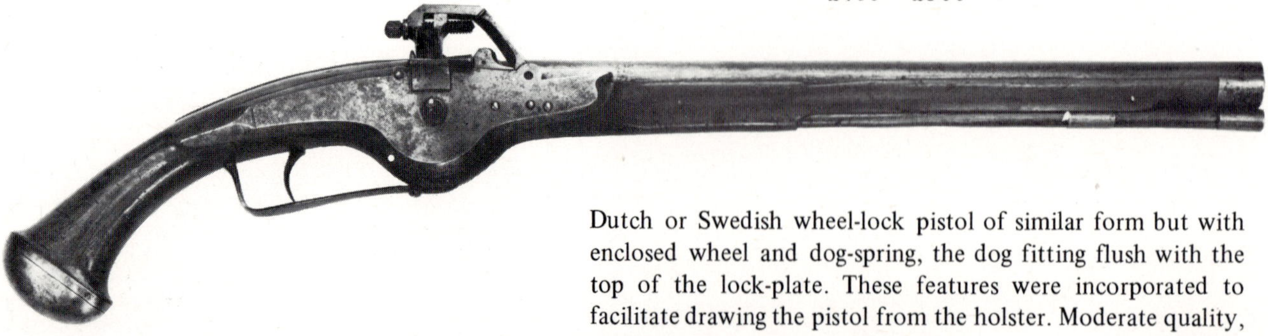

Dutch or Swedish wheel-lock pistol of similar form but with enclosed wheel and dog-spring, the dog fitting flush with the top of the lock-plate. These features were incorporated to facilitate drawing the pistol from the holster. Moderate quality, good condition. Circa 1670. 25½in. *Sotheby's*

£500 – £700

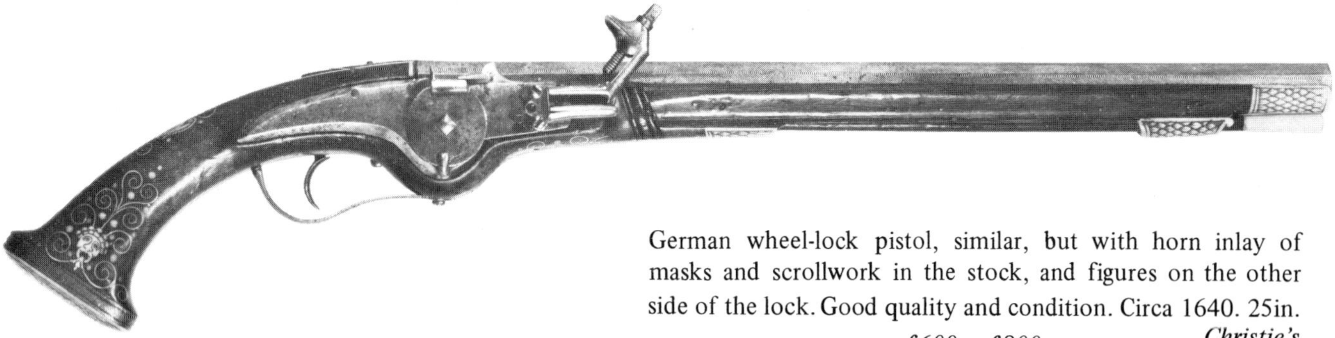

German wheel-lock pistol, similar, but with horn inlay of masks and scrollwork in the stock, and figures on the other side of the lock. Good quality and condition. Circa 1640. 25in.
£600 – £800 *Christie's*

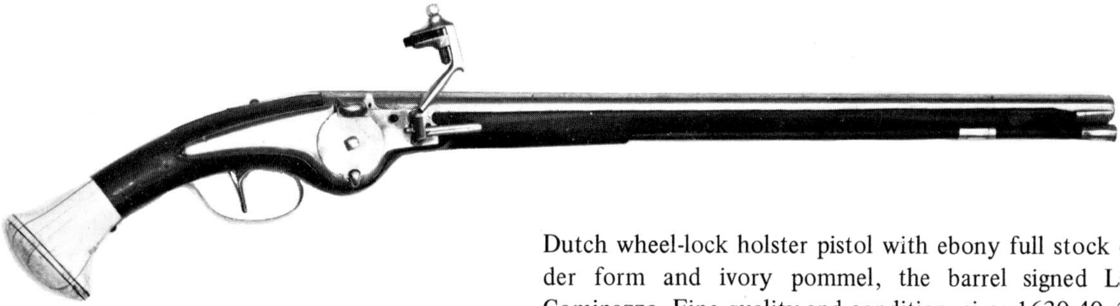

Dutch wheel-lock holster pistol with ebony full stock of slender form and ivory pommel, the barrel signed Lazarino Cominazzo. Fine quality and condition, circa 1630-40. 26in.
Christie's

Over £1,000

Wheel-lock military holster pistol in poor condition. Thought to be English, partly because it came from Petworth House, Sussex, partly because of the chevron pattern cut behind barrel tang and the English form of the butt. Circa 1640. 23½in. Despite condition it made *£475* in 1970. An English decorated wheel-lock is worth five figures, and is extremely rare.
Christie's

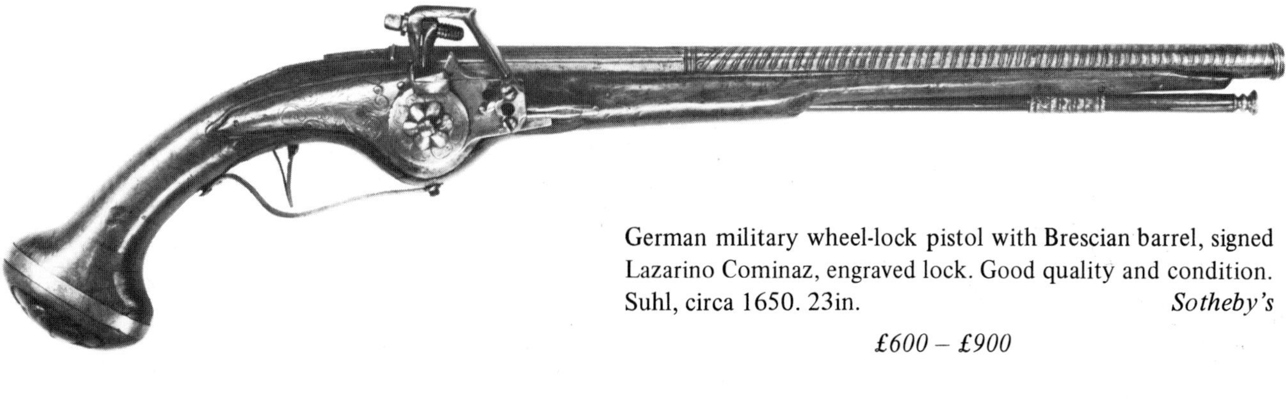

German military wheel-lock pistol with Brescian barrel, signed Lazarino Cominaz, engraved lock. Good quality and condition. Suhl, circa 1650. 23in. *Sotheby's*

£600 – £900

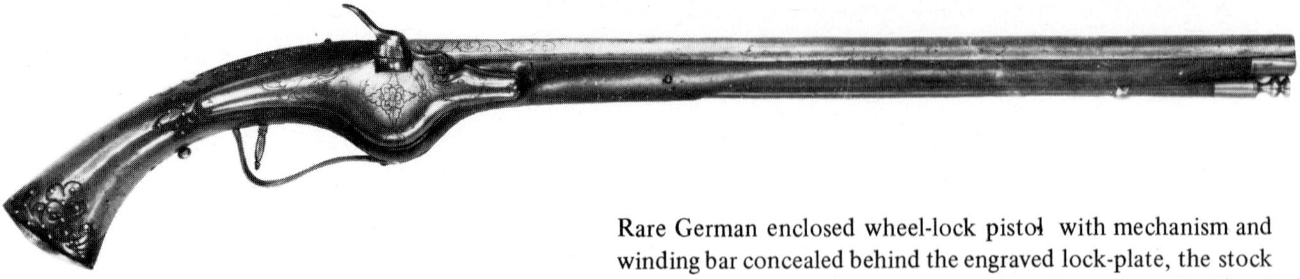

Rare German enclosed wheel-lock pistol with mechanism and winding bar concealed behind the engraved lock-plate, the stock engraved with leaves and enriched with steel studs. Good quality and condition. Circa 1660. 26in. *Sotheby's*

Over £1,000

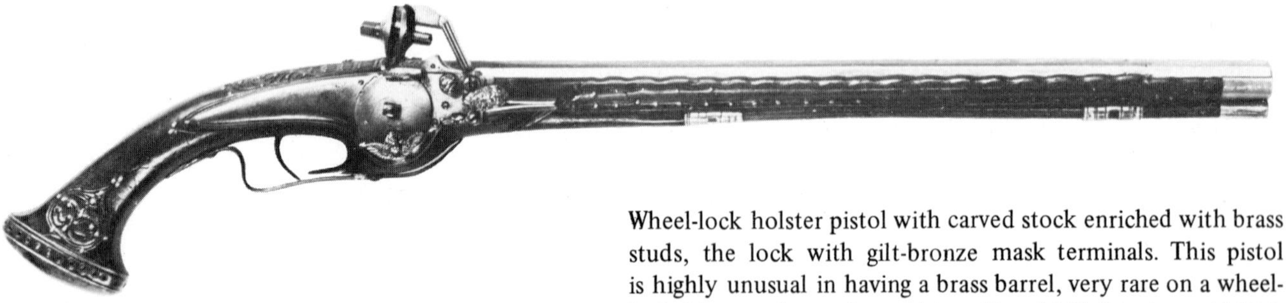

Wheel-lock holster pistol with carved stock enriched with brass studs, the lock with gilt-bronze mask terminals. This pistol is highly unusual in having a brass barrel, very rare on a wheel-lock. Fine quality and condition. Signed I.H. Lignitz, mid-17th century. 27¼in. *Sotheby's*

About £1,500

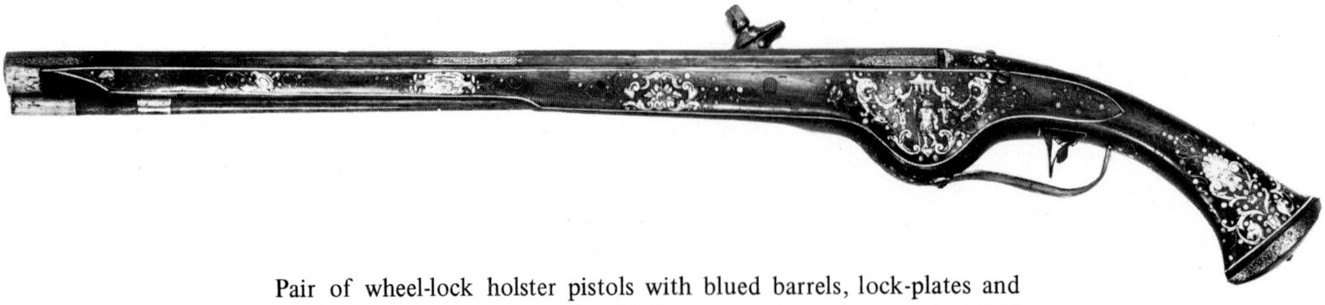

Pair of wheel-lock holster pistols with blued barrels, lock-plates and butt-caps each decorated with gold damascene, the walnut stocks inlaid with Diana and Acteon beneath canopies, together with masks, scrolls, pellets, and lines in engraved horn inlay, the remaining metal parts gilt. Exceptional quality, fine condition. Probably Dutch, circa 1650. 27¼in. *Sotheby's*

Over £10,000 the pair

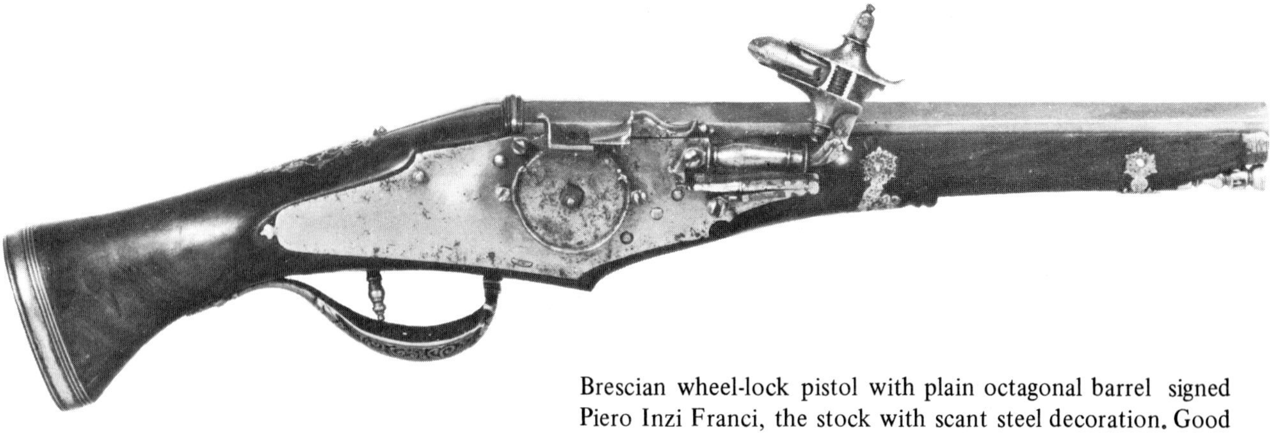

Brescian wheel-lock pistol with plain octagonal barrel signed Piero Inzi Franci, the stock with scant steel decoration. Good quality, not very good condition. Trigger-guard replaced, barrel possibly shortened. Circa 1640. 15½in. *Christie's*

£500 – £650

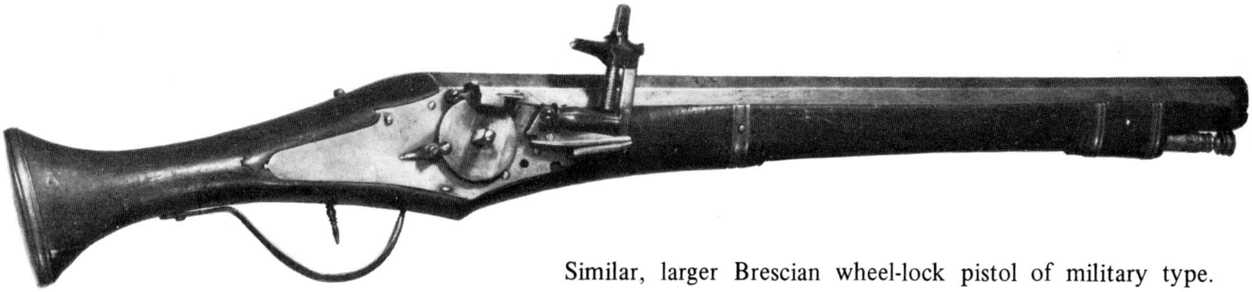

Similar, larger Brescian wheel-lock pistol of military type. Good quality and condition. Circa 1650. 24½in. *Christie's*

£700 – £900

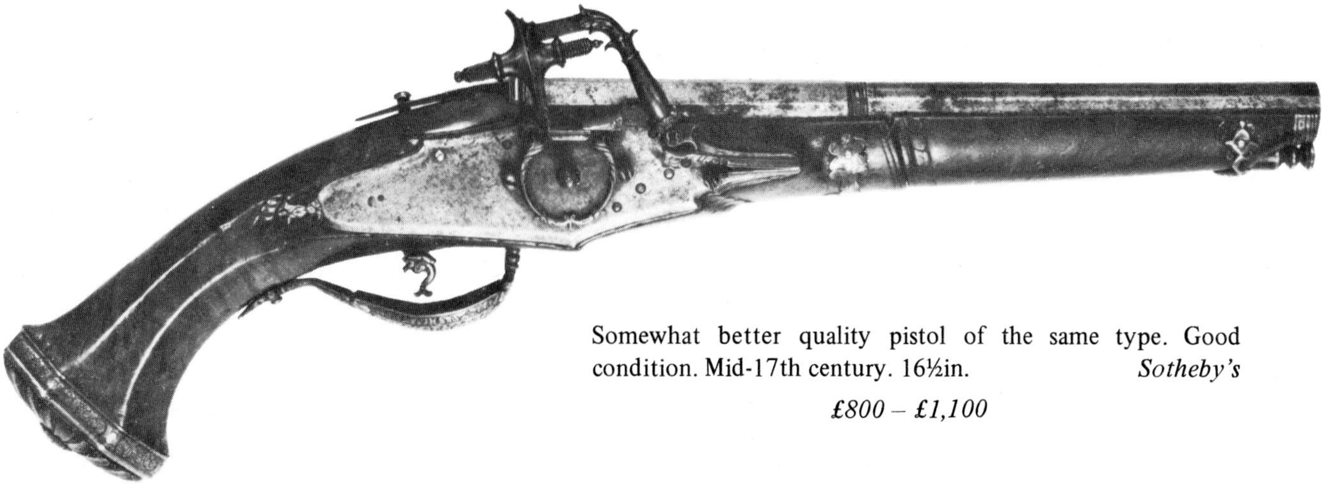

Somewhat better quality pistol of the same type. Good condition. Mid-17th century. 16½in. *Sotheby's*

£800 – £1,100

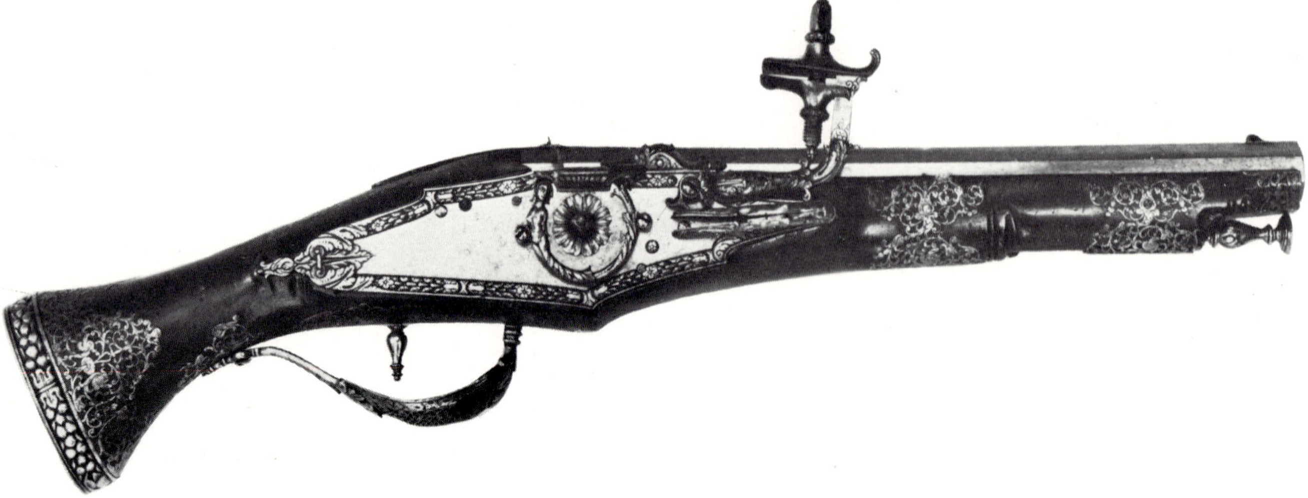

Highly elaborate pair of Brescian wheel-lock pistols with finely chiselled locks and mounts, the stocks inlaid with finely pierced steel. The price of this type of pistol depends on the quality of the piercing and chiselling: the best have the delicacy of lace. Fine quality and condition. Circa 1640. 15in. *Sotheby's*

£10,000 or more the pair

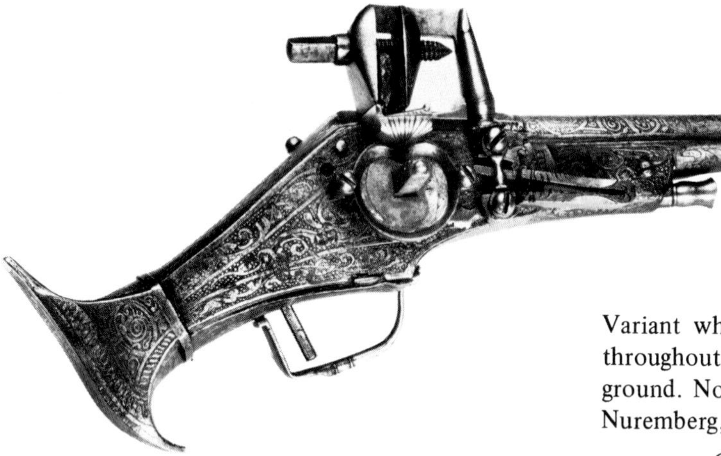

Variant wheel-lock pistol made entirely of steel and etched throughout with animals amidst scrolls on a granulated gilt ground. Note S-shaped butt-cap. Fine quality and condition. Nuremberg, circa 1570. 10in. *Sotheby's*

Over £3,000. Much less for a plain example

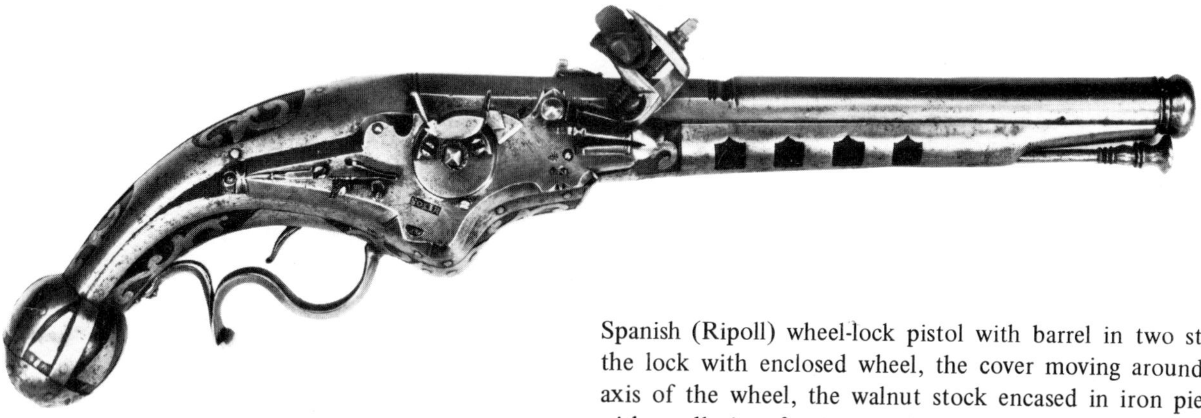

Spanish (Ripoll) wheel-lock pistol with barrel in two stages, the lock with enclosed wheel, the cover moving around the axis of the wheel, the walnut stock encased in iron pierced with scrolls, iron furniture and iron ramrod. Good quality, fine condition. Signed Soler. First half of the 17th century. 14½in. *Renwick Collection*

Over £4,000. Extremely rare.

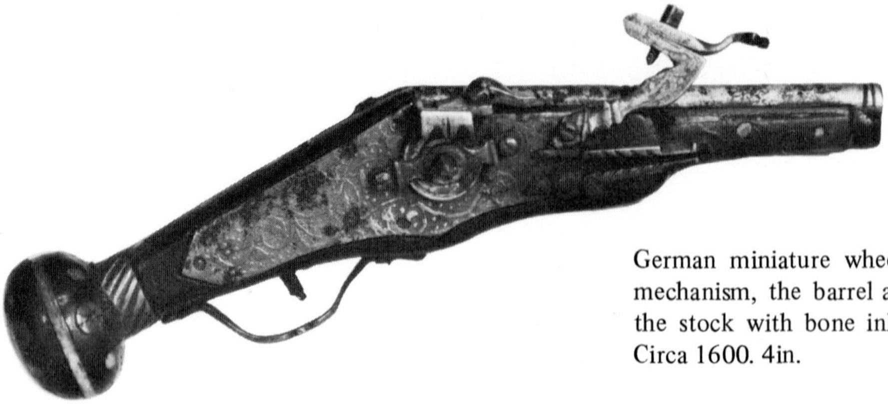

German miniature wheel-lock pistol complete with internal mechanism, the barrel and lock-plate decorated with etching, the stock with bone inlays. Moderate quality and condition. Circa 1600. 4in. *Christie's*

£300 – £500

Other examples of this type may be found entirely of metal, blued and gilt. These are attributed to Michael Mann of Nuremberg and range from *£200 to £400.*

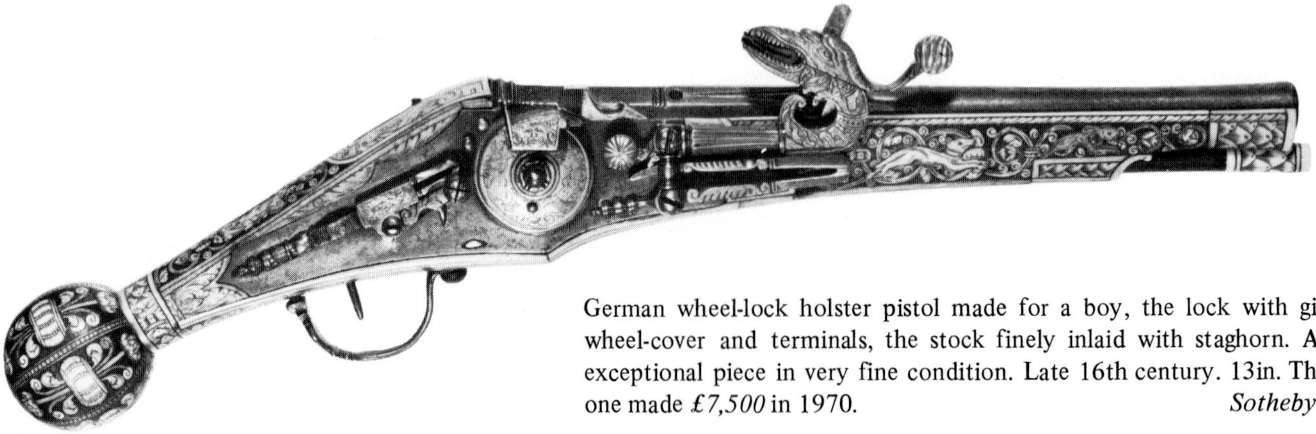

German wheel-lock holster pistol made for a boy, the lock with gilt wheel-cover and terminals, the stock finely inlaid with staghorn. An exceptional piece in very fine condition. Late 16th century. 13in. This one made *£7,500* in 1970. *Sotheby's*

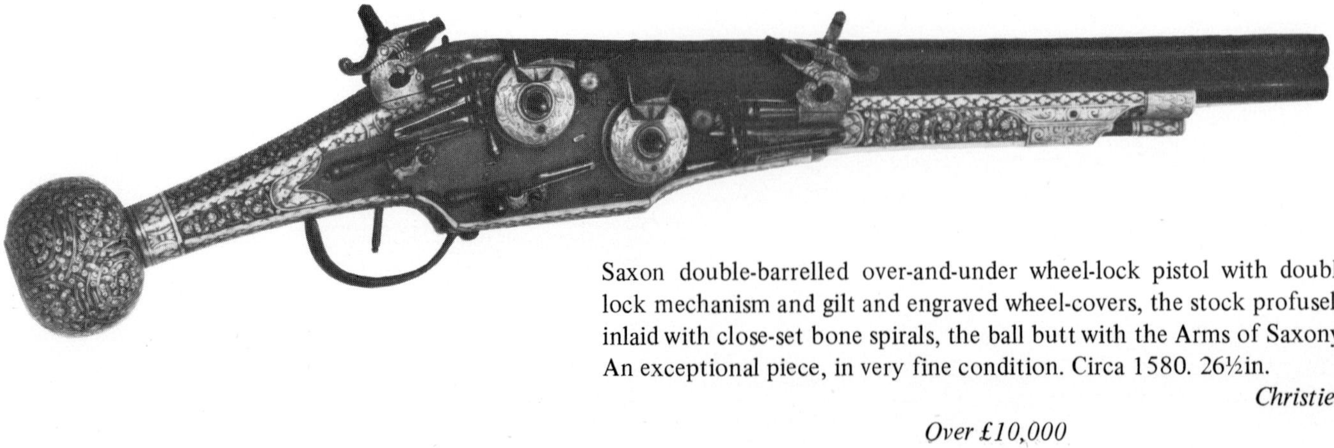

Saxon double-barrelled over-and-under wheel-lock pistol with double lock mechanism and gilt and engraved wheel-covers, the stock profusely inlaid with close-set bone spirals, the ball butt with the Arms of Saxony. An exceptional piece, in very fine condition. Circa 1580. 26½in. *Christie's*

Over £10,000

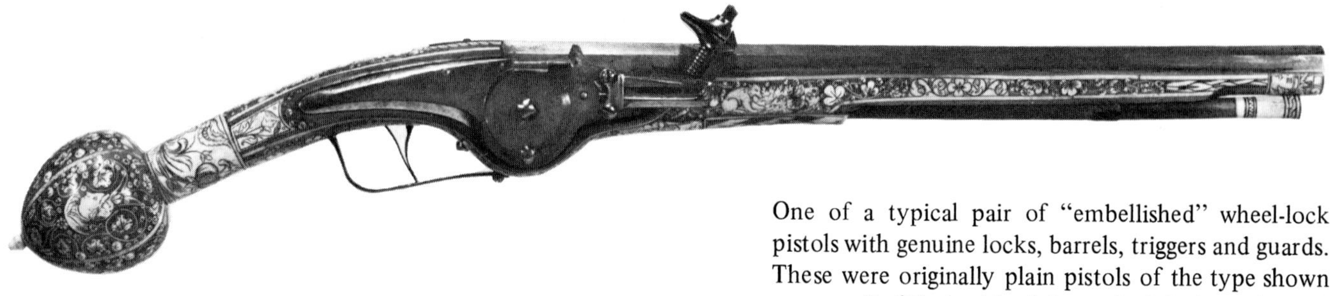

One of a typical pair of "embellished" wheel-lock pistols with genuine locks, barrels, triggers and guards. These were originally plain pistols of the type shown on page 8, fitted with elaborately inlaid stocks and lemon-shaped pommels during the 19th century or later. Note thin grip of circular section. Good condition. 25in. *Christie's*

Decorative value only, £1,000 – £1,300 the pair

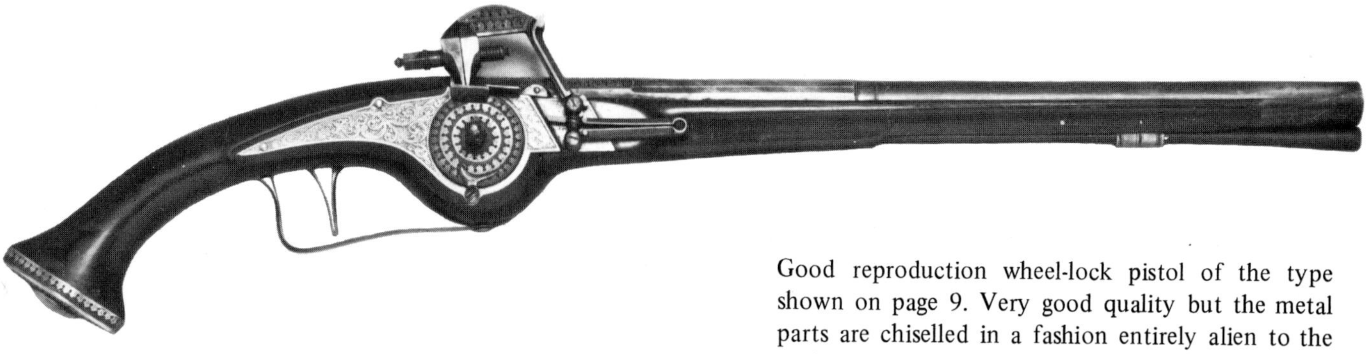

Good reproduction wheel-lock pistol of the type shown on page 9. Very good quality but the metal parts are chiselled in a fashion entirely alien to the 17th century. Fine condition. 23½in.

Knight, Frank & Rutley

£400 – £500

Snaphaunce Pistols

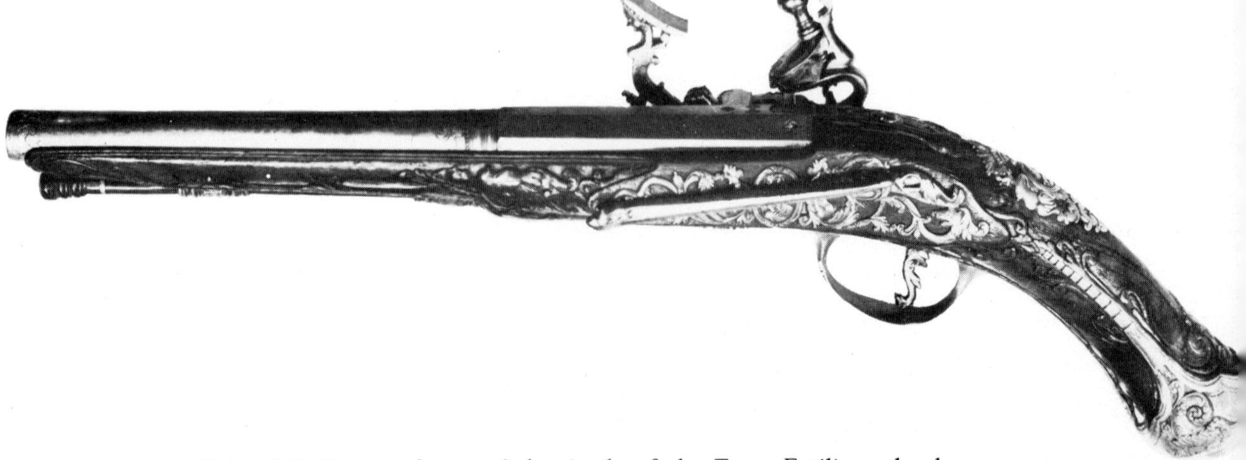

Pair of Italian snaphaunce belt pistols of the Tusco-Emilian school, fitted with Brescian barrels stamped with the mark of Gerolimo Mutti of Gardone. The locks signed Il Negroni (on one) and Brento (on the other). Carved walnut stocks and brass mounts, decorated with profile heads and terminal figures, the locks of steel finely chiselled en suite, Fine quality and condition. Probably late 17th century. 14¼in. Similar examples have chiselled steel furniture. *Sotheby's*

About £2,000 the pair

The price depends on the quality and the density of chiselled designs, also signature and date, usually on the inside of the lock-plate.

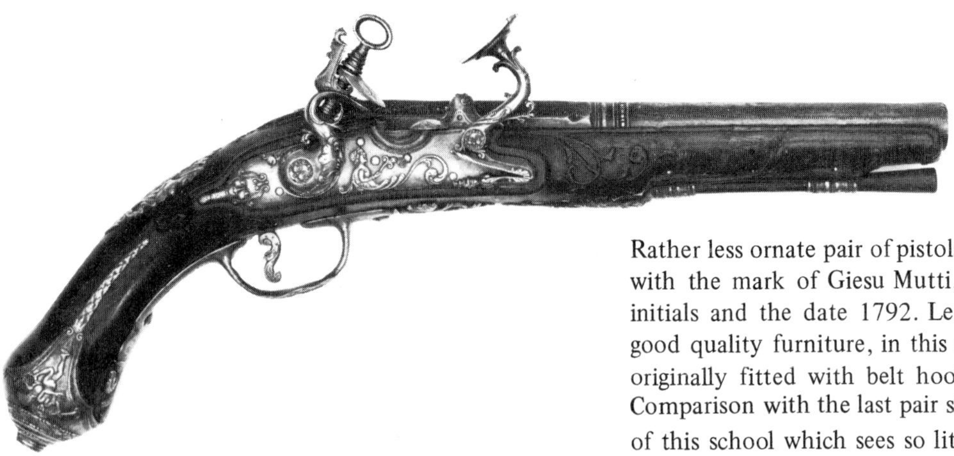

Rather less ornate pair of pistols of the same school, the barrels stamped with the mark of Giesu Mutti, the locks signed on the inside with his initials and the date 1792. Less elaborately carved walnut stocks, but good quality furniture, in this case of chiselled steel. Both pistols were originally fitted with belt hooks. Good quality and condition, 13½in. Comparison with the last pair shows how difficult it is to date examples of this school which sees so little change in a period of more than 100 years. *Sotheby's*

About £1,500 the pair

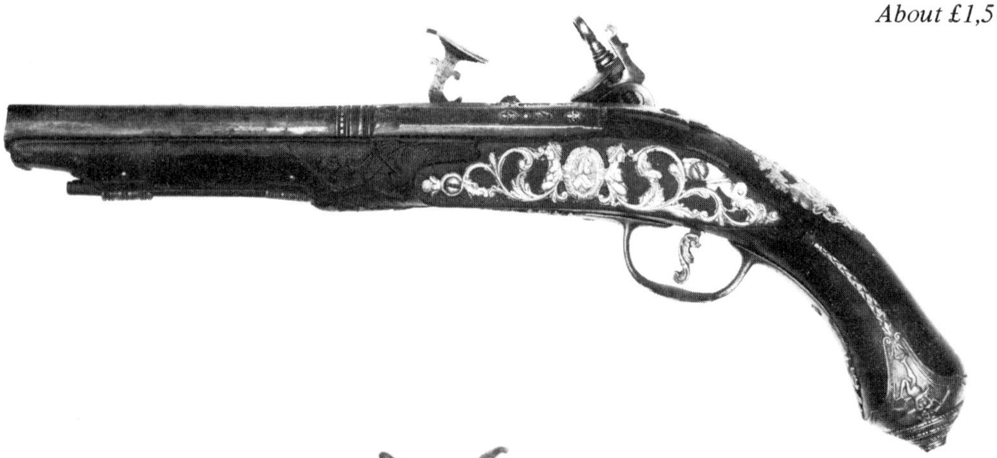

Small snaphaunce pistol showing the final development of the school, the lock with very little chiselling and dated 1826 on the inside. Walnut full stock with sparsely engraved steel furniture. Good quality and condition. 8½in. *Christie's*

£200 – £300

Central Italian snaphaunce belt pistol by Giovanni Beretta of Brescia. A long-barrelled version of the above. Lightly carved walnut stock with chiselled steel mounts. Good quality and condition. Probably late 17th century/early 18th century, but not dated. 19¼in. *Christie's*

£800 – £1,000, partly on the merit of the maker, still represented today.

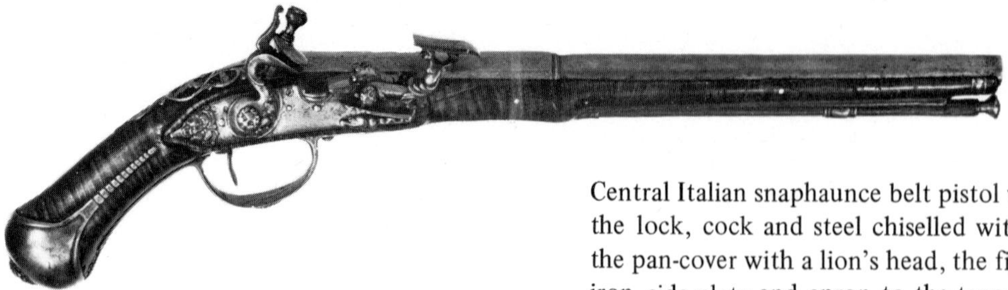

Central Italian snaphaunce belt pistol with barrel in two stages, the lock, cock and steel chiselled with masks and figures and the pan-cover with a lion's head, the figured stock with pierced iron side-plate and apron to the tang, the pommel and trigger-guard each with applied chiselled grotesque mask. Good quality and condition. Probably early 18th century, perhaps later. 18½ins. *Christie's*

About £800

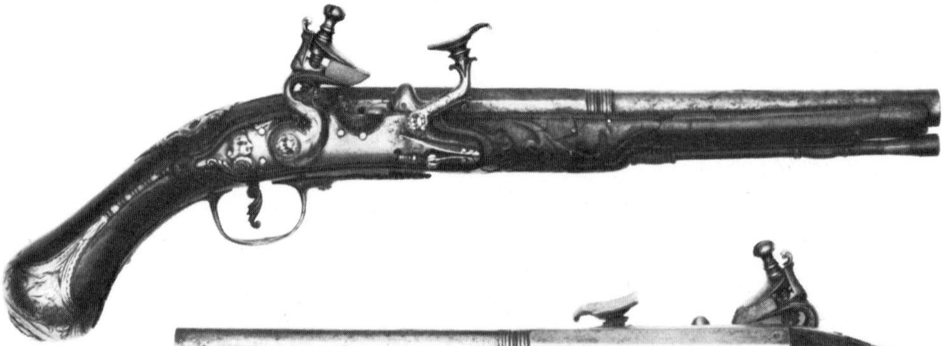

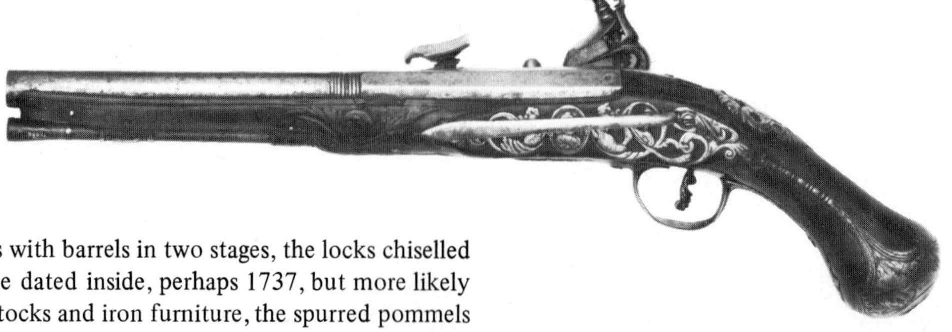

Pair of Tuscan belt pistols with barrels in two stages, the locks chiselled with profile heads and one dated inside, perhaps 1737, but more likely 1787. Carved walnut full stocks and iron furniture, the spurred pommels terminating in portrait heads. Good to fine quality, but several imperfections. 14in. *Sotheby's*

About £1,000 the pair

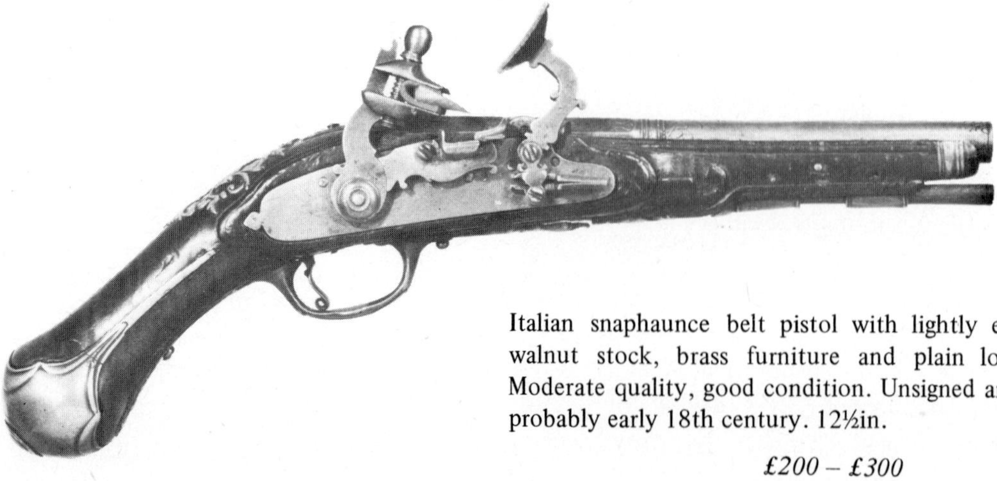

Italian snaphaunce belt pistol with lightly engraved barrel, walnut stock, brass furniture and plain lock mechanism. Moderate quality, good condition. Unsigned and undated, but probably early 18th century. 12½in. *Christie's*

£200 – £300

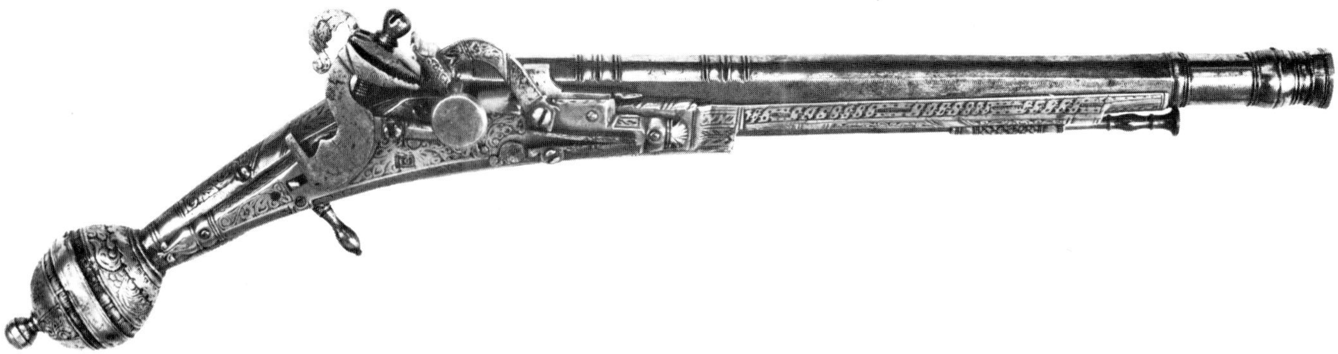

Scottish snaphaunce belt pistol with banded barrel faceted at the breech, the lock and stock of brass engraved with interlaced strapwork and foliate ornament, ovoid pommel. Fine quality, minor restorations. Signed IG (Gray of Dundee), about 1630. 17¼in. *Sotheby's*

Over £7,000. Extremely rare.

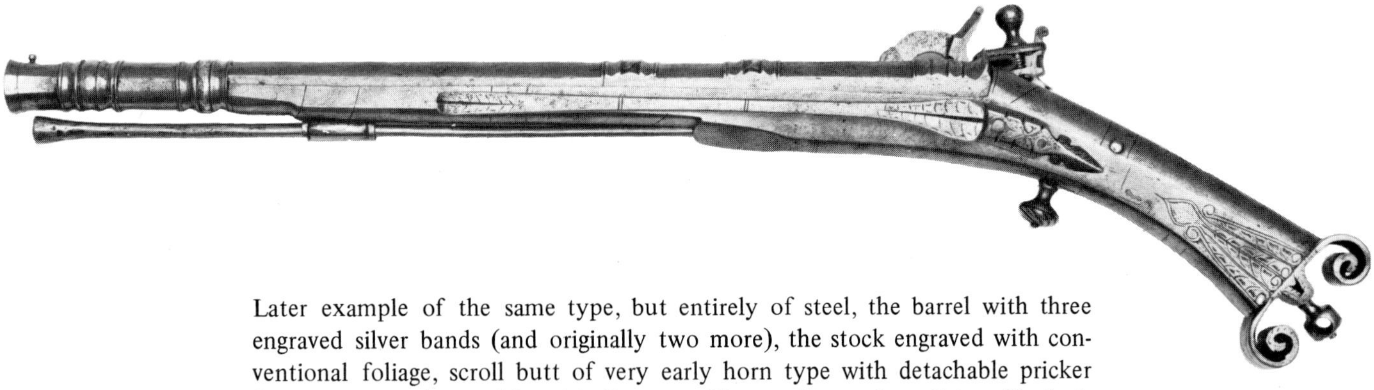

Later example of the same type, but entirely of steel, the barrel with three engraved silver bands (and originally two more), the stock engraved with conventional foliage, scroll butt of very early horn type with detachable pricker (cf. later Scottish pistols) and ball trigger. Fine quality and condition. The lock signed JS, possibly for John Stuart of Aberdeen, and dated 1683 on the circular fence to the pan. 20in. *Sotheby's*

About £5,000

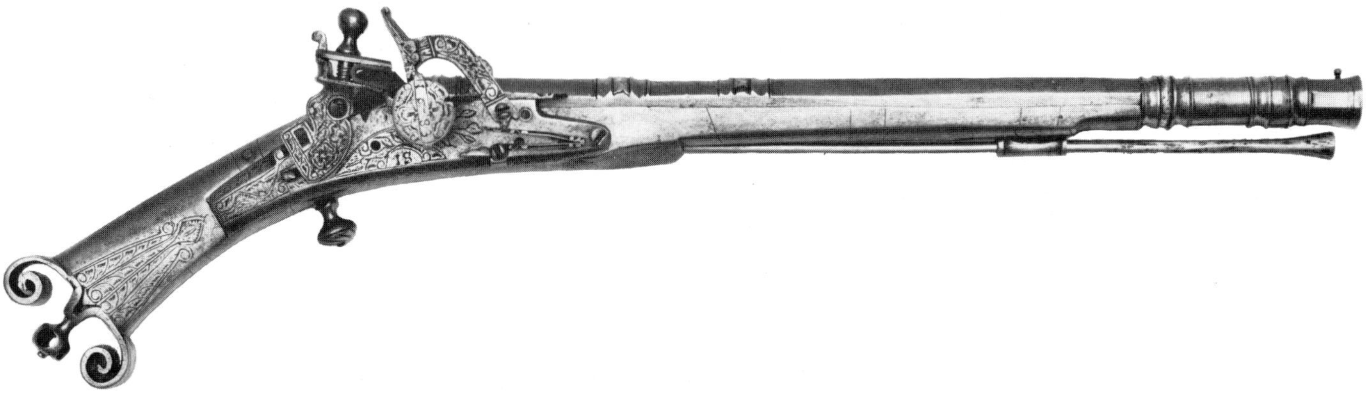

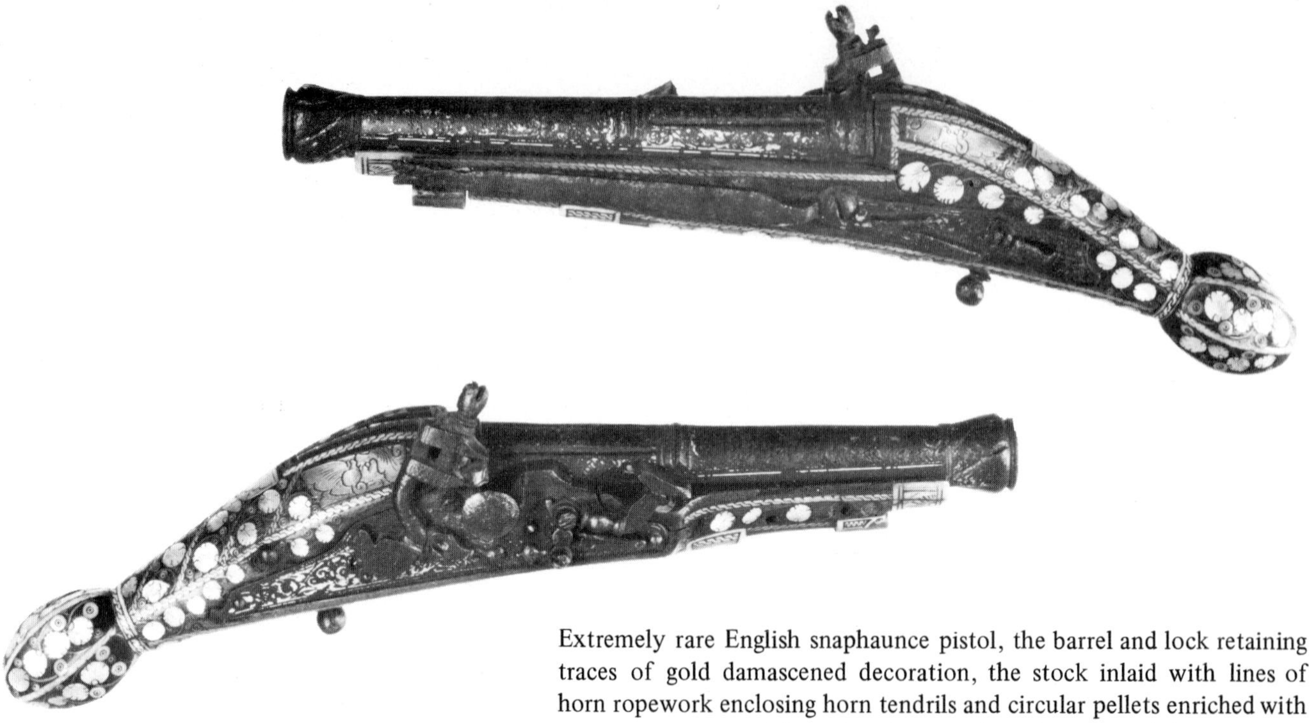

Extremely rare English snaphaunce pistol, the barrel and lock retaining traces of gold damascened decoration, the stock inlaid with lines of horn ropework enclosing horn tendrils and circular pellets enriched with numerous leaves and flowerheads in mother-of-pearl, with fluted lemon-shaped pommel en suite. Fine quality, imperfect, but untouched condition. Late 16th/early 17th century. 11¼in. *Christie's*

Over £10,000

19th century copy of a Scottish snaphaunce pistol, the stock and left-hand lock of engraved brass. Signed "R.G. Edr." and dated 1615 on the fence of the pan. 18in.
This pistol is of interest as it is a signed forgery of an earlier piece. It was made by Robert Glen (1835-1910/11), a bagpipe maker who established the firm of J. & R. Glen in 1866-7 at 2 North Bank Street, Edinburgh. Robert Glen produced numerous forgeries of Scottish weapons.
Wallis & Wallis

£500–£700

Miquelet-Lock Pistols

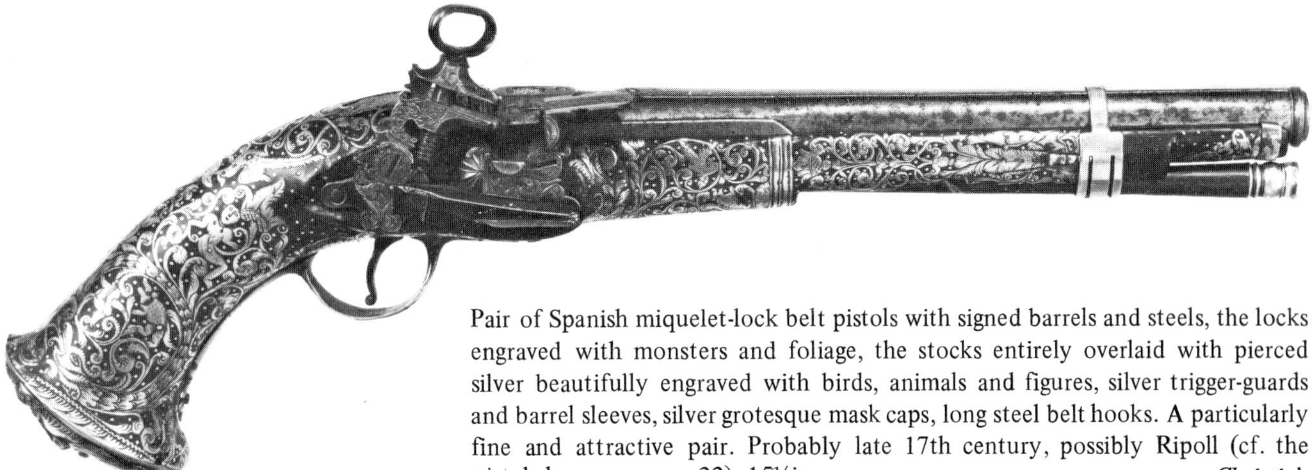

Pair of Spanish miquelet-lock belt pistols with signed barrels and steels, the locks engraved with monsters and foliage, the stocks entirely overlaid with pierced silver beautifully engraved with birds, animals and figures, silver trigger-guards and barrel sleeves, silver grotesque mask caps, long steel belt hooks. A particularly fine and attractive pair. Probably late 17th century, possibly Ripoll (cf. the pistol shown on page 22). 15½in. *Christie's*

Over £4,000.

Very rare. Less for a pair with brass inlay. Examples with this type of silver inlay were made up to about 1800.

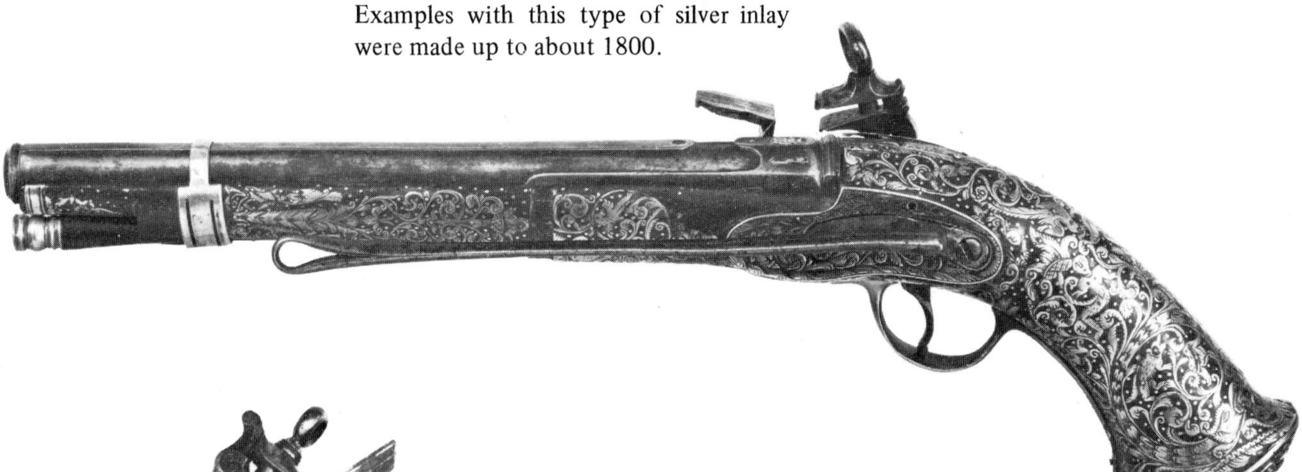

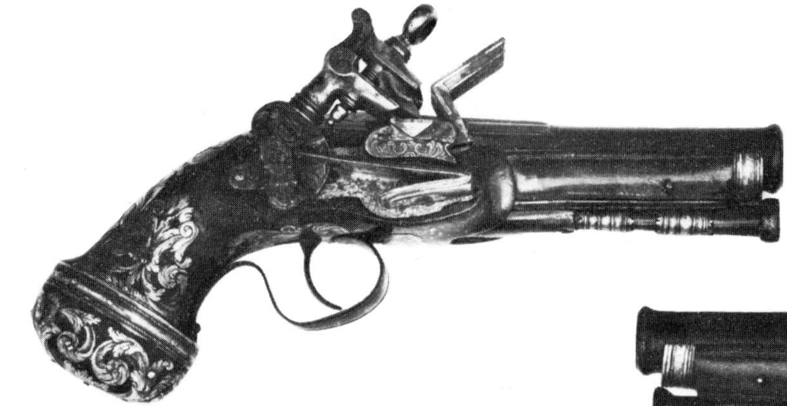

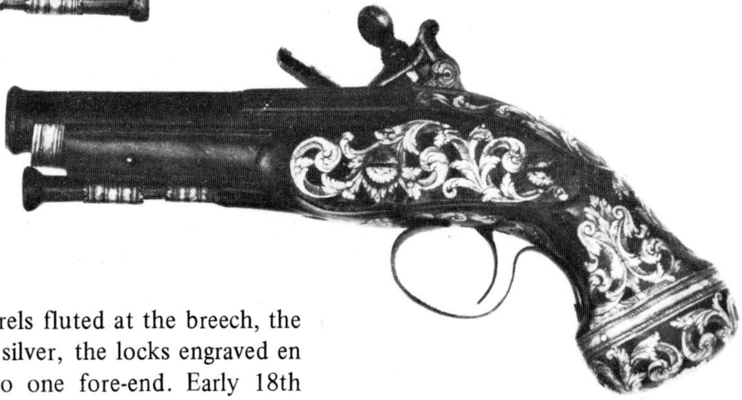

Pair of Ripoll miquelet-lock small pistols, the barrels fluted at the breech, the walnut full stocks inlaid with scrolling foliage in silver, the locks engraved en suite. Good quality and condition, but repair to one fore-end. Early 18th century. 8½in. *Sotheby's*

Over £1,000

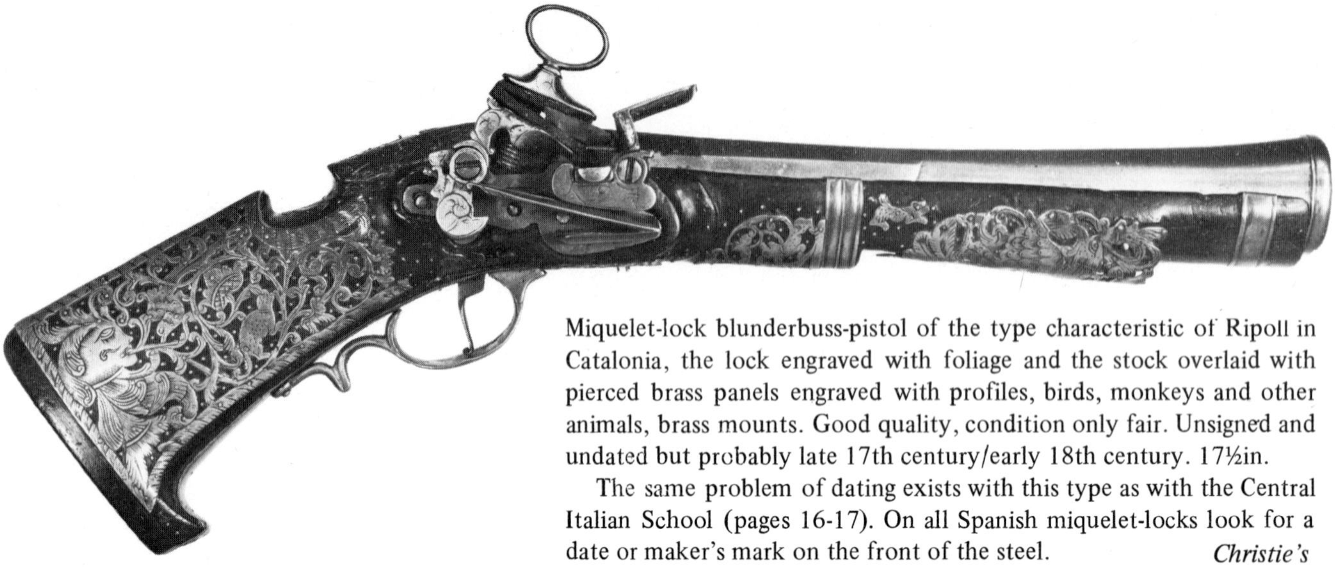

Miquelet-lock blunderbuss-pistol of the type characteristic of Ripoll in Catalonia, the lock engraved with foliage and the stock overlaid with pierced brass panels engraved with profiles, birds, monkeys and other animals, brass mounts. Good quality, condition only fair. Unsigned and undated but probably late 17th century/early 18th century. 17½in.

The same problem of dating exists with this type as with the Central Italian School (pages 16-17). On all Spanish miquelet-locks look for a date or maker's mark on the front of the steel. *Christie's*

£600 – £1,000

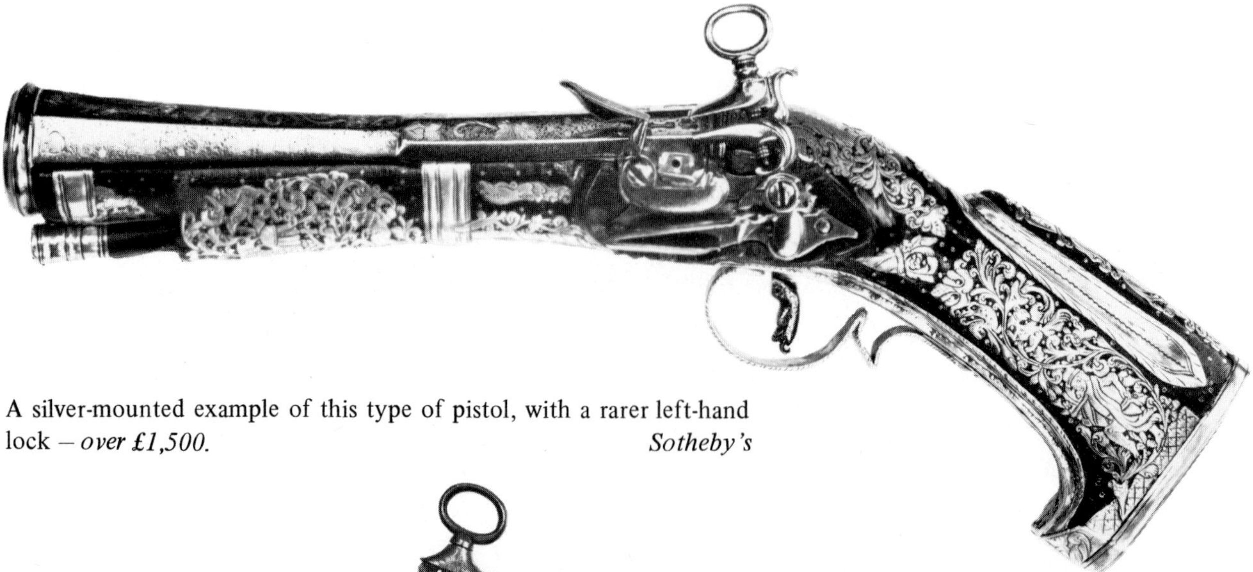

A silver-mounted example of this type of pistol, with a rarer left-hand lock – *over £1,500.* *Sotheby's*

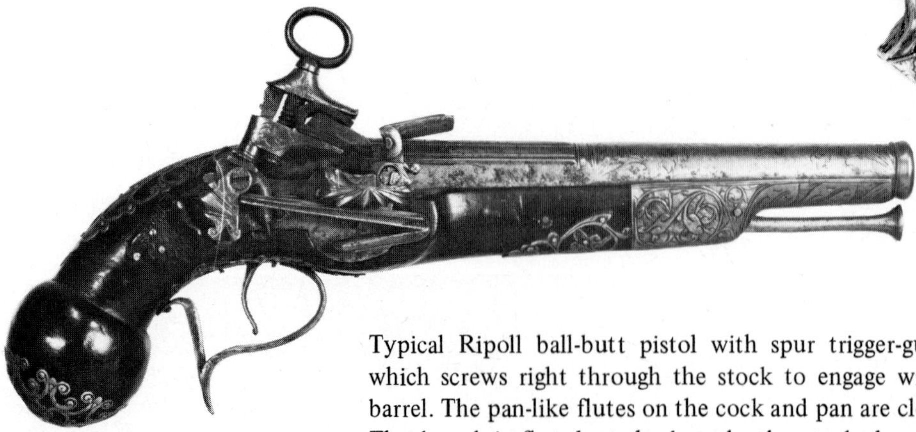

Typical Ripoll ball-butt pistol with spur trigger-guard, the front of which screws right through the stock to engage with the tang of the barrel. The pan-like flutes on the cock and pan are clear Ripoll pointers. The barrel is fluted at the breech, the stock decorated with pierced brass, the steel is stamped "Carbo" and engraved "Ripoll". Good quality and condition. Probably late 17th century, but similar pistols date from 100 years later. 11½in. *Christie's*

£400 – £800

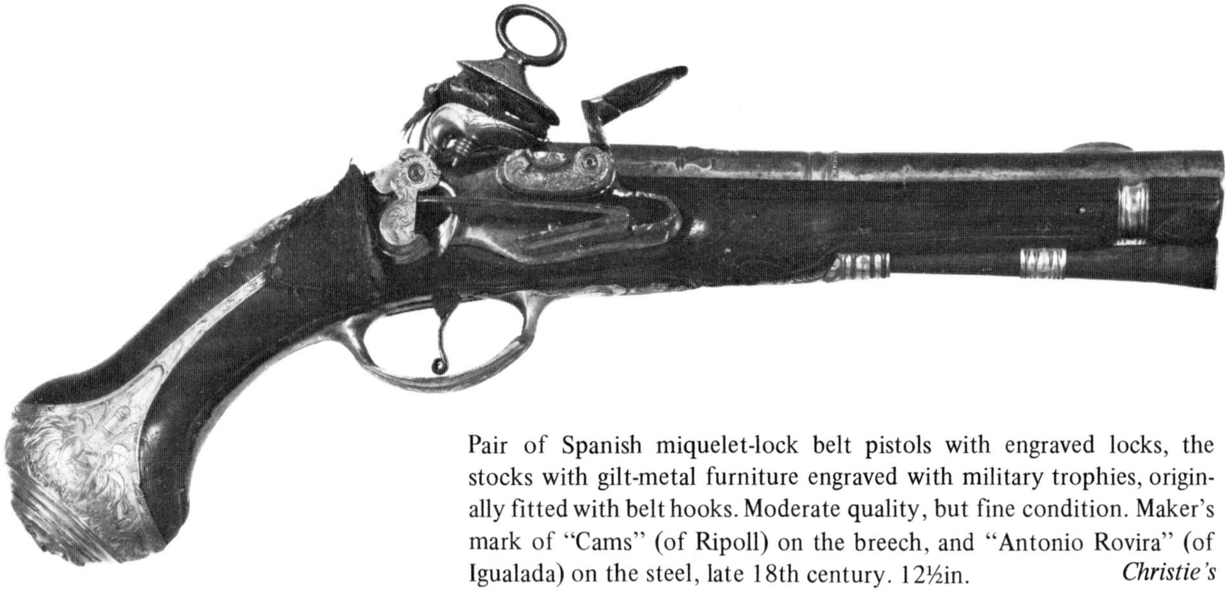

Pair of Spanish miquelet-lock belt pistols with engraved locks, the stocks with gilt-metal furniture engraved with military trophies, originally fitted with belt hooks. Moderate quality, but fine condition. Maker's mark of "Cams" (of Ripoll) on the breech, and "Antonio Rovira" (of Igualada) on the steel, late 18th century. 12½in. *Christie's*

Over £1,000

Spanish pistols and guns are found with a variety of gold maker's stamps ("punzones") on the lock, barrel and trigger-guard. Sometimes the maker's name is inscribed in gold letters on the barrel as well. These marks add to the value according to the merit of the maker and the key signature is usually to be found on the lock, a position apparently reserved for the man who assembled the weapon.

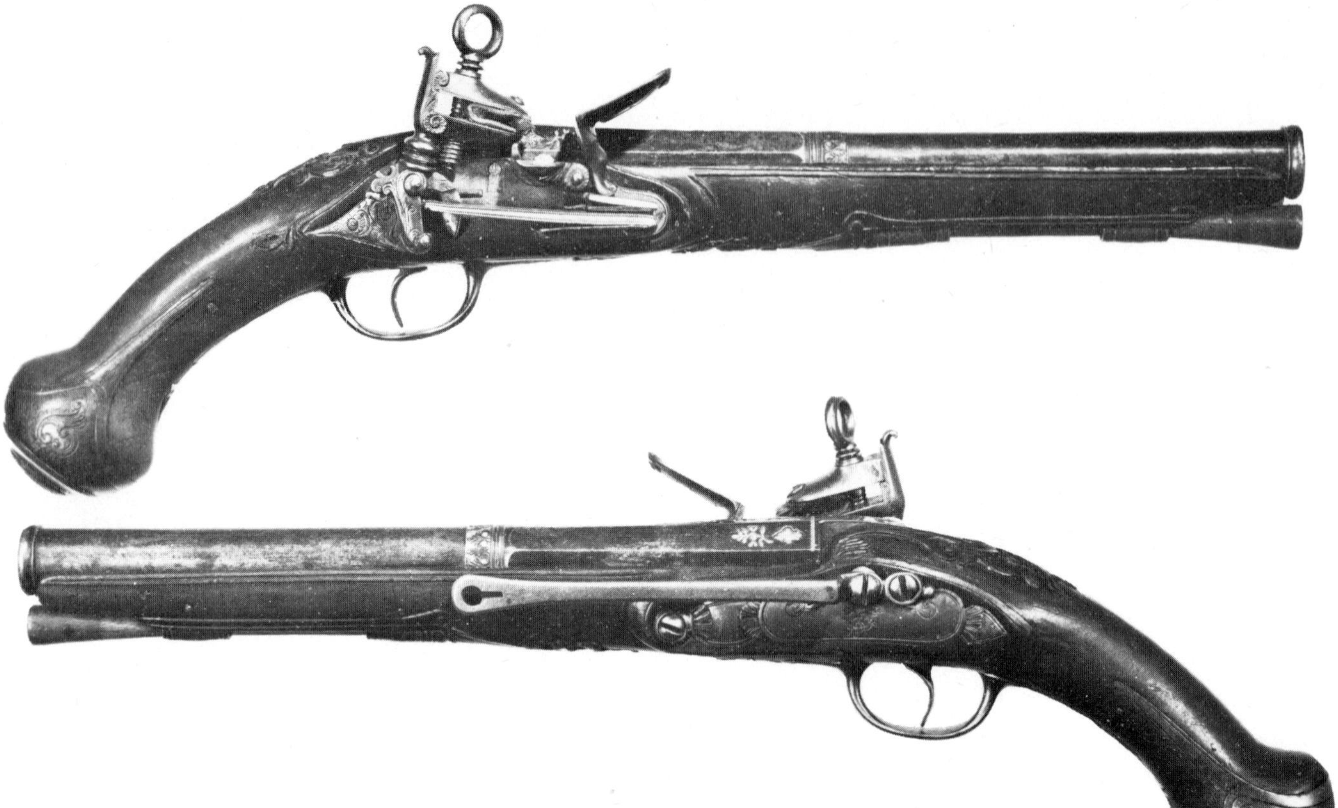

Pair of Spanish miquelet-lock belt pistols with typical barrels in two stages (called "Spanish form" after this type of pistol) with gold stamps at the breech and a chiselled girdle nearly half-way towards the muzzle. Lightly carved walnut stocks with engraved and partly chiselled steel furniture. Fine condition, good to fine quality. The barrels by Agostino Bustindui and the locks by Guisasola, late 18th century. 16¼in. *Christie's*

Over £1,000

One of a pair of Spanish miquelet-lock holster pistols of lesser quality, fitted with brass furniture. Condition less good than above, but the original barrel plugs sometimes found on Spanish pistols are an attractive feature. The barrels signed "Artura Echeberria", late 18th century. 16in. *Christie's*

About £1,000 the pair

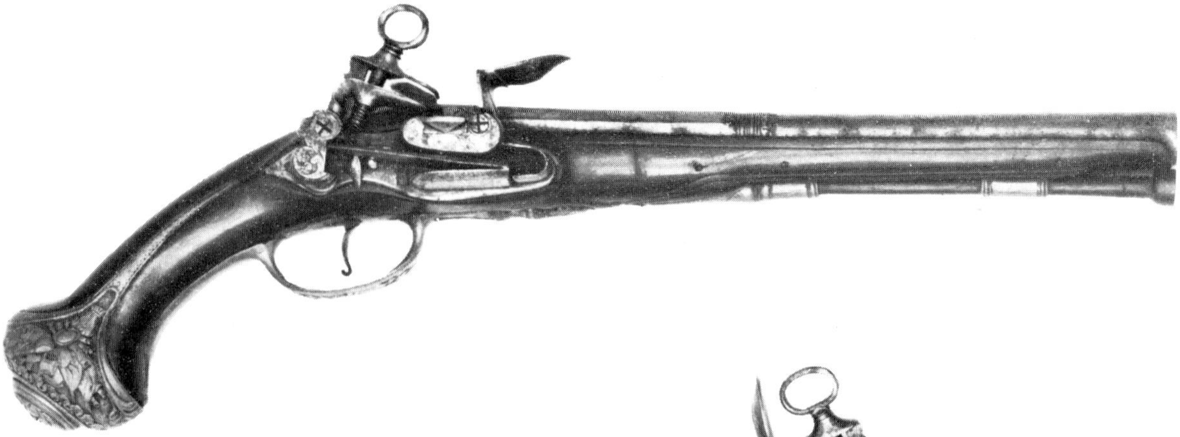

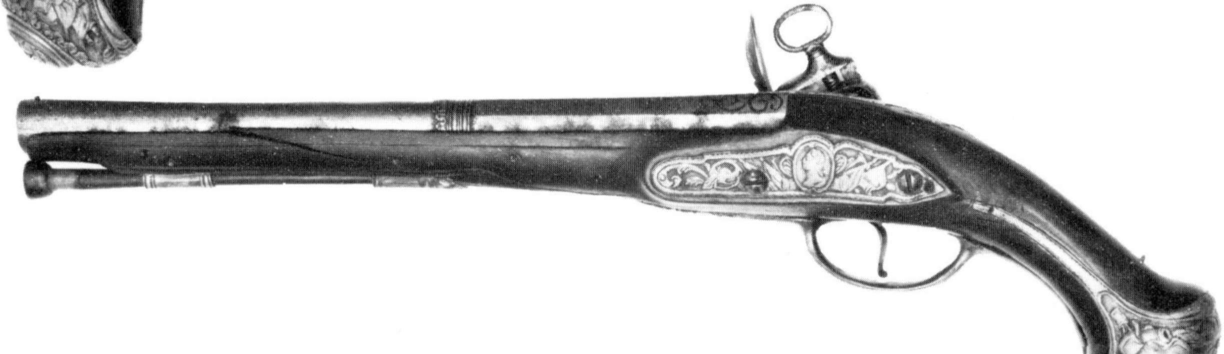

Pair of Spanish miquelet-lock holster pistols, the barrels with the mark of Eũdal Pous, the locks signed "Deop". Full stocks with brass mounts of poor to fair quality decorated with portrait medallions and military trophies. Condition only fair. Late 18th century. 17½in. *Sotheby's*

About £800 the pair

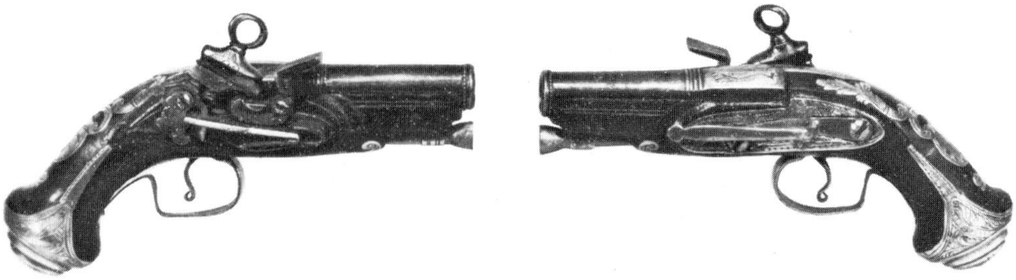

Pair of Spanish small miquelet-lock pistols with barrels of standard form inlaid with brass strips, the stocks decorated with coarsely engraved brass. Moderate quality, good condition. Provincial manufacture, late 18th century. 6¾in.

Christie's

£350 – £450 the pair

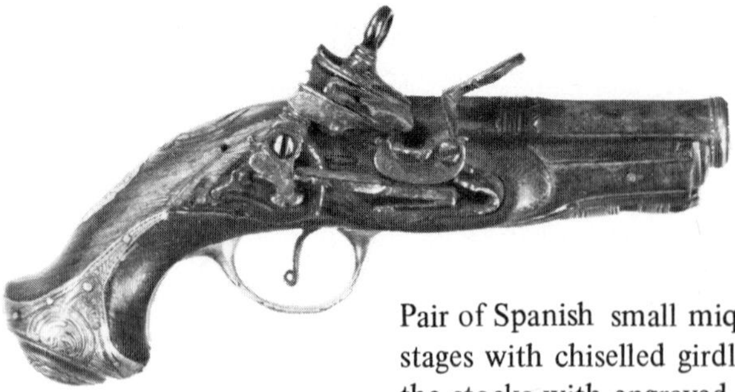

Pair of Spanish small miquelet-lock pistols, the barrels in two stages with chiselled girdle and inlaid with silver at the breech, the stocks with engraved brass mounts decorated with applied silver medallions typical of Barcelona (cf. page 25). Moderate quality, good uncleaned condition. Second half of the 18th century. $7\frac{1}{8}$in. *Christie's*

£400 – £500

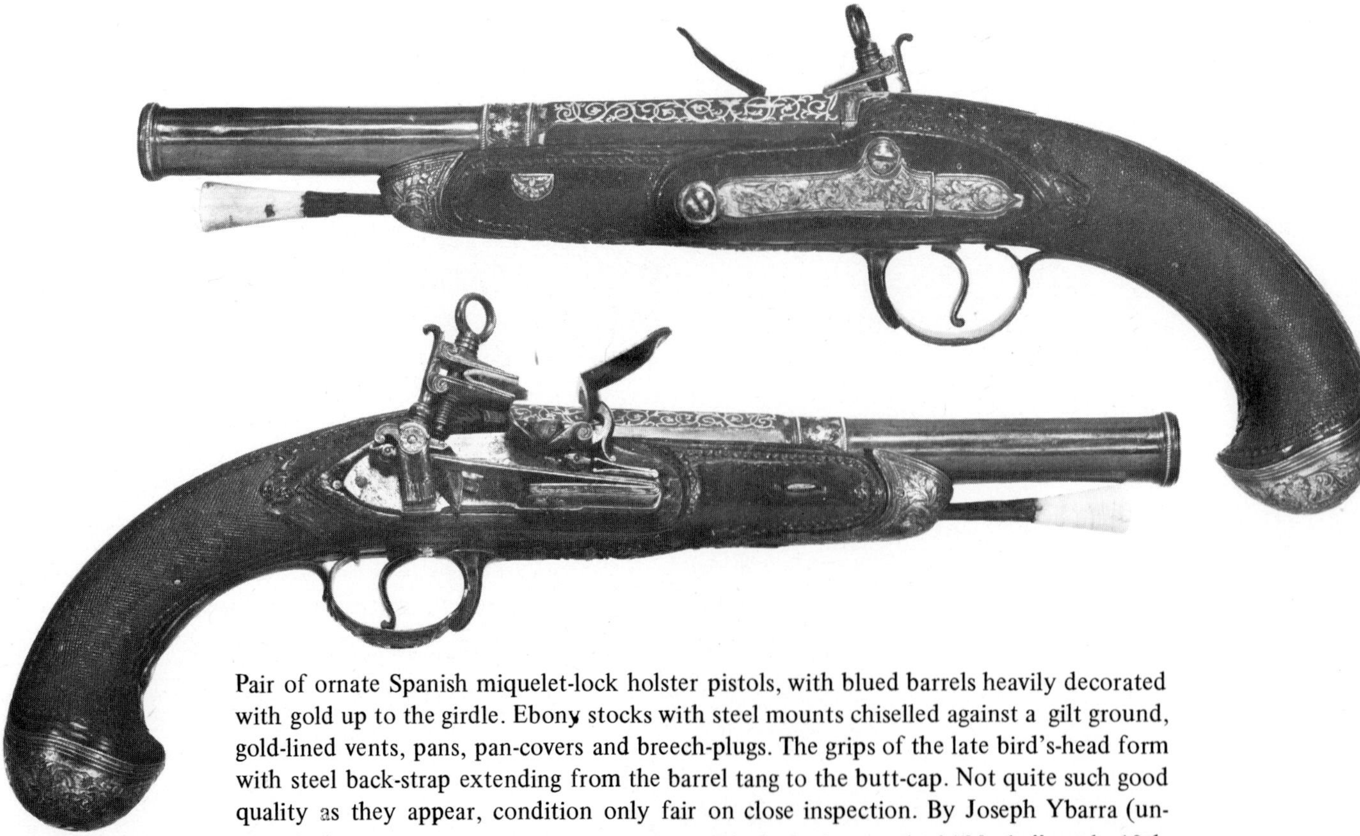

Pair of ornate Spanish miquelet-lock holster pistols, with blued barrels heavily decorated with gold up to the girdle. Ebony stocks with steel mounts chiselled against a gilt ground, gold-lined vents, pans, pan-covers and breech-plugs. The grips of the late bird's-head form with steel back-strap extending from the barrel tang to the butt-cap. Not quite such good quality as they appear, condition only fair on close inspection. By Joseph Ybarra (unrecorded), gold mark on breech and trigger-guard, the locks inscribed "Meabe", early 19th century. 15in. *Christie's*

About £2,000

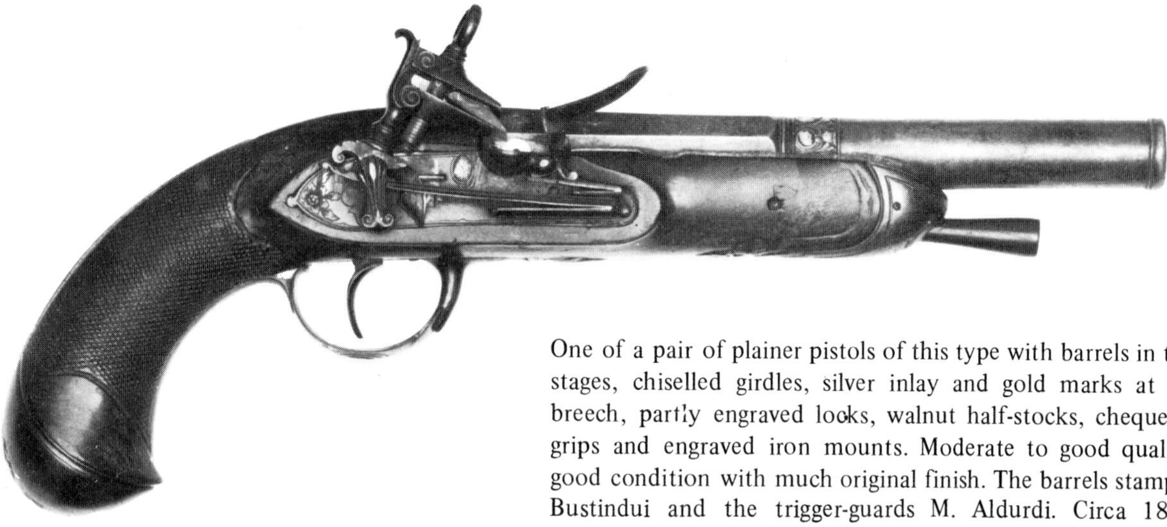

One of a pair of plainer pistols of this type with barrels in two stages, chiselled girdles, silver inlay and gold marks at the breech, partly engraved locks, walnut half-stocks, chequered grips and engraved iron mounts. Moderate to good quality, good condition with much original finish. The barrels stamped Bustindui and the trigger-guards M. Aldurdi. Circa 1820. 13¼in. *Sotheby's*

£500 – £600 the pair

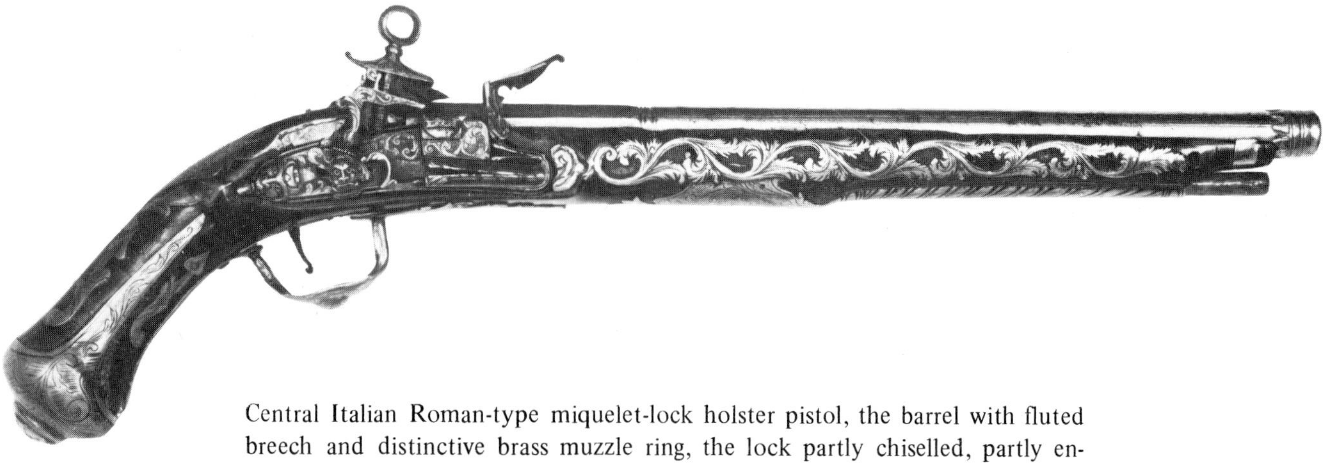

Central Italian Roman-type miquelet-lock holster pistol, the barrel with fluted breech and distinctive brass muzzle ring, the lock partly chiselled, partly engraved, the stock decorated with panels of engraved brass, brass furniture with mask applied to the pommel and trigger-guard. Moderate quality, good condition. Can only be dated to the 18th century, unless signed or dated inside the lock. 19½in. *Sotheby's*

£500 – £750

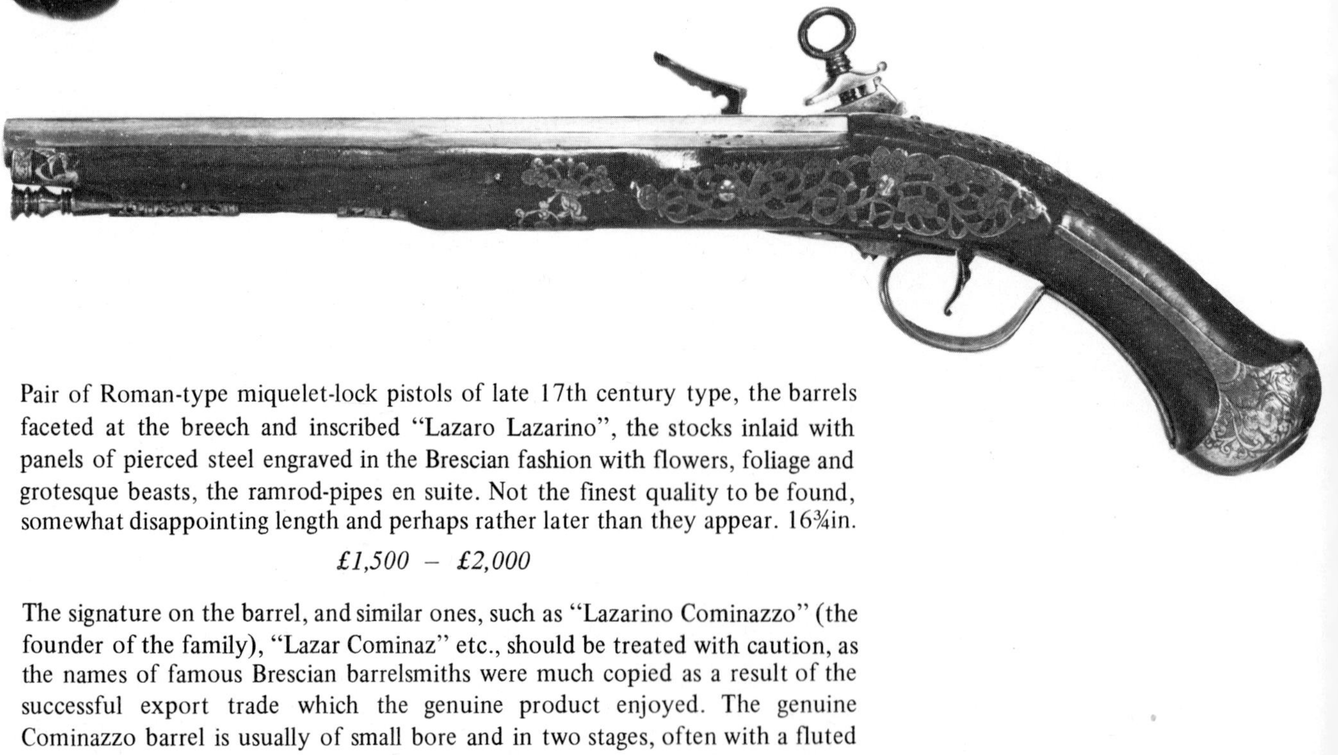

Pair of Roman-type miquelet-lock pistols of late 17th century type, the barrels faceted at the breech and inscribed "Lazaro Lazarino", the stocks inlaid with panels of pierced steel engraved in the Brescian fashion with flowers, foliage and grotesque beasts, the ramrod-pipes en suite. Not the finest quality to be found, somewhat disappointing length and perhaps rather later than they appear. 16¾in.

£1,500 – £2,000

The signature on the barrel, and similar ones, such as "Lazarino Cominazzo" (the founder of the family), "Lazar Cominaz" etc., should be treated with caution, as the names of famous Brescian barrelsmiths were much copied as a result of the successful export trade which the genuine product enjoyed. The genuine Cominazzo barrel is usually of small bore and in two stages, often with a fluted breech. The signature is accompanied by trefoil punches and is more often stamped than engraved. *Christie's*

Flintlock Pistols - 1650 - 1700

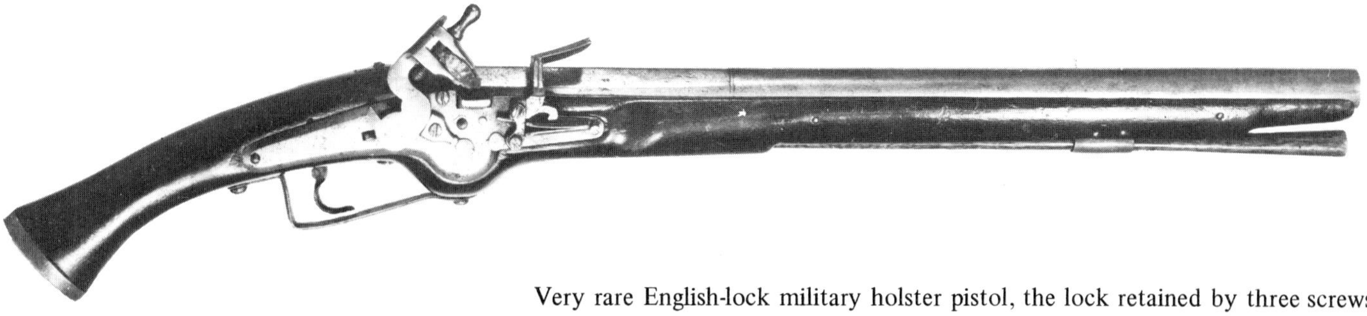

Very rare English-lock military holster pistol, the lock retained by three screws and fitted with a laterally operating sear as well as a buffer for the cock. Note the wheel-lock shape of the lock-plate. Plain stock and iron mounts, the stock in this case replaced. 23½in. Circa 1640. *Christie's*

About £500 owing to replaced stock.

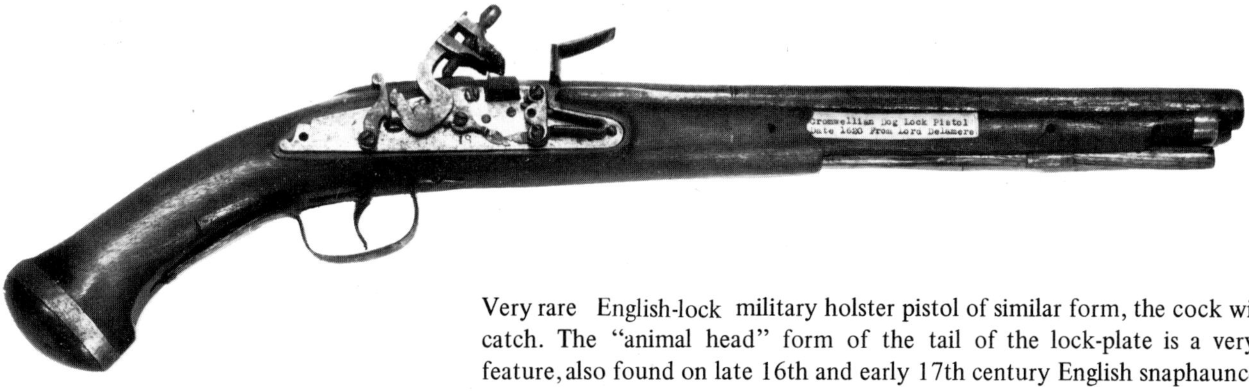

Very rare English-lock military holster pistol of similar form, the cock with dog catch. The "animal head" form of the tail of the lock-plate is a very early feature, also found on late 16th and early 17th century English snaphaunces. Untouched condition. Circa 1630-40 21in. This pistol is supposed to have been the first pistol used in the British Army. *Sotheby's*

£1,400 – £1,700

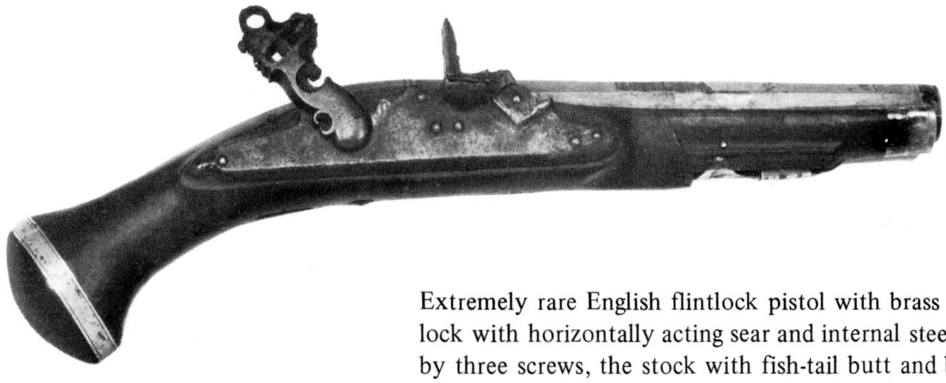

Extremely rare English flintlock pistol with brass octagonal barrel, the lock with horizontally acting sear and internal steel-spring and retained by three screws, the stock with fish-tail butt and brass mounts, button trigger without guard. Circa 1640. Good condition. 11½in. *Sotheby's*

About £600

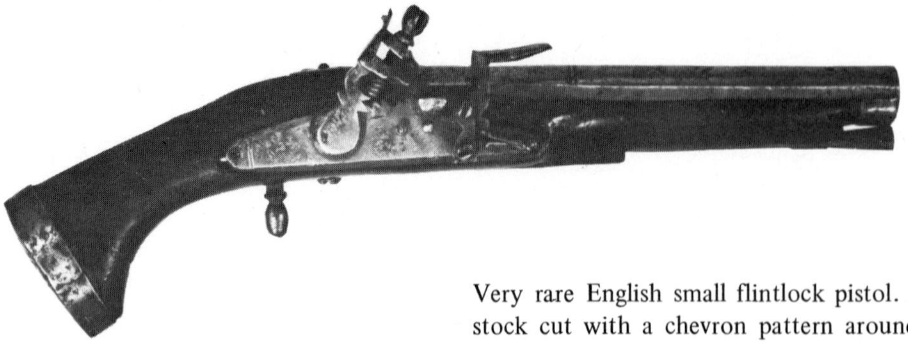

Very rare English small flintlock pistol. Flat lock secured by three screws, fu stock cut with a chevron pattern around the barrel tang, button trigger, iro band around the butt and fore-end. Poor condition. Mid-17th century c slightly later. 11¾in. *Christie*

About £400

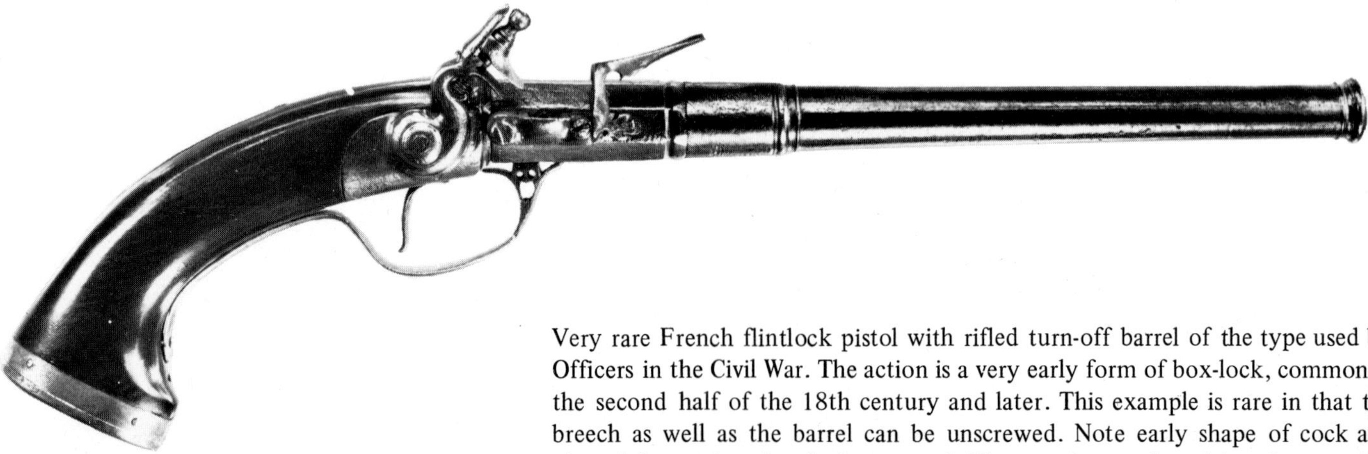

Very rare French flintlock pistol with rifled turn-off barrel of the type used b Officers in the Civil War. The action is a very early form of box-lock, common i the second half of the 18th century and later. This example is rare in that th breech as well as the barrel can be unscrewed. Note early shape of cock an pierced forward angle of trigger-guard. The wooden stock and iron butt-cap a later replacements. Signed Des Granges à Paris, circa 1660. 16in. *Christie*

About £400

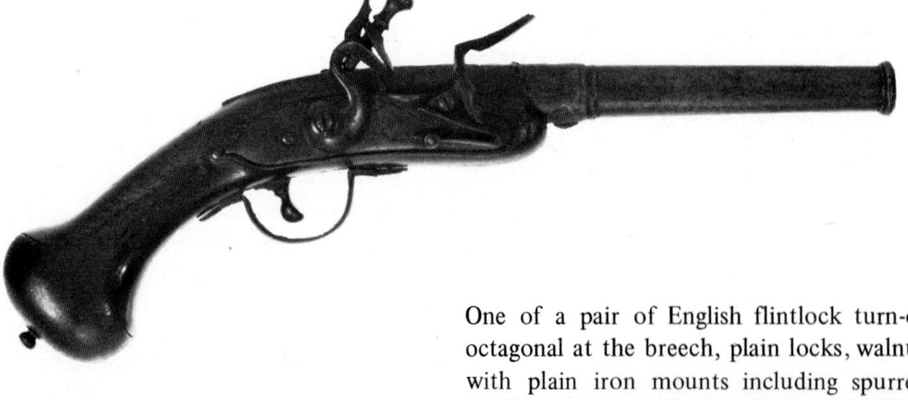

One of a pair of English flintlock turn-off pistols with rifled cannon barre octagonal at the breech, plain locks, walnut half-stocks moulded at the tang ar with plain iron mounts including spurred pommels with button finial, ar scroll side-plates. These pistols originally had button triggers without guard Moderate quality, fair condition. London, circa 1660. 12in. *Christi*

About £600 the pair. Very rare.

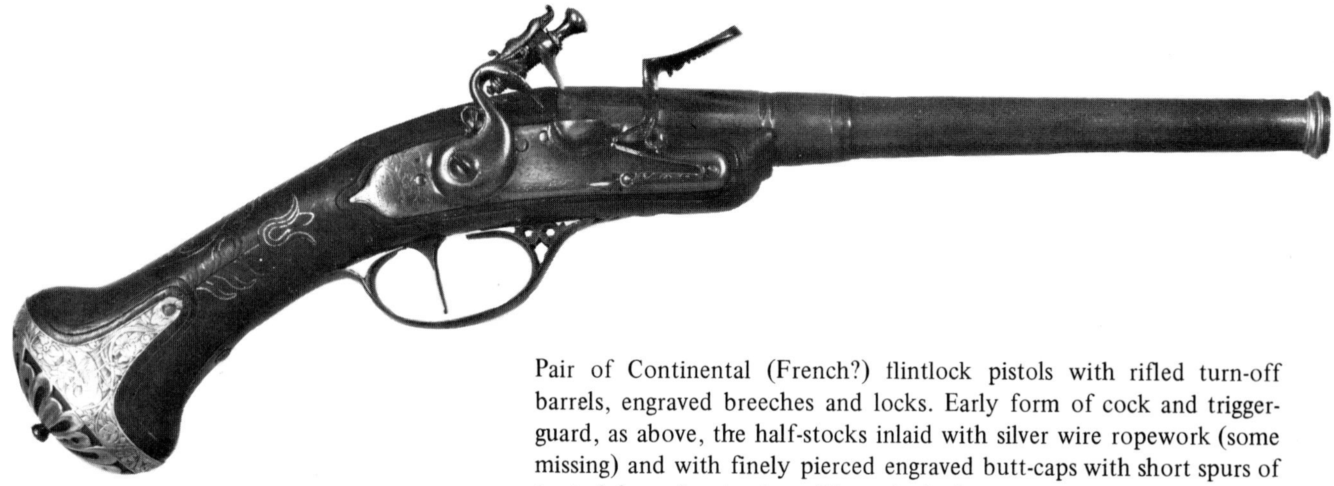

Pair of Continental (French?) flintlock pistols with rifled turn-off barrels, engraved breeches and locks. Early form of cock and trigger-guard, as above, the half-stocks inlaid with silver wire ropework (some missing) and with finely pierced engraved butt-caps with short spurs of typical form for the date. Through the butt-caps can be seen the blued liners over which they are set. Fine quality, good condition. By A. Lesconné, circa 1650. 16in. *Christie's*

About £3,000 the pair

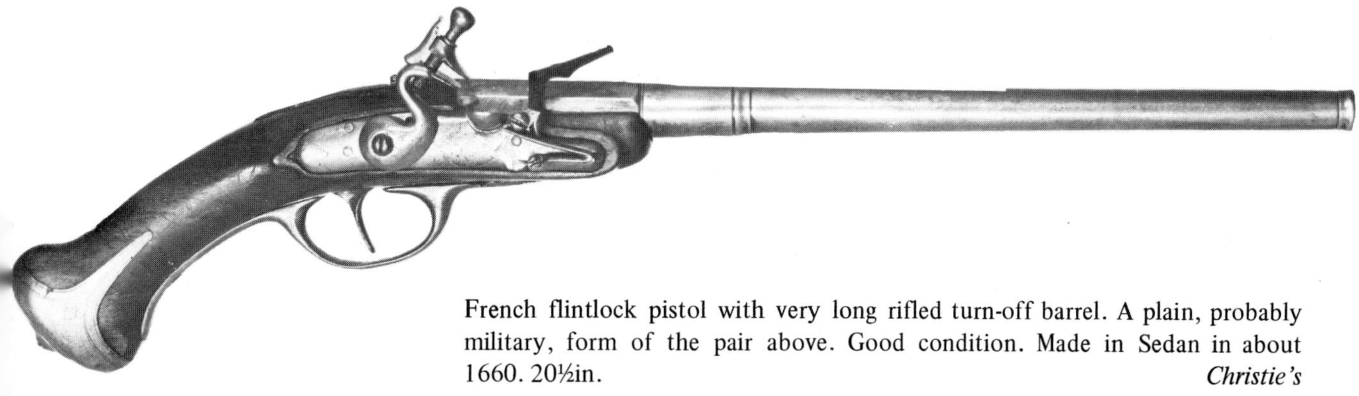

French flintlock pistol with very long rifled turn-off barrel. A plain, probably military, form of the pair above. Good condition. Made in Sedan in about 1660. 20½in. *Christie's*

£600 – £700

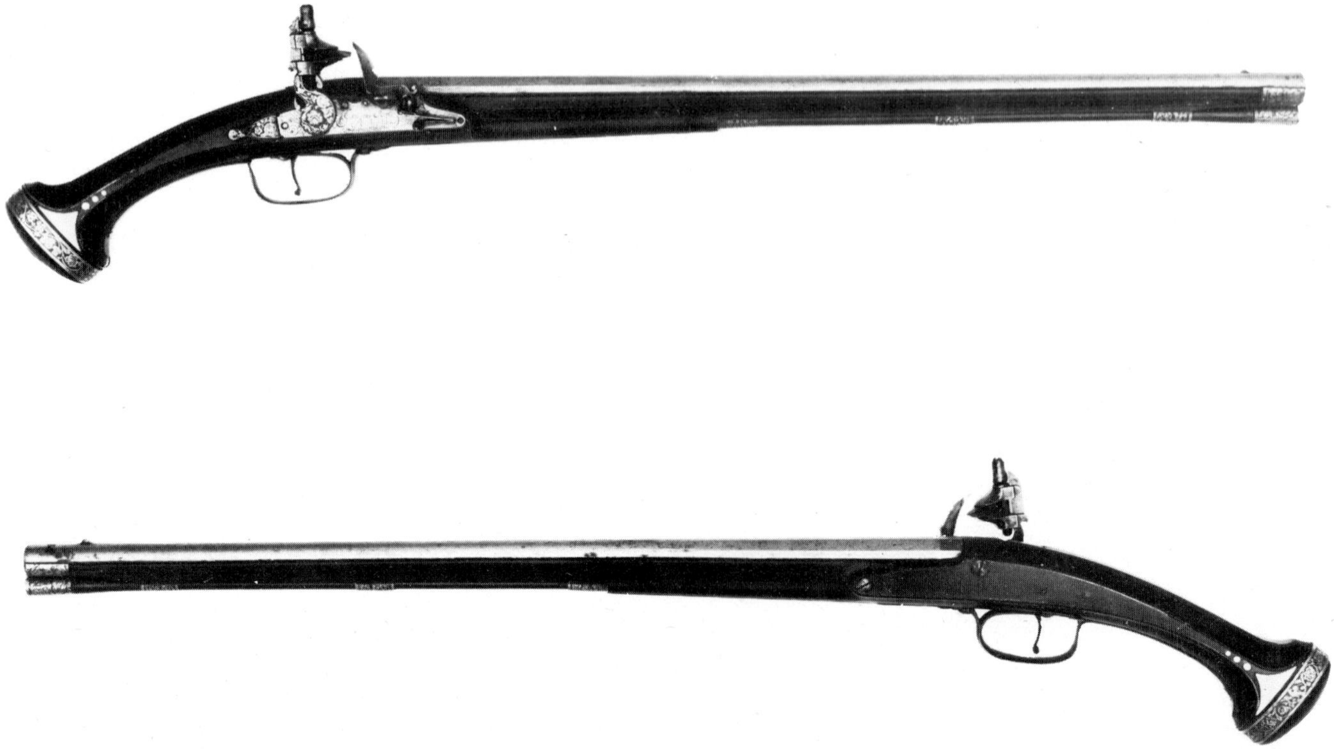

Exceptional pair of Dutch long flintlock holster pistols, the locks engraved with scrolls and a dragon, the ebony full stocks inlaid with twisted silver lines and with silver mounts finely engraved with flowers and scrolls, flattened butts and iron trigger-guards. Outstanding quality, fine condition. By Jan Aerts of Maastricht, circa 1650/60. 28¾in. *Renwick Collection*

About £20,000 the pair

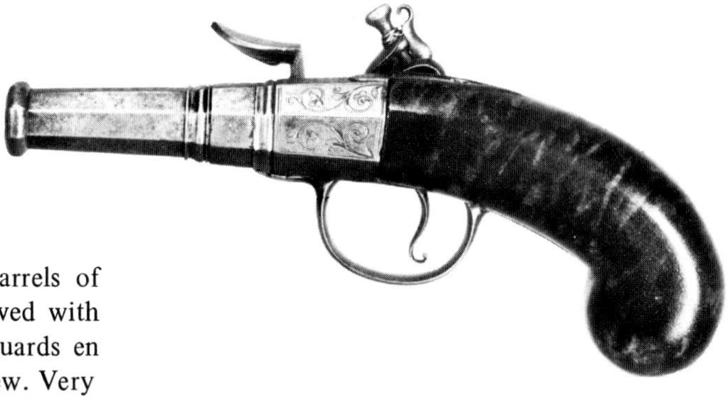

Pair of English flintlock turn-off pistols with octagonal barrels of baluster form and tapering octagonal breeches finely engraved with panels of strawberry leaves, the cocks, actions and trigger-guards en suite, the flat-sided rootwood butts retained by a single screw. Very fine quality, good condition, but one butt a replacement. By Sharpe, circa 1670-80. 7¼in. *Christie's*

£800 – £1,000 the pair

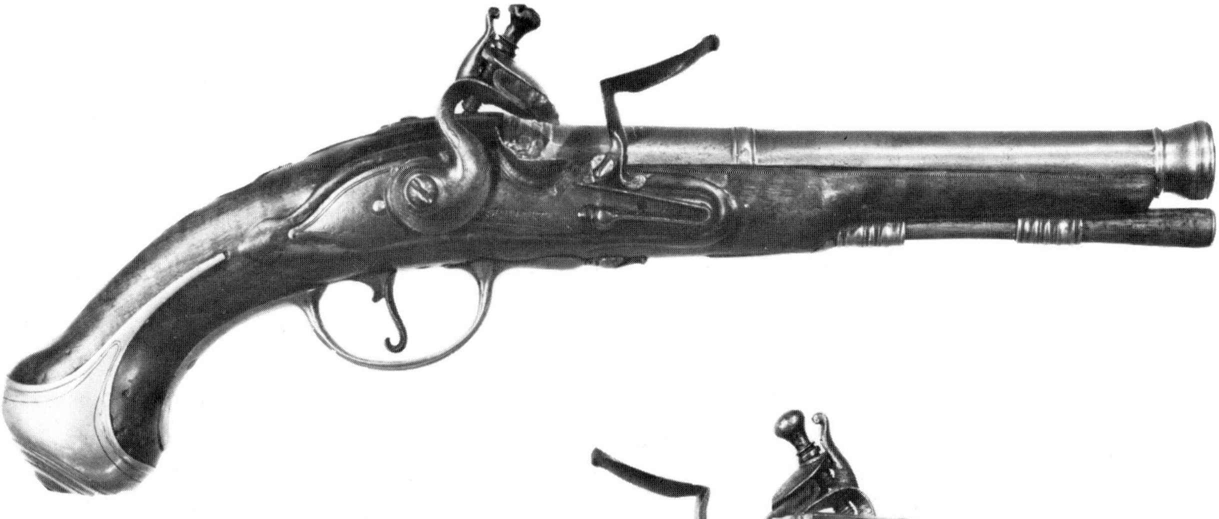

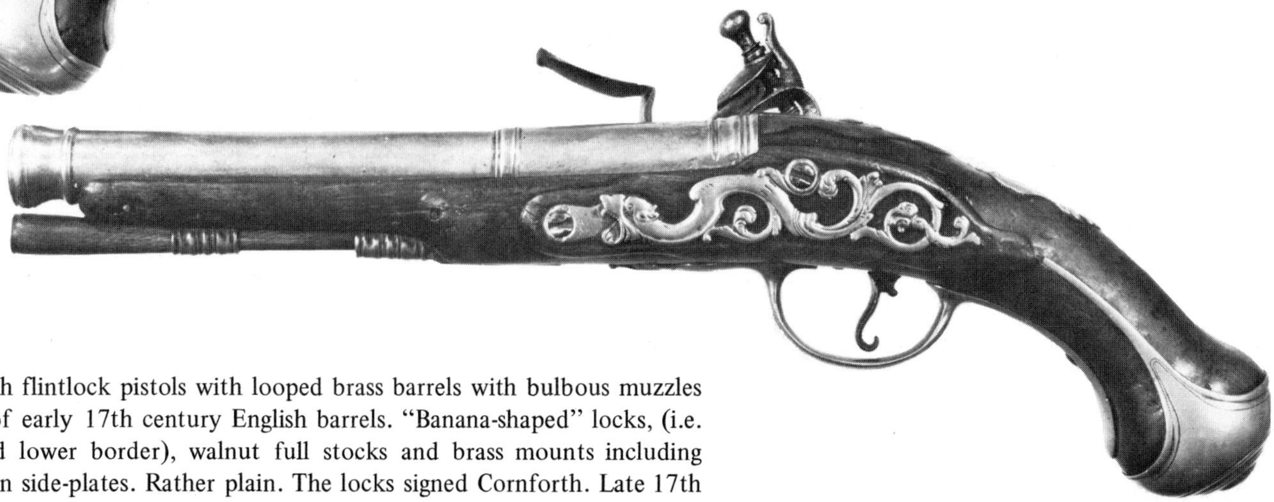

ıir of English flintlock pistols with looped brass barrels with bulbous muzzles miniscent of early 17th century English barrels. "Banana-shaped" locks, (i.e. ith incurved lower border), walnut full stocks and brass mounts including erced dragon side-plates. Rather plain. The locks signed Cornforth. Late 17th ntury/early 18th century. 14½in. *Christie's*

Over £1,000 the pair

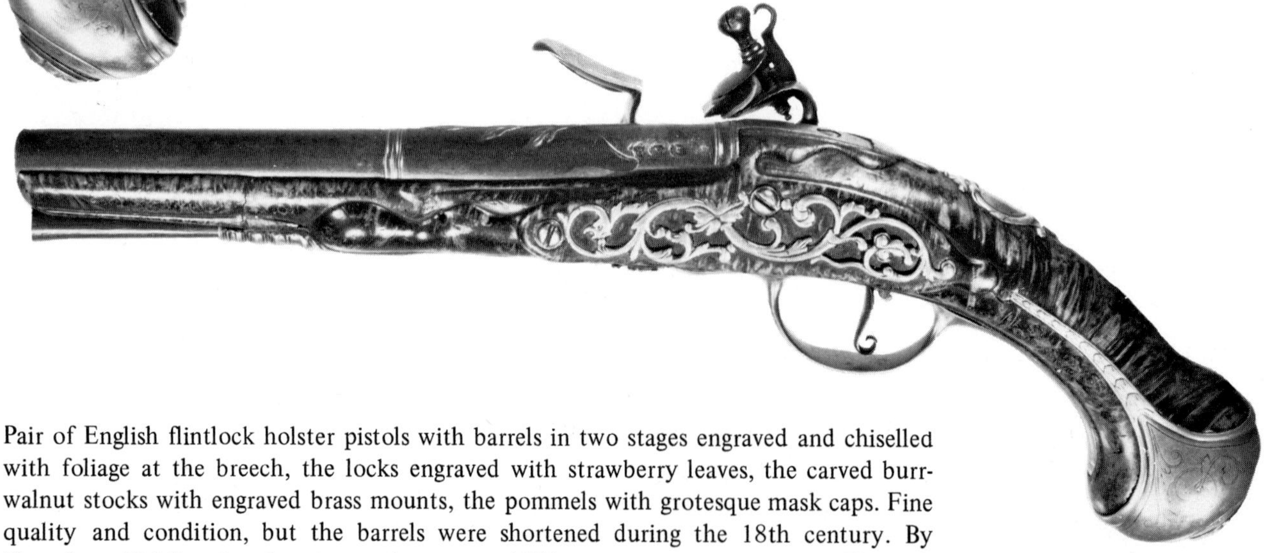

Pair of English flintlock holster pistols with barrels in two stages engraved and chiselled with foliage at the breech, the locks engraved with strawberry leaves, the carved burr-walnut stocks with engraved brass mounts, the pommels with grotesque mask caps. Fine quality and condition, but the barrels were shortened during the 18th century. By Humphrey Pickfatt, London, late 17th century, 15½in. *Christie's*

Over £1,000 the pair
Perhaps £3,000 had they not been shortened

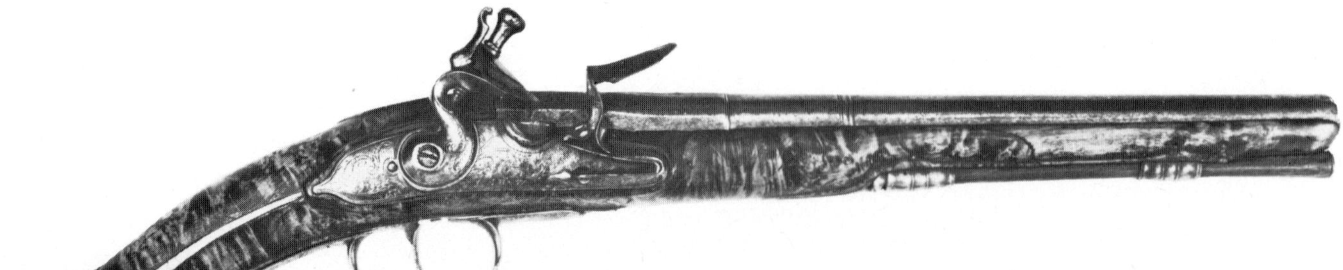

English flintlock holster pistol with steel barrel in three stages, the lock signed and engraved with foliage terminating in grotesque heads, engraved steel mounts, serpentine side-plate. Note the close figure of the stock, an attractive feature on 17th century English pistols, also the length of the spurs of the pommel extending to the very tail of the lock-plate. Good quality, but poor condition. By I. Shaw, late 17th century. 18½in. *Sotheby's*

About £500

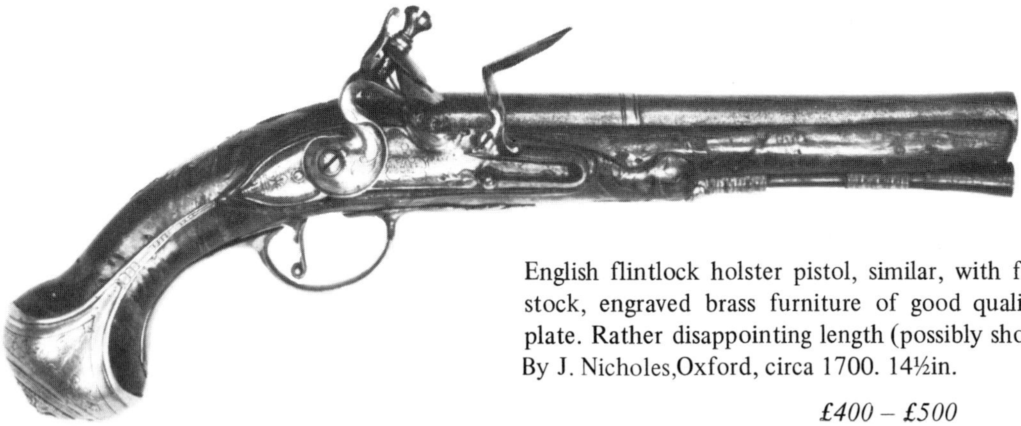

English flintlock holster pistol, similar, with finely figured burrwood stock, engraved brass furniture of good quality and serpentine sideplate. Rather disappointing length (possibly shortened). Fair condition. By J. Nicholes,Oxford, circa 1700. 14½in. *Sotheby's*

£400 – £500

Beware of barrel lengths on 17th century pistols, Many were brought up to date in the 18th century, and some have been restored to full length recently as this increases their value.

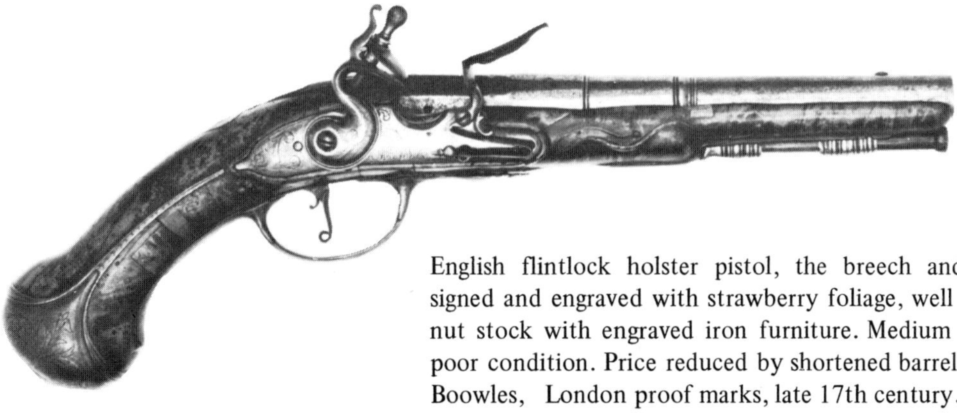

English flintlock holster pistol, the breech and lock each signed and engraved with strawberry foliage, well figured walnut stock with engraved iron furniture. Medium quality, but poor condition. Price reduced by shortened barrel. Signed R. Boowles, London proof marks, late 17th century. 15½in. *Sotheby's*

£200 – £300

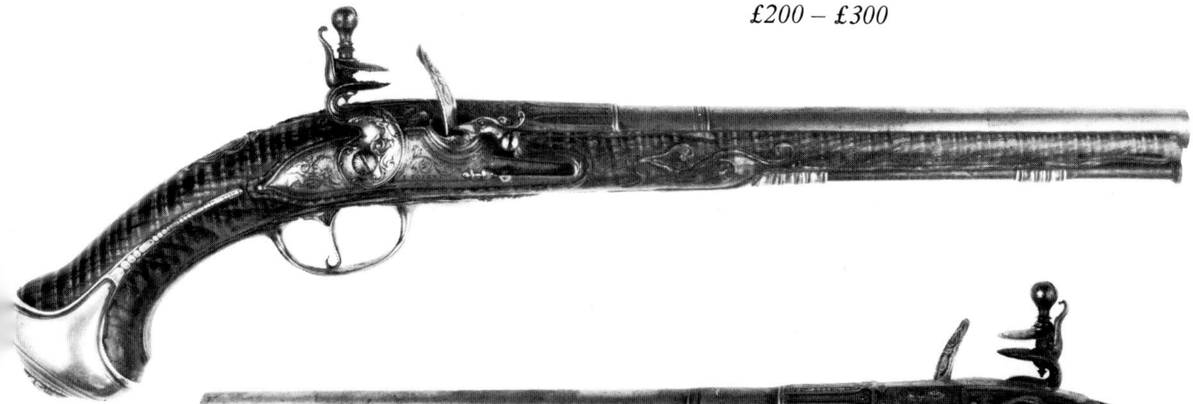

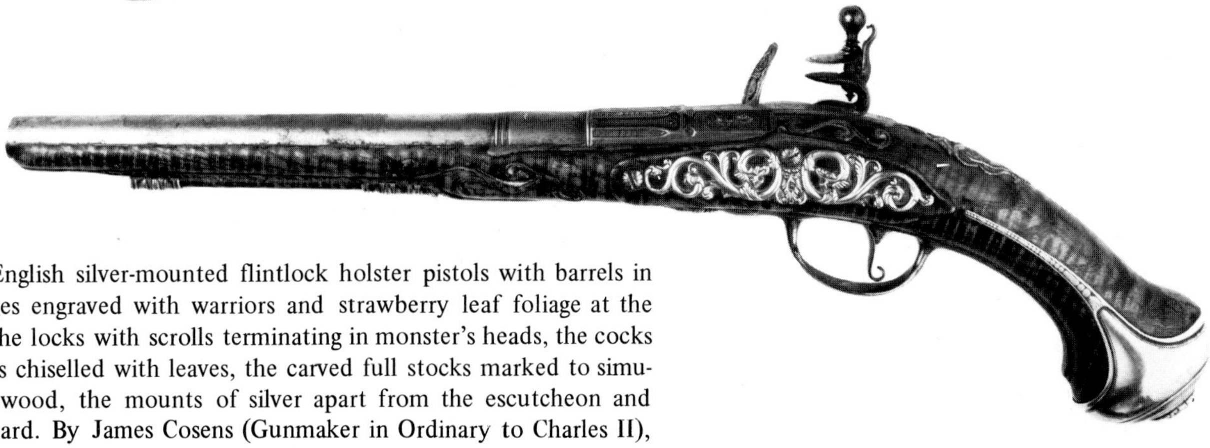

Pair of English silver-mounted flintlock holster pistols with barrels in four stages engraved with warriors and strawberry leaf foliage at the breech, the locks with scrolls terminating in monster's heads, the cocks and steels chiselled with leaves, the carved full stocks marked to simulate rootwood, the mounts of silver apart from the escutcheon and trigger-guard. By James Cosens (Gunmaker in Ordinary to Charles II), late 17th century. 18¾in. Fine quality and condition. *Sotheby's*

Over £5,000

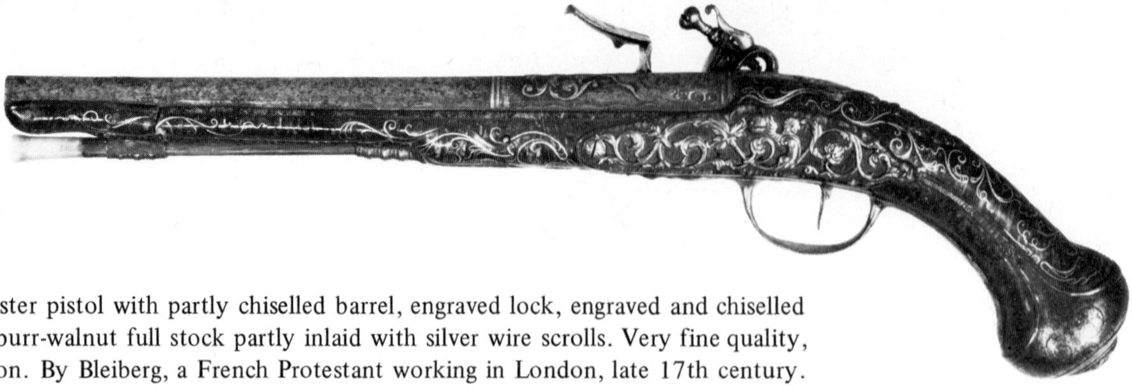

Flintlock holster pistol with partly chiselled barrel, engraved lock, engraved and chiselled mounts and burr-walnut full stock partly inlaid with silver wire scrolls. Very fine quality, poor condition. By Bleiberg, a French Protestant working in London, late 17th century. 19ins. *Christie's*

About £5,000 despite condition.

English flintlock pocket pistol with turn-off barrel, the barrel and lock signed and engraved with foliage, burr-walnut butt with engraved steel furniture and pierced serpentine side-plate. Fine quality, good condition. By T. Banister, circa 1700. 8in. *Sotheby's*

£500 – £750

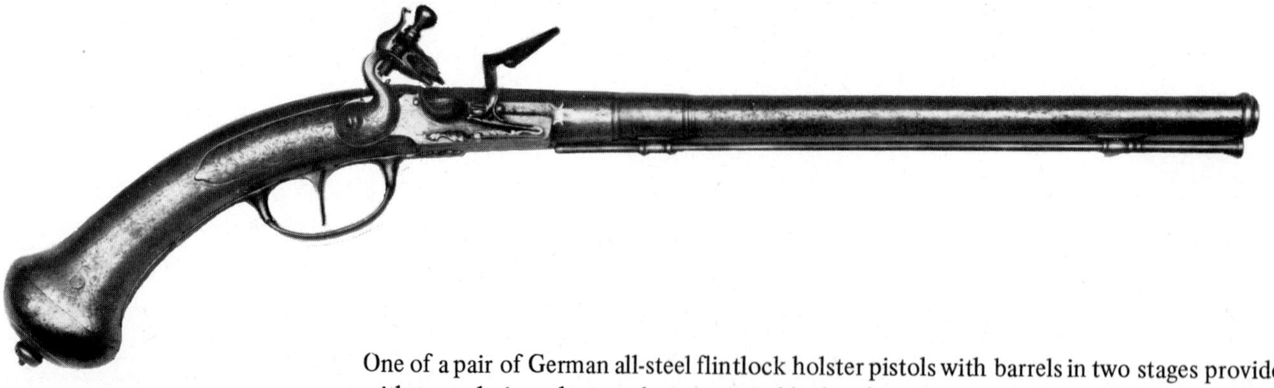

One of a pair of German all-steel flintlock holster pistols with barrels in two stages provided with turned pierced ramrod-pipes, signed locks, the grips engraved on either side to form a spurred pommel. Good quality and condition, but some wear. By Melchior Weschgin, Augsburg, late 17th century. 22in.

About £2,000 the pair

Most pistols of this type were made by the Cloeter family of Mannheim. *Christie's*

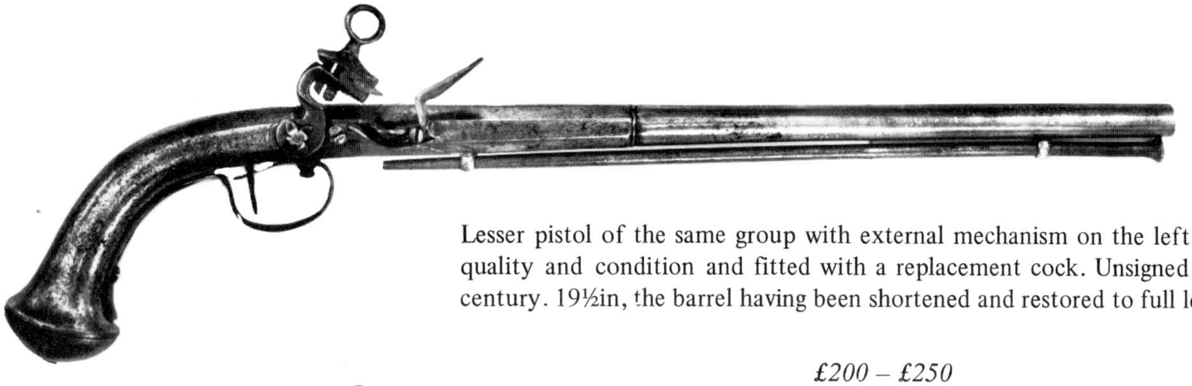

Lesser pistol of the same group with external mechanism on the left side. Poor quality and condition and fitted with a replacement cock. Unsigned, late 17th century. 19½in, the barrel having been shortened and restored to full length.
Sotheby's

£200 – £250

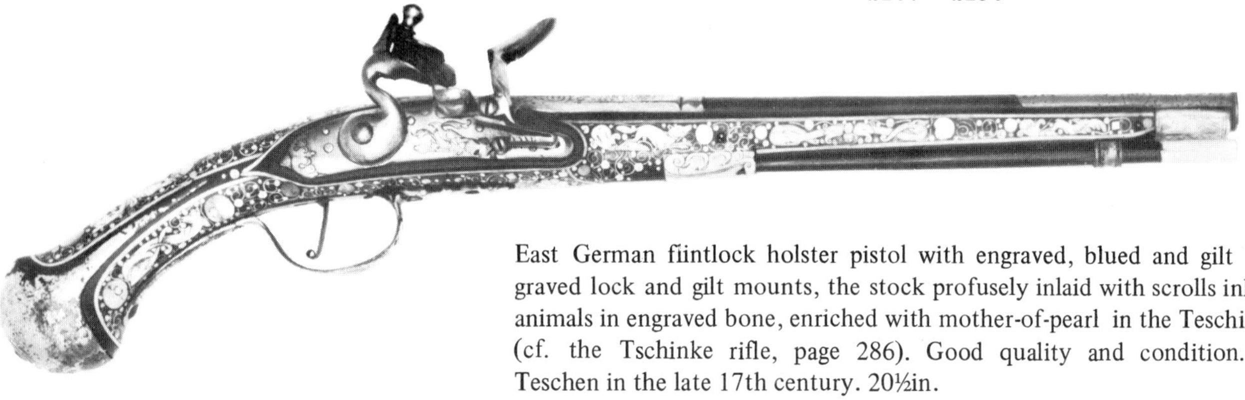

East German flintlock holster pistol with engraved, blued and gilt barrel, engraved lock and gilt mounts, the stock profusely inlaid with scrolls inhabited by animals in engraved bone, enriched with mother-of-pearl in the Teschian manner (cf. the Tschinke rifle, page 286). Good quality and condition. Made in Teschen in the late 17th century. 20½in. *Sotheby's*

About £1,000

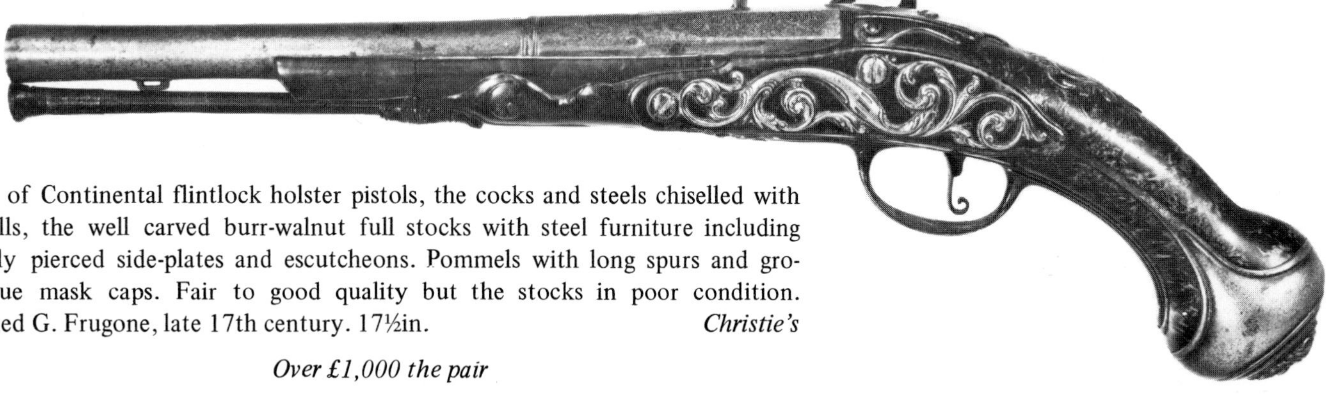

Pair of Continental flintlock holster pistols, the cocks and steels chiselled with scrolls, the well carved burr-walnut full stocks with steel furniture including finely pierced side-plates and escutcheons. Pommels with long spurs and grotesque mask caps. Fair to good quality but the stocks in poor condition. Signed G. Frugone, late 17th century. 17½in. *Christie's*

Over £1,000 the pair

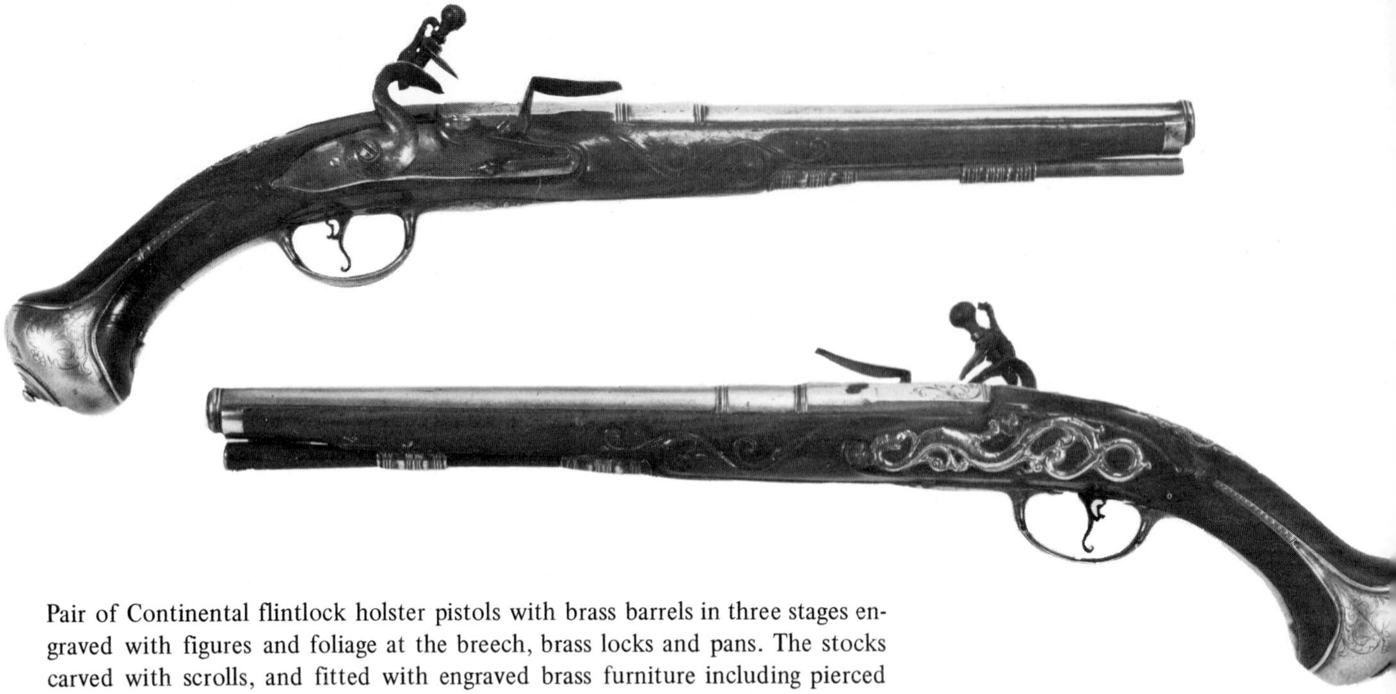

Pair of Continental flintlock holster pistols with brass barrels in three stages engraved with figures and foliage at the breech, brass locks and pans. The stocks carved with scrolls, and fitted with engraved brass furniture including pierced side-plates and escutcheons. Good quality and condition. Unsigned, circa 1700. 18¾in. *Christie's*

Over £1,000 the pair

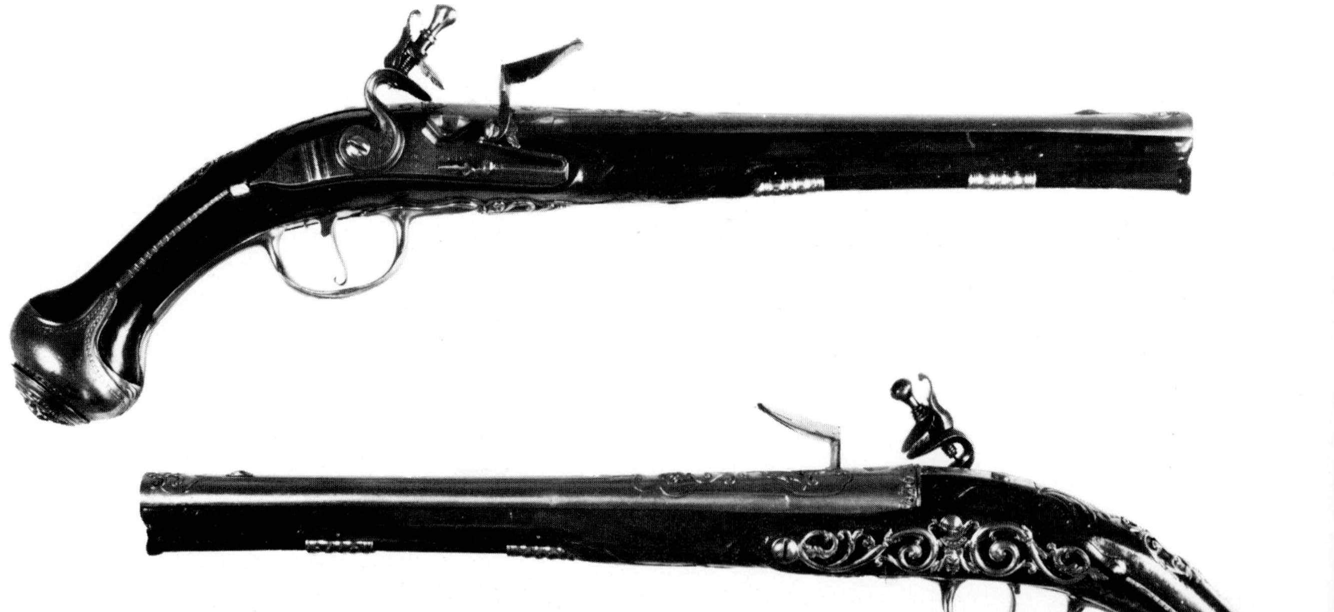

Pair of Dutch flintlock holster pistols with chiselled barrels engraved at the tang with the figure of Mars and struck with the town mark of Utrecht, engraved locks, carved full stocks and chiselled steel mounts including pierced side-plates and escutcheons. Fine quality, good but overcleaned condition. By Penterman, Utrecht, circa 1700.

£1,500 – £2,000 the pair

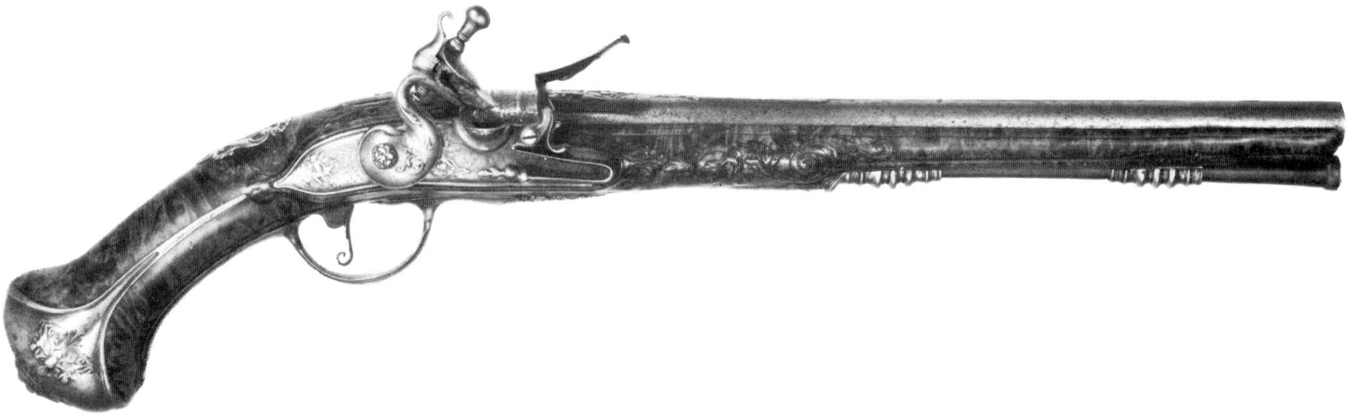

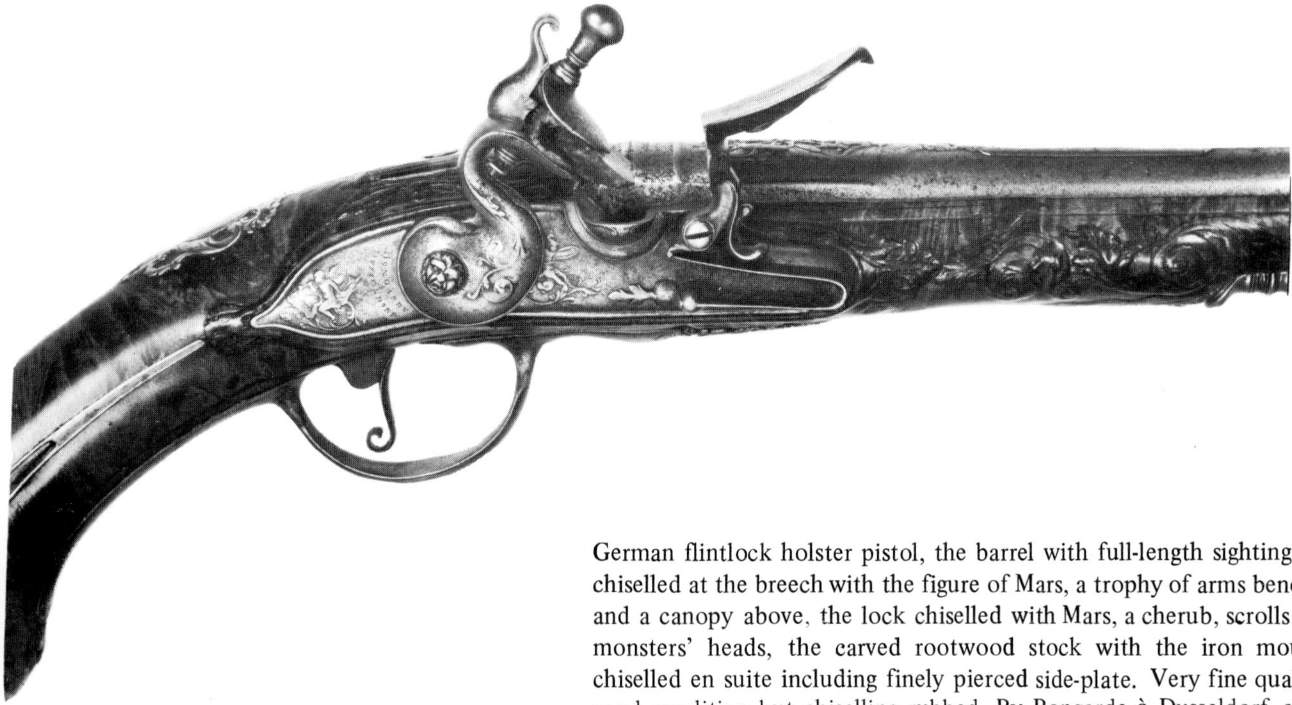

German flintlock holster pistol, the barrel with full-length sighting rib, chiselled at the breech with the figure of Mars, a trophy of arms beneath and a canopy above, the lock chiselled with Mars, a cherub, scrolls and monsters' heads, the carved rootwood stock with the iron mounts chiselled en suite including finely pierced side-plate. Very fine quality, good condition but chiselling rubbed. By Bongarde à Dusseldorf, circa 1700. 21in. *Private collection*

Over £1,500. Much more if condition were better.

Armand Bongarde was perhaps the most important German gunmaker at this time, noted especially for his chiselling (see detail of the lock).

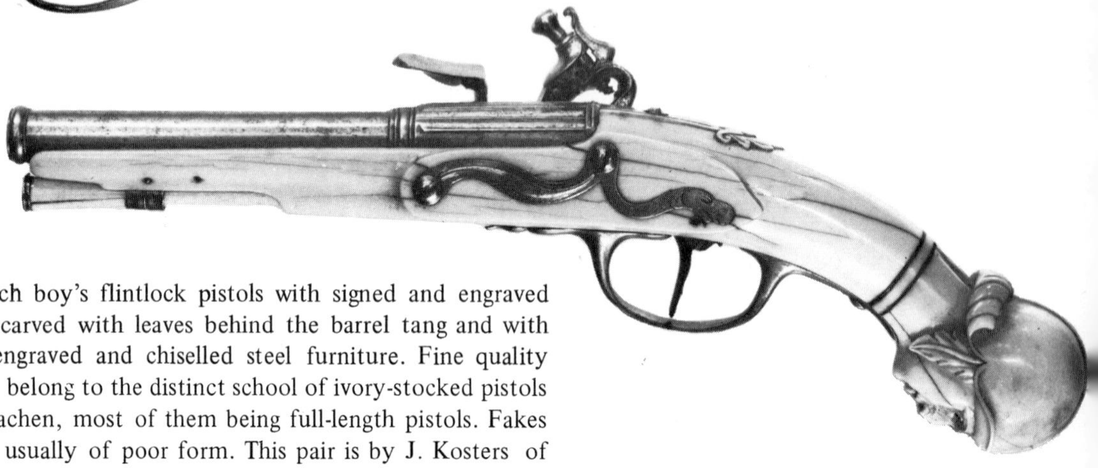

Pair of fine and rare Dutch boy's flintlock pistols with signed and engraved locks, the stocks of ivory carved with leaves behind the barrel tang and with warrior's head pommels, engraved and chiselled steel furniture. Fine quality and condition. These pistols belong to the distinct school of ivory-stocked pistols made in Maastricht and Aachen, most of them being full-length pistols. Fakes are not unknown, but are usually of poor form. This pair is by J. Kosters of Maastricht, late 17th century. 11in. *Sotheby's*

Over £10,000. Much more for a full-sized pair.

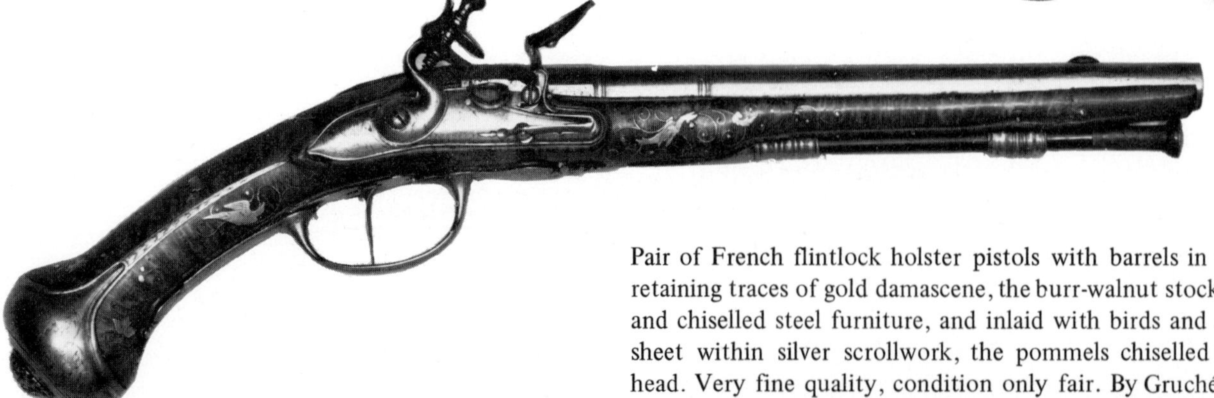

Pair of French flintlock holster pistols with barrels in three stages and retaining traces of gold damascene, the burr-walnut stocks with engraved and chiselled steel furniture, and inlaid with birds and animals in silver sheet within silver scrollwork, the pommels chiselled with a Medusa head. Very fine quality, condition only fair. By Gruché à Paris (one of the best Parisian makers of the late 17th century), circa 1680. 15½in. *Christie's*

Over £5,000

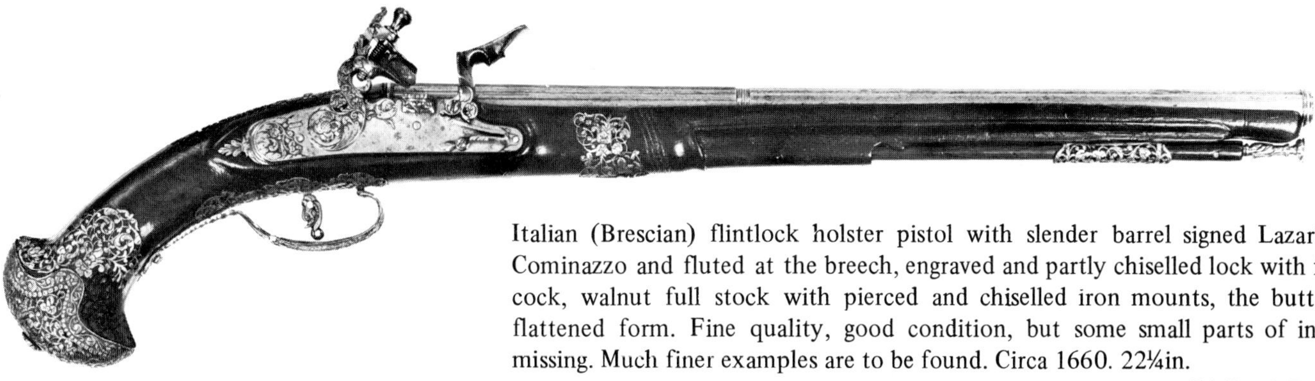

Italian (Brescian) flintlock holster pistol with slender barrel signed Lazarino Cominazzo and fluted at the breech, engraved and partly chiselled lock with flat cock, walnut full stock with pierced and chiselled iron mounts, the butt of flattened form. Fine quality, good condition, but some small parts of inlay missing. Much finer examples are to be found. Circa 1660. 22¼in.

Weller & Dufty

Over £2,000

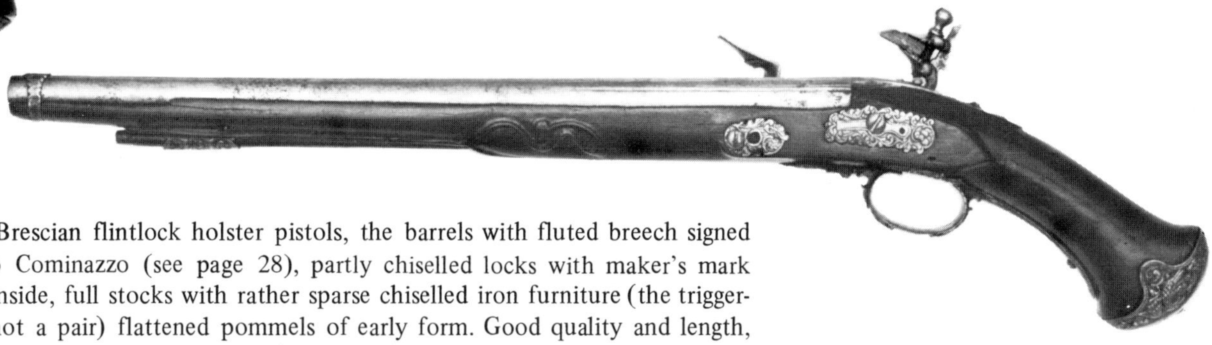

Pair of Brescian flintlock holster pistols, the barrels with fluted breech signed Lazarino Cominazzo (see page 28), partly chiselled locks with maker's mark on the inside, full stocks with rather sparse chiselled iron furniture (the trigger-guards not a pair) flattened pommels of early form. Good quality and length, but only fair condition. Circa 1660/1680. 22½in. *Sotheby's*

Over £2,000 the pair

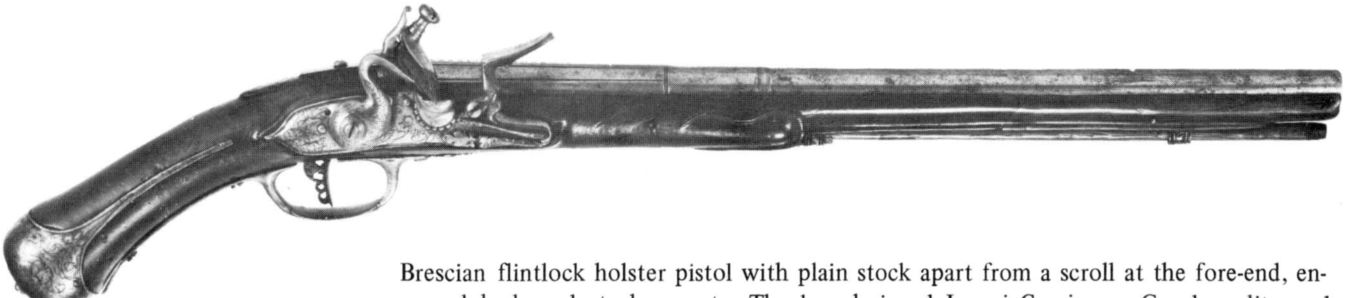

Brescian flintlock holster pistol with plain stock apart from a scroll at the fore-end, engraved lock and steel mounts. The barrel signed Lazari Cominazo. Good quality and condition, but the stock imperfect. Late 17th century. 15$\frac{1}{8}$in. *Christie's*

About £800

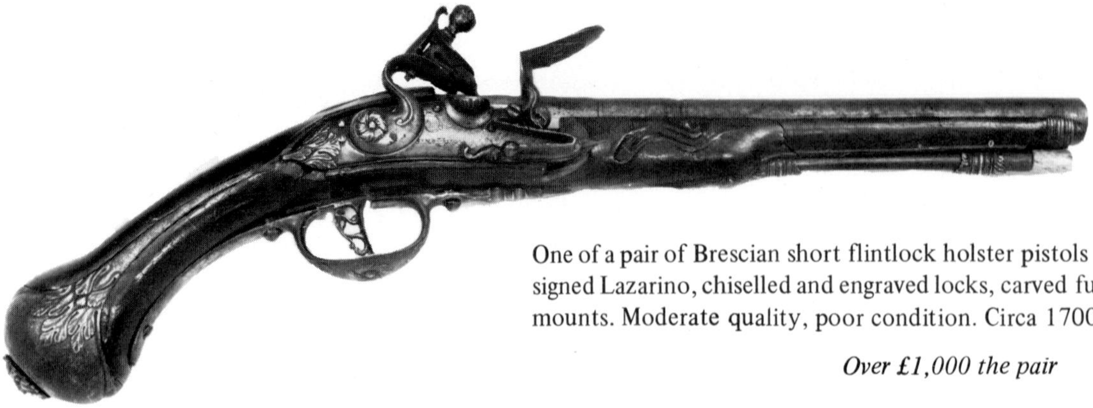

One of a pair of Brescian short flintlock holster pistols with barrels in three stages signed Lazarino, chiselled and engraved locks, carved full stocks and chiselled iron mounts. Moderate quality, poor condition. Circa 1700. 15in. *Sotheby's*

Over £1,000 the pair

Pair of Brescian export pistols, the barrels stamped Lazaro Lazari and chiselled with a mask and a band of foliage, the locks engraved and chiselled with masks, fitted with silver-gilt stocks cast and chased with masks, foliage and beading, false ramrods in the Turkish style. Possibly adapted from a pair of Brescian all-steel pistols. Good quality and condition, but some wear. Signed Azzoni in Brescia, circa 1700. 19¾in. *Christie's*

About £1,000 the pair

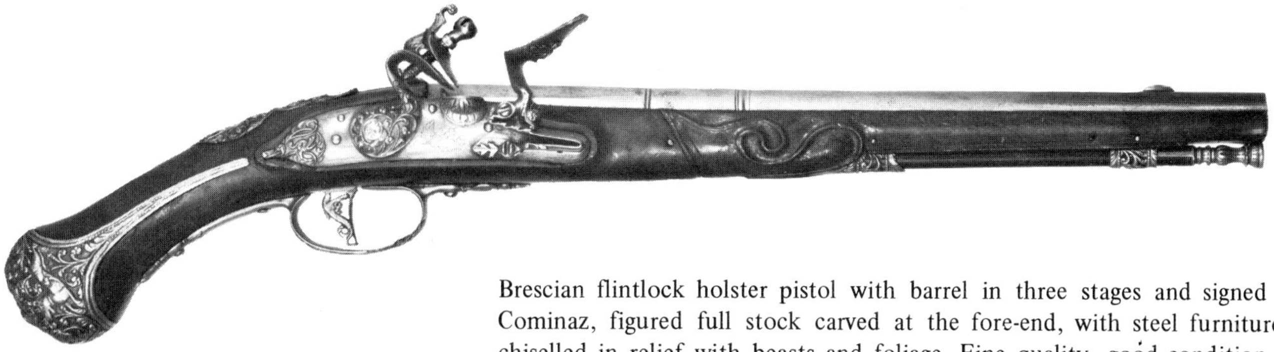

Brescian flintlock holster pistol with barrel in three stages and signed Lazar Cominaz, figured full stock carved at the fore-end, with steel furniture well chiselled in relief with beasts and foliage. Fine quality, good condition. Circa 1700. 18½in. *Christie's*

Over £1,000

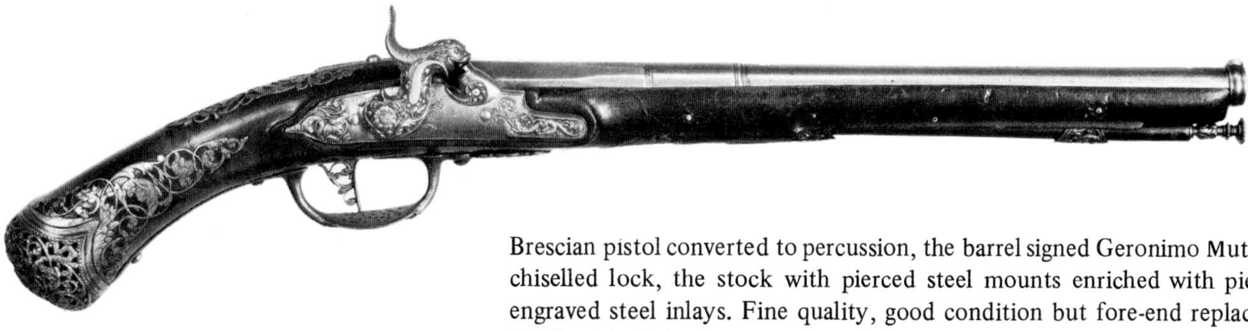

Brescian pistol converted to percussion, the barrel signed Geronimo Mutto, partly chiselled lock, the stock with pierced steel mounts enriched with pierced and engraved steel inlays. Fine quality, good condition but fore-end replaced. Circa 1700, with 19th century conversion. 18¾in. *Christie's*

About £500

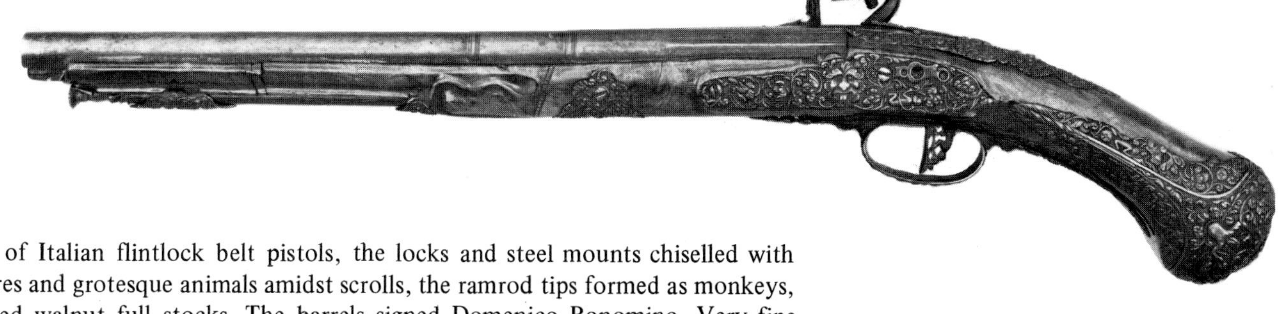

Pair of Italian flintlock belt pistols, the locks and steel mounts chiselled with figures and grotesque animals amidst scrolls, the ramrod tips formed as monkeys, carved walnut full stocks. The barrels signed Domenico Bonomino. Very fine quality, fine but uncleaned condition. Late 17th century. *Christie's*

Over £7,000 the pair

Pair of Italian flintlock holster pistols, the barrels with their original colour signed Lazarino Cominazzo, and chiselled with fluting, the walnut stocks profusely inlaid with pierced steel engraved with monsters amidst foliage, the locks, pommels and trigger-guards chiselled en suite. Very fine quality, fine condition. Late 17th century. *Christie's*

Over £10,000 the pair

English Flintlock Pistols - 1700 - 1750

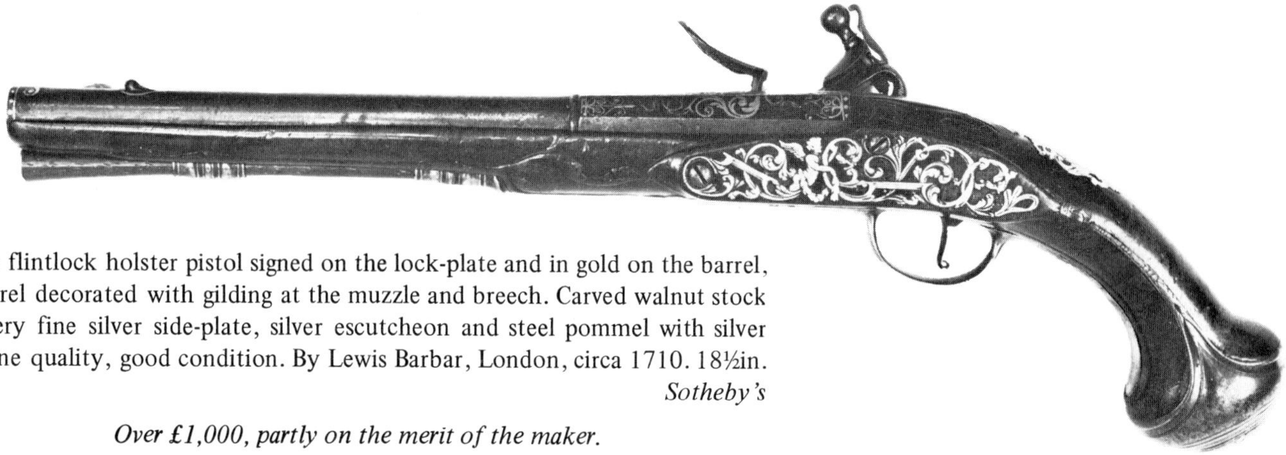

glish flintlock holster pistol signed on the lock-plate and in gold on the barrel, barrel decorated with gilding at the muzzle and breech. Carved walnut stock h very fine silver side-plate, silver escutcheon and steel pommel with silver ›. Fine quality, good condition. By Lewis Barbar, London, circa 1710. 18½in.

Sotheby's

Over £1,000, partly on the merit of the maker.

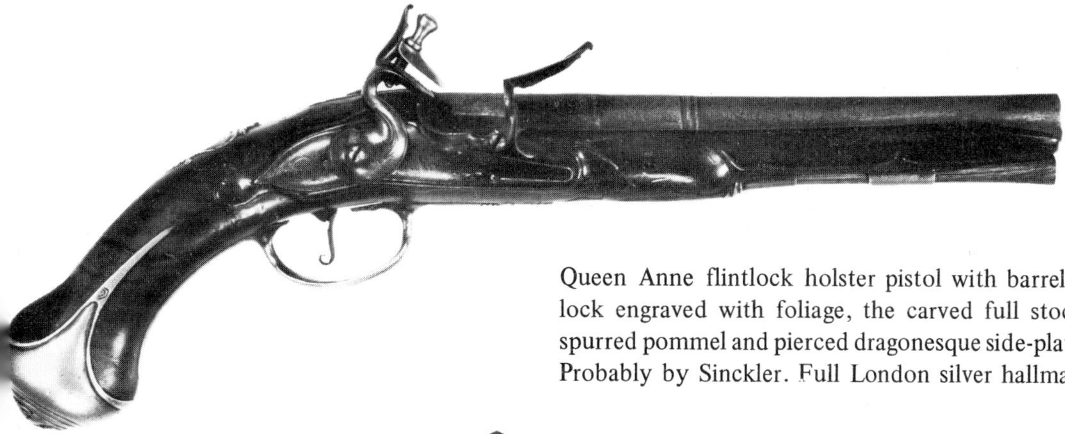

Queen Anne flintlock holster pistol with barrel in three stages, the breech and lock engraved with foliage, the carved full stock with silver mounts including spurred pommel and pierced dragonesque side-plate. Fine quality, good condition. Probably by Sinckler. Full London silver hallmarks for 1712, maker's mark BV.

Christie's

About £1,000. Very rare with this full early hallmark.

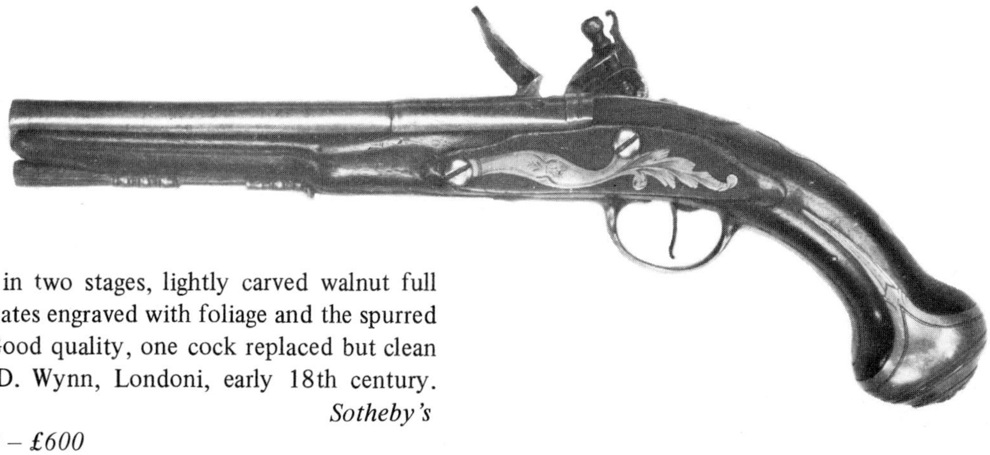

ır of flintlock pistols with barrels in two stages, lightly carved walnut full cks, full brass furniture, the side plates engraved with foliage and the spurred mmels with grotesque mask caps. Good quality, one cock replaced but clean ıdition, probably shortened. By D. Wynn, Londoni, early 18th century. ¾in.

Sotheby's

£500 – £600

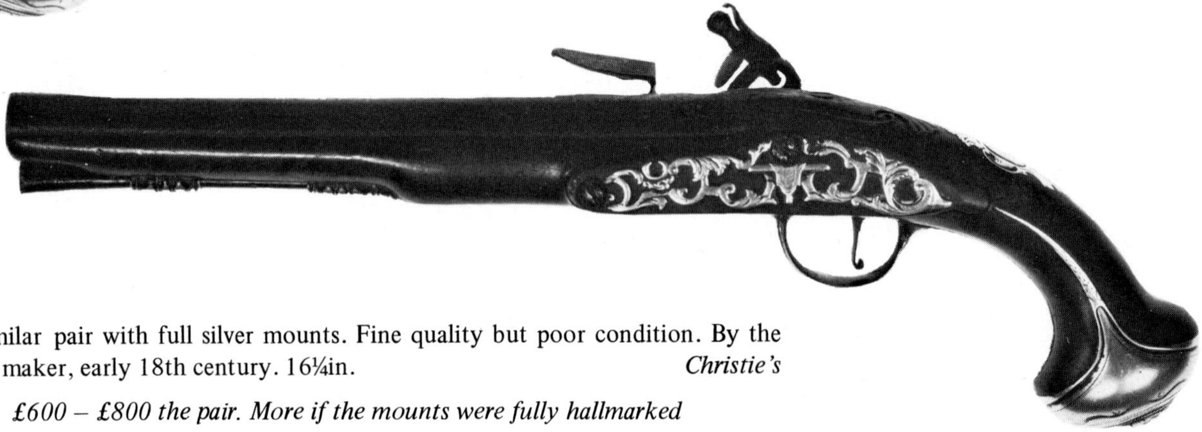

A similar pair with full silver mounts. Fine quality but poor condition. By the same maker, early 18th century. 16¼in. *Christie's*

£600 – £800 the pair. More if the mounts were fully hallmarked

English flintlock holster pistol with signed barrel and lock, the full stock carved around the brass mounts. Fine quality, fair condition. By the Huguenot maker Le Maire, London, circa 1720. 18¼in. *Sotheby's*

About £300
The same pistol with silver mounts, about £500

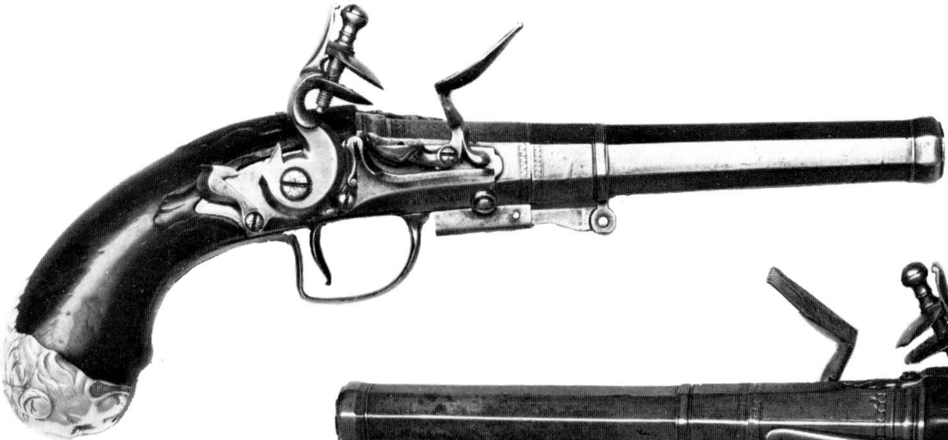

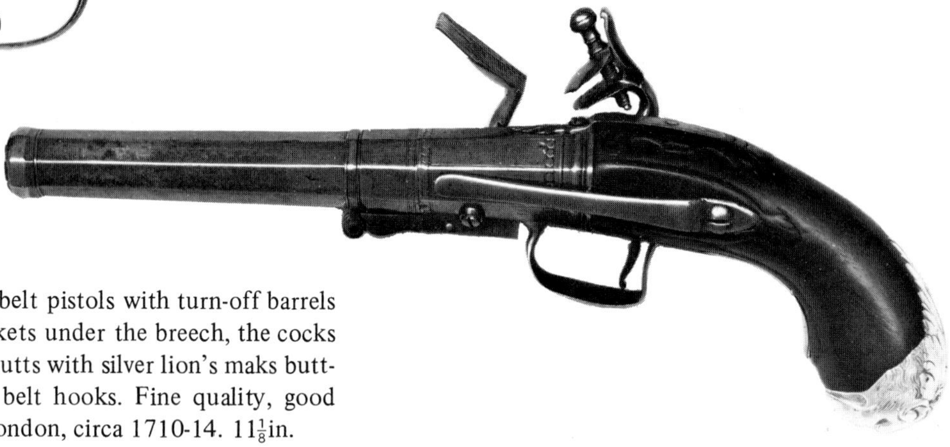

Pair of Queen Anne flintlock belt pistols with turn-off barrels and retaining links within sockets under the breech, the cocks with dog catches, the walnut butts with silver lion's maks butt-caps, iron trigger-guards and belt hooks. Fine quality, good condition. By Lewis Barbar, London, circa 1710-14. 11⅛in.

Over £2,000 the pair. True Queen Anne turn-off pistols are very rare.

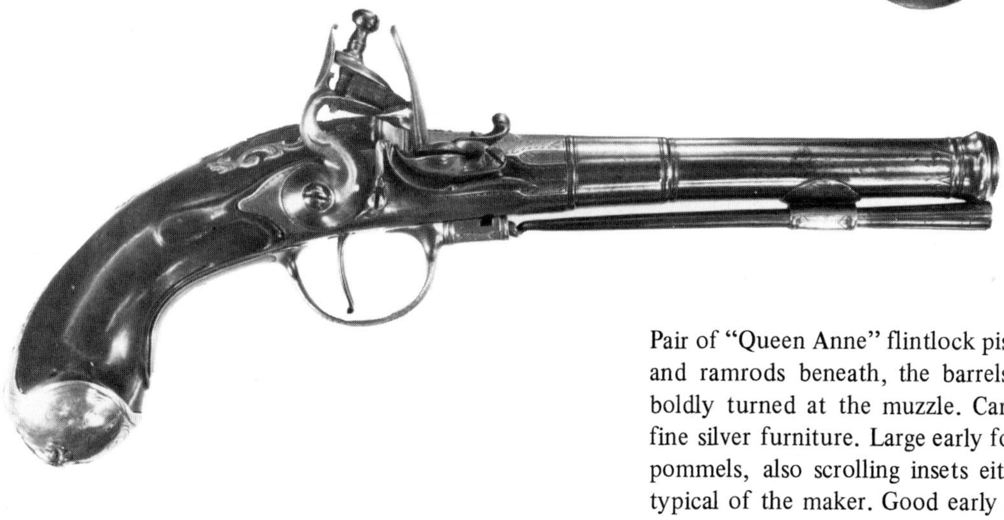

Pair of "Queen Anne" flintlock pistols fitted with fixed barrels and ramrods beneath, the barrels faceted at the breech and boldly turned at the muzzle. Carved walnut half-stocks with fine silver furniture. Large early form of foliate engraved silver pommels, also scrolling insets either side of the barrel tang, typical of the maker. Good early rounded cocks. Fine quality and condition. Signed James Freeman Londini. Circa 1715-20. 12½in. *Sotheby's*

Over £1,500 the pair

Similar pistol with turn-off cannon barrel. In not such good condition and not of such fine quality. By Robert Harvey, London, circa 1720/30. Cock replaced. 12½in.

Christie's

£300 – £400

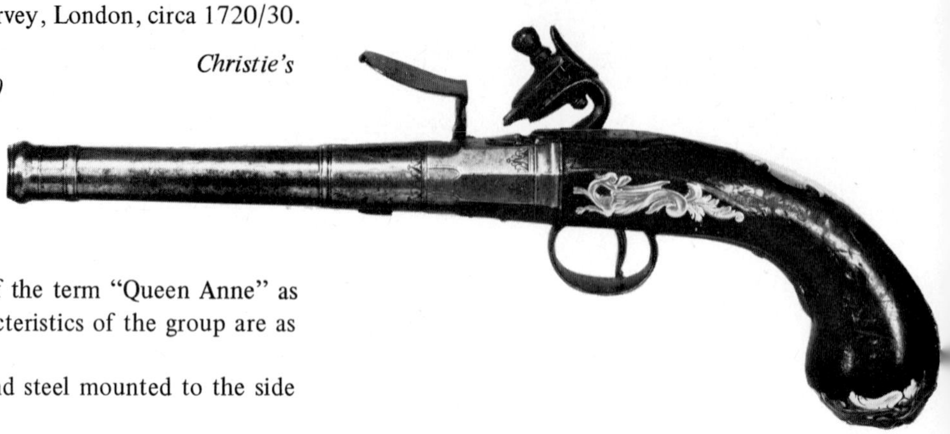

The last two examples show the misuse of the term "Queen Anne" as applied to pistols of this type. The characteristics of the group are as follows:-

1. Box-lock action with the cock and steel mounted to the side and with external steel-spring.
2. Cannon barrel usually unscrewing to allow loading at the breech.
3. Walnut butt with silver furniture, nearly always including a grotesque mask butt-cap, more rarely a spurred pommel.

The early examples tend to have a separate tang to the trigger-guard screwed onto the steel back-strap under the butt, whereas in later examples the trigger-guard is attached direct to the action, sometimes acting as safety-catch at half cock. A faceted breech is usually found on the early pistols and a round one on later ones.

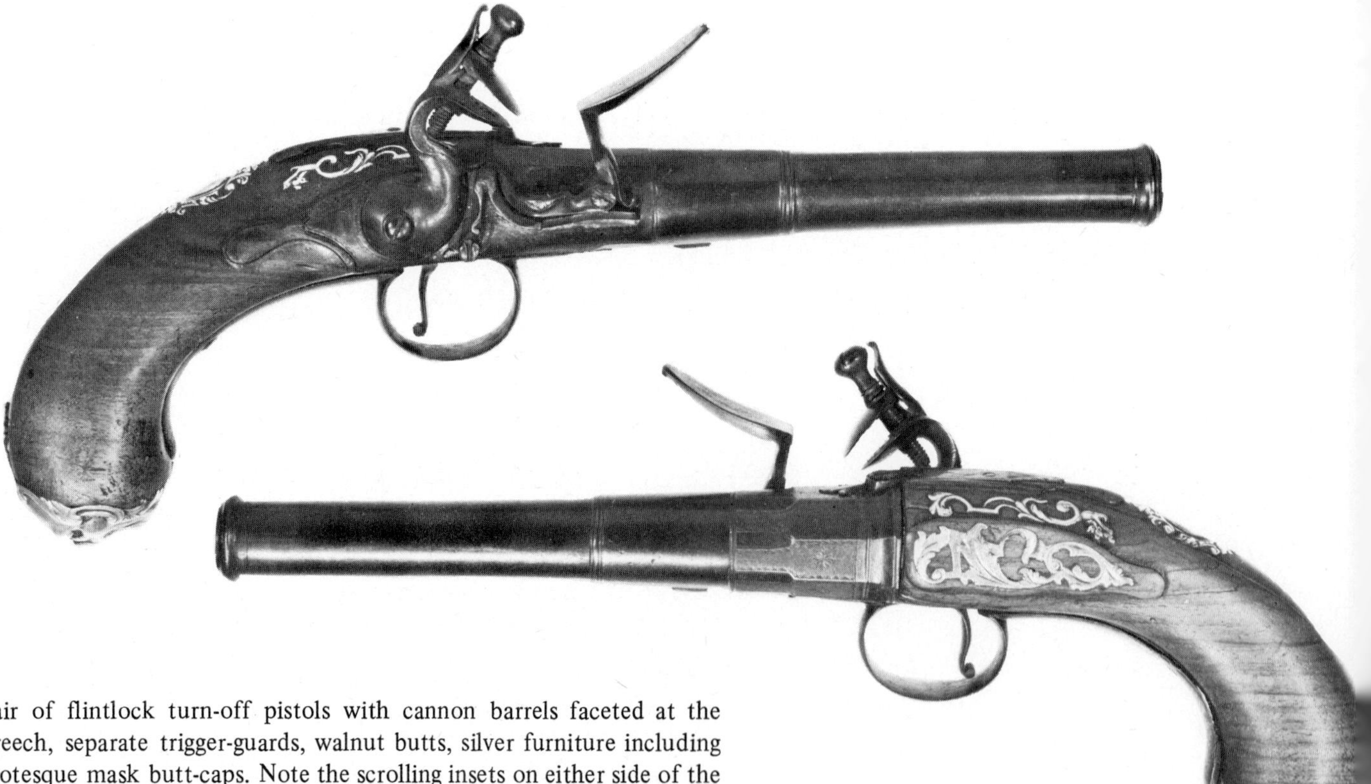

Pair of flintlock turn-off pistols with cannon barrels faceted at the breech, separate trigger-guards, walnut butts, silver furniture including grotesque mask butt-caps. Note the scrolling insets on either side of the barrel tang as in the pair by Freeman on page 47. Fine quality and condition. By James Freeman, London, about 1720. 12in. *Christie's*

About £1,200 the pair

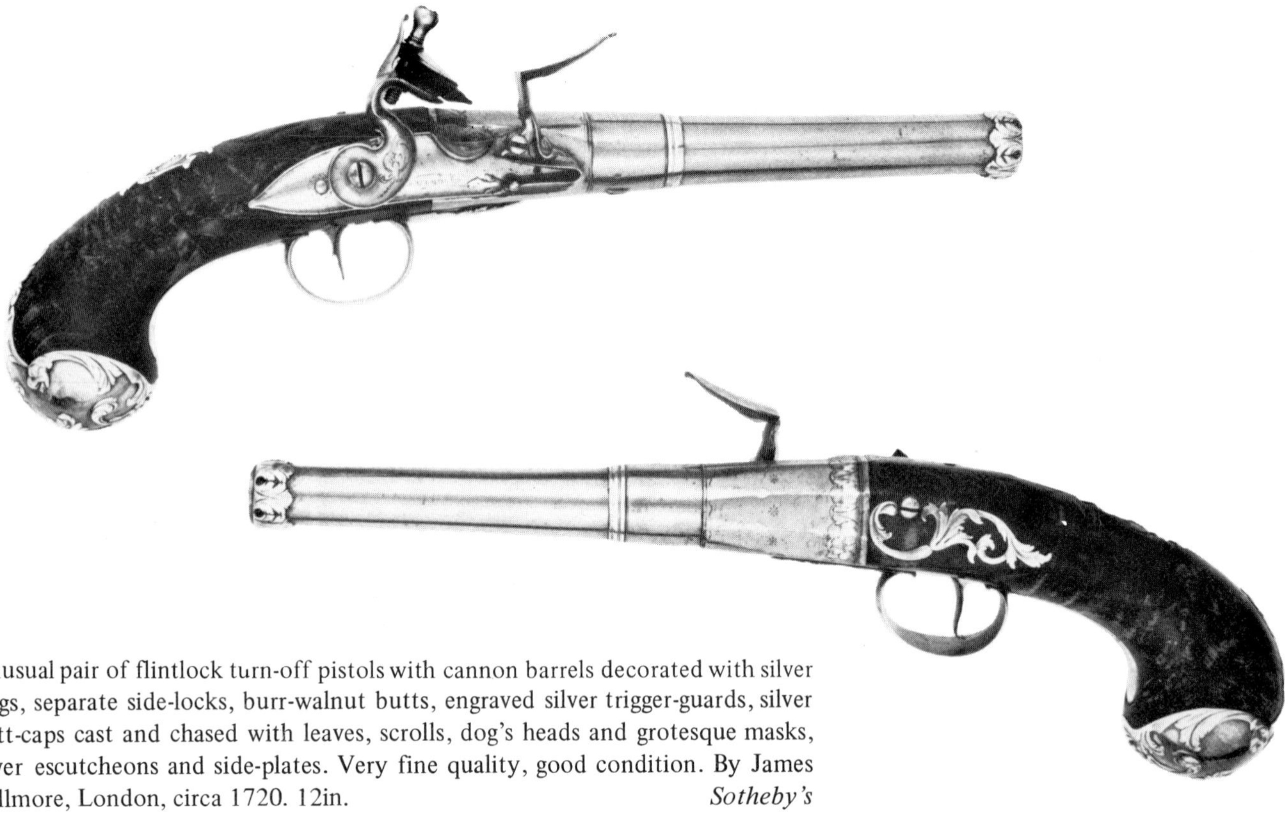

Unusual pair of flintlock turn-off pistols with cannon barrels decorated with silver rings, separate side-locks, burr-walnut butts, engraved silver trigger-guards, silver butt-caps cast and chased with leaves, scrolls, dog's heads and grotesque masks, silver escutcheons and side-plates. Very fine quality, good condition. By James Willmore, London, circa 1720. 12in. *Sotheby's*

Over £2,000 the pair. Of very individual design.

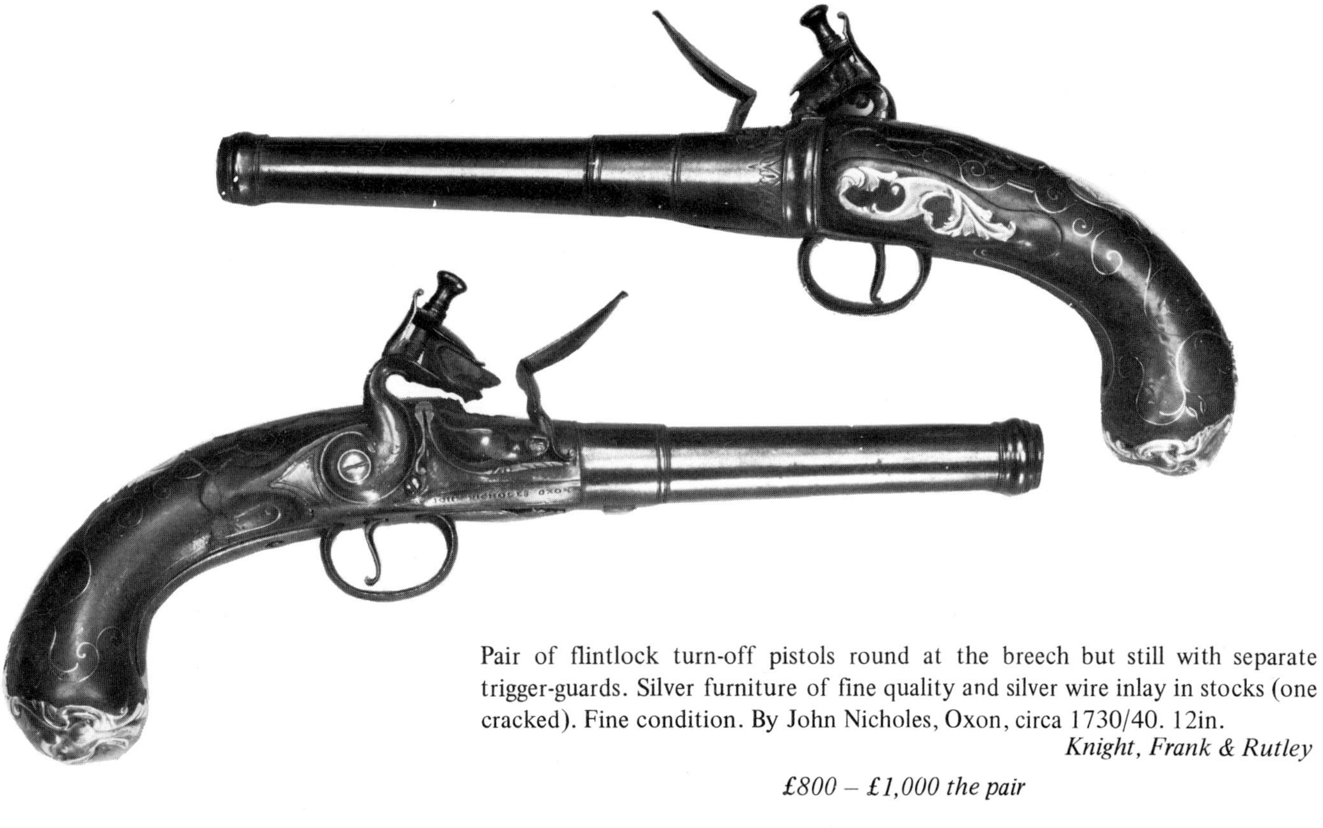

Pair of flintlock turn-off pistols round at the breech but still with separate trigger-guards. Silver furniture of fine quality and silver wire inlay in stocks (one cracked). Fine condition. By John Nicholes, Oxon, circa 1730/40. 12in. *Knight, Frank & Rutley*

£800 – £1,000 the pair

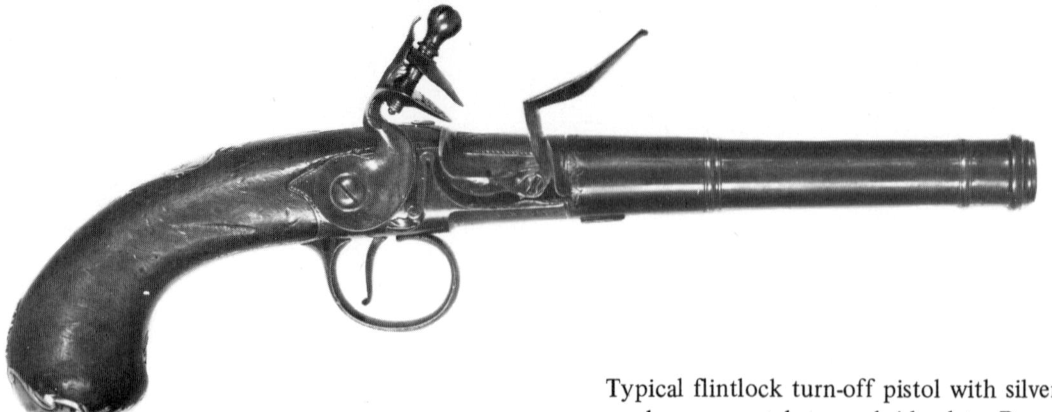

Typical flintlock turn-off pistol with silver mounts including grotesqu mask cap, escutcheon and side-plate. Round breech. This standard for of pistol dates from about 1730 to about 1760. This one is by Newto of Grantham, made in about 1750. 12in. *Christie*

£300 – £400 (£700 – £900 for a pair)

The price depends on condition, in this case very good. If worn, betwee £300 and £550 a pair. These are common enough for buyers to b choosy. Other good makers of this type of pistol are Turvey, Griffi Bumford and Clarkson.

Brass barrels and actions are worth more than iron ones.

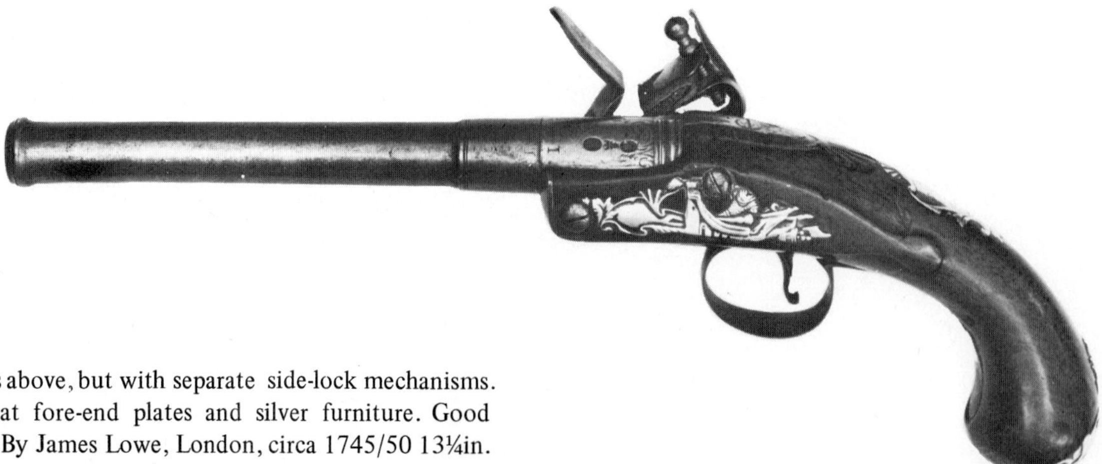

Pair of turn-off pistols, as above, but with separate side-lock mechanisms. The half-stocks have flat fore-end plates and silver furniture. Good quality, clean condition. By James Lowe, London, circa 1745/50 13¼in. *Sotheby's*

£600 – £800 the pair

Brass-mounted pistol of similar form. Good quality and condition. By Wilson, London, circa 1750. 12¼in. *Sotheby's*

About £300

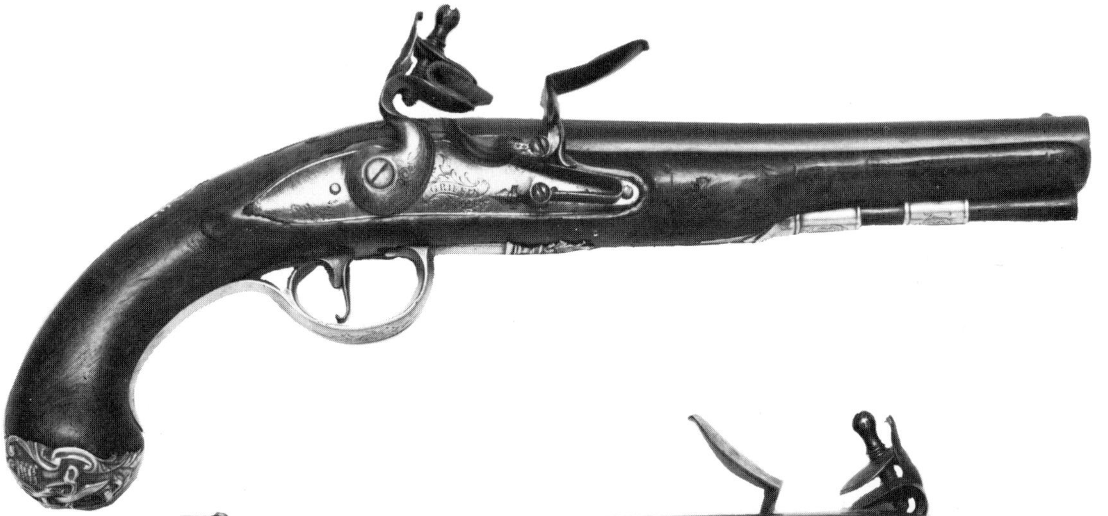

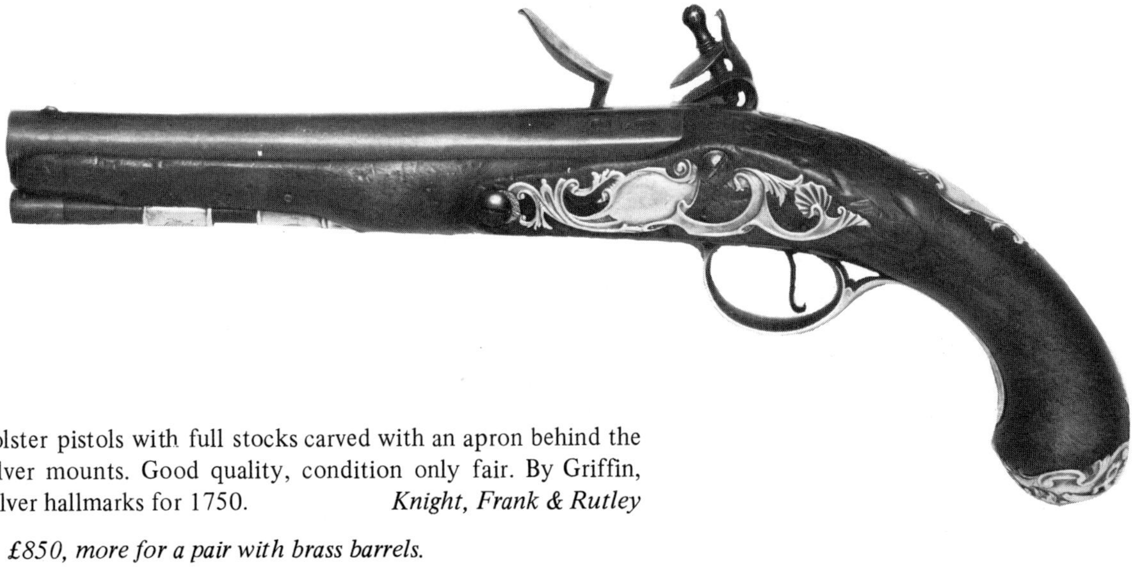

'air of flintlock holster pistols with full stocks carved with an apron behind the arrel tang, and silver mounts. Good quality, condition only fair. By Griffin, ,ondon, London silver hallmarks for 1750. *Knight, Frank & Rutley*

£600 – £850, more for a pair with brass barrels.

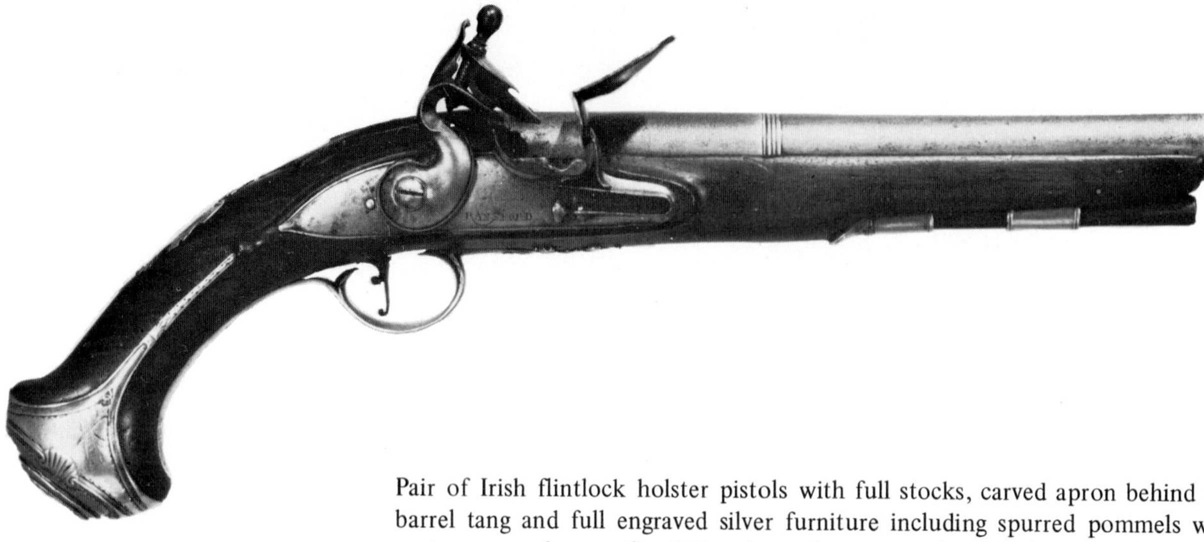

Pair of Irish flintlock holster pistols with full stocks, carved apron behind the barrel tang and full engraved silver furniture including spurred pommels with grotesque mask caps. Condition about the same as the pair above, but highly unusual in bearing Dublin silver hallmarks, struck on all the mounts except the forward ramrod-pipes. Irish hallmarks on firearms add considerably to the value. By Ransford, Dublin, circa 1745. 14in. *Christie's*

Over £1,000 the pair

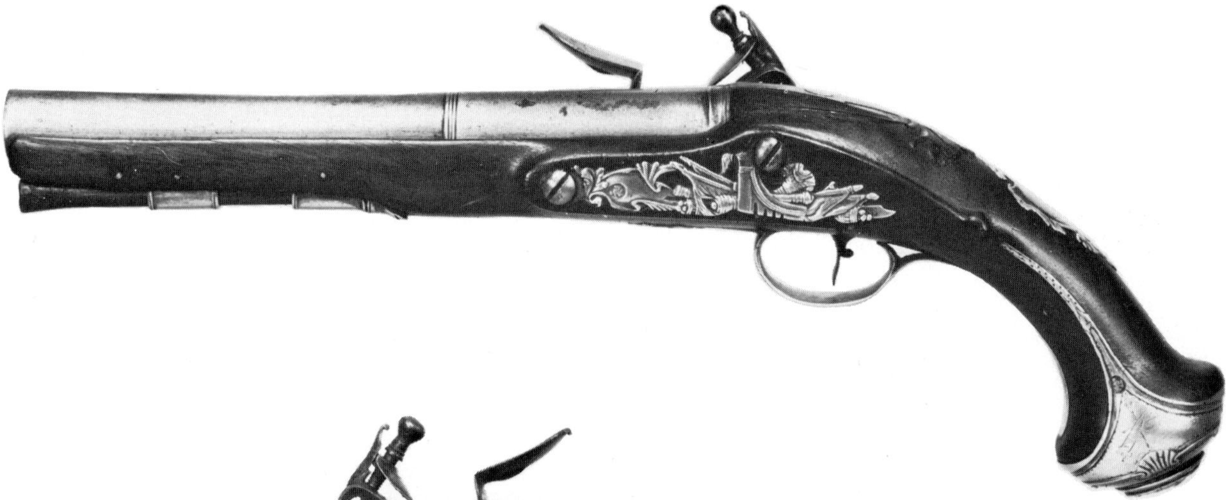

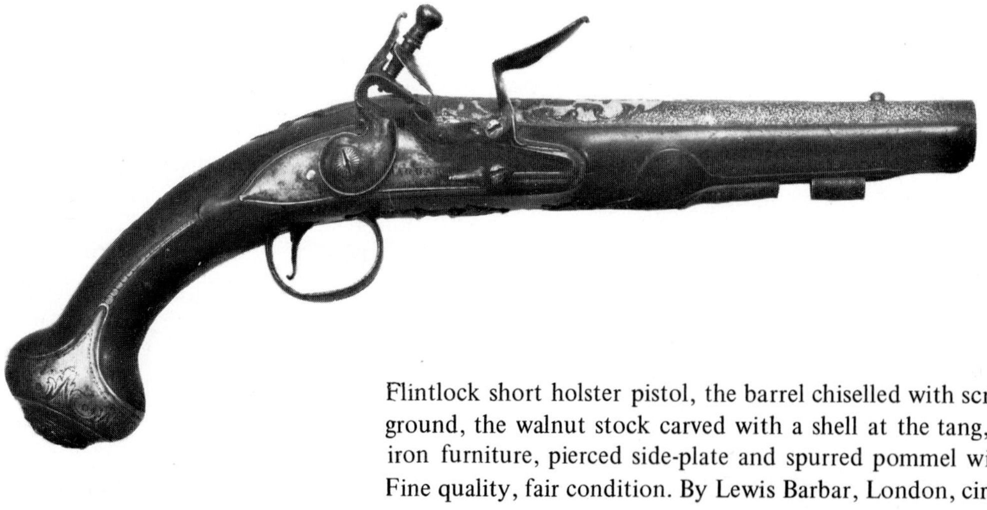

Flintlock short holster pistol, the barrel chiselled with scrolling foliage on a gold ground, the walnut stock carved with a shell at the tang, engraved and chiselled iron furniture, pierced side-plate and spurred pommel with chiselled floral cap. Fine quality, fair condition. By Lewis Barbar, London, circa 1740-50. 12½in.
Christie's

About £250

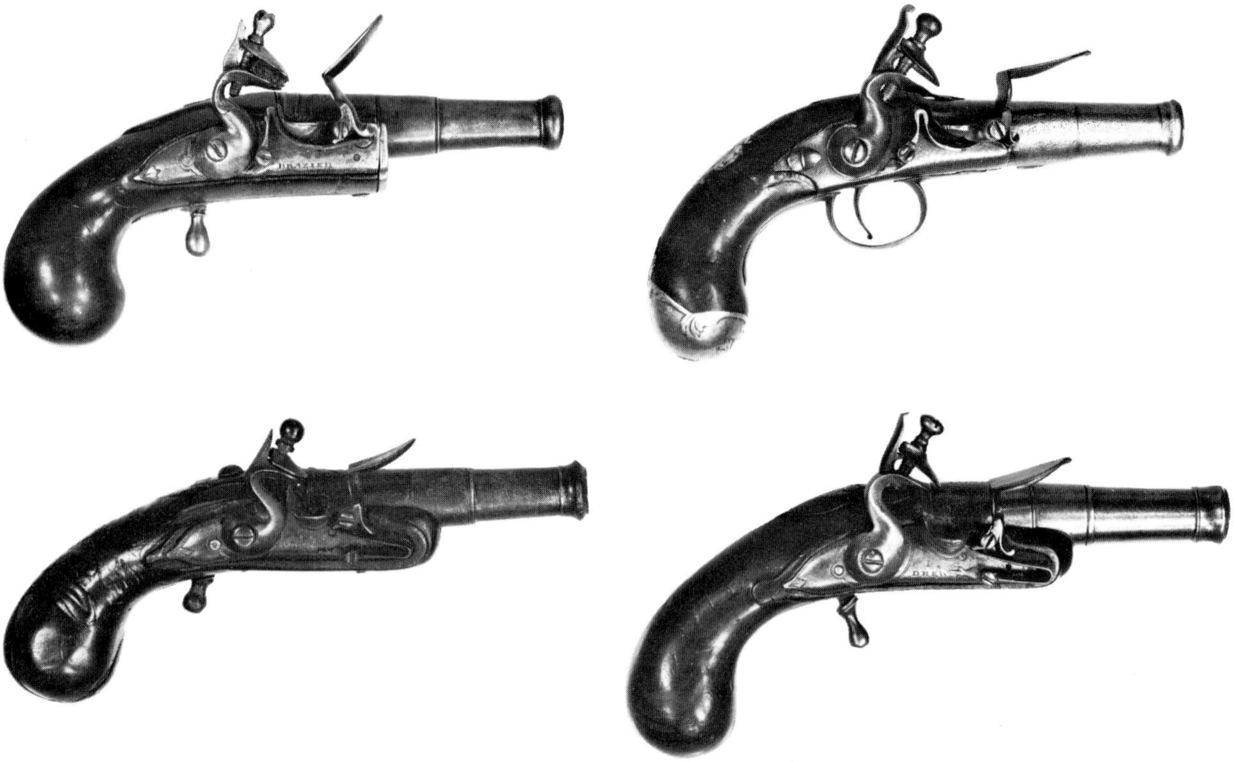

A group of English flintlock pocket pistols of good quality, each with short turn-off cannon barrel. Three have separate side-lock actions, button-triggers and plain globose butts, fitted only with a side-plate in each case. The fourth is of the "Queen Anne" type, with separate trigger-guard, and the butt has silver mounts. *Christie's*

Top Left:	By W. Brazier, London. Poor condition. Early 18th century. 7in. *£150 – £200*
Top Right:	London maker's signature effaced. Poor condition, cock replaced. Circa 1720. 6¾in. *About £150*
Bottom Left:	By I. Shorey. Stock repaired, cock replaced. Circa 1700. 7¼in. *£150 – £225*
Bottom Right:	By I. Drew, London. Each cock replaced, but condition otherwise good. This is one of a pair. Early 18th century. 7¼in. *£400 – £500 the pair*

Pair of flintlock pocket pistols with turn-off cannon barrels faceted at the breech, separate trigger-guards, carved walnut butts and silver mounts, the butt-caps similar in form to those on the pistols shown on page 47. Fine quality and untouched condition. By David Wynn, London, circa 1715/20. 7in. *Christie's*

About £800 the pair, as they are a particularly good example of this rare type. John Hosey made similar pistols without silver butt-caps.

Flintlock pocket pistol showing a later form of the same type. Turn-off cannon barrel and walnut butt with silver furniture. Note that the trigger-guard is attached direct to the action. Fine quality, good condition. By Stanton, London, mid-18th century. 7in. *Christie's*

About £200

Scottish Flintlock Pistols - 1700 - 1750

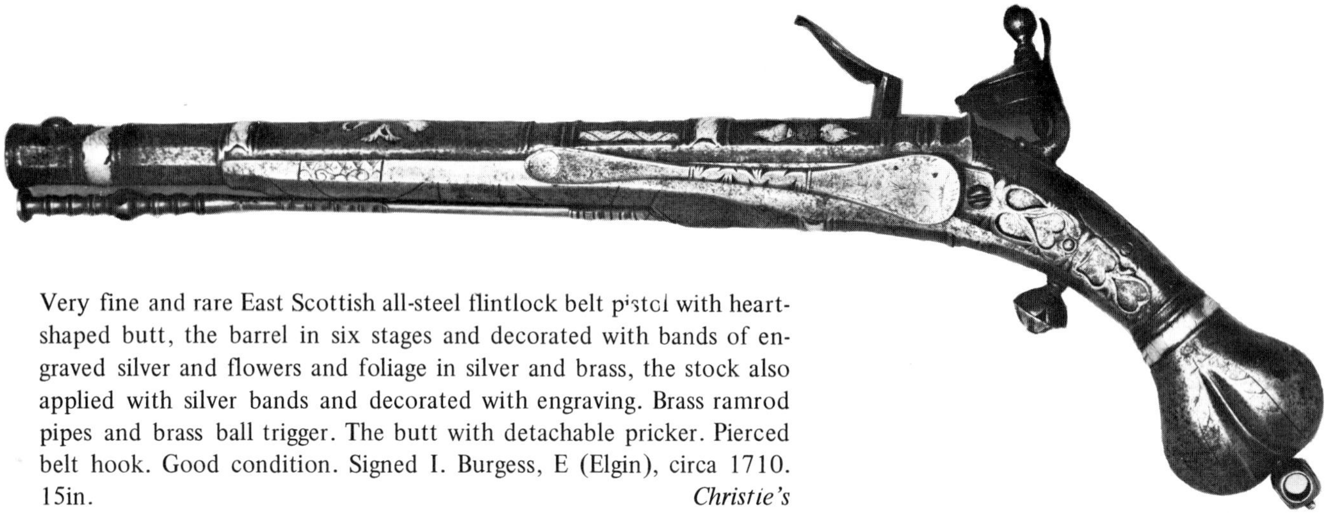

Very fine and rare East Scottish all-steel flintlock belt pistol with heart-shaped butt, the barrel in six stages and decorated with bands of engraved silver and flowers and foliage in silver and brass, the stock also applied with silver bands and decorated with engraving. Brass ramrod pipes and brass ball trigger. The butt with detachable pricker. Pierced belt hook. Good condition. Signed I. Burgess, E (Elgin), circa 1710. 15in. *Christie's*

Over £3,000

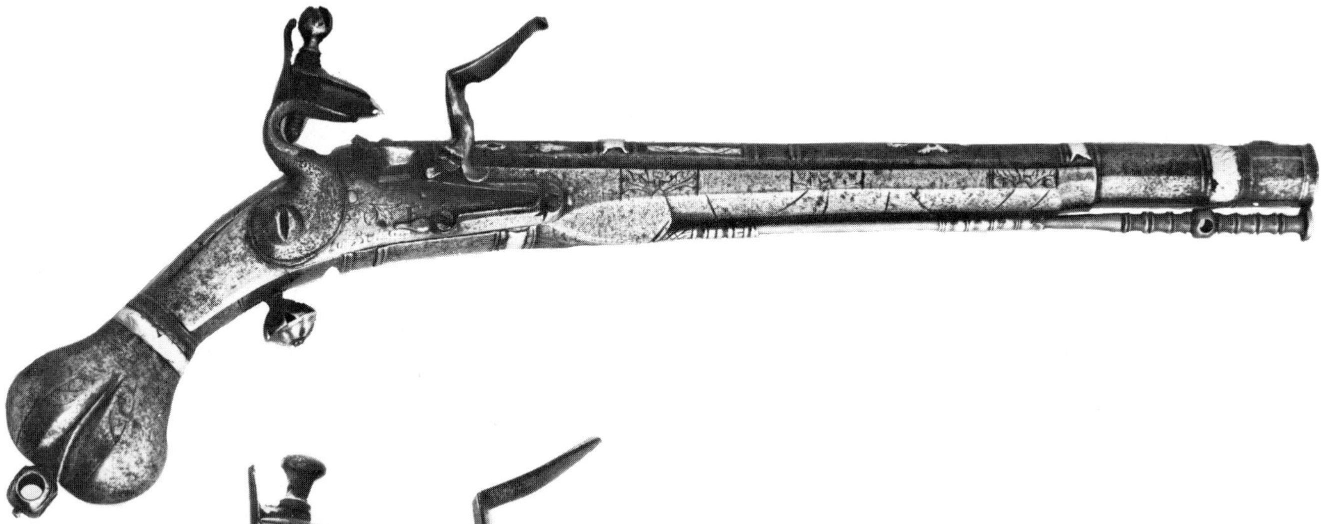

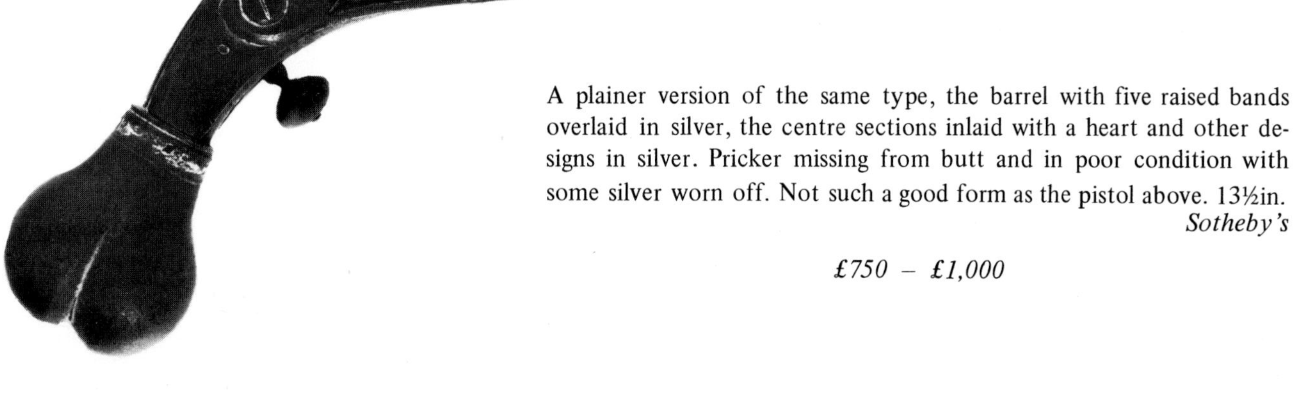

A plainer version of the same type, the barrel with five raised bands overlaid in silver, the centre sections inlaid with a heart and other designs in silver. Pricker missing from butt and in poor condition with some silver worn off. Not such a good form as the pistol above. 13½in. *Sotheby's*

£750 – £1,000

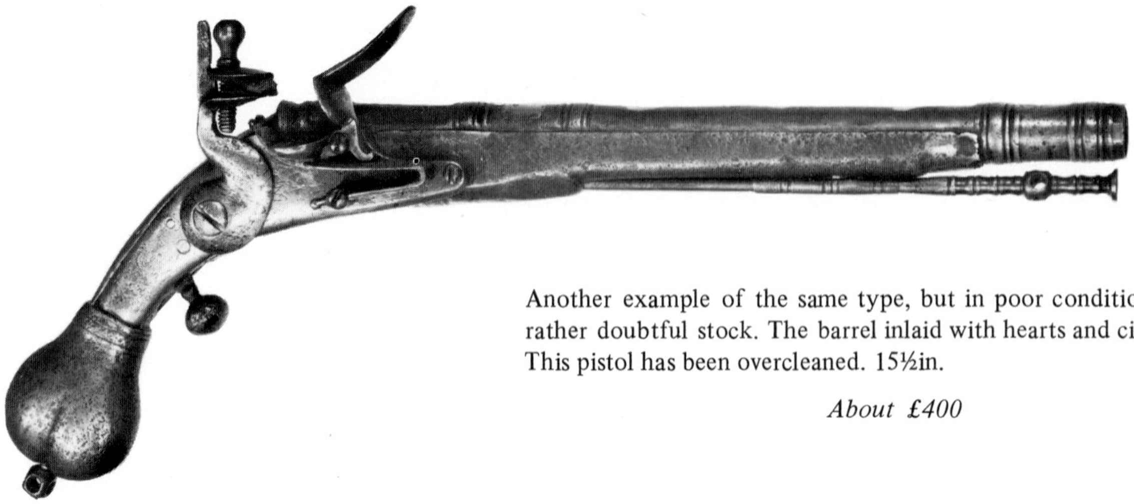

Another example of the same type, but in poor condition and with a rather doubtful stock. The barrel inlaid with hearts and circles in silver. This pistol has been overcleaned. 15½in. *Christie's*

About £400

Scottish all-steel flintlock belt pistol with ram's horn butt, a type found from the late 17th century right up to about 1840. Very good form with a nice squat rounded cock and the robust early type of stock (cf. page 19). Boldly decorated with stars and roses and a coat-of-arms, also rope twists and engraved bars in silver. Fine condition. Signed John Campbell,Downe (Doune), early 18th century. 16¼in. *Sotheby's*

Over £3,000. This is a particularly fine example.

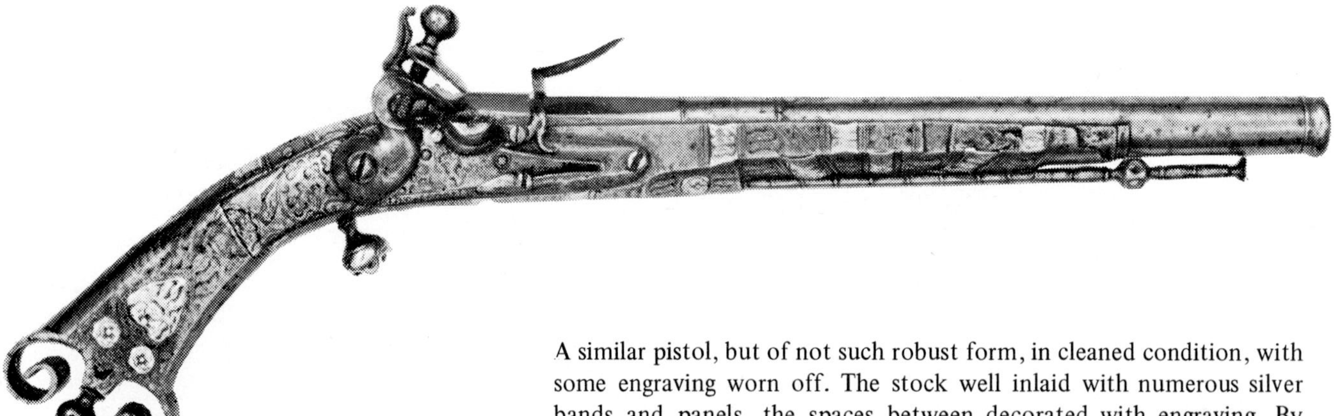

A similar pistol, but of not such robust form, in cleaned condition, with some engraving worn off. The stock well inlaid with numerous silver bands and panels, the spaces between decorated with engraving. By Thomas Caddell of Doune, second quarter of the 18th century. 16½in. *Sotheby's*

About £1,500

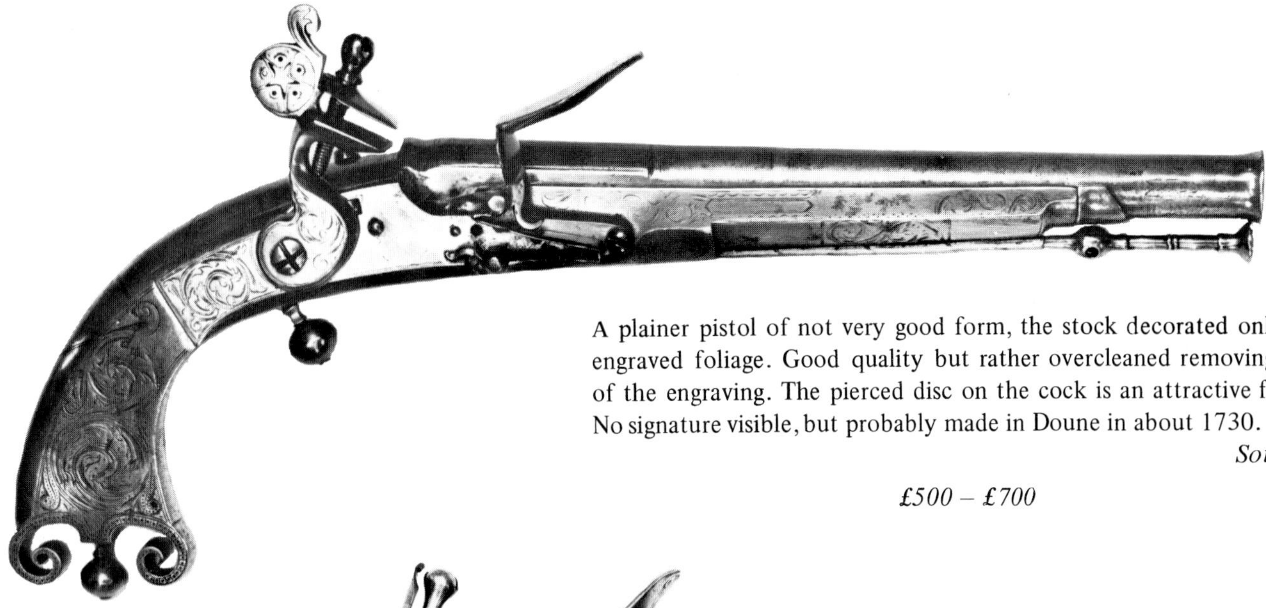

A plainer pistol of not very good form, the stock decorated only with engraved foliage. Good quality but rather overcleaned removing some of the engraving. The pierced disc on the cock is an attractive feature. No signature visible, but probably made in Doune in about 1730. 14¼in.

Sotheby's

£500 – £700

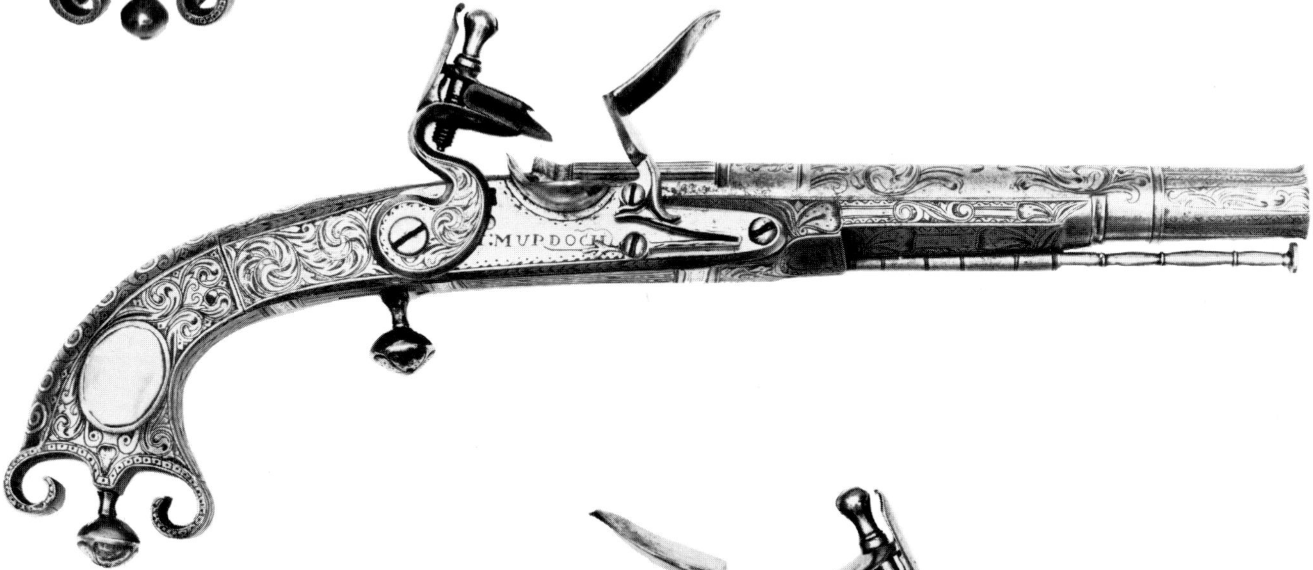

Typical pair of Scottish mid-18th century flintlock pistols, the barrels in four stages, fluted at the breech and octagonal at the muzzle and engraved with scrollwork, the stocks similarly engraved, with silver scrolls on the spine of the butt and on the underside with silver straps. Silver trigger and pricker heads engraved with an expanded flower. Oval silver escutcheon on either side of the butt, engraved with owner's name and date 1781. Pierced belt hook. Good quality, in good but perhaps slightly overcleaned condition. By I. Murdoch, Doune. 12½in.

Sotheby's

About £2,000 the pair

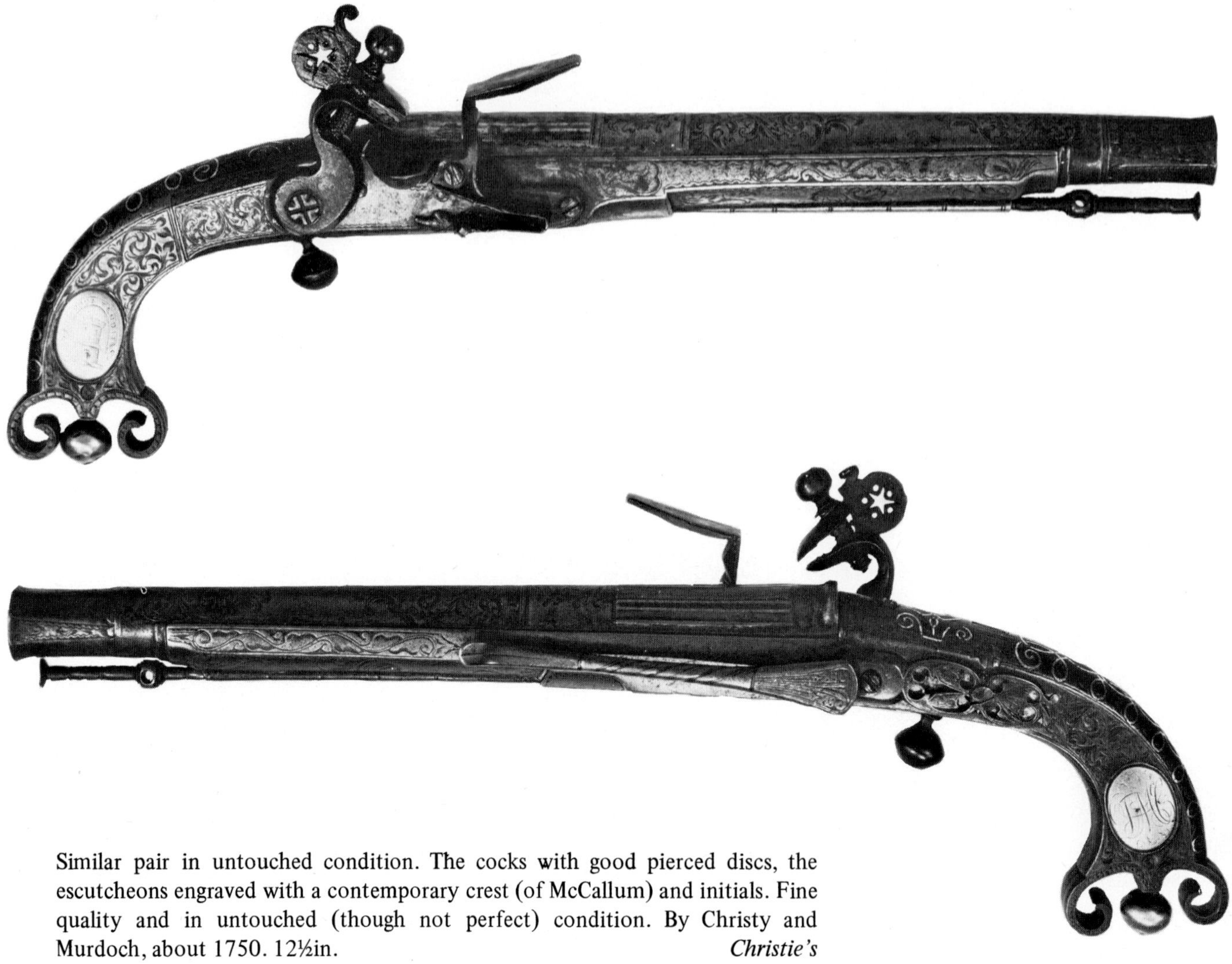

Similar pair in untouched condition. The cocks with good pierced discs, the escutcheons engraved with a contemporary crest (of McCallum) and initials. Fine quality and in untouched (though not perfect) condition. By Christy and Murdoch, about 1750. 12½in. *Christie's*

£2,000 – £2,500 the pair

Outstanding pair of flintlock pistols of this type, in quality, condition and form. In untouched original state throughout, even retaining some original blueing on the breeches. By Thomas Caddell of Doune, mid-18th century. 12½in.
Christie's

Over £5,000 the pair

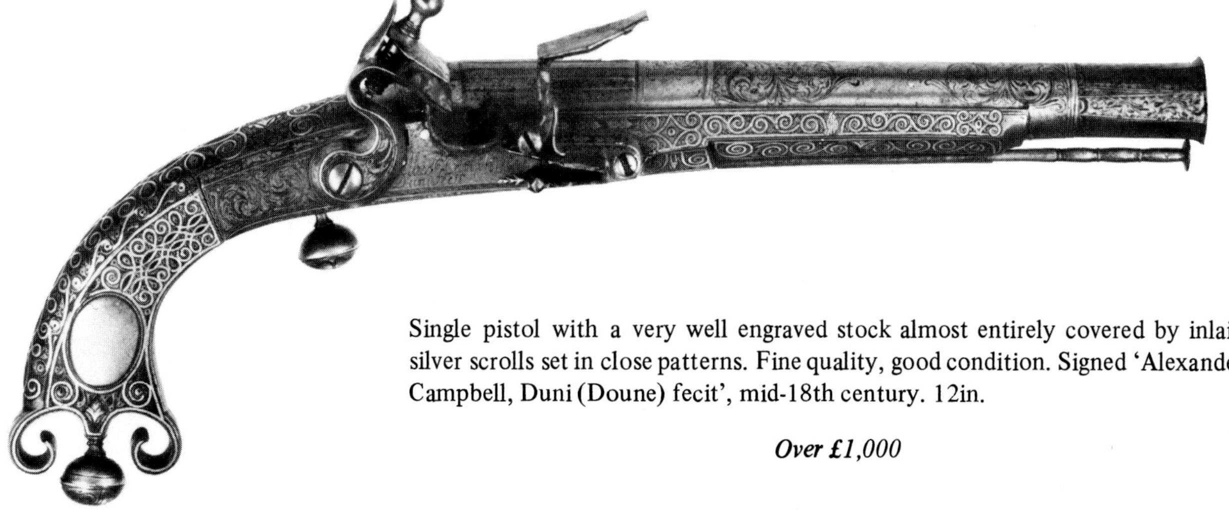

Single pistol with a very well engraved stock almost entirely covered by inlaid silver scrolls set in close patterns. Fine quality, good condition. Signed 'Alexander Campbell, Duni (Doune) fecit', mid-18th century. 12in.

Over £1,000

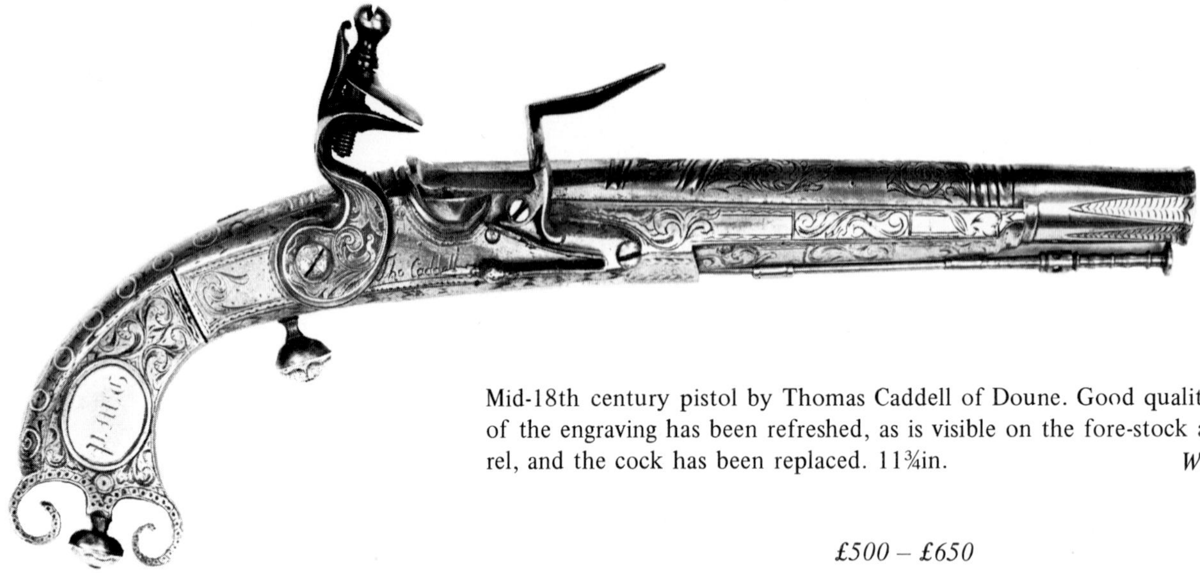

Mid-18th century pistol by Thomas Caddell of Doune. Good quality but some of the engraving has been refreshed, as is visible on the fore-stock and the barrel, and the cock has been replaced. 11¾in. *Weller & Dufty*

£500 – £650

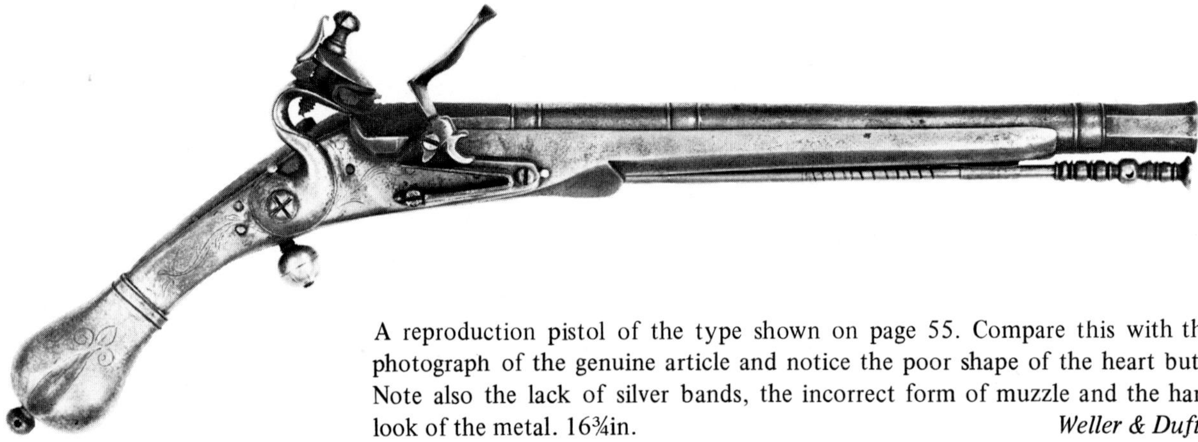

A reproduction pistol of the type shown on page 55. Compare this with the photograph of the genuine article and notice the poor shape of the heart butt. Note also the lack of silver bands, the incorrect form of muzzle and the hard look of the metal. 16¾in. *Weller & Dufty*

£200 – £250

Continental Flintlock Pistols - 1700 - 1750

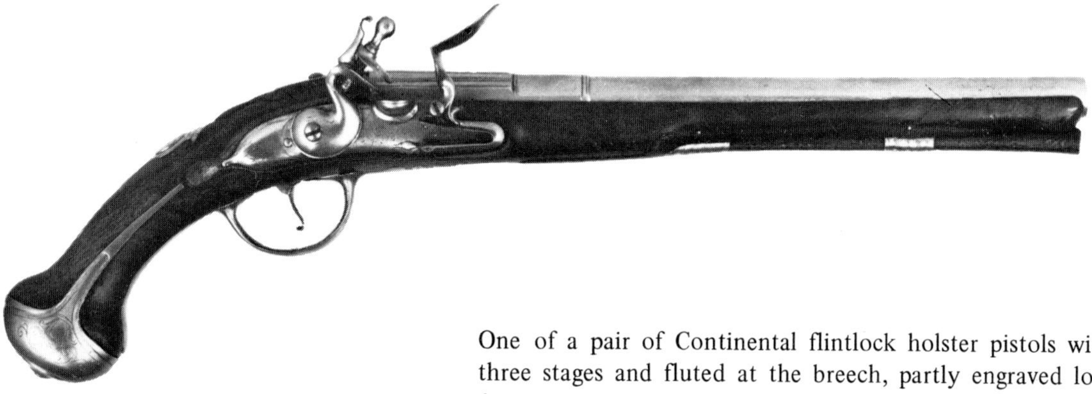

One of a pair of Continental flintlock holster pistols with barrels in three stages and fluted at the breech, partly engraved locks and iron furniture, full stocks and spurred pommels. Poor quality, but good condition. Unsigned, probably Liège, early 18th century. 20in.

Christie's

£600 – £750 the pair.

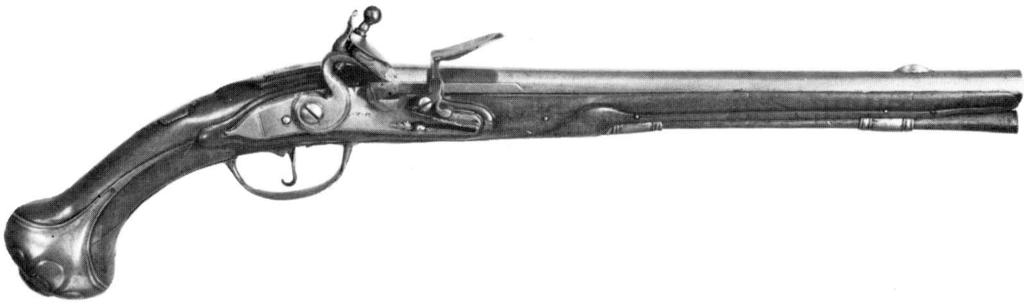

One of a pair of Continental flintlock holster pistols of similar quality but slightly more elegant form. Slight repairs to stocks. Unsigned, circa 1740. 20½in.

Christie's

£750 – £1,000 the pair.

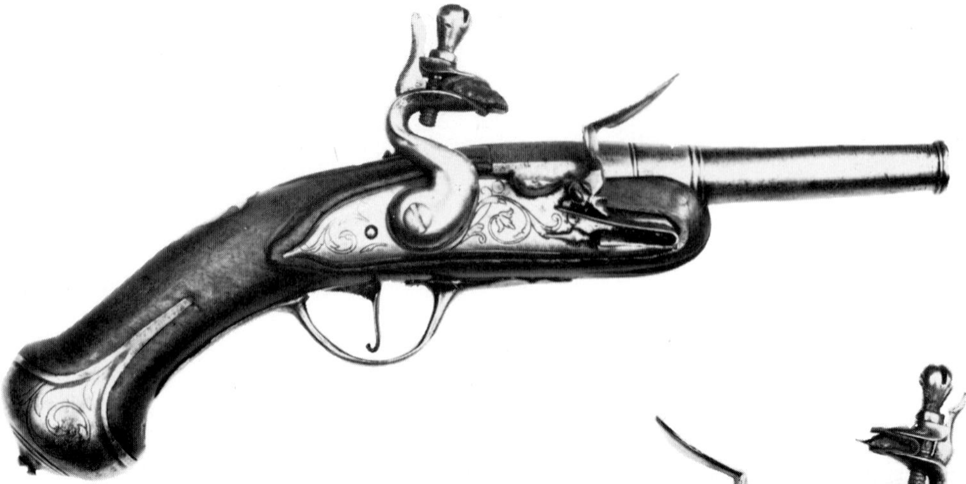

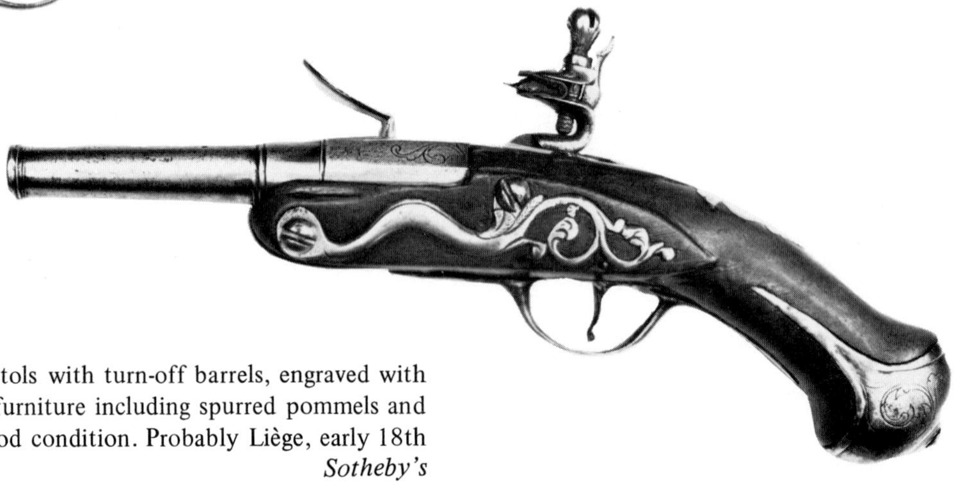

Pair of Continental flintlock rifled pistols with turn-off barrels, engraved with foliage on the lock and breech, steel furniture including spurred pommels and serpentine side-plates. Poor quality, good condition. Probably Liège, early 18th century. 10in. *Sotheby's*

£300 – £400 the pair

This type of pistol is often confused with English pistols of slightly earlier date. Note the poor shape of the cock and the stock, also the rather stiff engraving.

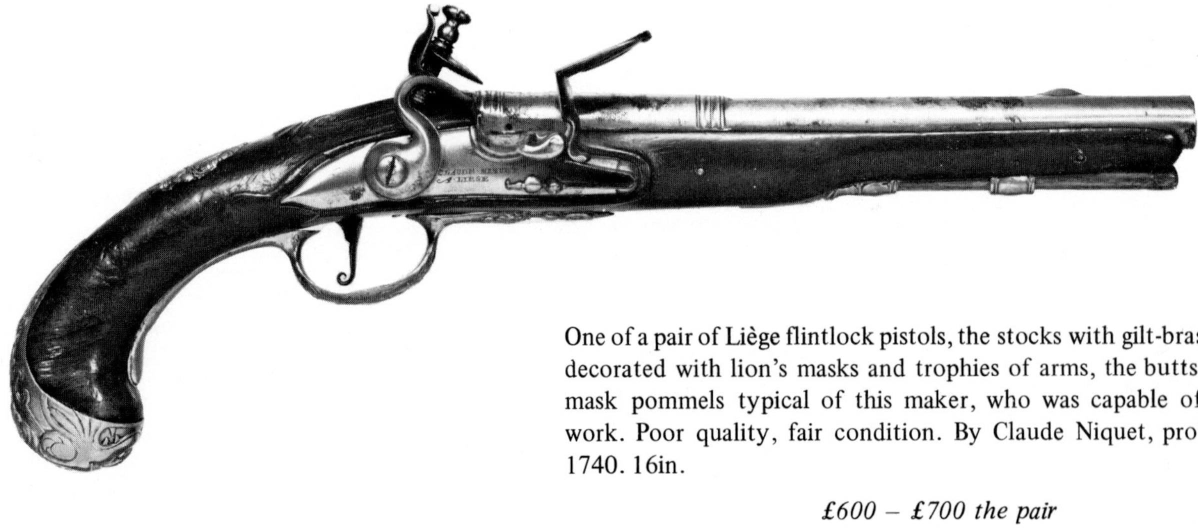

One of a pair of Liège flintlock pistols, the stocks with gilt-brass furnitur decorated with lion's masks and trophies of arms, the butts with lion' mask pommels typical of this maker, who was capable of far bette work. Poor quality, fair condition. By Claude Niquet, probably circ 1740. 16in. *Christie*

£600 – £700 the pair

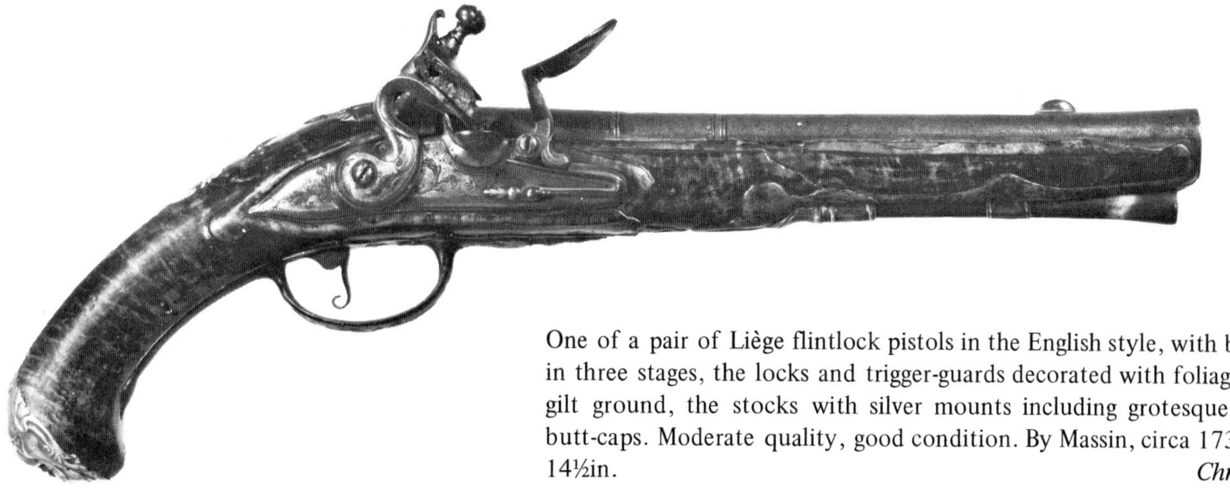

One of a pair of Liège flintlock pistols in the English style, with barrels in three stages, the locks and trigger-guards decorated with foliage on a gilt ground, the stocks with silver mounts including grotesque mask butt-caps. Moderate quality, good condition. By Massin, circa 1730/40. 14½in. *Christie's*

£400 – £500 the pair

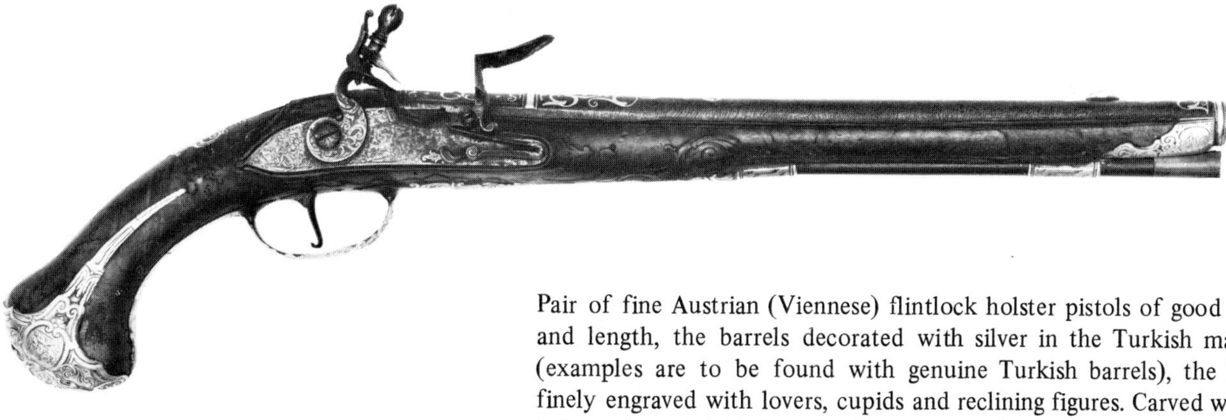

Pair of fine Austrian (Viennese) flintlock holster pistols of good form and length, the barrels decorated with silver in the Turkish manner (examples are to be found with genuine Turkish barrels), the locks finely engraved with lovers, cupids and reclining figures. Carved walnut full stocks and full silver furniture engraved with figures, and classical busts, the spurred pommels with female figures within scrollwork. Fine quality, good condition. Unsigned. Vienna hallmark for 1727. 20¾in. *Sotheby's*

About £4,000 the pair

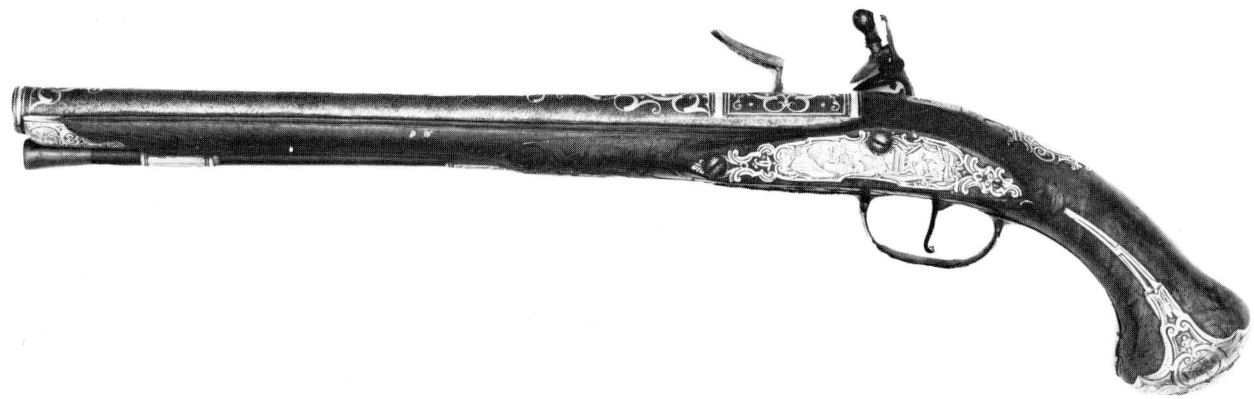

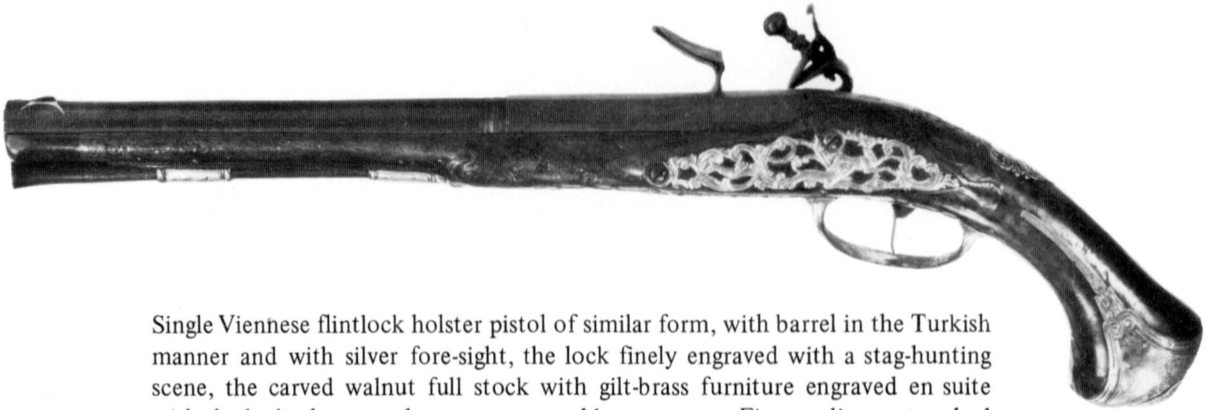

Single Viennese flintlock holster pistol of similar form, with barrel in the Turkish manner and with silver fore-sight, the lock finely engraved with a stag-hunting scene, the carved walnut full stock with gilt-brass furniture engraved en suite with the lock, the escutcheon surmounted by a coronet. Fine quality, untouched condition. Circa 1720. 20¼in. *Christie's*

£600 – £800

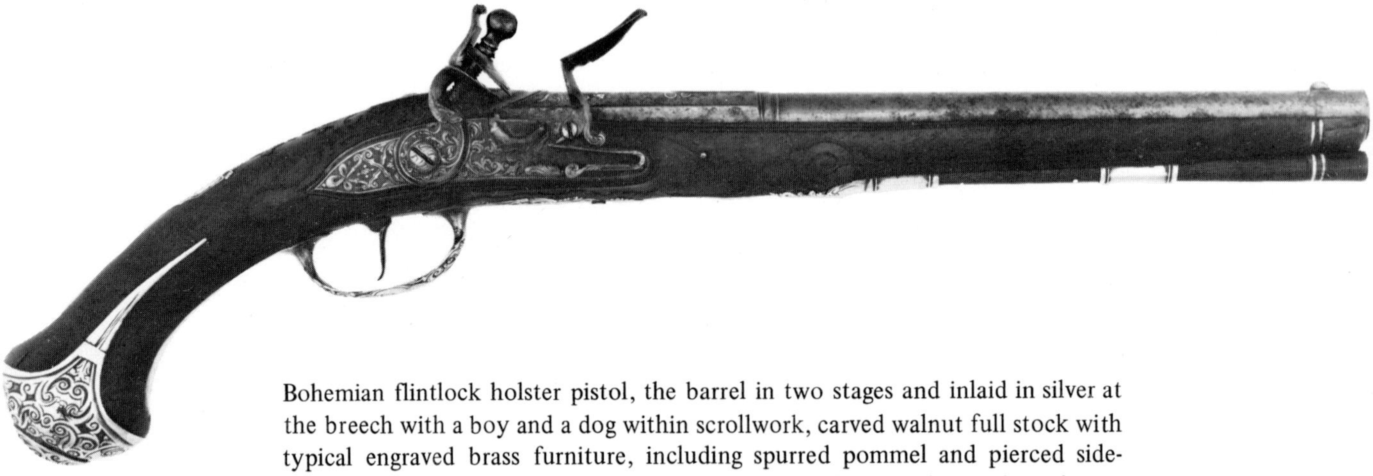

Bohemian flintlock holster pistol, the barrel in two stages and inlaid in silver at the breech with a boy and a dog within scrollwork, carved walnut full stock with typical engraved brass furniture, including spurred pommel and pierced side-plate, the lock finely engraved with scrolling foliage. Good quality and condition. Early 18th century. 20½in. *Sotheby's*

£300 – £500

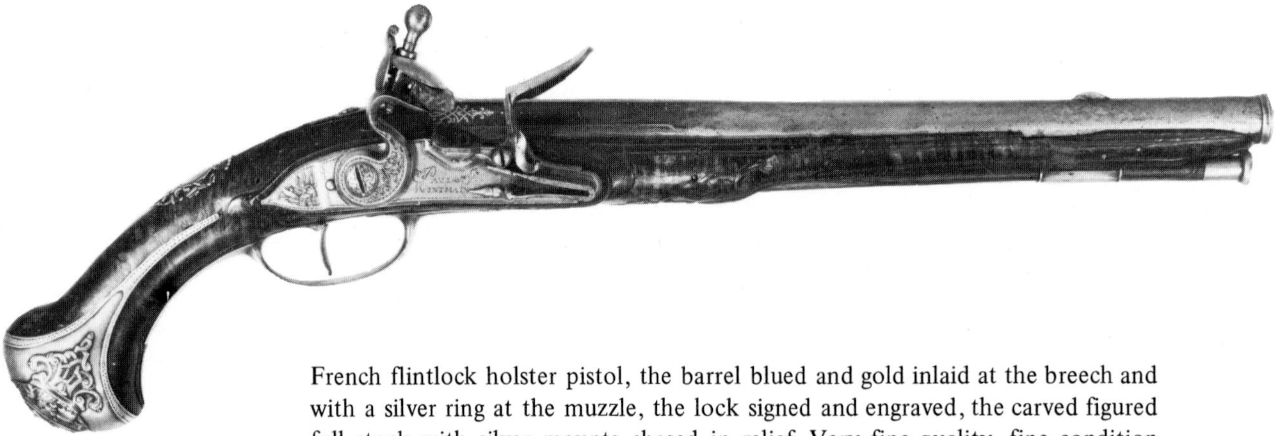

French flintlock holster pistol, the barrel blued and gold inlaid at the breech and with a silver ring at the muzzle, the lock signed and engraved, the carved figured full stock with silver mounts chased in relief. Very fine quality, fine condition despite minor defects. By Paul Montmain, circa 1720. *Christie's*

£1,500 – £2,000

From the Hesse-Darmstadt armoury.

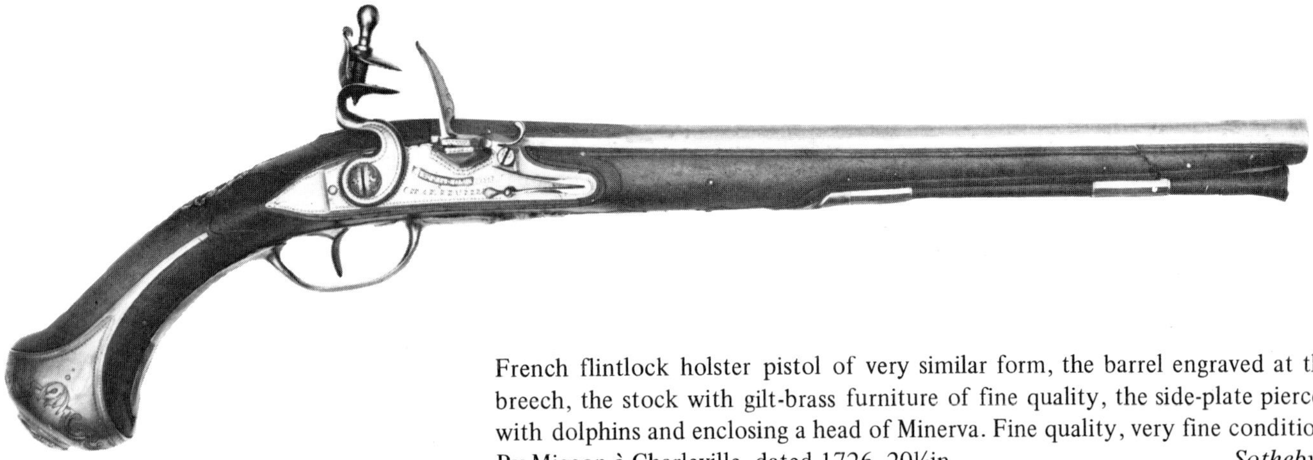

French flintlock holster pistol of very similar form, the barrel engraved at the breech, the stock with gilt-brass furniture of fine quality, the side-plate pierced with dolphins and enclosing a head of Minerva. Fine quality, very fine condition. By Migeon à Charleville, dated 1726. 20¼in. *Sotheby's*

£500 – £650

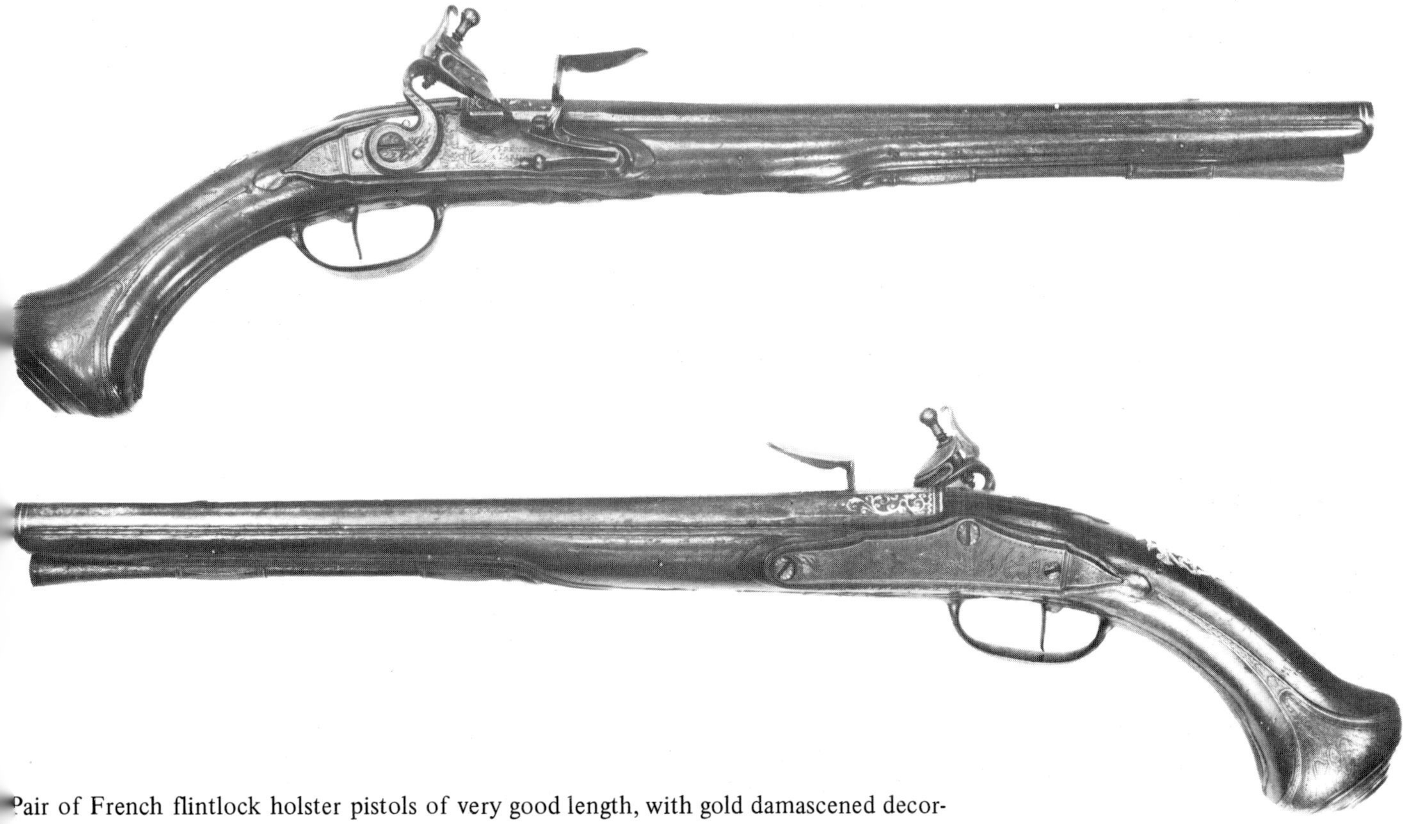

Pair of French flintlock holster pistols of very good length, with gold damascened decoration and signature on the barrels which retain their blueing, the locks signed and also engraved. Walnut full stocks carved around the steel mounts which are engraved with trophies of arms and scrollwork. Solid side-plates and spurred pommels with oval caps engraved with Roman busts, engraved silver escutcheons. Fine quality and condition. By Frenel, Paris, circa 1720. 21½in. *Sotheby's*

About £3,000 the pair, mainly on condition

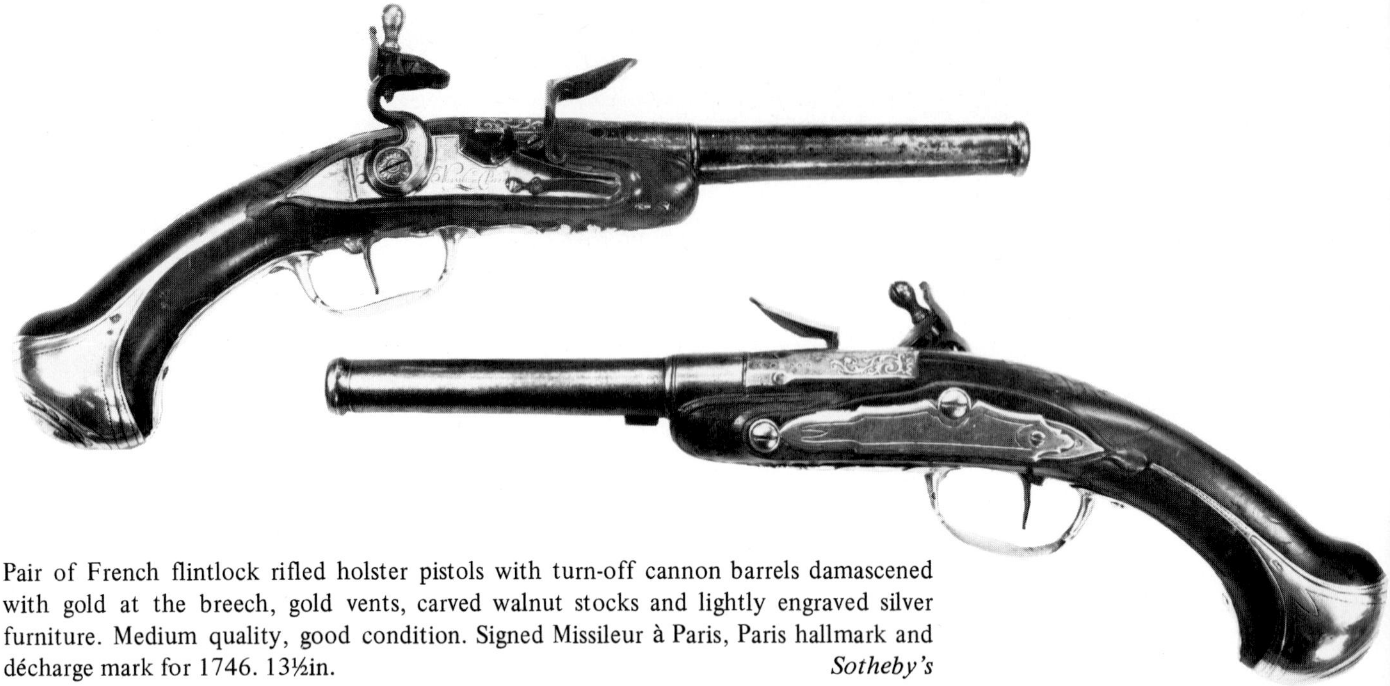

Pair of French flintlock rifled holster pistols with turn-off cannon barrels damascened with gold at the breech, gold vents, carved walnut stocks and lightly engraved silver furniture. Medium quality, good condition. Signed Missileur à Paris, Paris hallmark and décharge mark for 1746. 13½in. *Sotheby's*

Over £1,500

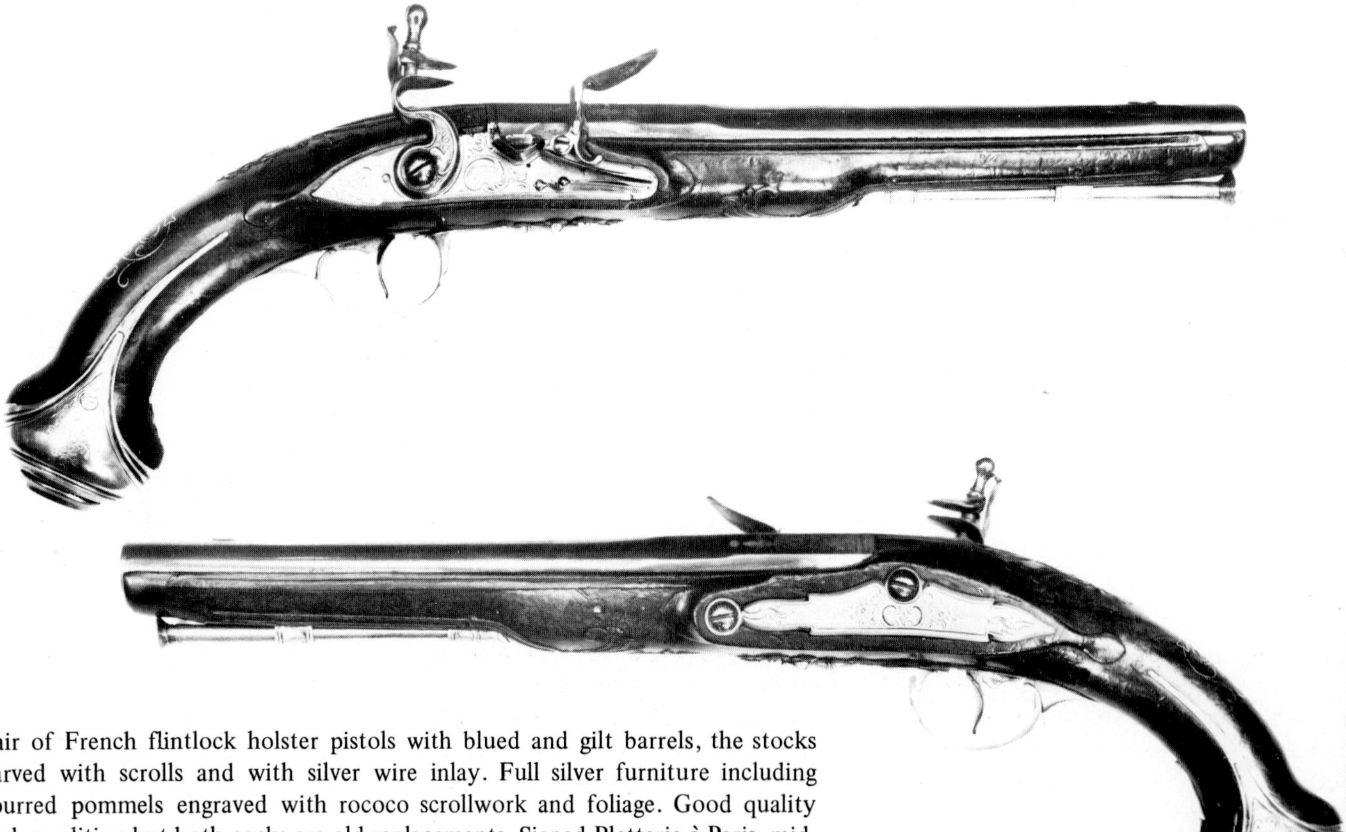

Pair of French flintlock holster pistols with blued and gilt barrels, the stocks carved with scrolls and with silver wire inlay. Full silver furniture including spurred pommels engraved with rococo scrollwork and foliage. Good quality and condition but both cocks are old replacements. Signed Bletterie à Paris, mid-18th century. 16in. *Sotheby's*

£700 – £900

A steel-mounted pair of similar quality between £500 and £700.

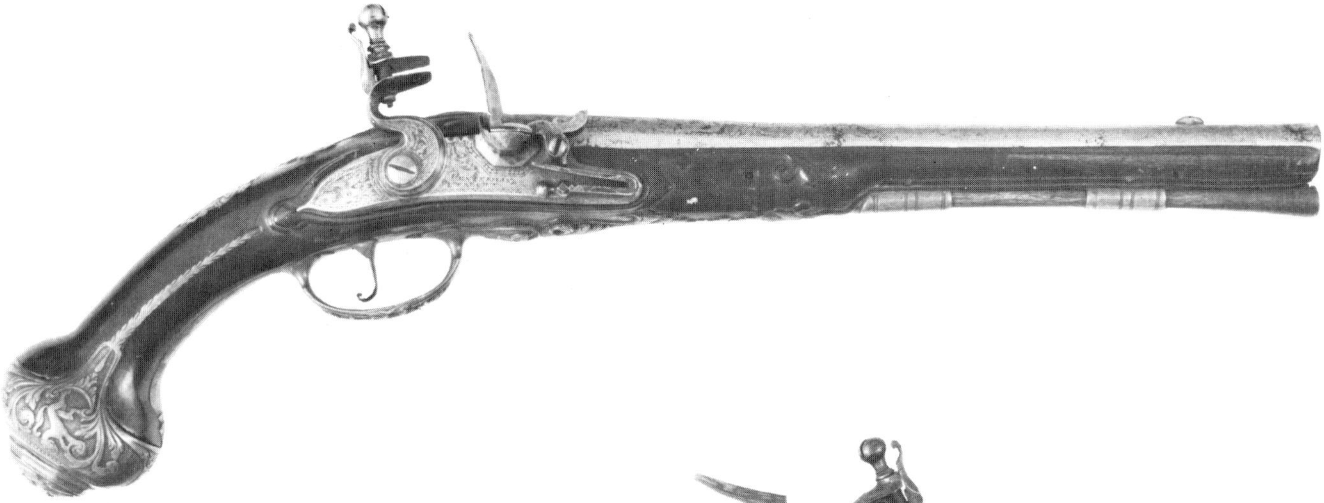

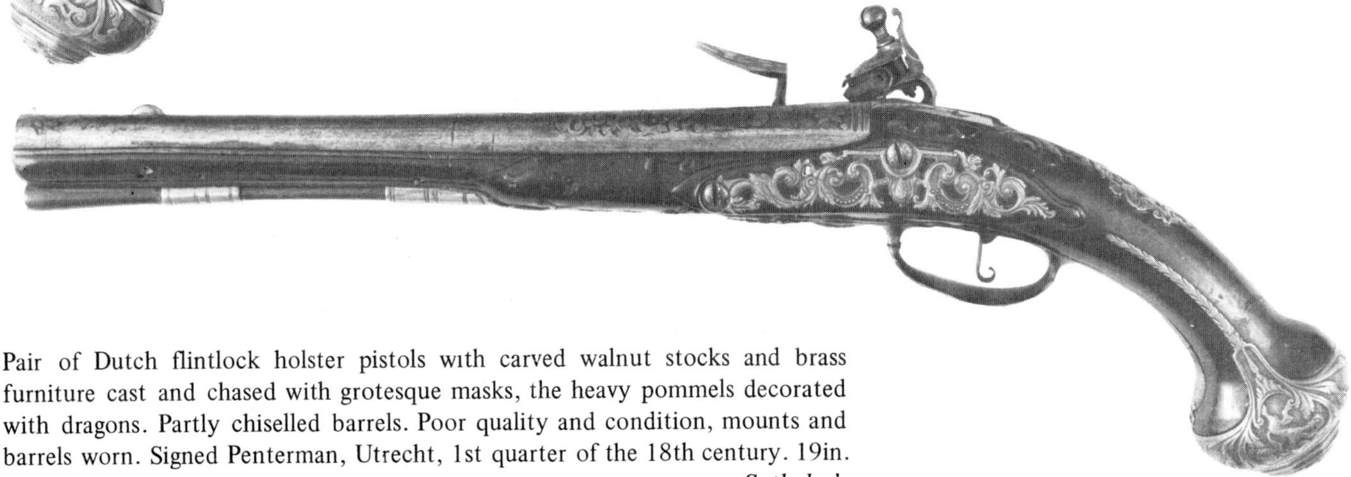

Pair of Dutch flintlock holster pistols with carved walnut stocks and brass furniture cast and chased with grotesque masks, the heavy pommels decorated with dragons. Partly chiselled barrels. Poor quality and condition, mounts and barrels worn. Signed Penterman, Utrecht, 1st quarter of the 18th century. 19in. *Sotheby's*

Over £1,200 the pair

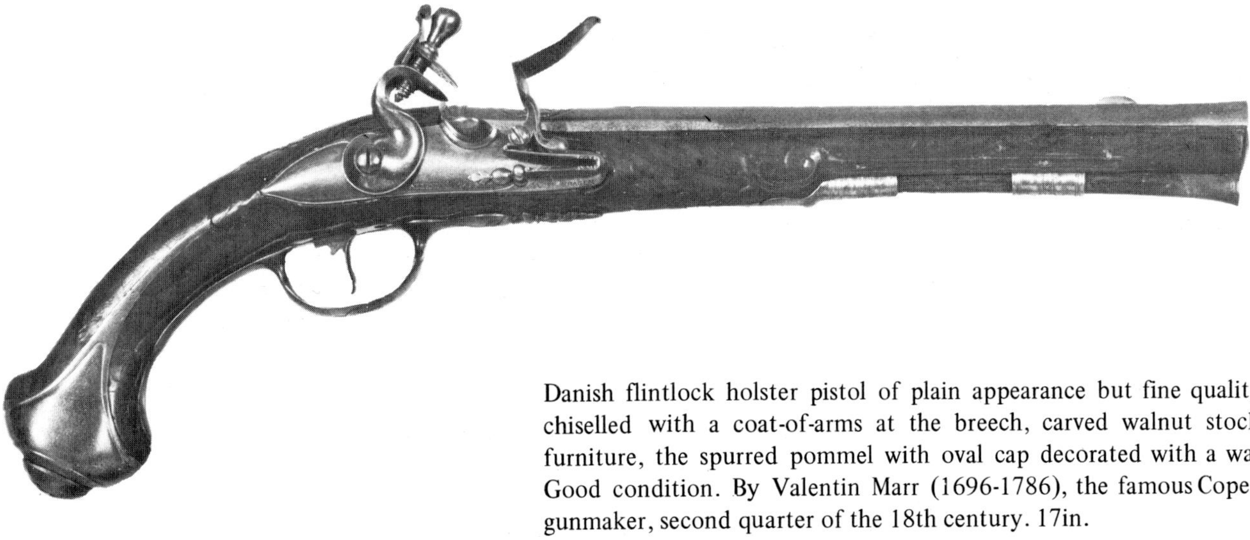

Danish flintlock holster pistol of plain appearance but fine quality, the barrel chiselled with a coat-of-arms at the breech, carved walnut stock with steel furniture, the spurred pommel with oval cap decorated with a warrior's head. Good condition. By Valentin Marr (1696-1786), the famous Copenhagen court gunmaker, second quarter of the 18th century. 17in. *Christie's*

£500 – £750

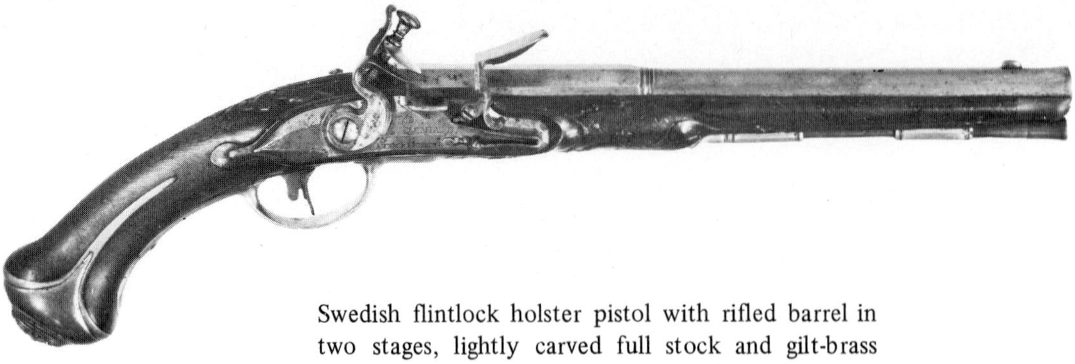

Swedish flintlock holster pistol with rifled barrel in two stages, lightly carved full stock and gilt-brass mounts. Fine quality but gilding worn. By A. Gerhardt, Stockholm, second quarter of the 18th century. 18½in. *Christie's*

About £500

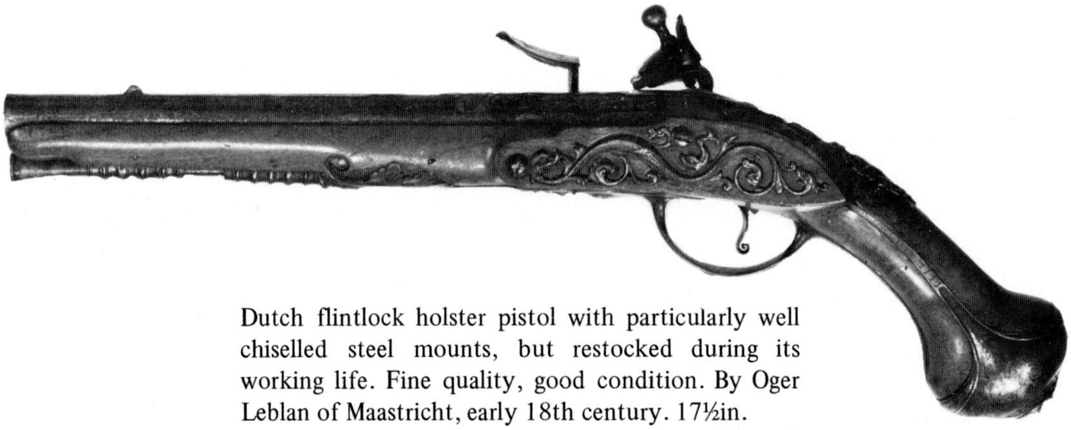

Dutch flintlock holster pistol with particularly well chiselled steel mounts, but restocked during its working life. Fine quality, good condition. By Oger Leblan of Maastricht, early 18th century. 17½in. *Christie's*

About £600

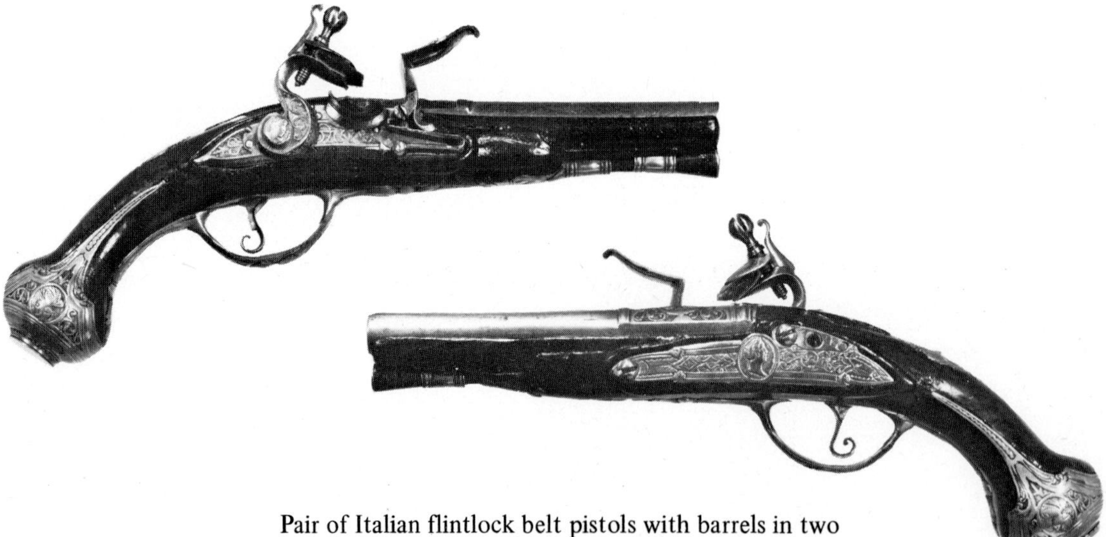

Pair of Italian flintlock belt pistols with barrels in two stages set with a female bust in brass and with two applied brass bands, the locks en suite, the full stocks with engraved brass furniture. Fine quality, but somewhat renovated condition. Signed C. Nicoli, early 18th century. 10¼in. *Christie's*

£500 – £600 the pair

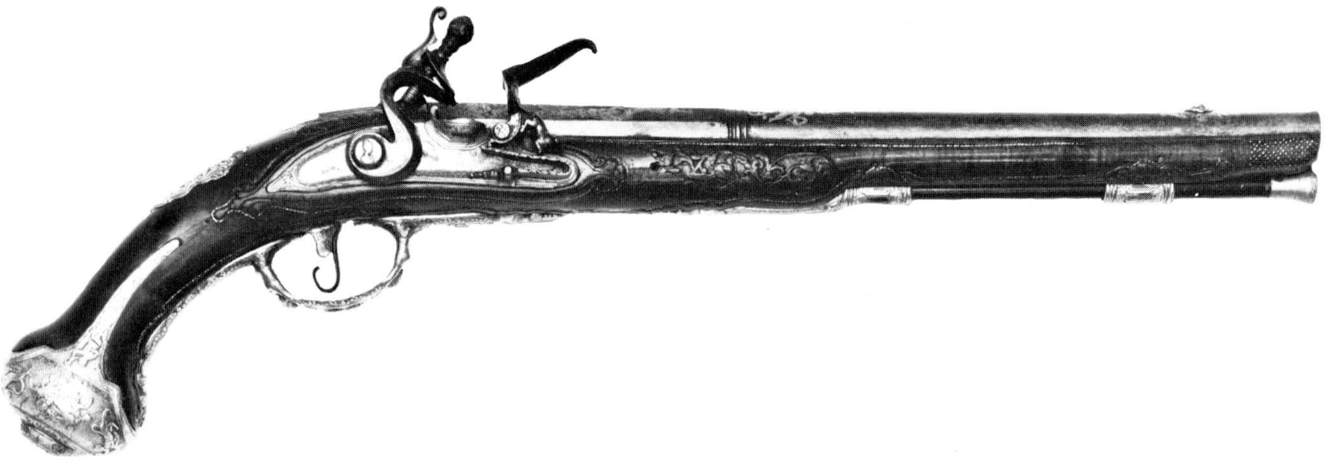

Single larger Italian flintlock pistol of the same type, the barrel decorated in silver with figures and trophies and stamped with gold maker's mark, the gilt-brass lock with silver figures. Carved full stock partly decorated with silver nails and with full gilt-brass mounts decorated with leaves, scrolls, figures, portrait heads, mythological scenes etc. Fine quality, good condition, circa 1750. 21¼ins. *Sotheby's*

Over £1,5000

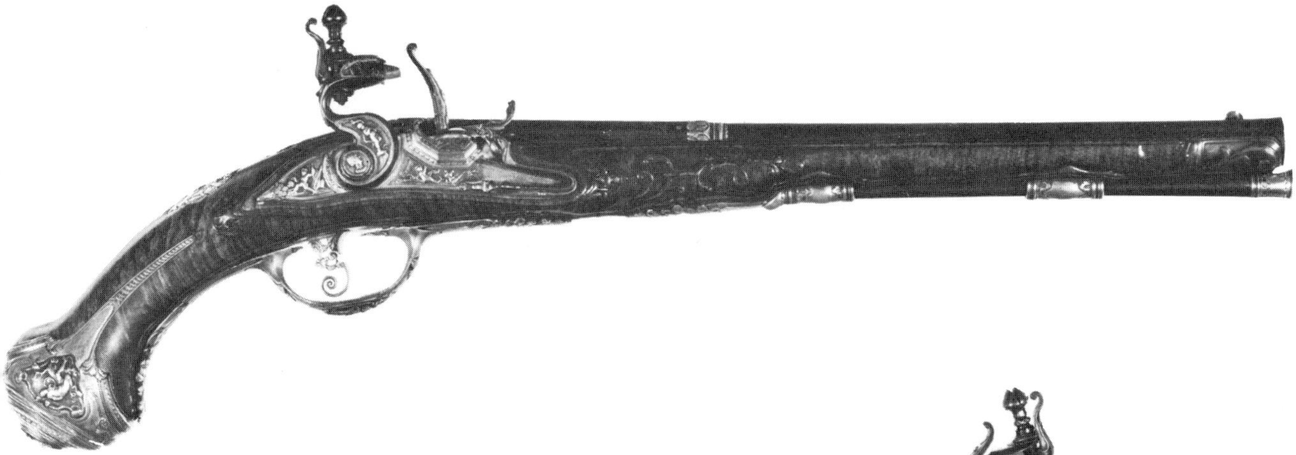

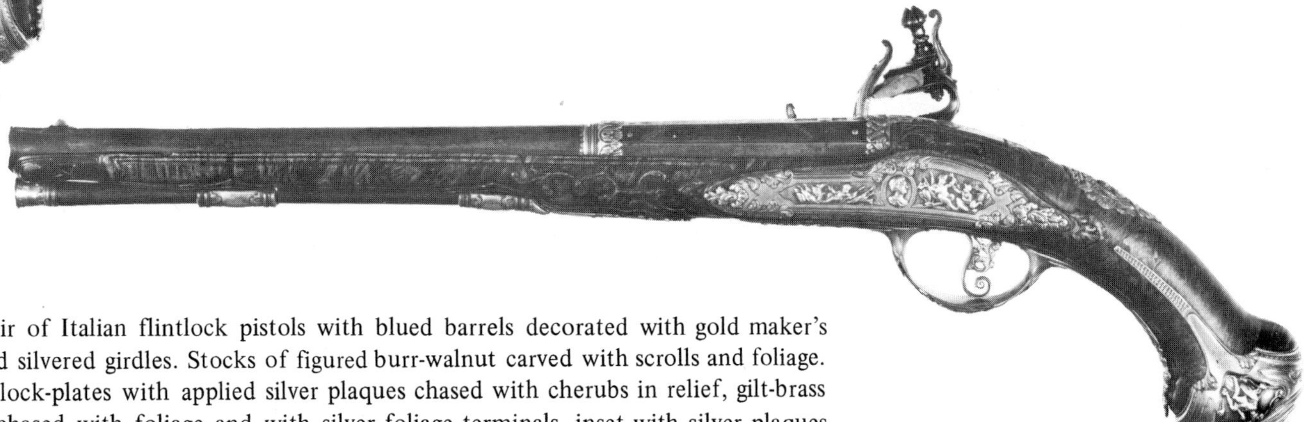

uperb pair of Italian flintlock pistols with blued barrels decorated with gold maker's tamps and silvered girdles. Stocks of figured burr-walnut carved with scrolls and foliage. ilt-brass lock-plates with applied silver plaques chased with cherubs in relief, gilt-brass urniture chased with foliage and with silver foliage terminals, inset with silver plaques ecorated in relief with numerous classical figures, the decoration on one pistol differing rom the other, as on other early 18th century pistols of the highest quality. The only crew apparent retains the barrel tang and the steel. Exceptional quality, fine condition. igned F. Bigoni in Brescia, first half of the 18th century. 21in. *Sotheby's*

Over £10,000 the pair

Pair of Spanish holster pistols with Madrid locks. This mechanism is a Spanish version of the French flintlock, a mixture between it and the miquelet-lock. The cock is held in the half-cock position by a bar which comes through the lock-plate and engages with the breast of the cock. The full cock position is held in a similar fashion on the tail of the cock.
Barrels of typical Spanish form inlaid with silver at the breech and with chiselled girdles, carved full stocks and full silver mounts decorated with rococo scrolls, the lock-plates engraved with foliage and scrolls against a gilt ground, and signed Joseph Deop (of Ripoll). Struck on the barrels with the mark of Pedro Esteva of Barcelona, mid-18th century. 17in. *Sotheby's*

Over £1,000 the pair, even in rubbed condition

The mounts of these pistols are typical of those produced in Barcelona, in this case somewhat worn but of medium to good quality. They are also found in brass, sometimes combined with silver or pewter, often of poor quality.

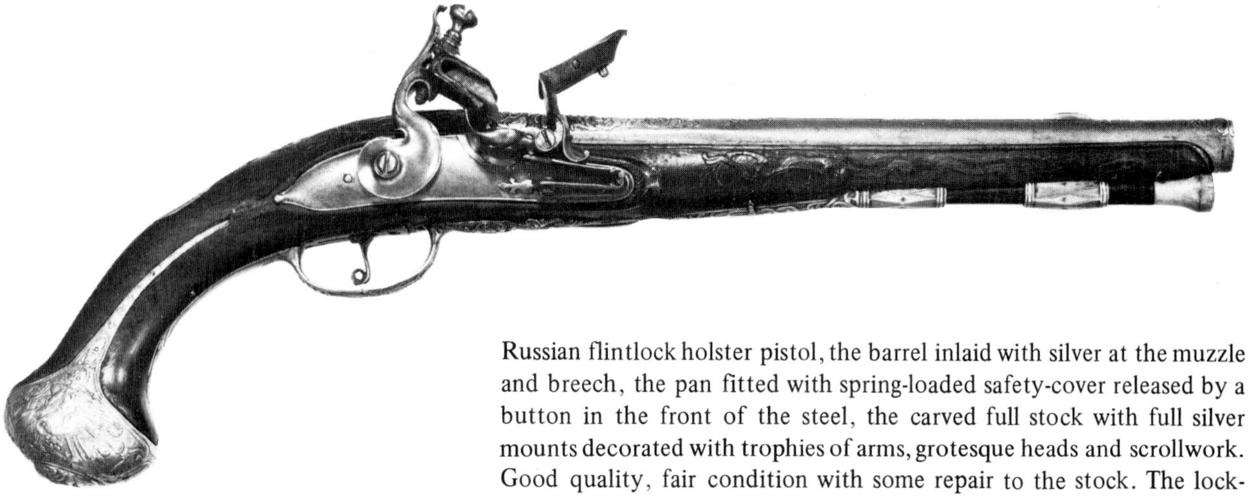

Russian flintlock holster pistol, the barrel inlaid with silver at the muzzle and breech, the pan fitted with spring-loaded safety-cover released by a button in the front of the steel, the carved full stock with full silver mounts decorated with trophies of arms, grotesque heads and scrollwork. Good quality, fair condition with some repair to the stock. The lock-plate engraved "Tula" with the date 1749. 18in. *Christie's*

£600 – £800. Very rare.

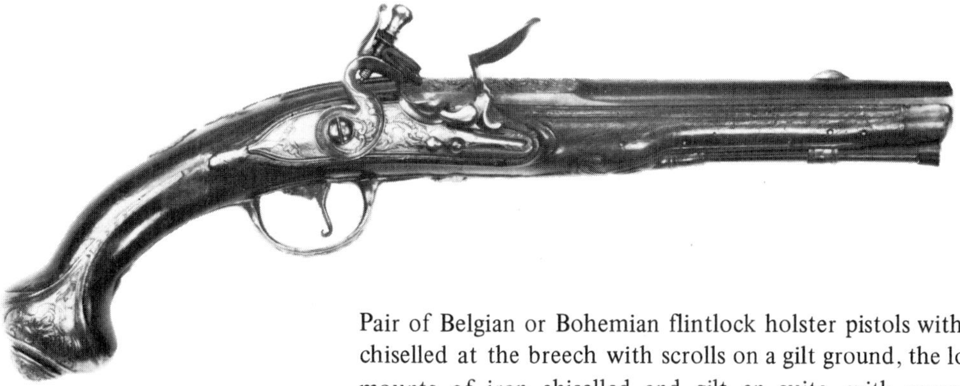

Pair of Belgian or Bohemian flintlock holster pistols with blued barrels chiselled at the breech with scrolls on a gilt ground, the lock-plates and mounts of iron chiselled and gilt en suite, with carved walnut full stocks and horn-tipped ramrods. Moderate to good quality, good condition. Unsigned, mid-18th century. 13½in. *Sotheby's*

About £1,000 the pair

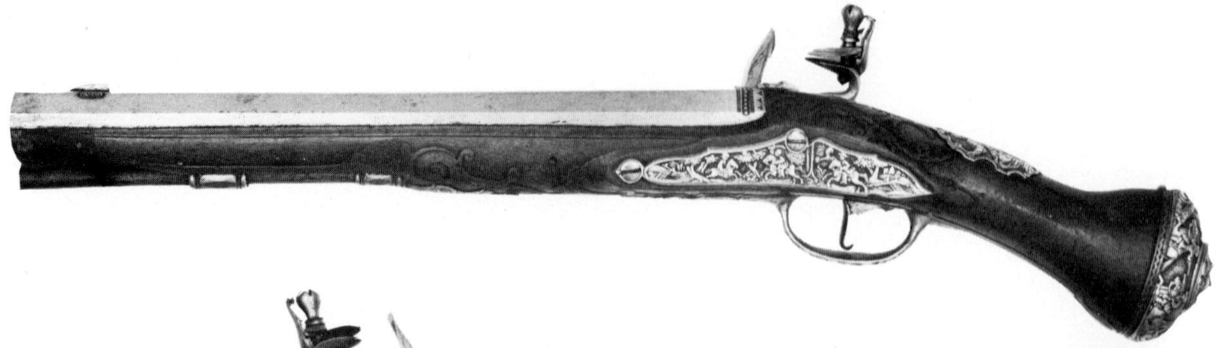

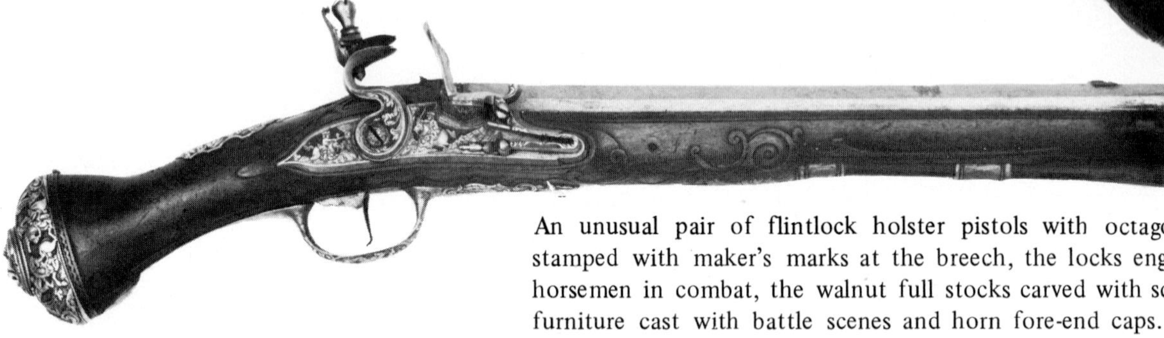

An unusual pair of flintlock holster pistols with octagonal barrels stamped with maker's marks at the breech, the locks engraved with horsemen in combat, the walnut full stocks carved with scrolls, brass furniture cast with battle scenes and horn fore-end caps. The ovoid pommels each detachable for the attachment of shoulder stocks (now missing). Fine quality, very fine condition. By Johann Andreas Hermann of Wiesenthal, second quarter of the 18th century. 19in.
Renwick Collection

About £4,000

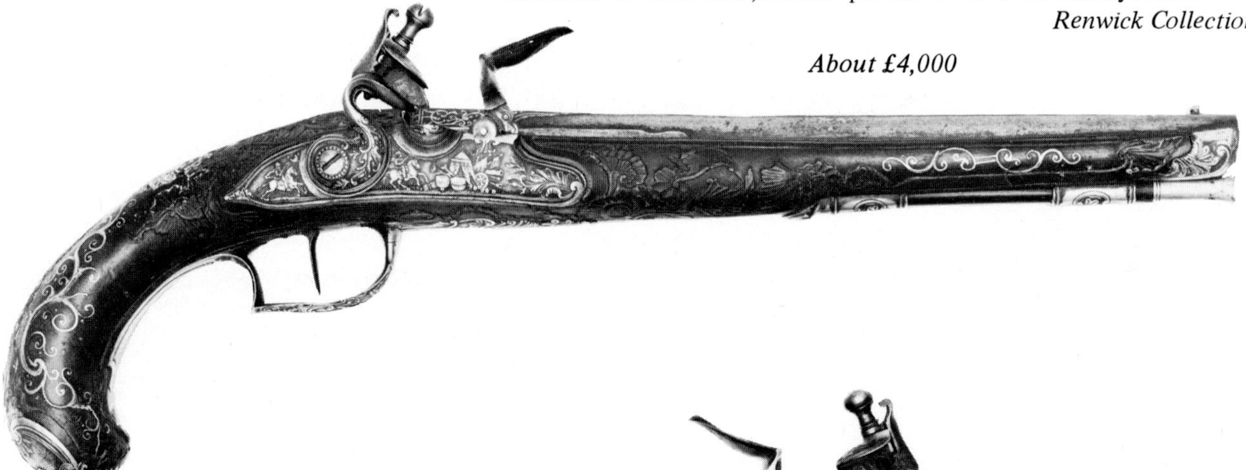

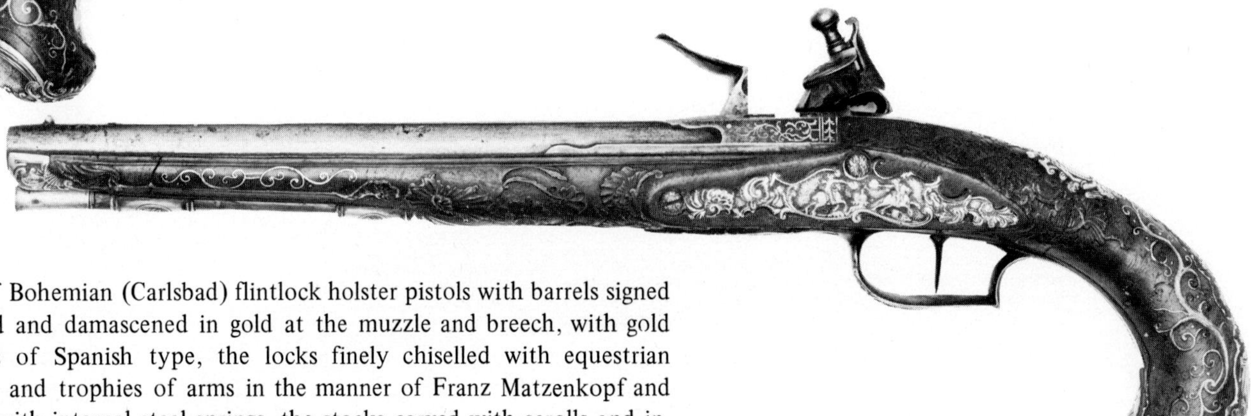

Pair of Bohemian (Carlsbad) flintlock holster pistols with barrels signed in gold and damascened in gold at the muzzle and breech, with gold stamps of Spanish type, the locks finely chiselled with equestrian figures and trophies of arms in the manner of Franz Matzenkopf and fitted with internal steel springs, the stocks carved with scrolls and inlaid with silver wire, the silver mounts cast and chased en suite with the locks within rococo scrollwork. Fine quality, good condition. By Leopold Becher. Mid-18th century. 17in. *Sotheby's*

Over £4,000 the pair

English Flintlock Pistols - 1750 - 1800

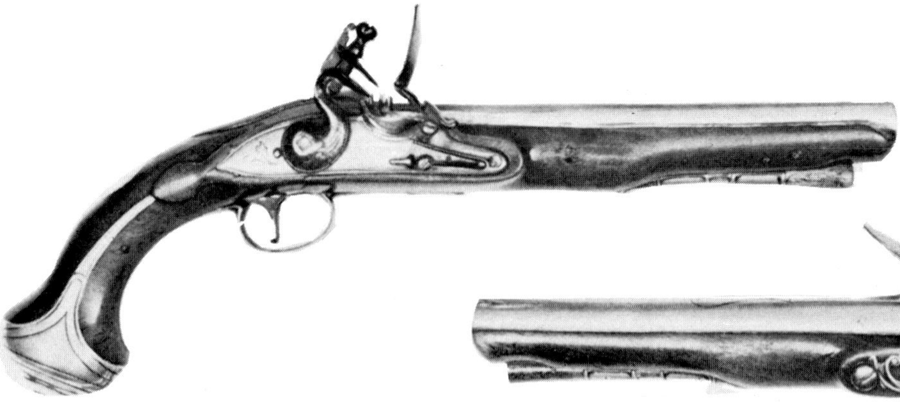

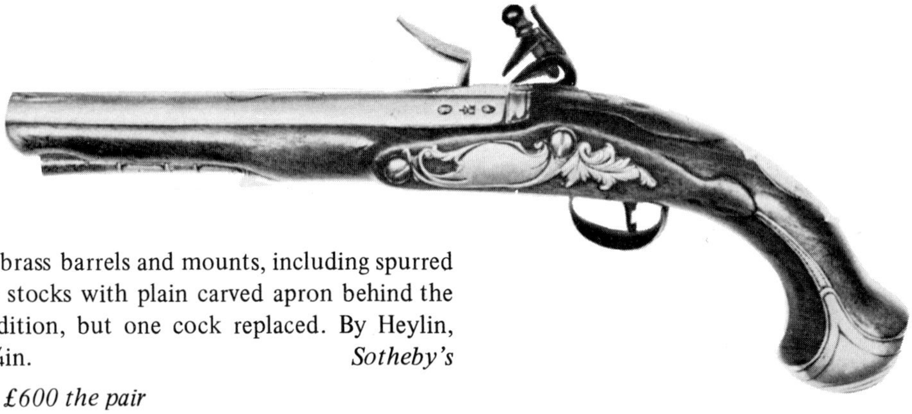

Pair of flintlock holster pistols with brass barrels and mounts, including spurred pommels and foliate side-plates. The stocks with plain carved apron behind the barrel tang. Good quality and condition, but one cock replaced. By Heylin, Cornhill, London, circa 1750-60. 14¼in. *Sotheby's*

£500 – £600 the pair

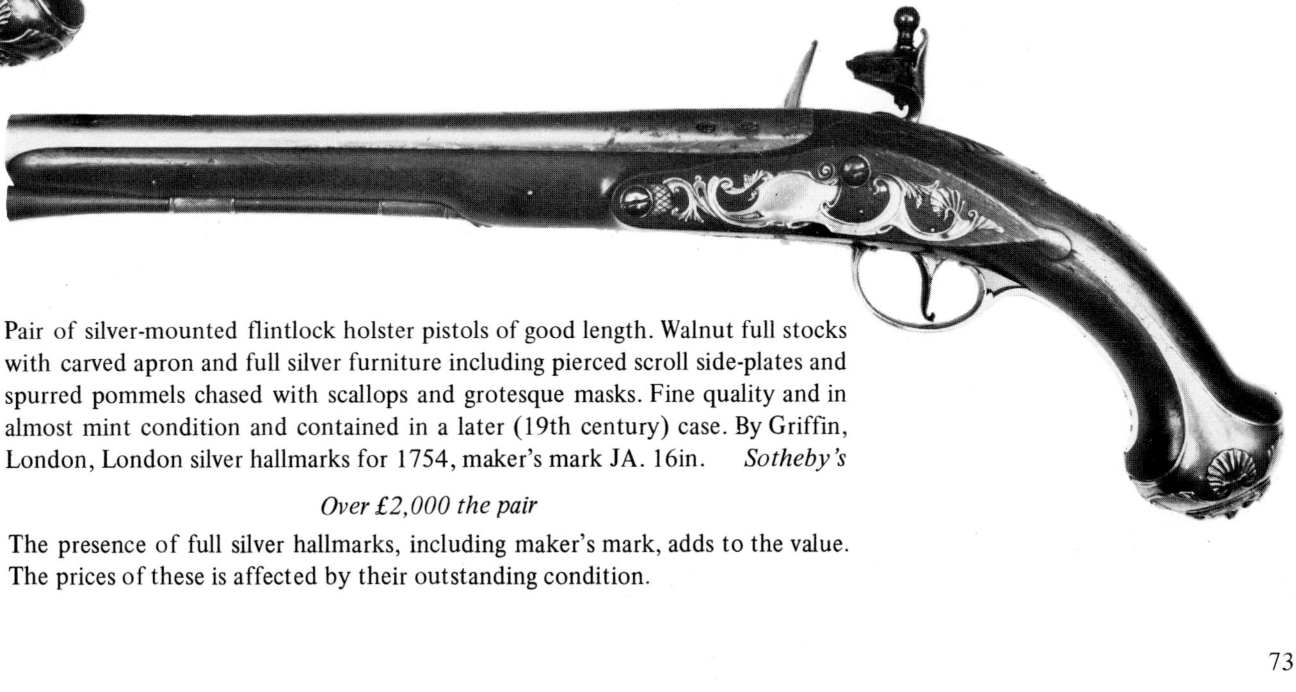

Pair of silver-mounted flintlock holster pistols of good length. Walnut full stocks with carved apron and full silver furniture including pierced scroll side-plates and spurred pommels chased with scallops and grotesque masks. Fine quality and in almost mint condition and contained in a later (19th century) case. By Griffin, London, London silver hallmarks for 1754, maker's mark JA. 16in. *Sotheby's*

Over £2,000 the pair

The presence of full silver hallmarks, including maker's mark, adds to the value. The prices of these is affected by their outstanding condition.

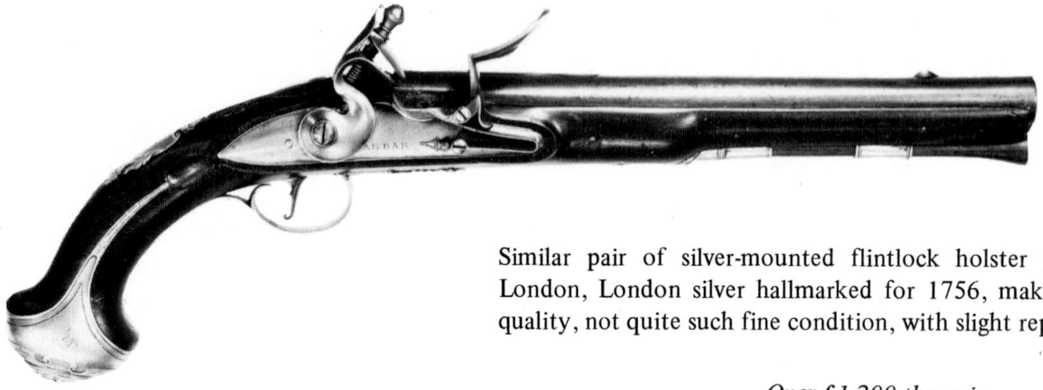

Similar pair of silver-mounted flintlock holster pistols. By Barbar, London, London silver hallmarked for 1756, maker's mark 1B. Fine quality, not quite such fine condition, with slight repairs, 16½in. *Christie's*

Over £1,200 the pair

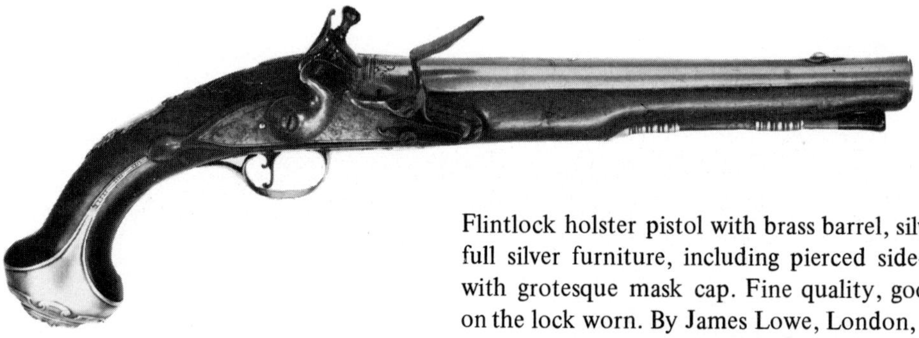

Flintlock holster pistol with brass barrel, silver fore-sight, full stock and full silver furniture, including pierced side-plate and spurred pommel with grotesque mask cap. Fine quality, good condition, but engraving on the lock worn. By James Lowe, London, London silver hallmarks for 1761, maker's mark JA. 15½in. *Christie's*

About £400. A pair would be worth £800 – £1,000

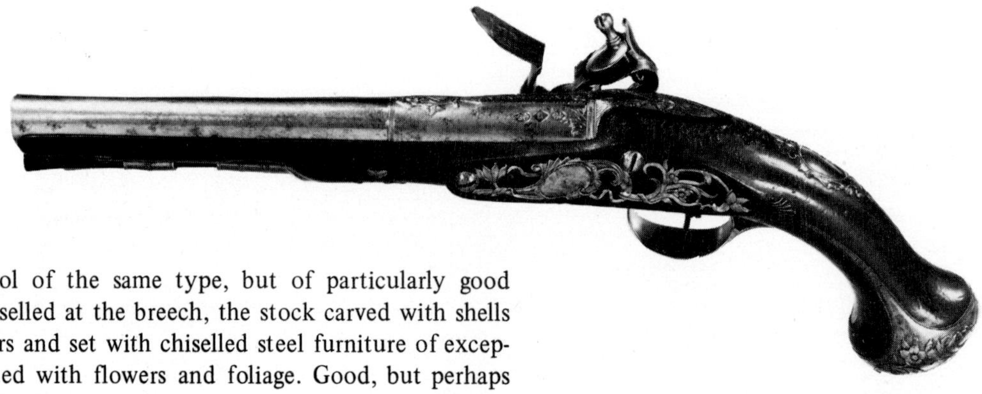

Flintlock holster pistol of the same type, but of particularly good quality, the barrel chiselled at the breech, the stock carved with shells and garlands of flowers and set with chiselled steel furniture of exceptional quality decorated with flowers and foliage. Good, but perhaps overcleaned condition, the jaws of the cock renewed. By E. North, London, circa 1750-60. 15in. *Christie's*

£800 – £1,000

The mounts of this pistol are perhaps finer than the silver mounts of the period, from which they draw their inspiration.

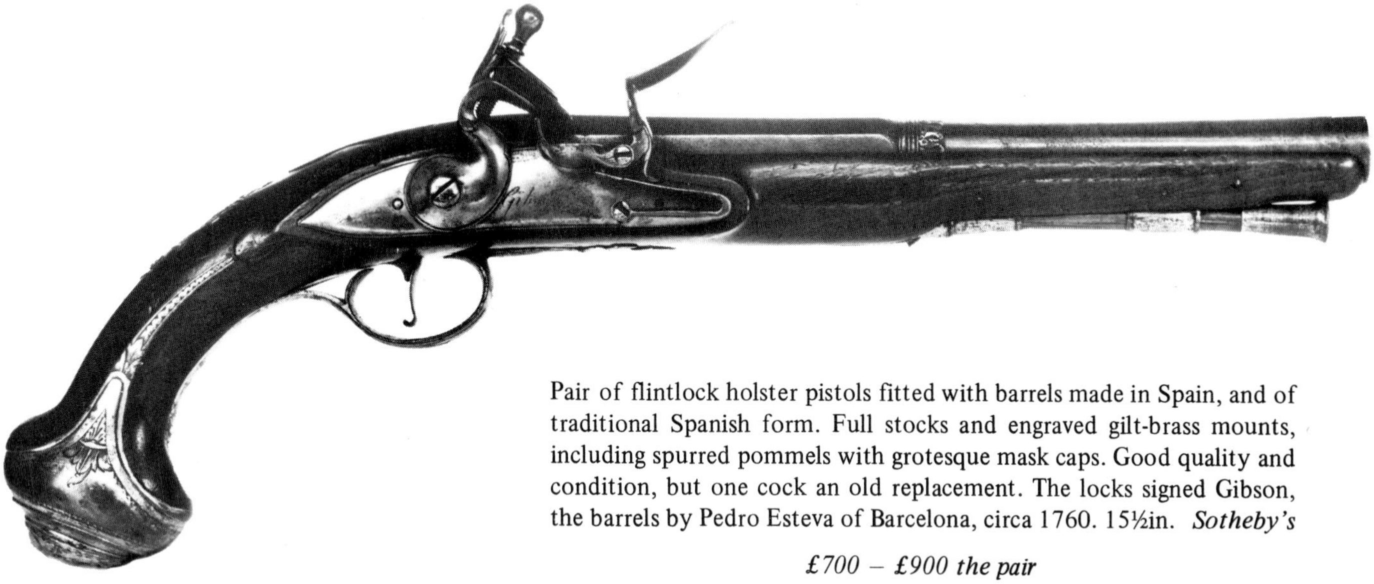

Pair of flintlock holster pistols fitted with barrels made in Spain, and of traditional Spanish form. Full stocks and engraved gilt-brass mounts, including spurred pommels with grotesque mask caps. Good quality and condition, but one cock an old replacement. The locks signed Gibson, the barrels by Pedro Esteva of Barcelona, circa 1760. 15½in. *Sotheby's*

£700 – £900 the pair

The Spanish barrels are an attractive feature. These enjoyed a great reputation at the time, but were used by English gunsmiths more commonly on guns than pistols.

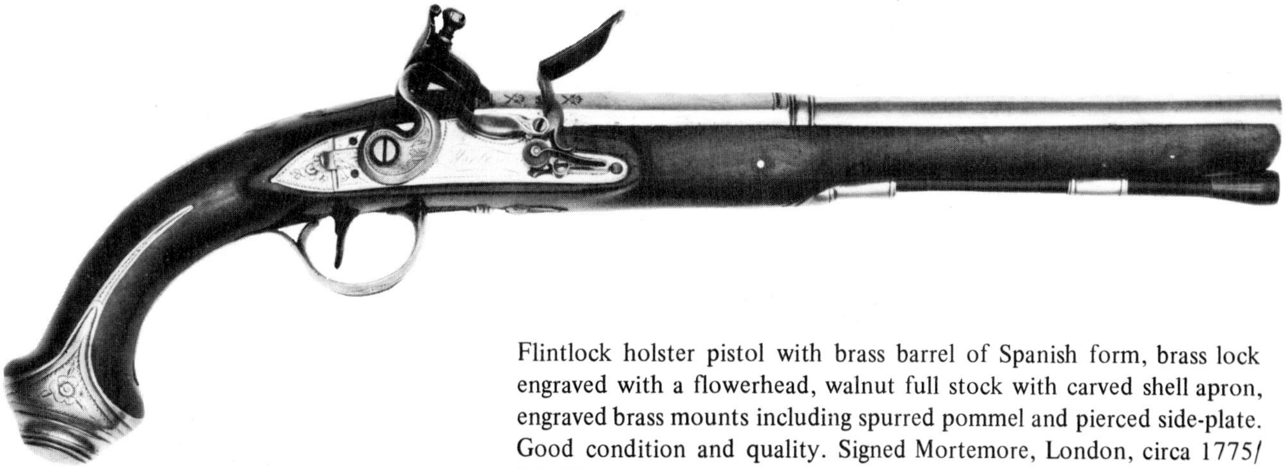

Flintlock holster pistol with brass barrel of Spanish form, brass lock engraved with a flowerhead, walnut full stock with carved shell apron, engraved brass mounts including spurred pommel and pierced side-plate. Good condition and quality. Signed Mortemore, London, circa 1775/80. 17in. *Sotheby's*

About £300 – £400

Pair of flintlock turn-off pistols with engraved central box-lock actions bearing the initials of the original owner, and trigger-guard safety-catches, the butts inlaid with fine quality silver wirework, silver trophy of arms escutcheons, and lion and rampart silver butt-caps. Fine quality, very good condition, but one cock repaired. More robust in form than most pistols of this group. By Joseph Adams, Birmingham proof marks, silver maker's mark JA, circa 1770. 12in.

£600 – £800 the pair

Although the earliest central box-lock pistols date from the 1720's, most examples were made after 1770. *Christie's*

One of a lesser pair of the same type with flat-sided butts and silver inlay of less elaborate form. Small butt-caps covering only the bottom flat and back. Moderate quality, condition not so good, engraving worn. By Barber, Newark, circa 1770. 11¾in. *Christie's*

£300 – £400 the pair

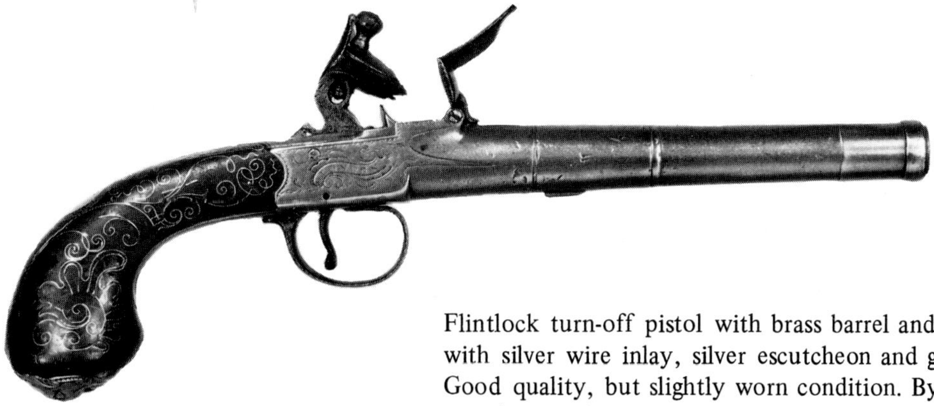

Flintlock turn-off pistol with brass barrel and action, the walnut butt with silver wire inlay, silver escutcheon and grotesque mask butt-cap. Good quality, but slightly worn condition. By Bunney, London, circa 1775/80. 12½in. *Christie's*

About £200

£150 – £175 for a similar example with iron barrel and action

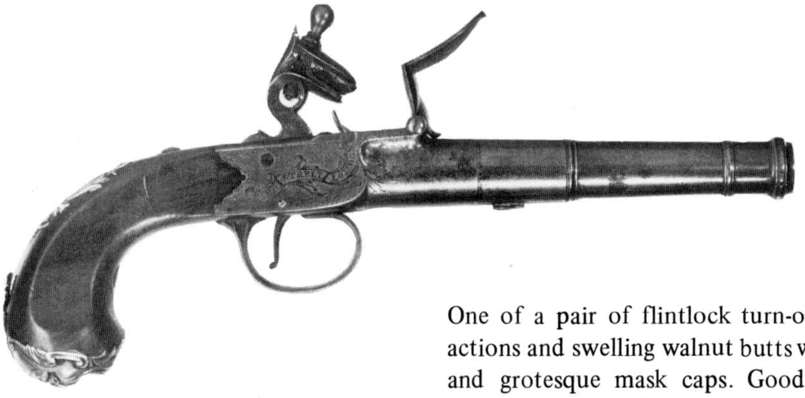

One of a pair of flintlock turn-off pistols with cannon barrels, signed actions and swelling walnut butts with silver trophy of arms escutcheons and grotesque mask caps. Good quality and condition, By Griffin, Bond Street, London, London silver hallmarks, maker's mark JA, circa 1780. 10in. *Christie's*

£300 – £400 the pair.

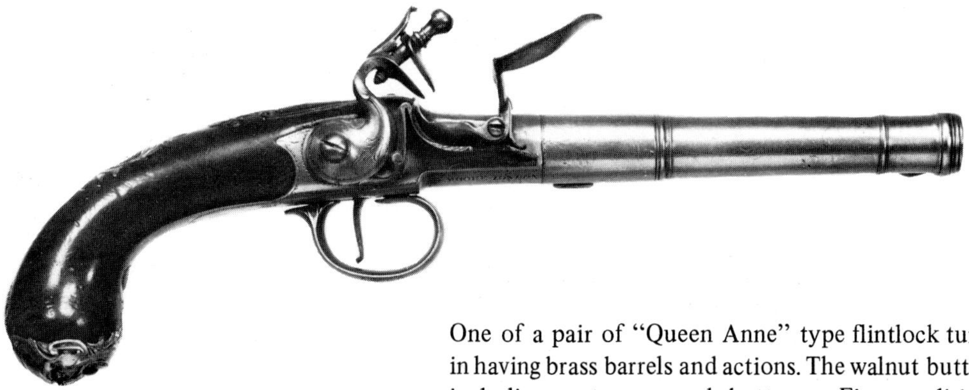

One of a pair of "Queen Anne" type flintlock turn-off pistols, unusual in having brass barrels and actions. The walnut butts with silver furniture, including grotesque mask butt-caps. Fine condition. By Daniel Moore, London, London silver maker's mark IK, circa 1760/1770. 13in. *Christie's*

£1,000 – £1,500 the pair

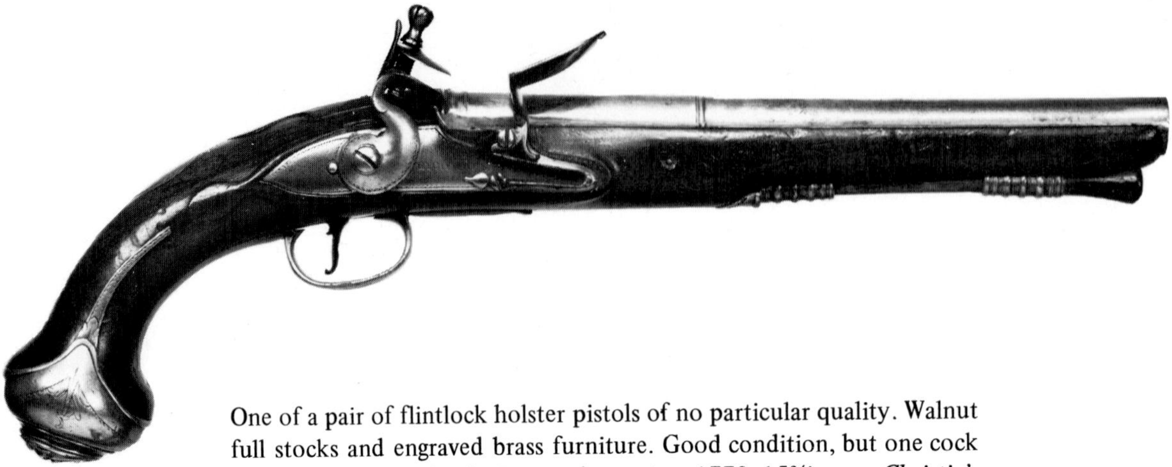

One of a pair of flintlock holster pistols of no particular quality. Walnut full stocks and engraved brass furniture. Good condition, but one cock replaced. By T. Richards, Birmingham, circa 1770. 15¾in. *Christie's*

£500 – £700 the pair

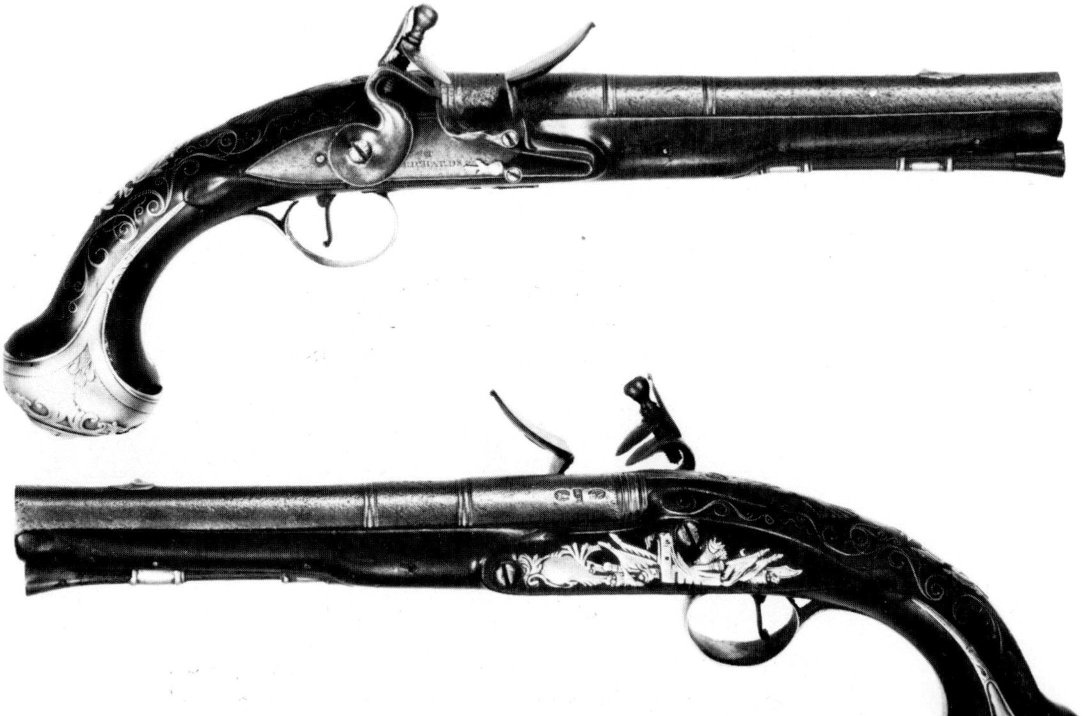

Pair of flintlock holster pistols with barrels in three stages, silver foresights, engraved breeches and tangs, the walnut stocks with carved shell aprons and silver mounts including trophy of arms side-plates and escutcheons and spurred pommels with grotesque mask caps, the butts inlaid with silver wire scrolls. Good quality, but worn condition with pitting and some restoration. By T. Richards, no silver hallmarks, circa 1770. 14¼in. *Christie's*

£600 – £800 the pair

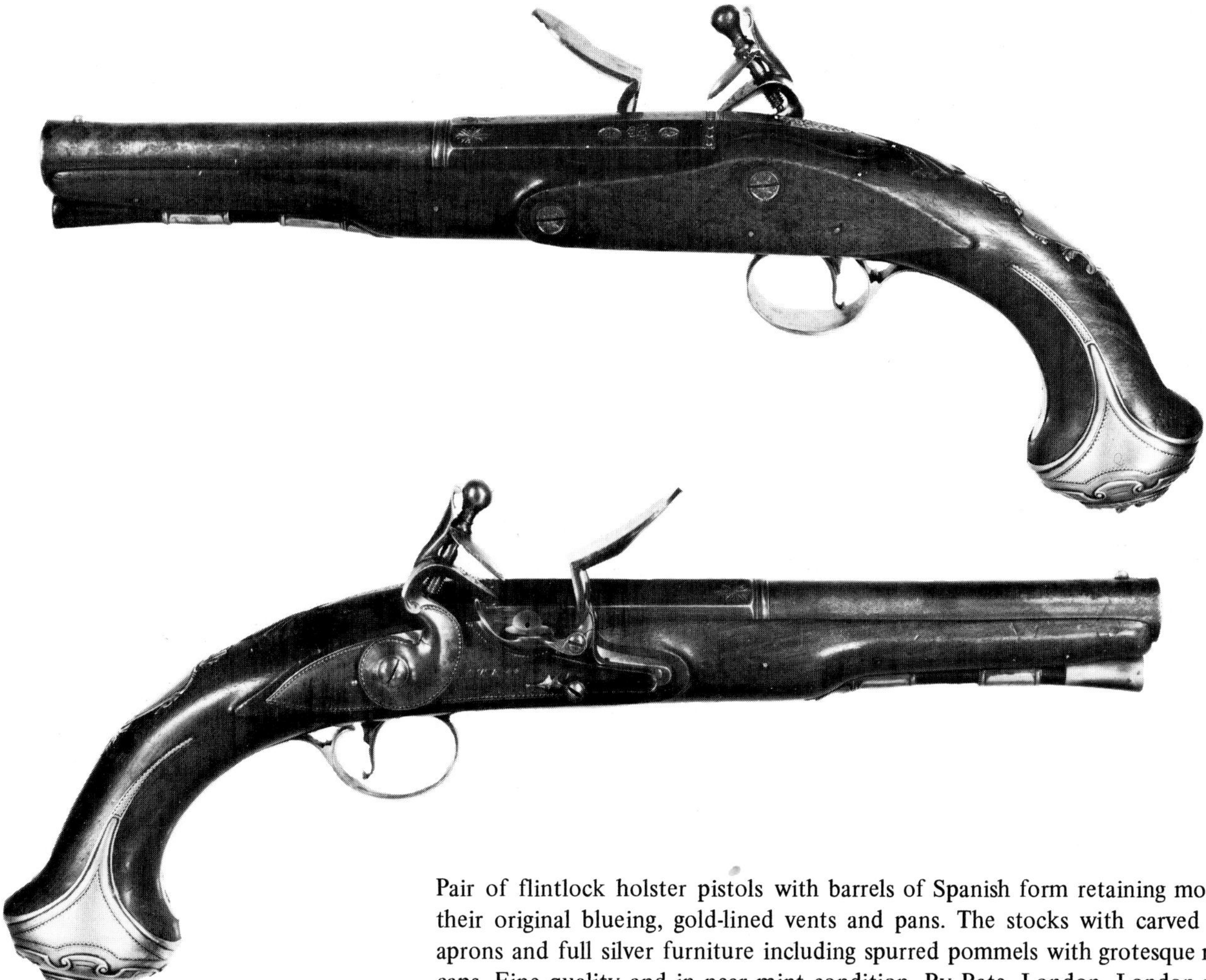

Pair of flintlock holster pistols with barrels of Spanish form retaining most of their original blueing, gold-lined vents and pans. The stocks with carved shell aprons and full silver furniture including spurred pommels with grotesque mask caps. Fine quality and in near mint condition. By Bate, London, London silver hallmarks for 1775, maker's mark IK. 14in. *Christie's*

Over £1,500 the pair. More if the pistols were a bit longer and had silver side-plates.

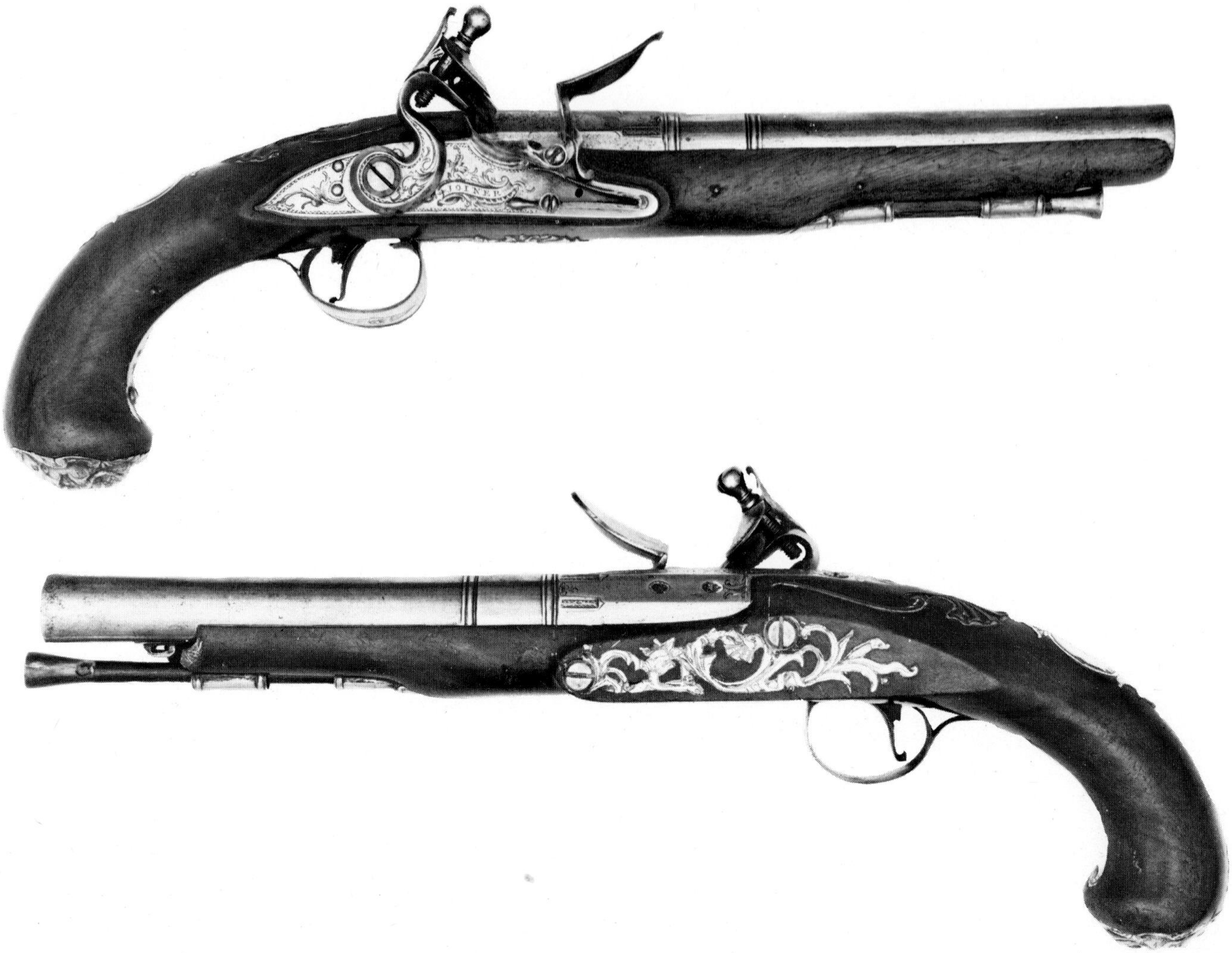

Pair of flintlock holster pistols with barrels in three stages, engraved locks and full stocks with carved aprons and full silver furniture including grotesque mask butt-caps. Medium to good quality, fair condition apart from damage to one fore-end. By Joiner, London, Birmingham silver hallmarks for 1778, maker's mark CF for Charles Freeth, 13¼in. *Sotheby's*

£700 – £900 the pair, a little more for a pair with brass barrels.

Pair of flintlock holster pistols with barrels of Spanish form retaining much original blueing, signed within a gold ribbon, with gold lines, vents, gold-lined pans and silver fore-sights, the locks deeply engraved and signed within a gold oval, fitted with safety-catches and roller bearings, the stocks with carved apron, exceptional silver furniture, and bone ramrods. Very fine quality, very fine untouched condition, but one butt broken through and one side-plate incomplete. By Bennett, Royal Exchange, London, London silver hallmarks for 1781, also Birmingham silver hallmarks for 1780 with several maker's marks. 15in.

Christie's

Over £3,000 the pair

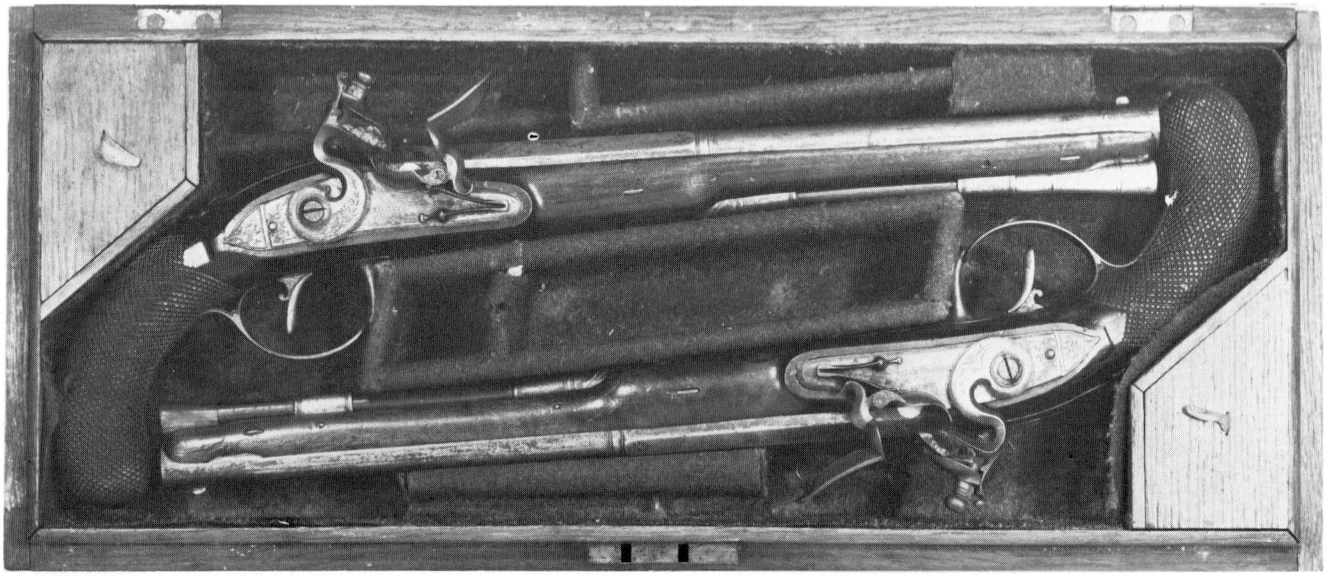

Cased pair of early flintlock duelling pistols with long barrels of Spanish form, silver fore-sights and gold vents, the stocks with carved aprons, (unusual in duelling pistols) and engraved steel furniture. Chequered flat-sided butts of early form. One ramrod tip is made of silver and unscrews to act as a powder measure. Fine quality, fair condition. The oak case is original, but has been re-lined and has none of the original fittings. By H.W. Mortimer, London, London proof marks, circa 1775/80. 16½in. *Christie's*

About £850

This form of pistol represents the development of the true duelling pistol from the holster pistol of the 1760s. Examples of true duelling pistols before 1780 are rare. H.W. Mortimer was one of the foremost makers of duelling pistols.

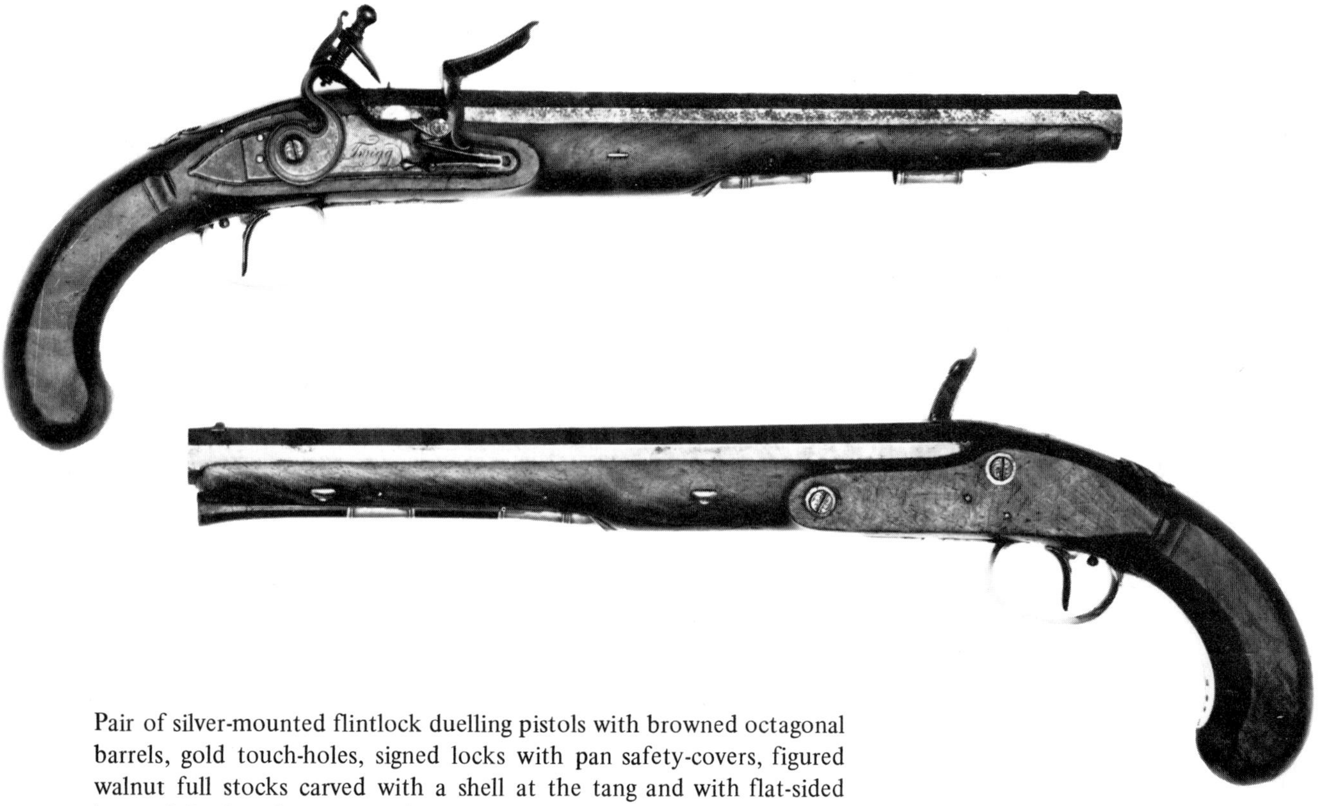

Pair of silver-mounted flintlock duelling pistols with browned octagonal barrels, gold touch-holes, signed locks with pan safety-covers, figured walnut full stocks carved with a shell at the tang and with flat-sided butts, full silver furniture and set triggers. Fine quality, fine untouched condition, but top of one cock missing. By Twigg, London, London silver hallmarks for 1771, with maker's mark IK. 15¼in. *Sotheby's*

Over £1,000 the pair. Very rare and by one of the best makers.

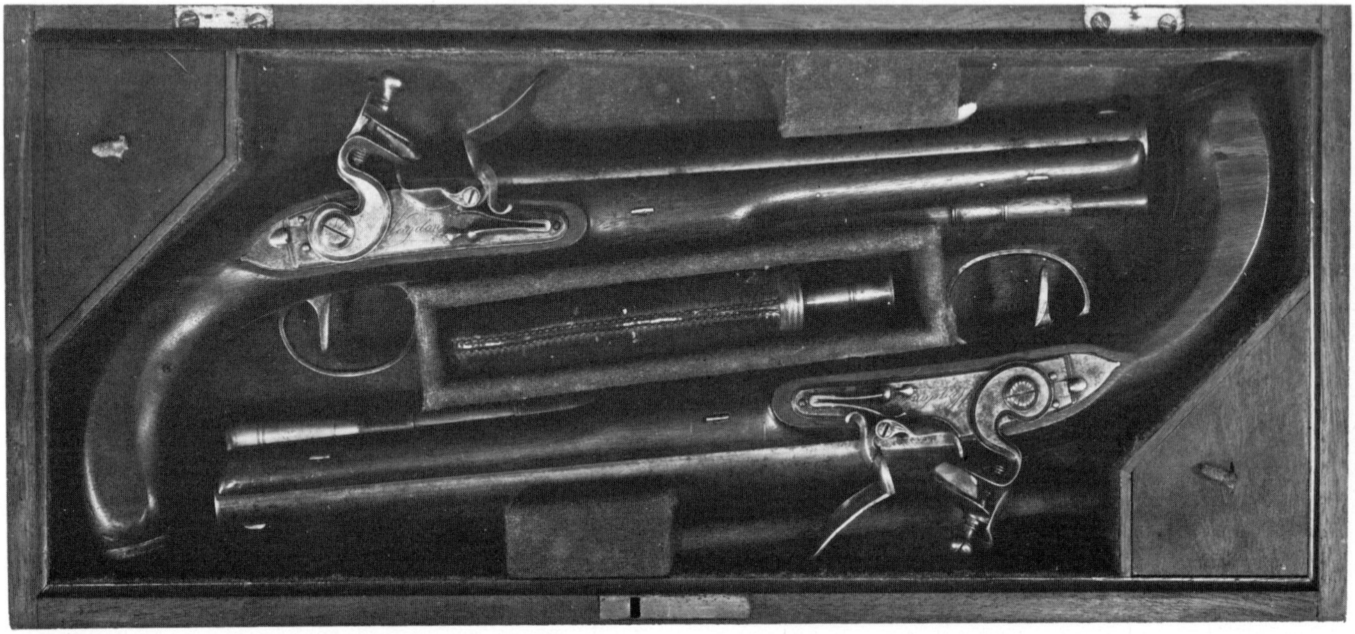

Typical cased pair of Wogdon flintlock duelling pistols with round barrels and top flats, signed locks with safety-catches, full stocks, flat-sided swelling butts and lightly engraved blued steel furniture. Of characteristically plain appearance but good quality and condition, with some original finish. In original lined and fitted mahogany case with original leather-covered flask (also typical of the maker). By Robert Wogdon, London, circa 1780. 14½in. *Christie's*

£700 – £900

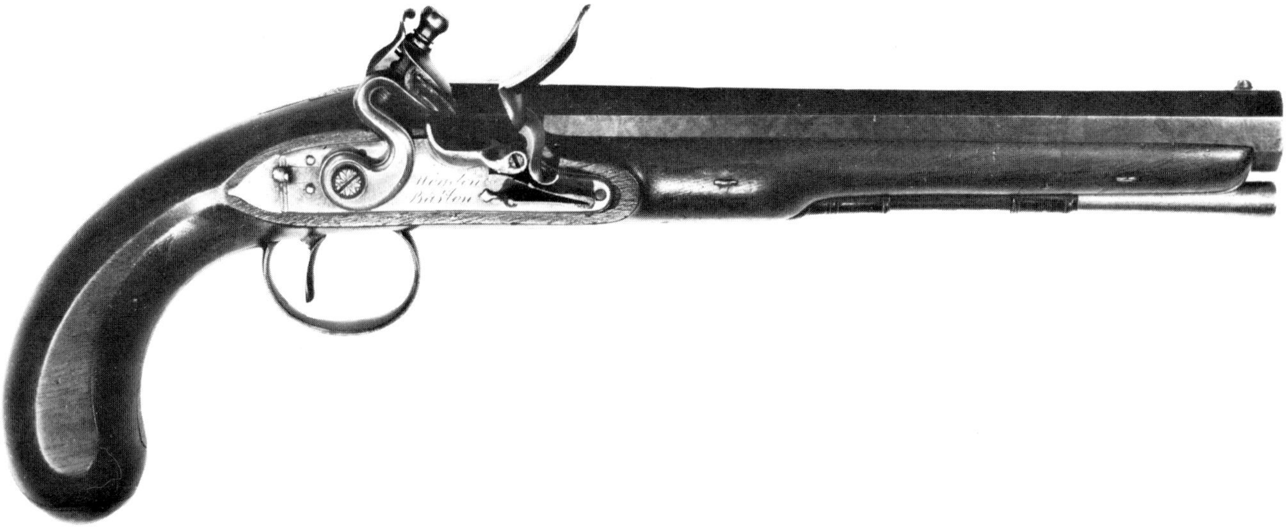

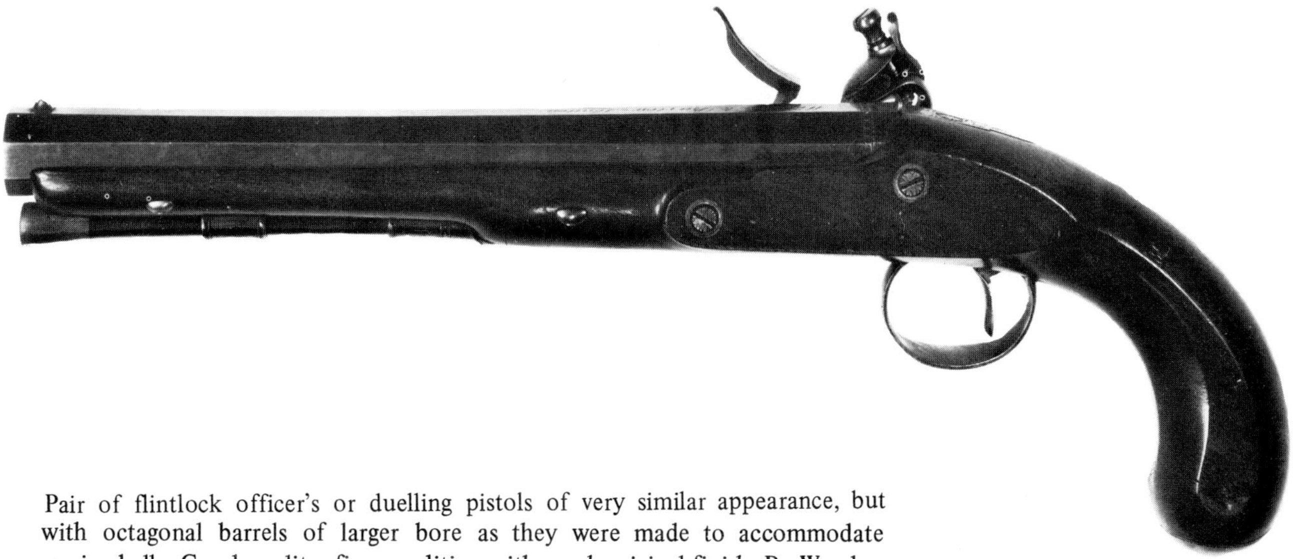

Pair of flintlock officer's or duelling pistols of very similar appearance, but with octagonal barrels of larger bore as they were made to accommodate service balls. Good quality, fine condition with much original finish. By Wogdon and Barton, London, circa 1790. 15in. *Christie's*

£500 – £600 the pair. A pair in original case with fittings, £600 – £800.

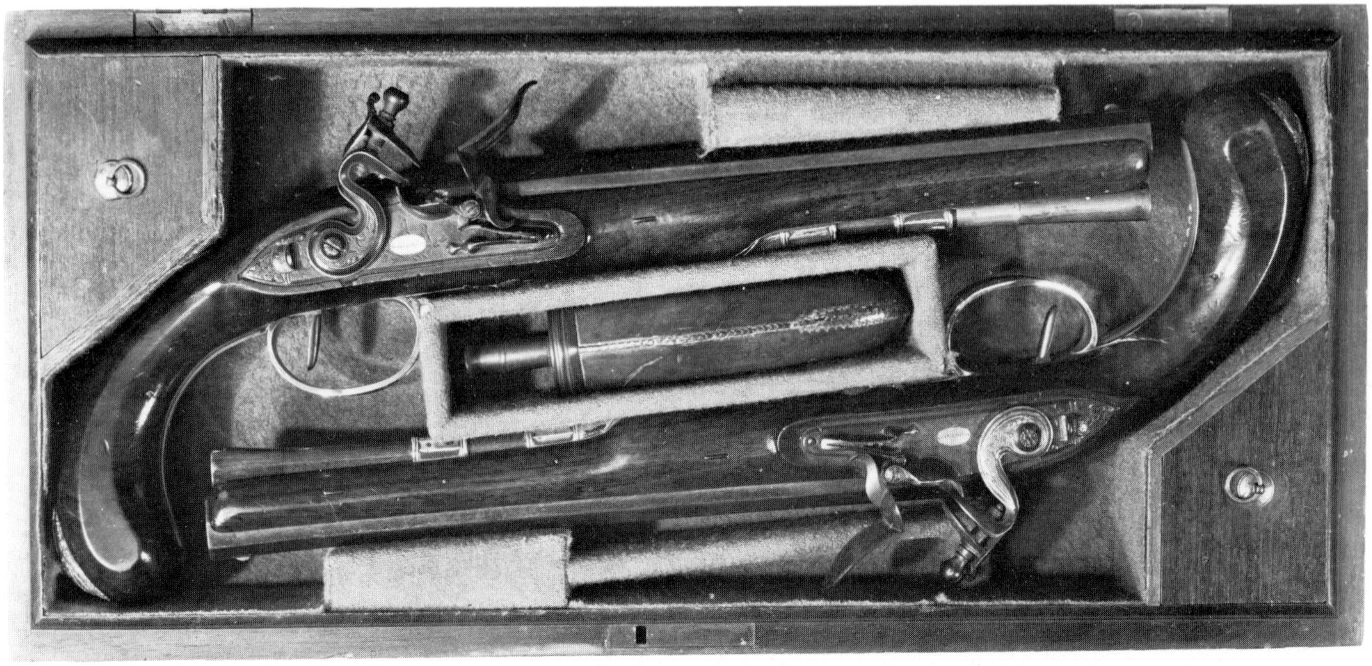

Cased pair of silver-mounted Wogdon flintlock duelling pistols of similar form, with octagonal barrels, gold vents and silver fore-sights, the locks engraved with flowers and foliage and signed within a gold oval. Full stocks with swelling flat-sided butts and silver Britannia butt-caps. Full stocks with engraved silver furniture including pierced side-plates. Very fine quality and in good condition apart from one broken butt and one badly repaired cock. The case and flask are original. By Robert Wogdon, London, London silver hallmarks for 1784, maker's mark MB for Moses Brent, 15in. *Christie's*

About £2,000

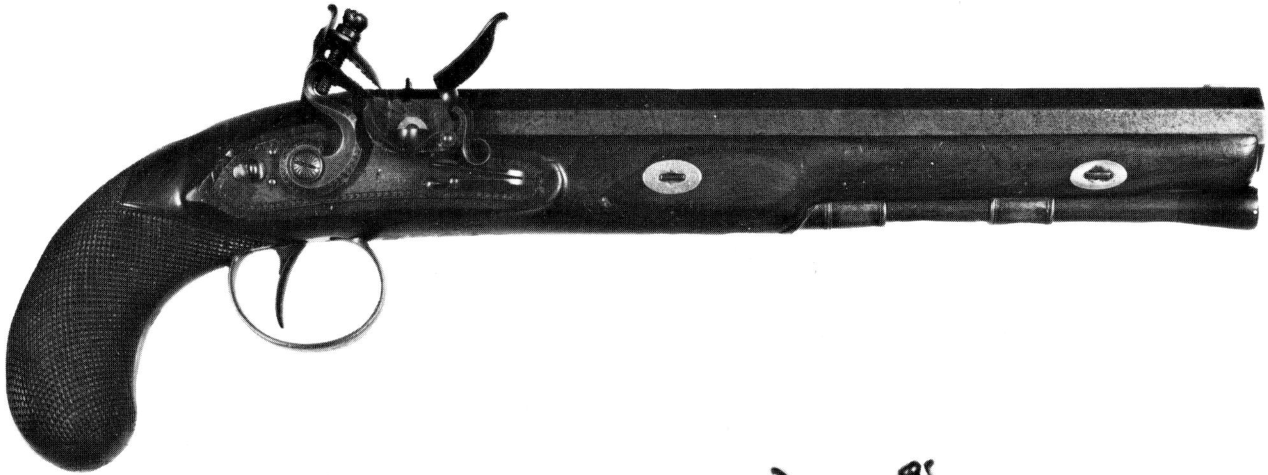

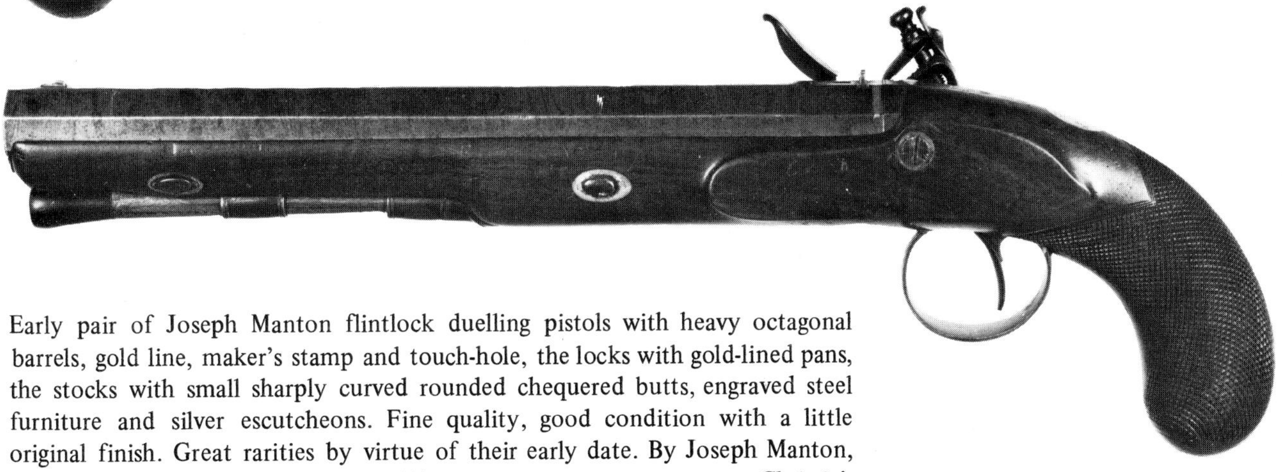

Early pair of Joseph Manton flintlock duelling pistols with heavy octagonal barrels, gold line, maker's stamp and touch-hole, the locks with gold-lined pans, the stocks with small sharply curved rounded chequered butts, engraved steel furniture and silver escutcheons. Fine quality, good condition with a little original finish. Great rarities by virtue of their early date. By Joseph Manton, London, serial no. 305, circa 1791. 14¾in. *Christie's*

About £1,400 the pair

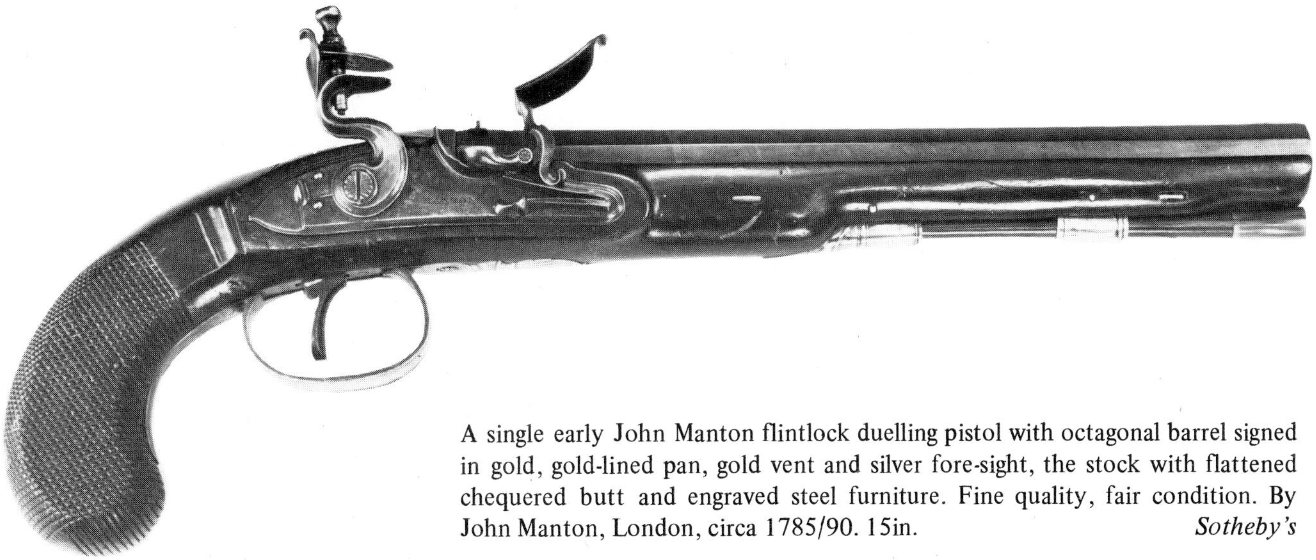

A single early John Manton flintlock duelling pistol with octagonal barrel signed in gold, gold-lined pan, gold vent and silver fore-sight, the stock with flattened chequered butt and engraved steel furniture. Fine quality, fair condition. By John Manton, London, circa 1785/90. 15in. *Sotheby's*

£400 – £600

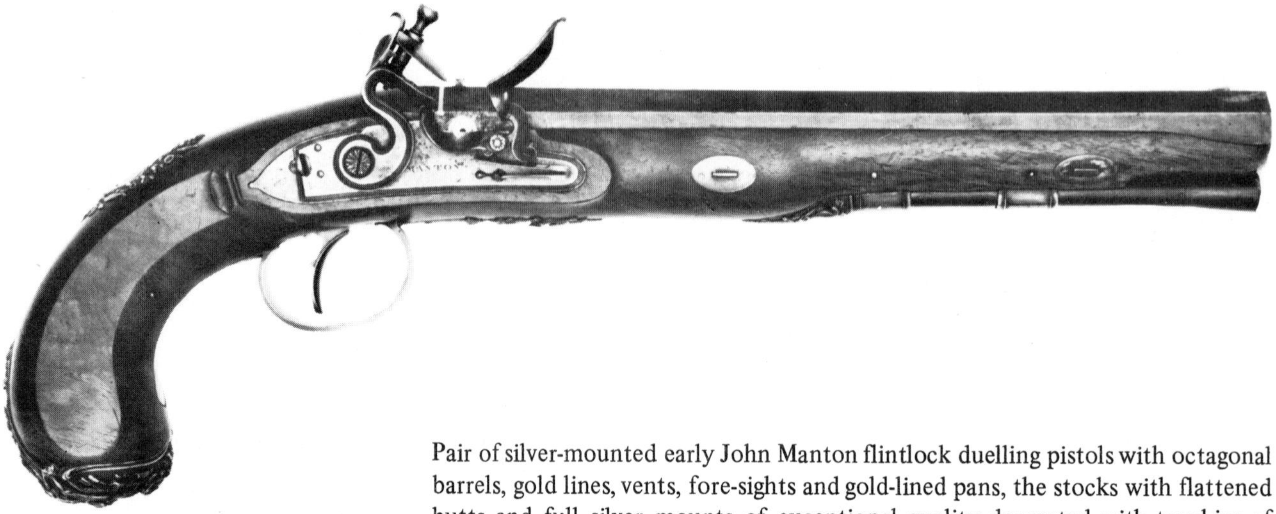

Pair of silver-mounted early John Manton flintlock duelling pistols with octagonal barrels, gold lines, vents, fore-sights and gold-lined pans, the stocks with flattened butts and full silver mounts of exceptional quality decorated with trophies of arms. In very fine untouched condition, complete with original case and most fittings. By John Manton, London, silver maker's mark MB for Moses Brent, and date letter for 1791. 15½in. *Sotheby's*

Over £6,000 the pair

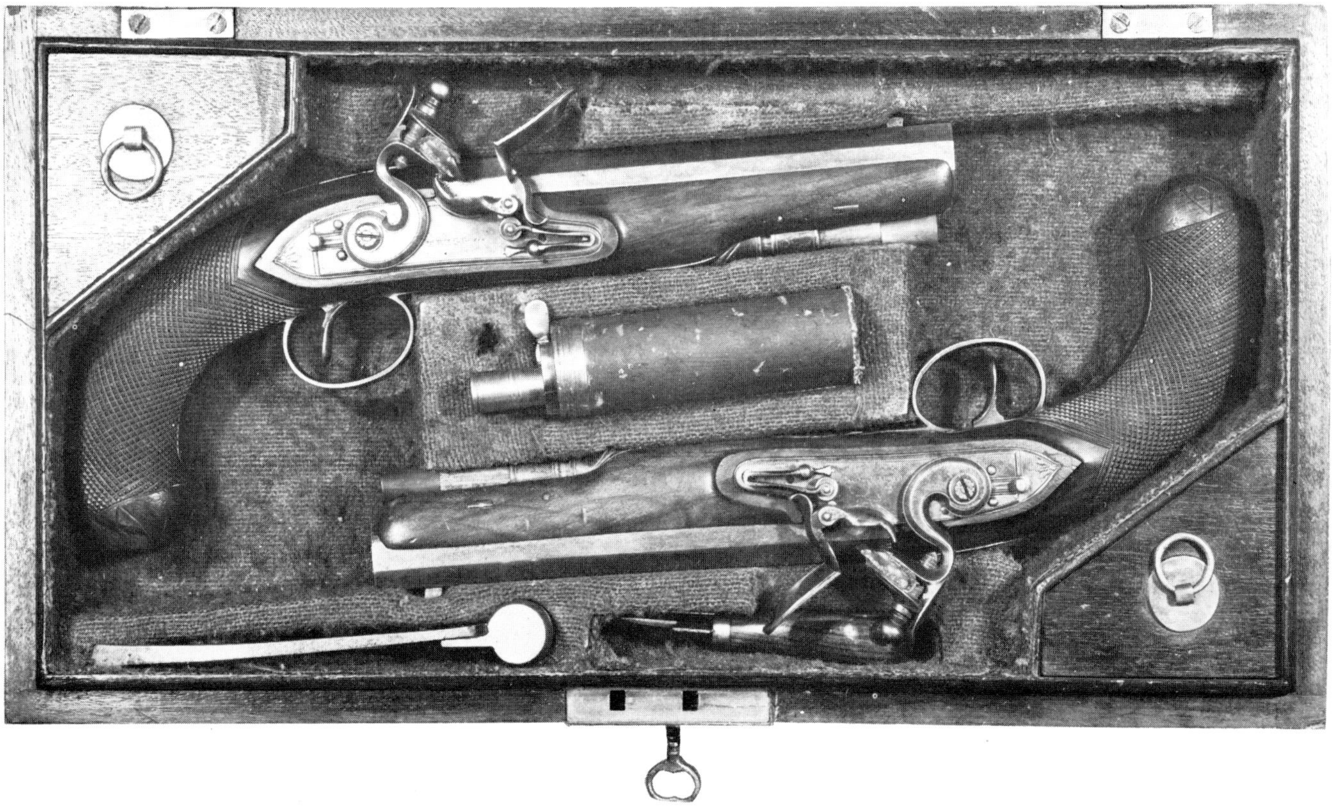

Cased pair of flintlock travelling pistols with octagonal barrels, gold vents and platinum lines, walnut full stocks, chequered butts and engraved blued steel furniture. Good quality, fine condition, in original fitted case with accessories. Signed Twigg, London, circa 1790/1800. 11in. *Christie's*

About £500

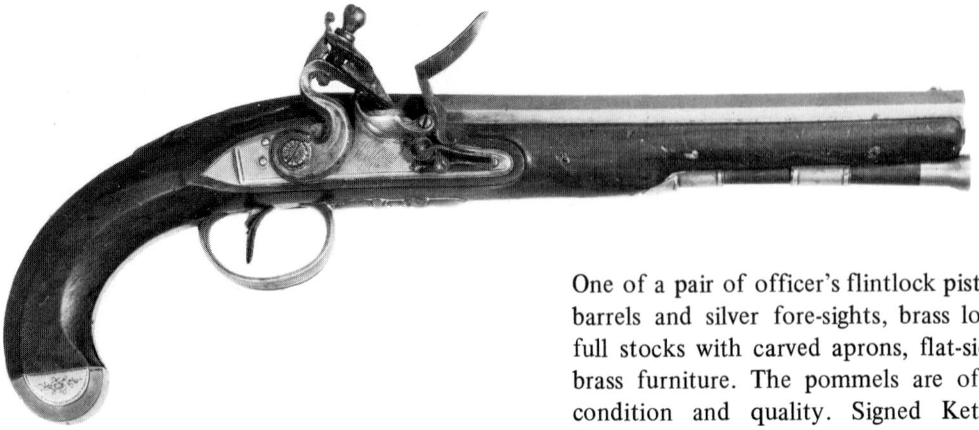

One of a pair of officer's flintlock pistols with brass octagonal barrels and silver fore-sights, brass lock-plates and pans and full stocks with carved aprons, flat-sided butts and engraved brass furniture. The pommels are of unusual design. Good condition and quality. Signed Ketland & Co., London, Birmingham proof marks, circa 1785. *Christie's*

£600 – £800 the pair

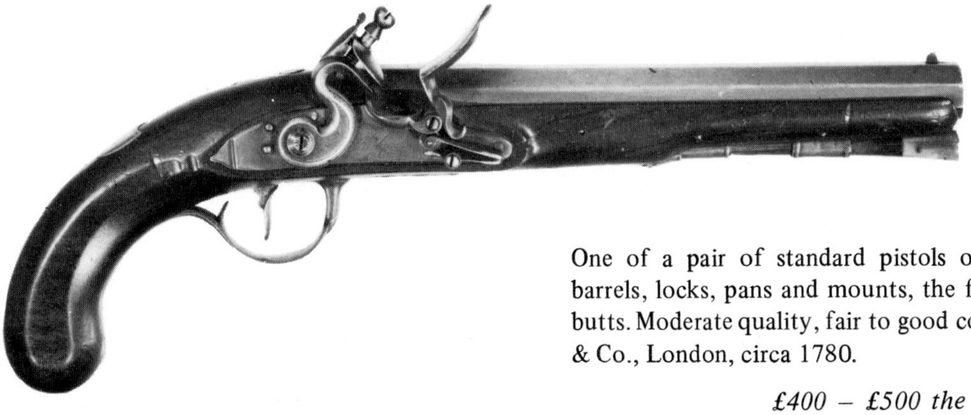

One of a pair of standard pistols of same type with brass barrels, locks, pans and mounts, the full stocks with flat-sided butts. Moderate quality, fair to good condition. Signed Ketland & Co., London, circa 1780. *Christie's*

£400 – £500 the pair

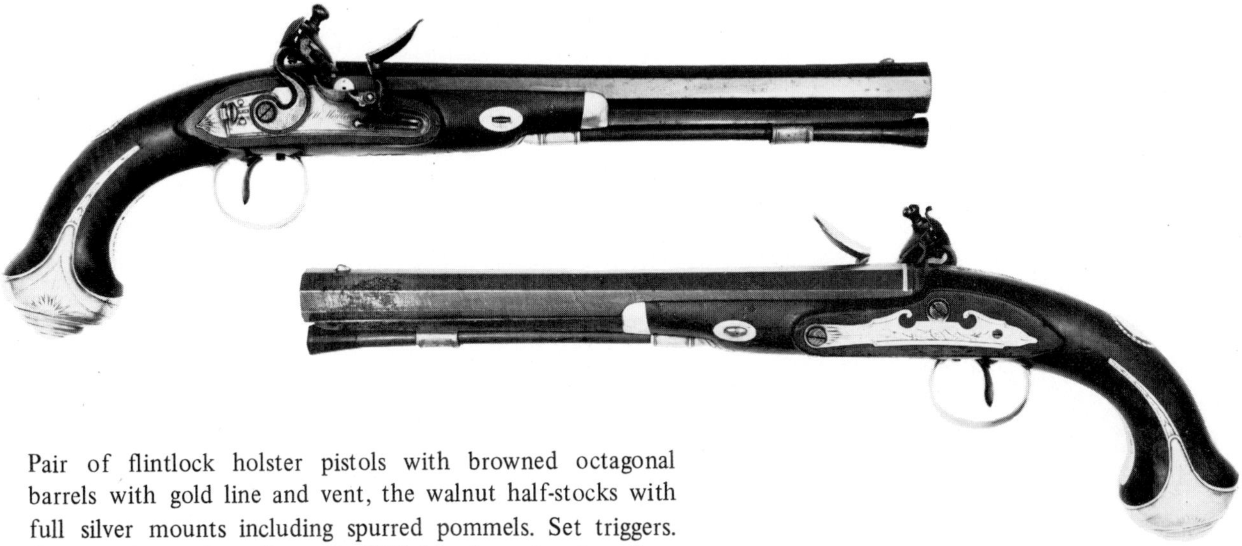

Pair of flintlock holster pistols with browned octagonal barrels with gold line and vent, the walnut half-stocks with full silver mounts including spurred pommels. Set triggers. Good quality and condition. By H.W. Mortimer, London, Gunmaker to His Majesty, London silver hallmarks for 1795, maker's mark of Moses Brent. 17in. *Sotheby's*

Over £1,000 the pair

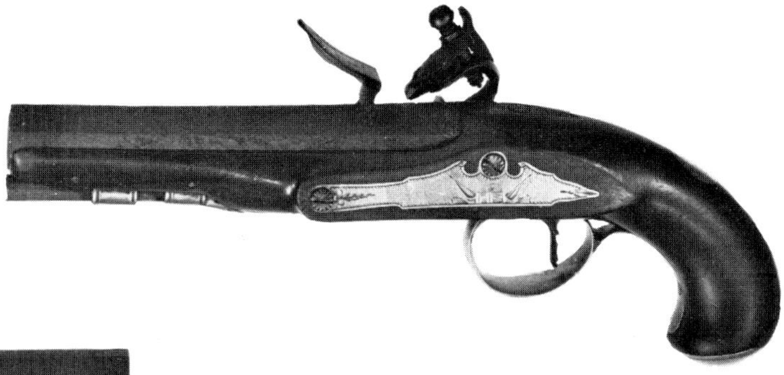

Pair of small flintlock pistols of similar quality, with octagonal barrels, full stocks and engraved silver mounts. Slight pitting on the barrels, but good condition. Signed Jackson, Maidstone, London proof marks, London silver hallmarks and maker's mark of Moses Brent, circa 1780/90. 9in. *Christie's*

About £400 the pair

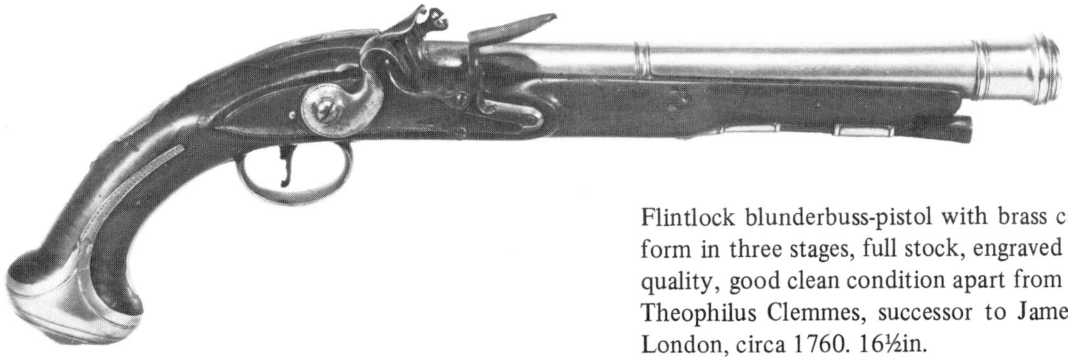

Flintlock blunderbuss-pistol with brass cannon barrel of good form in three stages, full stock, engraved brass furniture. Good quality, good clean condition apart from the repaired cock. By Theophilus Clemmes, successor to James Barbar, Shug Lane, London, circa 1760. 16½in. *Christie's*

£300 – £400
Less for a similar pistol with iron barrel.

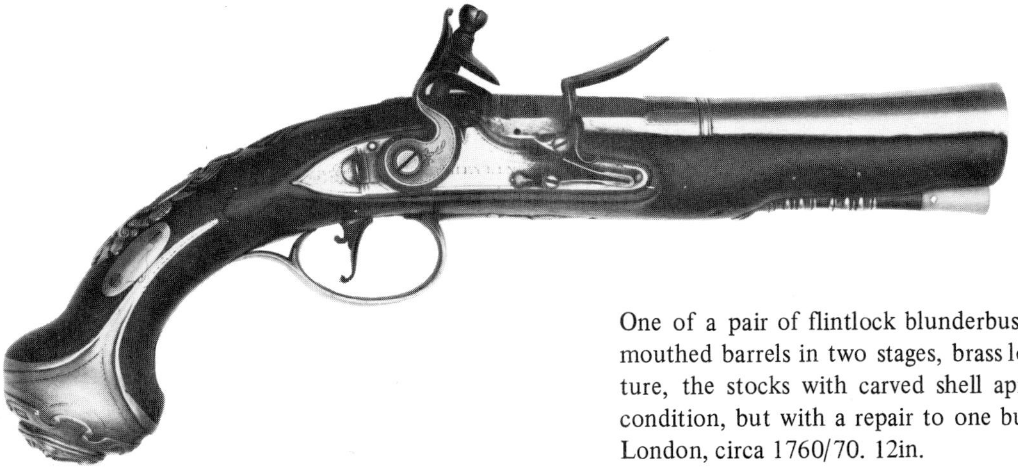

One of a pair of flintlock blunderbuss-pistols with brass bell-mouthed barrels in two stages, brass locks and full brass furniture, the stocks with carved shell aprons. Good quality and condition, but with a repair to one butt. By Heylin, Cornhill, London, circa 1760/70. 12in. *Sotheby's*

£800 – £1,000 the pair
A similar pair with similar mounts, about £1,250

Pair of flintlock box-lock blunderbuss-pistols with brass barrels and actions, spring bayonets beneath and ramrods to the side (one missing), sliding trigger-guards and flat-sided butts. Very good quality and condition. By W. Bond, London, circa 1790. 12¼in. *Christie's*

Over £1,000 the pair

Waters' patent flintlock pistol with brass blunderbuss barrel and signed brass action inscribed Waters & Co. Patent (with Patent number), spring bayonet, walnut butt and silver grotesque mask butt-cap. Good quality and condition. Birmingham silver hallmark for 1780. 13in. *Sotheby's*

About £400
A pair of Waters Patent pistols over £1,000 in equivalent condition

One of a pair of flintlock box-lock pistols with turn-off brass barrels mounted with spring bayonets to the side, engraved brass actions and walnut butts with silver escutcheons and retaining some silver wire inlay. Good quality, fair condition only. Signed Blake, London proof marks, late 18th century. *Christie's*

About £500 the pair

One of a pair of flintlock box-lock pocket pistols with short turn-off cannon barrels and engraved rounded actions, the walnut butts with silver wire inlay and silver butt-caps. Fine quality, but condition of one pistol poor. By Richard Wilson, London, circa 1760/70. 7in. *Christie's*

£300 – £400 the pair

One of a similar pair with actions of rectangular section well inlaid butts and silver grotesque mask butt-caps. Good quality and condition. By Godsall, Gloucester, circa 1780. 8in. *Christie's*

About £300 the pair

One of a similar pair with brass barrels and actions, the flat-sided butts decorated with silver wire and engraved silver escutcheons. Good quality and condition. By Bunney, London, circa 1770/80. 8¼in. *Christie's*

About £300 the pair

Fine and rare flintlock box-lock pistol with silver cannon barrel, action and engraved mounts, the butt inlaid with silver wire and with grotesque mask cap. Exceptional quality, fine condition. Signed Mortimer, London, Birmingham silver hallmarks for 1774, maker's mark CF, for Charles Freeth, 5in. *Sotheby's*

Over £800

Flintlock pocket pistol with rifled turn-off barrel, this and the action of light coloured brass, the butt inlaid with silver lines and with silver butt-cap. Fine quality and condition. By J. Richards, Strand, London, circa 1780. *Christie's*

About £300. Rare with rifled barrel.

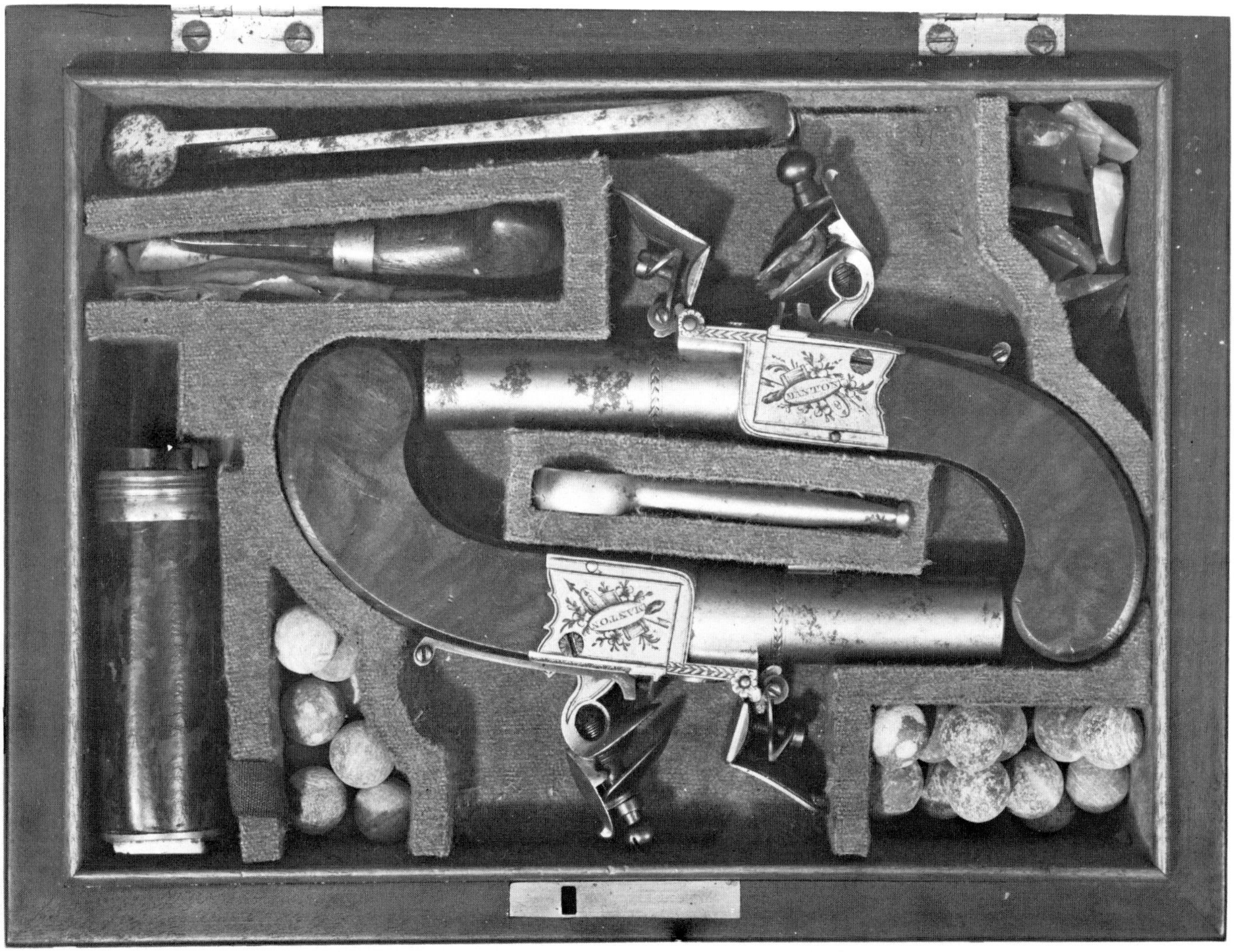

Cased pair of flintlock pocket pistols with finely engraved actions and plain flat-sided butts. Very fine quality, in exceptional condition and in original case complete with fittings. By John Manton, London, circa 1790. *Christie's*

About £1,000

Pair of all-steel flintlock box-lock pocket pistols with rifled turn-off cannon barrels, foliate engraved action and butts. Good condition and quality. By Barker, London, late 18th century. 8in. *Wallis & Wallis*

£400 – £500 the pair

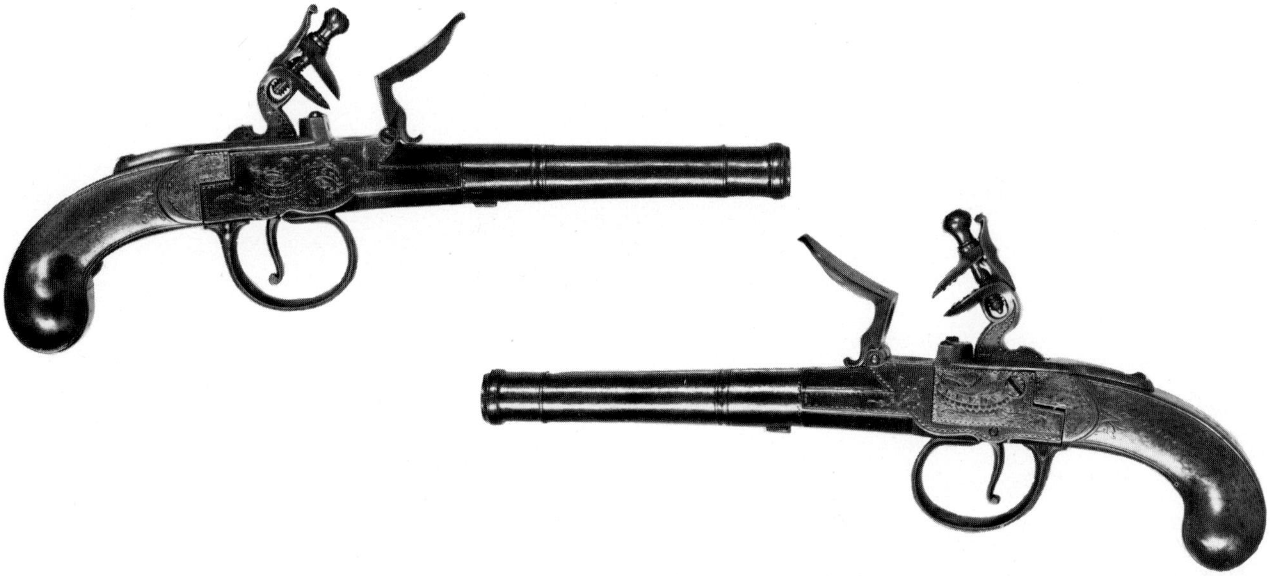

Another pair with turn-off barrels, engraved actions and butts. Fine quality and condition. Signed Reynolds, Leeds, Tower private proof marks, circa 1750/60. 9¼in. *Christie's*

£600 – £700 the pair

These can be distinguished from the group of Liège imitations (see page 106) by their superior quality and by the presence of genuine proof marks on the barrels.

Scottish Flintlock Pistols - 1750 - 1830

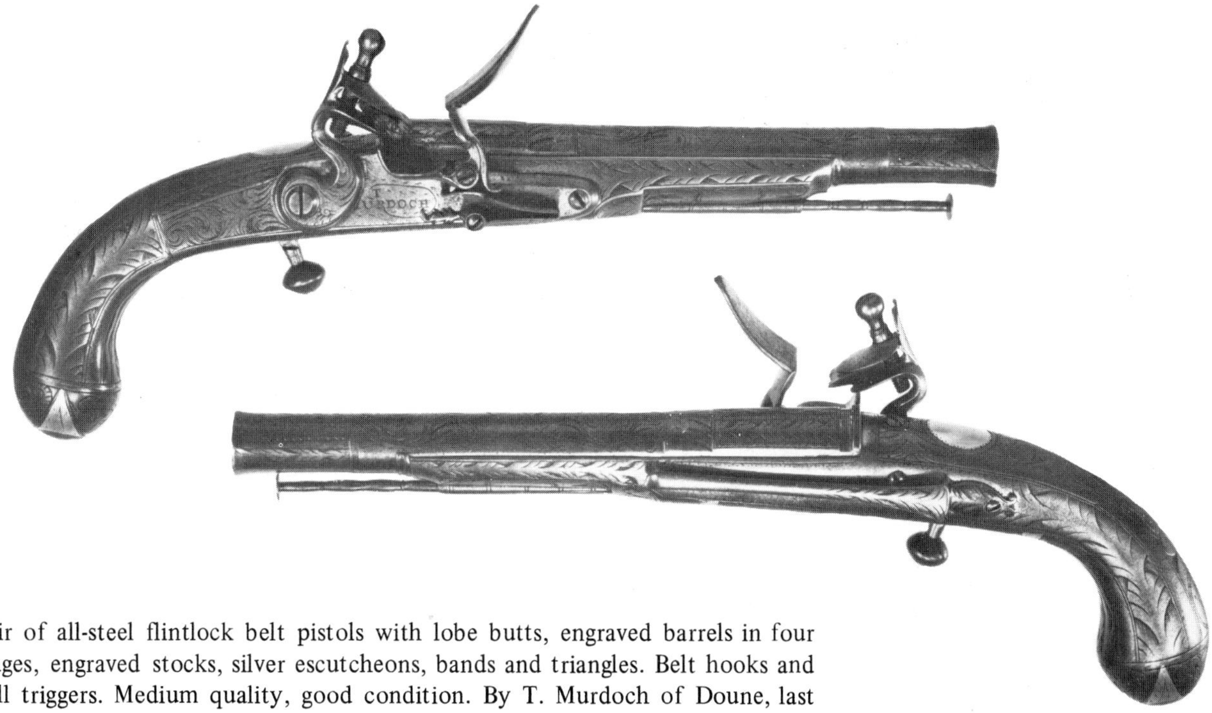

Pair of all-steel flintlock belt pistols with lobe butts, engraved barrels in four stages, engraved stocks, silver escutcheons, bands and triangles. Belt hooks and ball triggers. Medium quality, good condition. By T. Murdoch of Doune, last quarter of the 18th century. *Christie's*

About £1,200 the pair

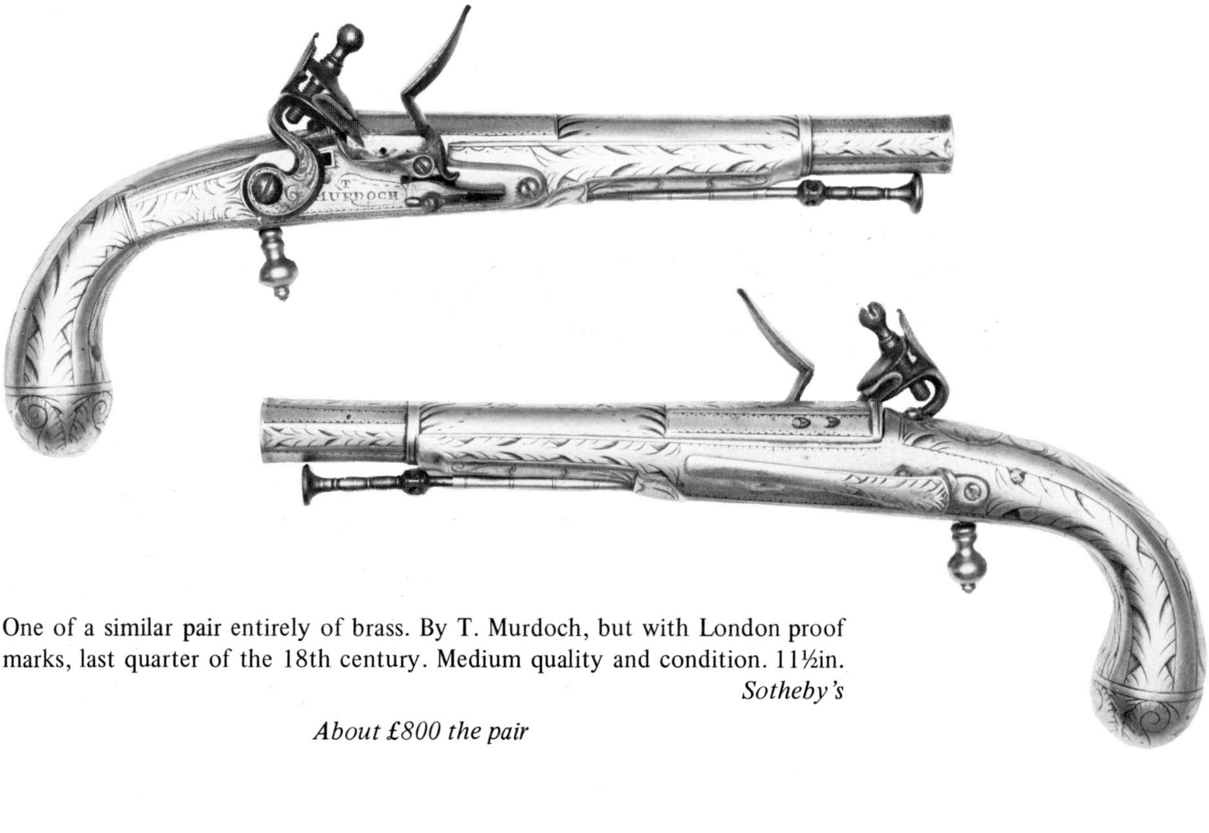

One of a similar pair entirely of brass. By T. Murdoch, but with London proof marks, last quarter of the 18th century. Medium quality and condition. 11½in. *Sotheby's*

About £800 the pair

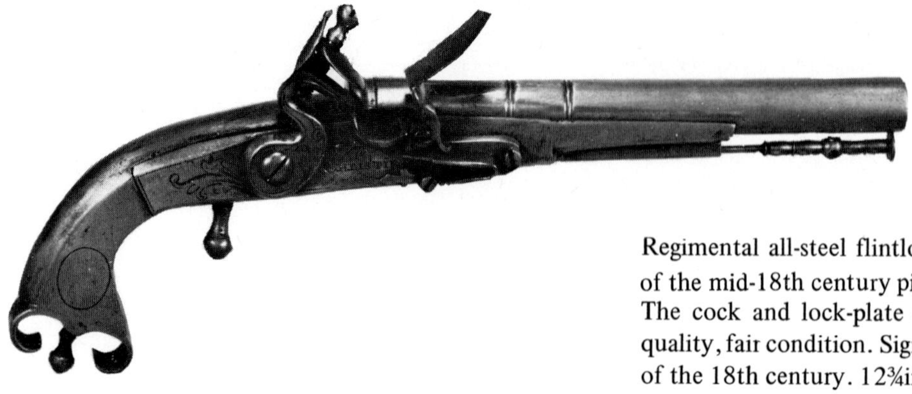

Regimental all-steel flintlock belt pistol, a plain form of the mid-18th century pistols with ram's horn butts. The cock and lock-plate engraved with foliage. Poor quality, fair condition. Signed Io. Christie, last quarter of the 18th century. 12¾in. *Christie's*

About £400

Many of these pistols were made in Birmingham by Isaac Bissell and are engraved R.H.R. (Royal Highland Regiment). The workmanship is usually poor.

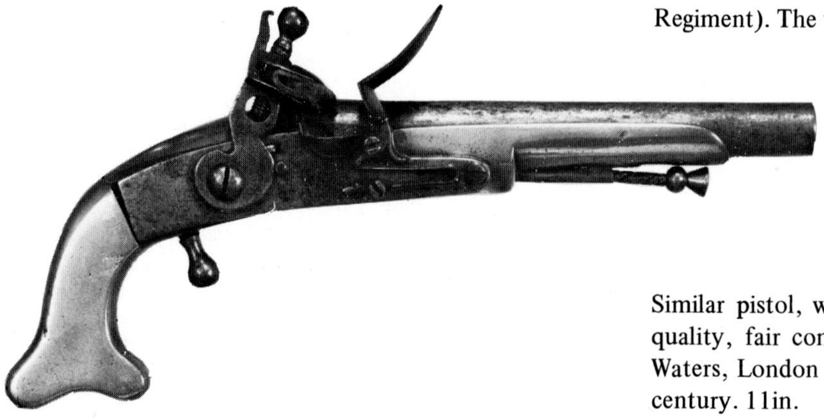

Similar pistol, with brass stock and solid butt. Poor quality, fair condition, but cock replaced. By John Waters, London proof marks, last quarter of the 18th century. 11in. *Christie's*

About £400

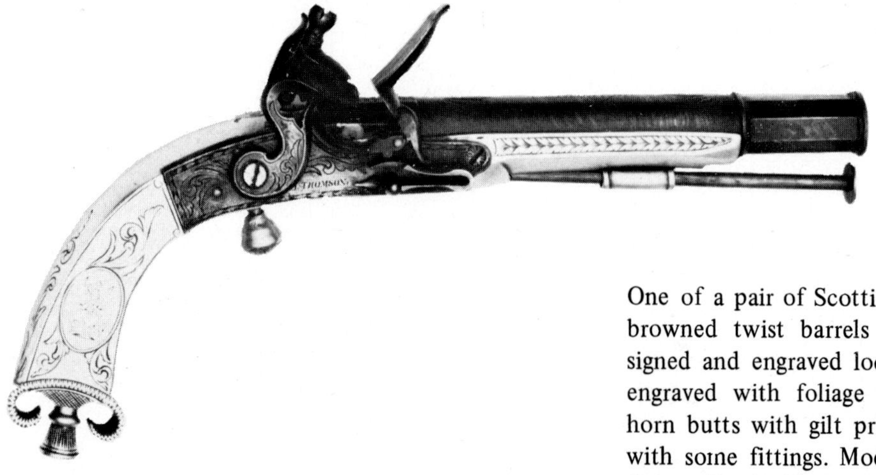

One of a pair of Scottish flintlock dress pistols with browned twist barrels in three stages, gold vents, signed and engraved locks, the German silver stocks engraved with foliage and two escutcheons, ram's horn butts with gilt prickets, gilt triggers. In a case with some fittings. Moderate quality, but good condition. By J. Thomson, Edinburgh, circa 1820/30. 10¼in. *Sotheby's*

About £800 the pair

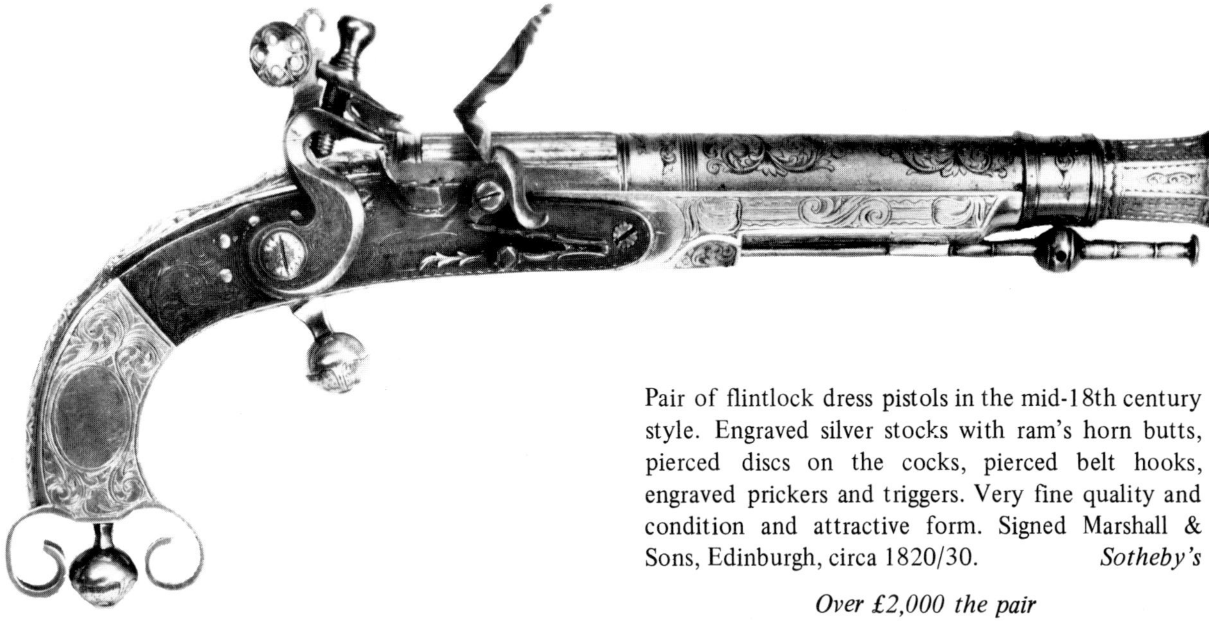

Pair of flintlock dress pistols in the mid-18th century style. Engraved silver stocks with ram's horn butts, pierced discs on the cocks, pierced belt hooks, engraved prickers and triggers. Very fine quality and condition and attractive form. Signed Marshall & Sons, Edinburgh, circa 1820/30. *Sotheby's*

Over £2,000 the pair

The finest pistols of this type have gold stocks.

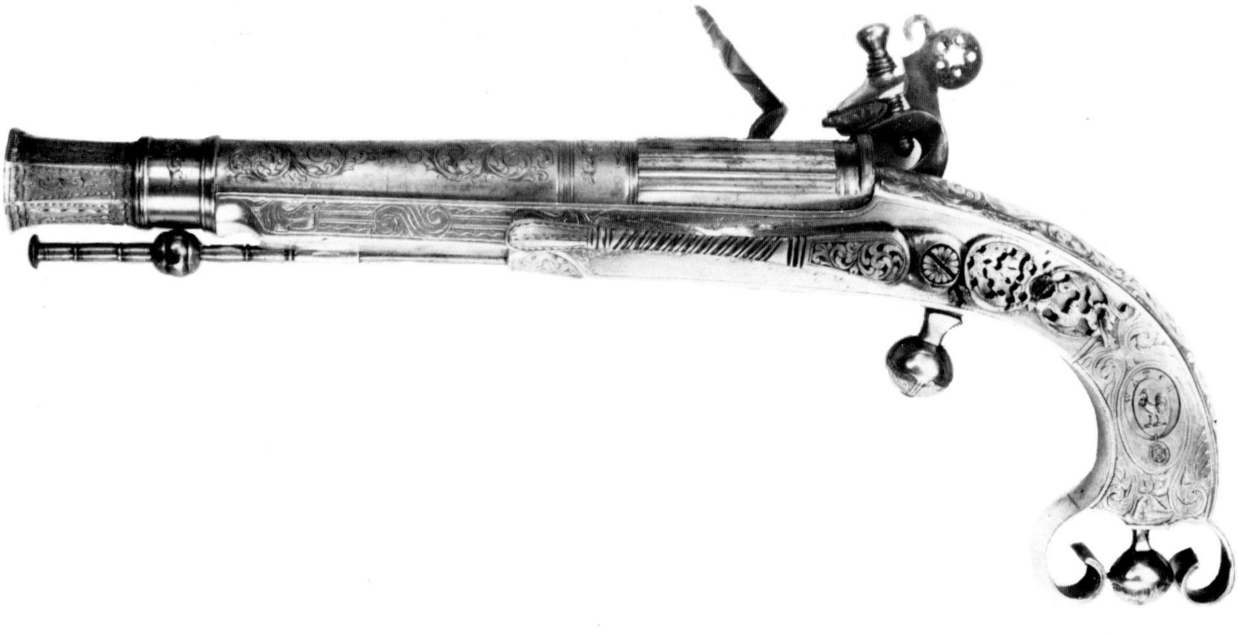

Continental Flintlock Pistols - 1750 - 1800

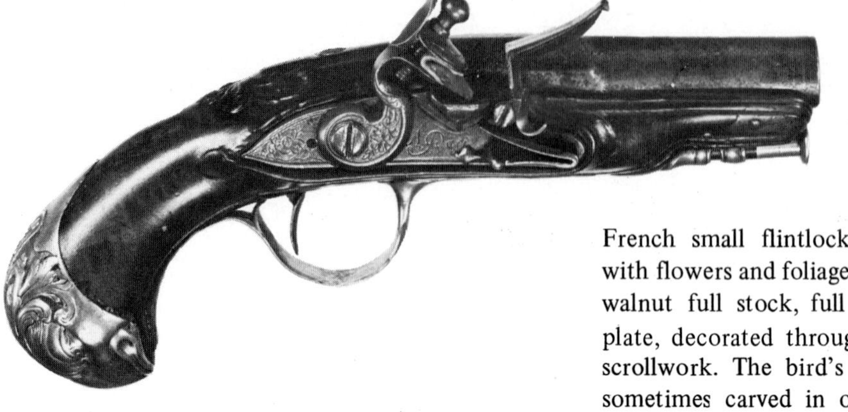

French small flintlock pistol, the barrel decorated with flowers and foliage in gold, engraved lock, carved walnut full stock, full silver mounts including side-plate, decorated throughout with shells, flowers and scrollwork. The bird's head pommel is typical, and sometimes carved in one with the grip rather than applied as a silver butt-cap. Good quality and condition. Unsigned, circa 1750/60. 7in. *Christie's*

£150 – £200

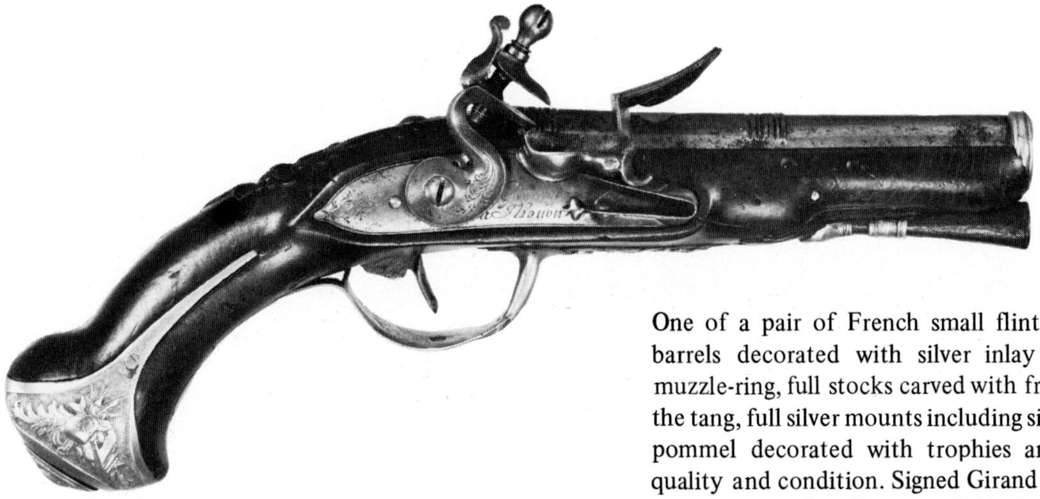

One of a pair of French small flintlock pistols, the barrels decorated with silver inlay and with silver muzzle-ring, full stocks carved with fruit and foliage at the tang, full silver mounts including side-plate, spurred pommel decorated with trophies and foliage. Good quality and condition. Signed Girand à Thonon, silver excise marks for 1775 to 1781, late 18th century. 8½in. *Christie's*

£350 – £400 the pair. £200 – £300 for a steel-mounted pair.

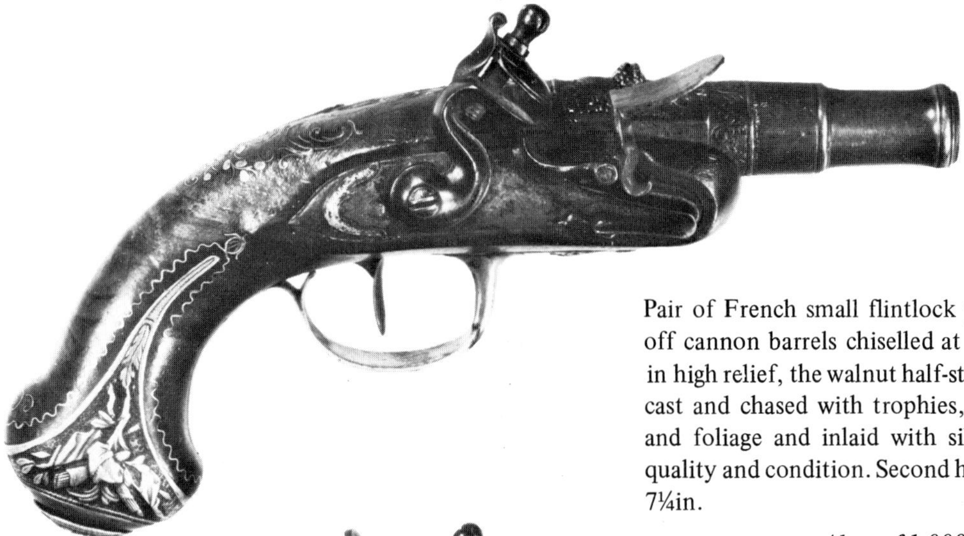

Pair of French small flintlock pistols with short turn-off cannon barrels chiselled at the breech with an urn in high relief, the walnut half-stocks with silver mounts cast and chased with trophies, portrait heads, flowers and foliage and inlaid with silver wire scrolls. Good quality and condition. Second half of the 18th century. 7¼in. *Christie's*

About £1,000 the pair.

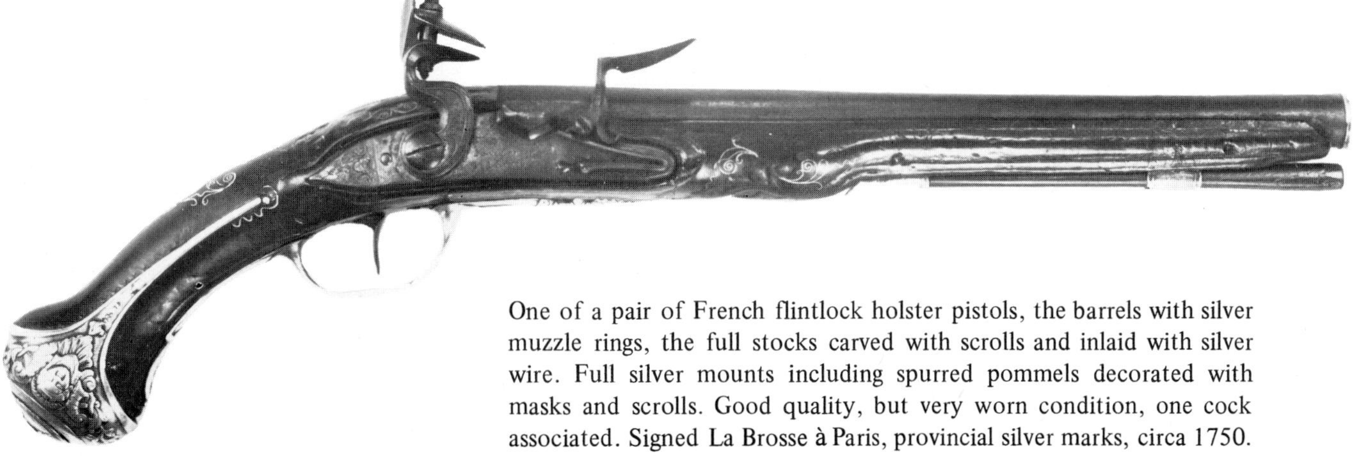

One of a pair of French flintlock holster pistols, the barrels with silver muzzle rings, the full stocks carved with scrolls and inlaid with silver wire. Full silver mounts including spurred pommels decorated with masks and scrolls. Good quality, but very worn condition, one cock associated. Signed La Brosse à Paris, provincial silver marks, circa 1750. 17in. *Sotheby's*

About £500 the pair. In fine condition perhaps £2,000.

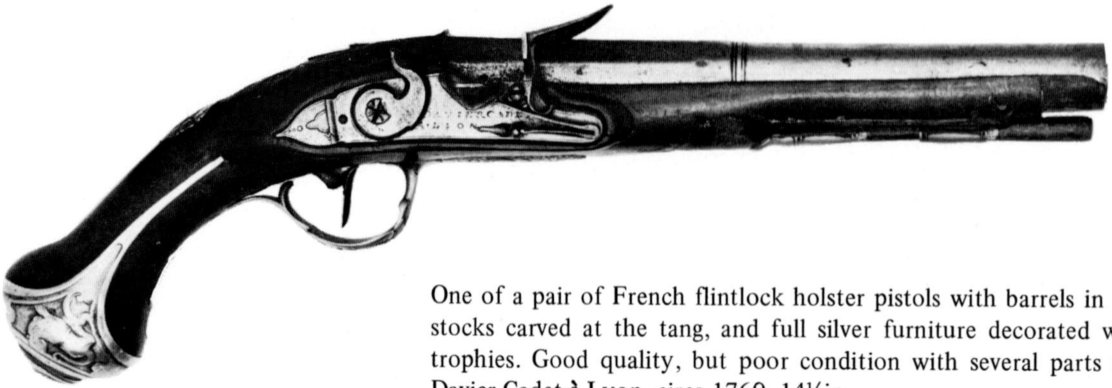

One of a pair of French flintlock holster pistols with barrels in two stages, full stocks carved at the tang, and full silver furniture decorated with scrolls and trophies. Good quality, but poor condition with several parts missing. Signed Davier Cadet à Lyon, circa 1760. 14¼in. *Sotheby's*

£300 – £450 the pair

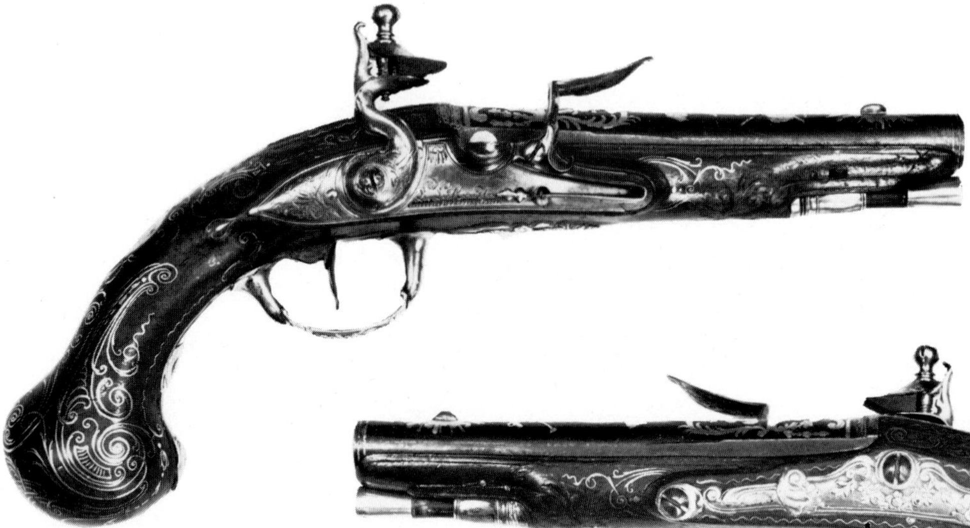

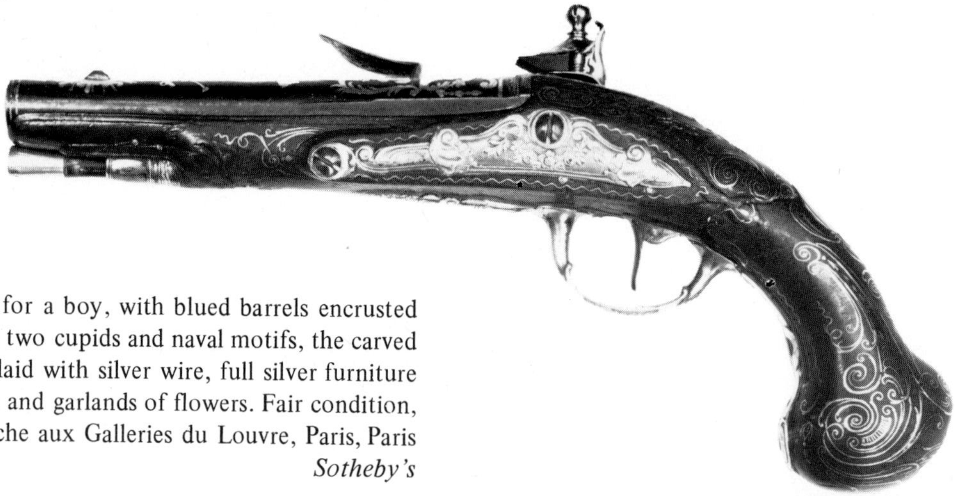

Pair of flintlock pistols made for a boy, with blued barrels encrusted with gold decoration including two cupids and naval motifs, the carved walnut full stocks profusely inlaid with silver wire, full silver furniture decorated with crossed torches and garlands of flowers. Fair condition, very fine quality. By Les Laroche aux Galleries du Louvre, Paris, Paris silver mark for 1750. 10in. *Sotheby's*

Over £3,000 the pair

This price rests to a large extent on the reputation of the Laroche family, who were Royal Gunmakers.

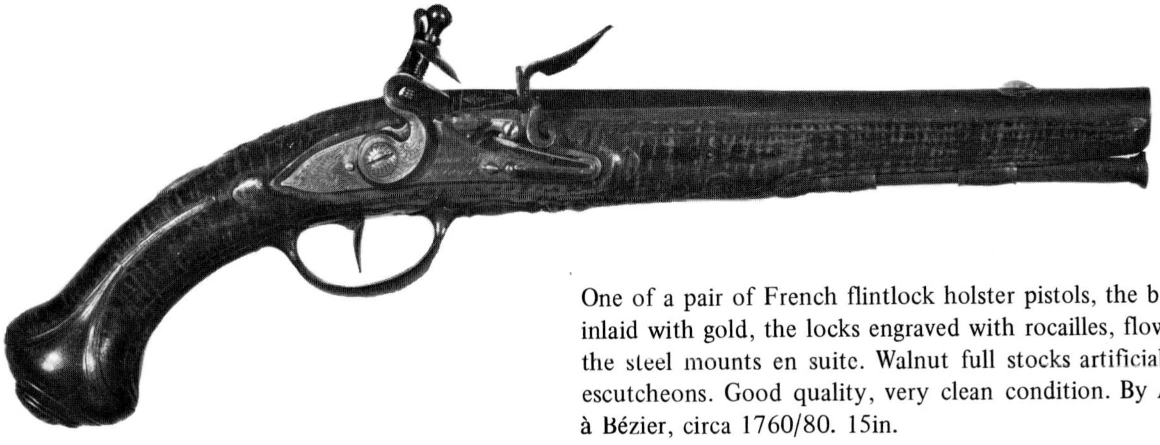

One of a pair of French flintlock holster pistols, the barrels blued and inlaid with gold, the locks engraved with rocailles, flowers and foliage, the steel mounts en suite. Walnut full stocks artificially flared. Silver escutcheons. Good quality, very clean condition. By Antoine Rebella à Bézier, circa 1760/80. 15in. *Christie's*

£600 – £700 the pair

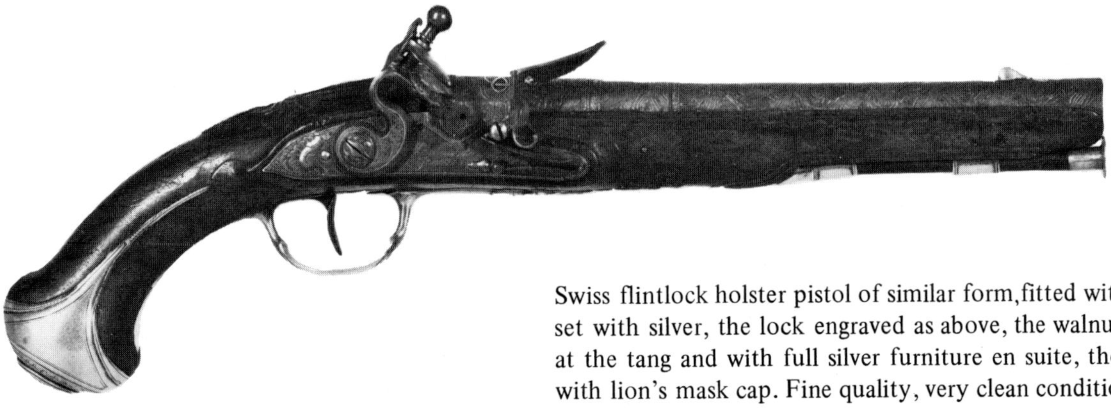

Swiss flintlock holster pistol of similar form, fitted with a Turkish barrel set with silver, the lock engraved as above, the walnut full stock carved at the tang and with full silver furniture en suite, the spurred pommel with lion's mask cap. Fine quality, very clean condition. By Montauban à Genève circa 1760/80. 15in. *Christie's*

About £600

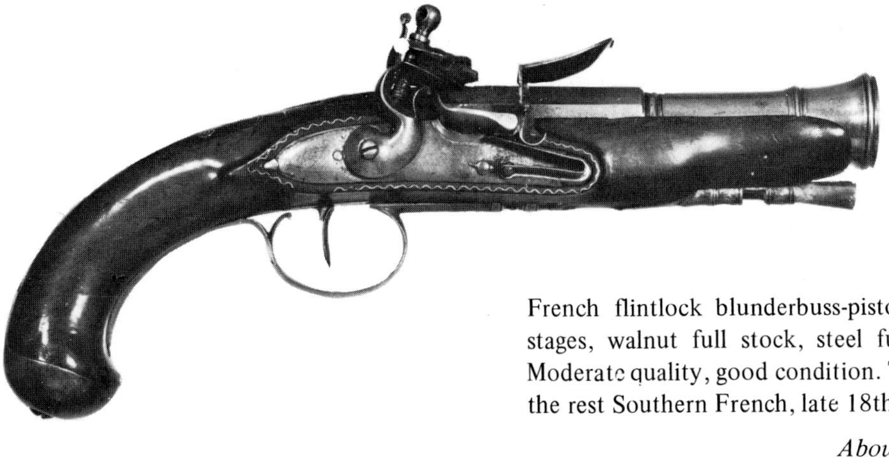

French flintlock blunderbuss-pistol with belled steel barrel in three stages, walnut full stock, steel furniture and slight silver wire inlay. Moderate quality, good condition. The barrel by Juan Santos of Madrid, the rest Southern French, late 18th century. 11½in. *Christie's*

About £300.

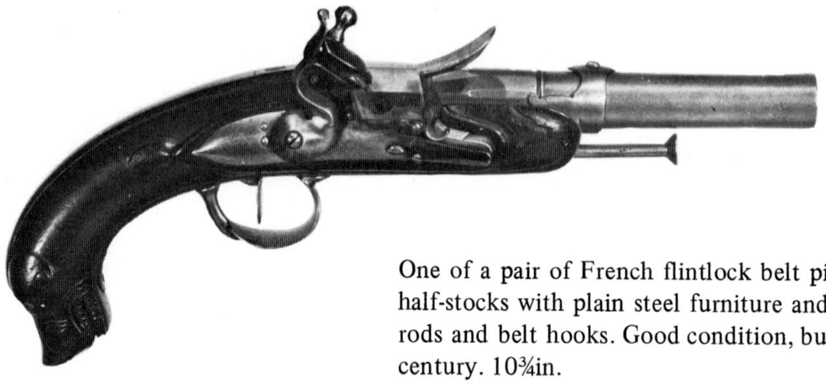

One of a pair of French flintlock belt pistols with barrels in two stages, walnut half-stocks with plain steel furniture and carved dog's head pommels, steel ramrods and belt hooks. Good condition, but poor quality. Signed Desaca, late 18th century. 10¾in. *Christie's*

£250 – £350 the pair

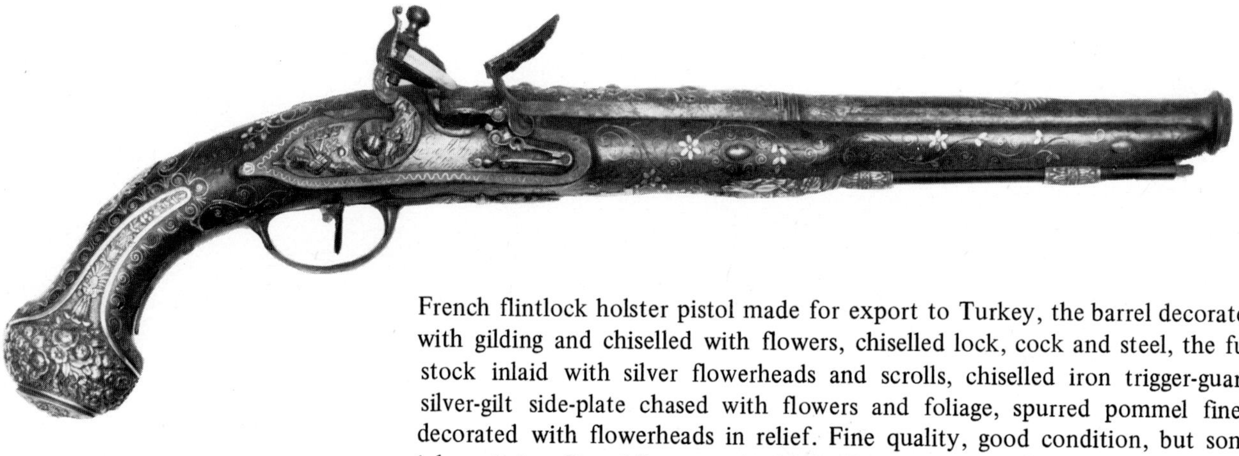

French flintlock holster pistol made for export to Turkey, the barrel decorated with gilding and chiselled with flowers, chiselled lock, cock and steel, the full stock inlaid with silver flowerheads and scrolls, chiselled iron trigger-guard, silver-gilt side-plate chased with flowers and foliage, spurred pommel finely decorated with flowerheads in relief. Fine quality, good condition, but some inlay missing. Signed Lamotte Ainé à St. Etienne, circa 1800. 20in.

£500 – £700

This is a well above average example of a large group of such export pistols. Many are of poor quality, worth perhaps only half as much.

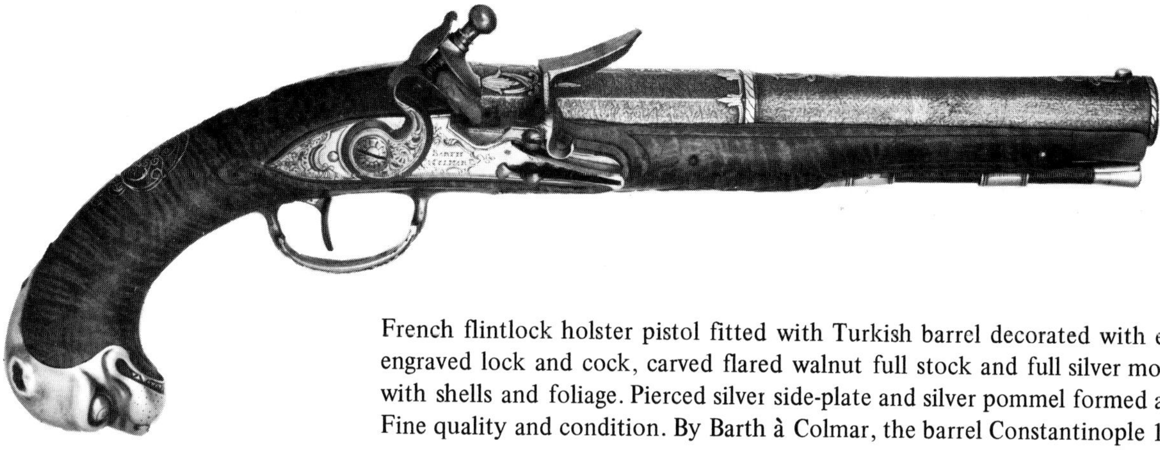

French flintlock holster pistol fitted with Turkish barrel decorated with encrusted gold, engraved lock and cock, carved flared walnut full stock and full silver mounts decorated with shells and foliage. Pierced silver side-plate and silver pommel formed as a dog's head. Fine quality and condition. By Barth à Colmar, the barrel Constantinople 1783. 14½in.

About £1,000, a most attractive and unusual form.

Pair of flintlock blunderbuss-pistols modelled on similar English examples. Brass barrels and actions, spring bayonets, walnut butts with silver wire decoration. Ramrods mounted to the side (cf. page 92). Moderate quality, fair condition. French or Belgian, circa 1800. 11in. *Sotheby's*

About £400 the pair

These can be distinguished from the English ones by the shape of the butts, also the lack of quality.

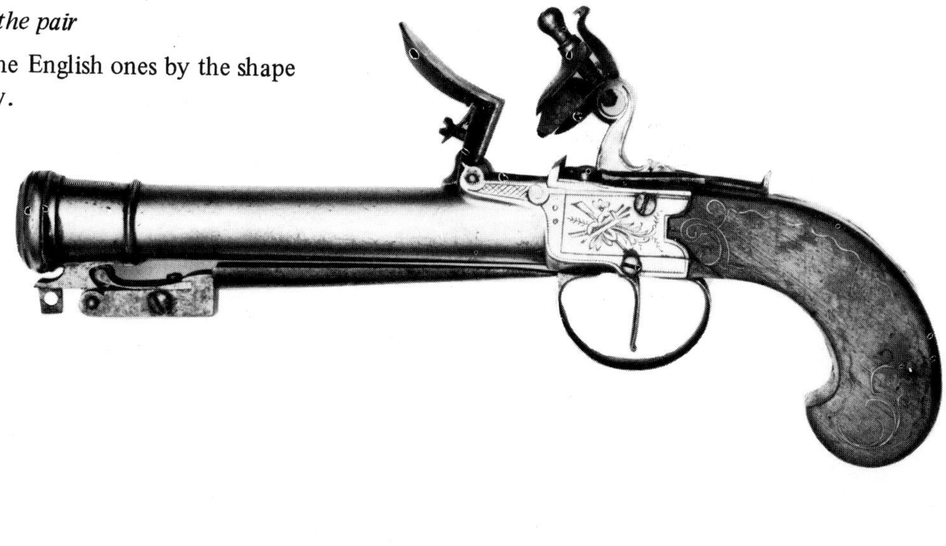

Liège cannon-barrelled flintlock pistol, the Belgian equivalent of the English "Queen Anne" type pistol. The barrel does not turn off and therefore has a ramrod below. Walnut butt and brass furniture. Poor quality, fair condition, but fitted with a later cock. Unsigned, but of the type made by Devillers of Liège in about 1750. 15in. *Sotheby's*

£150 – £200

Similar, smaller pistol of better quality fitted with engraved silver stock. Fine quality and condition. 8in. *Christie's*

£500 – £600

Liège copy of a "Queen Anne" type flintlock pistol with cannon barrel and walnut butt inlaid with silver wire and with English-type silver grotesque mask butt-cap. Good quality and condition. By H. Petitjean, late 18th century. 9¾in. *Sotheby's*

£200 – £250

One of a pair of Belgian all-steel flintlock pocket pistols with central box-lock mechanisms, short turn-off barrels, engraved swelling butts with volute pommels, trigger-guard safety-catches. These pistols belong to a large group made in the third quarter of the 18th century. They often bear spurious London proof marks and the actions are engraved "London" or with variations of the maker's name "Segallas", "Seglas" or "Gallas" (based on the London gunmaker Israel Segalas). They are nearly always of moderate quality (cf. pages 175 and 192). The pistols illustrated are signed Velut à Liège. Good condition, poor quality. 5¾in. *Christie's*

About £200 the pair
£80 – £100 for a single pistol

One of a pair of Liège English-type flintlock turn-off pistols with cannon barrels, signed and engraved central box-lock actions, the walnut butts inlaid with silver wire. Poor quality, fair condition. Signed I. Perry, late 18th century. 11½in. *Christie's*

£150 – £200 the pair

These can be distinguished from an English pair by the engraving on the actions and the silver decoration on the butts. Liège was an immensely productive arms making centre and far more copies of English firearms were made there than is commonly realised.

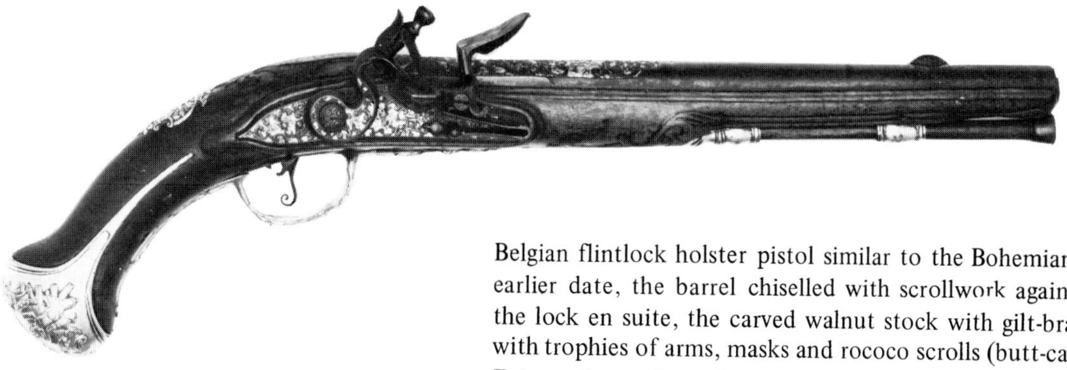

Belgian flintlock holster pistol similar to the Bohemian type of slightly earlier date, the barrel chiselled with scrollwork against a gilt ground, the lock en suite, the carved walnut stock with gilt-brass furniture cast with trophies of arms, masks and rococo scrolls (butt-cap finial missing). Fair quality and condition. Pistols of this type can be distinguished by the lack of definition in the chiselling of the iron and the moulding of the brass. They are usually, like this one, unsigned. Circa 1750. 18½in. *Sotheby's*

£500 – £800

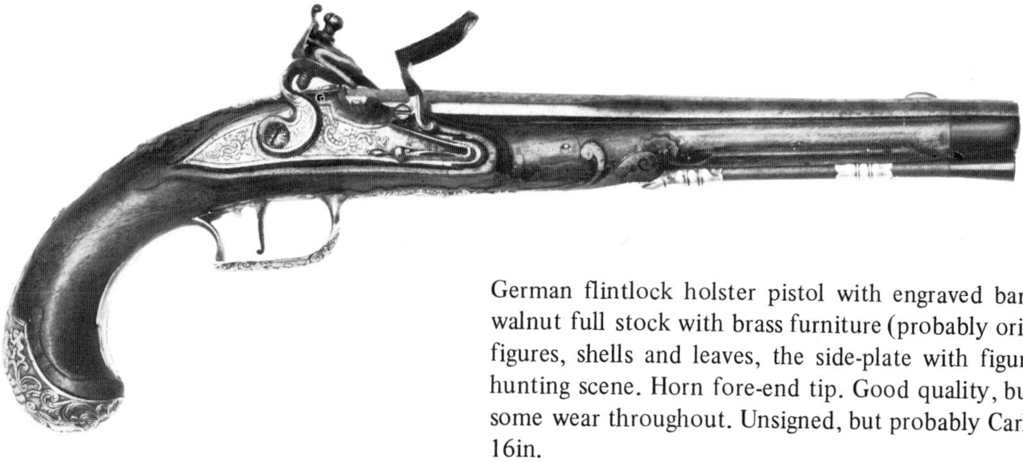

German flintlock holster pistol with engraved barrel and lock, carved walnut full stock with brass furniture (probably originally gilt) cast with figures, shells and leaves, the side-plate with figures and hounds in a hunting scene. Horn fore-end tip. Good quality, but condition fair with some wear throughout. Unsigned, but probably Carlsbad, circa 1750/60. 16in. *Sotheby's*

£300 – £400

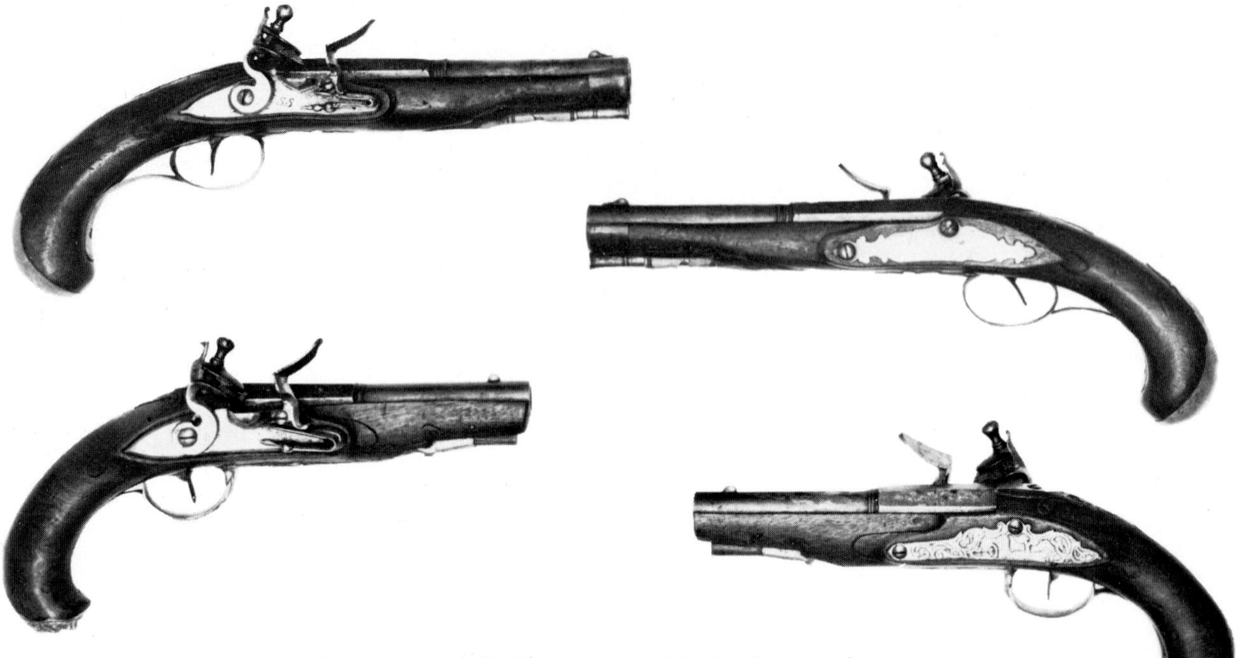

Two pairs of Austrian or German flintlock pistols of similar form, each with blued barrels in two stages (rifled on one pair), full stocks and brass mounts, plain in the top pair and decorated in the bottom pair. Moderate quality, fair condition. Circa 1760/70. 11in. and 9½in. *Sotheby's*

About £300 each pair

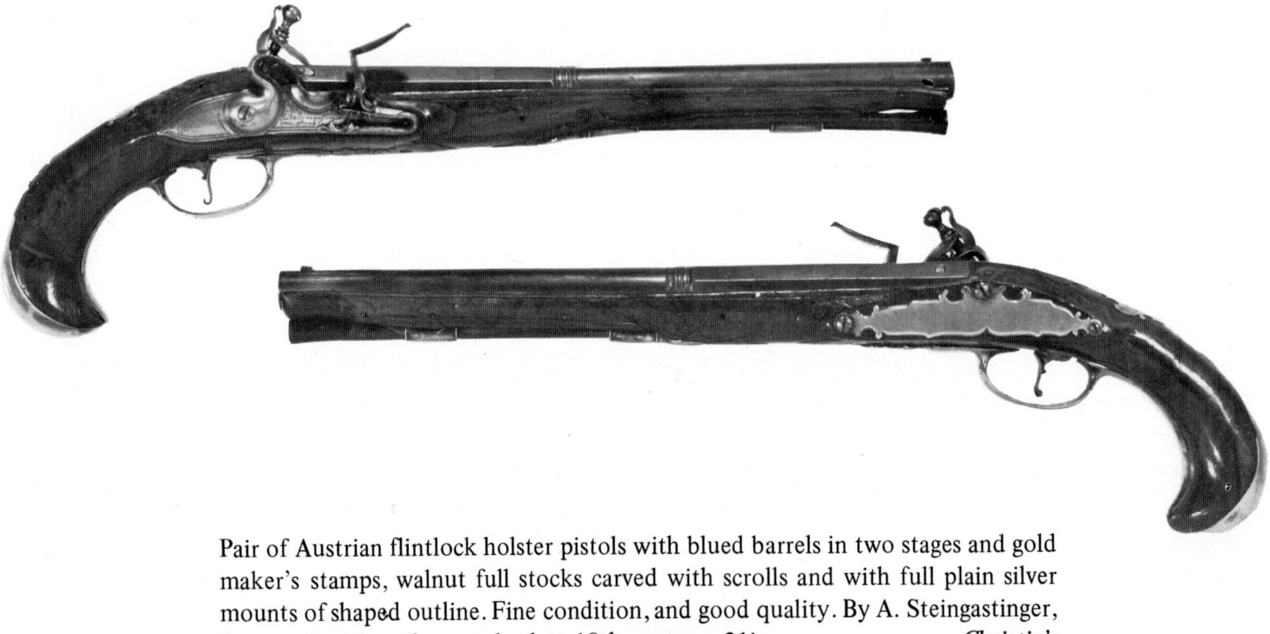

Pair of Austrian flintlock holster pistols with blued barrels in two stages and gold maker's stamps, walnut full stocks carved with scrolls and with full plain silver mounts of shaped outline. Fine condition, and good quality. By A. Steingastinger, Prague, Austrian silver marks, late 18th century. 21in. *Christie's*

Over £1,000 the pair

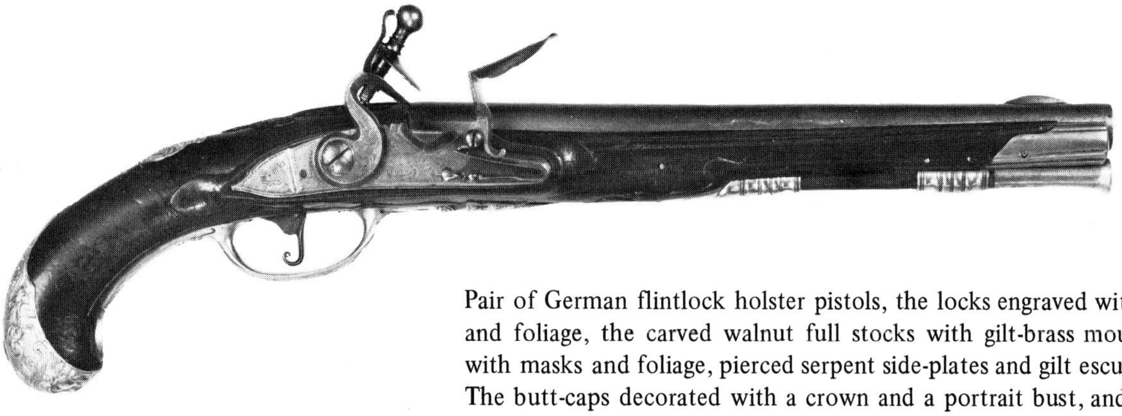

Pair of German flintlock holster pistols, the locks engraved with beasts and foliage, the carved walnut full stocks with gilt-brass mounts cast with masks and foliage, pierced serpent side-plates and gilt escutcheons. The butt-caps decorated with a crown and a portrait bust, and terminating in a lion's mask. Gilt fore-end caps and ramrod tips. Fine quality and condition. Unsigned, circa 1750/60. 18in. *Christie's*

Over £1,000 the pair

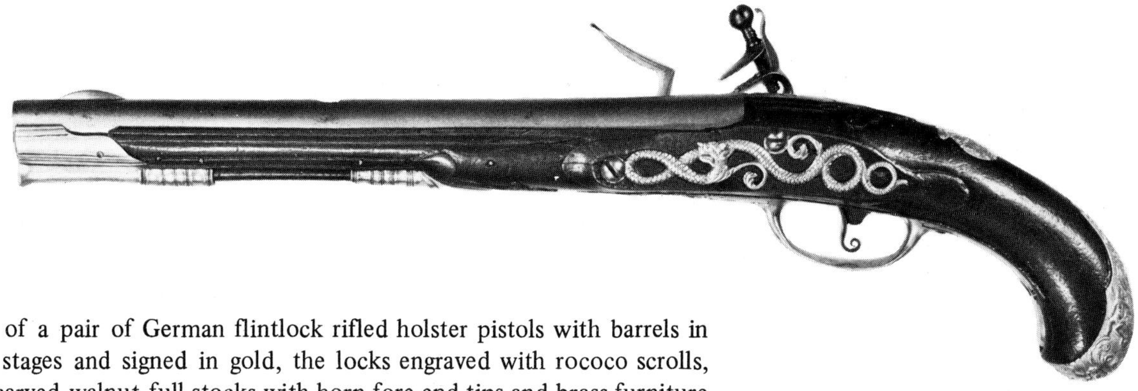

One of a pair of German flintlock rifled holster pistols with barrels in two stages and signed in gold, the locks engraved with rococo scrolls, the carved walnut full stocks with horn fore-end tips and brass furniture decorated with further scrolls. Fair condition, good quality. By Johann Jacob Kuchenreiter of Regensburg, late 18th century. 17in. *Sotheby's*

Over £1,000 the pair

The price reflects the reputation of this gunmaker.

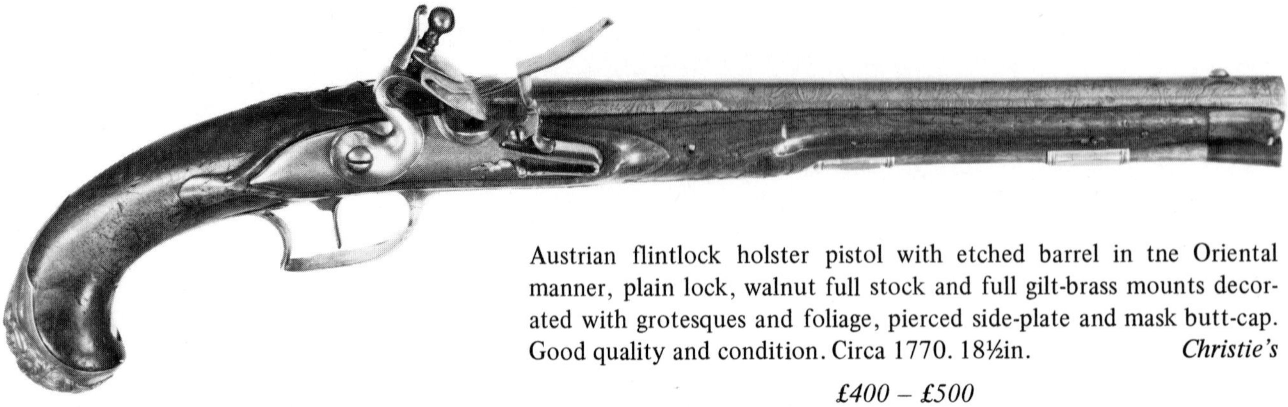

Austrian flintlock holster pistol with etched barrel in tne Oriental manner, plain lock, walnut full stock and full gilt-brass mounts decorated with grotesques and foliage, pierced side-plate and mask butt-cap. Good quality and condition. Circa 1770. 18½in. *Christie's*

£400 – £500

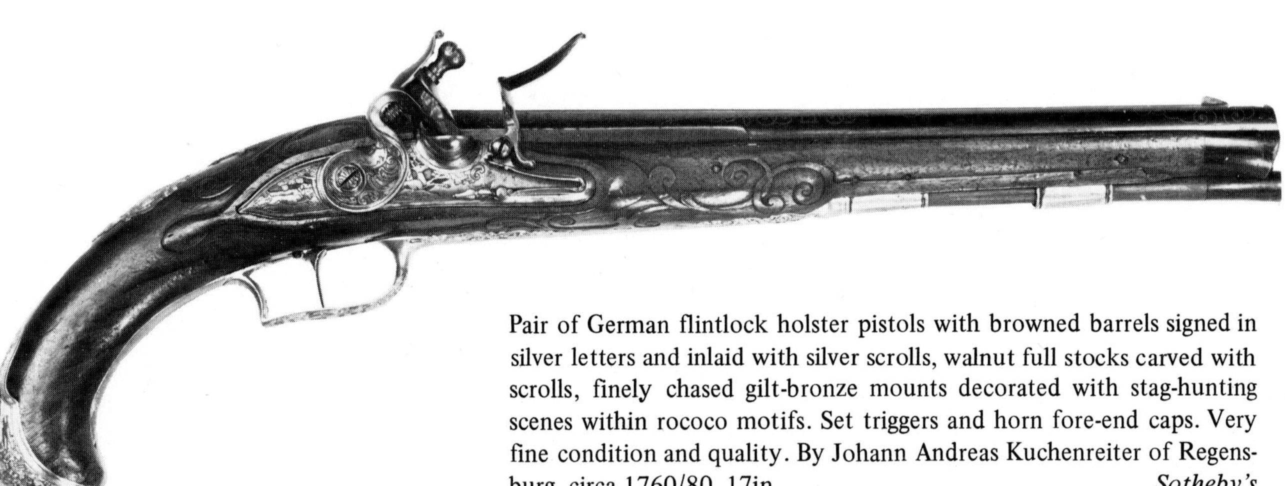

Pair of German flintlock holster pistols with browned barrels signed in silver letters and inlaid with silver scrolls, walnut full stocks carved with scrolls, finely chased gilt-bronze mounts decorated with stag-hunting scenes within rococo motifs. Set triggers and horn fore-end caps. Very fine condition and quality. By Johann Andreas Kuchenreiter of Regensburg, circa 1760/80. 17in. *Sotheby's*

About £2,000 the pair

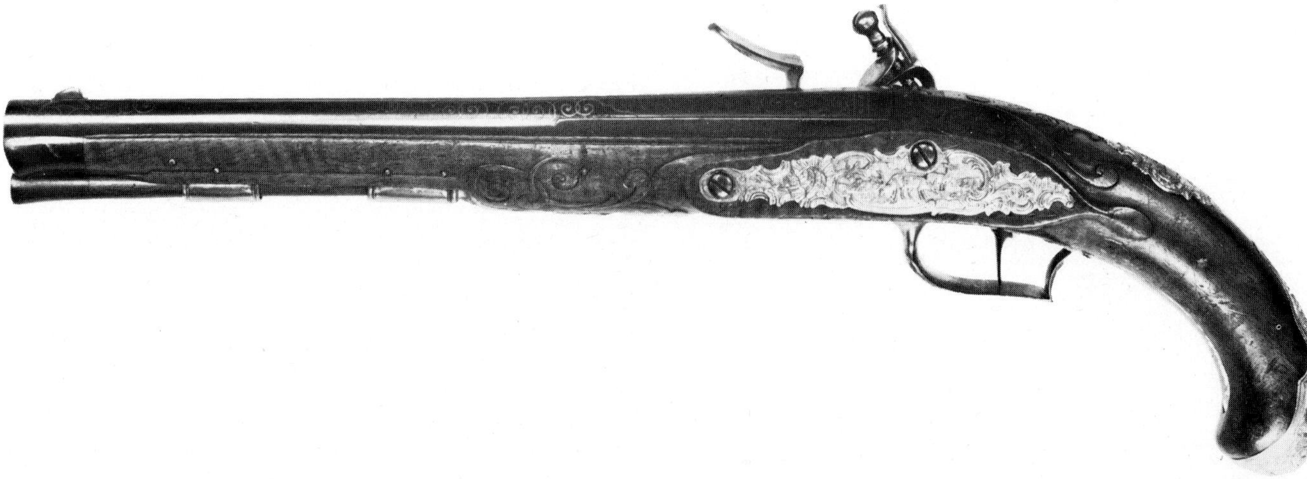

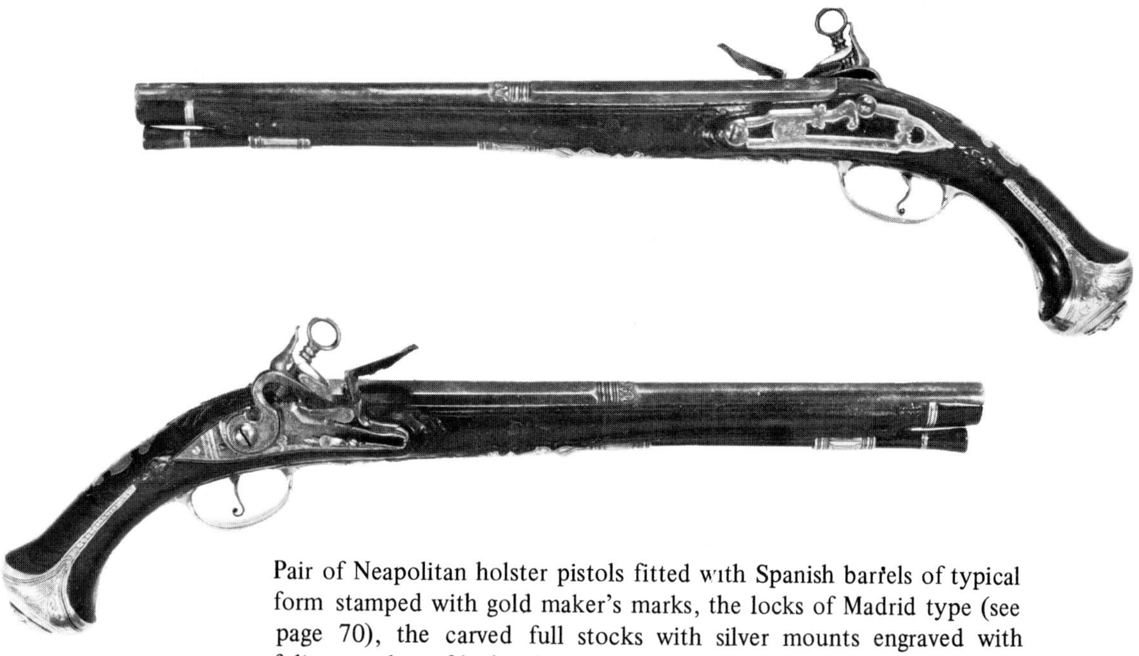

Pair of Neapolitan holster pistols fitted with Spanish barrels of typical form stamped with gold maker's marks, the locks of Madrid type (see page 70), the carved full stocks with silver mounts engraved with foliage and profile heads, pierced escutcheons and side-plates. Fine quality and condition. The barrels by Pedro Esteva of Barcelona, the mounts with numerous Naples silver marks, the steels dated 1761. 19½in. *Christie's*

About £1,500 the pair

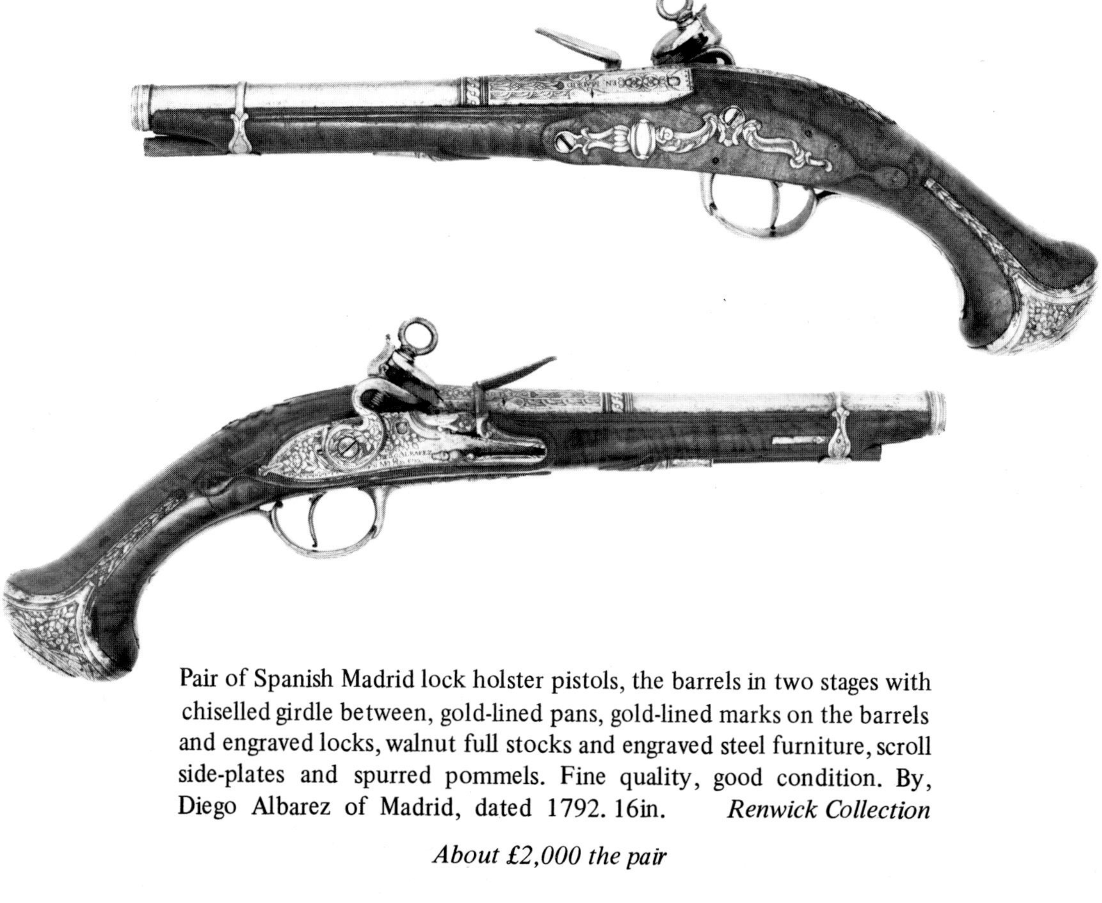

Pair of Spanish Madrid lock holster pistols, the barrels in two stages with chiselled girdle between, gold-lined pans, gold-lined marks on the barrels and engraved locks, walnut full stocks and engraved steel furniture, scroll side-plates and spurred pommels. Fine quality, good condition. By, Diego Albarez of Madrid, dated 1792. 16in. *Renwick Collection*

About £2,000 the pair

English Flintlock Pistols - 1800 - 1830

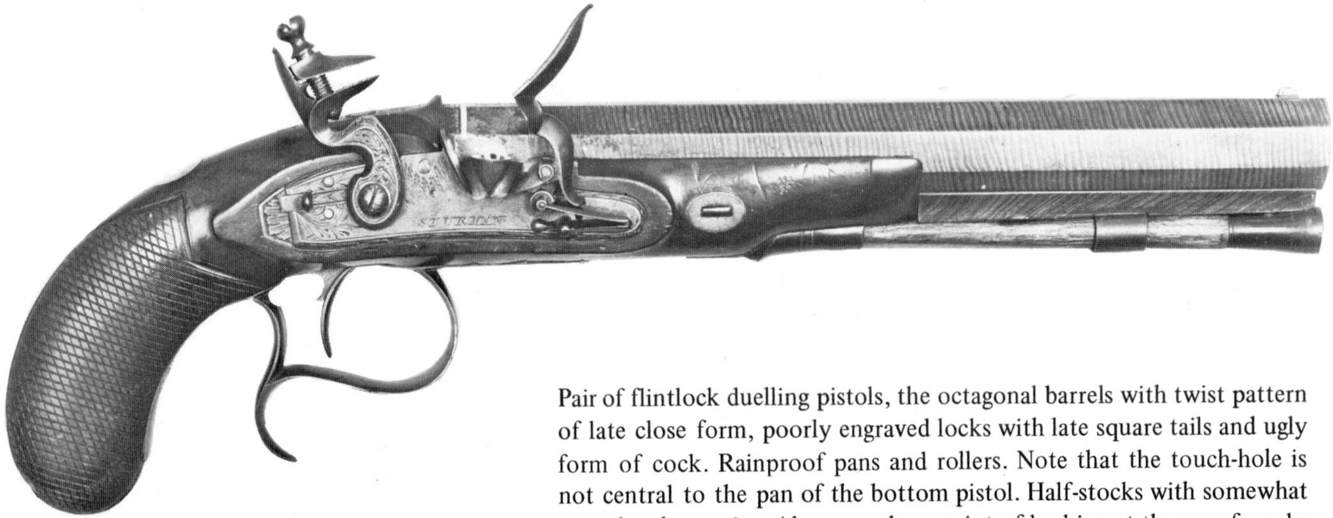

Pair of flintlock duelling pistols, the octagonal barrels with twist pattern of late close form, poorly engraved locks with late square tails and ugly form of cock. Rainproof pans and rollers. Note that the touch-hole is not central to the pan of the bottom pistol. Half-stocks with somewhat irregular chequering. Always make a point of looking at the proof marks under the breech of this type of pistol, many were made in Birmingham for retail in London. Poor quality, fair condition. Signed Sturman, Boro' Market, probably about 1825. 9in. barrels.

Knight, Frank & Rutley

About £450 the pair

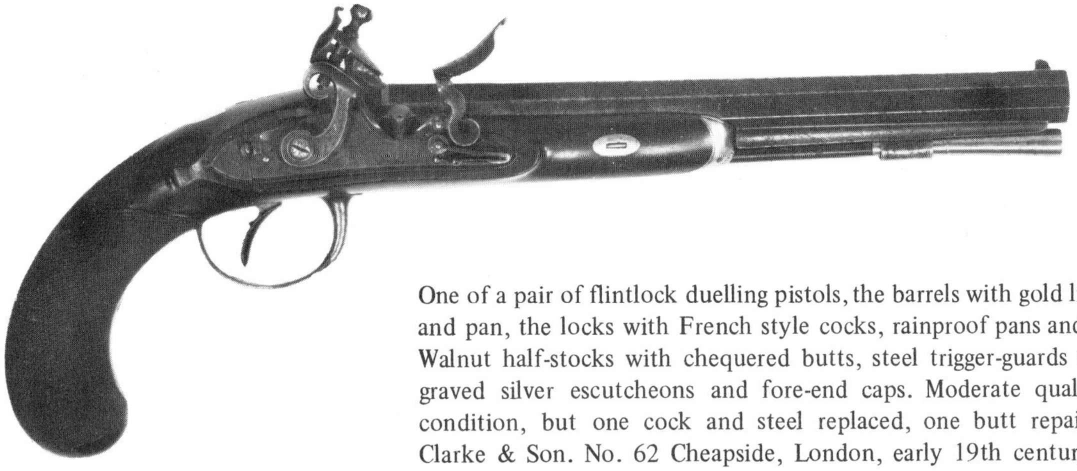

One of a pair of flintlock duelling pistols, the barrels with gold line, vent and pan, the locks with French style cocks, rainproof pans and rollers. Walnut half-stocks with chequered butts, steel trigger-guards and engraved silver escutcheons and fore-end caps. Moderate quality, fair condition, but one cock and steel replaced, one butt repaired. By Clarke & Son. No. 62 Cheapside, London, early 19th century. 15in.
Christie's

£500 – £600 the pair

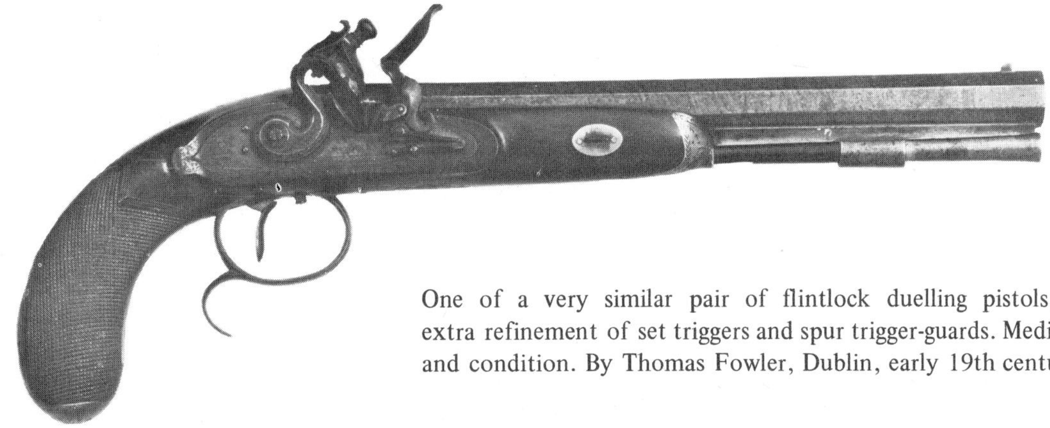

One of a very similar pair of flintlock duelling pistols, with the extra refinement of set triggers and spur trigger-guards. Medium quality and condition. By Thomas Fowler, Dublin, early 19th century. 15½in.
Christie's

About £600 the pair

Irish duelling pistols are popular and Fowler was one of the top Irish makers.

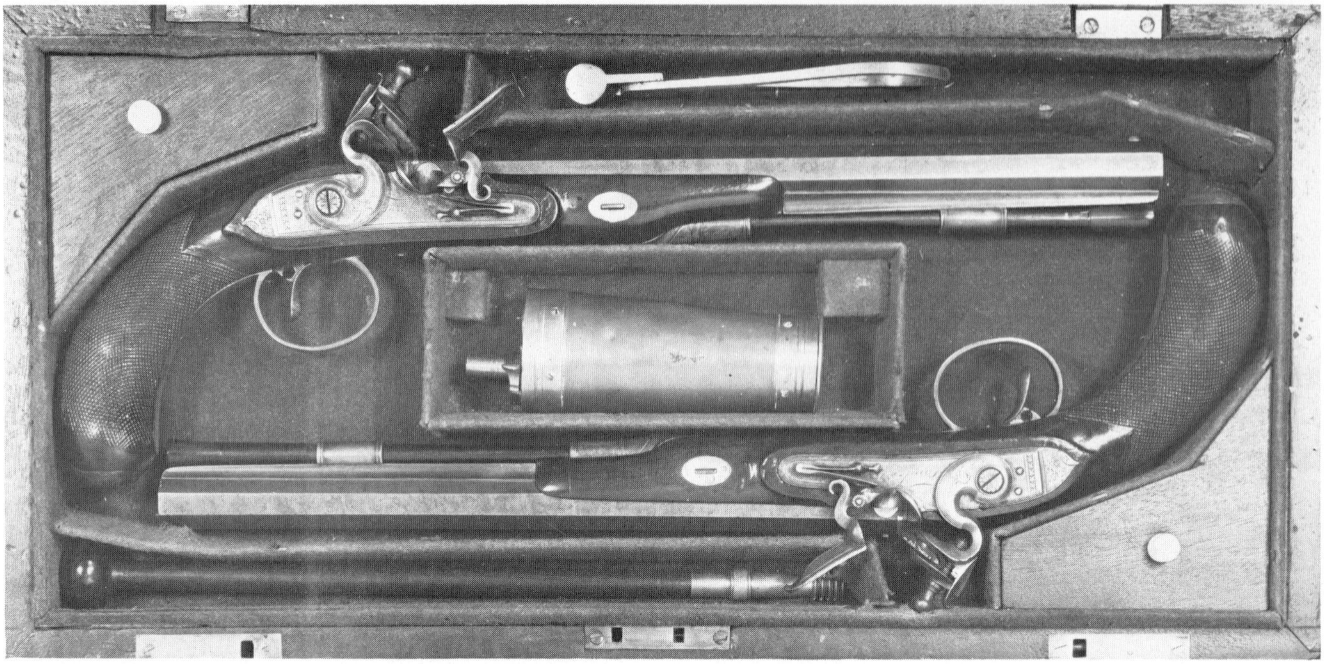

Pair of Irish flintlock duelling pistols of similar type, the barrels with gold line and vent, engraved locks, walnut half-stocks, engrave steel mounts and horn fore-end tips. Medium quality and condition. The case is not original (note shape of corner compartments, tha the central compartment does not reach the front of the trigger-guards and that there is no recess for the steel), nor is the powder flask By Fowler, Dublin, circa 1800. 16½in. *Christie*

£600 – £750

There is all the difference in the world between a complete original cased set and an assemblage such as this. The range in value is be tween 75% and 100%.

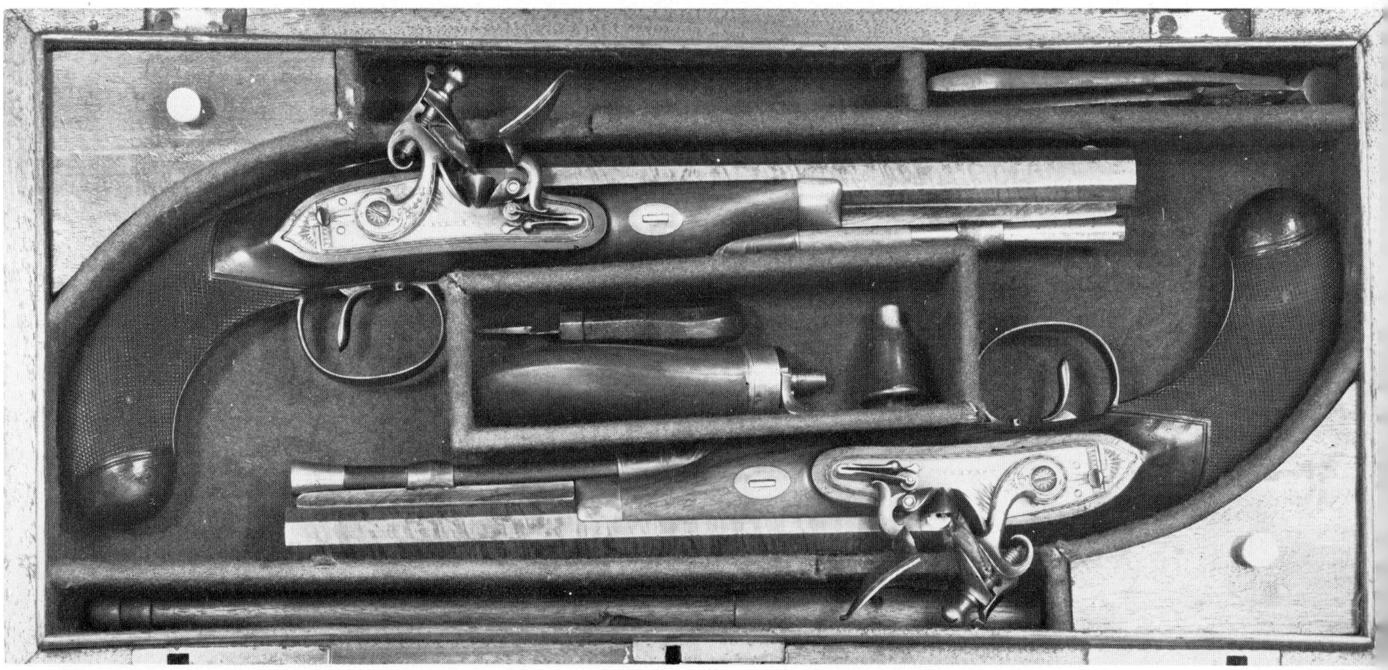

Cased pair of provincial flintlock duelling pistols, the barrels with gold lines and platinum vent, the locks with French style cocks a rainproof pans. Walnut half-stocks with blued steel furniture and silver escutcheons, set triggers and horn fore-end tips. Mediu quality, good condition, but poor form and length. The case is probably original but the powder flask associated. By Sykes, Oxfor early 19th century. 14¼in. *Christi*

£700 – £850

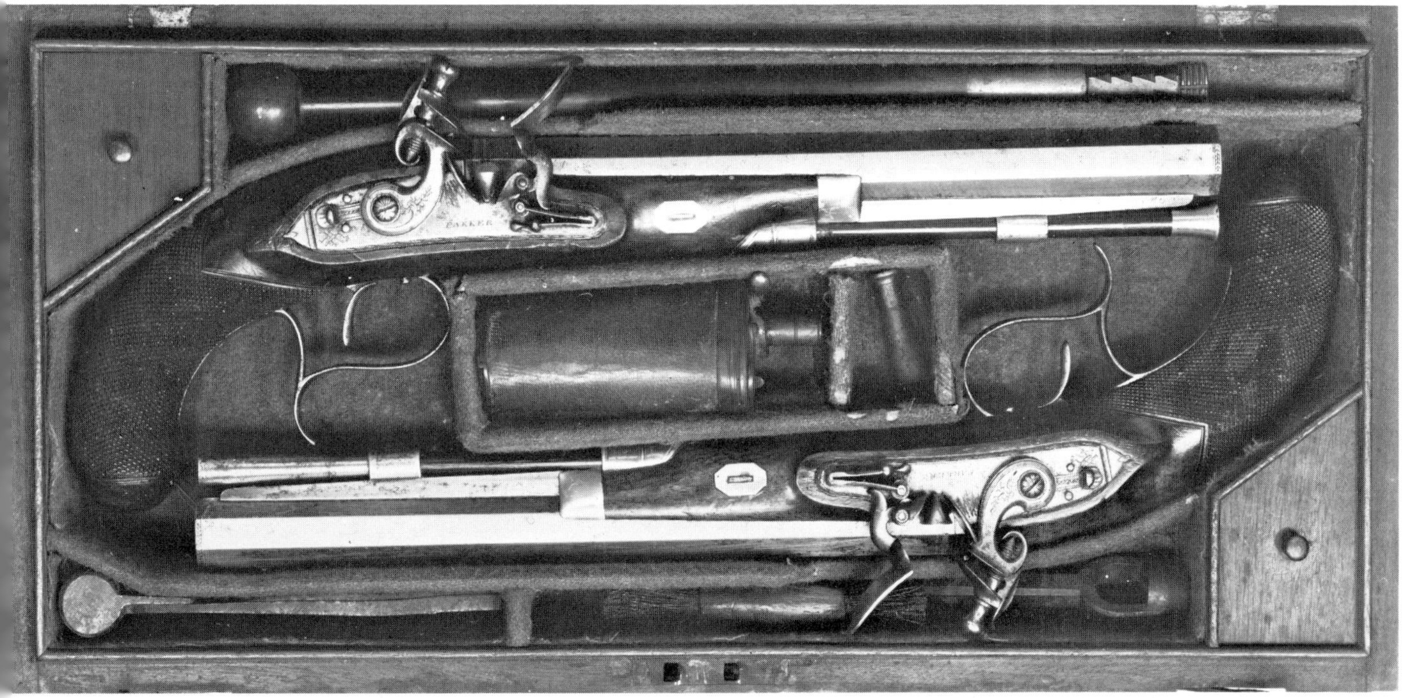

Cased pair of London flintlock duelling pistols of good quality but in poor condition, having no original finish. The case is original and has its trade label in the lid. By W. Parker, High Holborn, London, circa 1815. 15½in. *Christie's*

£600 – £750

These would be worth more than the pair by Sykes if the condition were better.

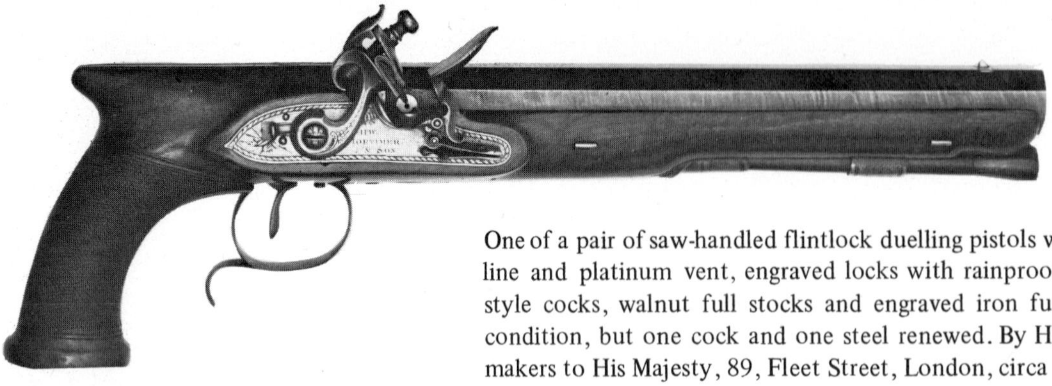

One of a pair of saw-handled flintlock duelling pistols with octagonal barrels, gold line and platinum vent, engraved locks with rainproof pans and rollers, French style cocks, walnut full stocks and engraved iron furniture. Good quality and condition, but one cock and one steel renewed. By H.W. Mortimer & Son, Gunmakers to His Majesty, 89, Fleet Street, London, circa 1815. 15¼in. *Sotheby's*

£600 – £700 the pair

Mortimer made a number of similar saw-handled pistols.

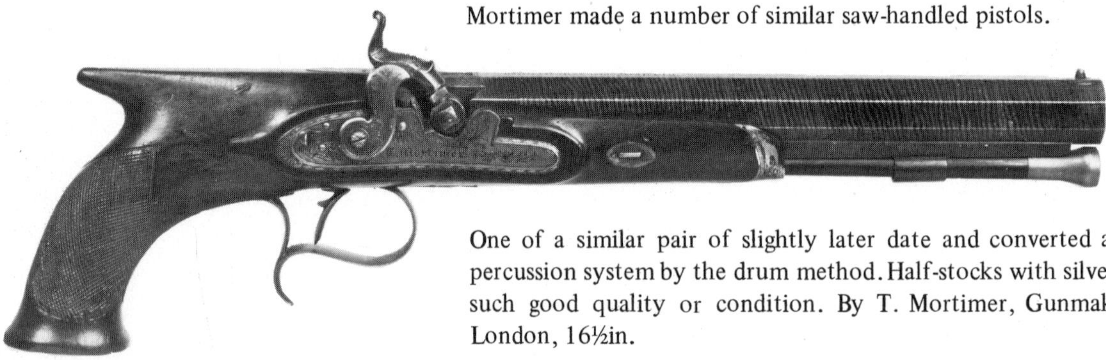

One of a similar pair of slightly later date and converted around 1830 to the percussion system by the drum method. Half-stocks with silver fore-end caps. Not such good quality or condition. By T. Mortimer, Gunmaker to His Majesty, London, 16½in. *Christie's*

£300 – £400 the pair

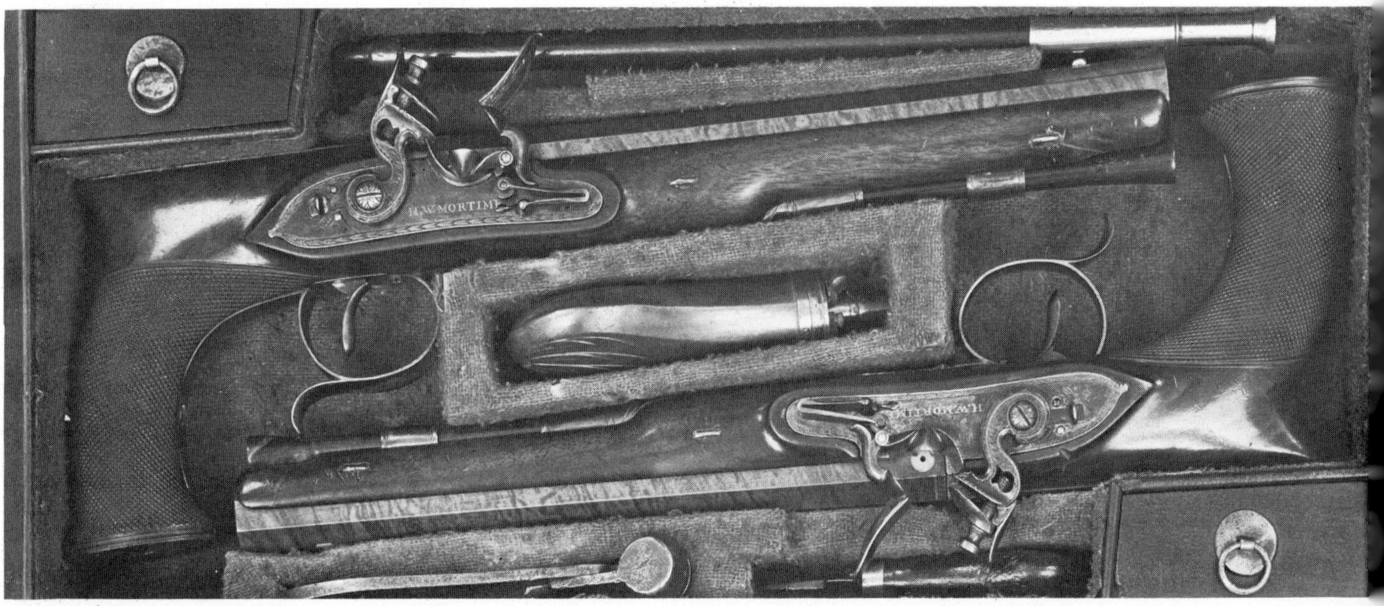

Cased pair of H.W. Mortimer saw-handled flintlock pistols which were converted to percussion in about 1830, and have recently be re-converted to flint in an effort to double their value. Note poor shape of cocks, week gold signatures on locks, the ends of which a obscured by the steel springs. You can tell much from the colour of the metal, also by looking at the pan on the inside of the lock.

About £450

These would be worth more than double if they were original flints.

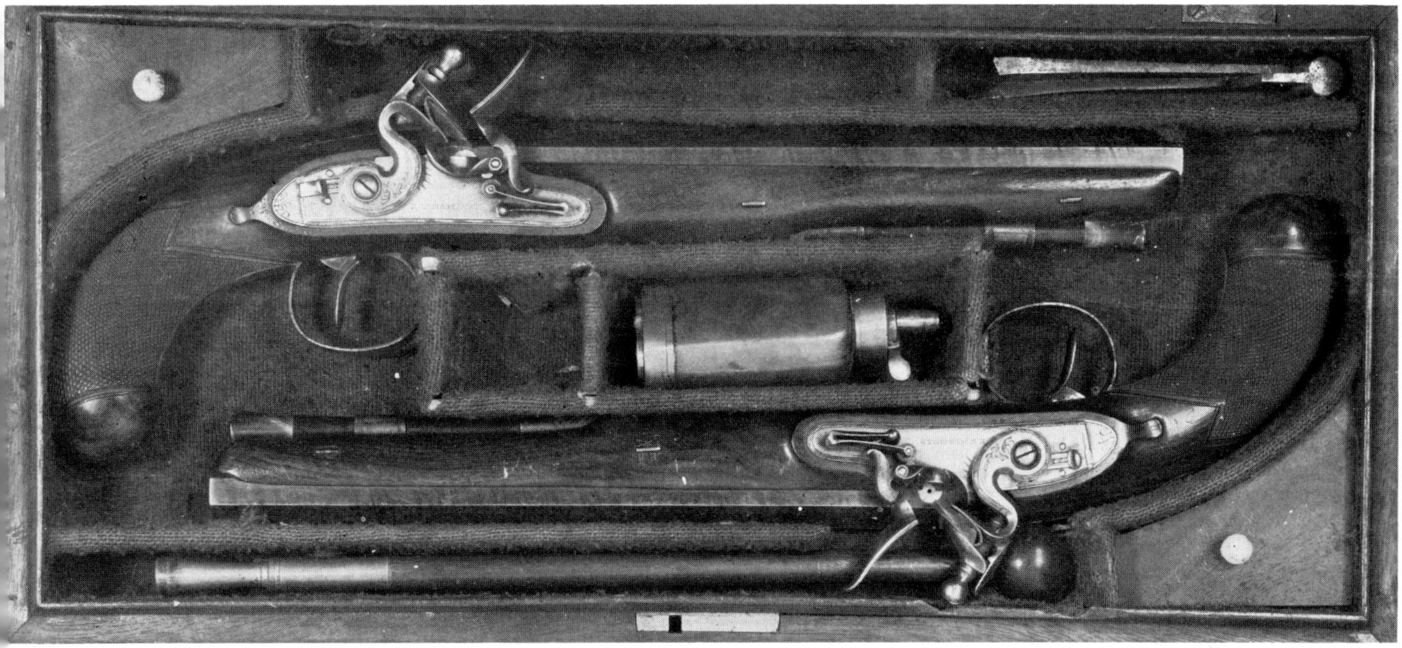

Cased pair of flintlock duelling pistols engraved H.W. Mortimer on the barrels and locks, but not by this maker. Genuine Mortimer pistols of this full-stocked variety have spirally fluted pommels, and are of finer quality. Medium quality, good condition. The case may be original but the H.W. Mortimer label in the lid is certainly not. Early 19th century. 15in. *Christie's*

£400 – £500

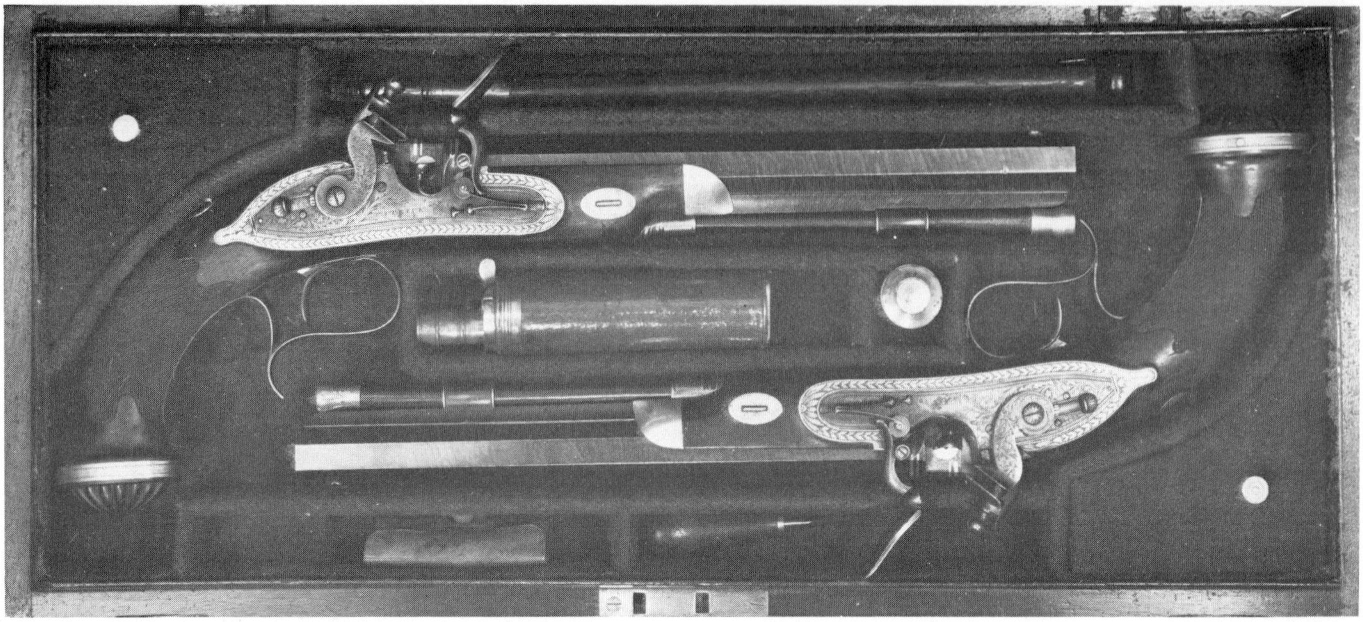

Cased pair of flintlock duelling pistols of very distinctive form. Octagonal barrels with patent recessed breech, gold lines, platinur vents and swept rainproof pans, engraved locks with flat cocks and large rollers, bordered in engraved silver. Walnut half-stocks wit silver fore-end tips and fluted wooden pommels. Fine quality and condition with some re-finishing. In fitted case, probably original bu relined, with accessories. By Patrick, Liverpool, circa 1830. 15½in. *Christie's*

Over £1,500

The firm of Patrick is of interest because it was one of the few in the history of gunmaking to be run by a woman.

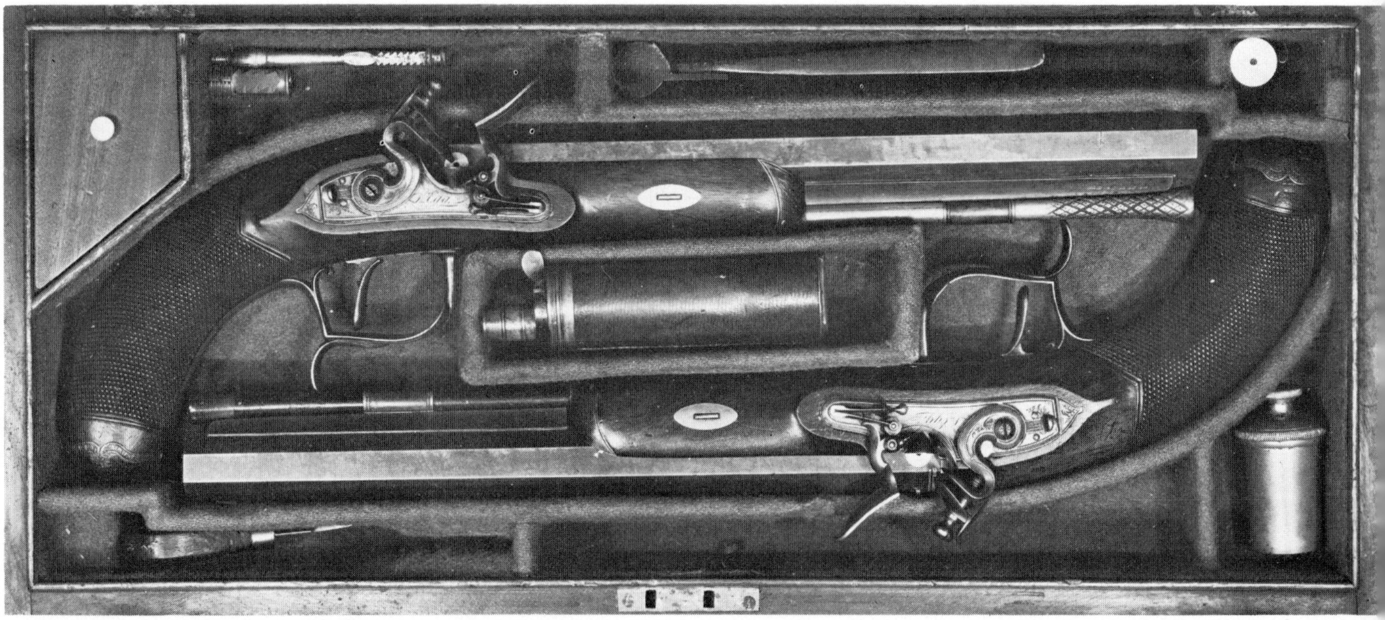

Cased pair of flintlock duelling pistols by a top London maker, with browned octagonal barrels, gold signatures, lines, fore-sights an vents, signed and engraved locks with rollers and gold-lined pans. Walnut half-stocks with finely engraved blued steel furniture, gol escutcheons, set triggers and original ramrods. Fine quality and condition with much original finish. In original case with mos accessories and trade label. By Durs Egg, London, circa 1800. *Christie*

About £2,000

D. Egg and the Manton brothers are probably the best London gunmakers of the early 19th century, but the value of pistols such a these depends to a very large extent on the condition.

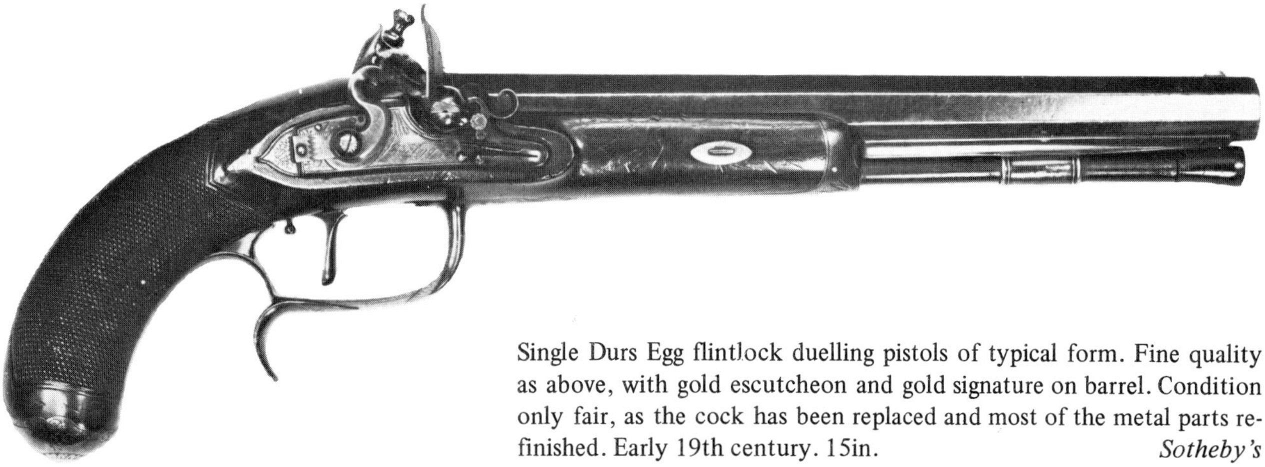

Single Durs Egg flintlock duelling pistols of typical form. Fine quality as above, with gold escutcheon and gold signature on barrel. Condition only fair, as the cock has been replaced and most of the metal parts refinished. Early 19th century. 15in. *Sotheby's*

About £300

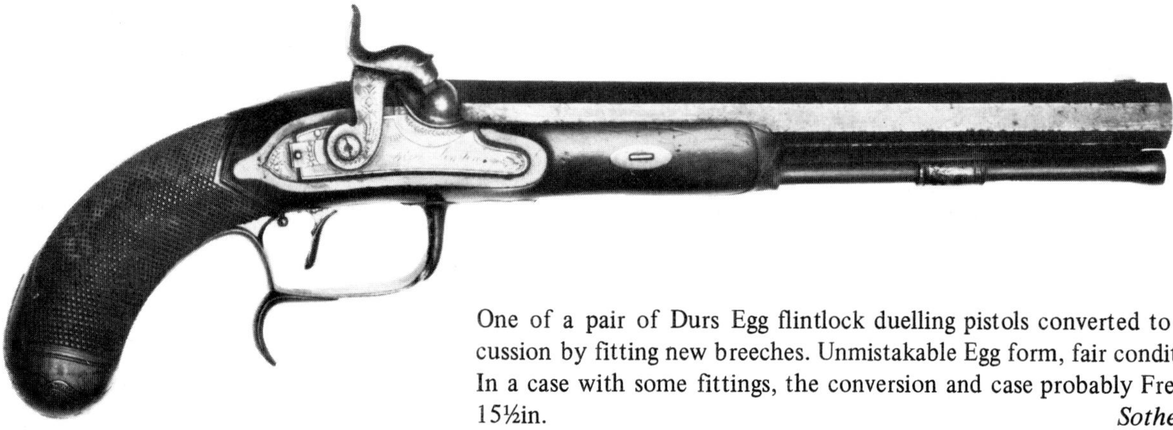

One of a pair of Durs Egg flintlock duelling pistols converted to percussion by fitting new breeches. Unmistakable Egg form, fair condition. In a case with some fittings, the conversion and case probably French. 15½in. *Sotheby's*

£400 – £500 the pair

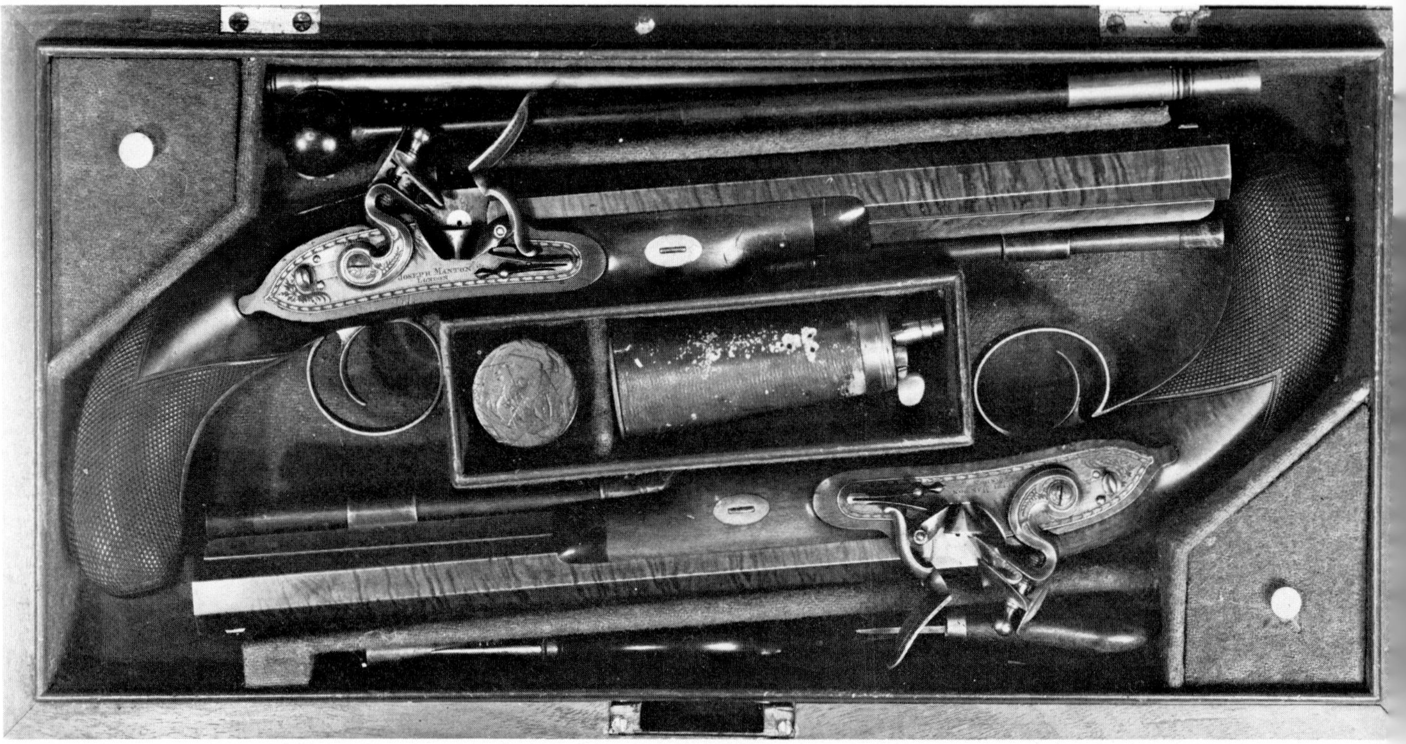

Cased pair of flintlock duelling pistols with octagonal twist barrels, patent recessed breech, platinum line, vent and maker's stamp, engraved locks with rainproof pans. Walnut half-stocks with engraved blued steel furniture and silver escutcheons. Very fine quality and almost new condition. In original case with accessories and label. By Joseph Manton, Davies Street, Berkeley Square, No. 6585, circa 1815. 15in. *Christie's*

Over £2,000

The price depends entirely on condition and originality. A similar pair in less good or refinished condition may be worth about half as much.

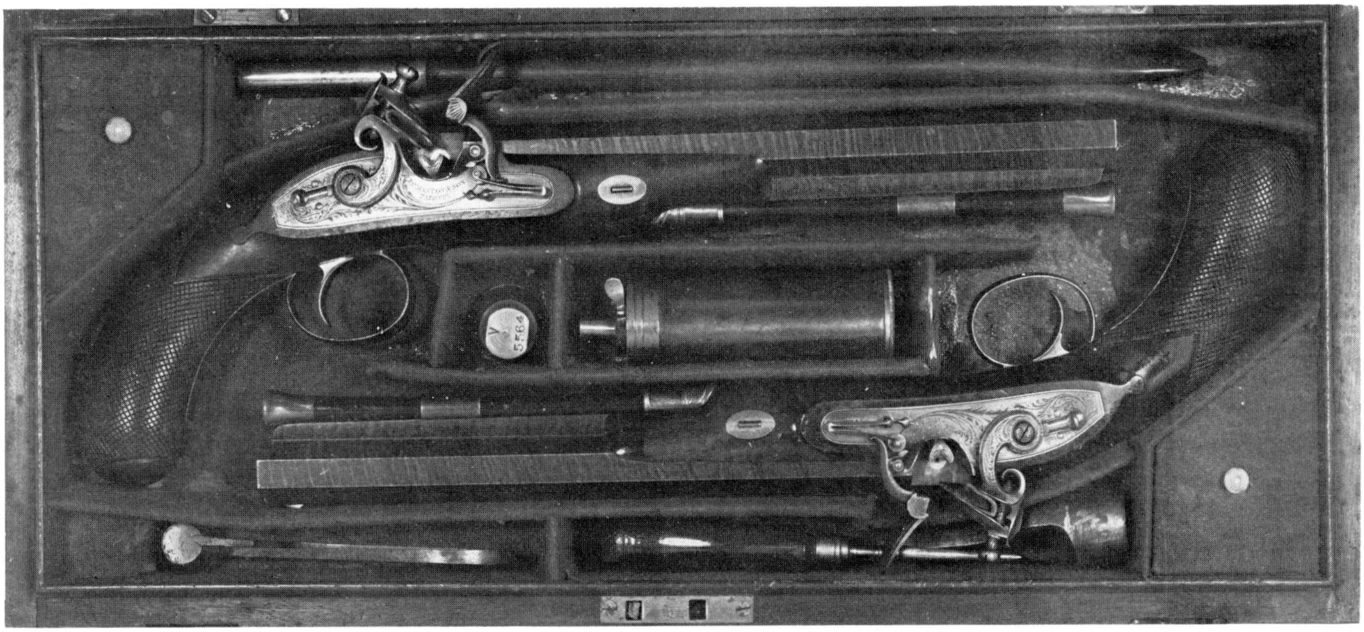

Cased pair of flintlock duelling pistols by John Manton, very similar to the work of Joseph Manton, but with square-backed lock-plates, French style cocks and patent V-shaped pans. Very fine quality and fine condition, apart from the lining of the case. By John Manton & Son, Dover Street, No.9733, circa 1828. 15in. *Christie's*

£1,500 – £2,000

Condition not quite so good as in the preceding pair.

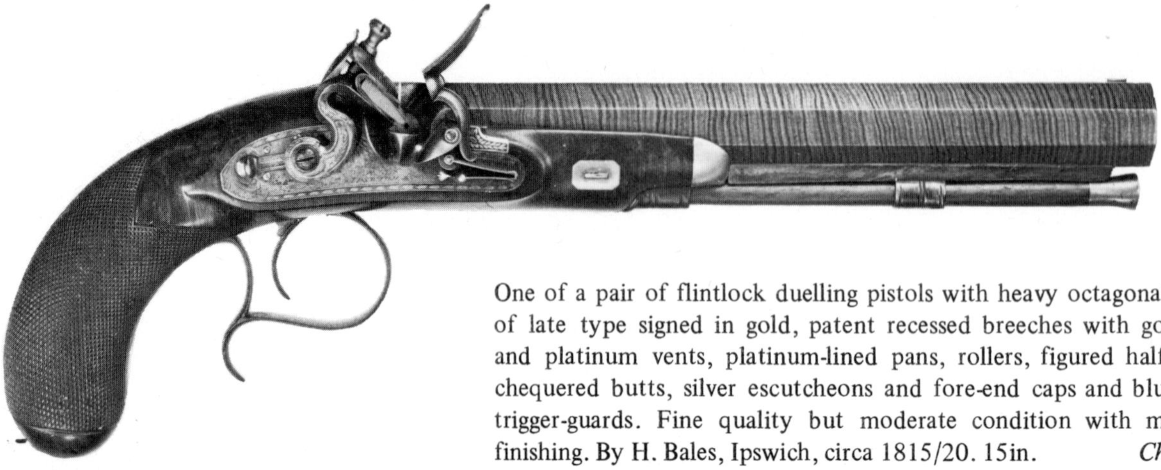

One of a pair of flintlock duelling pistols with heavy octagonal barrels of late type signed in gold, patent recessed breeches with gold lines and platinum vents, platinum-lined pans, rollers, figured half-stocks, chequered butts, silver escutcheons and fore-end caps and blued spur trigger-guards. Fine quality but moderate condition with much re-finishing. By H. Bales, Ipswich, circa 1815/20. 15in. *Christie's*

£600 – £800 the pair

One of a pair of officer's flintlock pistols with heavy octagonal barrels, platinum lines and vents, engraved locks with rollers and safety-catches, full stocks, chequered butts, engraved blued steel furniture, stirrup ramrods and bone fore-end tips. Medium quality, but excellent condition. In original velvet-lined case. Signed Hawkes Mosely & Co., London, circa 1830. 13½in. *Christie's*

£600 – £750

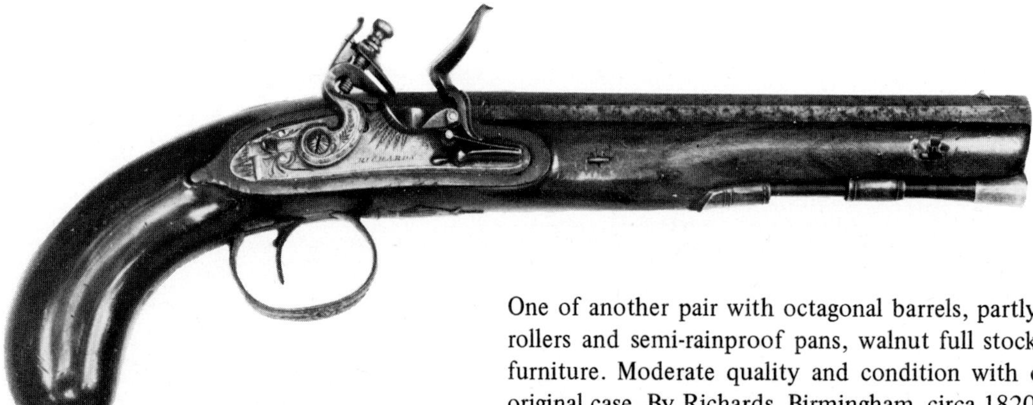

One of another pair with octagonal barrels, partly engraved locks with rollers and semi-rainproof pans, walnut full stocks with engraved steel furniture. Moderate quality and condition with one cock replaced. In original case. By Richards, Birmingham, circa 1820. 14½in. *Sotheby's*

£500 – £750

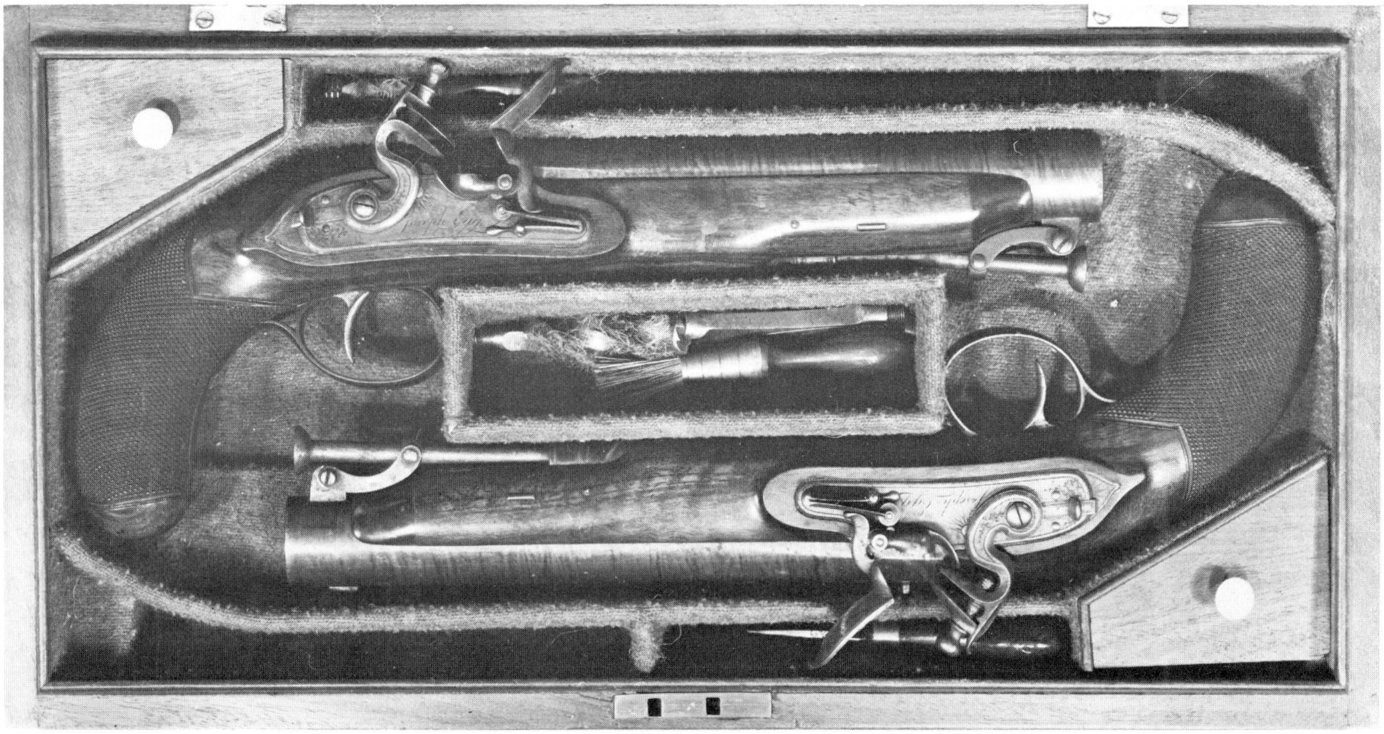

Cased pair of officer's flintlock pistols with heavy barrels made to accommodate a musket ball, gold line and platinum vent, the locks with semi-rainproof pans and rollers. Full stocks and engraved blued steel furniture, silver escutcheons and stirrup ramrods. Fine quality and condition. Original case complete with label, the flask missing. By Joseph Egg, No.1, Piccadilly, London, early 19th century. 13¼in. *Christie's*

About £1,500

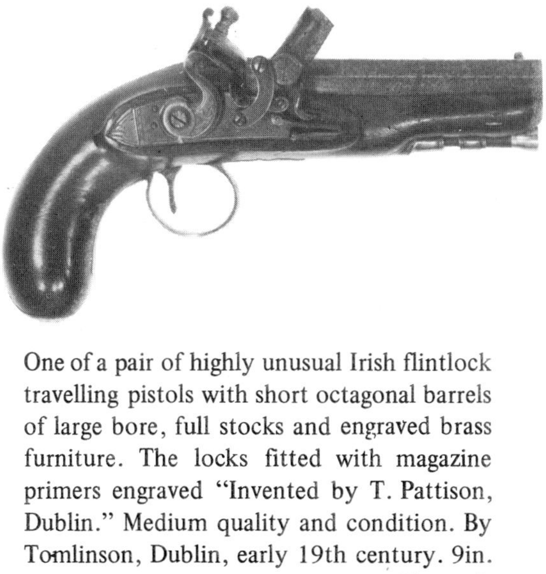

One of a pair of highly unusual Irish flintlock travelling pistols with short octagonal barrels of large bore, full stocks and engraved brass furniture. The locks fitted with magazine primers engraved "Invented by T. Pattison, Dublin." Medium quality and condition. By Tomlinson, Dublin, early 19th century. 9in. *Christie's*

£800 – £900 the pair

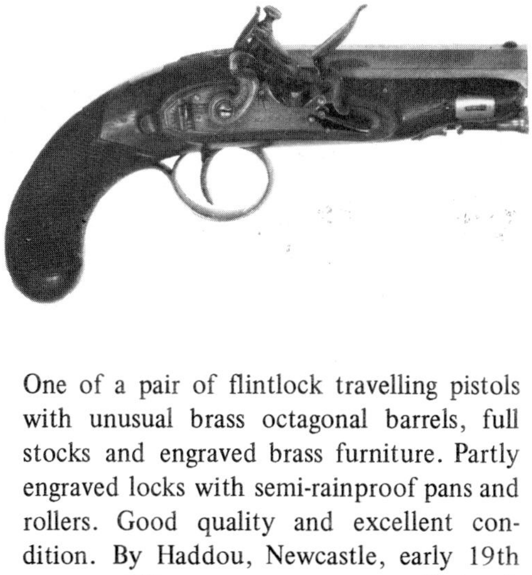

One of a pair of flintlock travelling pistols with unusual brass octagonal barrels, full stocks and engraved brass furniture. Partly engraved locks with semi-rainproof pans and rollers. Good quality and excellent condition. By Haddou, Newcastle, early 19th century. 8¼in. *Christie's*

£500 – £600 the pair

Cased pair of flintlock travelling pistols with octagonal barrels, platinum lines and vent, engraved locks and engraved steel furniture full stocks and chequered butts. Original oak case with fittings and label. Fine quality and condition. By Staudenmayer, London, earl 19th century. 11½in. *Christie*

£500 – £600

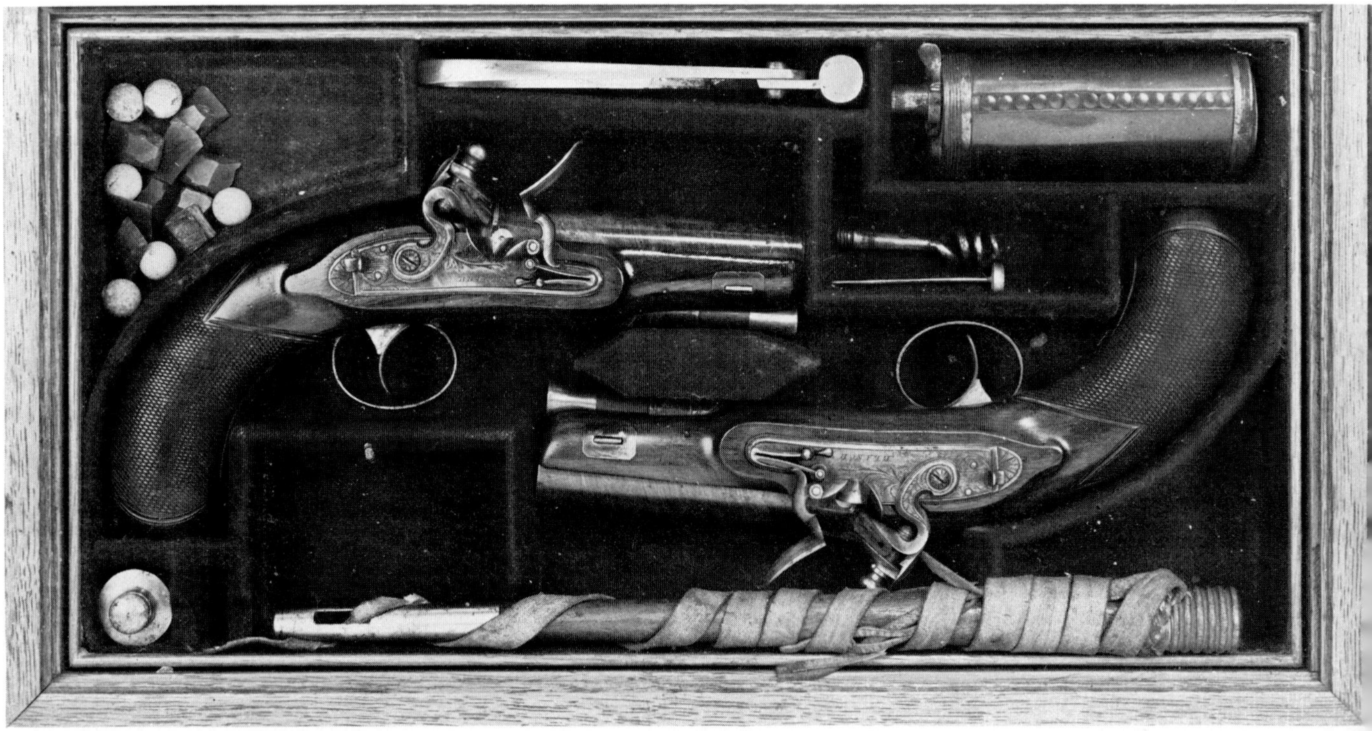

Cased pair of small full-stocked flintlock pistols with browned barrels, engraved locks, rollers and engraved steel furniture. Fine quali and very fine condition. In original case with accessories. Signed Blanch, London, early 19th century. 4in. barrels. *Knight, Frank & Rut*

£500 – £650

Plain flintlock box-lock pistol with turn-off barrel, signed action and flat-sided walnut butt. No roller, no safety-catch. Moderate quality and condition. By Heaton & Smith, London, early 19th century. 6¾in.

£75 – £100

One of a pair of flintlock box-lock pocket pistols with iron turn-off barrels and engraved brass actions, rollers, chequered butts, brass escutcheons and lion's mask butt-caps, folding triggers and safety-catches. Good quality, moderate condition. Signed H. Nock, London, early 19th century. 6½in. *Christie's*

About £200 the pair

One of a pair of flintlock box-lock pocket pistols with turn-off barrels, engraved rounded actions, rollers, chequered butts, silver escutcheons, folding triggers and thumbpiece safety-catches. Good quality, fair condition. Signed Smith, London, early 19th century. 6 in. *Christie's*

£175 – £200 the pair

One of a pair of flintlock pocket pistols, the engraved brass actions with rainproof pans, rollers, safety catches and folding triggers, the butts decorated with scrolls, flowers and foliage in silver and with silver lion's mask butt-caps. Fine quality and condition. Signed Smith, London, Birmingham proof marks, early 19th century. 6in. *Christie's*

£400 – £500 the pair

Cased pair of flintlock pistols with blued actions well engraved with trophies of arms, turn-off barrels, folding triggers, rollers, thumbpiece safety-catches, chequered butts and silver escutcheons. Fine quality, fine condition. In velvet-lined case, probably original, with mould, barrel key and turnscrew (no flask). By Staudenmayer, London, early 19th century. 6in. *Christie's*

£500 – £750

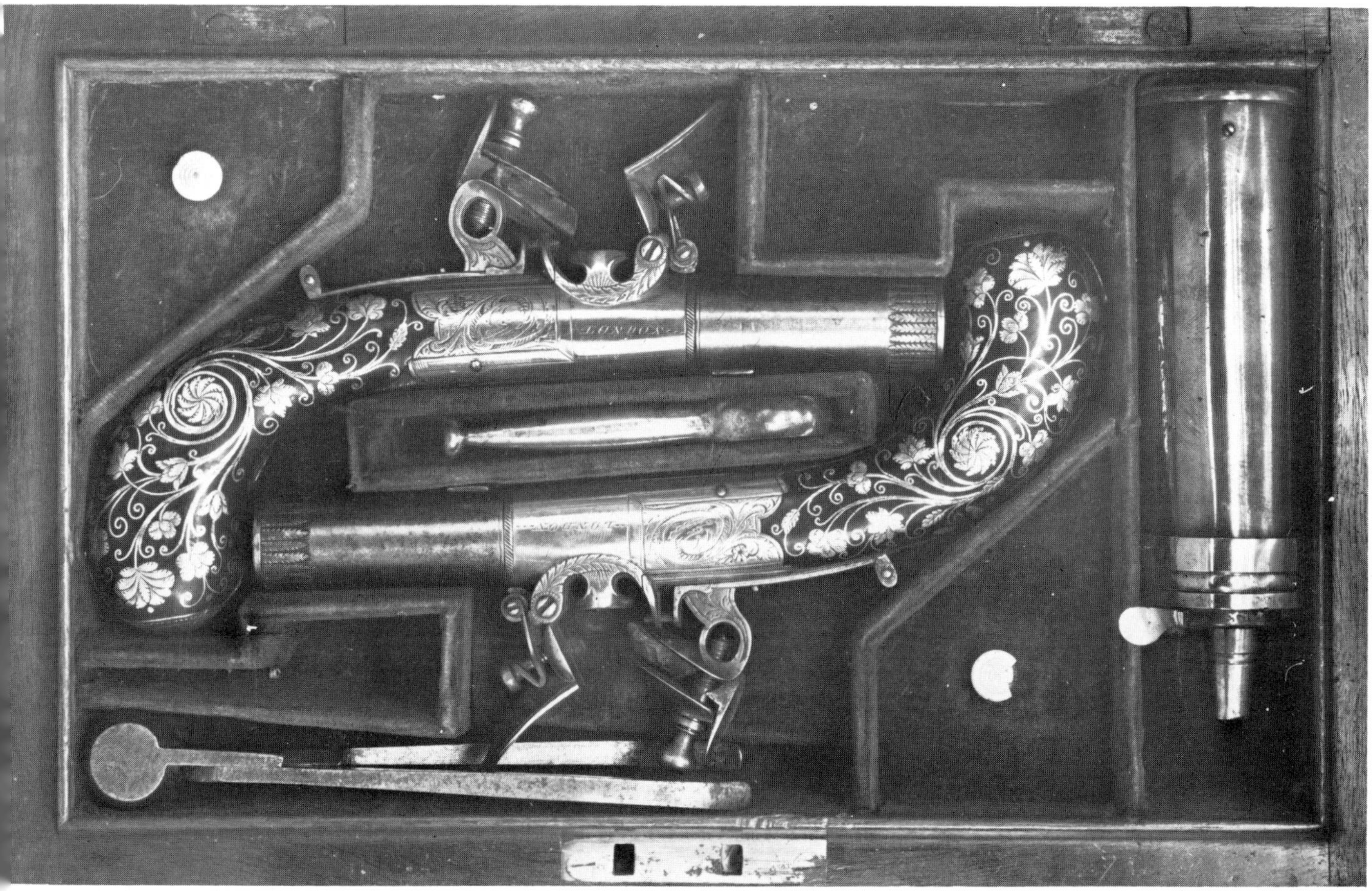

Cased pair of flintlock pocket pistols with steel barrels and engraved gun-metal actions with rainproof pans, rollers, folding triggers and thumbpiece safety-catches. The butts with particularly fine silver wire inlay and silver caps. Original-velvet-lined mahogany case with label decorated with hunting and archery scenes, complete with mould and flask. Very fine quality, excellent condition. By E. & W. Bond, Cornhill, London, early 19th century. 6½in.

Sotheby's

Over £1,000

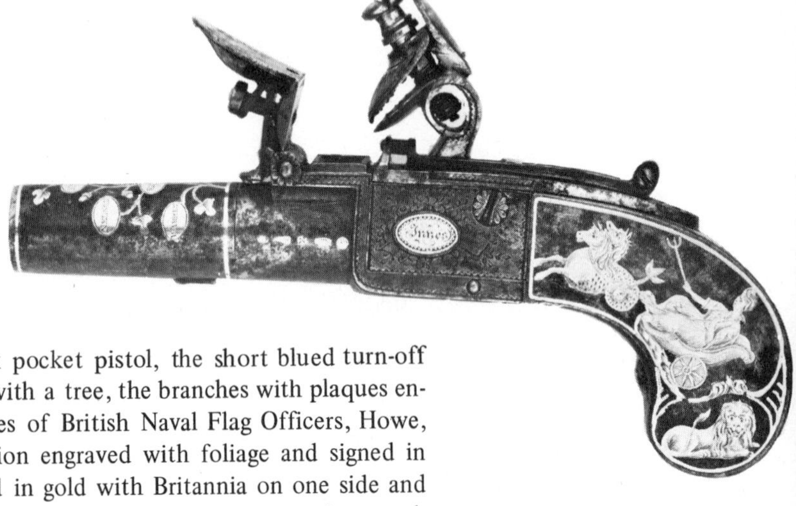

Presentation flintlock pocket pistol, the short blued turn-off barrel inlaid in gold with a tree, the branches with plaques engraved with the names of British Naval Flag Officers, Howe, Nelson, etc., the action engraved with foliage and signed in gold. Iron butt inlaid in gold with Britannia on one side and Galatea on the other, folding trigger, thumbpiece safety-catch and roller. Exceptional quality, fine condition. By Innes, Maker to His Majesty, Edinburgh, circa 1800. 4 $\frac{1}{8}$in. *Sotheby's*

Over £1,500

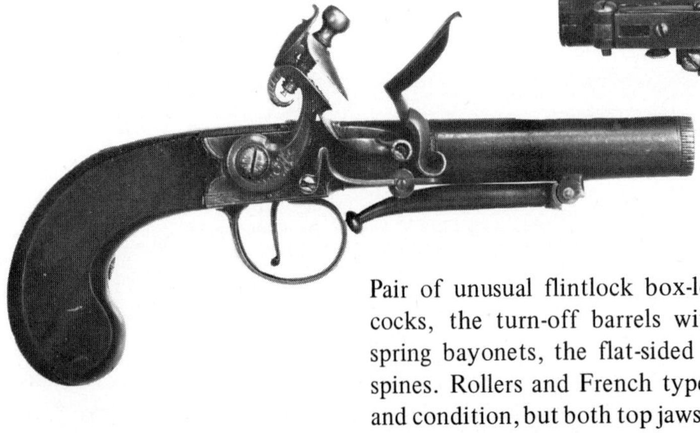

Pair of unusual flintlock box-lock pistols with side-cocks, the turn-off barrels with folding levers and spring bayonets, the flat-sided butts with chequered spines. Rollers and French type cocks. Good quality and condition, but both top jaws replaced. By Hewson, London, circa 1820. *Christie's*

£400 – £500 the pair.

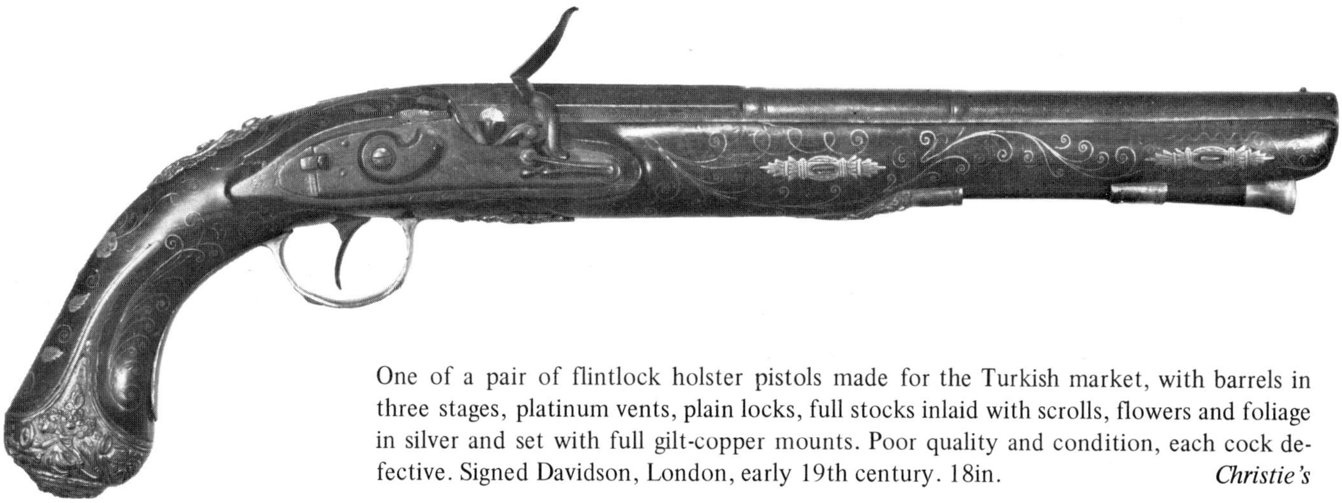

One of a pair of flintlock holster pistols made for the Turkish market, with barrels in three stages, platinum vents, plain locks, full stocks inlaid with scrolls, flowers and foliage in silver and set with full gilt-copper mounts. Poor quality and condition, each cock defective. Signed Davidson, London, early 19th century. 18in. *Christie's*

About £600 the pair

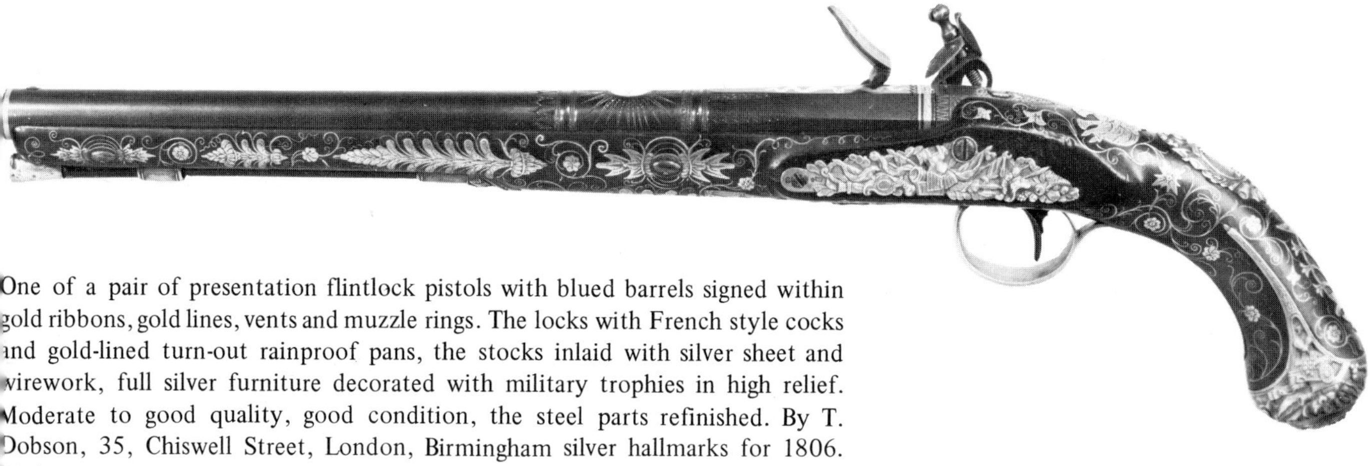

One of a pair of presentation flintlock pistols with blued barrels signed within gold ribbons, gold lines, vents and muzzle rings. The locks with French style cocks and gold-lined turn-out rainproof pans, the stocks inlaid with silver sheet and wirework, full silver furniture decorated with military trophies in high relief. Moderate to good quality, good condition, the steel parts refinished. By T. Dobson, 35, Chiswell Street, London, Birmingham silver hallmarks for 1806. 20½in. *Christie's*

Over £1,500 the pair

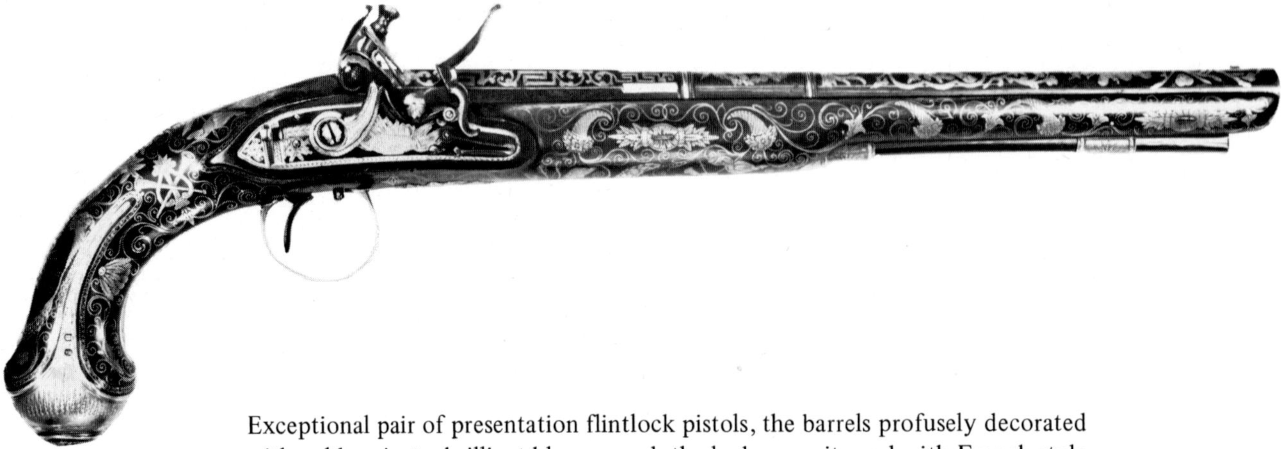

Exceptional pair of presentation flintlock pistols, the barrels profusely decorated with gold against a brilliant blue ground, the locks en suite and with French style cocks, rainproof pans and rollers. Full stocks with exceptional silver inlay incorporating cornucopiae, classical vases and Turkish trophies. Full silver furniture, spurred pommels and set triggers. Excellent quality and condition. By Bennett and Lacy, 67, Royal Exchange, London, Makers to H.R.H. Prince Regent, Birmingham silver hallmark for 1811. 20in. *Sotheby's*

Over £4,000 the pair

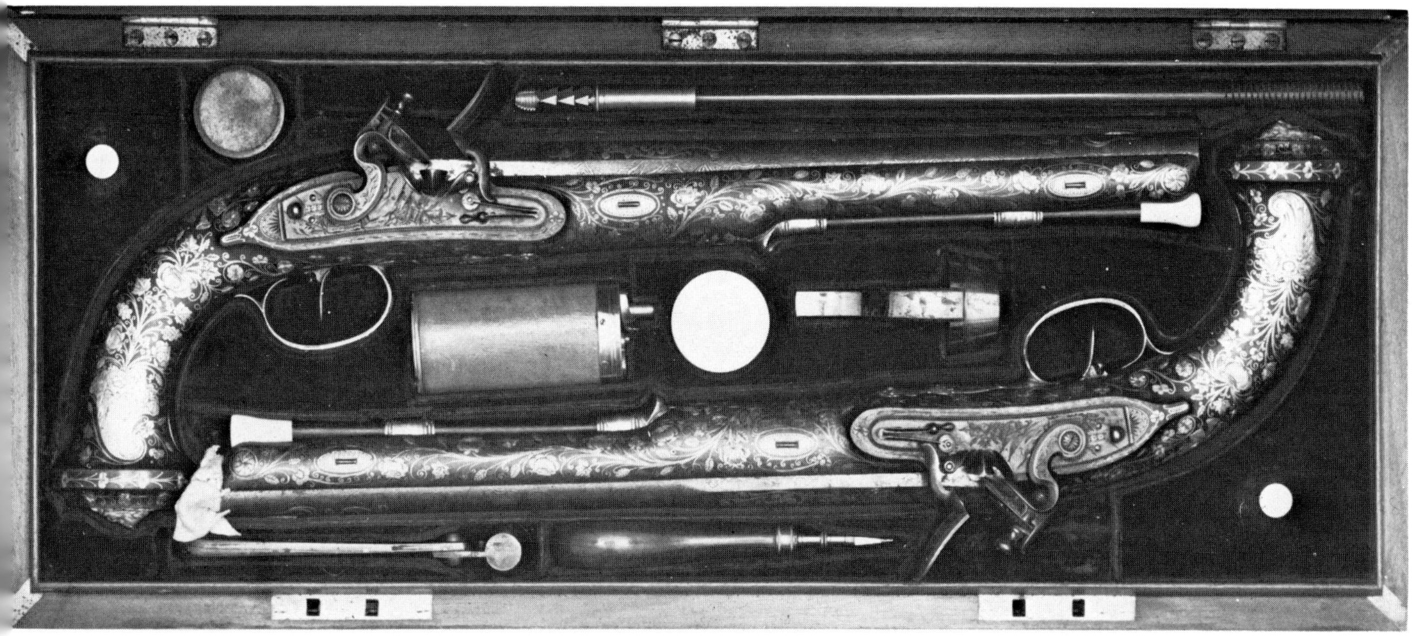

Exceptional cased pair of presentation flintlock pistols with Turkish barrels decorated with silver and gold, gold vents and gold-lined pans. The locks engraved with trophies of arms, the full stocks entirely inlaid with trophies of arms, foliage and flowers in silver, full gilt-brass mounts embossed with further trophies, the butt-caps formed as lion's masks. Fine quality, particularly the inlay on the stocks, the pistols, case and accessories in virtually new condition. Circa 1830. 18in. *Sotheby's*

Over £6,000, mainly on condition

Continental Flintlock Pistols 1800 - 1830

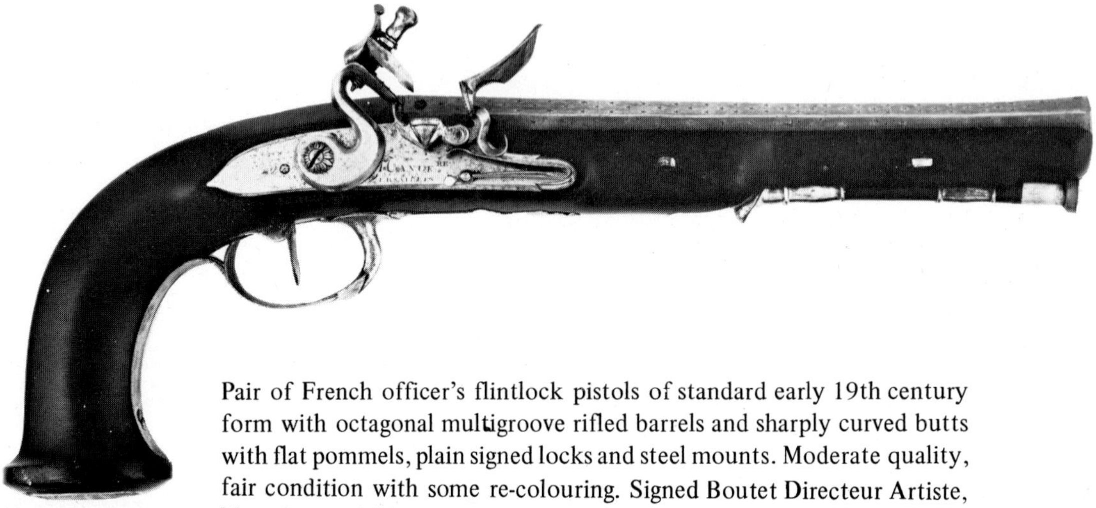

Pair of French officer's flintlock pistols of standard early 19th century form with octagonal multigroove rifled barrels and sharply curved butts with flat pommels, plain signed locks and steel mounts. Moderate quality, fair condition with some re-colouring. Signed Boutet Directeur Artiste, Manufacture à Versailles. Circa 1800-10. 13½in. *Sotheby's*

About £750, mainly for the name.

Plain pistols of similar design were made in large numbers. With lesser signatures they are worth £250 – £500 a pair.

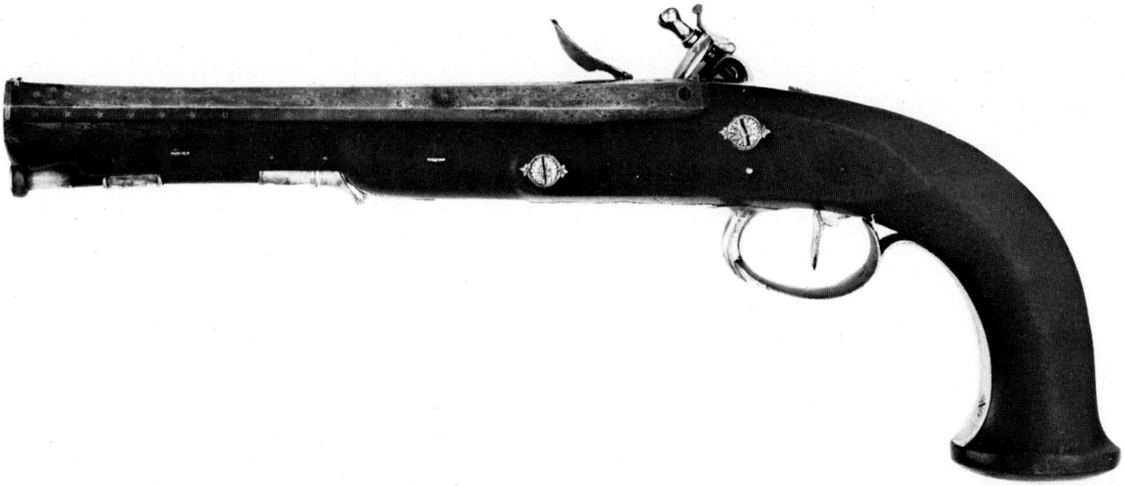

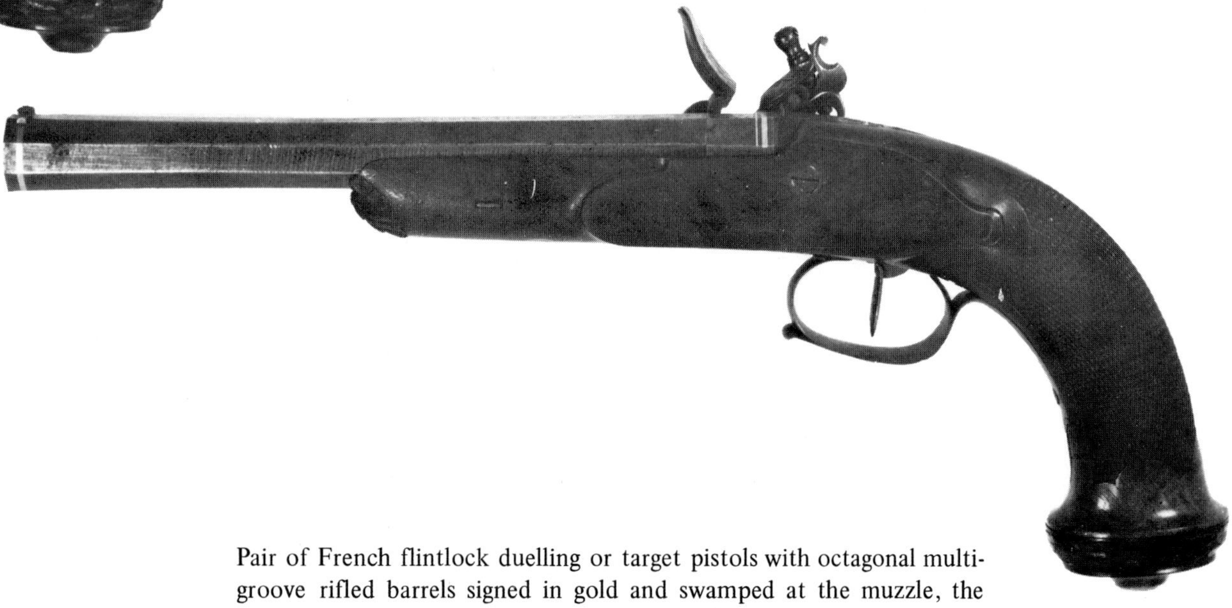

Pair of French flintlock duelling or target pistols with octagonal multi-groove rifled barrels signed in gold and swamped at the muzzle, the locks with rainproof pans and rollers, the half-stocks carved with a shell at the fore-end and with carved ebony pommels. Case-hardened engraved steel furniture and set triggers. Poor quality for this maker, but fine condition. By Le Page, Arqu. er du Roi, each dated 1827 on the breech. 15in. *Christie's*

Over £1,000

Le Page and Boutet both worked for Napoleon, and are the most important French makers of the early 19th century. Boutet has the greater reputation today and is therefore the more expensive to buy.

Very fine pistol with blued and gilt barrel decorated with stars, pennants and a trophy of arms, the breech with gold poinçons, the lock engraved with winged monsters. Walnut stock with silver-gilt mounts decorated with trophies in relief, the butt studded with silver nails. Superb quality and condition. The barrel by Boutet and the lock by Le Page, silver hallmarks as used between 1807 and 1819 with what is probably Boutet's own silver mark, circa 1815. 15¼in. *Christie's*

£2,000 – £3,000

Liège copy of this type of pistol, the barrel with a little gold decoration, the stock with silver mounts. Fair quality and condition. By A. Rongé, Belgian silver mark in use from 1814 to 1831, circa 1820. 13½in. *Sotheby's*

£300 – £400

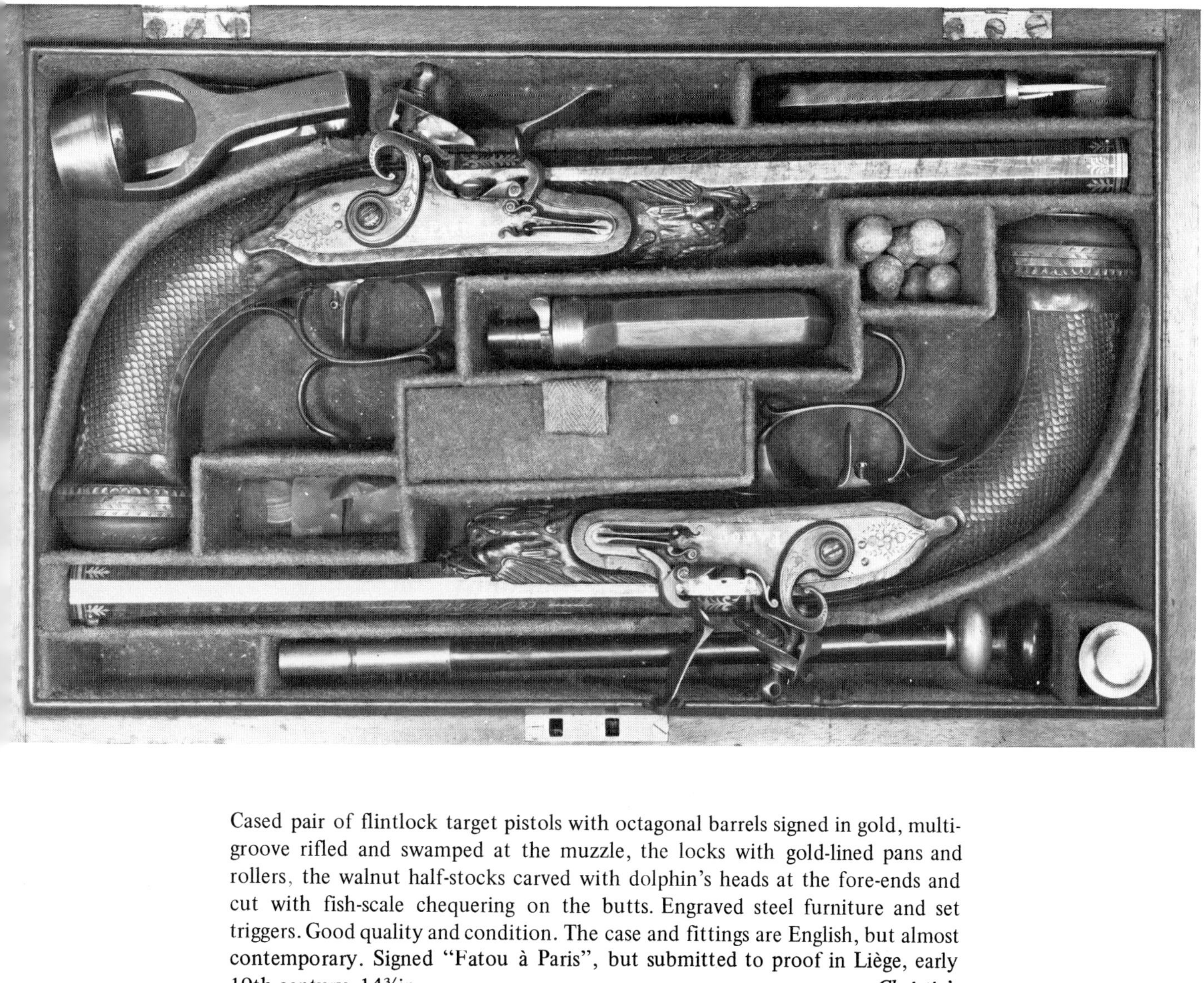

Cased pair of flintlock target pistols with octagonal barrels signed in gold, multi-groove rifled and swamped at the muzzle, the locks with gold-lined pans and rollers, the walnut half-stocks carved with dolphin's heads at the fore-ends and cut with fish-scale chequering on the butts. Engraved steel furniture and set triggers. Good quality and condition. The case and fittings are English, but almost contemporary. Signed "Fatou à Paris", but submitted to proof in Liège, early 19th century. 14¾in. *Christie's*

About £1,500

Always take the barrels off pistols like these and look for Liège proof marks. Many Paris makers used Liège components, even the esteemed Boutet. Belgian origin lowers the value unless the quality is impeccable.

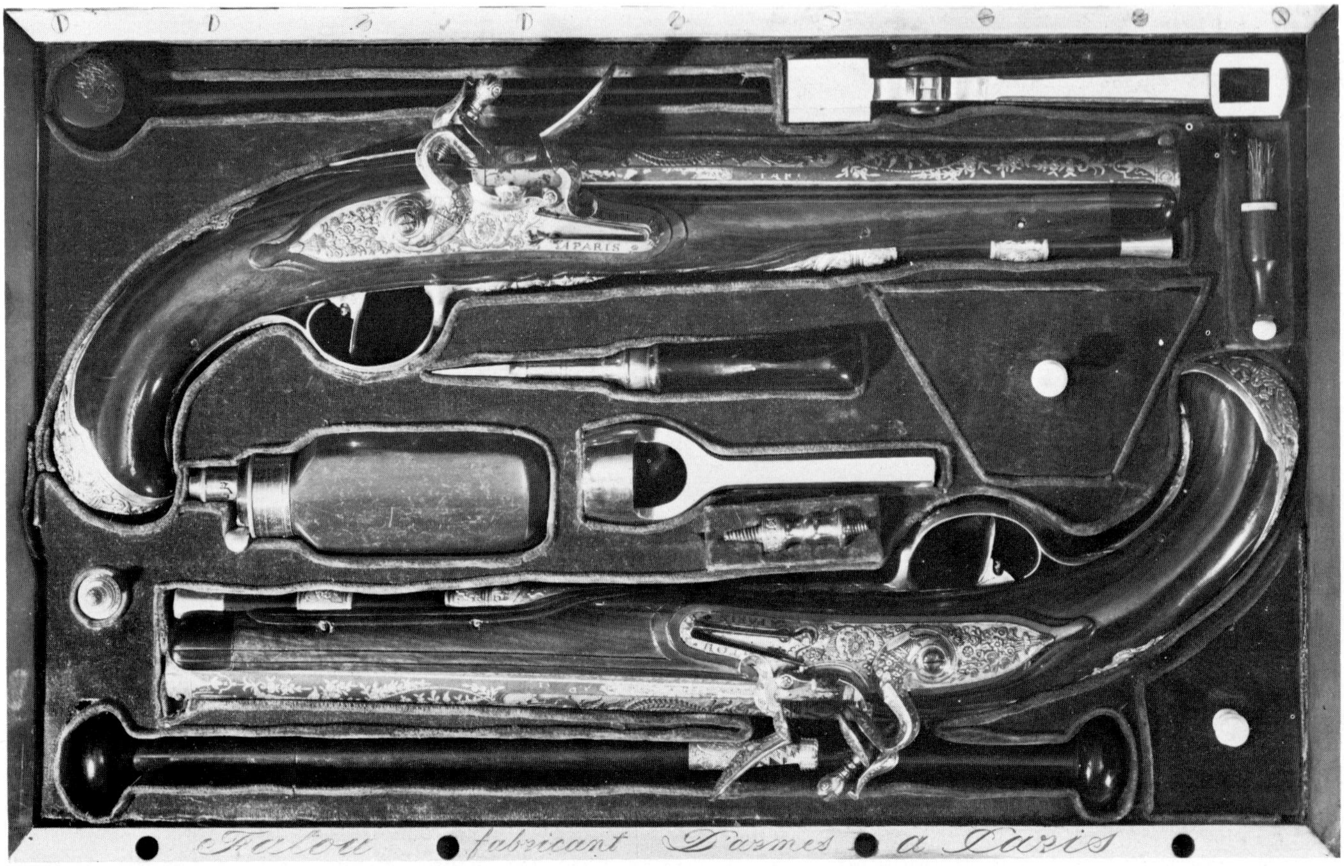

Elaborate cased pair of presentation flintlock pistols with chiselled and gilt barrels, locks, cocks and steels, set triggers and gold-lined pans, the full stocks with silver mounts decorated rococo scrolls enclosing huntsmen and hounds against a gilt fish-roe ground. In finely veneered case lined in mauve velvet with accessories and signed in full on the lock, the lid finely mounted with ormolu and set with a large coat-of-arms. Fair quality, good condition. By Fatou, Paris, dated 1818. 15in. *Christie's*

Over £3,000

The case finer than the pistols.

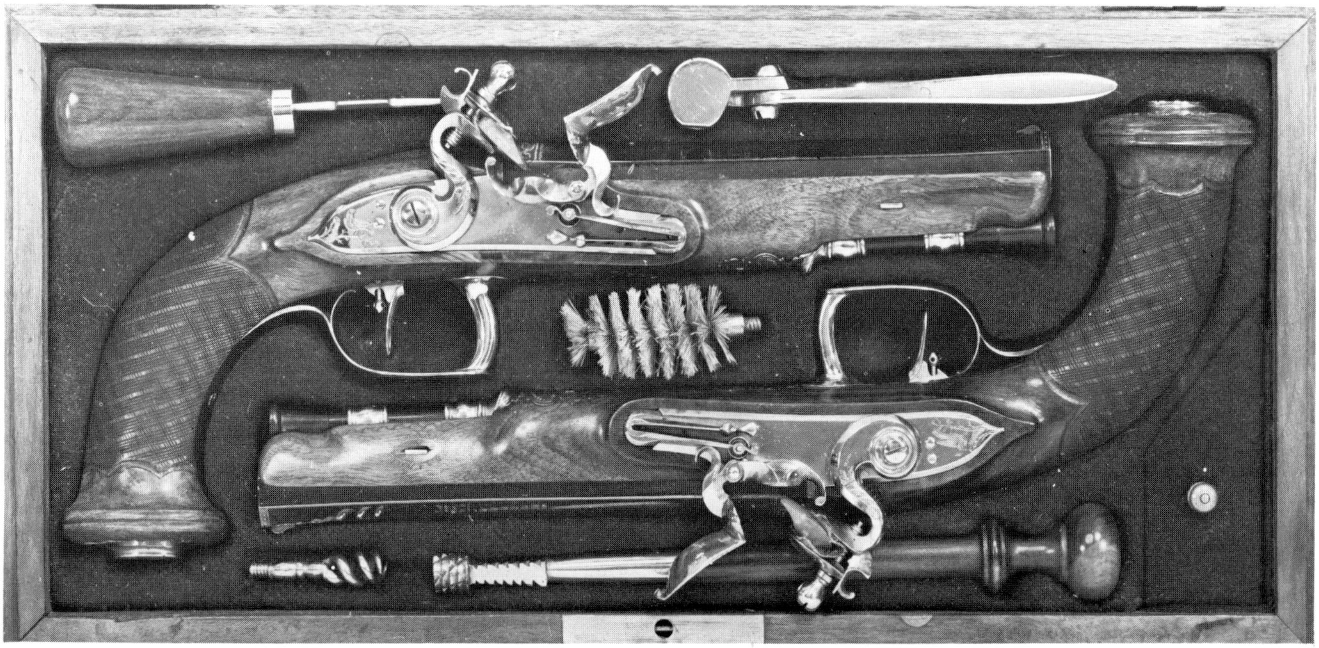

Another example of Liège export work – a cased pair of flintlock rifled target pistols, similar to the type produced in Italy. Blued octagonal barrels inlaid with gold, full stocks, engraved steel furniture bordered with silver wire, the butts studded with small silver nails. Complete with accessories. Fair quality, but excellent condition. Signed P. Rouma, Liège proof marks, early 19th century, 11¾in. *Christie's*

About £1,500 mainly on condition

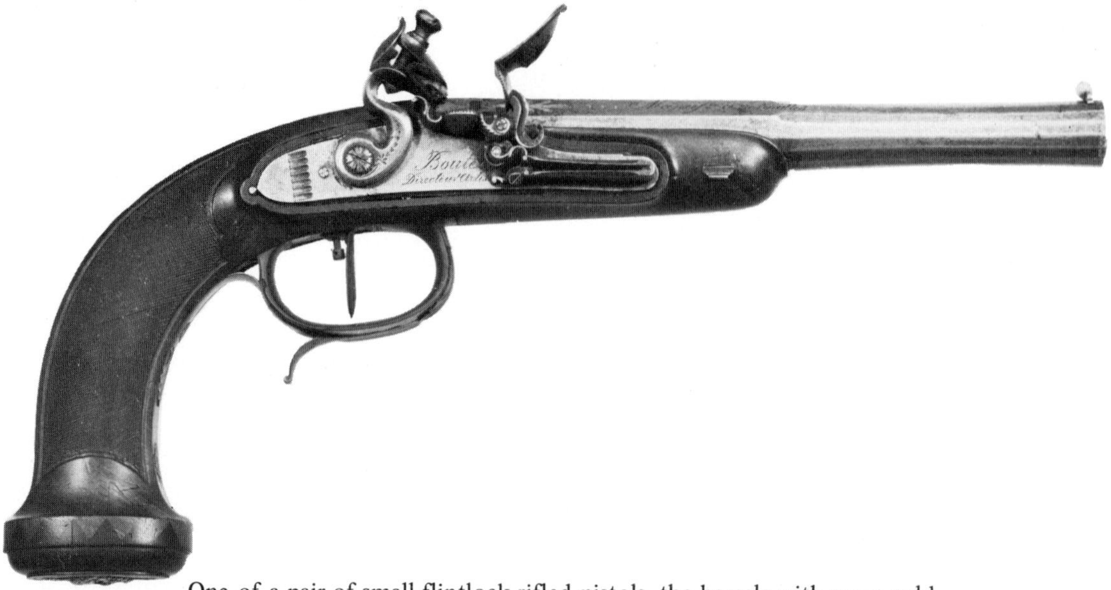

One of a pair of small flintlock rifled pistols, the barrels with some gold inlay, the stocks with chequered flat-sided butts, finely chiselled steel mounts, bone trigger-guards reinforced with steel, ebony pommels with silver caps decorated with the head of Hercules. Fine quality but only fair condition with both cocks replaced. By Boutet, early 19th century. 12½in. *Christie's*

Over £1,000 the pair

One of a pair of Swiss rifled flintlock duelling or target pistols with blued octagonal barrels, gold line, vents and pans, carved full stocks and blued steel furniture and silver foliage pommels. Good quality and condition with most of the original finish. By F. Ulrich, Bern., early 19th century. 13in. *Christie's*

£600 – £800 the pair

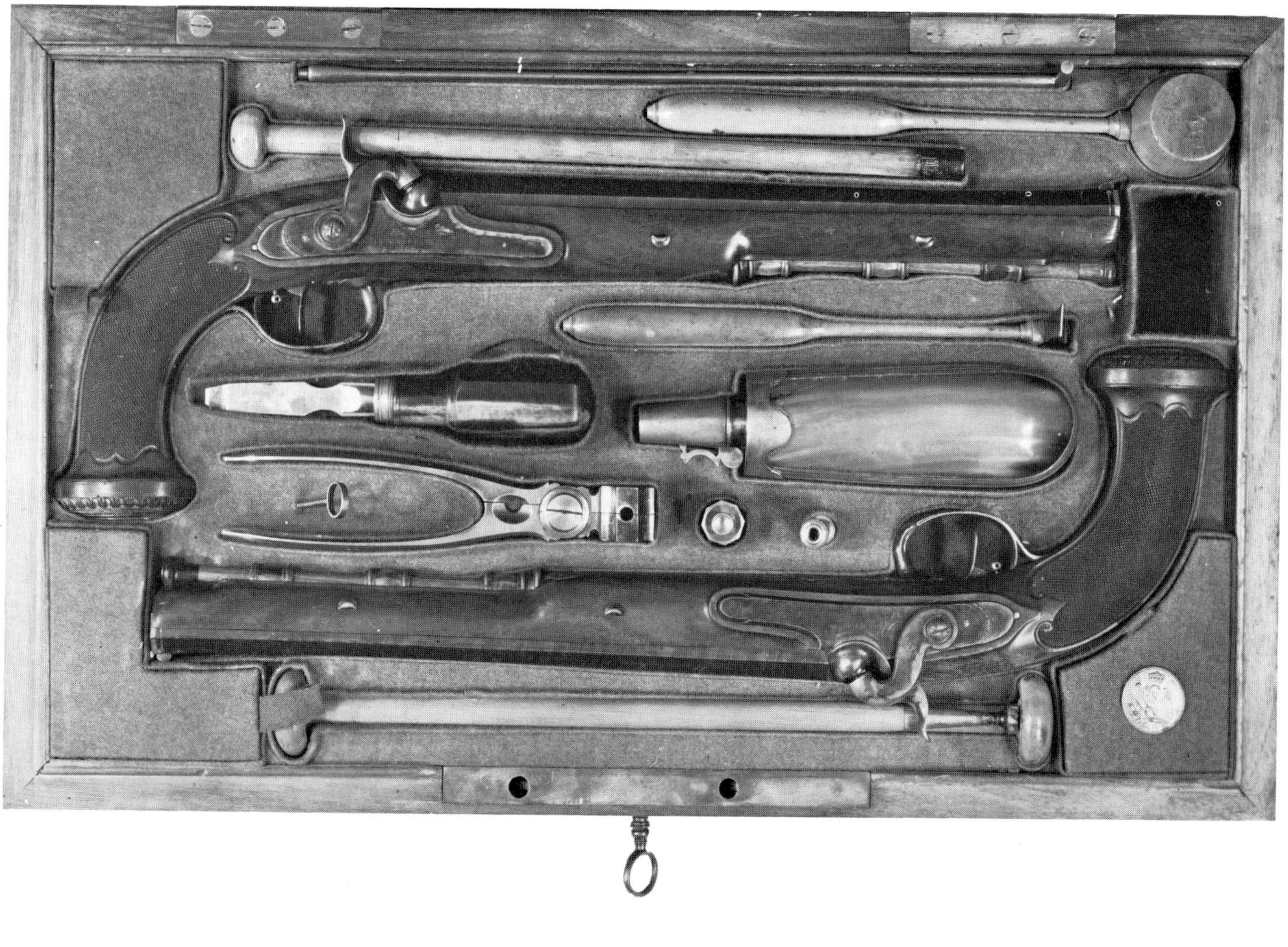

Cased pair of percussion target pistols, converted from flintlock, with plain browned barrels and partly engraved iron mounts, the stocks with chequered butts and carved pommels. Complete with accessories. Fine quality and condition. By Boutet, Versailles, circa 1800. 16in. *Christie's*

Over £,1000

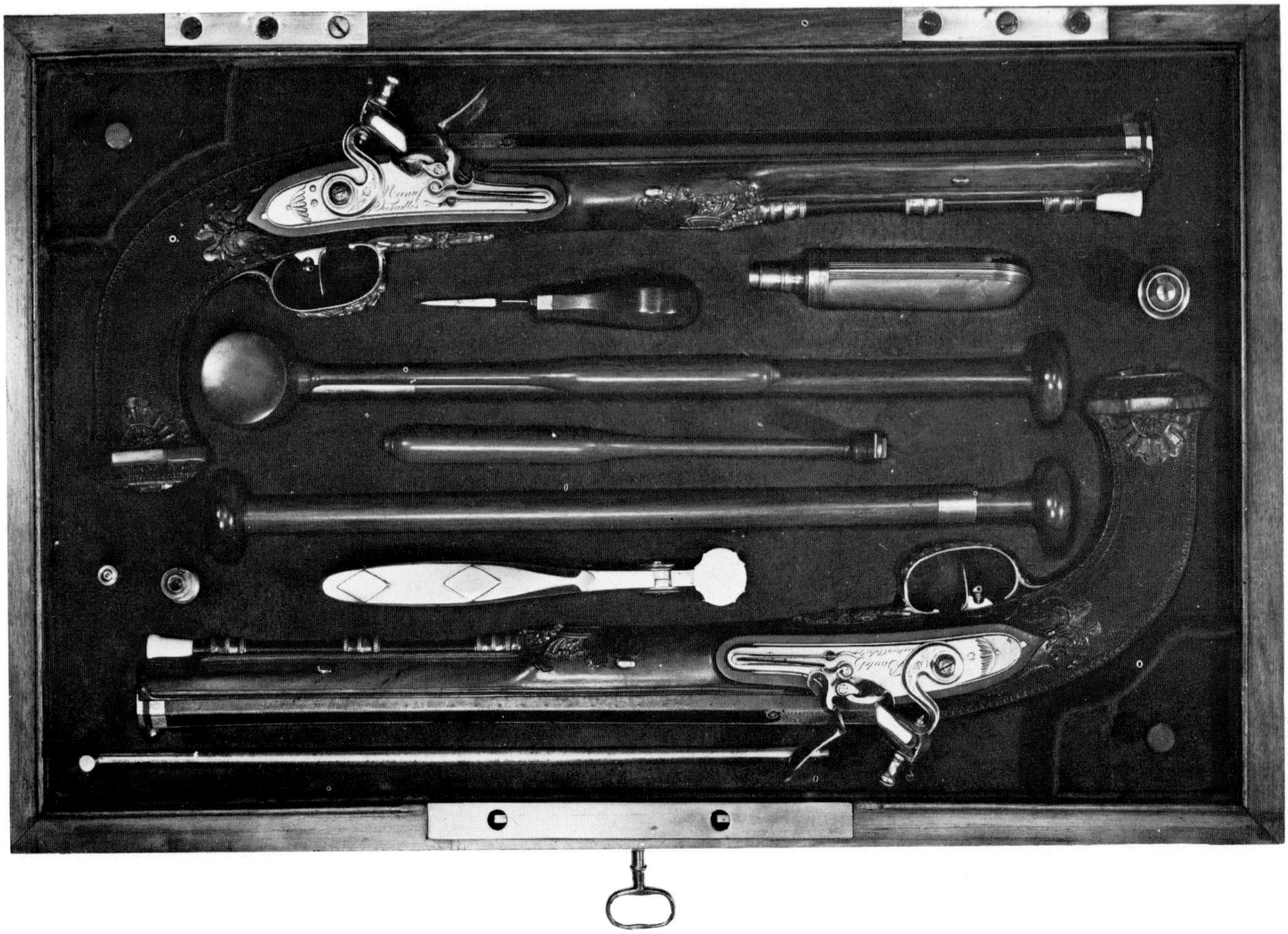

Cased pair of flintlock presentation pistols of the same form, with blued and gilt octagonal multigroove rifled barrels signed in gold and punched with stars. Figured walnut full stocks carved with foliage and ropework, cast and chased silver mounts decorated with helmets, trophies, swords and garlands of flowers. Set triggers and ivory-tipped bone ramrods. Complete with accessories including original flask. Superb quality although somewhat refinished. By Boutet, Versailles. 16½in. *Christie's*

Over £14,000

Presented by Napoleon to the Austrian General Joseph de St. Julien in July 1800.

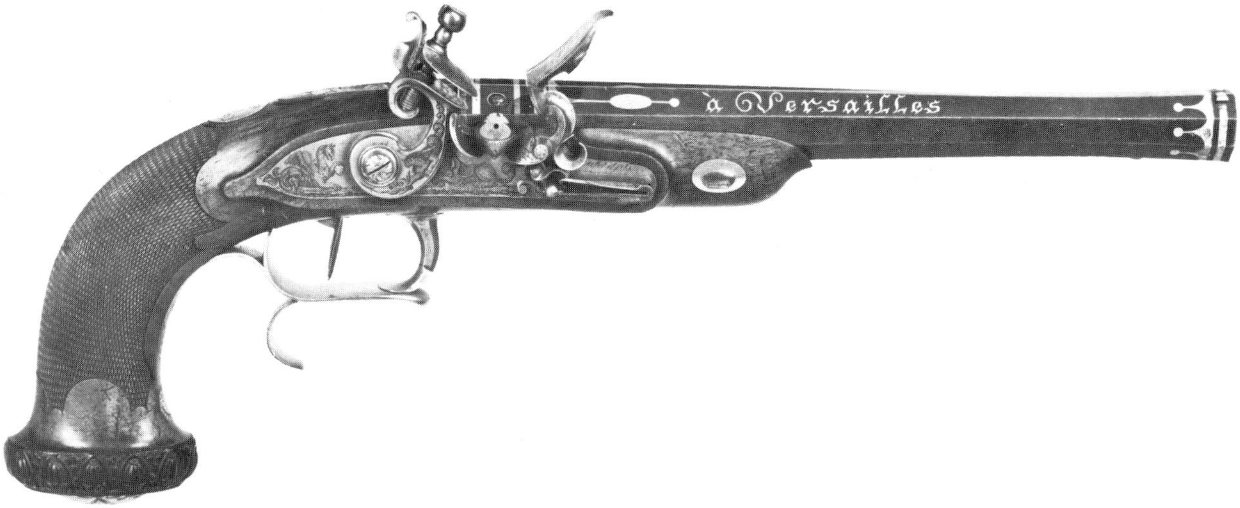

Pair of flintlock target pistols with multigroove rifled swamped browned barrels signed and inlaid in gold, gold lines and vent, the cocks engraved with mythical beasts and with gold-lined rainproof pans. Late style of half-stocks with carved ebony pommels and engraved and cut steel mounts, spur trigger-guards and set triggers. Gold escutcheons and ovals around the barrel bolts. Exceptional quality and condition. By Boutet et Fils, Versailles, circa 1815/18. 15in. *Christie's*

Over £5,000 the pair

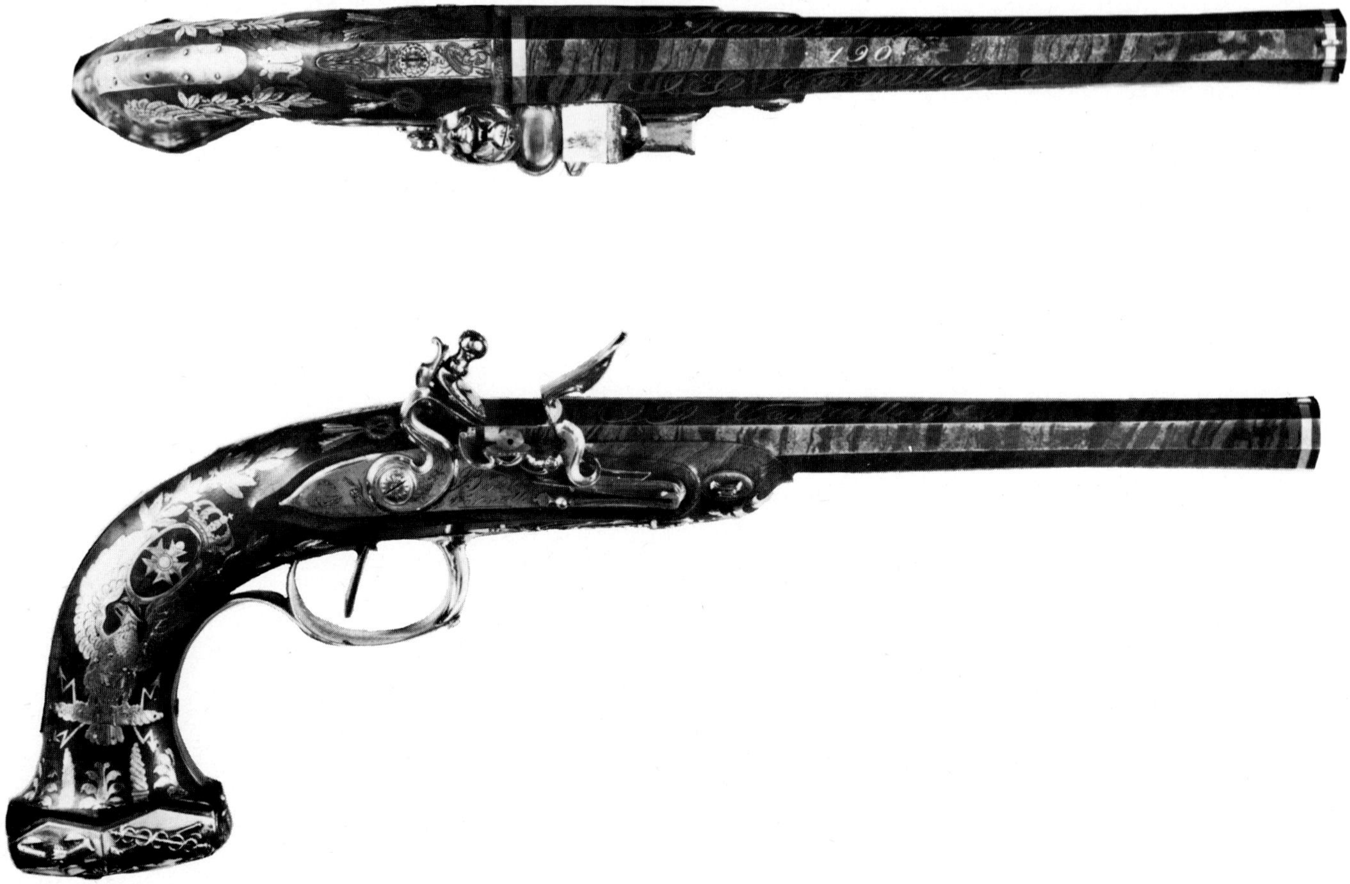

Cased pair of flintlock presentation pistols of similar form but with elaborate silver mounts decorated with emblems of sovereignty and of various virtues, the trigger-guards with the figure of Zeus. The half-stocks iniaid with Empire ornament and on each side of the butts with an eagle supporting a crowned cartouche enclosing the cross of the Légion d'Honneur. In original lined and fitted case with full accessories. Exceptional quality and condition. By Boutet, Versailles, the mounts with Paris marks used up to 1809. 15in. *Christie's*

£15,000 – £20,000

Traditionally presented by Napoleon to his brother in about 1808.

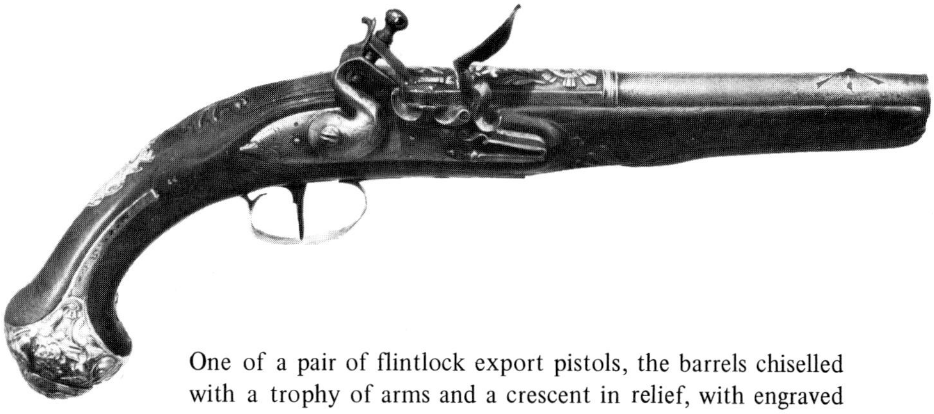

One of a pair of flintlock export pistols, the barrels chiselled with a trophy of arms and a crescent in relief, with engraved locks, full stocks and parcel-gilt silver mounts decorated with trophies, flowers and foliage. False ramrods of Turkish type. Moderate quality and condition. St. Etienne proof marks, provincial silver marks in use between 1809 and 1819. 14½in.

Christie's

£300 – £500 the pair

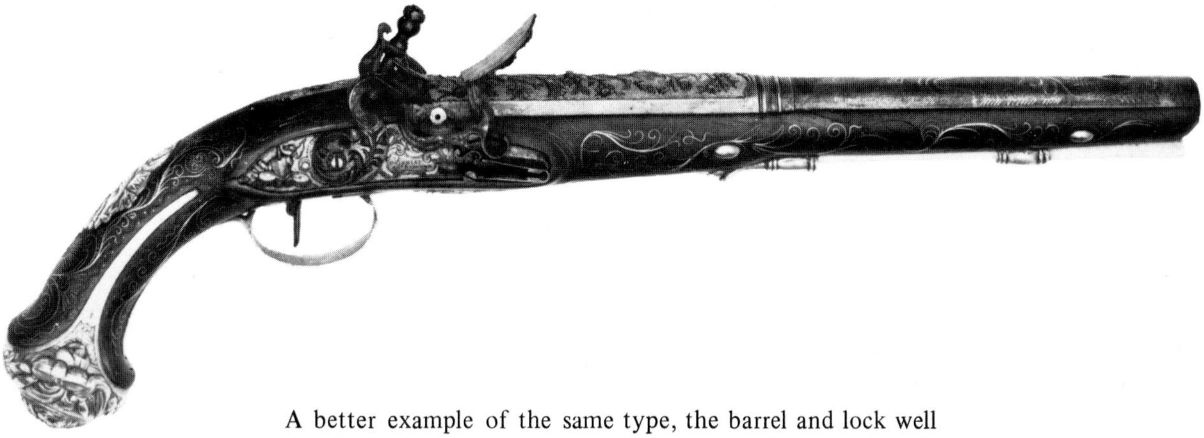

A better example of the same type, the barrel and lock well chiselled with flowers and trophies against a gilt ground, gold-lined vent and pan, walnut full stock with silver wire inlay and full silver furniture decorated with arms and scrolls in relief. Signed H. Vigniat à St. Etienne. Early 19th century. 19in.

Sotheby's

£400 – £600

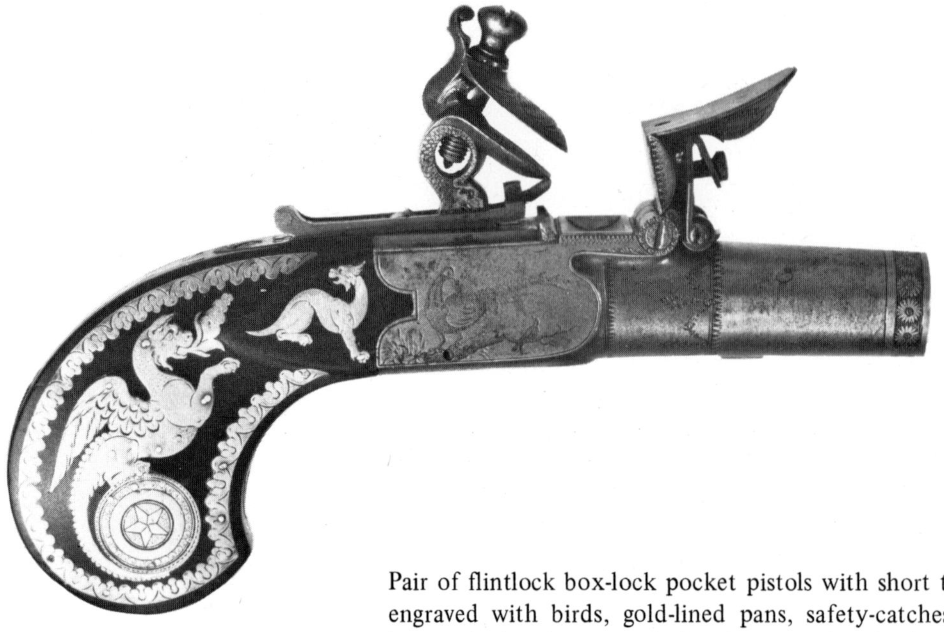

Pair of flintlock box-lock pocket pistols with short turn-off barrels, the actions engraved with birds, gold-lined pans, safety-catches and folding triggers, the butts inlaid with engraved silver beasts and with silver borders of running foliage. Very fine quality, good condition only. By Le Page, Paris, early 19th century. 5½in. *Christie's*

£1,500 – £2,000 the pair

Detonator Pistols

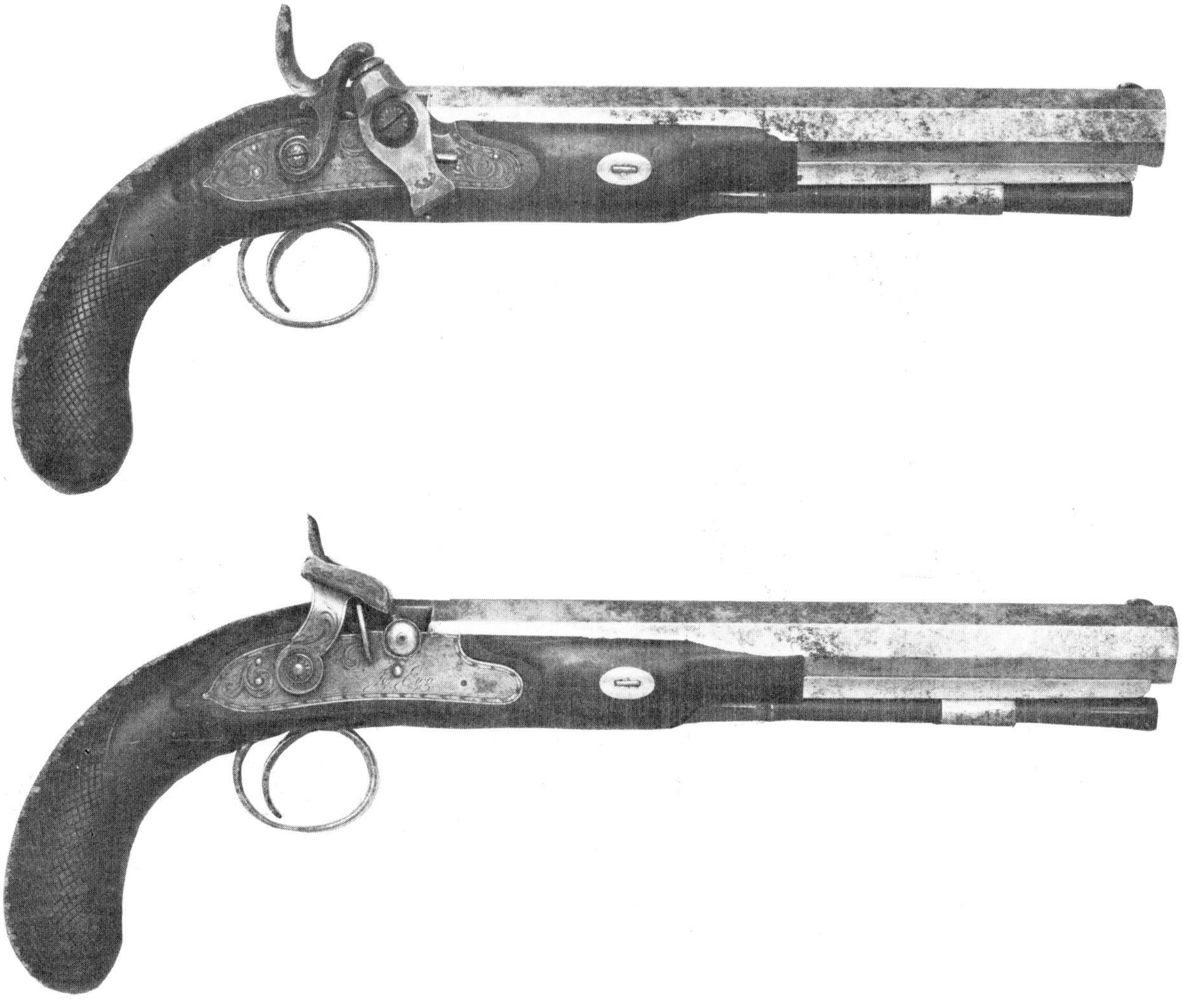

Cased pair of flintlock duelling pistols by Joseph Manton, one converted to Forsyth's detonating system (often referred to as the "scent bottle" lock) and the other converted to percussion cap by Joseph Egg. Fine quality, but poor condition. By Joseph Manton, London, No. 3227 (for 1805). 14¾in. *Knight, Frank & Rutley*

About £2,000. Rarity value.

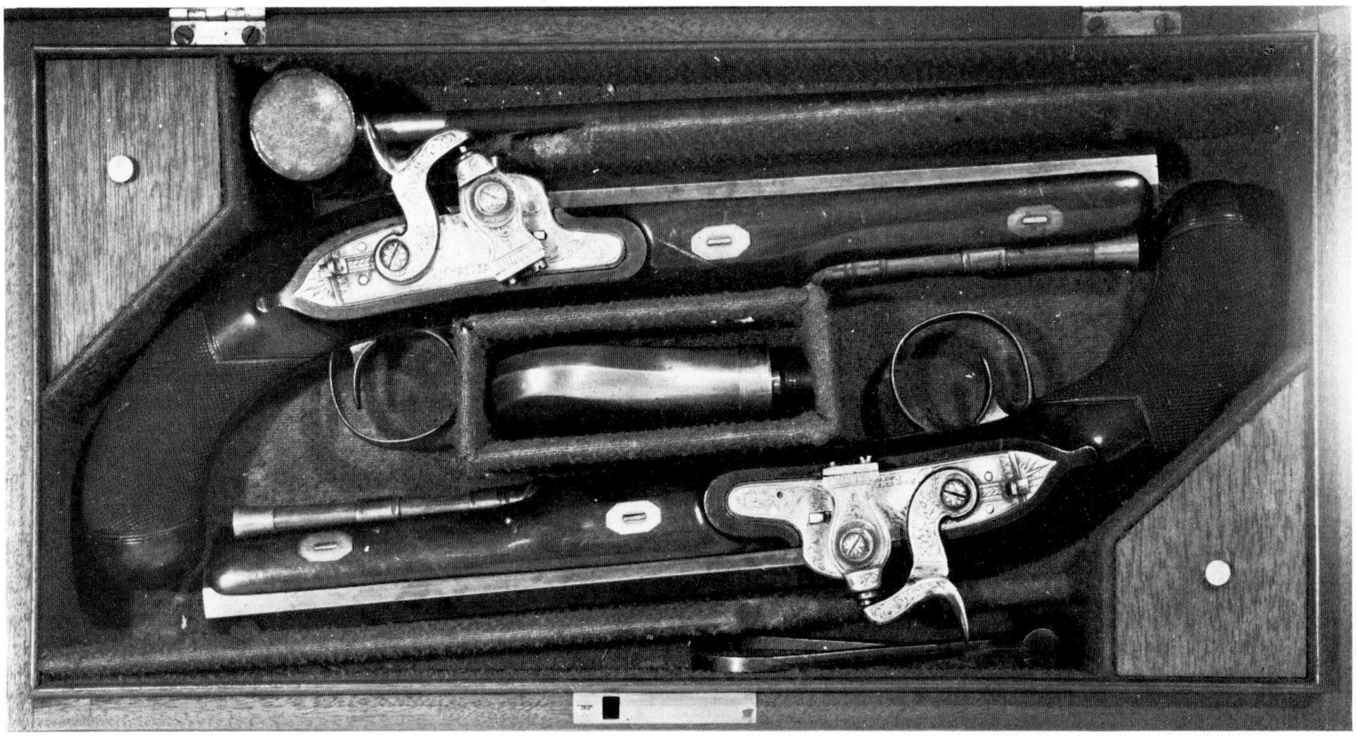

Cased pair of spurious Forsyth pistols. These have been adapted from a pair of moderate quality flintlock duelling pistols of about 1810. Compare the shape of the lock mechanisms with the top pistol of the previous pair. The engraving is of very poor quality. Numerous such imitations were made earlier this century, both guns and pistols.

No value to collectors.

Market value perhaps £800

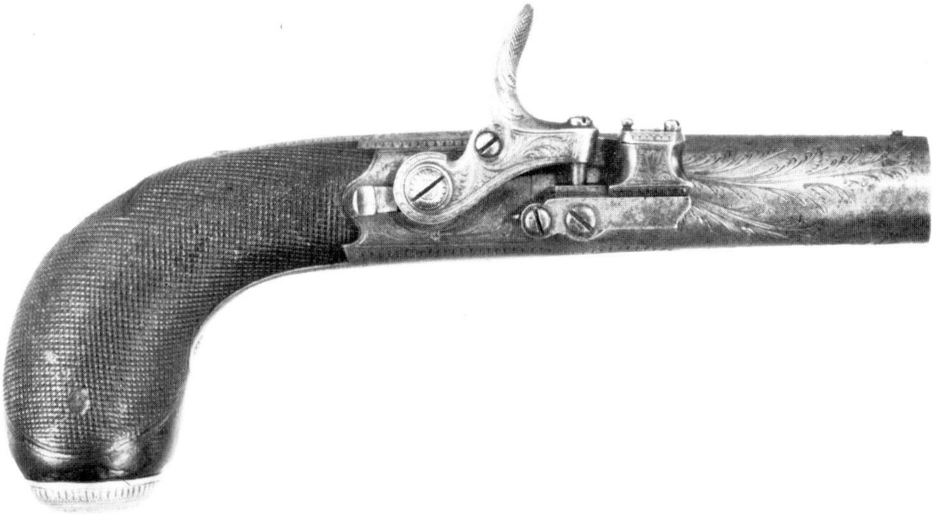

Forsyth patent pocket pistol with improved detonating system employing a sliding magazine. Iron body and barrel in one piece, each engraved with foliage, folding trigger and sliding safety-catch. Fine quality and condition. Signed Forsyth & Co., Patent Gunmakers, London. Circa 1824. 6¾in. *Christie's*

About £800. Extremely rare.

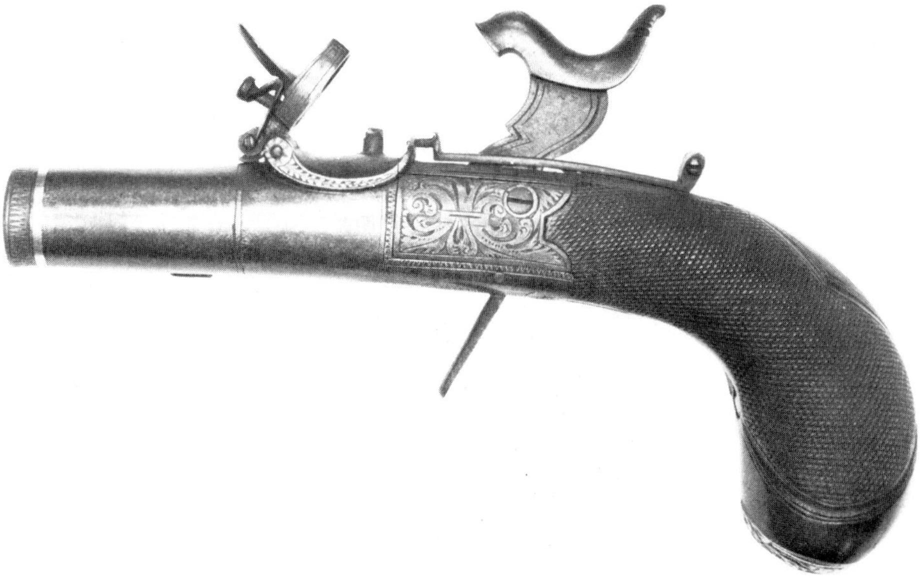

One of a pair of pocket pistols made to use top-hat percussion caps. Turn-off barrels with gold ring at the muzzle, engraved rounded box-lock actions, folding triggers, thumbpiece safety-catches and chequered butts. Good quality and condition. Unsigned. 5¾in. *Corry Collection*

£200 – £250 the pair

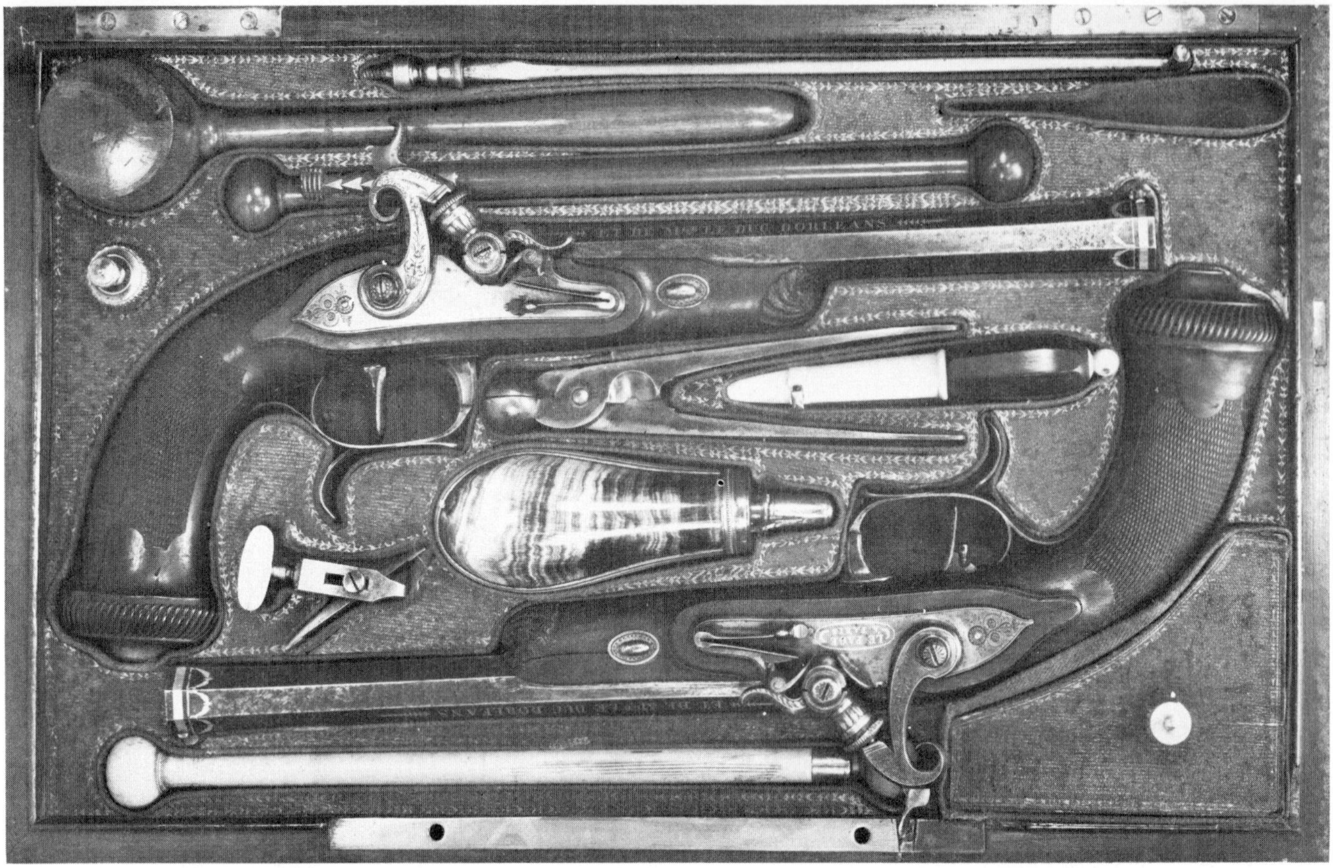

Cased pair of pellet-lock target pistols, the barrels and locks signed in gold, the stocks carved with shells and with engraved steel furniture, spur trigger-guards, and set triggers. The case lined with tooled red morocco leather, complete with fittings. Fine quality and good condition. By Le Page arqu. r du Roi et de Mgr. le Duc d'Orléans, circa 1822-28. 14¼in. *Sotheby's*

Over £1,500

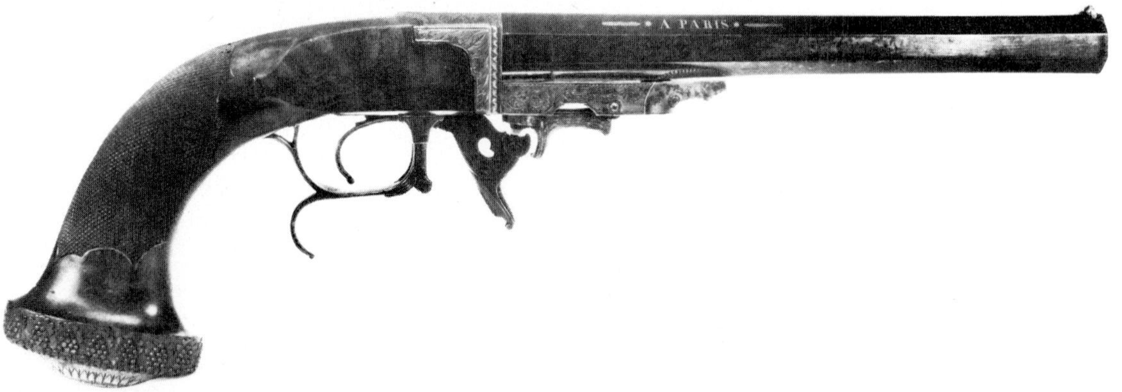

One of a pair of under-hammer tube-lock pistols with multigroove rifled octagonal barrels inlaid in gold, walnut butts, the pommels carved with bunches of grapes, finely engraved steel furniture. Fine quality and condition. By Gosset à Paris, circa 1815-20. 15½in. *Sotheby's*

Over £1,000 the pair

English Percussion Cap Pistols 1830 - 1860

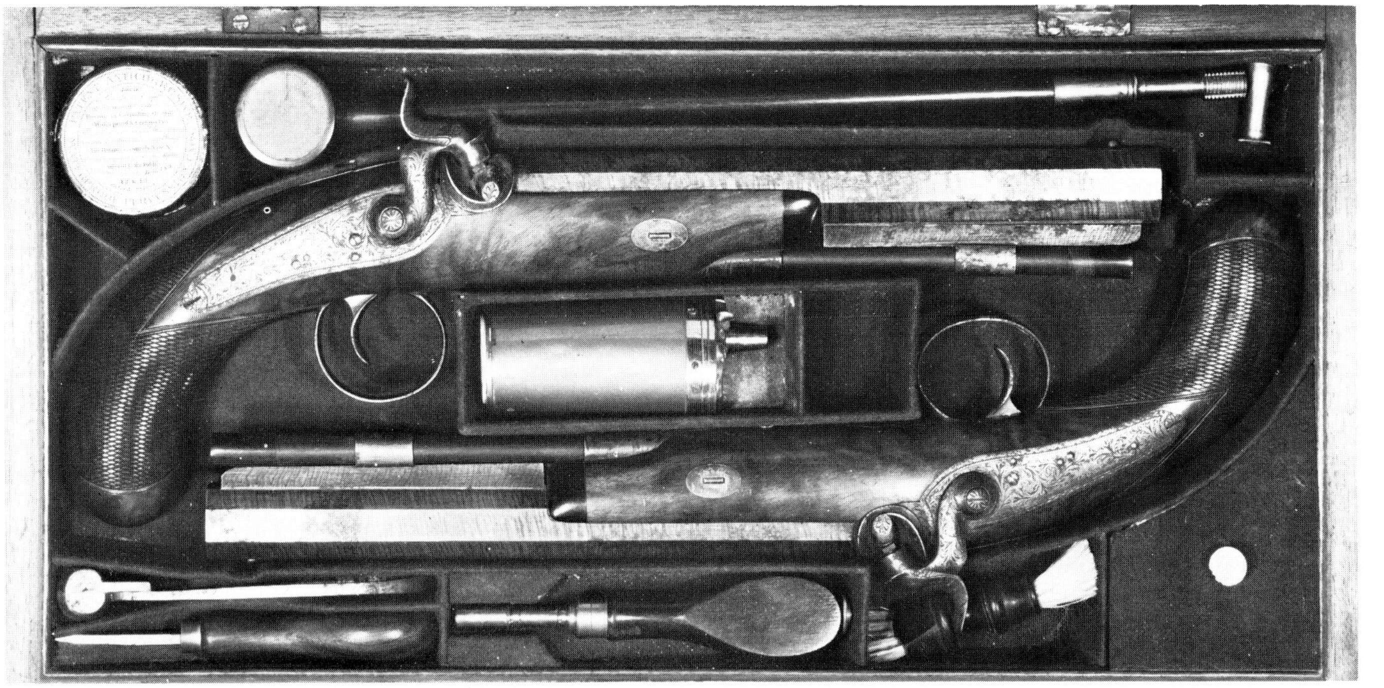

Cased pair of percussion duelling or target pistols with octagonal barrels, scroll engraved back-action locks and hammers, figured walnut half-stocks with silver escutcheons and engraved iron furniture. In original case with most accessories and label. Moderate quality, but good untouched condition with much original finish. By Alexander Wilson, London, circa 1830. *Christie's*

£450 – £650

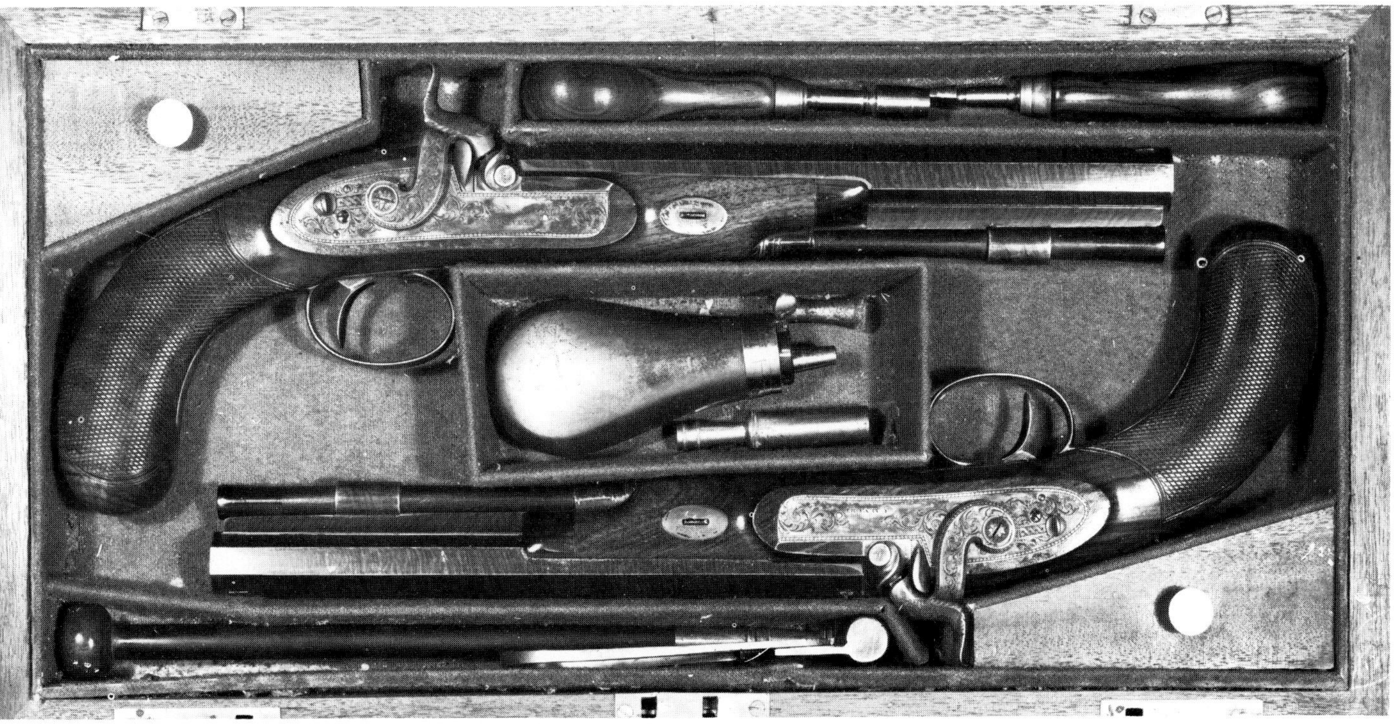

Cased pair of provincial percussion pistols with browned twist barrels, engraved locks and hammers, walnut half-stocks and engraved blued steel furniture. Good quality and outstanding condition, retaining all original finish, original case with fittings. By Calvert, Leeds, circa 1840. 14½in. *Christie's*

£600 – £800

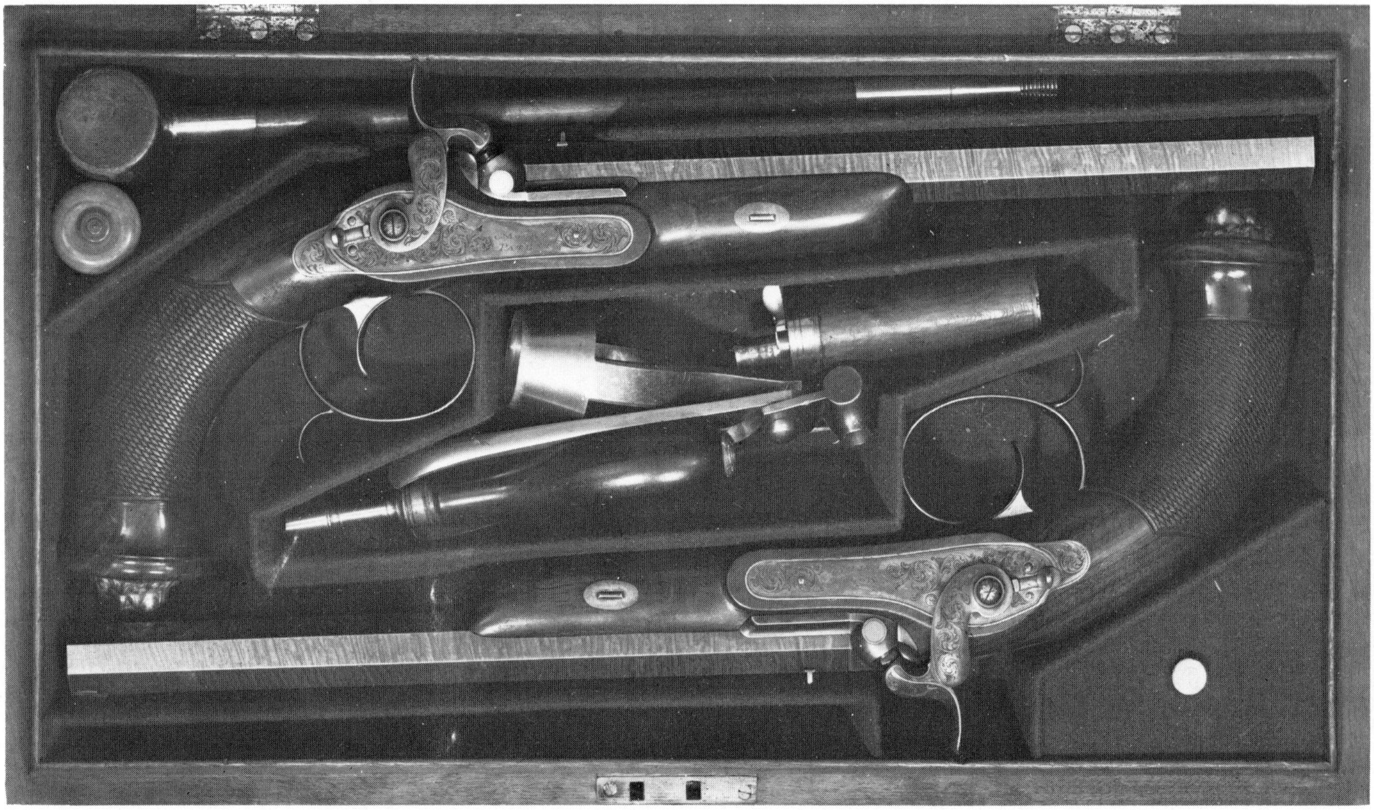

Cased pair of percussion target pistols with rifled barrels, platinum plugs, engraved locks and hammers, the half-stocks with silver escutcheons and lion's mask butt-caps and engraved blued steel trigger-guards. Original case with fittings and label. Fine quality, very fine condition with all original finish. By Charles Moore, 77 St. James's Street, London, circa 1840. 15½in. *Christie's*

Over £1,000

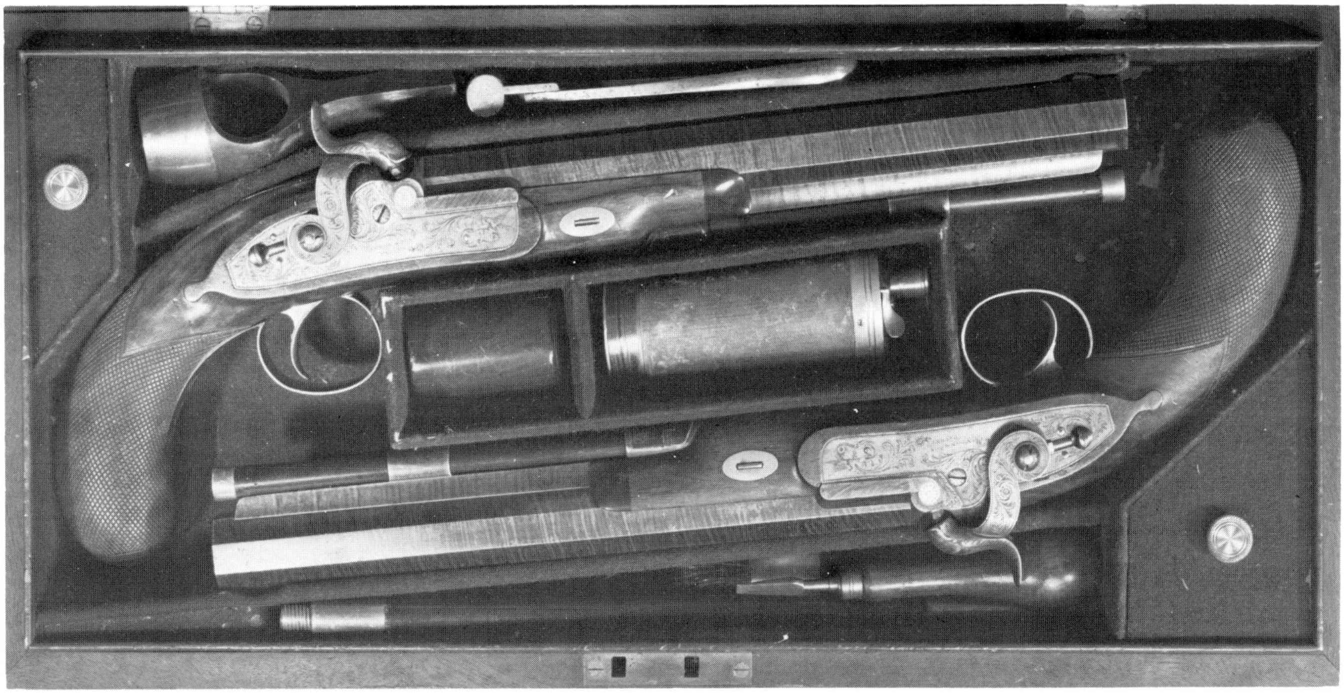

Cased pair of percussion target pistols with heavy octagonal barrels, platinum plugs and silver fore-sights, the engraved locks with blued safety-catches, the half-stocks with engraved blued steel furniture and silver escutcheons. Original case with fittings and label, fine quality and near new condition. By John Manton & Son, Gunmakers to the Royal Family, No. 6, Dover Street, London, No. 10136, circa 1831.

About £2,000

These were made for the Duke of Cambridge, seventh son of George III, but even without the history they are worth over £1,000. *Christie's*

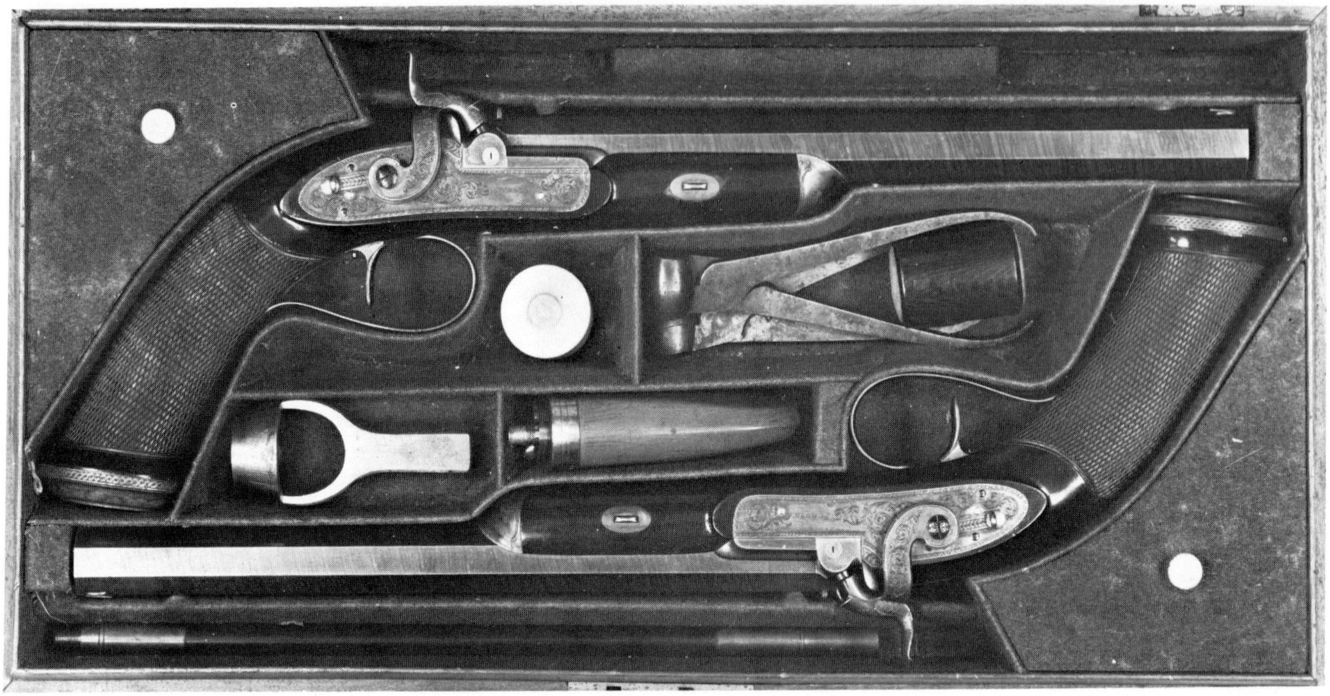

Cased pair of percussion target pistols with rifled octagonal barrels, platinum line and plug, engraved locks and hammers, set triggers ebonised half-stocks and engraved blued and case-hardened steel furniture. Fine quality and condition with nearly all original finish Original case with some fittings and trade label. By J. Purdey, 314½ Oxford Street, London, Nos. 2707 and 2708, circa 1836. 16½in

Over £1,200 *Sotheby's*

Similar cased pair of percussion target pistols, but with interchangeable rifled and smooth bore barrels. Fine quality and excellent condition. By J. Purdey, 314½ Oxford Street, London, Nos. 2837 and 2838, circa 1837. *Christie*

Over £2,000

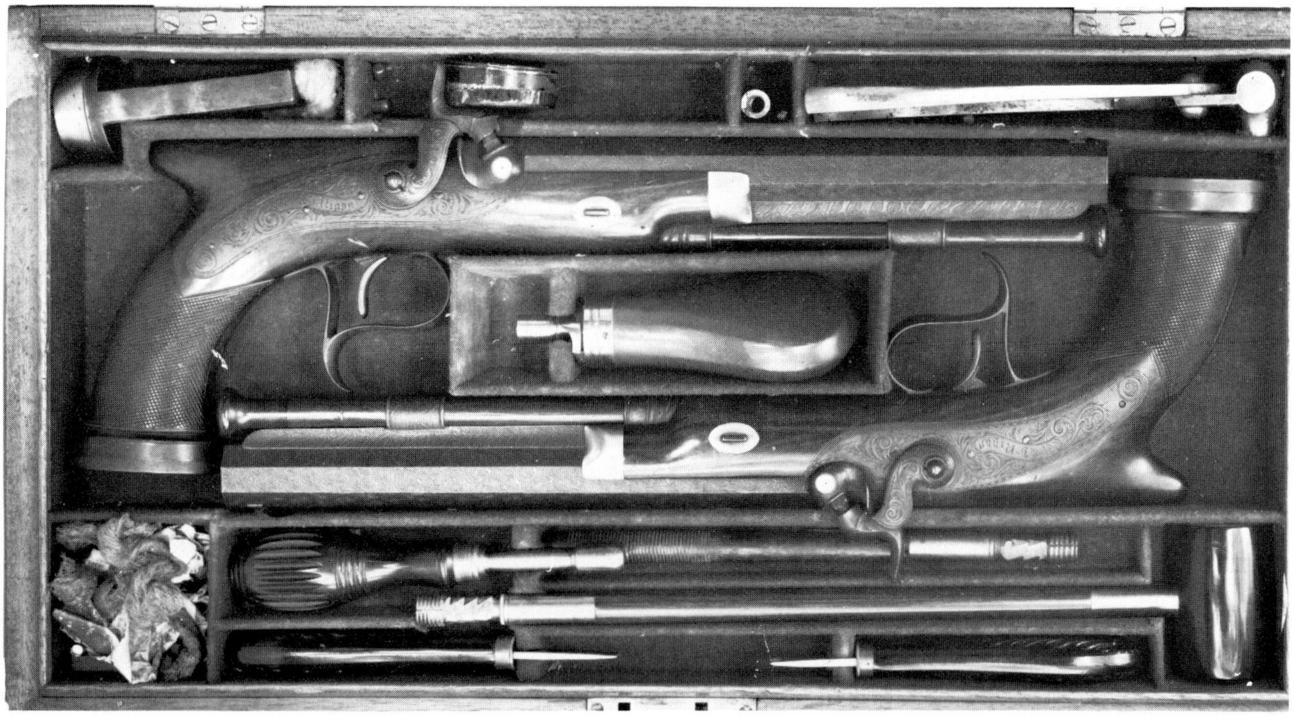

Pair of saw-handled percussion duelling pistols with etched twist octagonal barrels, platinum line and plug, engraved hammers and back-action locks, engraved blued steel furniture, spur trigger-guards and set triggers, silver fore-end caps and escutcheons. Fine quality and condition. Original case with complete fittings and label. By W. & J. Rigby, Dublin, circa 1830. 14½in. *Sotheby's*

Over £1,200

Rigby was one of the best makers of the percussion era.

Two pairs of percussion pistols to show the difference in price between original complete sets and their component parts.

One of a cased pair of saw-handled duelling pistols similar to the pair above, but in not such good condition. By W. & J. Rigby, Dublin, circa 1830. 14in. *Sotheby's*

£500 – £700 the pair

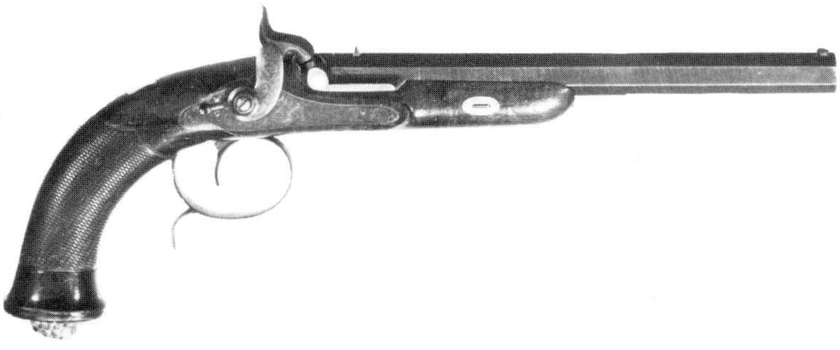

One of a pair of target pistols by Charles Moore, circa 1840. No case and not such good condition as the pair on page 150. 15½in. *Christie's*

£400 – £600 the pair

Cased pair of percussion travelling pistols with octagonal barrels, gold line, platinum plug, engraved hammers and locks, the full stocks with engraved steel furniture and stirrup ramrods. Moderate quality, good condition. Original velvet-lined case with fittings but no label. Signed Clive. Circa 1835. 11in. *Corrv Collection*

£300 – £450

One of a pair of percussion duelling pistols, converted from flintlock, with octagonal barrels, platinum plug, full stocks, engraved blued steel furniture and engraved silver escutcheons. Fair quality and condition. By Innes, Edinburgh, early 19th century. *Christie's*

£250 – £300 the pair

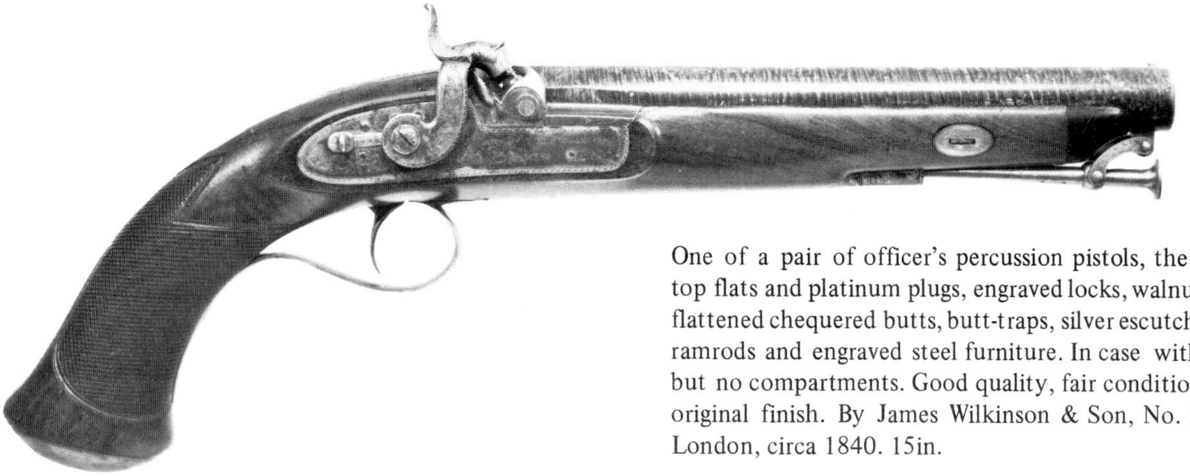

One of a pair of officer's percussion pistols, the barrels with top flats and platinum plugs, engraved locks, walnut full stocks, flattened chequered butts, butt-traps, silver escutcheons, stirrup ramrods and engraved steel furniture. In case with trade label, but no compartments. Good quality, fair condition, with some original finish. By James Wilkinson & Son, No. 27 Pall Mall, London, circa 1840. 15in. *Christie's*

£400 – £500 the pair

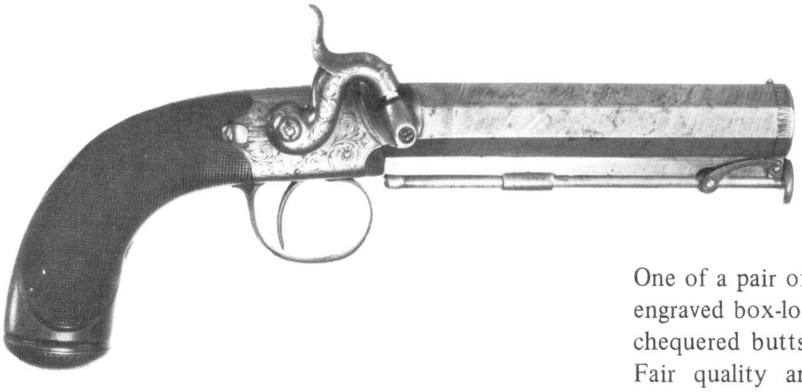

One of a pair of percussion belt pistols with octagonal barrels, engraved box-lock actions with side hammers and safety-catch, chequered butts with butt-traps at the base, stirrup ramrods. Fair quality and condition, but no finish. By Wilkinson, London, circa 1840. 10in. *Christie's*

£200 – £250 the pair

In case, complete with finish and fittings, £400 – £500

One of a pair of back-action percussion overcoat pistols with octagonal barrels, engraved locks and hammers, full stocks and stirrup ramrods. Poor, but untouched condition and poor quality. Birmingham proof marks, circa 1850. 8¼in. *Christie's*

£100 – £150 the pair

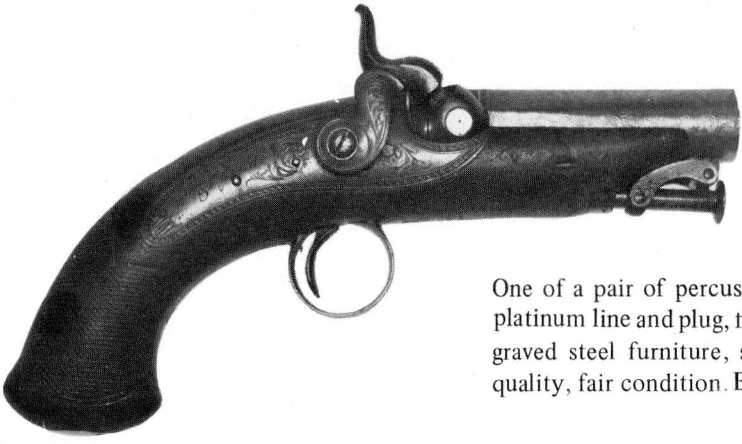

One of a pair of percussion travelling pistols with etched twist barrels, platinum line and plug, full stocks with flattened chequered butts and engraved steel furniture, stirrup ramrods and plain silver butt-caps. Fine quality, fair condition. By W. & J. Rigby, Dublin, circa 1850. 7½in.
Corry Collection

£300 – £350 the pair

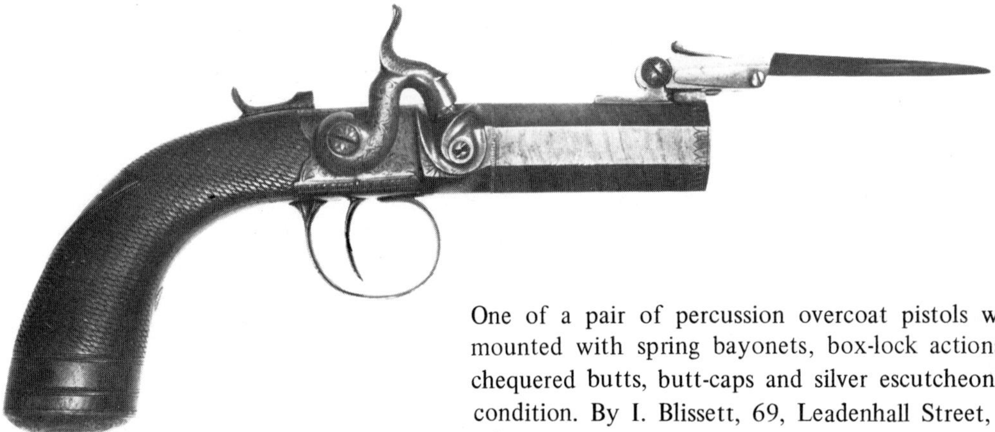

One of a pair of percussion overcoat pistols with octagonal barrels mounted with spring bayonets, box-lock actions with side hammers, chequered butts, butt-caps and silver escutcheons. Good quality and condition. By I. Blissett, 69, Leadenhall Street, London, circa 1840. 7½in. *Corry Collection*

£200 – £300 the pair

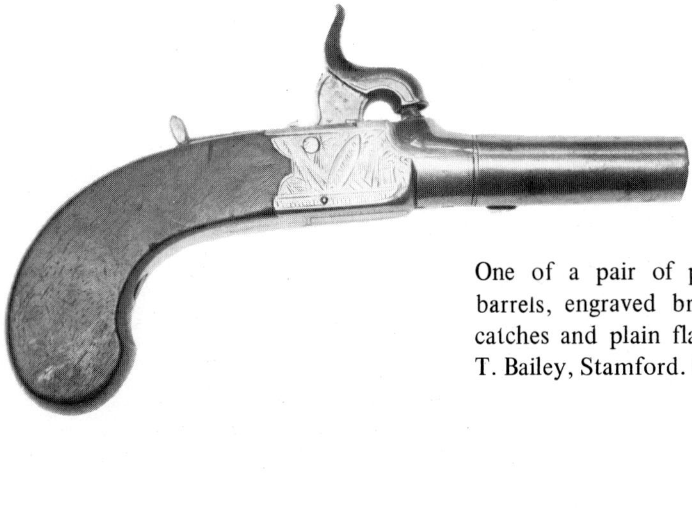

One of a pair of percussion box-lock pocket pistols with turn-off barrels, engraved brass actions, folding triggers, thumbpiece safety-catches and plain flat-sided butts. Poor quality, fair condition. Signed T. Bailey, Stamford. Circa 1840. 6½in. *Corry Collection*

£80 – £100 the pair

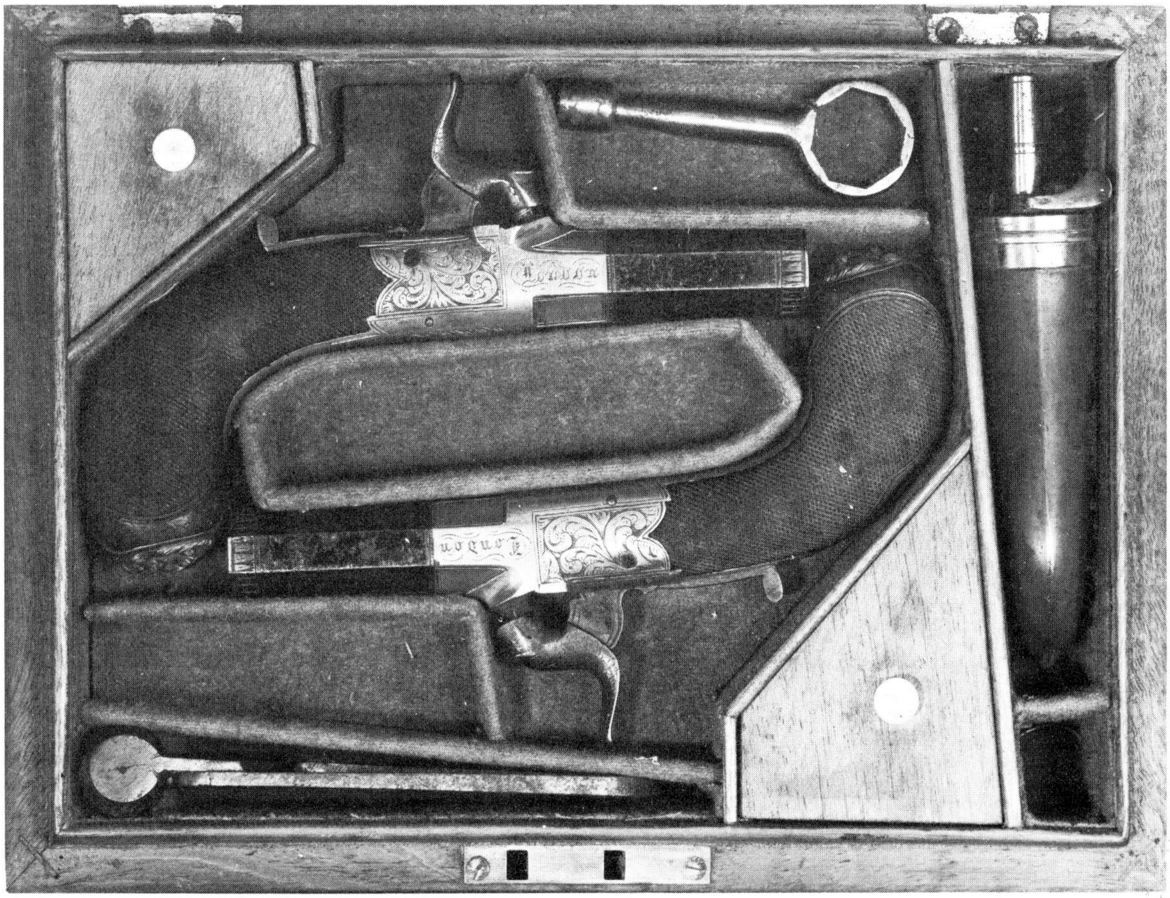

Cased pair of percussion box-lock pocket pistols with blued octagonal turn-off barrels, engraved silvered actions with folding triggers and thumbpiece safety-catches, chequered butts, silver escutcheons and lion's mask butt-caps. Original case with fittings. Good quality, fine condition. Signed Blanch, London. Circa 1840. 5¾in. *Christie's*

About £400 the pair

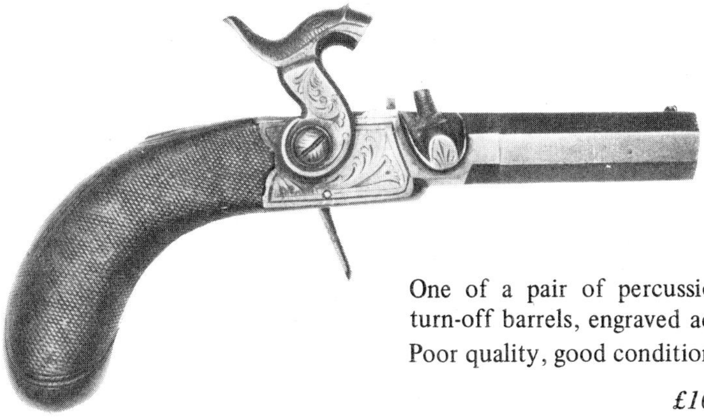

One of a pair of percussion box-lock pocket pistols with octagonal turn-off barrels, engraved actions, folding triggers and chequered butts. Poor quality, good condition. 5in. *Corry Collection*

£100 – £120 the pair

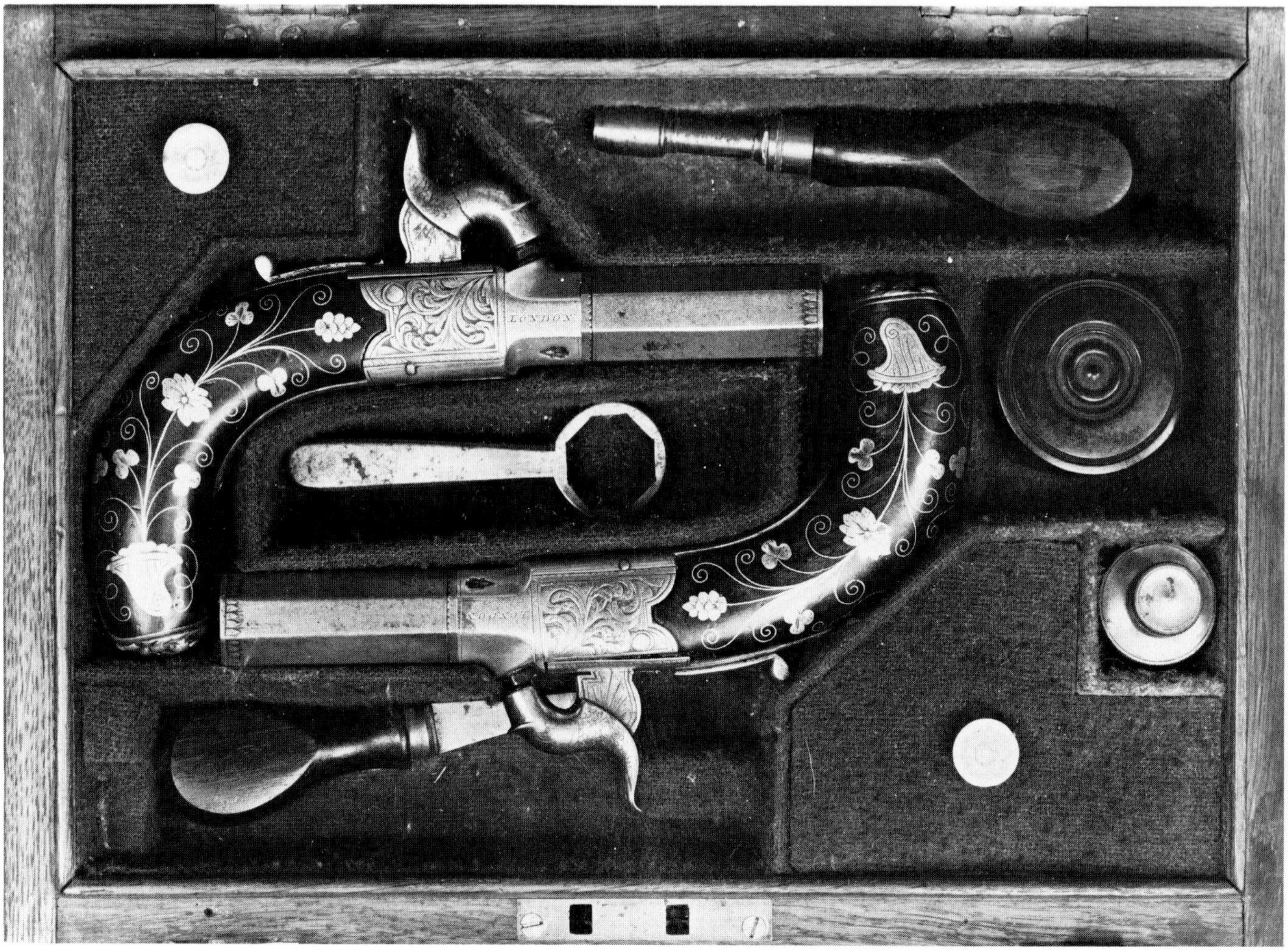

Cased pair of percussion box-lock pocket pistols with engraved brass actions, folding triggers and thumbpiece safety-catches, the butts inlaid with scrolls and foliage in silver and with silver lion's mask caps. Oak case with accessories (no flask) and trade label of Edward London. Moderate quality, fair condition. The pistols signed Smith, London. Circa 1840. 5¾in. *Christie's*

About £400
£800 for a really fine pair

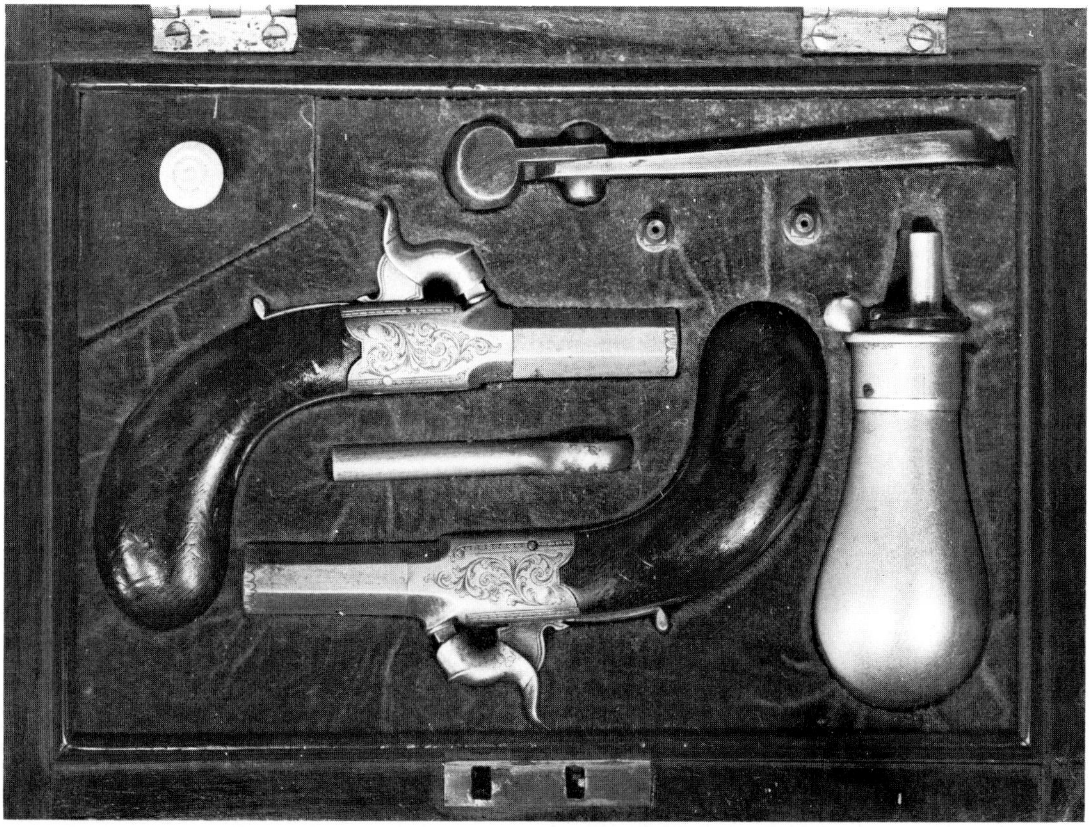

Cased pair of percussion box-lock muff pistols with foliate engraved actions, folding triggers and thumbpiece safety-catches, the ebonised butts with silver escutcheons. Fine quality and condition. Original velvet-lined case with label and fittings. By Samuel Nock, Gunmaker to His Majesty, London, circa 1845. 3½in.

Christie's

£400 – £600

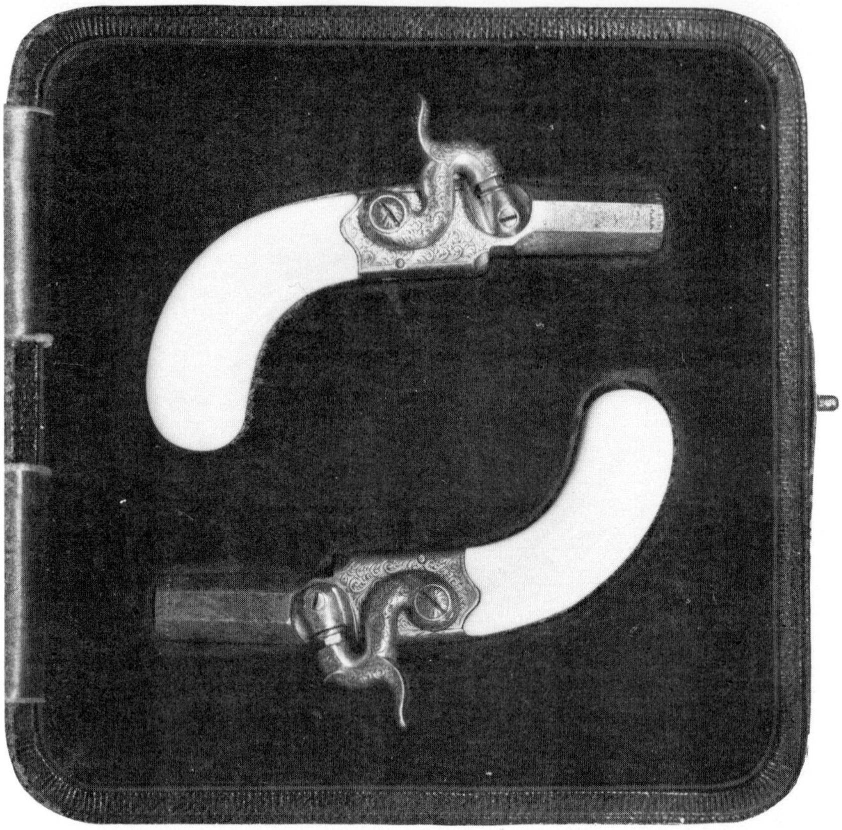

Cased pair of percussion muff pistols with octagonal barrels, box-lock side-hammer actions, scroll engraved and retaining most of their original gilding, folding triggers and ivory butts. In original velvet-lined glazed display case. Fine quality, good condition. Circa 1860 (possibly made for the Paris Universal Exhibition of 1867). 3in. *Christie's*

£400 – £500

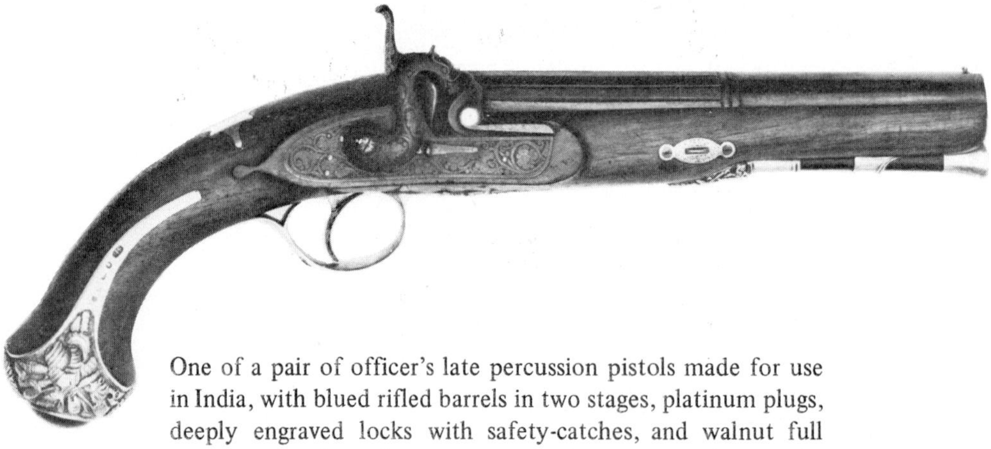

One of a pair of officer's late percussion pistols made for use in India, with blued rifled barrels in two stages, platinum plugs, deeply engraved locks with safety-catches, and walnut full stocks with embossed silver mounts including spurred pommels. Fine quality and condition. Birmingham silver hallmarks for 1863. 14½in. *Christie's*

£600 – £900 the pair

Scottish Percussion Cap Pistols 1830 - 1860

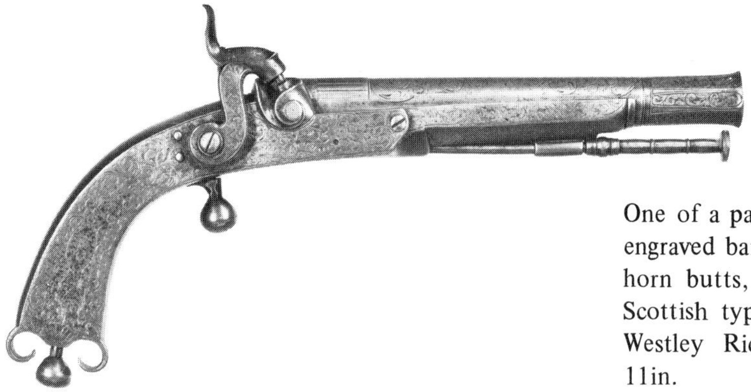

One of a pair of all-steel percussion belt pistols with engraved barrels, locks and stocks, ball triggers, ram's horn butts, prickers, belt hooks and ramrods all of Scottish type. Moderate quality and condition. By Westley Richards, Birmingham, mid-19th century. 11in. *Christie's*

About £400 the pair

One of a pair of percussion dress pistols, the blued barrels engraved with scrollwork, with silver stocks and trigger-guards engraved with foliage, the pommels set with a cairngorm. Good quality and condition. Signed J. Beattie, London. Circa 1830. 10½in. *Sotheby's*

Over £800 the pair

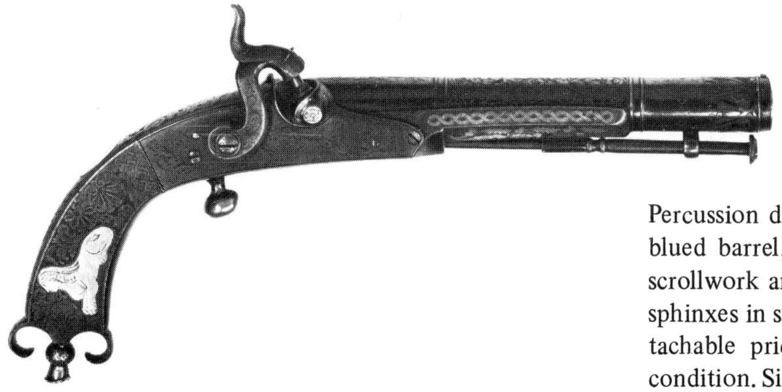

Percussion dress pistol of Scottish type, with engraved blued barrel, the steel stock engraved with shells and scrollwork and inlaid with thistles, strapwork and two sphinxes in silver, engraved silver escutcheon, silver detachable pricker and ball trigger. Good quality, fine condition. Signed Mortimer . Mid-19th century. 11in. *Christie's*

About £300

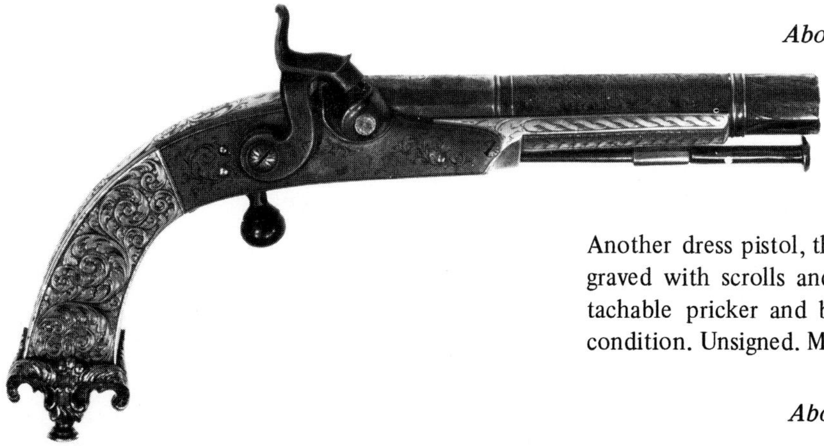

Another dress pistol, the stock entirely of paktong engraved with scrolls and overlapping foliage, with detachable pricker and ball trigger. Good quality, fine condition. Unsigned. Mid-19th century. 9¾in. *Christie's*

About £300

Continental Percussion Cap Pistols

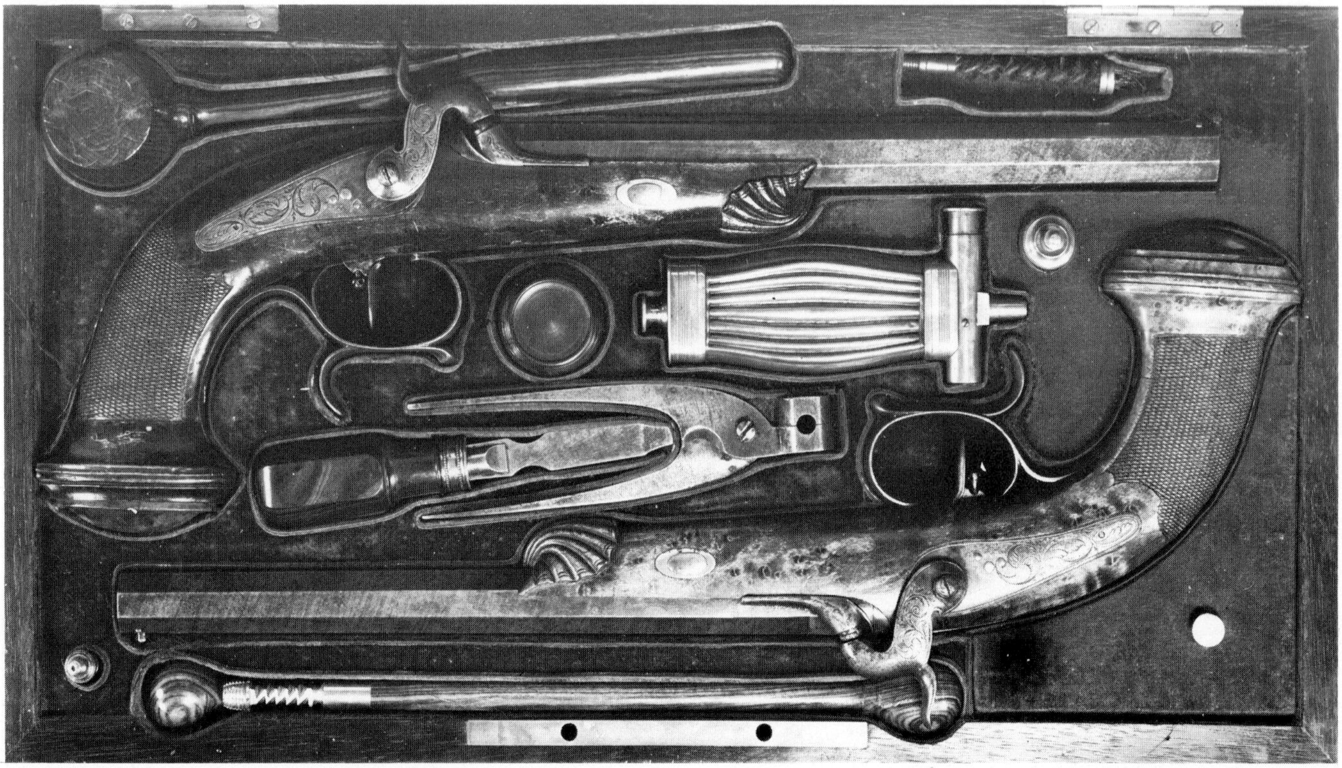

Cased pair of back-action percussion target pistols with rifled octagonal barrels, engraved locks and hammers, walnut half-stocks with carved scallop fore-ends and oval escutcheons, spur trigger-guards and set triggers. Poor quality, but good condition. Original case lined in velvet (worn) with complete fittings. Note weakness of layout, with some accessories let into the side of the case. Unmarked but probably Liège, mid-19th century. 16in. *Christie's*

£600 – £750

The same pistols without the case and fittings £300 – £400. Single pistol £120 – £150.

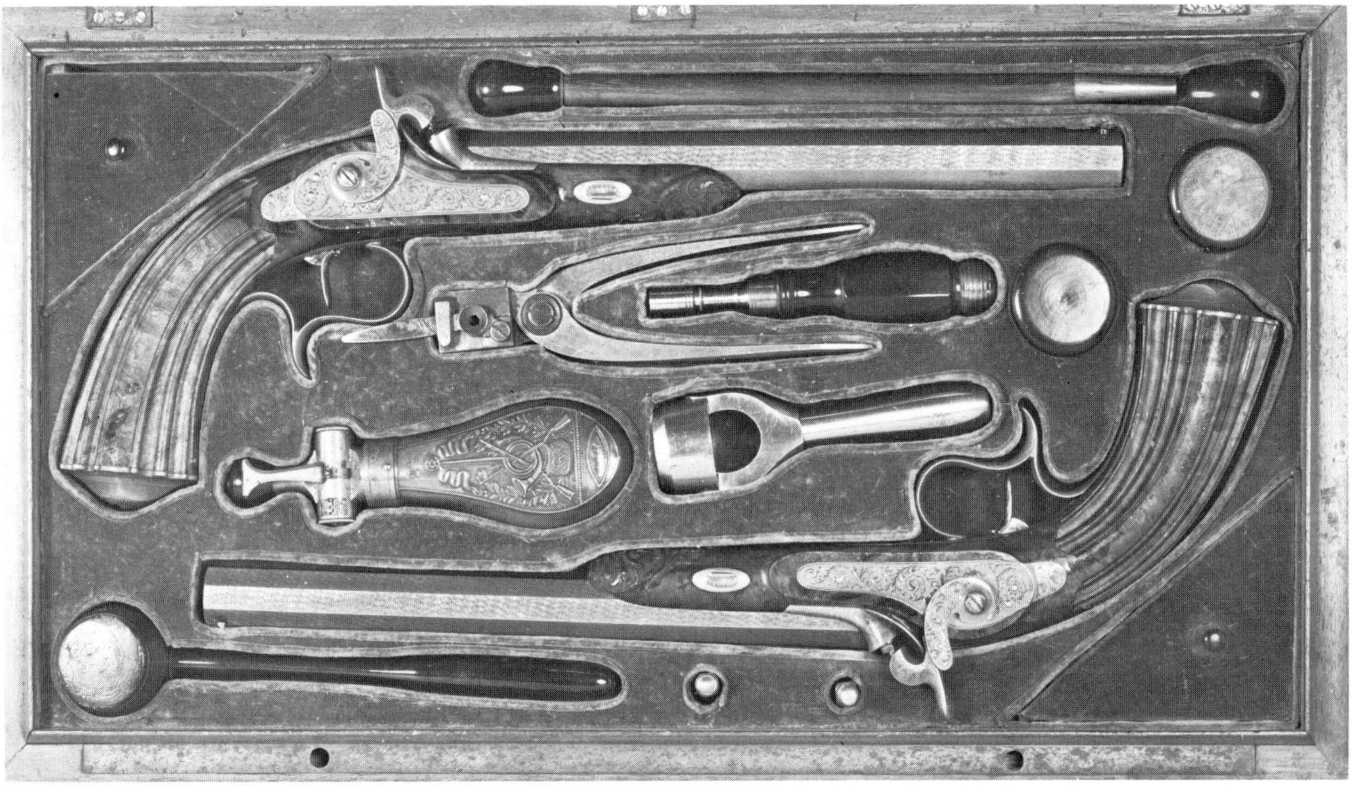

Cased pair of Swiss percussion rifled target pistols with twist octagonal barrels, engraved locks and hammers, carved walnut half-stocks with fluted butts. Original case with full accessories. Good quality, fine condition. By J. Vannod, Lausanne, circa 1840. *Christie's*

£750 – £1,000

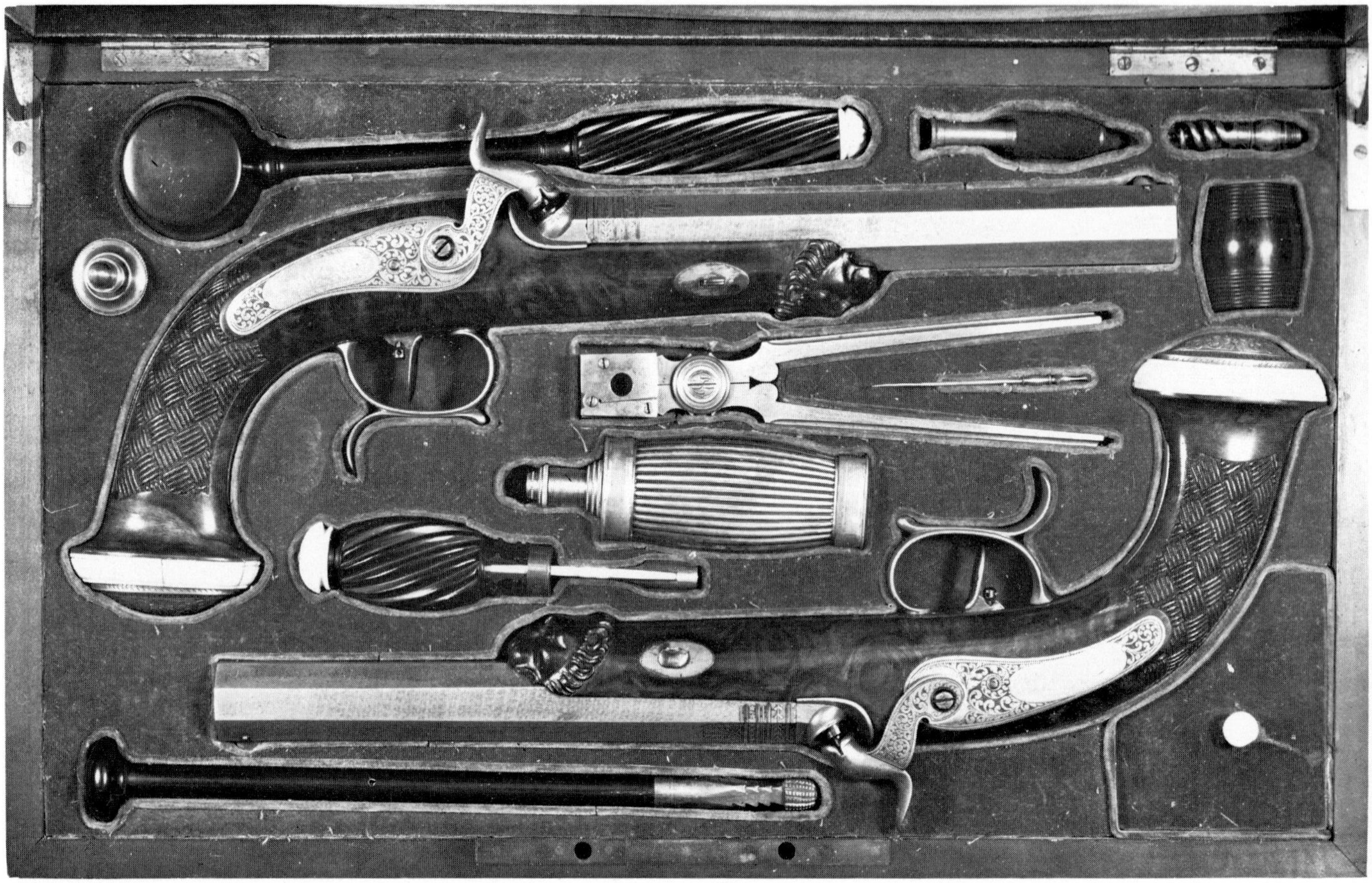

Cased pair of back-action percussion rifled target pistols signed in gold on the barrels and lock-plates, with twist silver and gold inlaid barrels, figured walnut half-stocks with carved lion's mask fore-ends, set triggers, spur trigger-guards, steel and ebony pommels. Fine quality and condition, original case with full accessories. Signed Le Page à Paris. Circa 1840. 4½in. *Christie's*

£1,500 – £2,000

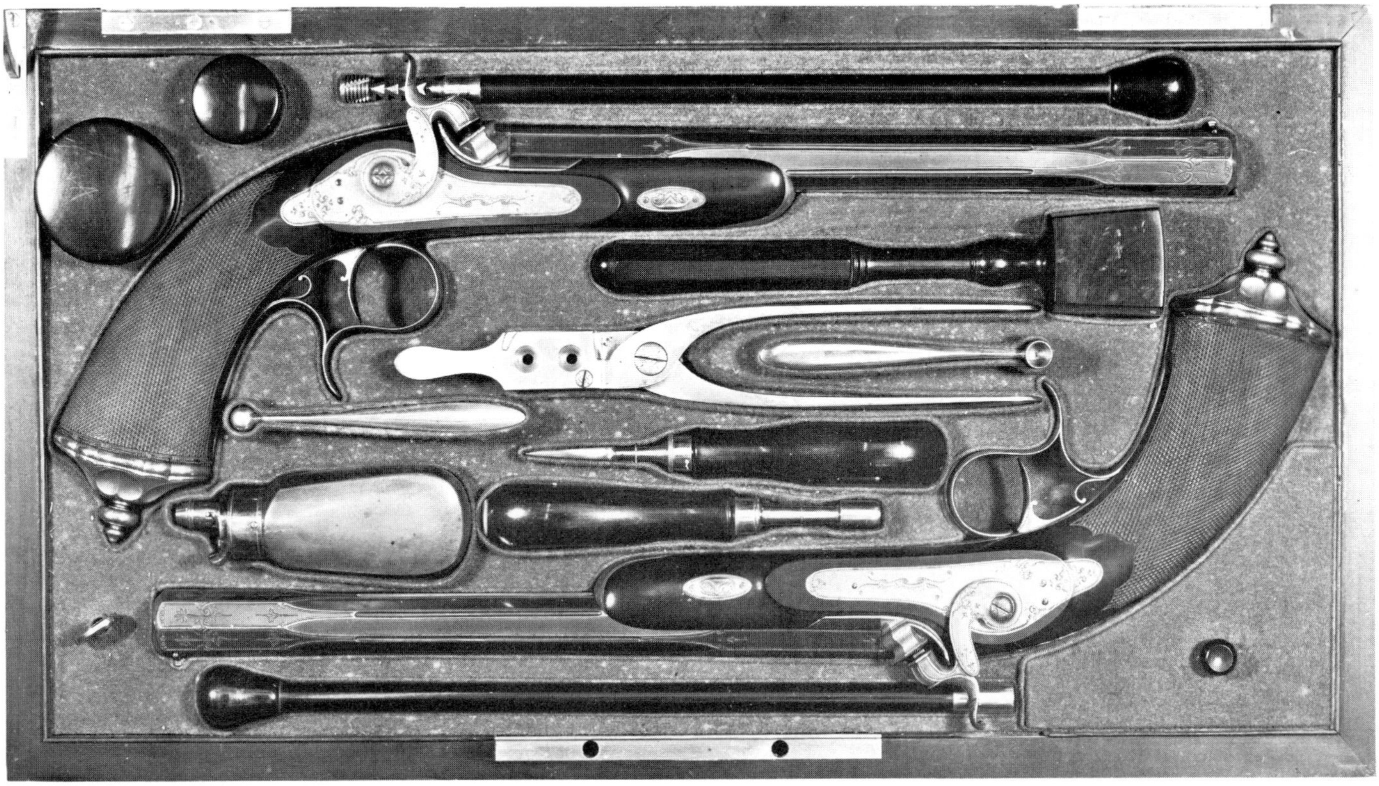

Cased pair of percussion rifled target pistols with browned fluted octagonal barrels, finely engraved locks and hammers, ebony half-stocks and bright steel furniture. Fine quality and condition. Original ebonised case with full accessories, the lid inlaid with a scroll cartouche, complete with leather outer cover. By Gastinne Renette, Arq. de L'Empereur à Paris, mid-19th century. 16½in.

Christie's

Over £1,500

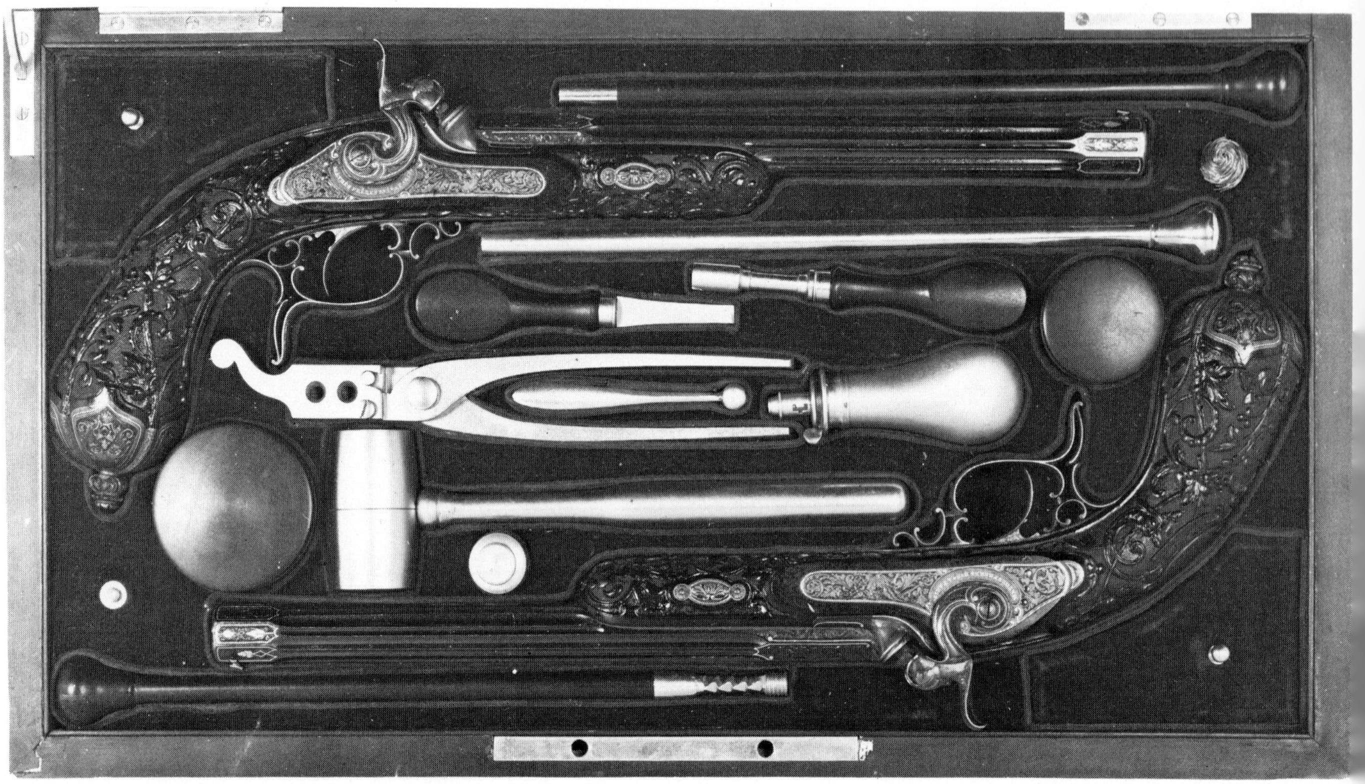

Cased pair of percussion rifled target pistols with engraved and gold inlaid fluted octagonal barrels, signed locks inlaid and engraved en suite, ebony half-stocks finely carved with grotesque beasts and foliage, gold-inlaid steel mounts. Very fine quality and condition. Original velvet-lined case with full plated accessories. By Mathès Frères à Paris. 16½in. *Christie's*

Over £4,000. Made for the Paris Exhibition of 1878.

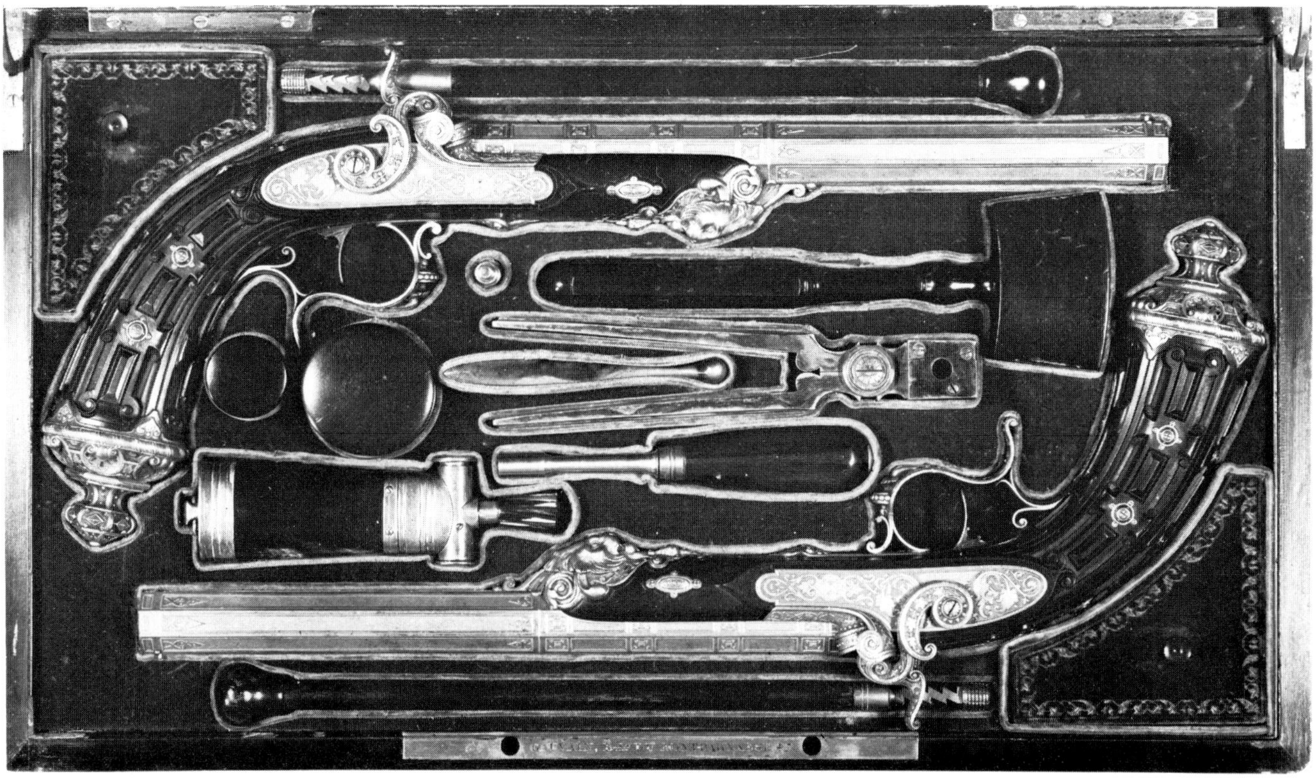

Cased pair of percussion rifled target pistols with octagonal barrels inlaid with gold, deeply engraved locks with chiselled hammers and gold lined borders signed in gold, finely carved ebony stocks in the Gothic style with iron furniture with gold borders deeply chiselled with foliate decoration, chiselled lion's head fore-end caps. Superb quality and condition. Original red velvet lined case with full accessories and inlaid lid stamped with gold signature on the inside. By Gauvain, Paris, the case inscribed "Exposition Universelle 1849". 16in. *Sotheby's*

Over £6,000

The highest price so far recorded at auction for pistols of this type is £8,200 for a pair of more elaborate pistols by Gastinne Renette.

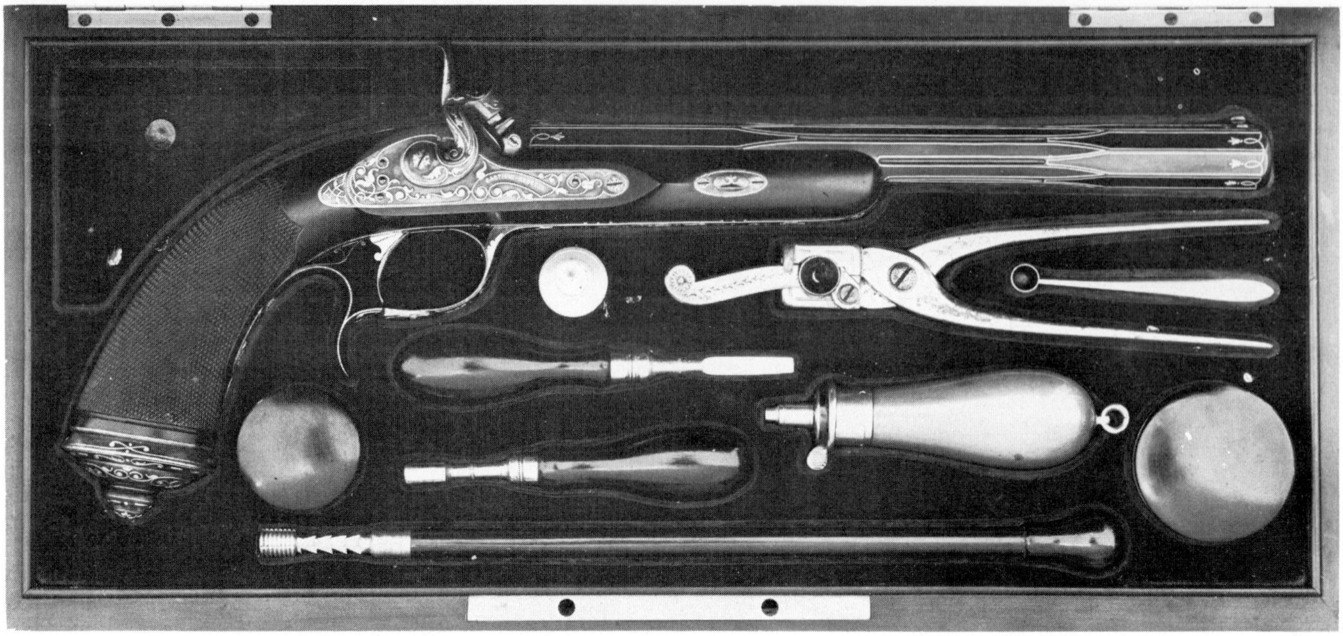

Cased percussion breech-loading target pistol with fluted octagonal barrel with gold borders, the lock and hammer decorated with foliage in gold, the ebony half-stock with steel mounts en suite. The trigger-guard comes apart, the forward part acting as a lever to slide the barrel forward. Very fine quality and exceptional condition. Original velvet-lined ebony case with full accessories. By Gastinne Renette à Paris, circa 1860. 16in. *Sotheby's*

Over £1,000

Cased pair of percussion saloon pistols with concealed hammers and break actions, blued sighted barrels, foliate engraved frames and fluted walnut grips. Moderate quality and condition. Original lined and fitted case (nipple key missing). By A. Caron, Arquebusier du Roi, Passage de l'Opéra 20, Paris, circa 1850. 12¾in. *Christie's*

£400 – £500

Small bore saloon pistols such as these were made for indoor target shooting.

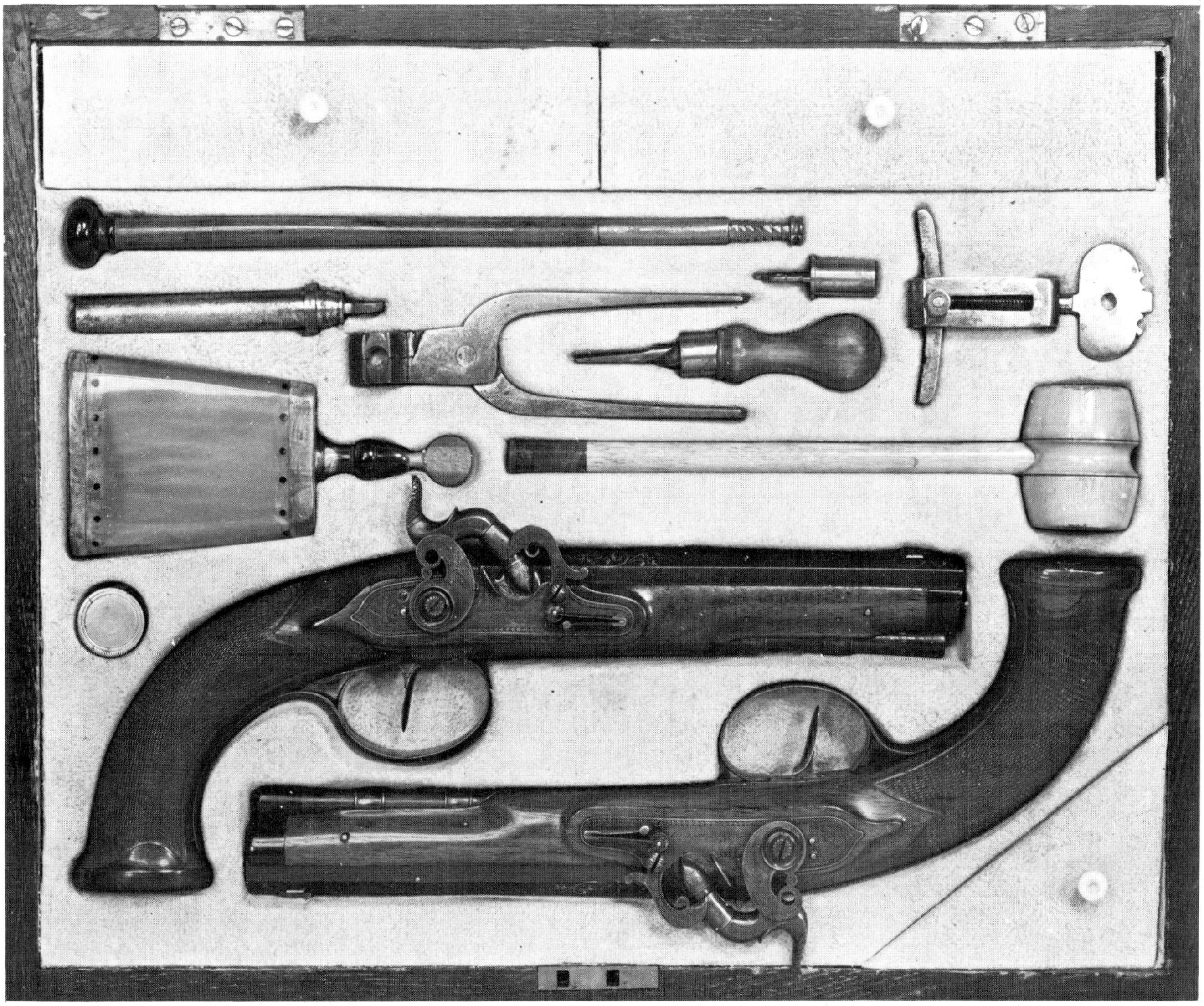

Cased pair of German percussion pistols, converted from flintlock, with browned barrels signed in silver, walnut full stocks, engraved steel furniture and bone fore-end caps. The locks with spring-loaded nipple covers. Fine quality and condition. In chamois leather lined case with fittings. By Johann Christoph Kuchenreiter, Regensburg, early 19th century. 12in. *Christie's*

£800 – £1,200

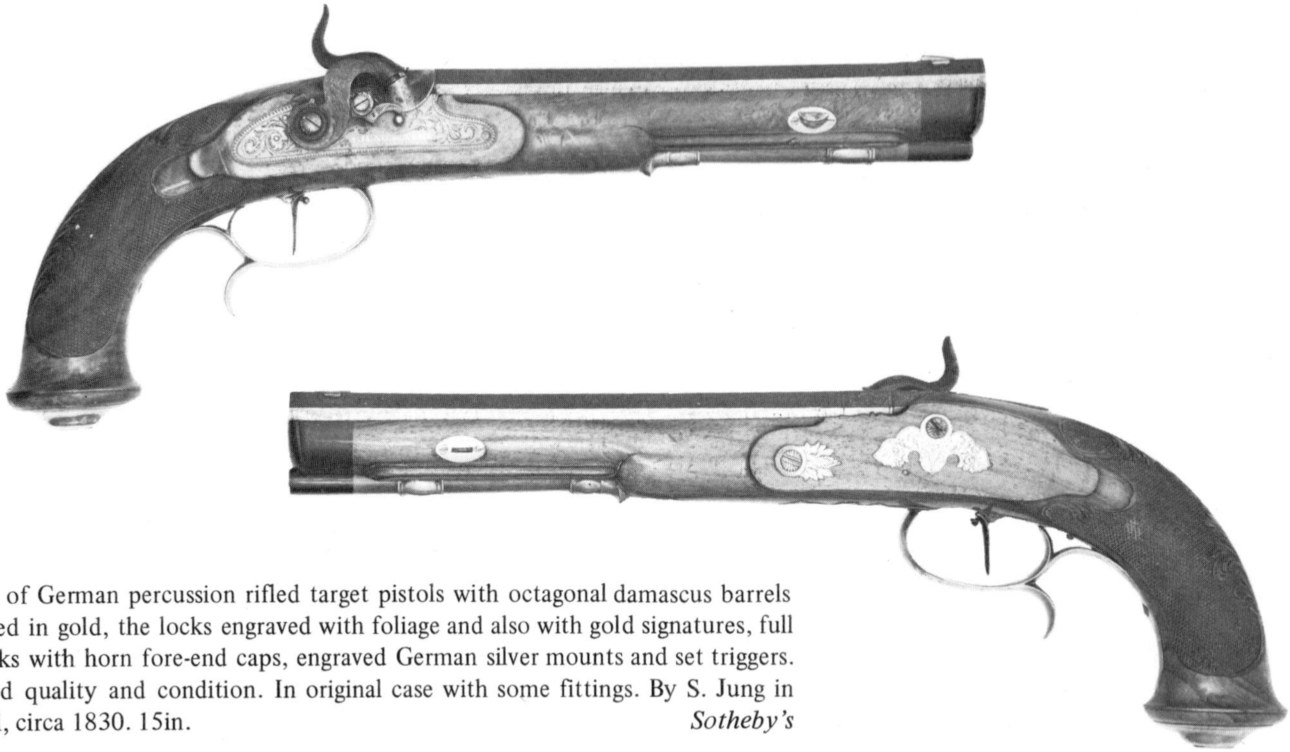

Pair of German percussion rifled target pistols with octagonal damascus barrels signed in gold, the locks engraved with foliage and also with gold signatures, full stocks with horn fore-end caps, engraved German silver mounts and set triggers. Good quality and condition. In original case with some fittings. By S. Jung in Suhl, circa 1830. 15in. *Sotheby's*

£500 – £750

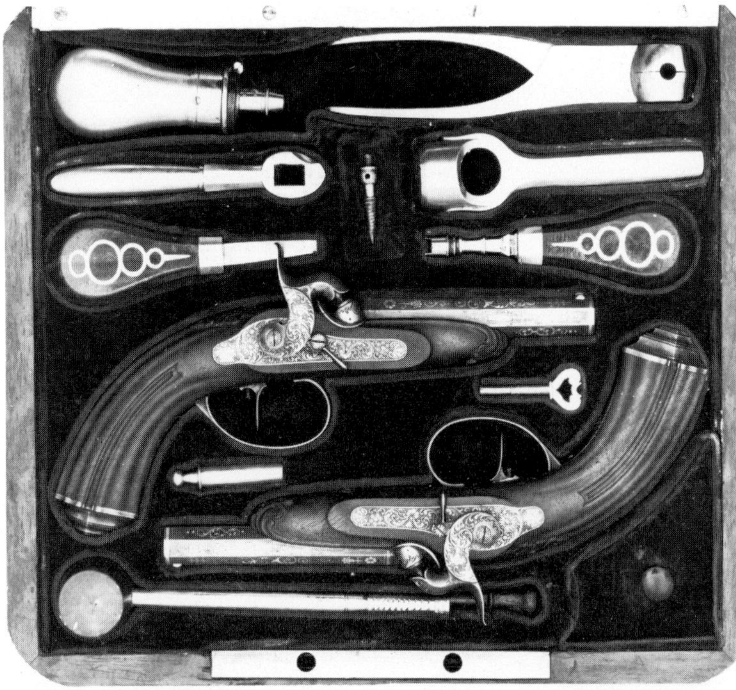

Very fine pair of small percussion pistols, the barrels signed and inlaid in gold and silver with flowerheads, cornucopiae, scrolls and birds, finely engraved locks picked out in silver and gold, carved walnut half-stocks with fluted butts, patent safety-catches on the locks. Excellent quality and condition. Original silver-bound case lined in velvet with full fittings. By J. Adam Kuchenreiter of Regensburg, circa 1830. 6¾in. *Sotheby's*

Over £2,000

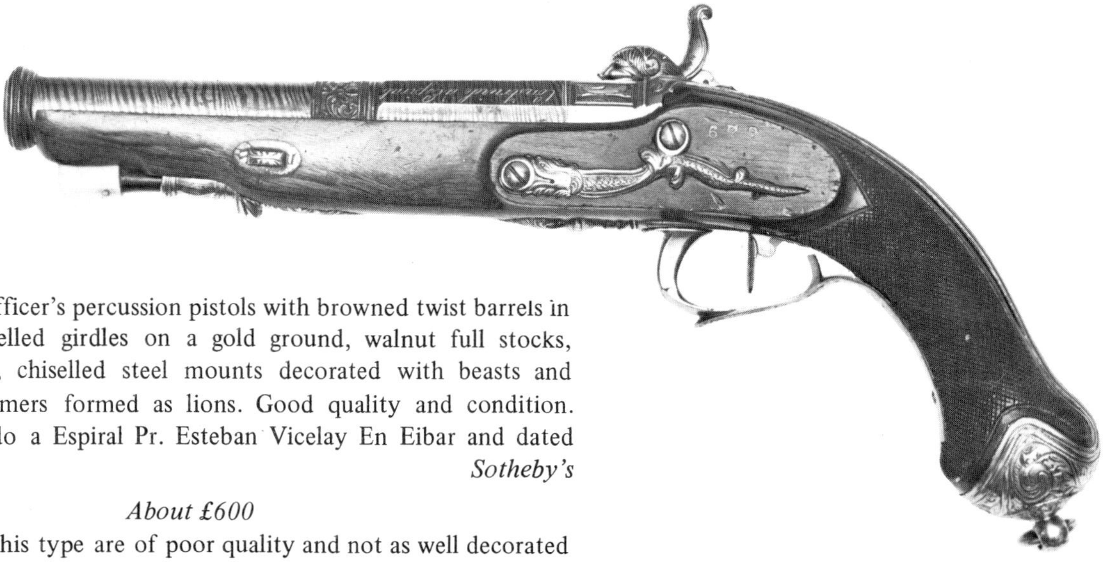

Pair of Spanish officer's percussion pistols with browned twist barrels in two stages, chiselled girdles on a gold ground, walnut full stocks, chequered butts, chiselled steel mounts decorated with beasts and scrolls, the hammers formed as lions. Good quality and condition. Signed Construido a Espiral Pr. Esteban Vicelay En Eibar and dated 1836. 14in. *Sotheby's*

About £600

Many pistols of this type are of poor quality and not as well decorated as these. Lesser ones £200 – £300 a pair

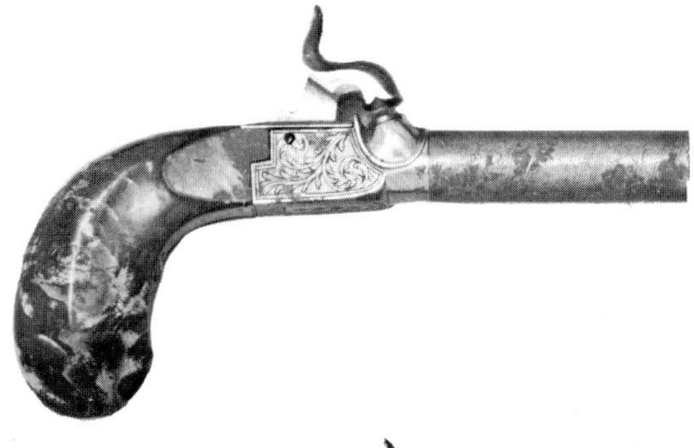

One of a pair of typical Liège percussion pocket pistols with turn-off barrels, engraved actions, simulated rootwood butts of flattened form, and folding triggers. Poor quality, fair condition. Unsigned, Liège proof marks. Circa 1840. 6in. *Knight, Frank & Rutley*

About £100 the pair

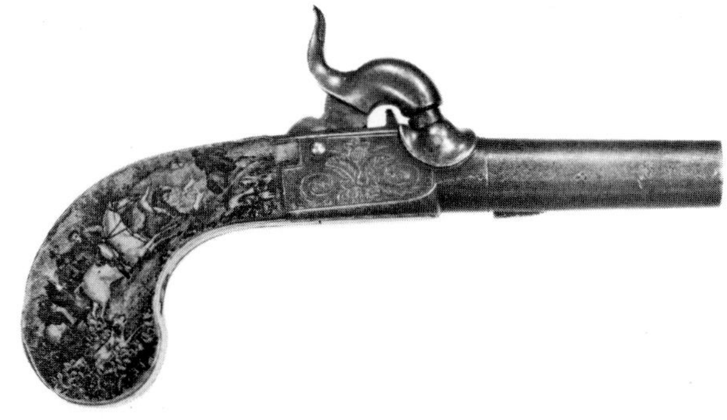

One of an attractive pair of Liège pocket pistols of similar form, the butts decorated with transfers of sporting prints. Fair quality and condition. Unsigned, Liège proof marks. Circa 1840. 6¼in. *Christie's*

£200 – £250 the pair

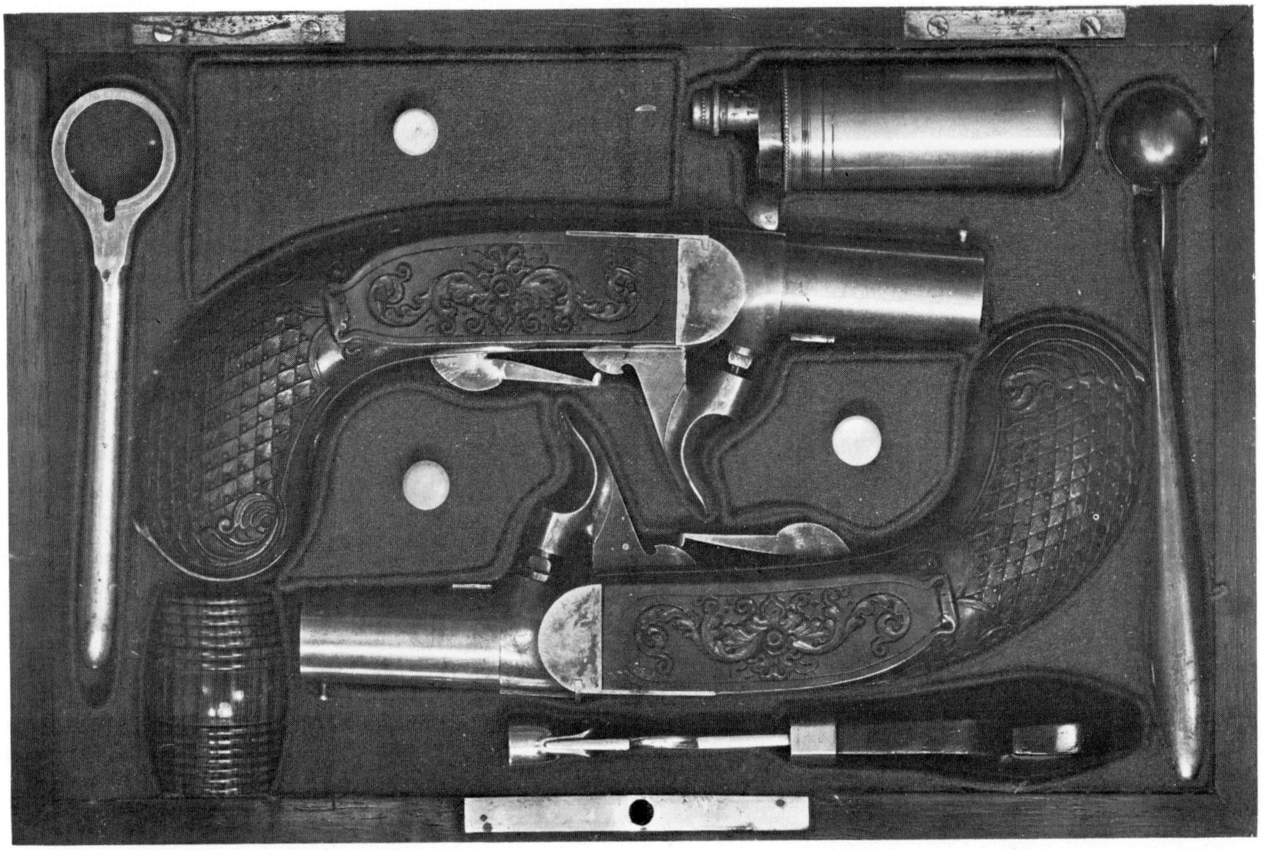

Pair of cased French percussion pocket pistols with multigroove rifled turn-off barrels, under-hammers and folding triggers also acting as safety-catches, finely carved butts with hinged butt-traps. Fine quality and excellent condition. Original mahogany case with full accessories and trade label. By Pirmet, 15 Allée D'Antin, Champs Elysées, Paris, circa 1840/50. 6¼in. *Christie's*

£800 – £1,000

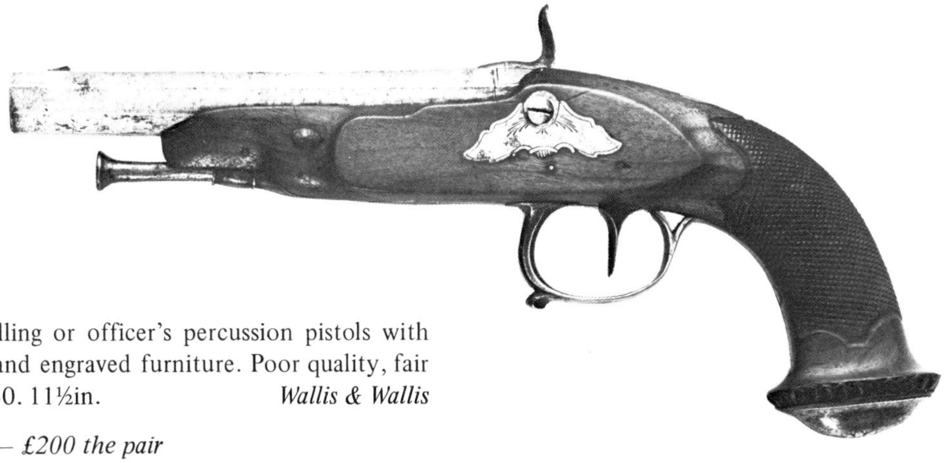

One of a pair of Liège travelling or officer's percussion pistols with octagonal barrels, half-stocks and engraved furniture. Poor quality, fair condition. Unsigned. Circa 1830. 11½in. *Wallis & Wallis*

£150 – £200 the pair

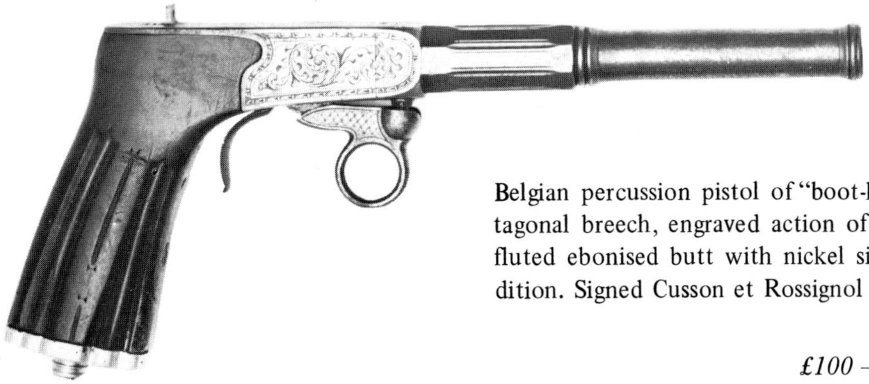

Belgian percussion pistol of "boot-leg" type, the barrel with fluted octagonal breech, engraved action of square section, ring under-hammer fluted ebonised butt with nickel silver butt-cap. Fair quality and condition. Signed Cusson et Rossignol Breveté, circa 1830. 11in.
Sotheby's

£100 – £140

Double-Barrelled Flintlock Pistols

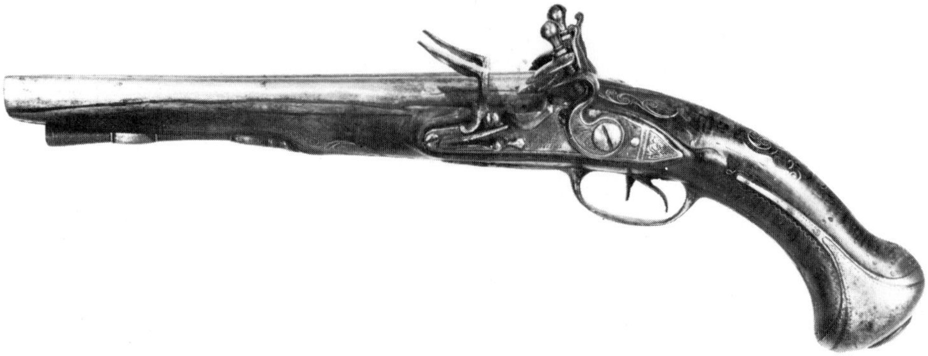

One of a pair of French officer's flintlock pistols with sighted barrels, engraved lock-plates, cocks and steels, lightly carved walnut full stocks retaining most of their silver wire inlay, steel furniture and spurred pommels. Good quality, but condition poor. By Joseph Lamotte, circa 1730/40. 16in. *Christie's*

£600 – £750 the pair, owing to the condition

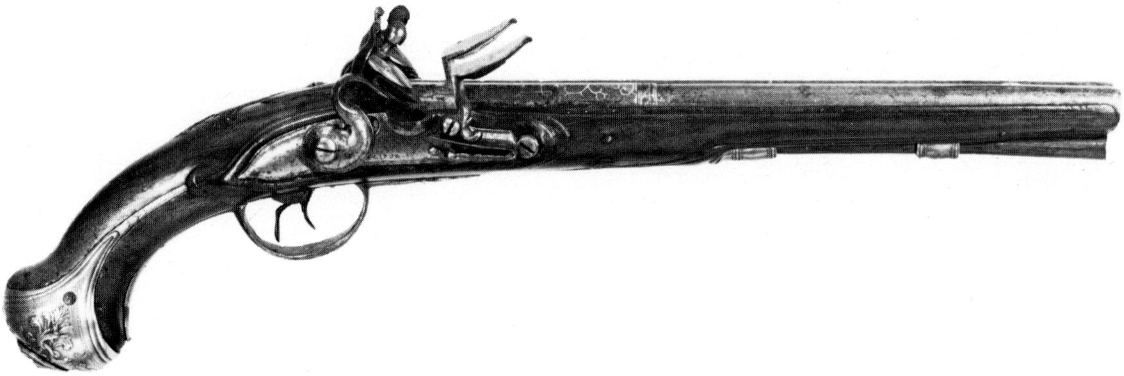

Liège flintlock pistol, the barrel octagonal at the breech and inlaid with silver scrolls, lightly carved full stock with brass furniture sparsely engraved, spurred pommel with grotesque mask cap. Moderate quality and condition. By Florkin, circa 1740. 19½in. *Christie's*

£500 – £600

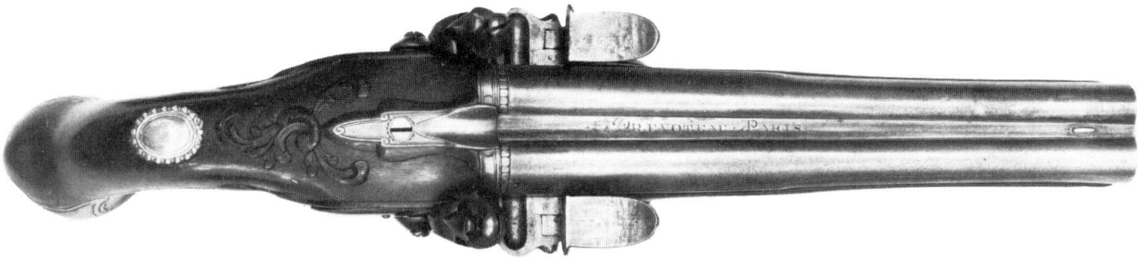

Cased pair of French flintlock travelling pistols with carved stocks and steel furniture including spurred pommels, silver escutcheons. Good quality and condition, but the barrels should be blued. Original case with some fittings. By Prevoteau à Paris, circa 1770/80. 15in. *Christie's*

Over £1,500

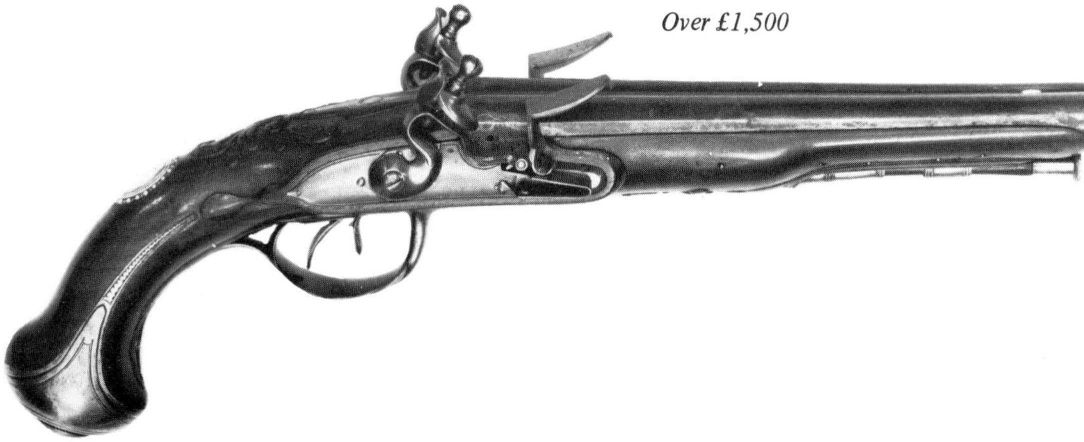

One of a pair of Liège all-steel flintlock pocket pistols of typical type, with trigger-guard safety-catches, double cocks, steels and triggers and foliate engraved swelling butts. Poor quality, good condition. Signed Seglas, London, late 18th century. 5¾in. *Christie's*

About £500 the pair

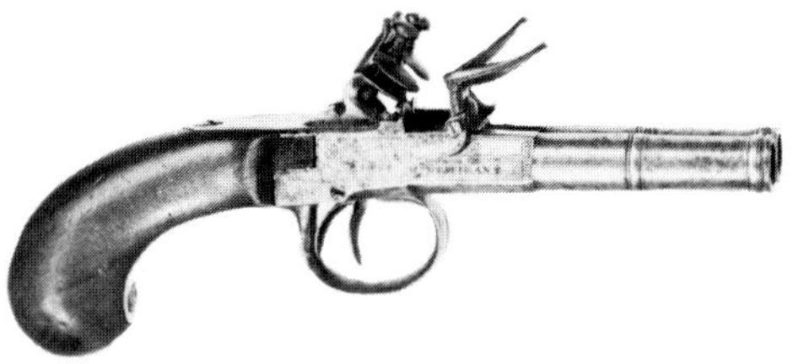

One of a pair of Liège pistols of similar form but with wooden butts. Poor quality, good condition. Signed H. Petitjean, Liège, late 18th century. 8½in. *Christie's*

About £400 the pair

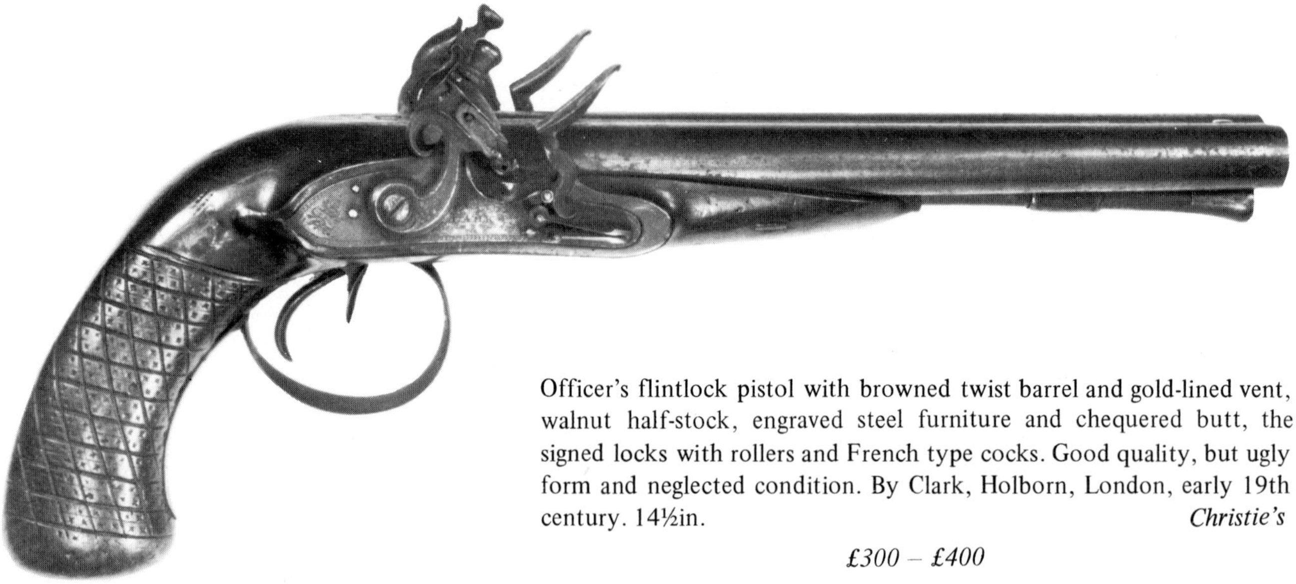

Officer's flintlock pistol with browned twist barrel and gold-lined vent, walnut half-stock, engraved steel furniture and chequered butt, the signed locks with rollers and French type cocks. Good quality, but ugly form and neglected condition. By Clark, Holborn, London, early 19th century. 14½in. *Christie's*

£300 – £400

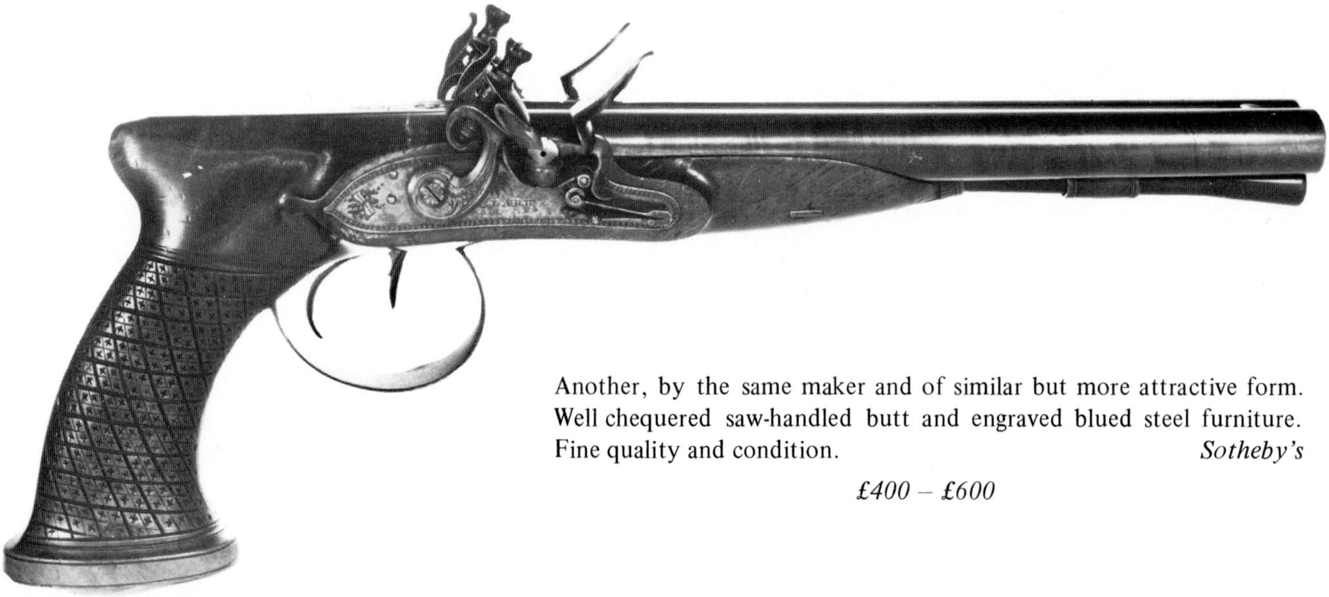

Another, by the same maker and of similar but more attractive form. Well chequered saw-handled butt and engraved blued steel furniture. Fine quality and condition. *Sotheby's*

£400 – £600

Pair of officer's pistols with signed barrels and locks, gold-lined vents and pans, safety-steels, walnut full stocks carved with a shell at the tang, silver mounts including escutcheons and spurred pommels. Very fine quality, fine condition despite one cracked butt. By Twigg, London, London silver hallmarks for 1773, maker's mark IK. 16½in. *Renwick Collection*

Over £4,000

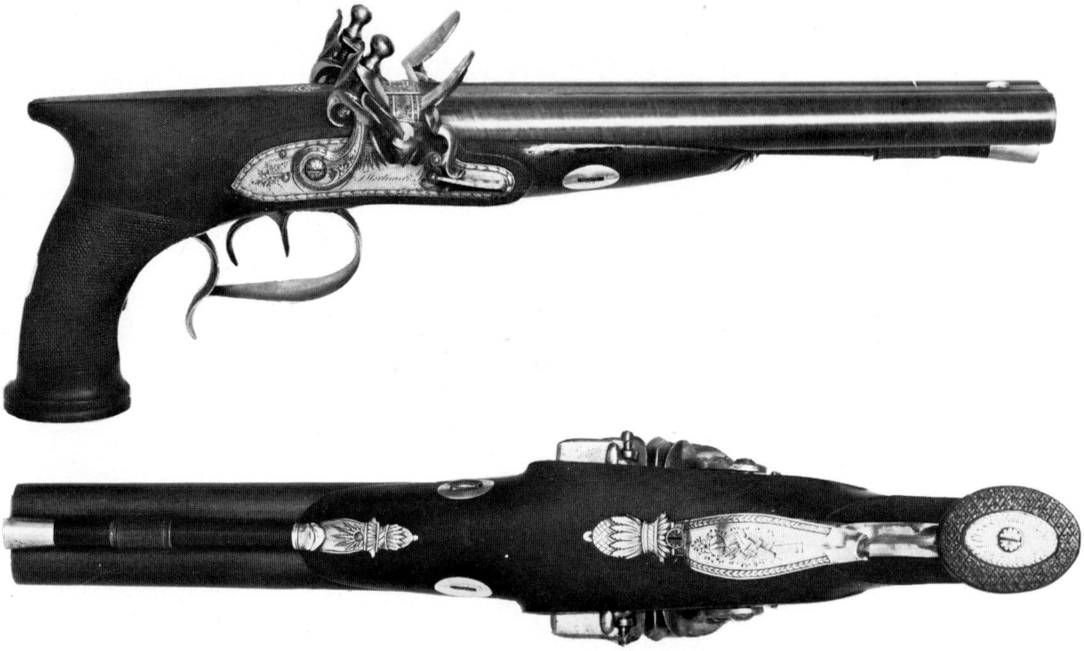

Pair of large saw-handled pistols, the barrels with gold lines and platinum vents, the engraved locks with rainproof pans, the stocks with engraved silver mounts. In original case (re-lined). Fine quality, but somewhat restored condition. By T. Mortimer & Son, Gunmaker to His Majesty, London, early 19th century. 15¾in.
Christie's

About £2,000 the pair

Dutch over-and-under flintlock holster pistol with barrels in three stages, signed locks, burr-walnut full stock and steel furniture including spurred pommel engraved with birds and with chiselled mask cap. Fine quality, fair condition. By T. Micharius, Breda, late 17th century. 19½in. *Sotheby's*

About £1,500

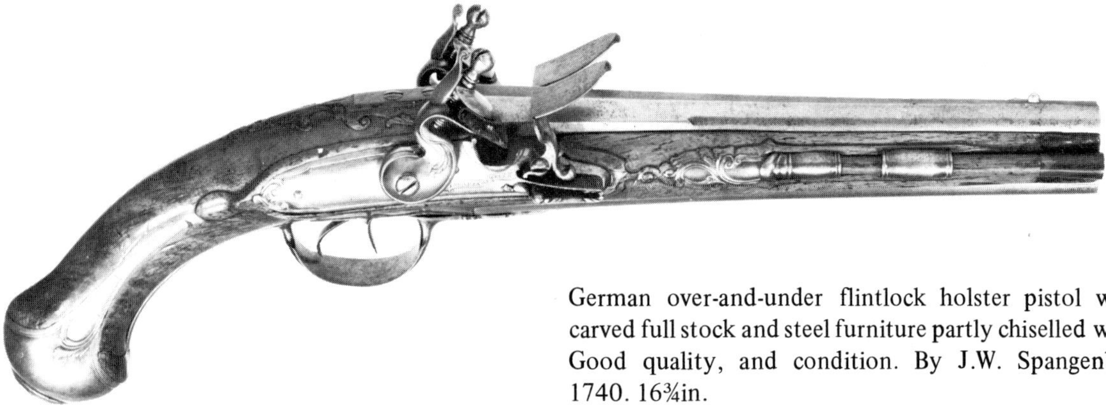

German over-and-under flintlock holster pistol with lightly carved full stock and steel furniture partly chiselled with foliage. Good quality, and condition. By J.W. Spangenburg, circa 1740. 16¾in. *Christie's*

£800 – £1,000

One of a pair of over-and-under flintlock holster pistols with signed barrels and locks, the latter with external actions, the butts carved with shell aprons at the tang, with silver escutcheons and silver spurred pommels and grotesque mask caps. Fine quality, fair condition, the mounts somewhat worn. By Griffin, Bond Street, London, circa 1750. 16½in. *Sotheby's*

About £2,000 the pair

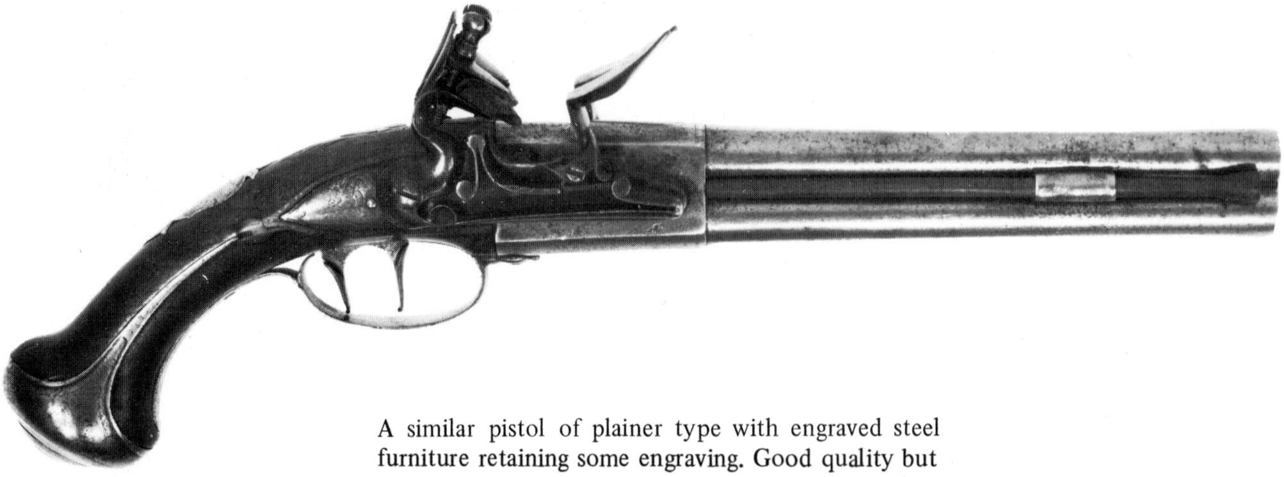

A similar pistol of plainer type with engraved steel furniture retaining some engraving. Good quality but poor condition. By Griffin, London, circa 1760. 16½in. *Christie's*

£300 – £400

Over-and-under flintlock pocket pistol with turn-off cannon barrels, chiselled cocks and steels mounted on either side of the barrels and silver butt finely chased with scrollwork on a matted ground. Fine quality, good condition, despite one restored cock. By Devillers, Liège, circa 1740. 5in. *Christie's*

Over £1,000

Over-and-under flintlock pistol with browned octagonal barrels signed in gold and with gold line and platinum vent, the locks with external actions and safety-catches, the pommel engraved Josh. Egg's Improvement. Complete with detachable skeleton carbine stock. Fine quality and condition. By Joseph Egg, No. 1, Piccadilly, London, circa 1820. The pistol 10½in. *Christie's*

Over £1,500

Over-and-under flintlock pistol with single trigger action, browned octagonal barrels with gold signatures and lines, fore-sight and vents, engraved locks with safety-catches, gold-lined pans, gold escutcheon and blued steel furniture. Fine quality and condition with much original finish. Ramrod replaced. By Durs Egg, London, early 19th century. 9in. *Christie's*

Over £1,000

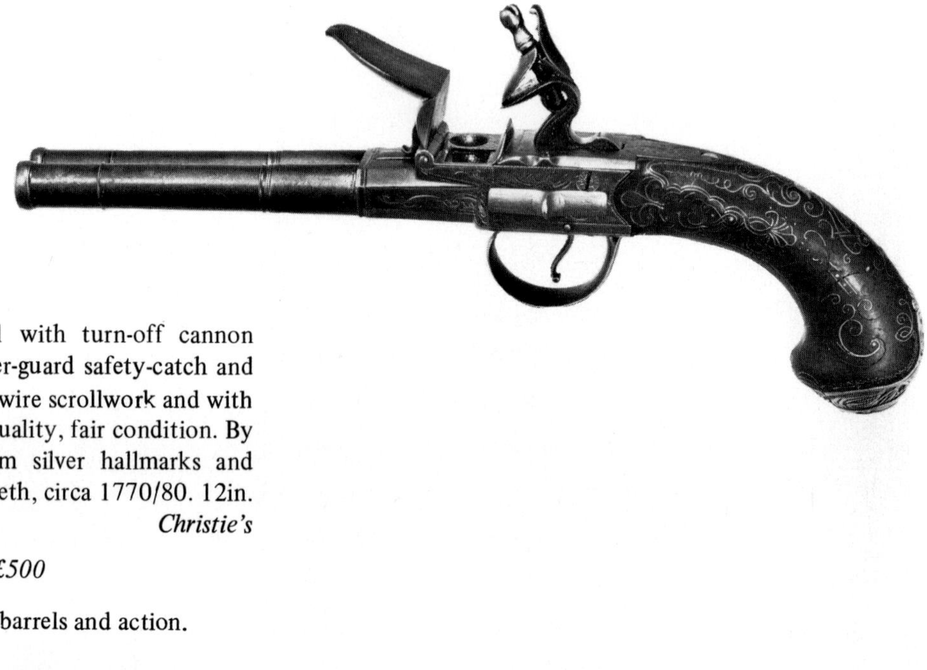

Side-by-side flintlock pistol with turn-off cannon barrels, sliding cut-off, trigger-guard safety-catch and walnut butt inlaid with silver wire scrollwork and with silver floral butt-cap. Good quality, fair condition. By Ketland & Co., Birmingham silver hallmarks and maker's mark of Charles Freeth, circa 1770/80. 12in. *Christie's*

£400 – £500

More for one with brass barrels and action.

Another, smaller, the butt inlaid with silver flowers and scrolls, with silver grotesque mask butt-cap. Good quality, fair condition. By Bunney, London, Birmingham silver hallmarks, circa 1780. 8¾in. *Christie's*

£500 – £600

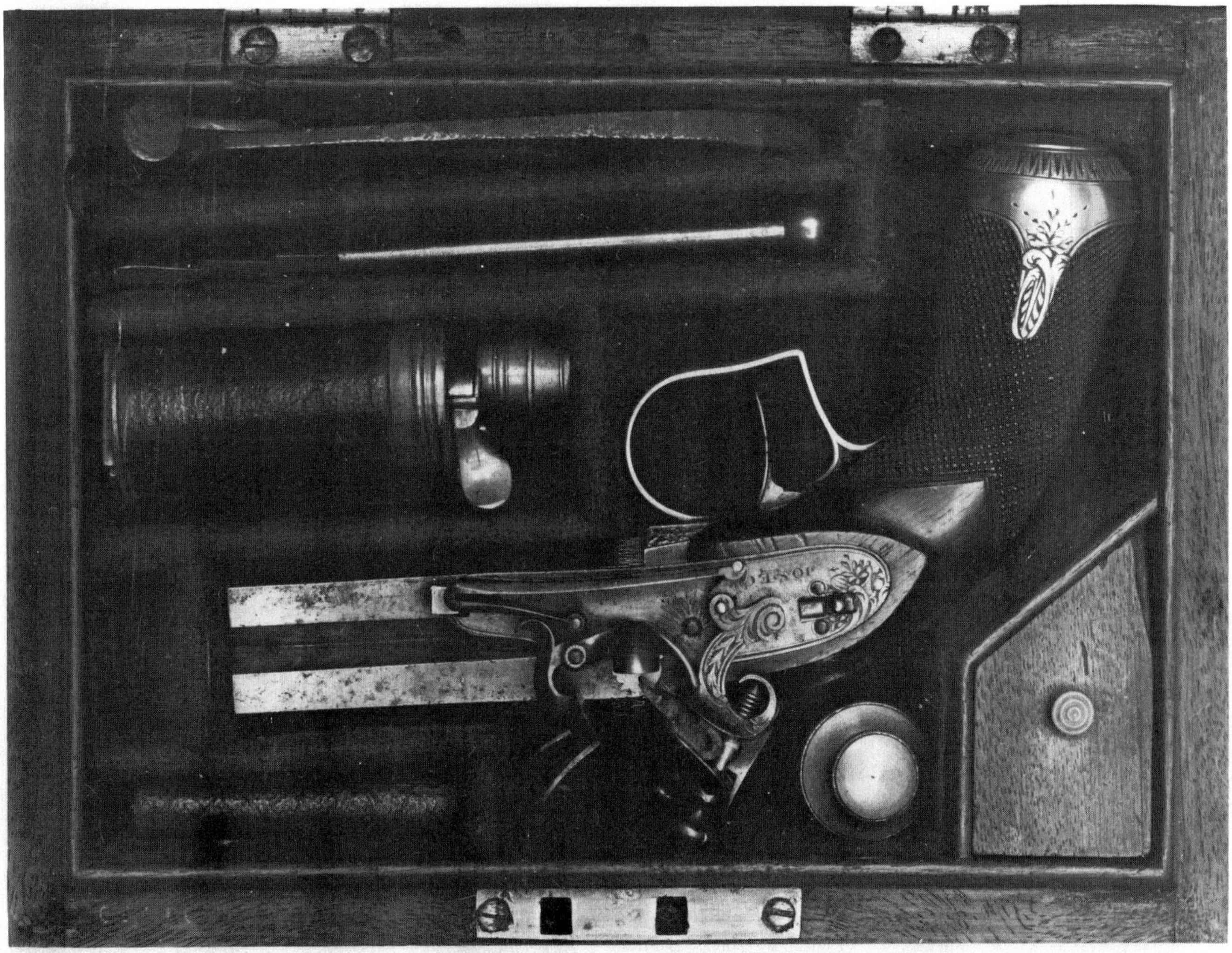

Over-and-under flintlock pocket pistol with blued octagonal barrels signed in gold, platinum line and vent, external actions with safety-catches, single trigger mechanism, the butt with engraved silver mounts, gold escutcheon and butt-cap. In original lined and fitted case with accessories. By Joseph Egg, No.1 Piccadilly, London, circa 1820-25. Fine quality and condition. 5½in. *Christie's*

Over £2,000

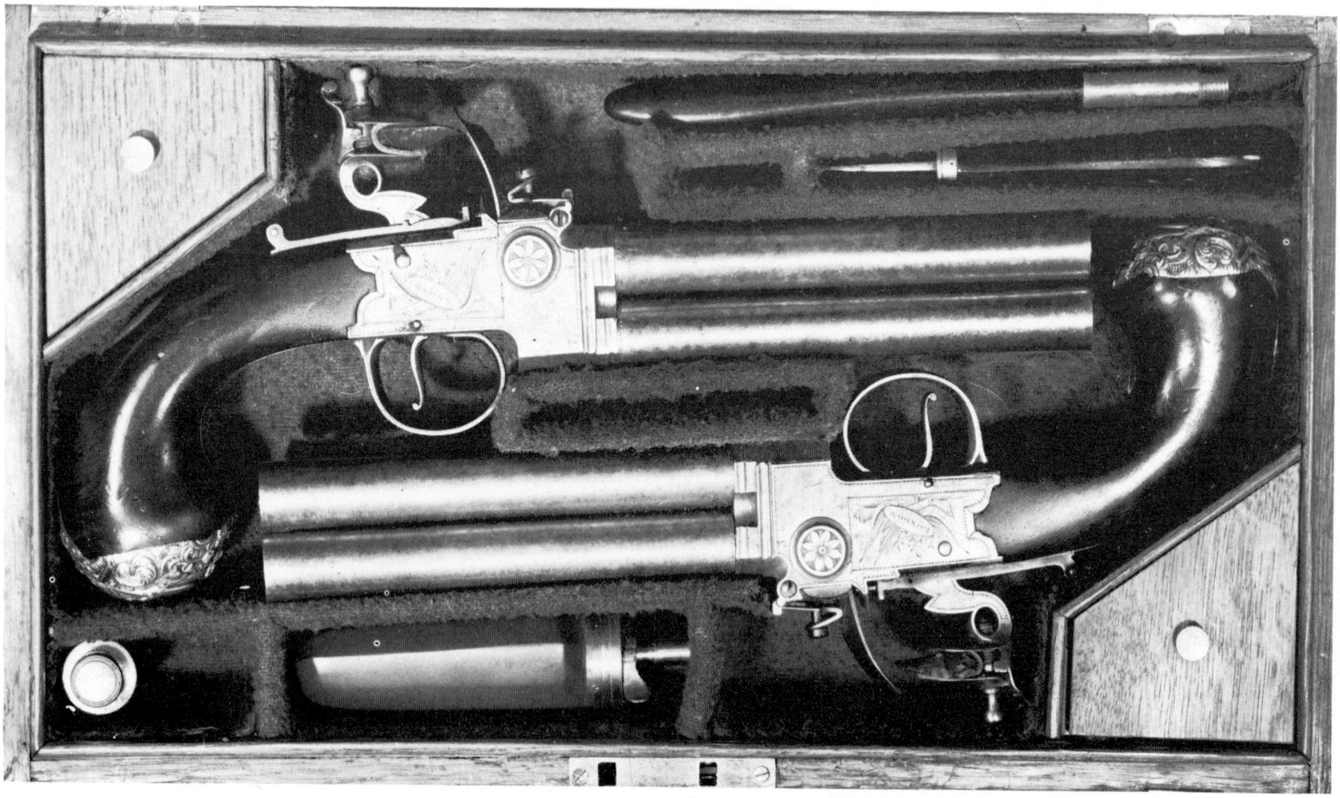

Cased pair of flintlock over-and-under tap-action pistols with long turn-off barrels, engraved actions signed within trophies of arms, swelling walnut butts with silver escutcheons and large silver butt-caps cast and chased with trophies of arms, flowers and foliage. In slightly later oak case with accessories and John Blanch label. By D. Goff, London, silver maker's mark of Moses Brent, late 18th century. Fine quality, good condition with minor restoration. 11¾in.
Christie's

Over £1,000

Flintlock over-and-under tap-action pistol with turn-off cannon barrels, engraved action, trigger-guard safety-catch, silver escutcheon and grotesque mask butt-cap. Good quality and condition. Signed Henshaw, Strand, London. Birmingham silver hallmark for 1776. 9in. *Christie's*

£400 – £500

Another, with plain turn-off barrels and swelling flat-sided butt, the action signed within pendant husks, Good quality, fair condition. Signed Ketland & Co. London, late 18th century, 8¼in.

£200 – £300

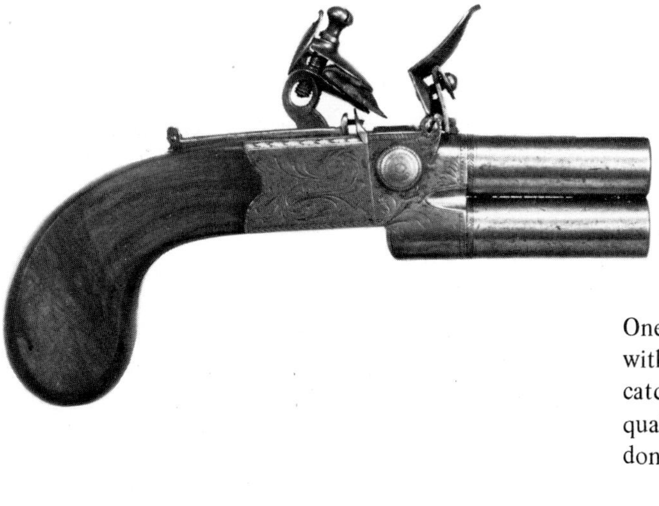

One of a pair of over-and-under tap-action pistols with foliate engraved actions, thumbpiece safety-catches, silver escutcheon and plain butts. Good quality and condition. Signed Joseph Manton, London. Early 19th century. 7in.

£500 – £650 the pair, mainly for the name.

Tap-action pistol with well engraved action, the butt decorated with silver wire inlay and an engraved silver plaque on either side. Fair quality, good condition. By Smith, London, late 18th century. 8½in. *Christie's*

£300 – £400

Side-by-side pistols with tap actions rather than sliding cut-offs (page 182) are rarer than the over-and-under variety, but beware of fakes made from single pistols. This one has steel barrels and engraved brass action and the butt is inlaid with silver wire (which may be a later addition). Fair quality only but good condition. Signed John Jones & Co. Late 18th century. 6½in. *Christie's*

About £300

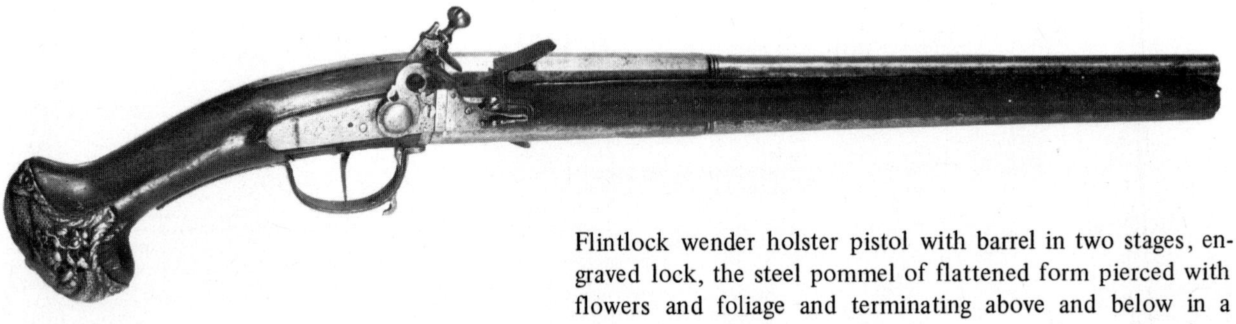

Flintlock wender holster pistol with barrel in two stages, engraved lock, the steel pommel of flattened form pierced with flowers and foliage and terminating above and below in a grotesque mask. Good quality, but poor condition. French or Dutch, circa 1660. 23in. *Christie's*

£600 – £800 even in this condition

This is a rare early type of which very fine examples exist.

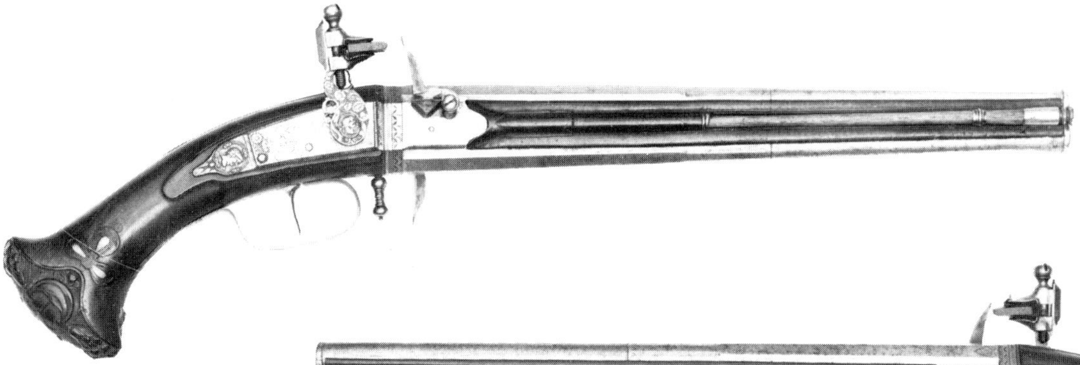

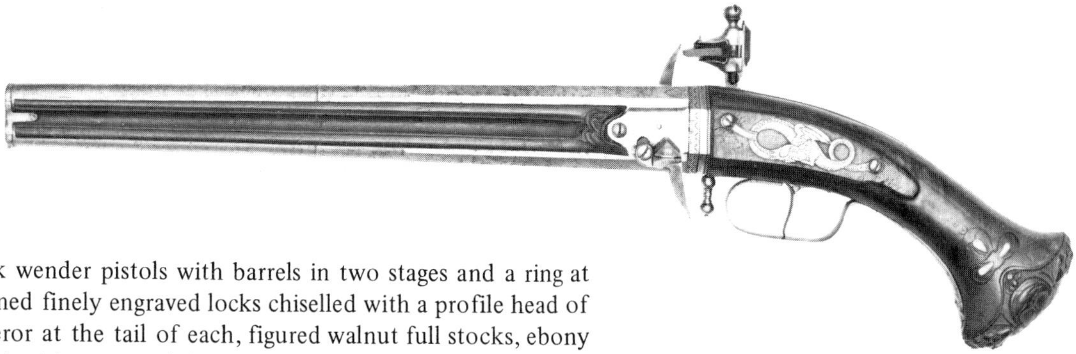

Pair of flintlock wender pistols with barrels in two stages and a ring at the muzzle, signed finely engraved locks chiselled with a profile head of a Roman Emperor at the tail of each, figured walnut full stocks, ebony butt-caps carved with swags of fruit, the butts inlaid with ebony and ivory. Very fine quality, fine condition although perhaps shortened. By J.S. Charlet à Lyon. circa 1660/70. 20½in. *Renwick Collection*

Over £6,000 the pair

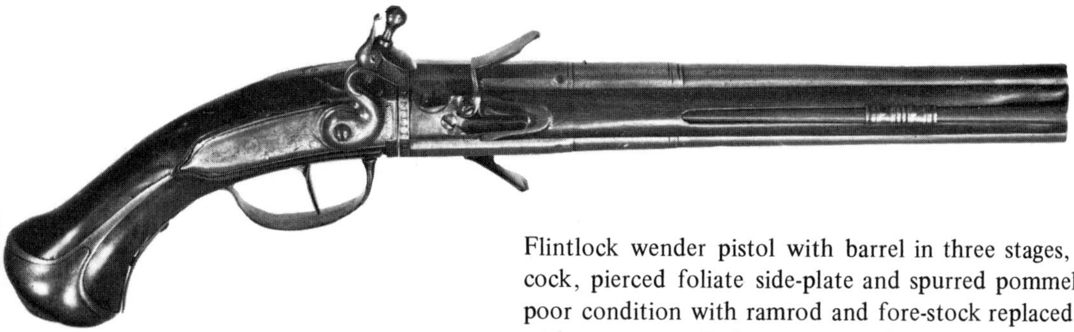

Flintlock wender pistol with barrel in three stages, engraved lock and cock, pierced foliate side-plate and spurred pommel. Fair quality, but poor condition with ramrod and fore-stock replaced, the lock engraved with a spurious Dolep signature. Probably Dutch, early 18th century. 18in. *Christie's*

£300 – £400

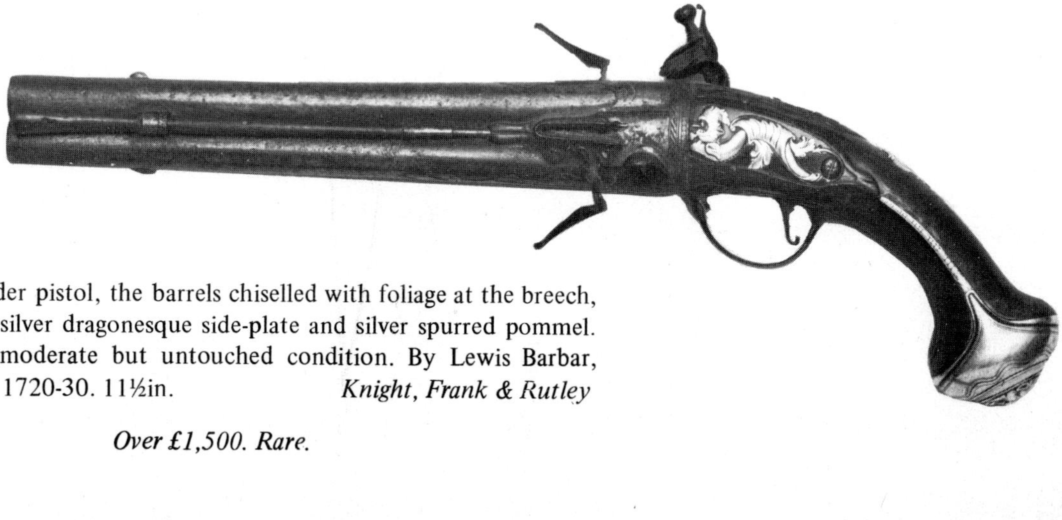

Flintlock wender pistol, the barrels chiselled with foliage at the breech, the butt with silver dragonesque side-plate and silver spurred pommel. Fine quality, moderate but untouched condition. By Lewis Barbar, London, circa 1720-30. 11½in. *Knight, Frank & Rutley*

Over £1,500. Rare.

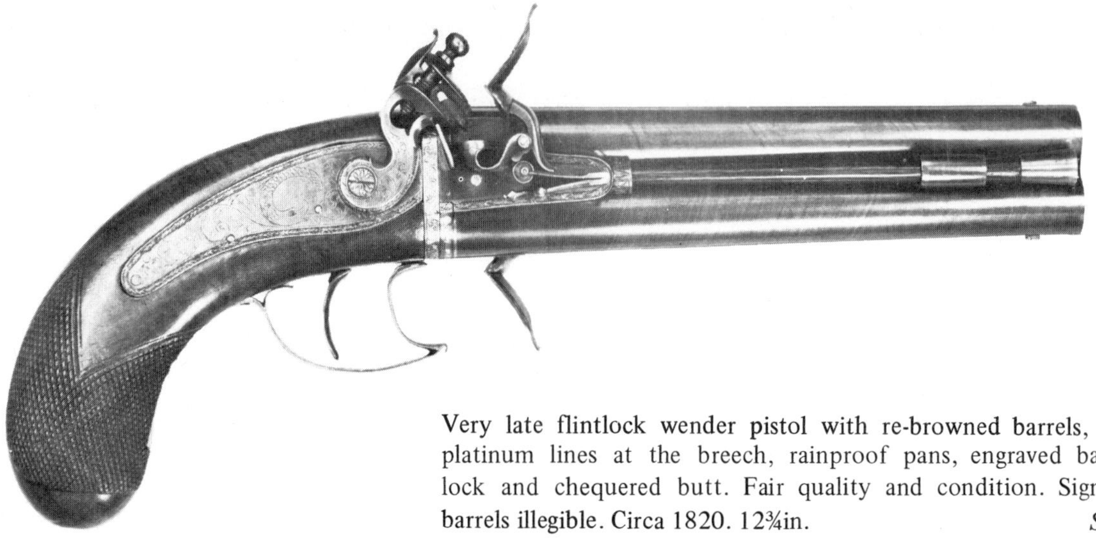

Very late flintlock wender pistol with re-browned barrels, gold and platinum lines at the breech, rainproof pans, engraved back-action lock and chequered butt. Fair quality and condition. Signature on barrels illegible. Circa 1820. 12¾in. *Sotheby's*

£600 – £800

An unusually late example of the flintlock wender system.

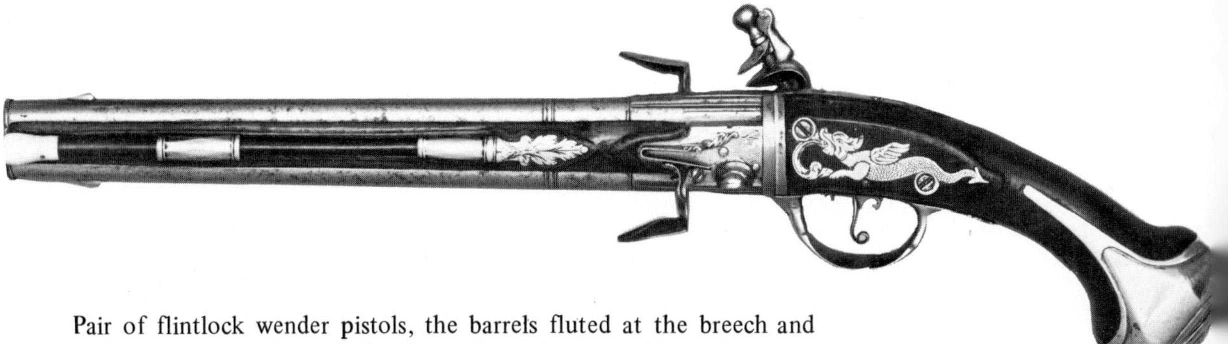

Pair of flintlock wender pistols, the barrels fluted at the breech and with brass ring to the muzzle, the stocks with engraved brass furniture, dragon side-plates and faceted spurred pommels. Good quality and condition, but slight restorations. Probably Dutch, late 17th century/ early 18th century. 18½in. *Christie's*

About £2,000

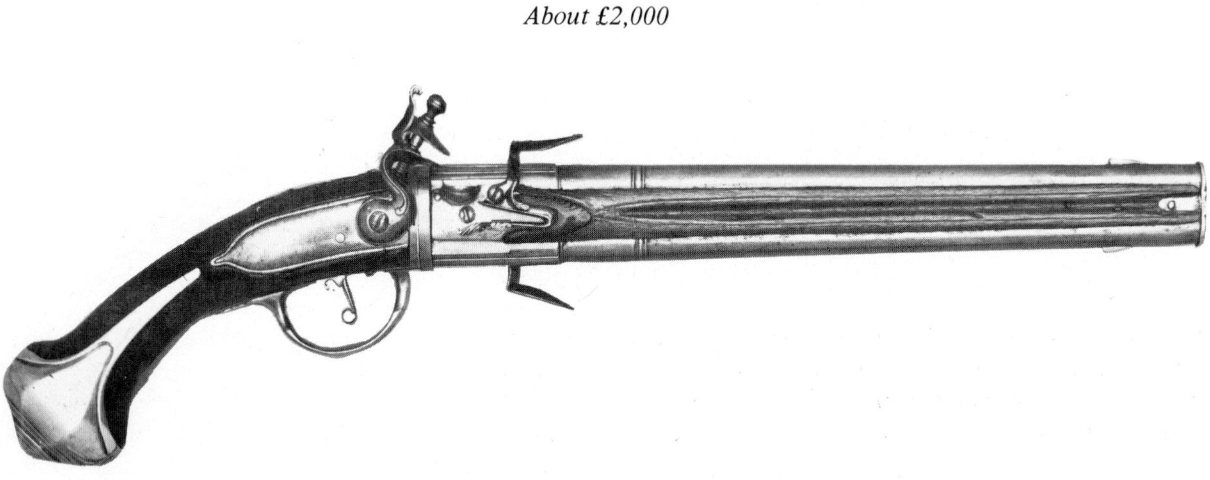

Flintlock Multishot, Revolving, Repeating and Breech-Loading Pistols

Three-barrel tap-action pocket pistol with steel barrels and action, plain butt and silver escutcheon. Fair quality, poor condition. Signed McBurnie, London. Early 19th century. 6¾in. *Christie's*

£250 – £300

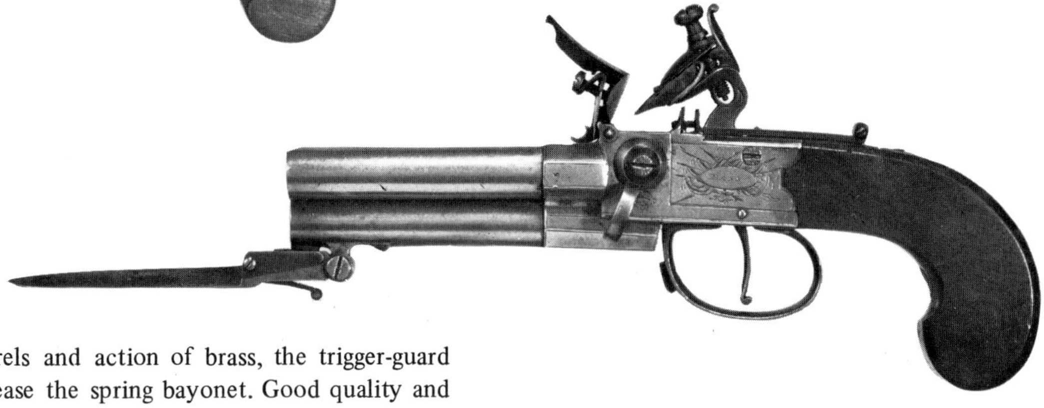

Another, with barrels and action of brass, the trigger-guard sliding back to release the spring bayonet. Good quality and condition. By Bass, London, late 18th century. 8½in. *Christie's*

£300 – £400

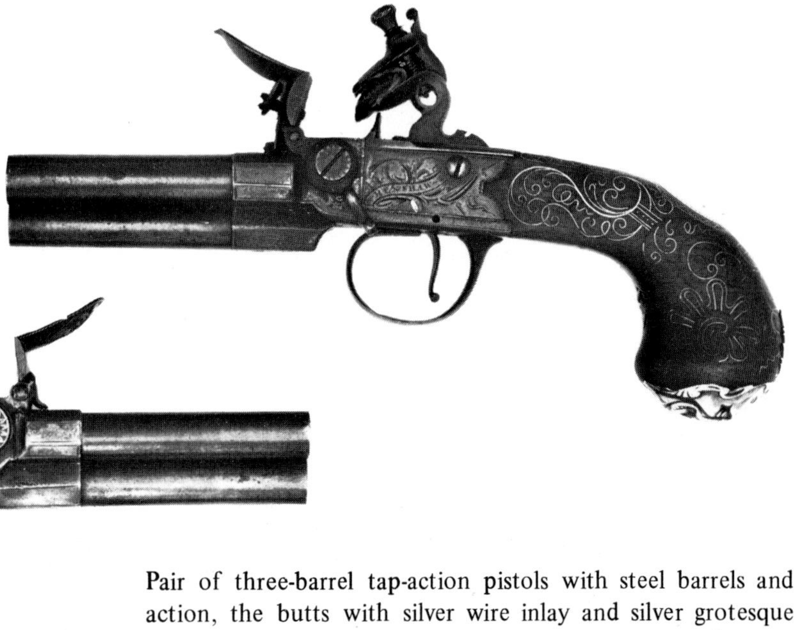

Pair of three-barrel tap-action pistols with steel barrels and action, the butts with silver wire inlay and silver grotesque mask caps. Good quality but some parts missing, others replaced. Signed Henshaw, Cambridge, Tower proof marks, Birmingham silver hallmarks for 1783. 9in. *Sotheby's*

£800 – £1,000 the pair

Three-barrel tap-action pocket pistol with barrels in vertical row numbered 4, 5 and 6, engraved box-lock action signed within a trophy of arms on each side, thumbpiece safety-catch, folding trigger, chequered butt and silver escutcheon. Fine quality, good condition. By Prosser, Charing Cross, London, early 19th century, 5¾in.
Weller & Dufty

Pistol made £900 in 1970.
Genuine examples are extremely rare.

Four-barrel tap-action pistol with steel barrels and action, the latter well engraved with trophies, sliding cut-off on the right side, plain butt, thumbpiece safety-catch and silver escutcheon. Good quality and condition. Signed Catchpool, Dover. London proof marks, early 19th century. *Christie's*

About £500

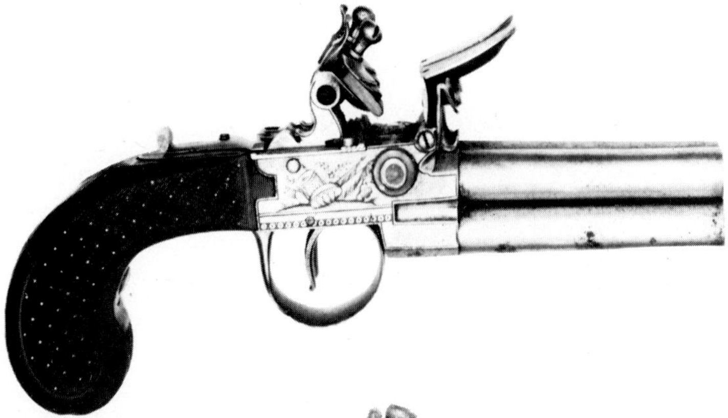

The Belgian four-barrel tap-action pistol of this type is worth about half as much.
Sotheby's

Another, the barrels and actions of brass, the latter finely engraved with trophies, trigger-guard safety-catch, walnut butt, engraved silver escutcheon and chased silver butt-cap. Fine quality, but grip loose and steel missing. By Perry, London, London silver hallmarks for 1782. *Christie's*

£600 – £700, even with defects

Brass examples are popular.

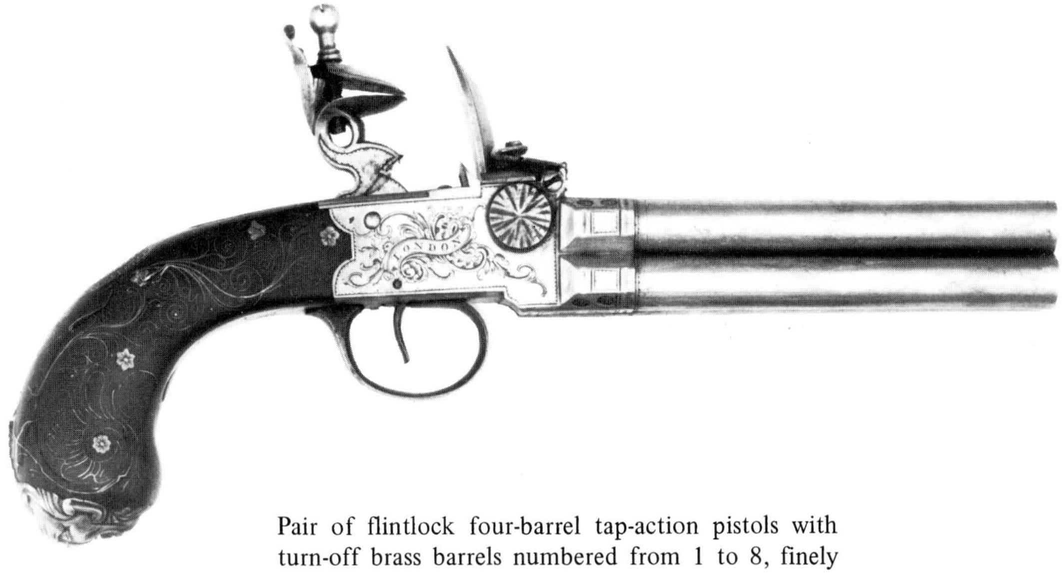

Pair of flintlock four-barrel tap-action pistols with turn-off brass barrels numbered from 1 to 8, finely engraved brass actions, walnut butts with silver wire inlay terminating in flowerheads, silver escutcheons and silver grotesque mask caps. Very fine quality and condition. By Barbar, London, London private proof marks, silver maker's mark of Charles Freeth, circa 1770/80. 11½in. *Renwick Collection*

Over £2,000 the pair

Belgian all-steel four-barrel wender pistol with turn-off cannon barrels, each with its own steel and pan, the action engraved with a trophy on either side, the swelling butt with flowers and scalework. Poor but typical quality. Fair condition. Liège, late 18th century. 6½in.

£400 – £500

Like the single and double-barrel all-steel Liège pistols (see pages 106 and 175) these often bear spurious London (Segalas) signatures.

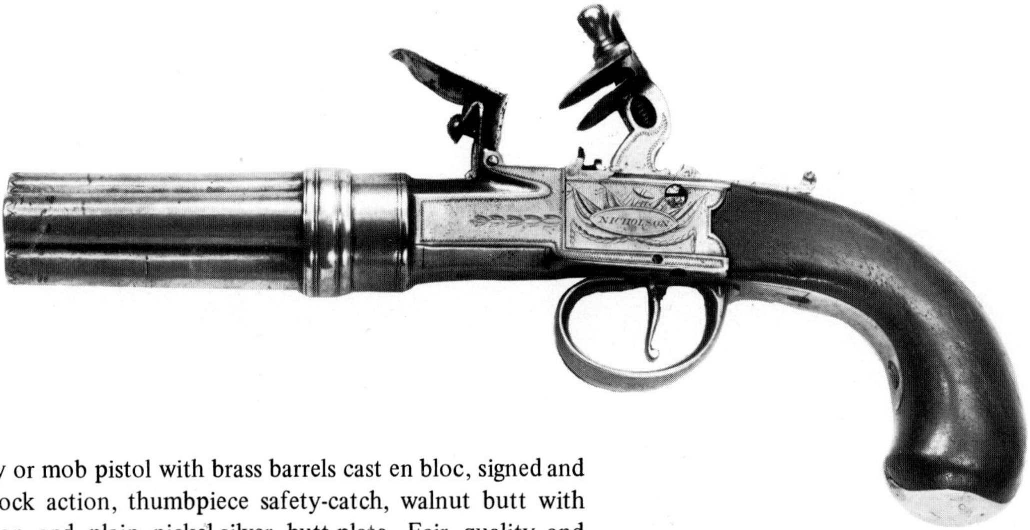

Flintlock volley or mob pistol with brass barrels cast en bloc, signed and engraved box-lock action, thumbpiece safety-catch, walnut butt with silver escutcheon and plain nickel-silver butt-plate. Fair quality and condition. By Nicholson, No. 75 Cornhill, London, circa 1800. 11in.

Sotheby's

£500 – £750

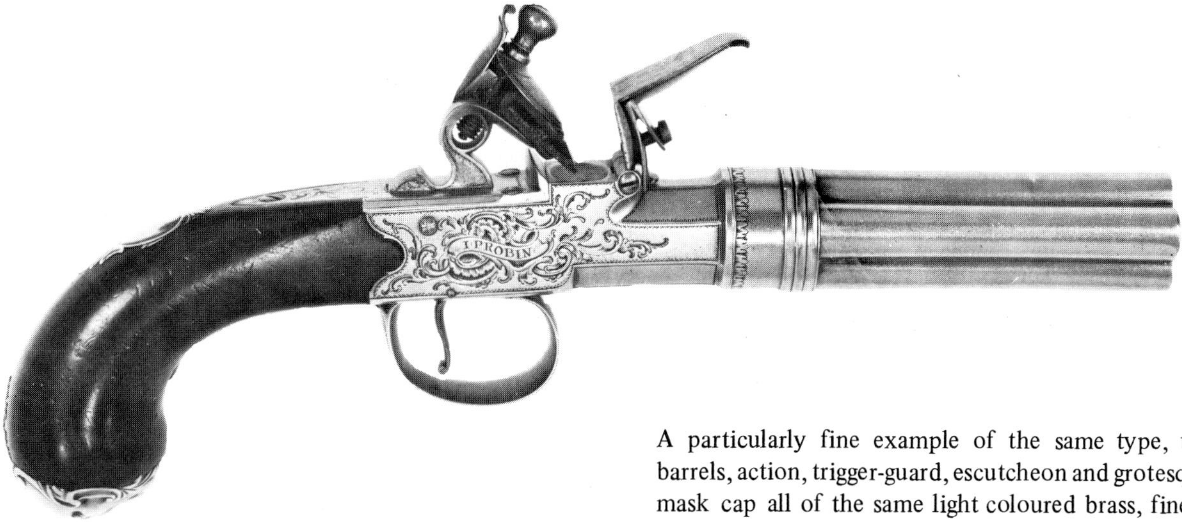

A particularly fine example of the same type, the barrels, action, trigger-guard, escutcheon and grotesque mask cap all of the same light coloured brass, finely engraved with rococo scrolls and foliage. By Probin, London, circa 1770/80. 11¾in. *Christie's*

Over £1,000

"Duck's foot" pistol with four splayed steel barrels, the brass action signed and engraved, chequered butt. Good quality, fair condition with cock repaired and safety-catch missing. Signed G. Goodwin & Co., London. Early 19th century. *Sotheby's*

Over £1,000

Genuine examples of these pistols are extremely rare and several fakes have been on the market recently, including a pair with five barrels, and a pocket-sized example of the type illustrated.

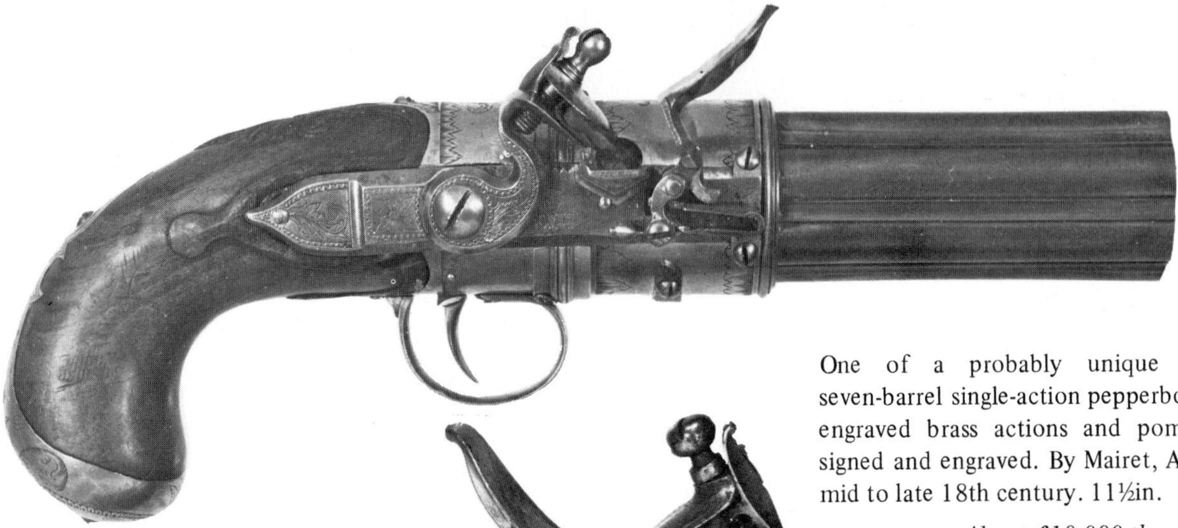

One of a probably unique pair of Swiss seven-barrel single-action pepperbox revolvers with engraved brass actions and pommels, the locks signed and engraved. By Mairet, Artiste aux Ponts, mid to late 18th century. 11½in. *Christie's*

About £10,000 the pair

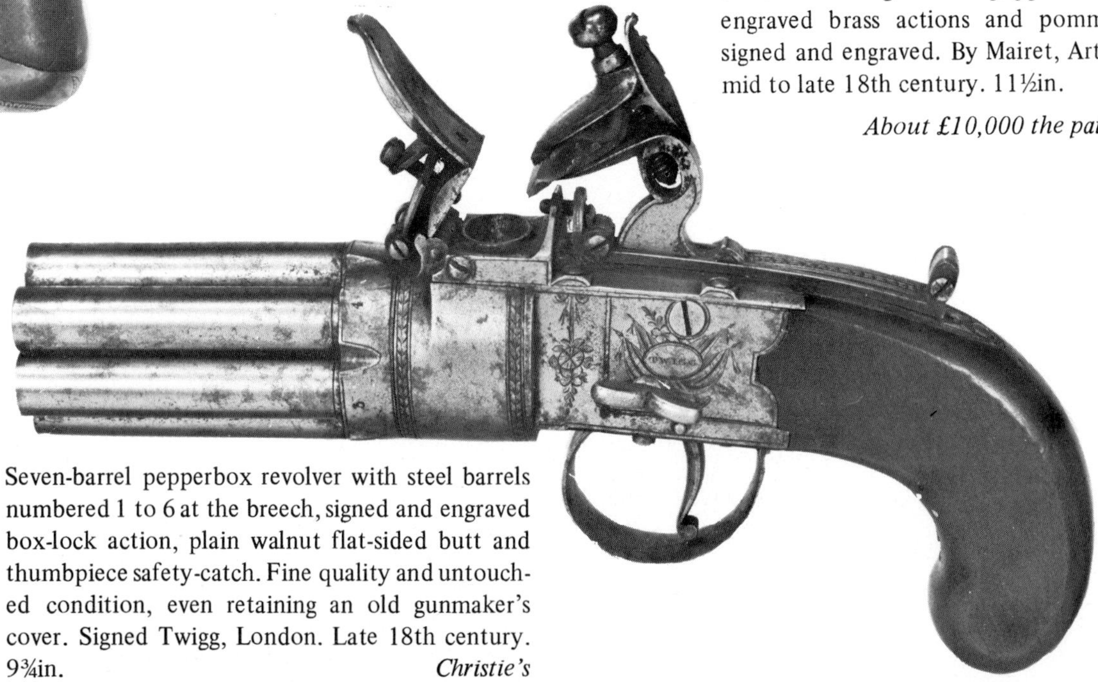

Seven-barrel pepperbox revolver with steel barrels numbered 1 to 6 at the breech, signed and engraved box-lock action, plain walnut flat-sided butt and thumbpiece safety-catch. Fine quality and untouched condition, even retaining an old gunmaker's cover. Signed Twigg, London. Late 18th century. 9¾in. *Christie's*

About £3,000, mainly on condition.

Most examples of this rare type which come on the market are in poor or refinished condition.

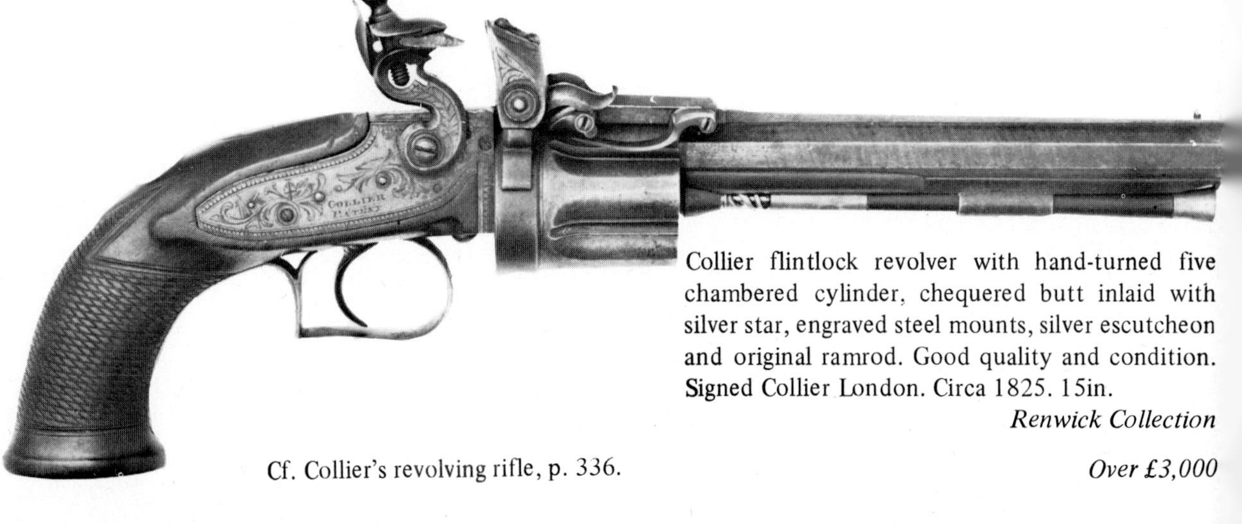

Collier flintlock revolver with hand-turned five chambered cylinder, chequered butt inlaid with silver star, engraved steel mounts, silver escutcheon and original ramrod. Good quality and condition. Signed Collier London. Circa 1825. 15in. *Renwick Collection*

Cf. Collier's revolving rifle, p. 336.

Over £3,000

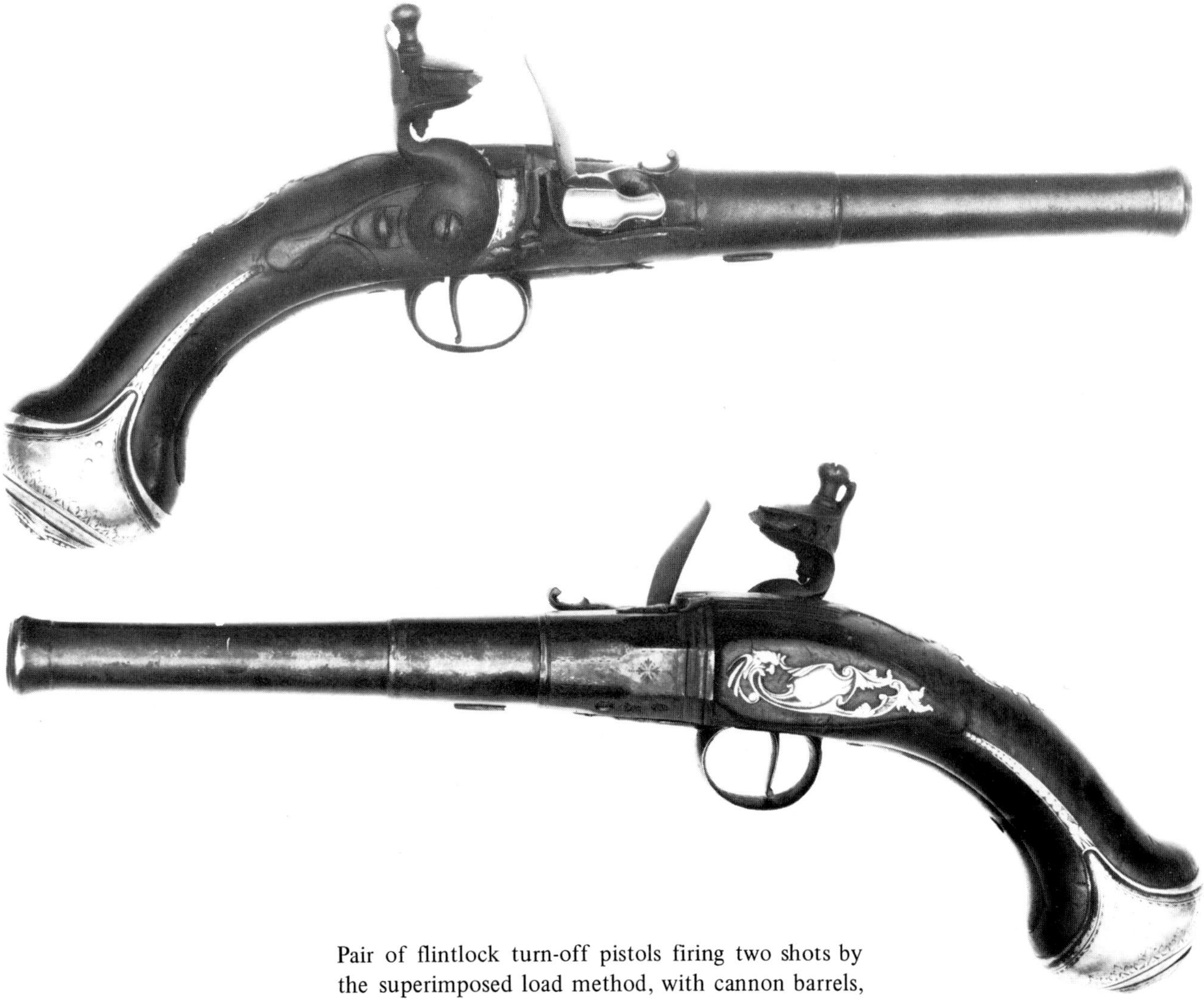

Pair of flintlock turn-off pistols firing two shots by the superimposed load method, with cannon barrels, the locks fitted with silver cut-offs to allow operation of the forward and rear vents, the walnut butts with silver mounts including spurred pommels, the caps decorated with a head of Mars. Fine quality, moderate condition. By James Freeman. Circa 1730. 14½in.

Renwick Collection

Over £2,000 the pair

Breech-loading repeating magazine pistol on the Lorenzoni system with turn-off cannon barrel, the action, lock, and cock chiselled with scallop shells, trophies and foliage on a gilt ground, the butt finely inlaid with silver decoration including putti, silver spurred pommel engraved with trophies of arms. Very fine quality, condition only fair. Signed Barbar, London. Circa 1760/70. 13¾in. *Sotheby's*

Over £4,000

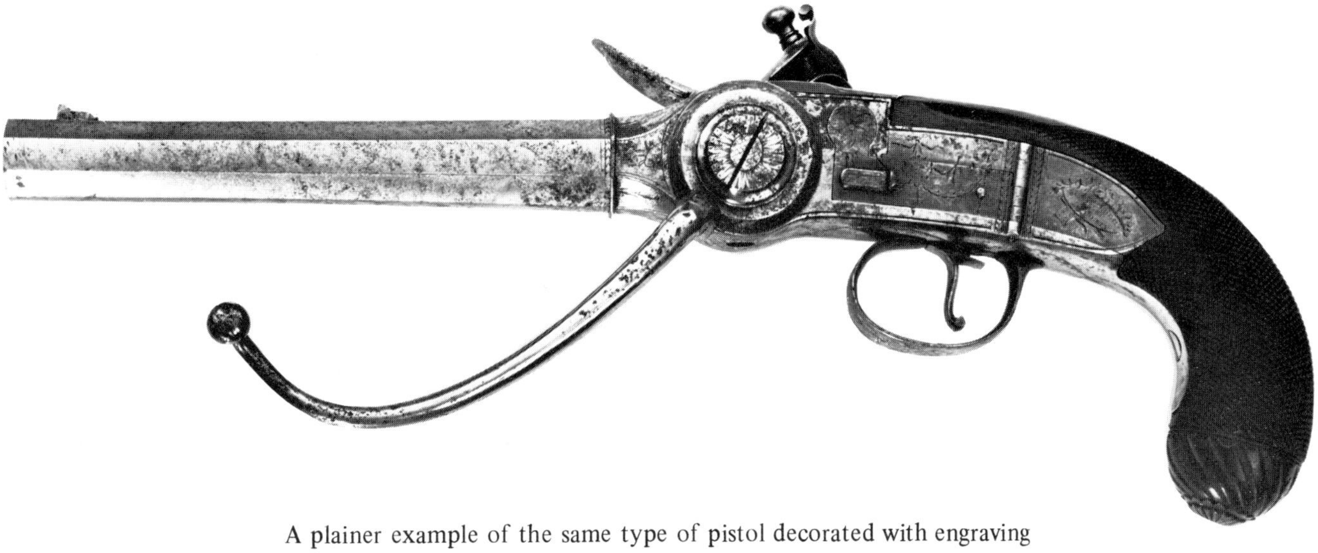

A plainer example of the same type of pistol decorated with engraving and signed on the lock, chequered butt with spirally fluted pommel. Fine quality, but only fair condition with some pitting. By H.W. Mortimer, London, late 18th century, 15½in. *Wallis & Wallis*

About £2,000

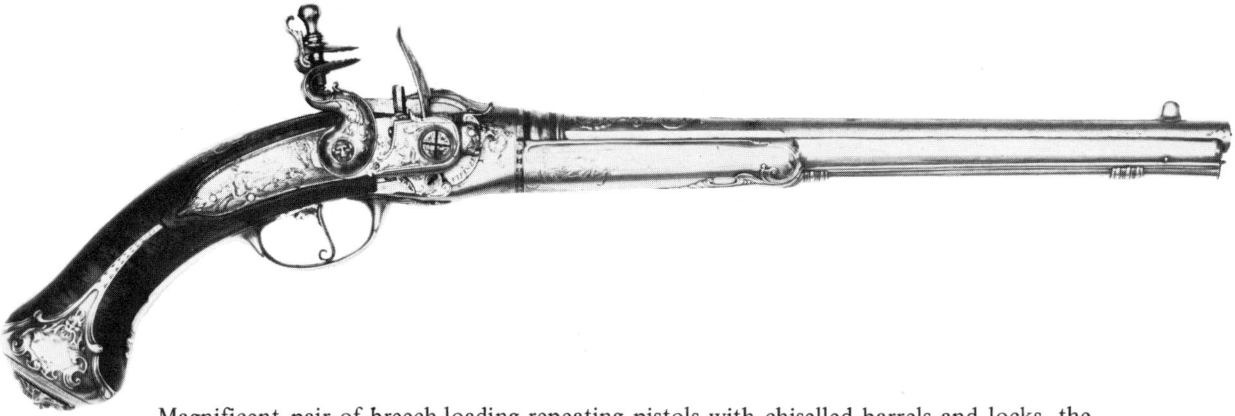

Magnificent pair of breech-loading repeating pistols with chiselled barrels and locks, the latter finely engraved with battle scenes, the butts of figured root walnut inlaid around the tang with silver wire, silver mounts and fore-stocks, foliate side-plates and spurred pommels cast and chased with cartouches and terminating in mask caps. Exceptional quality and condition. By Michele Lorenzoni of Florence, early 18th century. The silver signed Cocchi. 20in.

Renwick Collection

Over £40,000 the pair

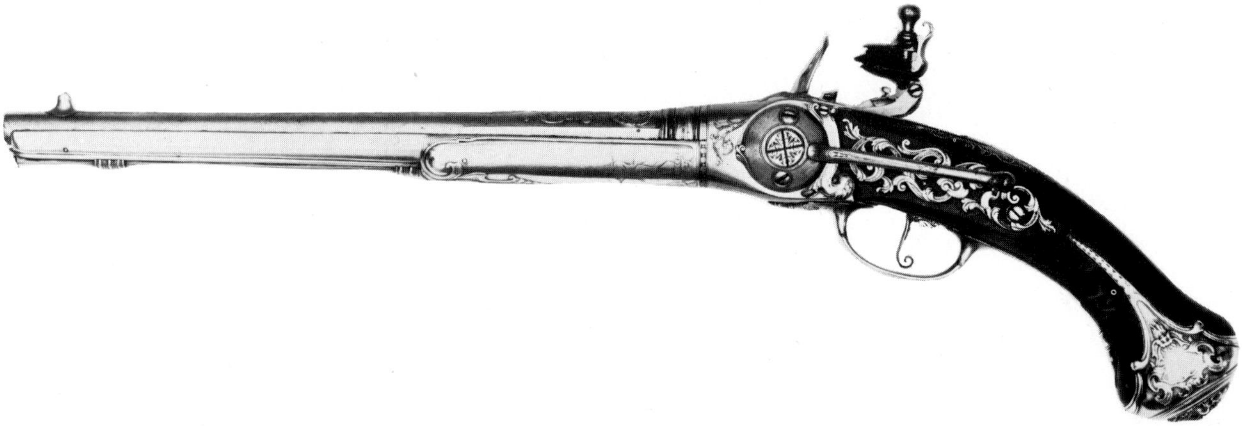

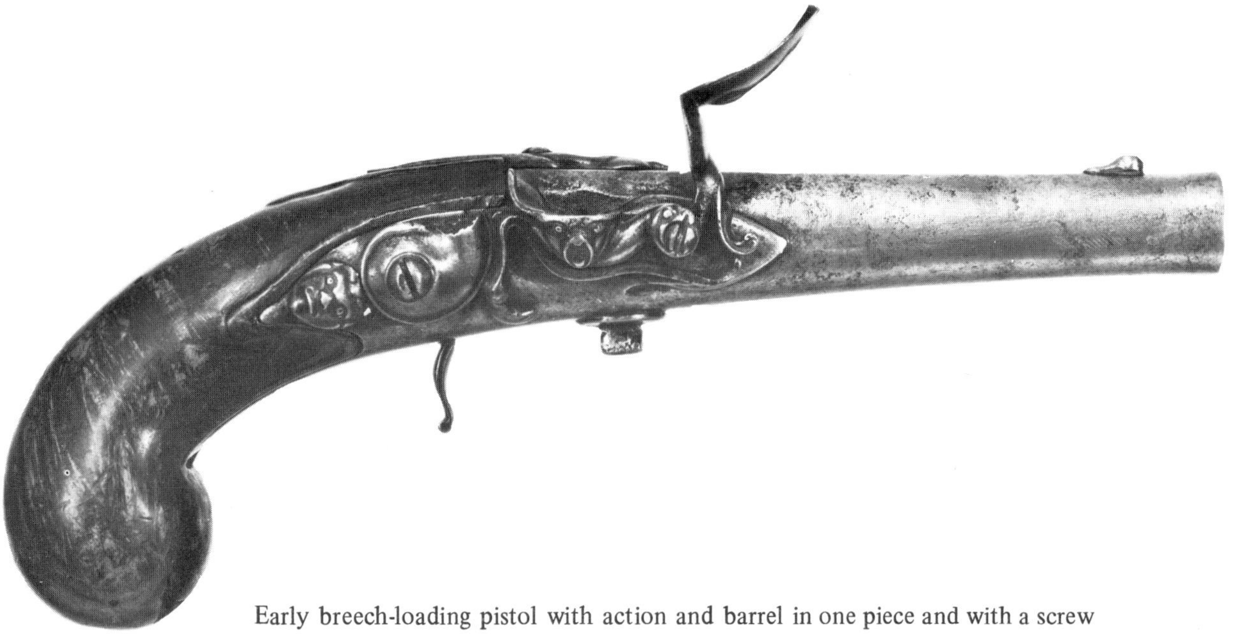

Early breech-loading pistol with action and barrel in one piece and with a screw plug in the base permitting loading from beneath, the lock decorated with male masks chiselled in relief, the burr-wood butt retained by a single screw in the barrel tang. Fine quality, moderate condition with top half of cock missing. Unsigned, probably English, late 17th century, 9½in. *Christie's*

Over £1,000. Extremely rare.

Breech-loading pistol of "Queen Anne" type with cannon barrel in three stages engraved with foliage at the breech, the trigger-guard with screw plug in front allowing loading from beneath, the walnut butt with silver grotesque mask cap and silver escutcheon. Fine quality, untouched but poor condition with several parts missing. By R. Rowland, London, early 18th century. *Sotheby's*

£800 – £1,000 owing to condition.

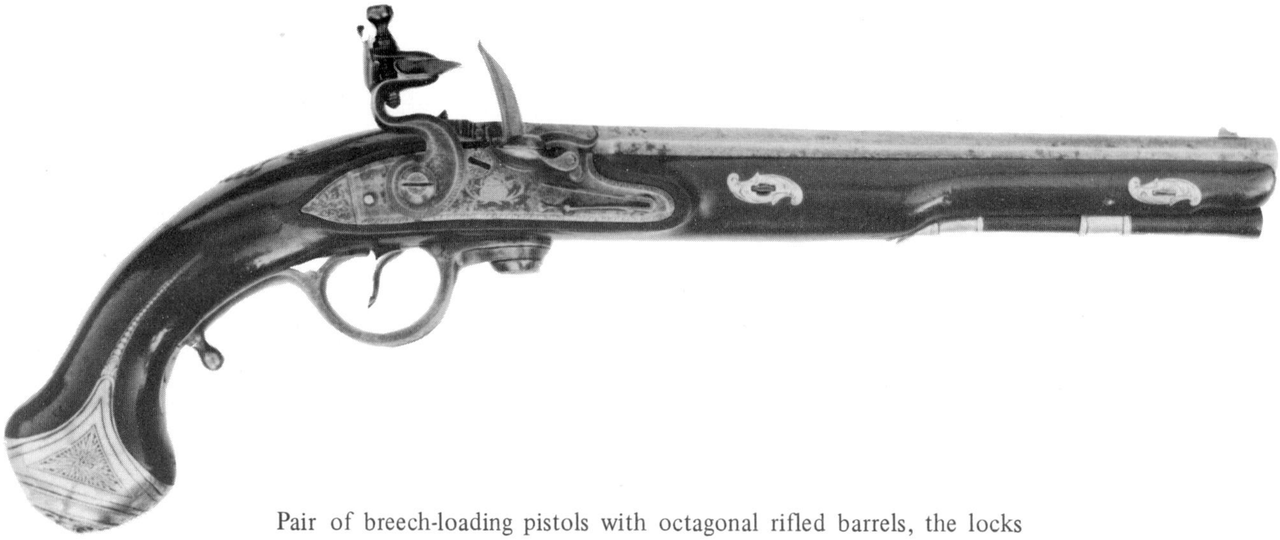

Pair of breech-loading pistols with octagonal rifled barrels, the locks signed within a gold oval and fitted with rollers, the trigger-guards constructed to unscrew allowing loading from the top. Engraved silver mounts including pommels with grotesque mask caps, and engraved silver escutcheons. Fine quality, good condition but one cock repaired. By Jover, London, circa 1780. 15in.

Over £8,000. Extremely rare.

Double-Barrelled Percussion Cap Pistols

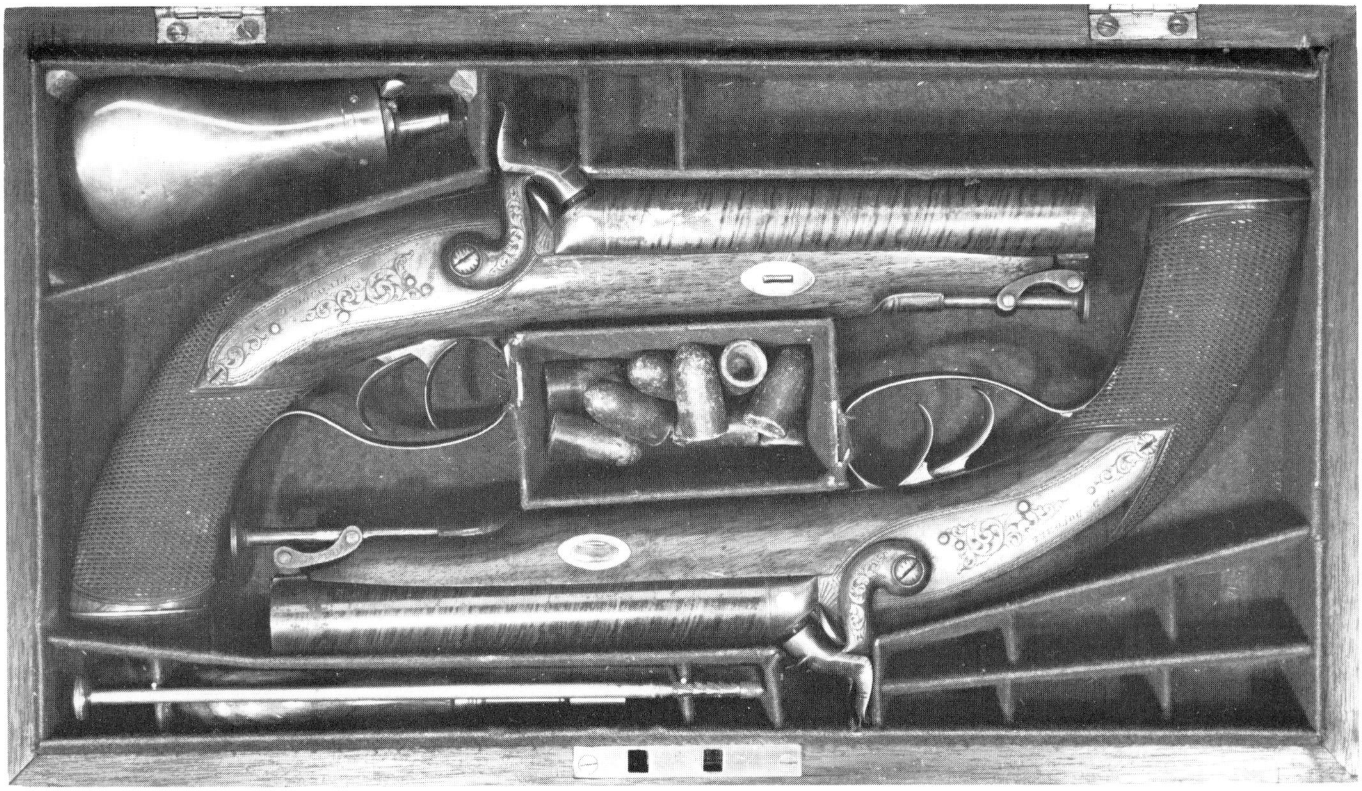

Cased pair of double-barrelled officer's or travelling pistols with browned barrels, platinum plugs, engraved back-action locks and steel furniture, chequered butts with butt-traps. Original case. Good quality and condition. By J.D. Dougall, Glasgow, circa 1840. 12¼in. *Christie's*

£600 – £700

Cased pair of double-barrelled pistols converted from flintlock, with browned twist barrels, platinum plugs, engraved bolted locks and walnut half-stocks with flat-sided chequered butts. Good quality and condition, the case associated. Signed Beckwith, London. *Christie's*

About £500

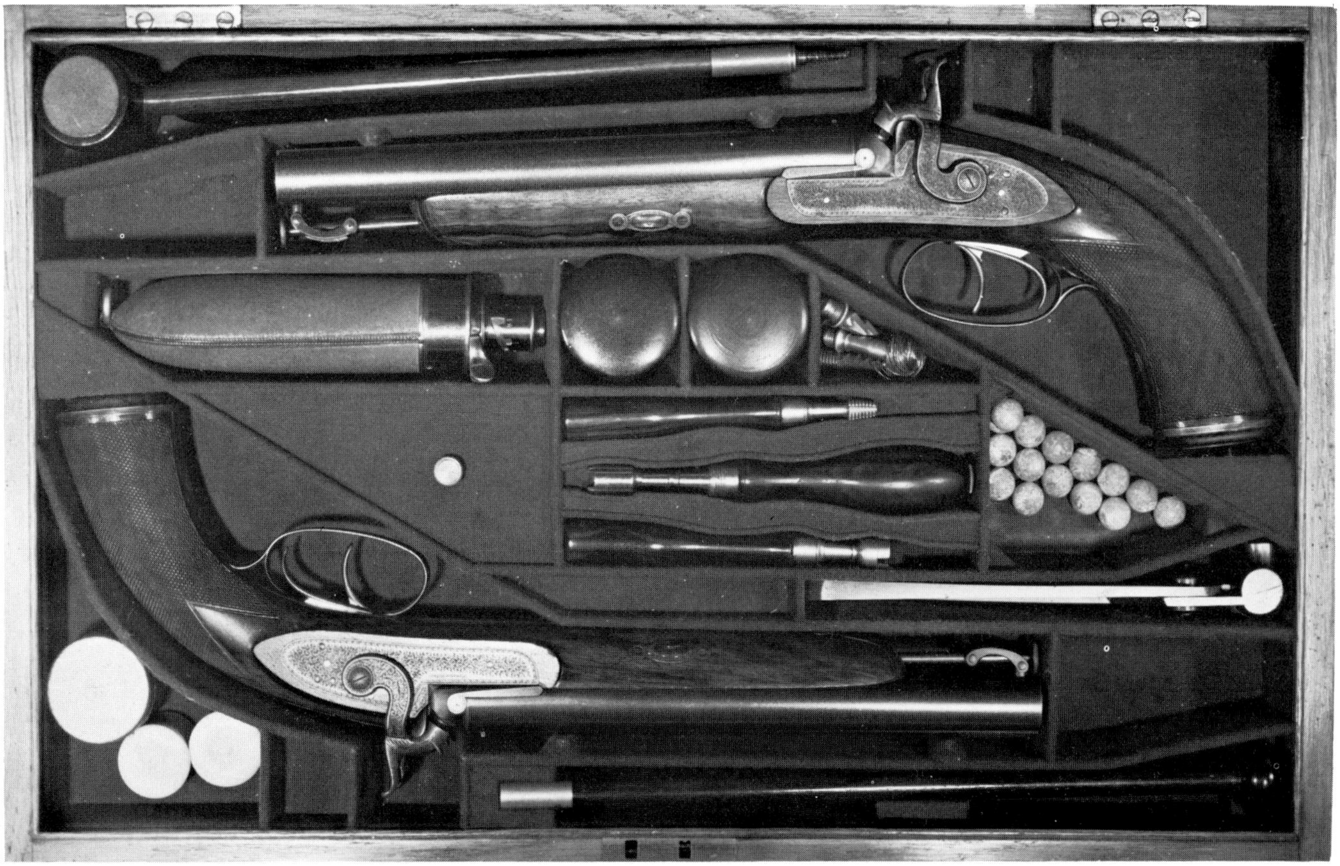

Cased pair of double-barrelled howdah pistols with browned twist barrels rifled with six grooves and with engraved platinum plugs, finely engraved case-hardened locks, hammers and mounts. Original oak case with fittings and label. Fine quality, condition as new. By Joseph Harkom, Edinburgh, circa 1860. 14¾in.

Christie's

About £2,000

Mainly on condition, but howdah pistols have a certain cachet.

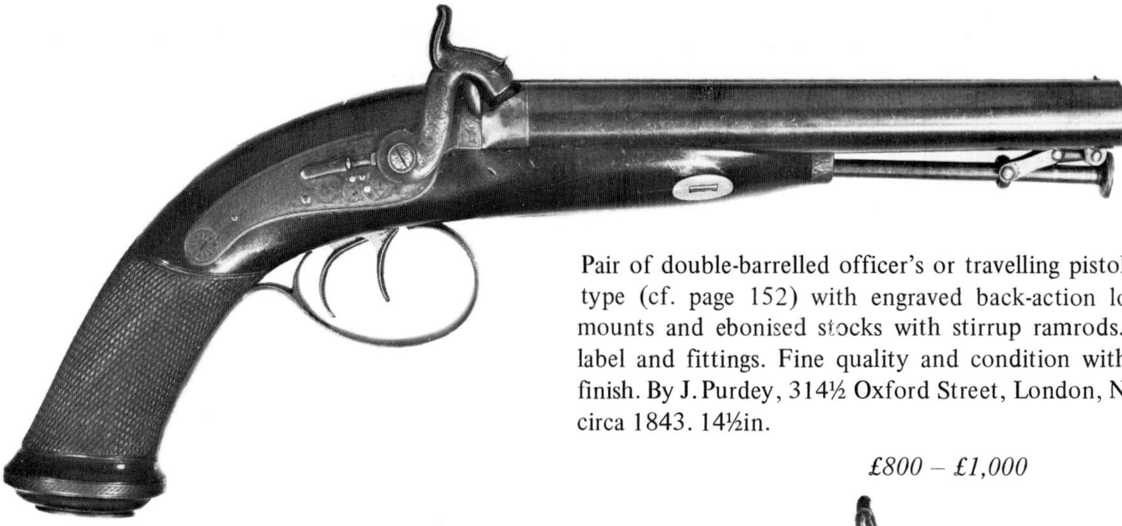

Pair of double-barrelled officer's or travelling pistols of typical Purdey type (cf. page 152) with engraved back-action locks, hammers and mounts and ebonised stocks with stirrup ramrods. Original case with label and fittings. Fine quality and condition with nearly all original finish. By J. Purdey, 314½ Oxford Street, London, Nos. 3843 and 3844, circa 1843. 14½in. *Christie's*

£800 – £1,000

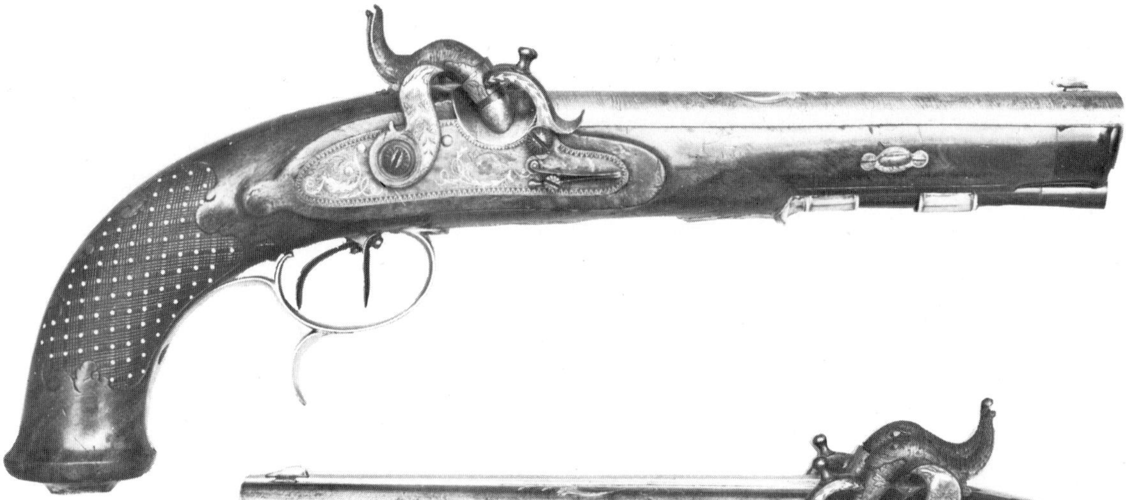

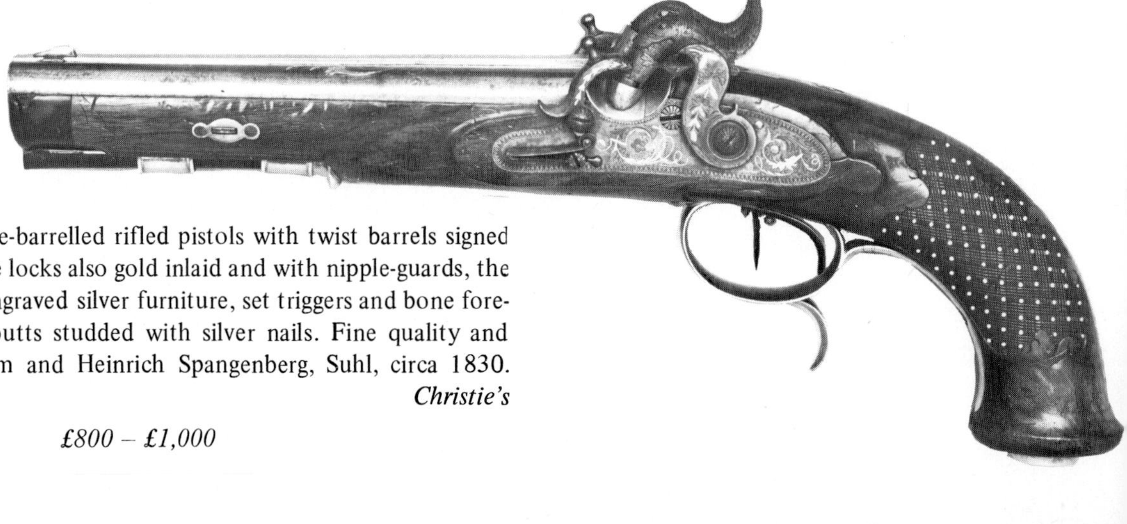

Pair of German double-barrelled rifled pistols with twist barrels signed and inlaid in gold, the locks also gold inlaid and with nipple-guards, the figured stocks with engraved silver furniture, set triggers and bone fore-end tips, chequered butts studded with silver nails. Fine quality and condition. By Wilhelm and Heinrich Spangenberg, Suhl, circa 1830. 13¾in. *Christie's*

£800 – £1,000

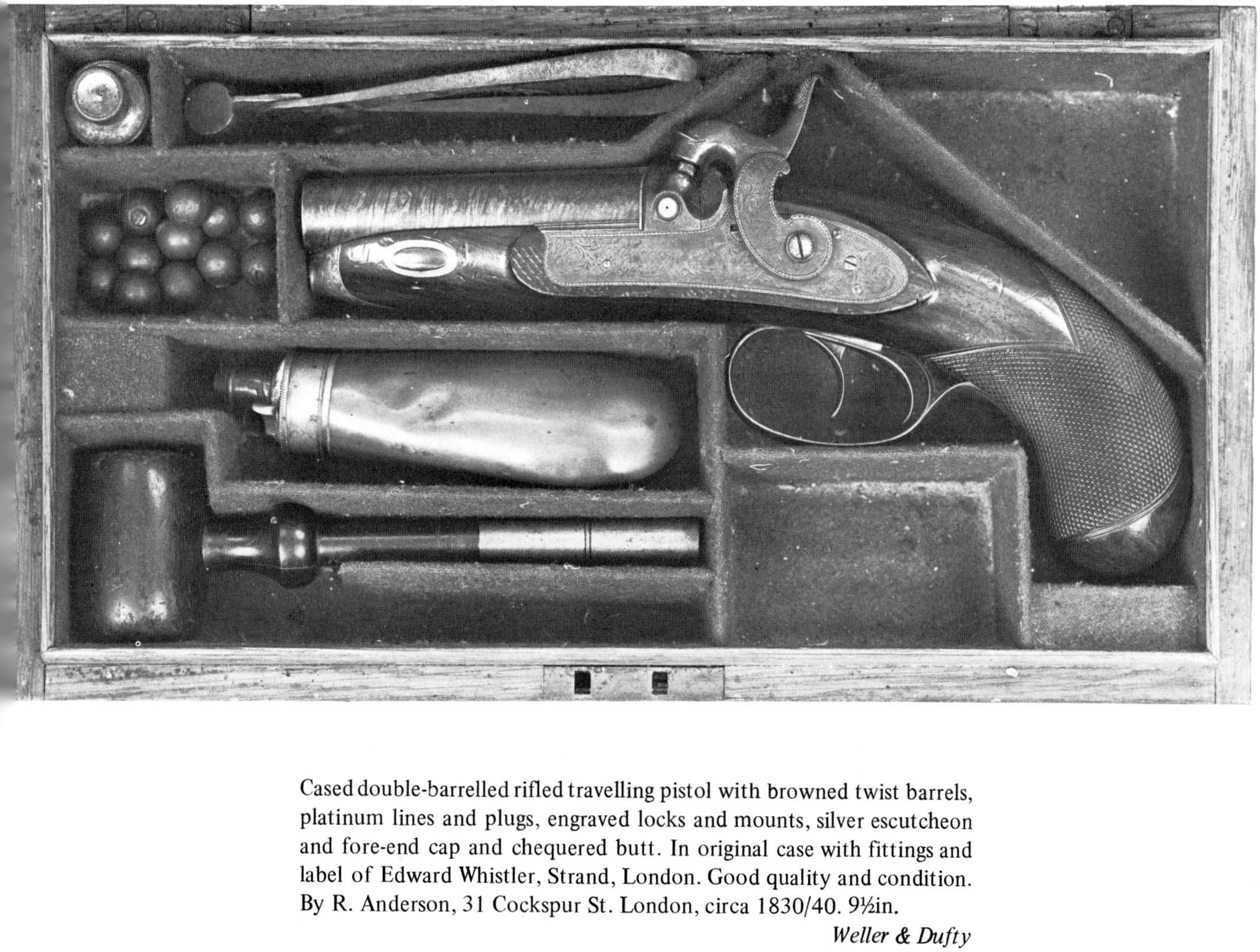

Cased double-barrelled rifled travelling pistol with browned twist barrels, platinum lines and plugs, engraved locks and mounts, silver escutcheon and fore-end cap and chequered butt. In original case with fittings and label of Edward Whistler, Strand, London. Good quality and condition. By R. Anderson, 31 Cockspur St. London, circa 1830/40. 9½in.

Weller & Dufty

About £300. Without case £200 – £220.

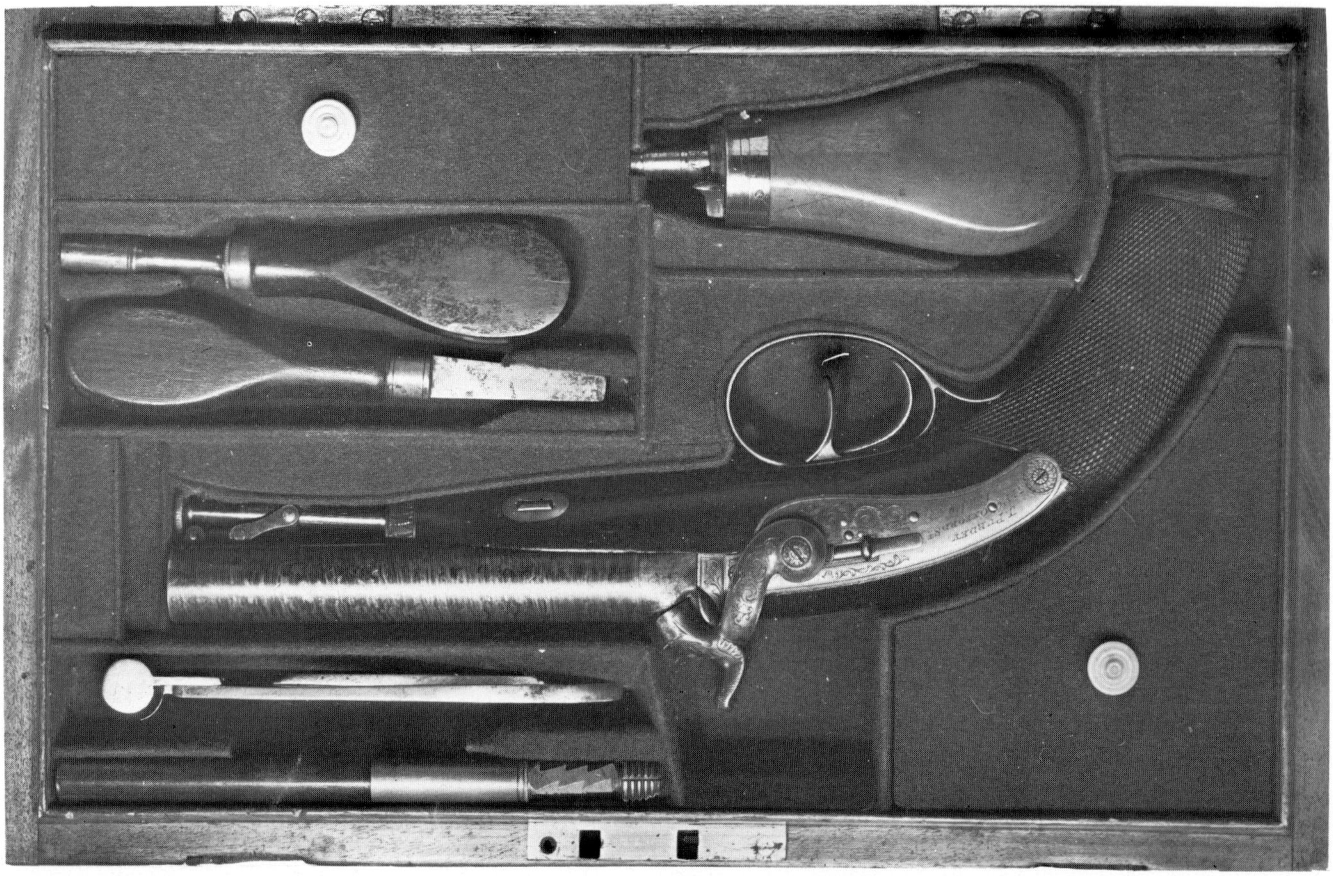

Cased double-barrelled pistol, a small version of the pair on page 204, in original case with fittings and label. Fine quality and condition. By J. Purdey, 314½ Oxford Street, circa 1837. 10½in. *Christie's*

About £500

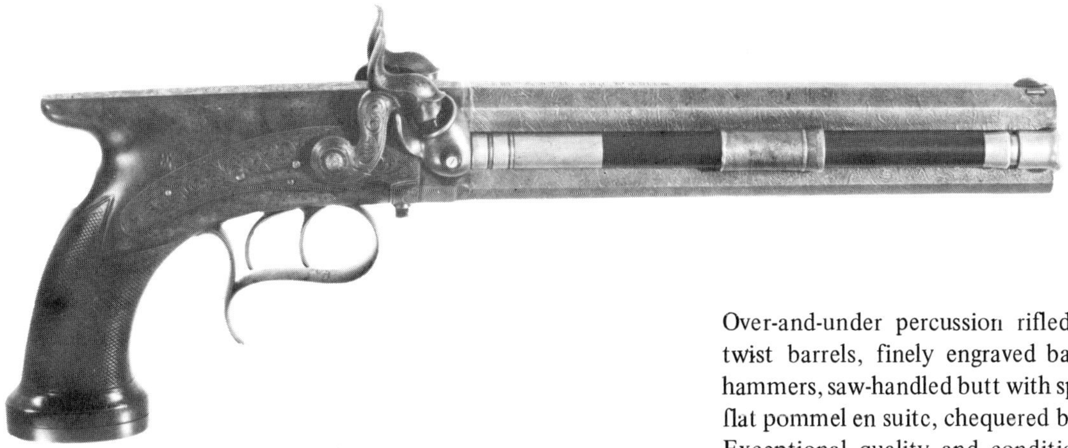

Over-and-under percussion rifled pistol with etched twist barrels, finely engraved back-action locks and hammers, saw-handled butt with spur trigger-guard and flat pommel en suite, chequered butt, original ramrod. Exceptional quality and condition. By Wm. and Jn. Rigby, Dublin, circa 1843. 15in. *Christie's*

£800 – £1,000

Over-and-under single-trigger pocket pistol with blued octagonal barrels, engraved platinum plugs, engraved locks and hammers, engraved silver trigger-guard and butt-plate with gold cap, gold escutcheon. By Joseph Egg, No. 1 Piccadilly, London, London silver hallmarks for 1831. 6¼in. *Christie's*

£500 – £750

This is an original percussion version, not a converted example of the flint type shown on page 183.

Over-and-under pistol made for Smith's Imperial Patent caps, with platinum plugs, chequered butt, engraved bolted back-action locks and silver escutcheon, the rammer housed within the grip. Good quality, fair condition. By Samuel and Charles Smith, Princes St. Leicester Square, London, circa 1830/35. 7½in. *Christie's*

£200 – £300. A rare system of ignition

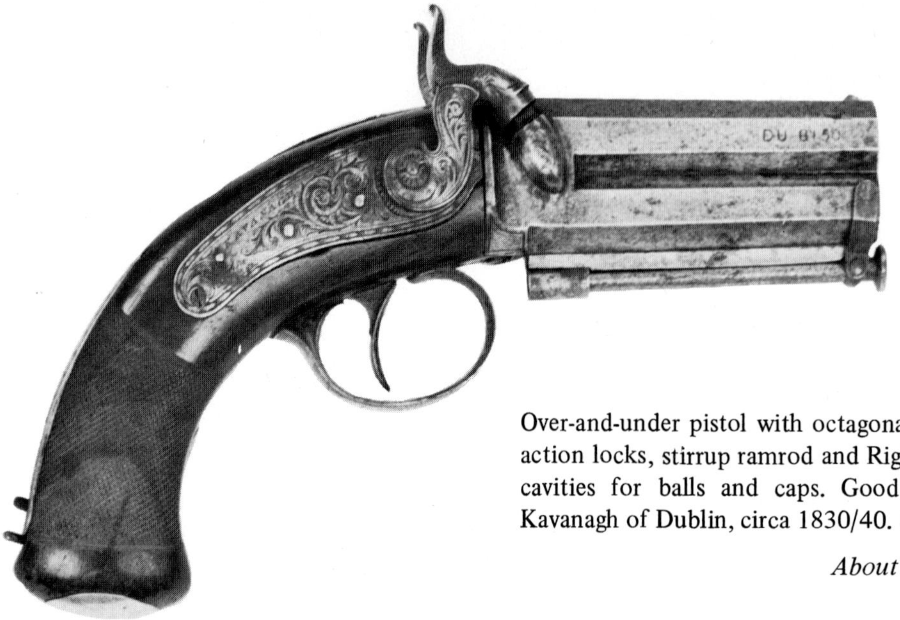

Over-and-under pistol with octagonal barrels, engraved hammers, back-action locks, stirrup ramrod and Rigby-type hinged back-strap revealing cavities for balls and caps. Good quality, only fair condition. By Kavanagh of Dublin, circa 1830/40. 8in. *Weller & Dufty*

About £200

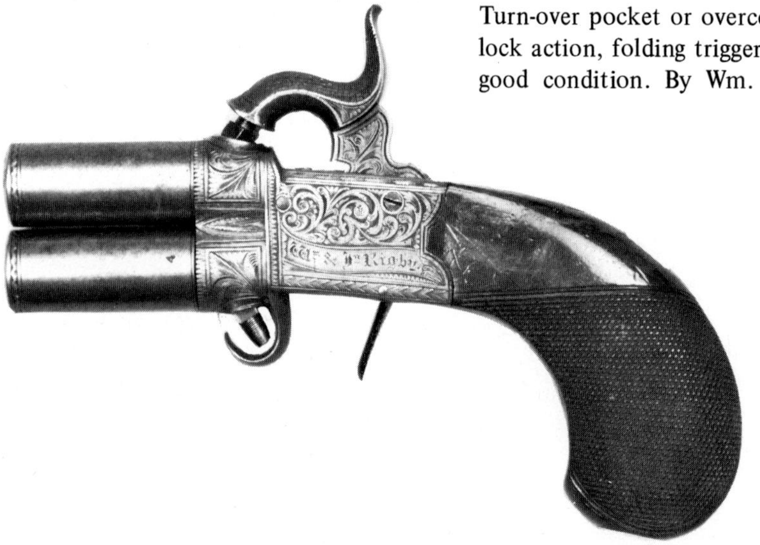

Turn-over pocket or overcoat pistol with turn-off barrel, engraved box-lock action, folding trigger and flattened chequered butt. Fine quality, good condition. By Wm. and Jn. Rigby, Dublin, circa 1830. 6¼in. *Knight, Frank & Rutley*

£200 – £250

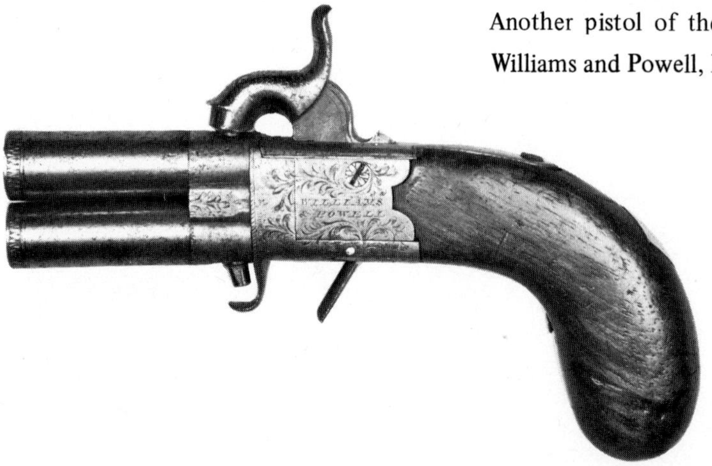

Another pistol of the same type. Poor quality, fair condition. Signed Williams and Powell, London. Circa 1840. 6in. *Knight, Frank & Rutley*

£100 – £150

Cased pair of turn-over percussion pocket pistols, the round barrels with top flats, engraved actions and trigger-guards. Original case with fittings and Robert Adams, 76 King William Street, trade label. Poor quality, but fine condition. The pistols unsigned, Birmingham proof marks. Circa 1850. 7in. *Weller & Dufty*

£300 – £400

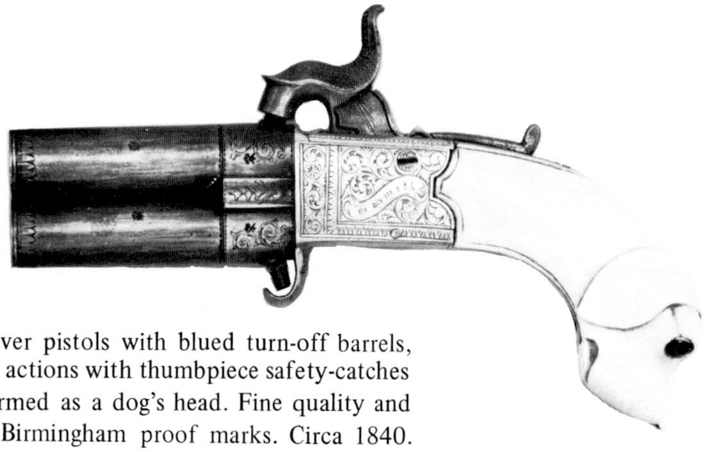

Unusual pair of double-barrelled turn-over pistols with blued turn-off barrels, signed and scroll engraved German silver actions with thumbpiece safety-catches and folding triggers, the ivory butts formed as a dog's head. Fine quality and condition. Signed H. Smith, London, Birmingham proof marks. Circa 1840. 6½in. *Christie's*

£800 – £1,000

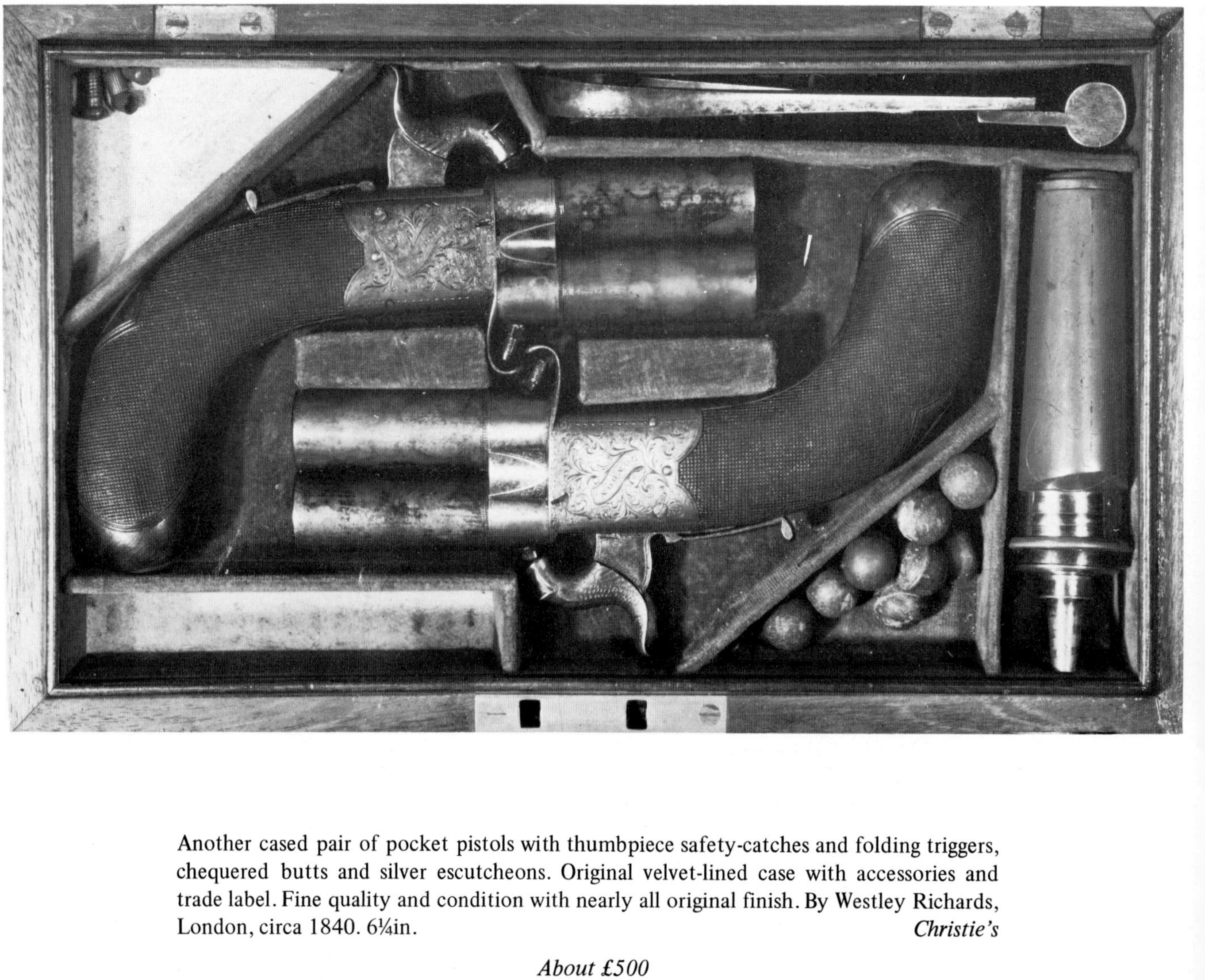

Another cased pair of pocket pistols with thumbpiece safety-catches and folding triggers, chequered butts and silver escutcheons. Original velvet-lined case with accessories and trade label. Fine quality and condition with nearly all original finish. By Westley Richards, London, circa 1840. 6¼in. *Christie's*

About £500

Unusually fine cased pair of turn-over pocket pistols with turn-off barrels, engraved actions, folding triggers and thumbpiece safety-catches, the butts inlaid with silver flowers and foliage and silver wire scrolls. Original case with fittings and label. Very fine condition. By Lang, 7 Haymarket, London, circa 1840. 5½in. *Sotheby's*

£1,200 – £1,500

Percussion Cap Multishot Pistols

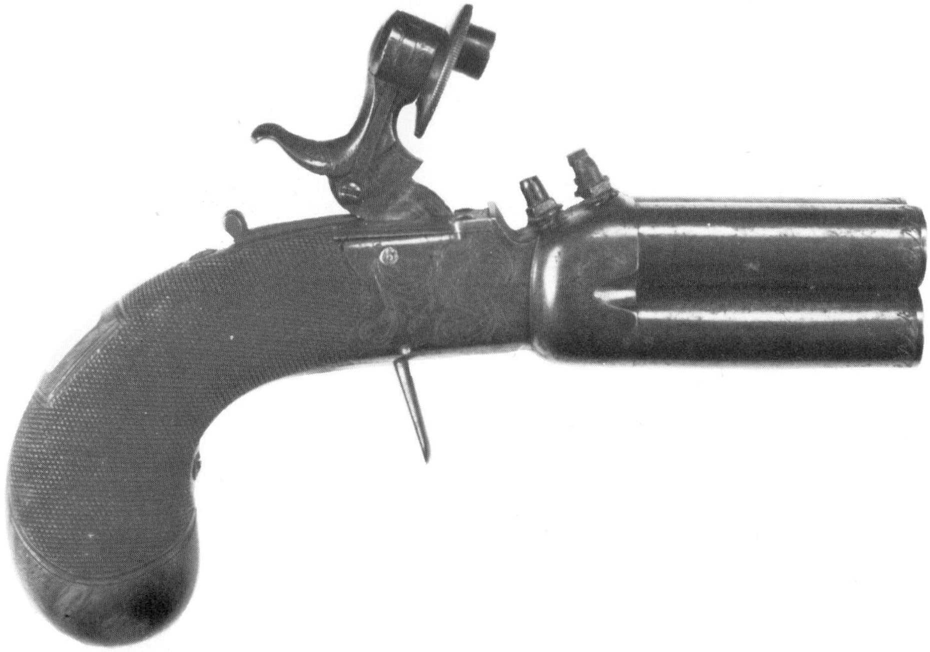

Three-barrel pocket pistol with turn-off barrels, signed and engraved action, chequered butt, folding trigger and silver escutcheon, the hammer with revolving nose of Rigby type for firing each of the barrels in turn. Fair quality, good condition. Signed Pether, Oxford. Circa 1830. 6in.
Knight, Frank & Rutley

About £300

Rigby made an all-steel version of this type – value £400 to £500 in equivalent condition.

Four-barrel turn-over pocket pistol with two hammers, engraved box-lock action, chequered butt, safety-catch and silver escutcheon, the ram-rod housed within the grip, good quality, fair condition. By J. Lang & Son, 22 Cockspur St. London, circa 1840. 7½in. *Weller & Dufty*

£200 – £250

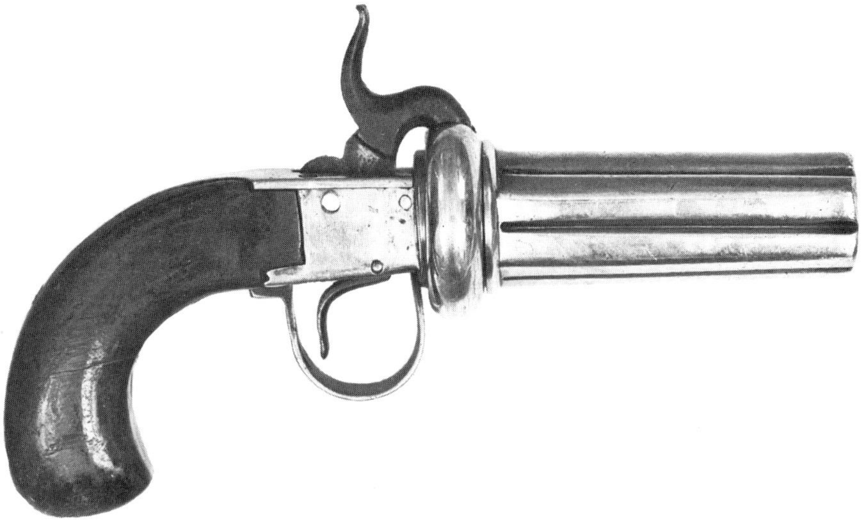

Six-barrel hand-rotated pepperbox pistol with brass barrels and action, brass trigger-guard and one-piece butt. Poor quality, fair condition. Circa 1830. *Weller & Dufty*

About £150

Mariette patent six-shot pepperbox revolver with etched twist barrels, foliate engraved action, under-hammer, ring trigger and fluted grips. Fair quality and condition. Stamped Mariette Breveté, Liège proof, Circa 1840. 7¾in. *Christie's*

£120 – £160

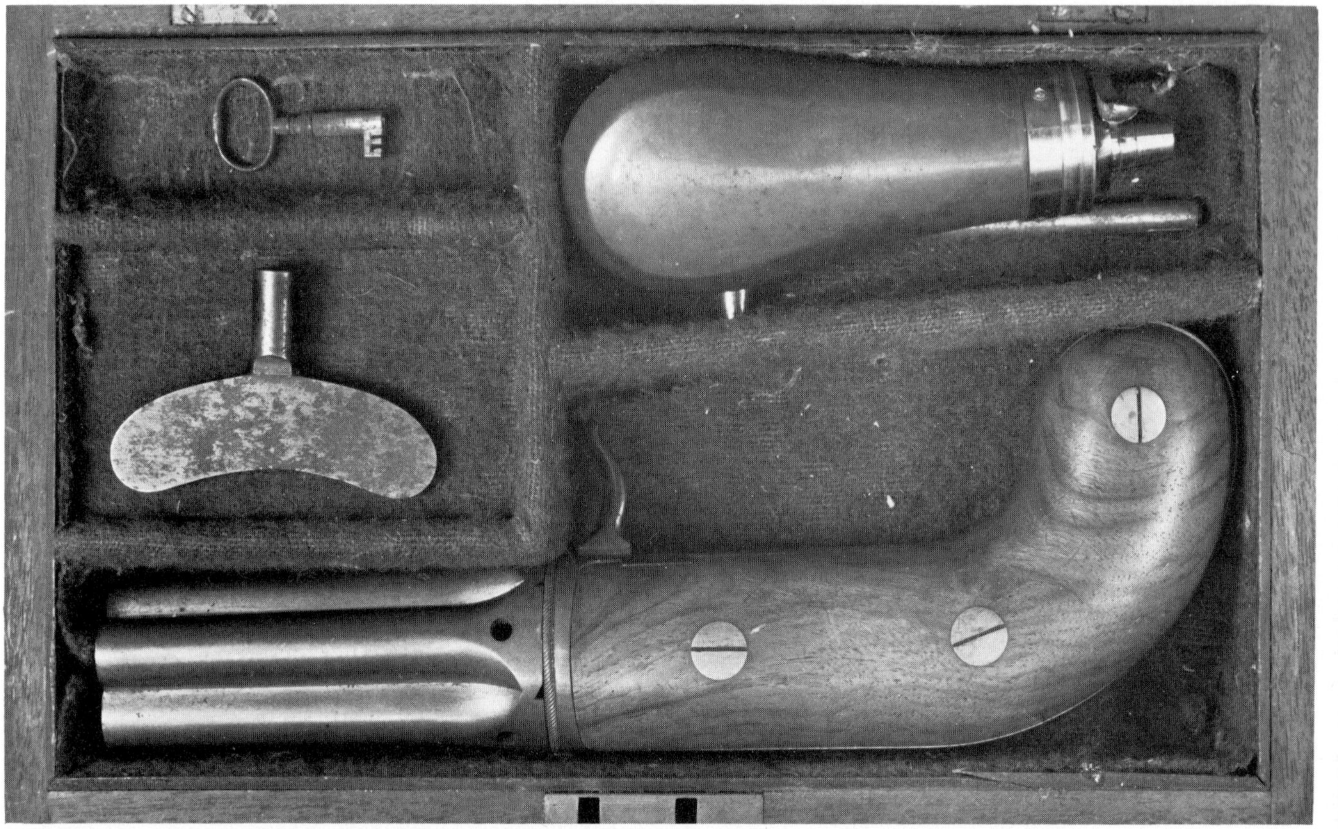

Cased Budding patent hand-rotated pepperbox revolver with brass frame and barrels, walnut grips and blued trigger. Original case with flask, nipple and barrel key, the lid with instruction label. Very rare and in fine condition. Signed Budding, Maker, Birmingham proof marks, made in Stroud, Gloucestershire, circa 1830. 8¼in. *Sotheby's*

£600 – £700

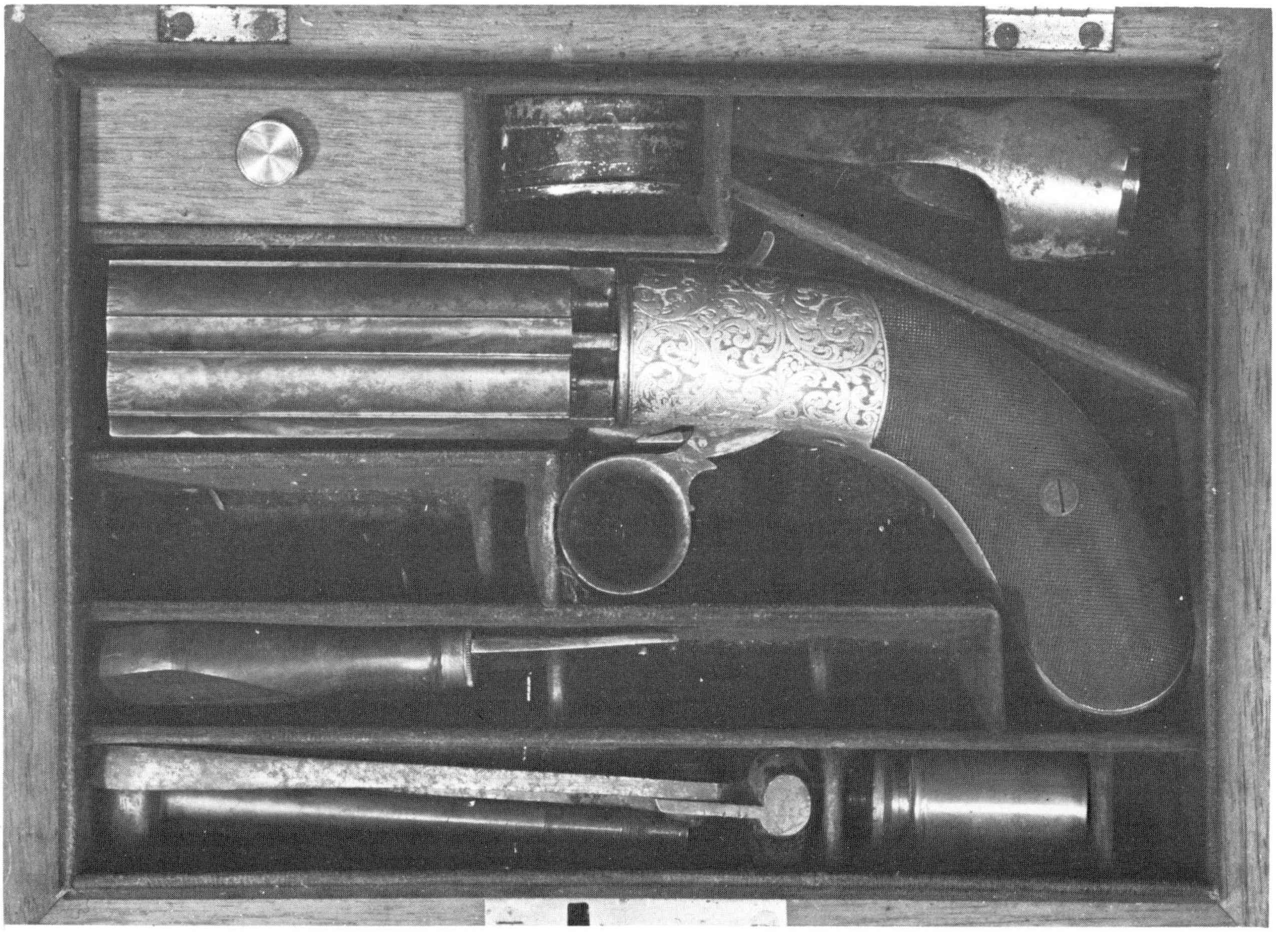

Cased Cooper's patent six-shot pepperbox revolver, with engraved German silver action and back-strap, blued safety-catch, barrels and ring trigger, chequered grips. In original fitted case with accessories (flask missing). Good quality, fine condition. Signed J.R. Cooper, Patentee, Birmingham proof marks. Circa 1855. 13¼in. *Christie's*

£300 – £400

A plain Cooper's patent six-shot pepperbox revolver with steel action uncased is worth about £75 – £100.

Six-shot pepperbox revolver with engraved action and walnut grips. Poor quality, fair condition. Unsigned, Birmingham proof marks. Circa 1830/40. 8 in. *Christie's*

£60 – £80

Similar pistol with German silver action. Poor quality, fair condition. Unsigned, Birmingham proof marks. Circa 1830/40. 8in. *Christie's*

£80 – £100

Six-shot pepperbox revolver with well engraved German silver action and blued hammer, thumbpiece safety-catch and chequered butt. Medium to good quality, good condition. Signed Tipping and Lawden, London. Circa 1840. 7in. *Christie's*

£100 – £150

Rigby six-shot pepperbox with detachable barrels, bold scroll engraving, chequered grips. Fine quality, and condition with all original finish, circa 1830. 6½in. *Christie's*

About £500

The very best are cased with a spare barrel block, and a special powder measure.

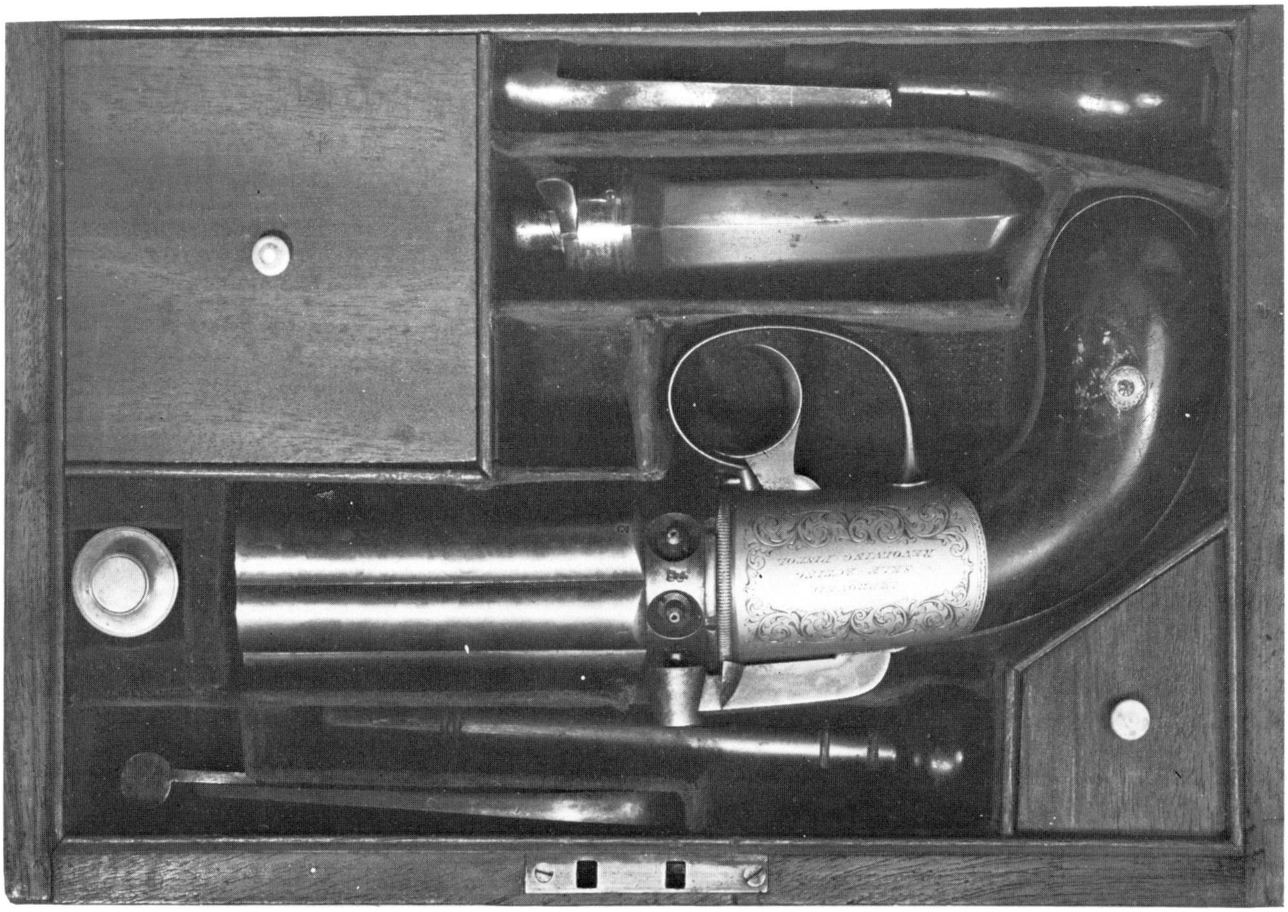

Cased six-shot pepperbox revolver with German silver action engraved "Improved Self-acting Revolving Pistol" within scrollwork, engraved back-strap, trigger-guard and bar hammer, and walnut grips. Original case with fittings and label. Fine quality and condition. By Thomas Jackson, 29 Edwards Street, Portman Square, London, circa 1840. 8½in. *Christie's*

About £400

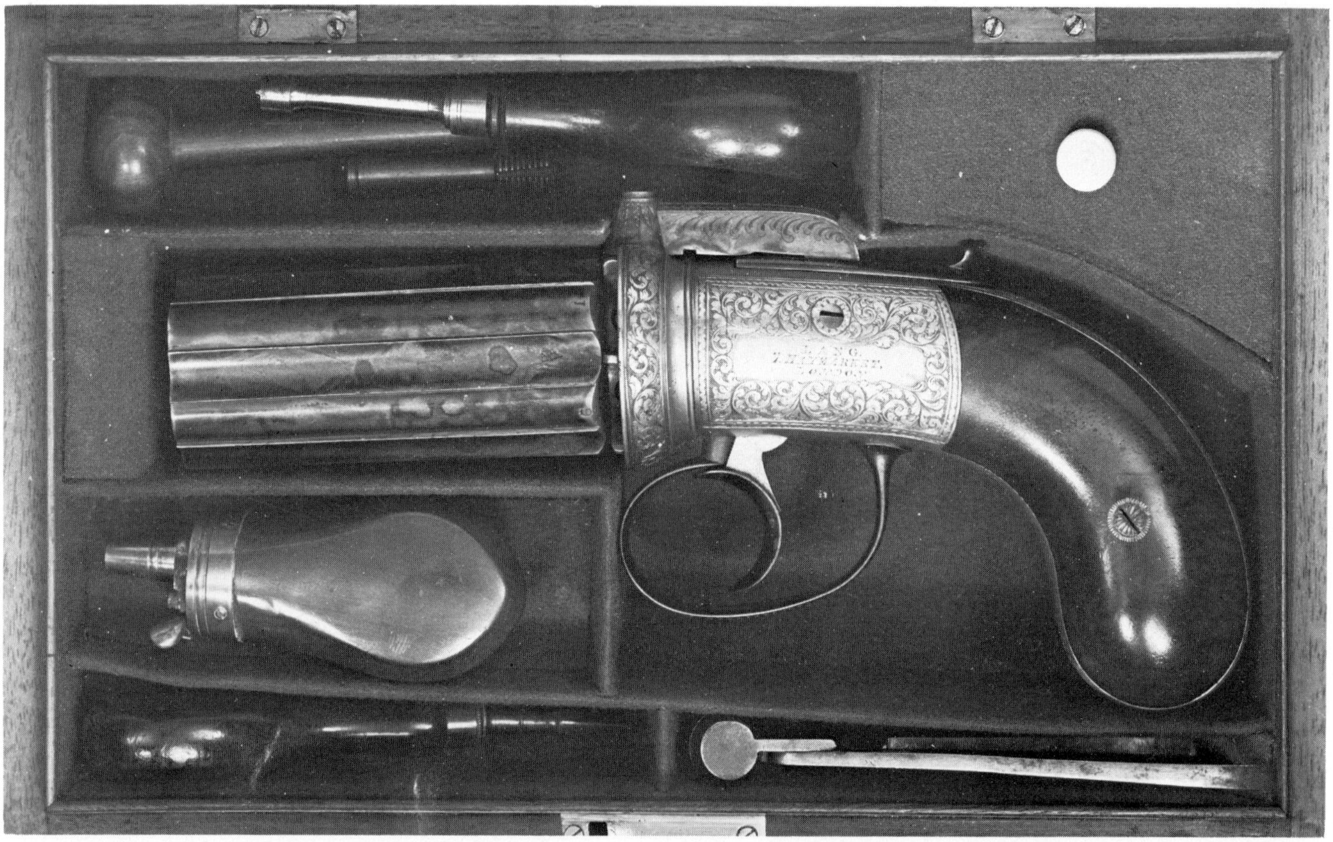

Cased six-shot pepperbox revolver with signed and engraved German silver action, blued and engraved steel mounts and figured grips. Original case with fittings and label. Fine quality, almost new condition. By J. Lang, 7 Haymarket, London, circa 1840. 8½in. *Christie's*

About £500 owing to condition

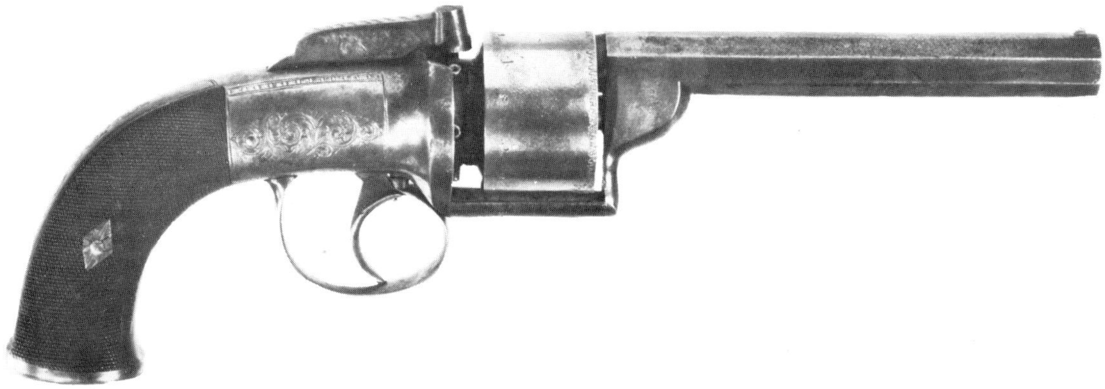

Six-shot transitional revolver with octagonal barrel, engraved action and bar hammer and chequered grips. Poor quality, good condition. Unsigned, Birmingham proof marks, circa 1830. 12¾in. *Christie's*

£70 – £100

Similar revolver, the barrel fitted with spring bayonet. Poor quality, fair condition. Birmingham proof marks. Circa 1830. 12½in. *Christie's*

£100 – £140

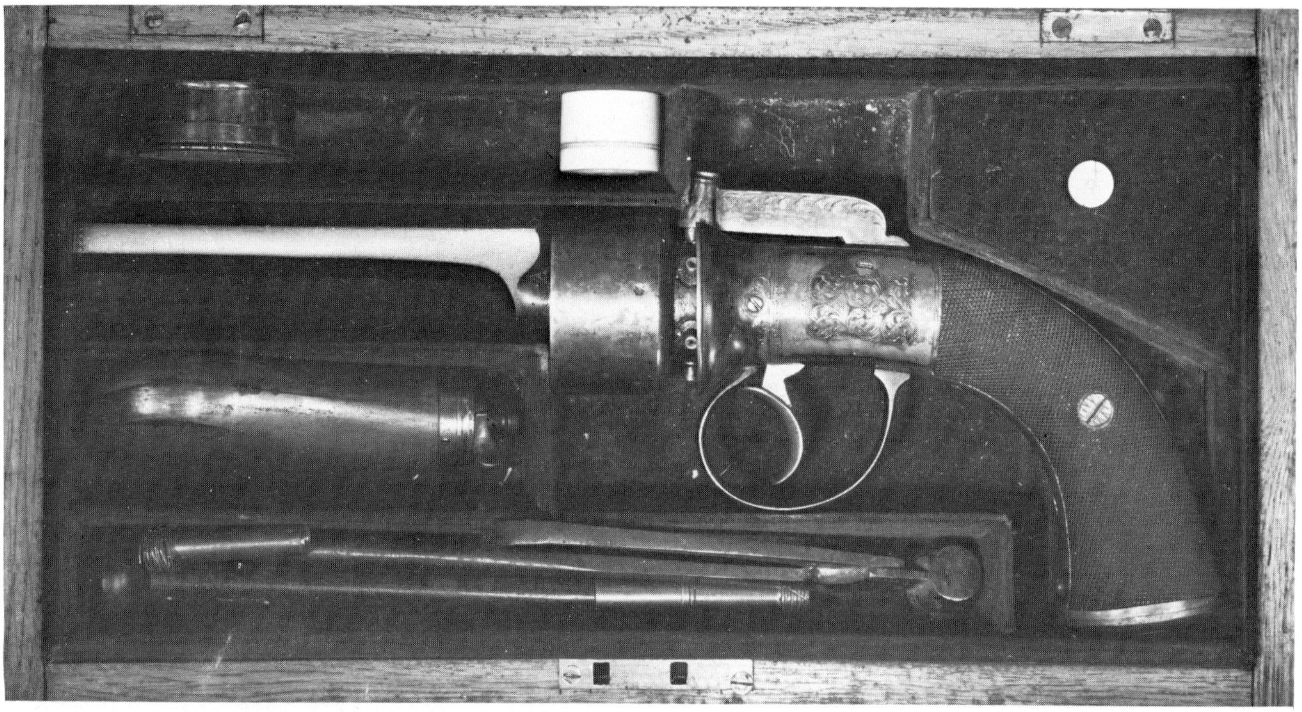

Cased six-shot transitional revolver with blued octagonal barrel, engraved case-hardened action and chequered grips. Original oak case with fittings, the lid with trade label. Fair quality, good condition. By Frederick Barnes & Co., No. 109 Fenchurch Street, London, circa 1830. 12in. *Christie's*

£250 – £300

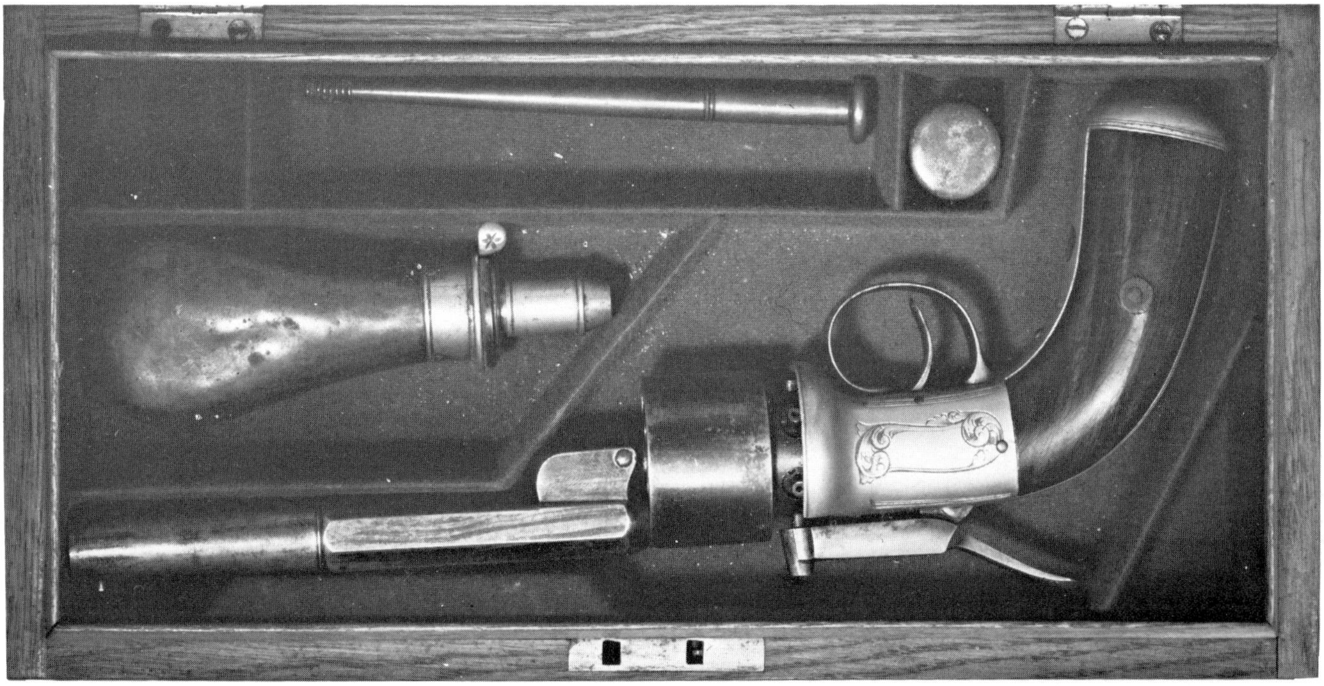

Cased Baker's patent six-shot transitional revolver with barrel in two stages, engraved German silver action and walnut grips. Original case with fittings and instructions label in lid. Fair quality, fine condition. Stamped "Registered April 24th, 1852". Birmingham proof. 11½in. *Christie's*

About £250

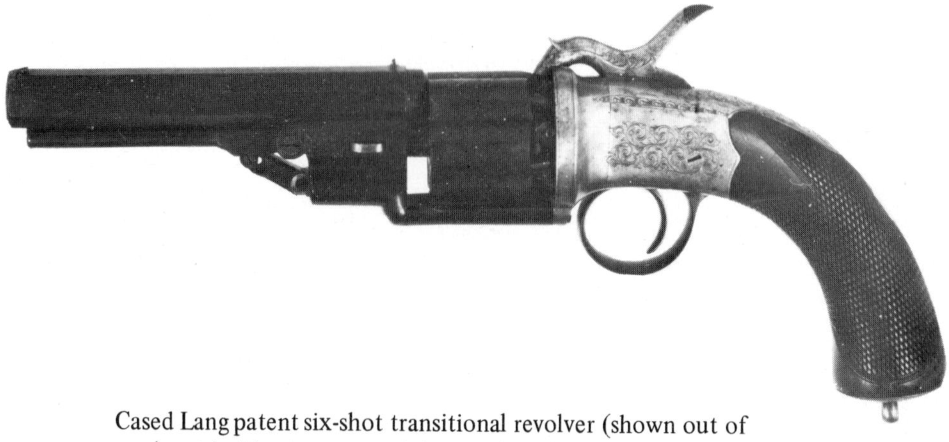

Cased Lang patent six-shot transitional revolver (shown out of case) with blued octagonal barrel and fluted cylinder, off-set hammer, engraved action and chequered butt. Original case with fittings and trade label. Good quality, fair condition but refinished. By J. Lang, 22 Cockspur Street, London, circa 1835. 12½in. *Christie's*

About £200 owing to condition.
£400 – £500 for a really good one.

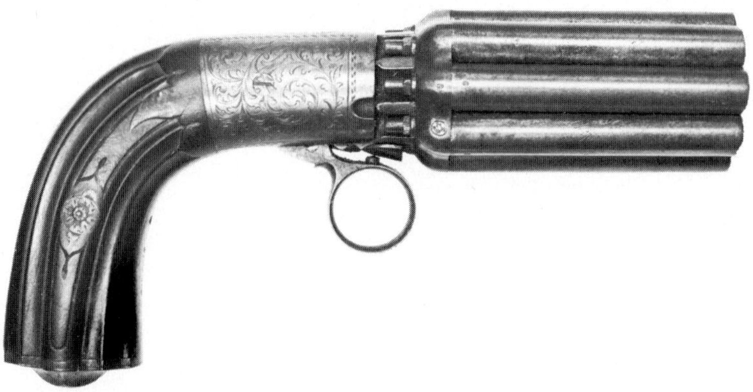

Mariette patent eight-shot pepperbox revolver of exactly the same form as that shown on page 213. Fair quality, good condition. Circa 1830. *Christie's*

£200 – £300. Rare.

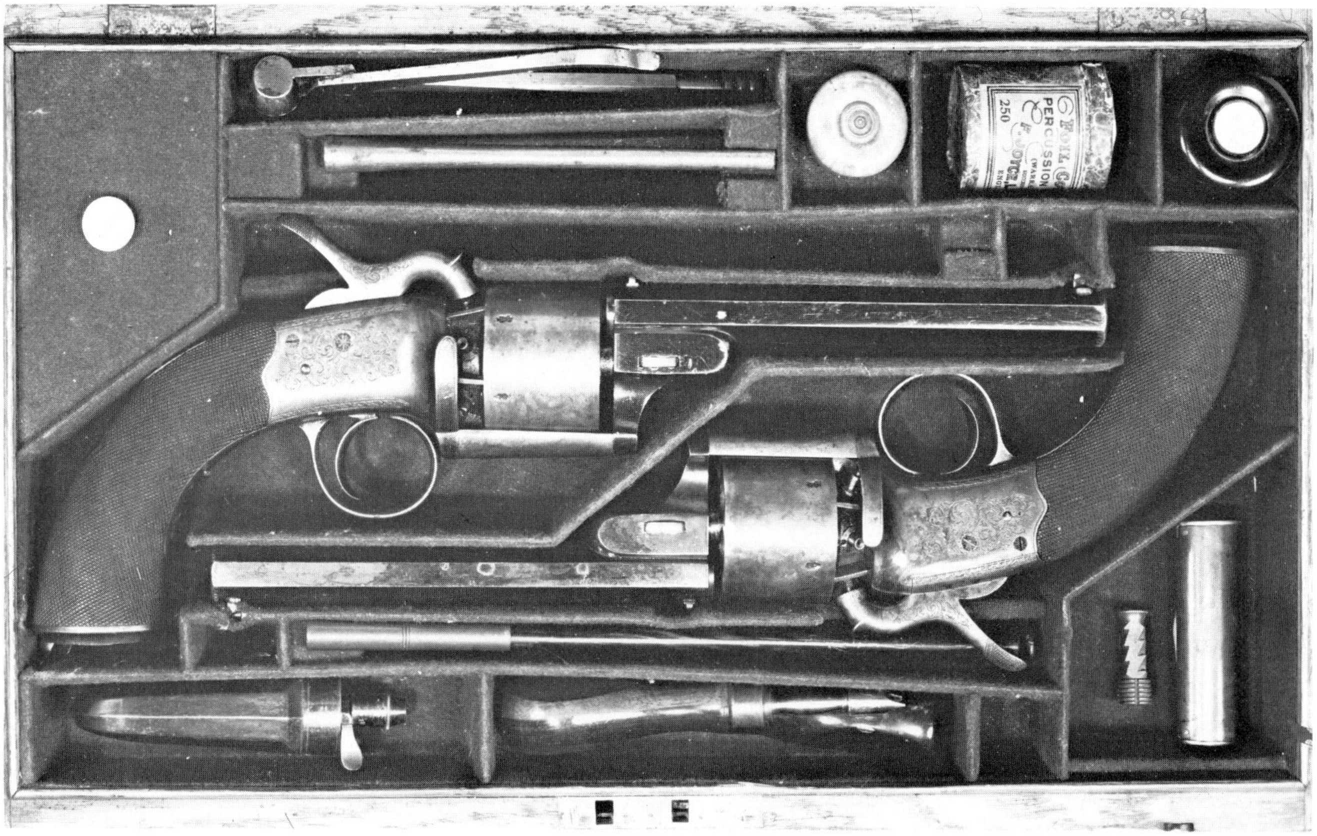

Rare cased pair of Blissett patent six-shot transitional revolvers, with blued barrels, case-hardened cylinders, engraved actions and chequered butts. Original case with fittings. Fine quality and condition with much original finish. Engraved John Blissett's Newest Improvement, 322 High Holborn, London. Circa 1840/50. 12¾in. *Christie's*

£800 – £1,000

Percussion Cap Patent Revolvers

Collier-type revolver with octagonal barrel, fluted five-shot cylinder, engraved lock and steel furniture. Moderate quality, fair condition, barrel and cylinder refinished. Signed J. Smith, London. Circa 1830-40. 12in. *Christie's*

About £800

Collier patent five-shot revolver, the lock engraved with foliage and trophies, and "Collier & Co. Patent". Fine quality, good condition. By Collier & Co., 54, Strand, London. Circa 1830. *Christie's*

Over £1,000

Cased Adams 1851 model "Dragoon" double-action revolver with accessories, the barrel engraved "Deane, Adams & Deane, 30 King William St., London Bridge". 13¼in.
These range from over £300 for one with all original finish to about £150 for a tired or refinished set. *Christie's*

This one £250 – £300

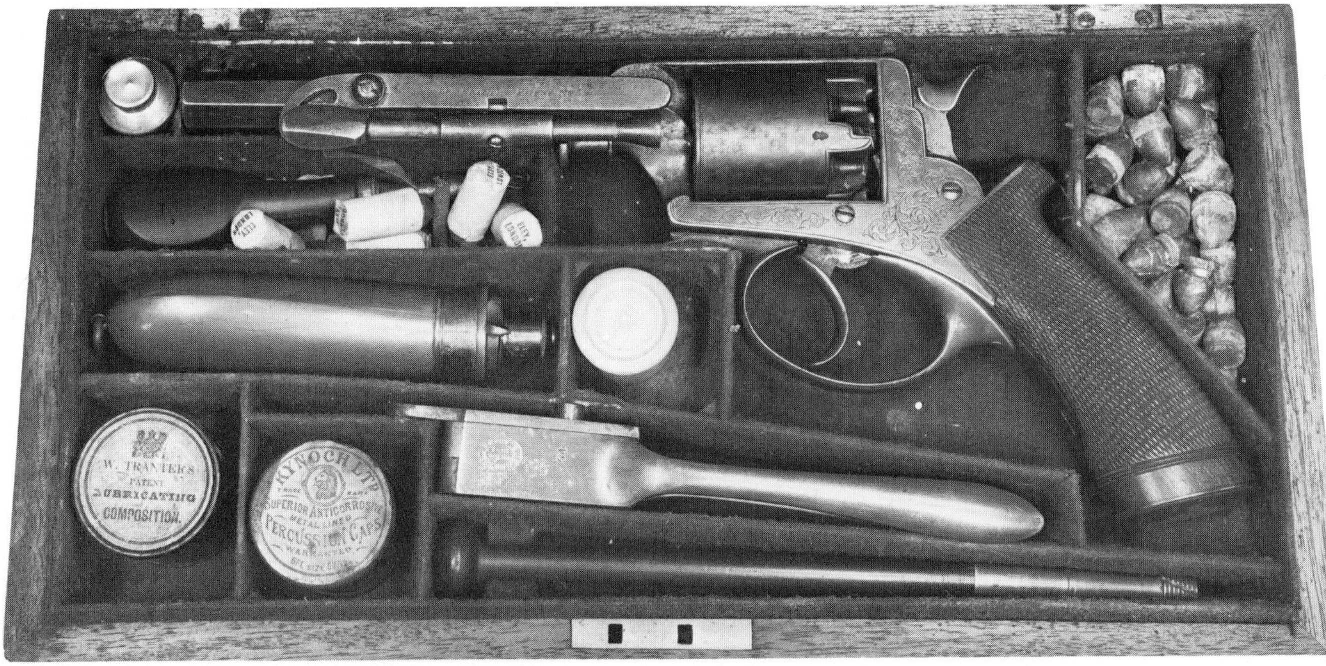

Cased Adams Patent revolver fitted with Joseph Brazier's patent rammer. Original case with fittings. 12in. *Corry Collection*

Over £300 for a clean one down to £150 for a poor one. This one is average.

About £200

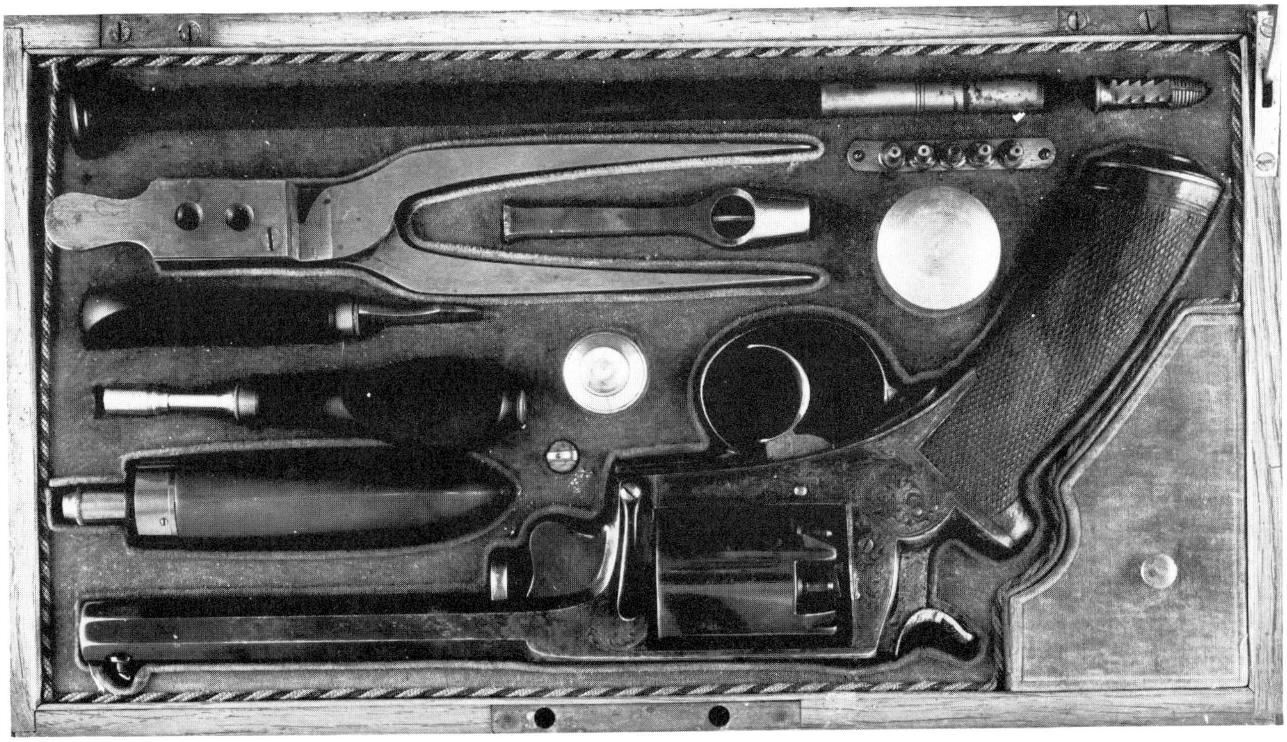

Rare cased German copy of a Beaumont-Adams revolver, with Kerr-type rammer, inscribed "Imperial Patent Revolver" on the top strap, engraved frame. Original case with velvet lining and all accessories. Fine condition. 13in. *Sotheby's*

Over £500

Kerr's patent single-action side-hammer revolver, stamped London Armoury on the lock. 11in.

Weller & Dufty

Over £150 for a clean example with finish to £80 for a poor one.

This one about £100

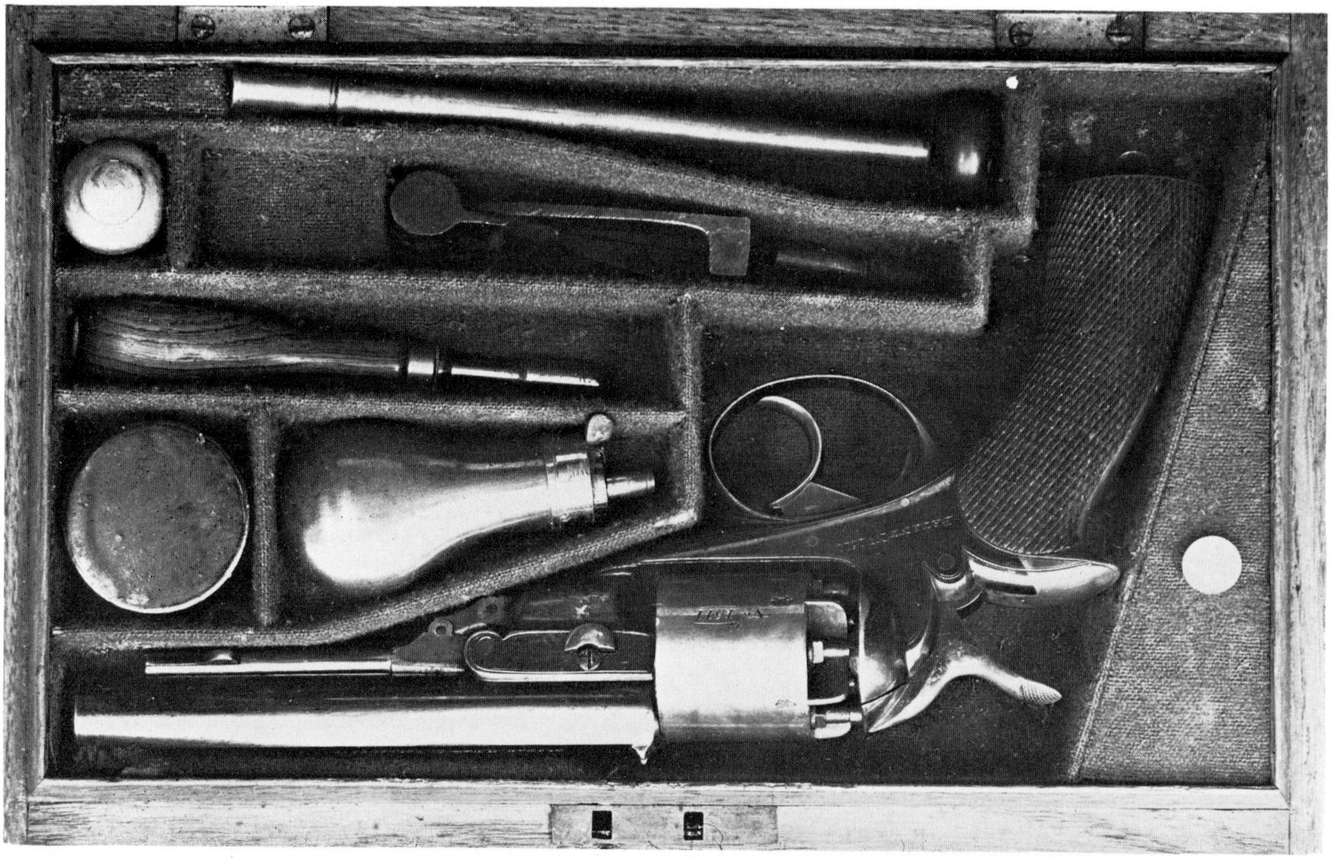

Cased Daw's patent double-action revolver, the barrel engraved "George H. Daw, 57 Threadneedle Street, London". 10in. *Wallis & Wallis*

These are worth between £300 and under £200. They were the best of the "hand-made" revolvers produced to compete with the factory-made Adams and Tranter weapons.

This one £200 – £250

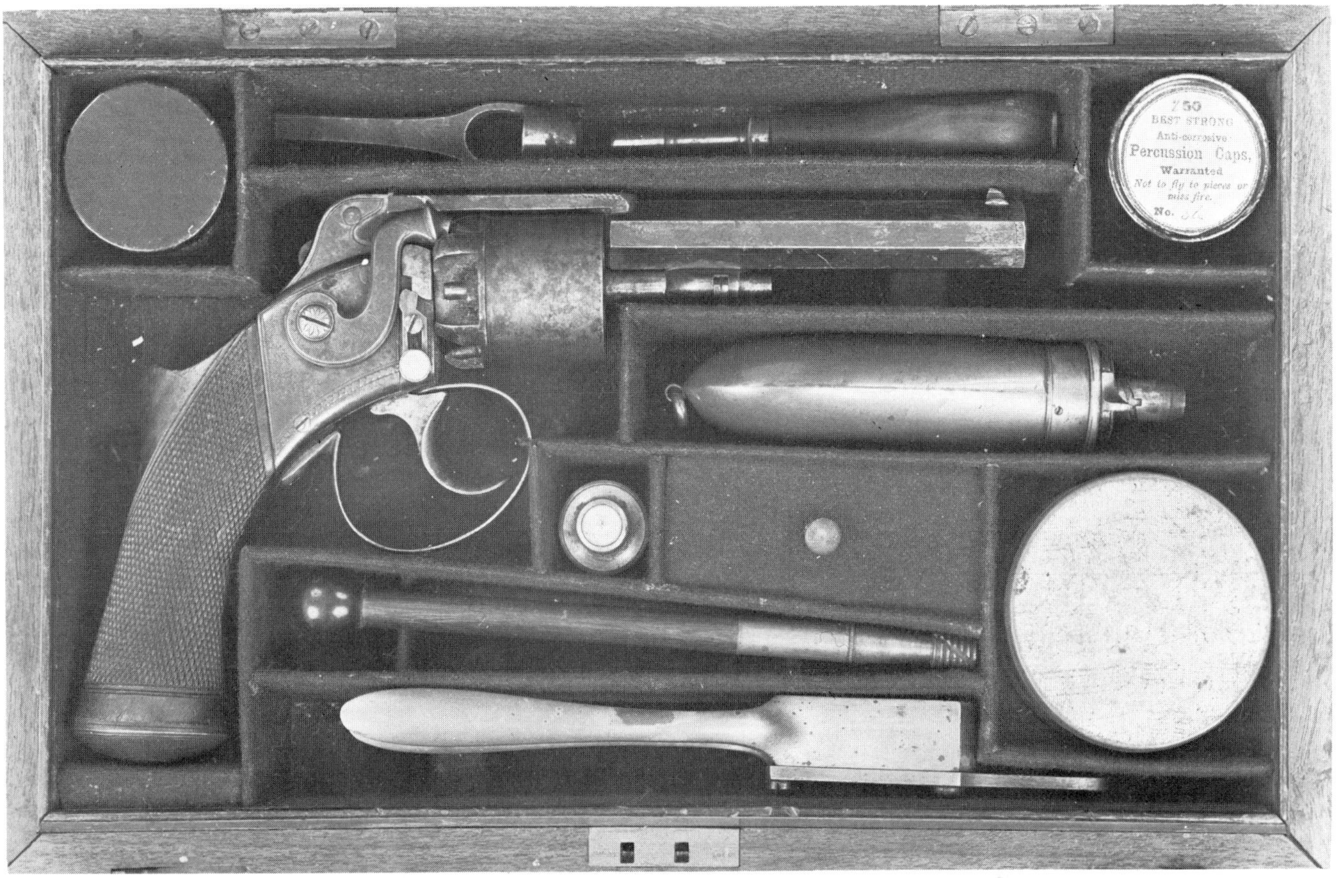

Cased Westley Richards double-action revolver, the barrel flat marked "Westley Richards, 170 New Bond Street, London", partly engraved and with platinum-filled safety-catch, complete with accessories and label in lid. The serial numbers on these are usually of three figures only, and they are accordingly rare items. 9½in. *Weller & Dufty*

Price ranges from over £400 down to about £200 according to condition.

This one £300 – £350

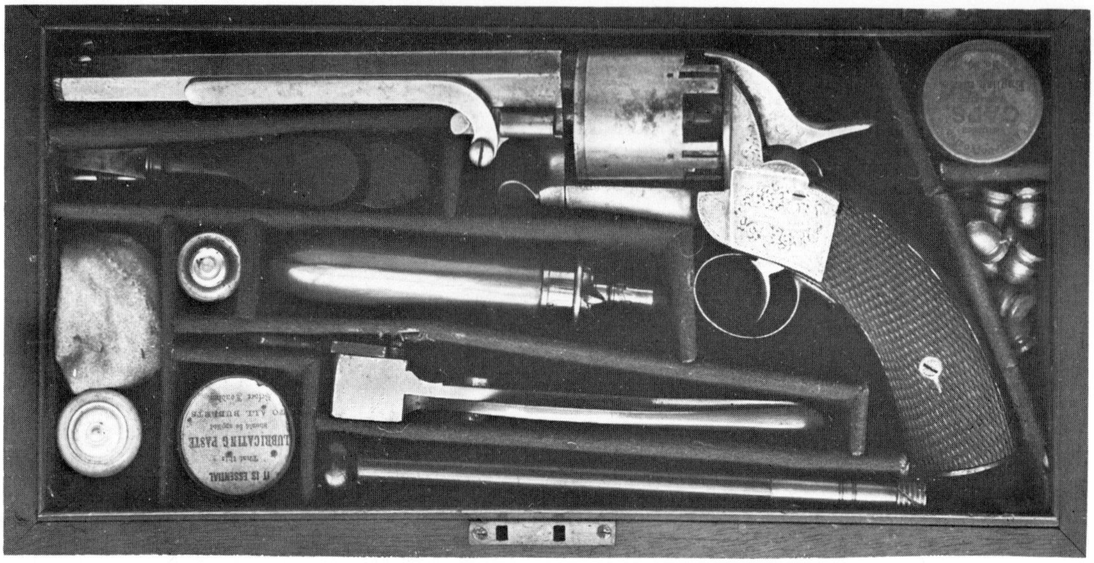

Cased Webley Long Spur 3rd Model revolver, the barrel and frame engraved "Webley's Patent". 12½in. *Wallis & Wallis*

This one £200 – £250 as the casing is complete and the pistol has some original finish.

Cased Tranter Patent double-action revolver with single trigger, presented to H.R.H. The Prince of Wales in 1862, with accessories. 12in. This is a very fine example in fine condition. *Knight, Frank & Rutley*

About £600

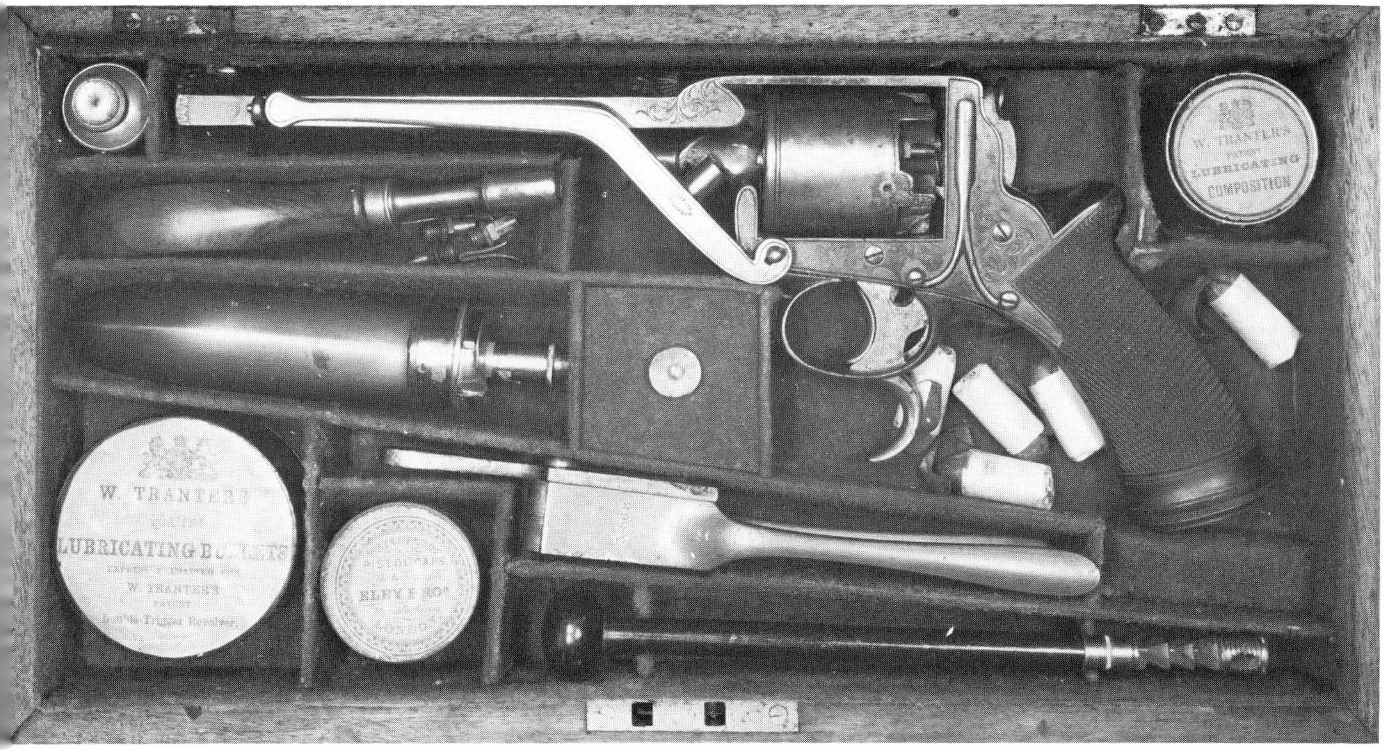

A regular example of a cased Tranter Patent revolver in very fine condition is worth about £350, in poor state under £150. Without a case they are worth between £80 and £150 according to condition. This one is good. *Corry Collection*

£200 – £250

Deane-Harding Patent double-action revolver, the barrel engraved "Deane & Son. London Bridge", with hinged rammer and side safety-catch. Fine condition with much original blue. 12¼in. *Christie's*

£120 – £150

Webley "wedge-frame" revolver with scroll engraved action. Good condition but no finish. 10in. *Christie's*

£100 – £120

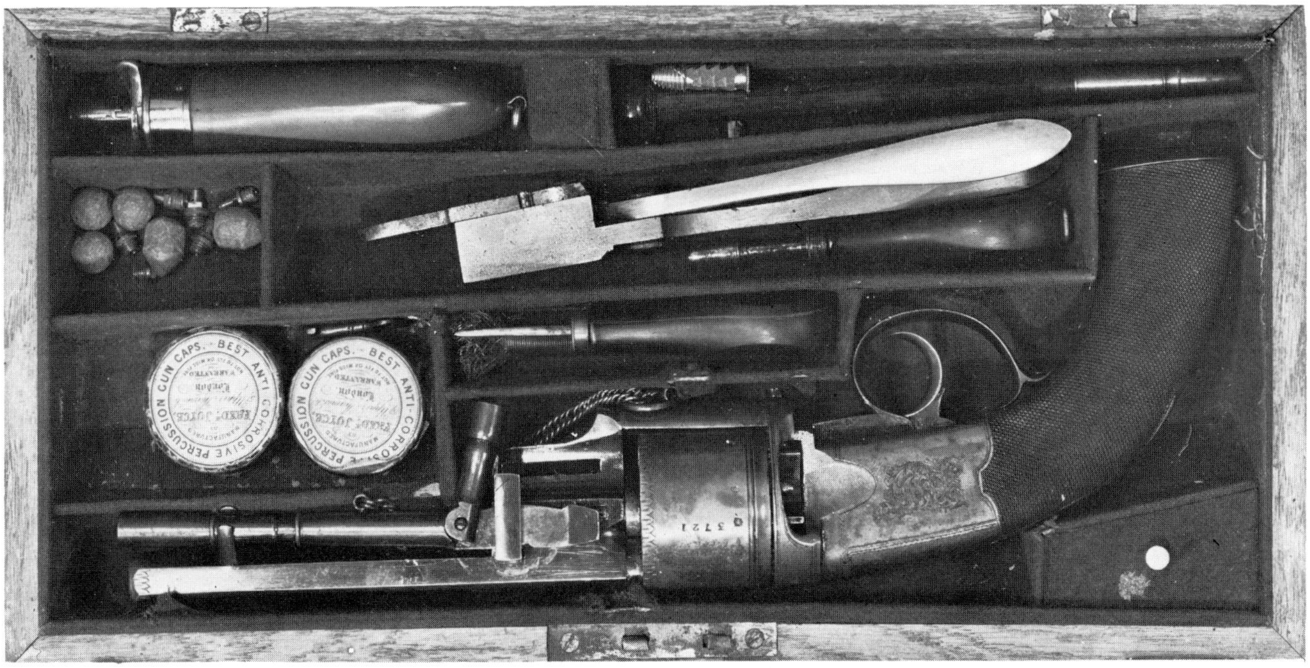

Cased Harvey's Patent "hammerless" revolver, the barrel rifled with two grooves, fitted with combination turnscrew, nipple-key and loading rod. Full accessories and original case. 13½in. A rare item in outstanding condition. *Christie's*

Over £600
An uncased example in good condition is worth £300 – £400

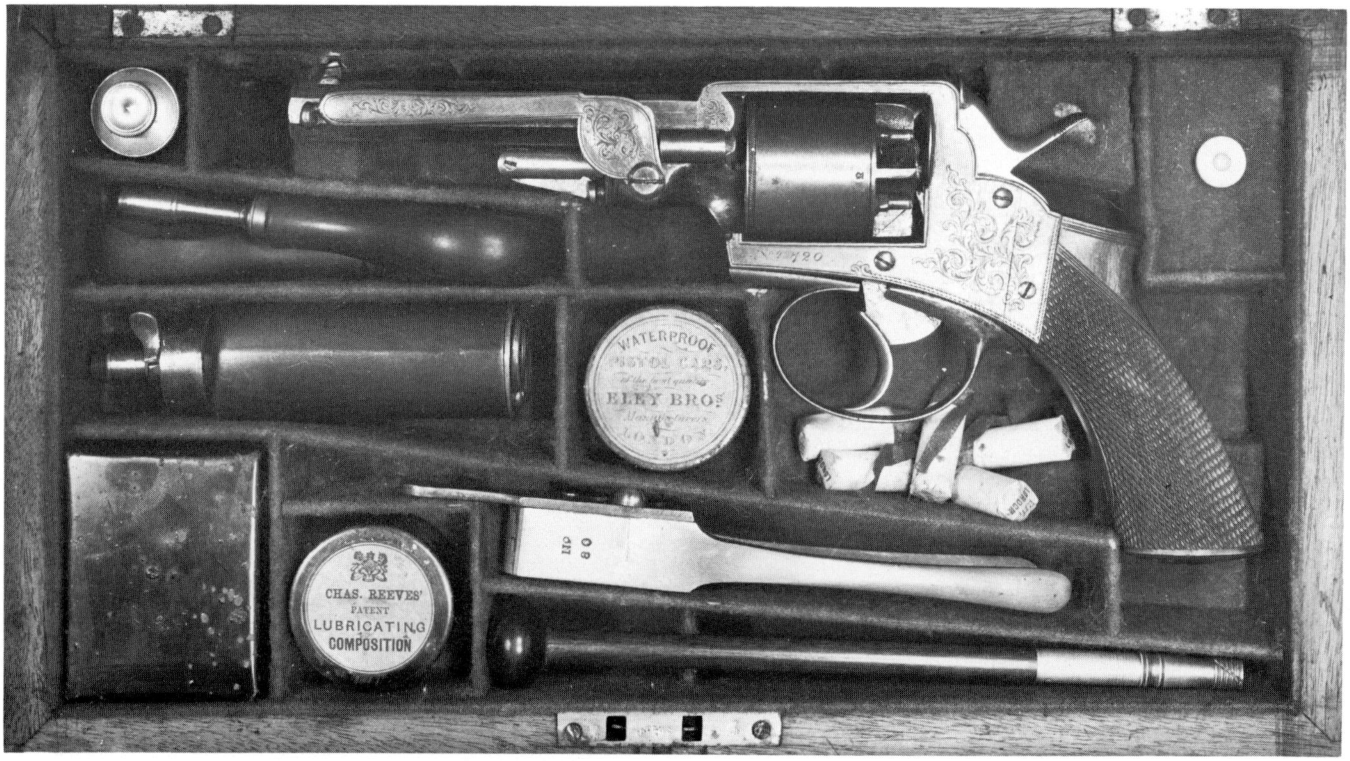

Cased Reeve's Patent revolver. In original case with fittings. 9¼in. The price range for these is between £300 and about £100. *Corry Collection*

This one about £200

Le Mat Patent revolver, the barrel inscribed "Col. Le Mat Bte., s. g. d. g. Paris". 13½in. *Sotheby's*

Over £600 for a fine example, about £300 for an average one, as illustrated.

Flintlock Service Pistols

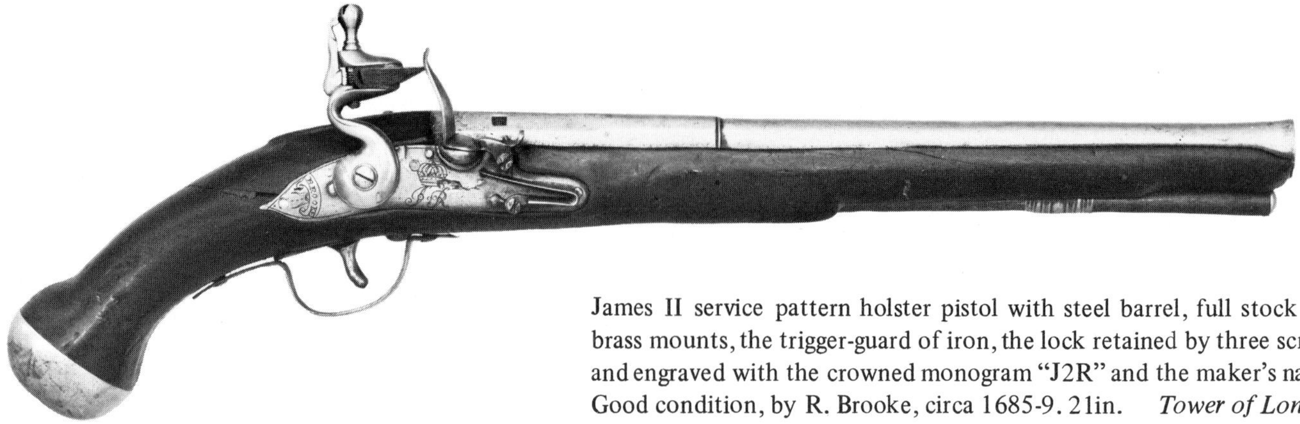

James II service pattern holster pistol with steel barrel, full stock and brass mounts, the trigger-guard of iron, the lock retained by three screws and engraved with the crowned monogram "J2R" and the maker's name. Good condition, by R. Brooke, circa 1685-9. 21in. *Tower of London*

Over £1,000

Early regulation pistols are extremely rare and several fakes have appeared on the market in recent years. Provenance is all-important.

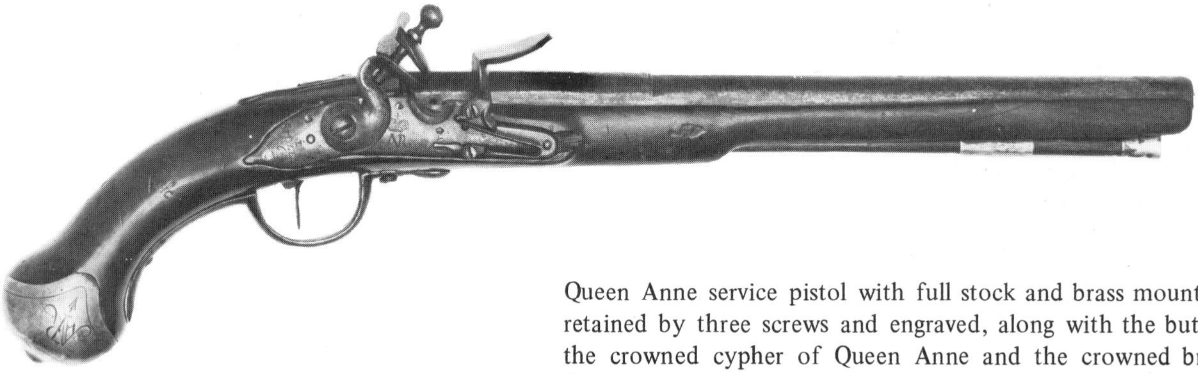

Queen Anne service pistol with full stock and brass mounts, the lock retained by three screws and engraved, along with the butt-cap, with the crowned cypher of Queen Anne and the crowned broad arrow Ordnance mark. The tail of the lock-plate is engraved with maker's name and an abbreviated date. Fair condition. This one siged "I. Sibley, '6" (for 1706). 21in. *Sotheby's*

£750 – £1,000

Beware, the same applies as to the James II pistol.

George II Light Dragoon service pistol with full stock and brass mounts, the lock engraved with "GR" crowned and the signature "Edge, 1760". Good condition. 9in. barrel. *Tower of London*

Over £500. The signature and the date adds to the value.

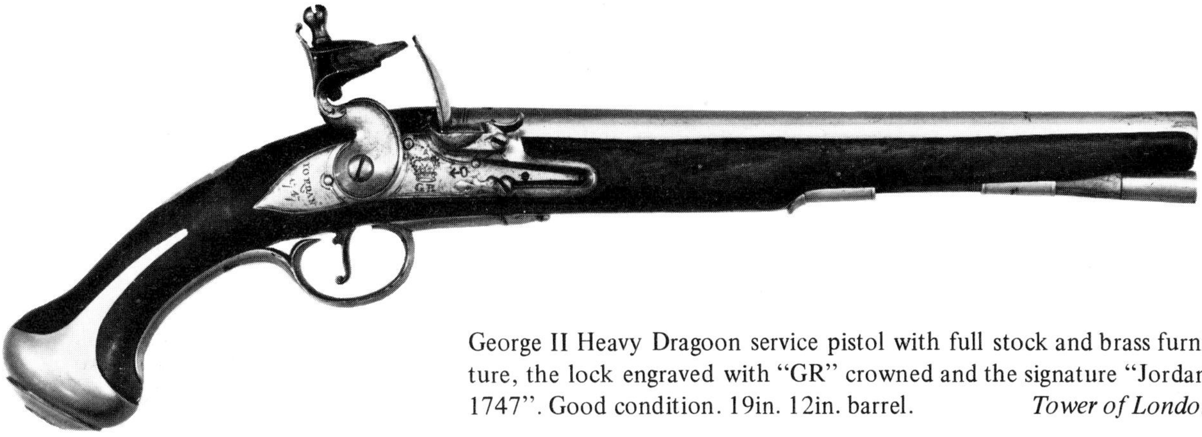

George II Heavy Dragoon service pistol with full stock and brass furniture, the lock engraved with "GR" crowned and the signature "Jordan, 1747". Good condition. 19in. 12in. barrel. *Tower of London*

Over £600

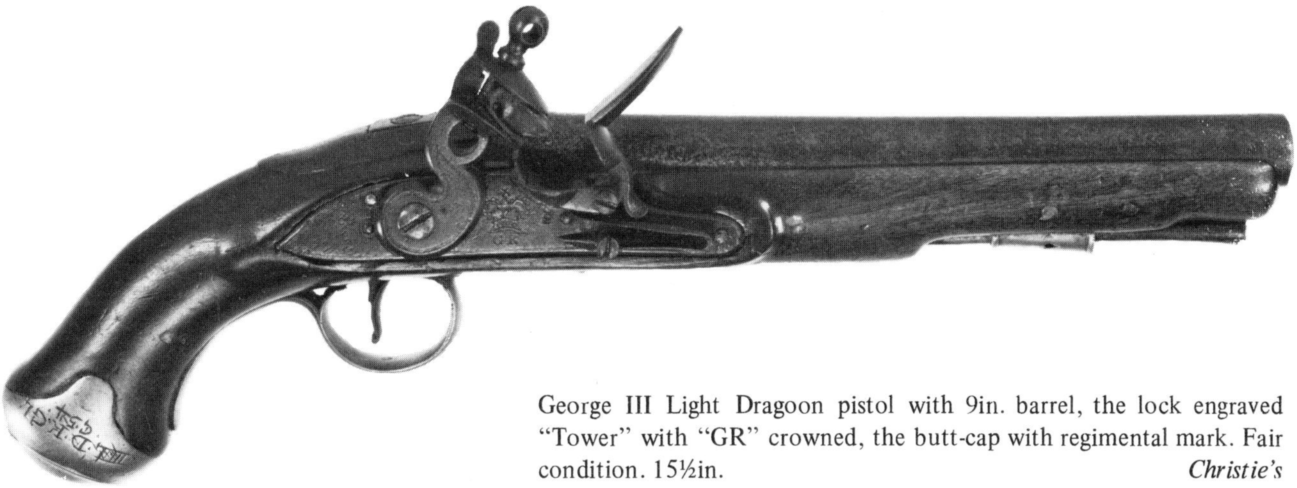

George III Light Dragoon pistol with 9in. barrel, the lock engraved "Tower" with "GR" crowned, the butt-cap with regimental mark. Fair condition. 15½in. *Christie's*

£100 – £120

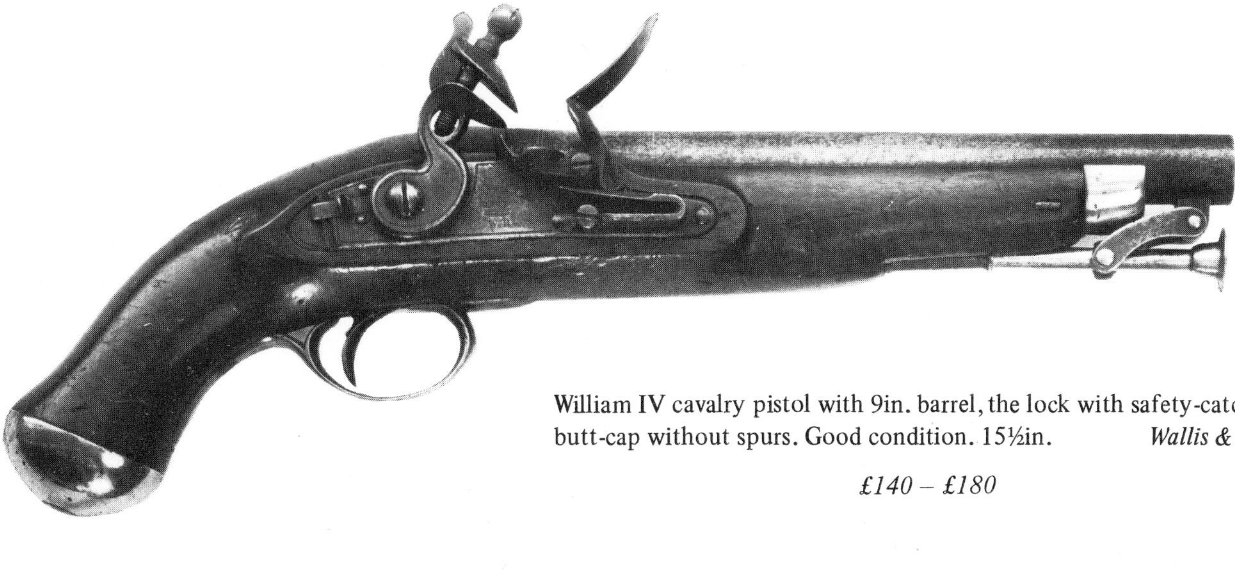

William IV cavalry pistol with 9in. barrel, the lock with safety-catch, the butt-cap without spurs. Good condition. 15½in. *Wallis & Wallis*

£140 – £180

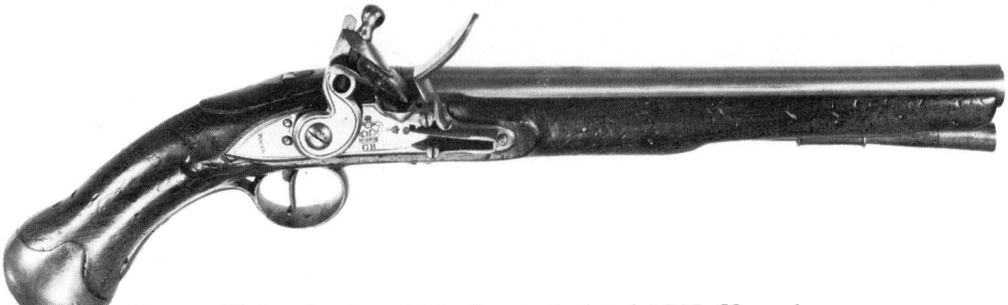

George III Sea Service pistol, the stock dated 1805. Very clean condition. 19¼in. overall. 12in. barrel. *Christie's*

£200 – £250

William IV Sea Service pistol with 9in. barrel. Very clean condition. 15¼in. overall. *Wallis & Wallis*

£150 – £180

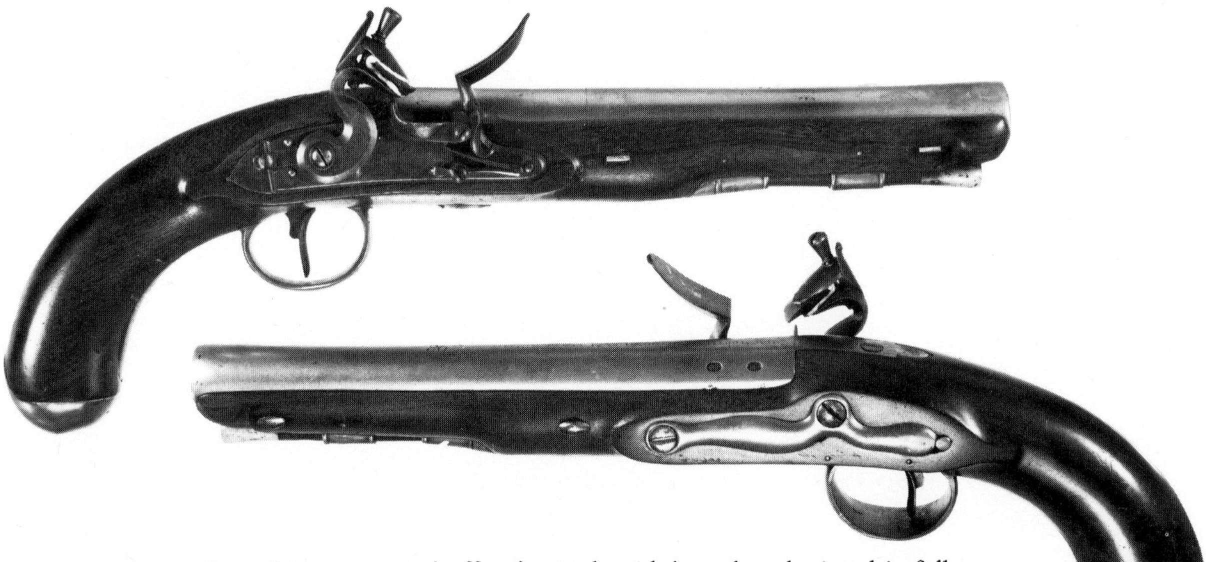

Pair of brass-mounted officer's pistols with brass barrels signed in full and engraved "98th" (now Argyll and Sutherland Highlanders), signed locks with safety-catches. Good quality, condition only fair. Cocks not a pair. By H.W. Mortimer, London, circa 1800. 15¼in. *Christie's*

£500 – £600 the pair

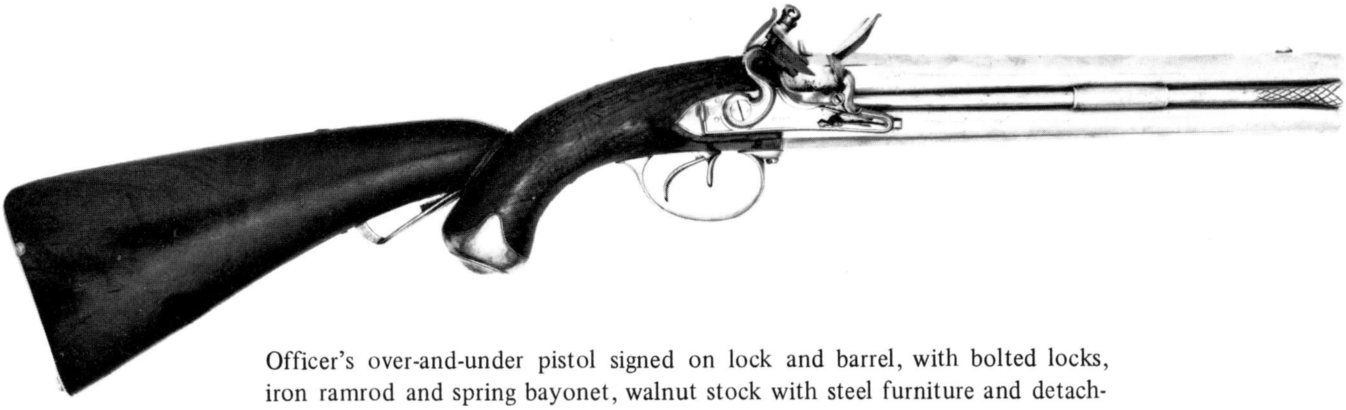

Officer's over-and-under pistol signed on lock and barrel, with bolted locks, iron ramrod and spring bayonet, walnut stock with steel furniture and detachable carbine butt, the butt-plate engraved "Egg's Patent Butt". Good condition. By Durs Egg, circa 1800. 34¾in. *Sotheby's*

Over £1,000

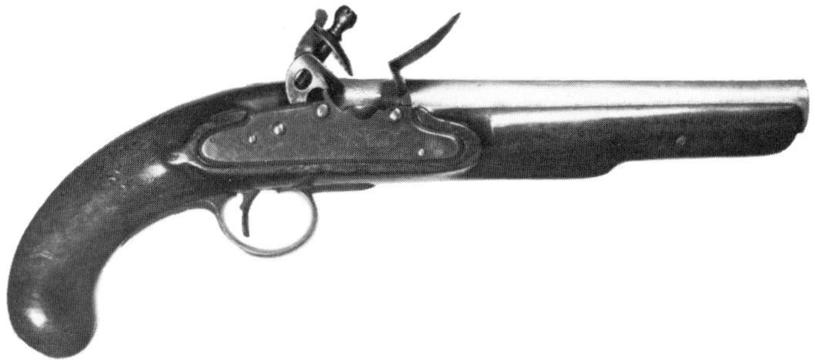

Henry Nock patent enclosed lock pistol with 9in. brass barrel, the lock signed H. Nock, walnut full stock without ramrod, and brass trigger-guard. Good condition. 15½in. *Tower of London*

About £400. Very rare.

Victorian Mail Coach Guard's pistol with brass barrel signed and numbered, and engraved around the muzzle "For Her Majesty's Mail Coaches", signed bolted lock, full stock and brass mounts. Fine condition. By J. Harding & Son, London. Dated 1837. 14¾in. *Christie's*

£500 – £600. A Victorian flintlock example is rare.

Durs Egg pistol made for Philip d'Auvergne, Prince de Bouillon, Captain of the Royal Naval Force based in the Channel Islands. Full stock and brass mounts. Good condition. Circa 1796. 12in. *Sotheby's*

About £300

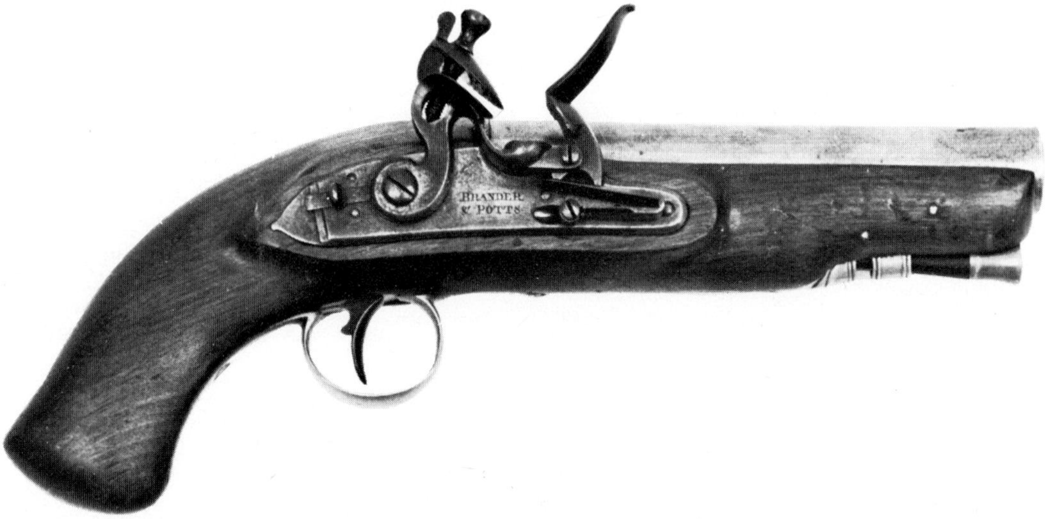

Coastguard or Police pistol with full stock and plain brass furniture, signed bolted lock and brass-tipped ramrod. Good condition. Signed Brander and Potts. Circa 1825. 11½ins. *Wallis & Wallis*

£100 – £120

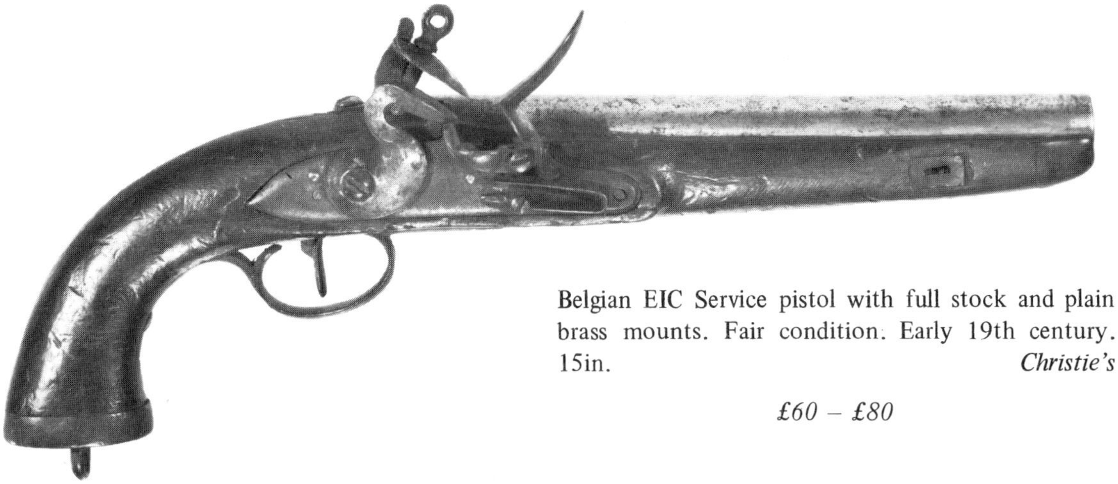

Belgian EIC Service pistol with full stock and plain brass mounts. Fair condition. Early 19th century. 15in. *Christie's*

£60 – £80

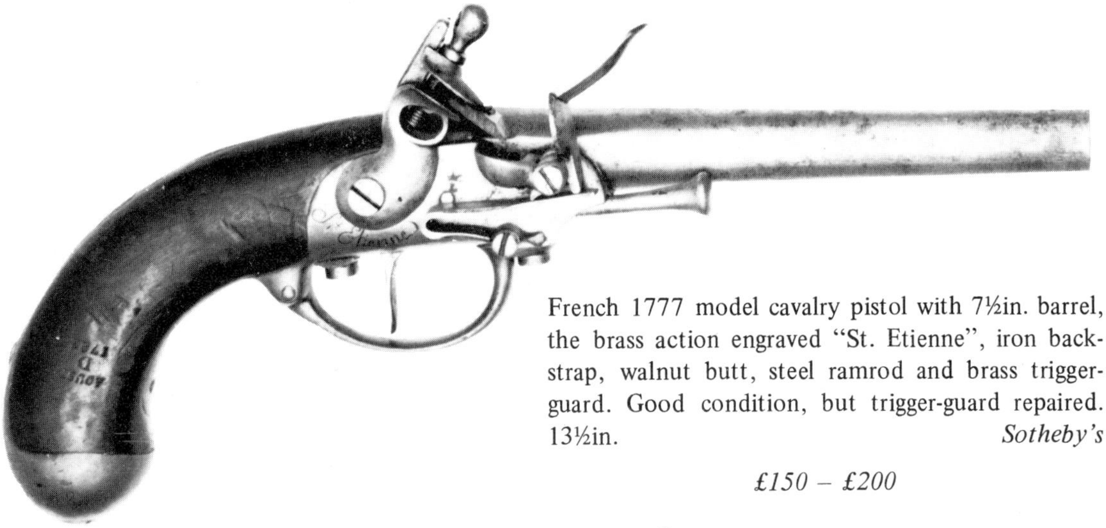

French 1777 model cavalry pistol with 7½in. barrel, the brass action engraved "St. Etienne", iron backstrap, walnut butt, steel ramrod and brass trigger-guard. Good condition, but trigger-guard repaired. 13½in. *Sotheby's*

£150 – £200

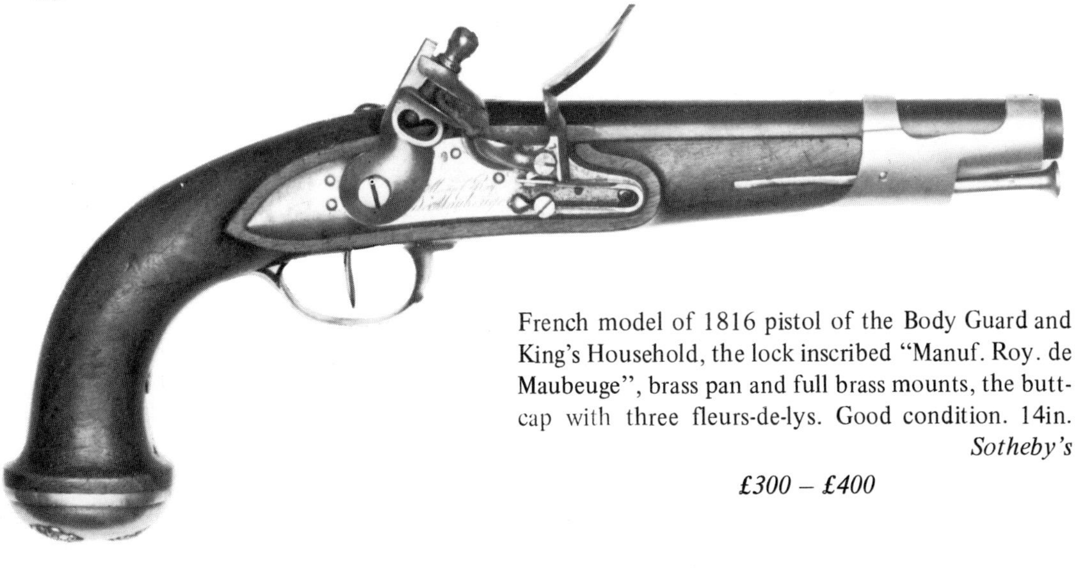

French model of 1816 pistol of the Body Guard and King's Household, the lock inscribed "Manuf. Roy. de Maubeuge", brass pan and full brass mounts, the butt-cap with three fleurs-de-lys. Good condition. 14in. *Sotheby's*

£300 – £400

Percussion Cap Service Pistols

Percussion cap Naval and Coastguard pistol, the lock with Victorian cypher, and engraved "Tower, 1849". Good condition. 11½in.

Tower of London

£80 – £120

Police pocket pistol, engraved "Tower, 1848". Good condition. 9½in.

Tower of London

£80 – £100.

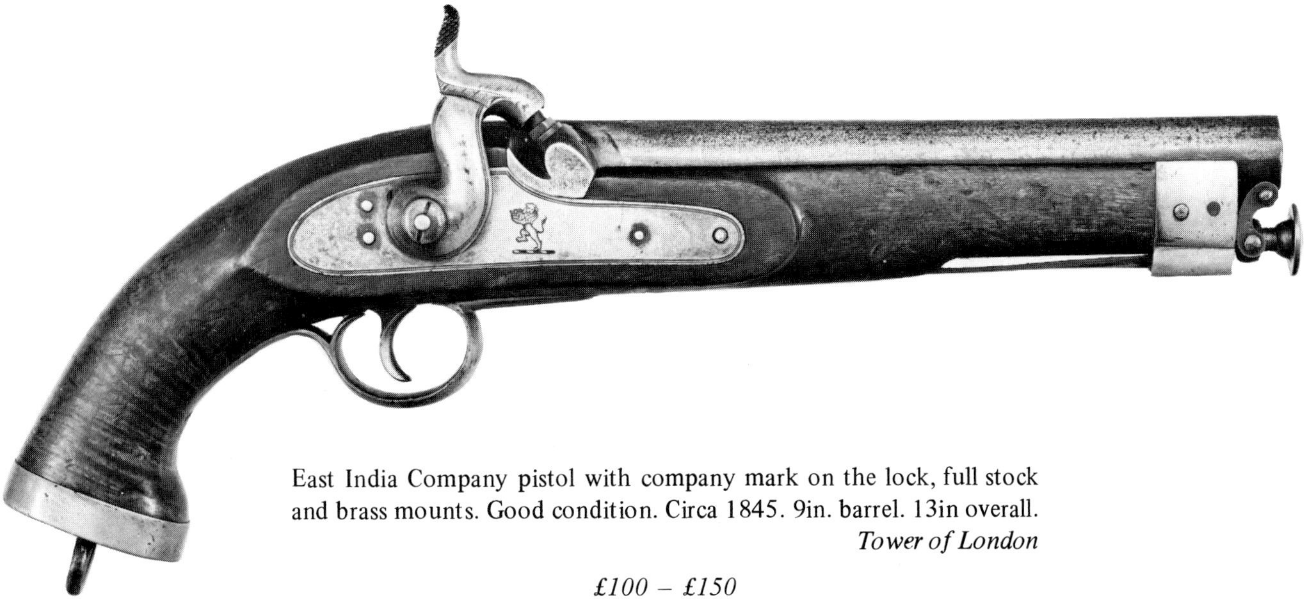

East India Company pistol with company mark on the lock, full stock and brass mounts. Good condition. Circa 1845. 9in. barrel. 13in overall.
Tower of London

£100 – £150

Many of these have recently been imported from Indian Armouries and some have new stocks –

£40 – £50

1842 pattern cavalry pistol, the lock with "VR" and crown, and inscribed "Tower 1843". Good condition, 9in.barrel, 15½in. overall.
Tower of London

£150 – £200

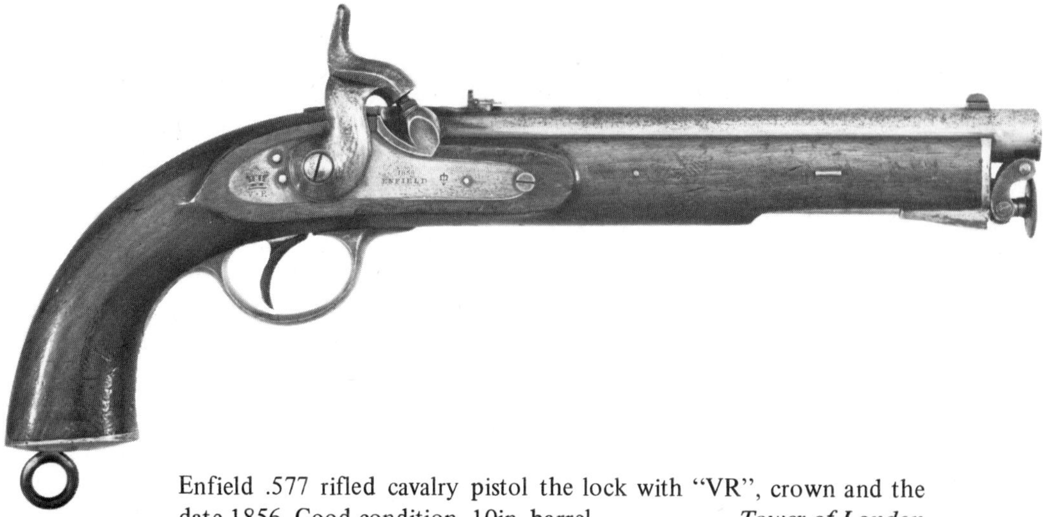

Enfield .577 rifled cavalry pistol the lock with "VR", crown and the date 1856. Good condition. 10in. barrel. *Tower of London*

Over £200

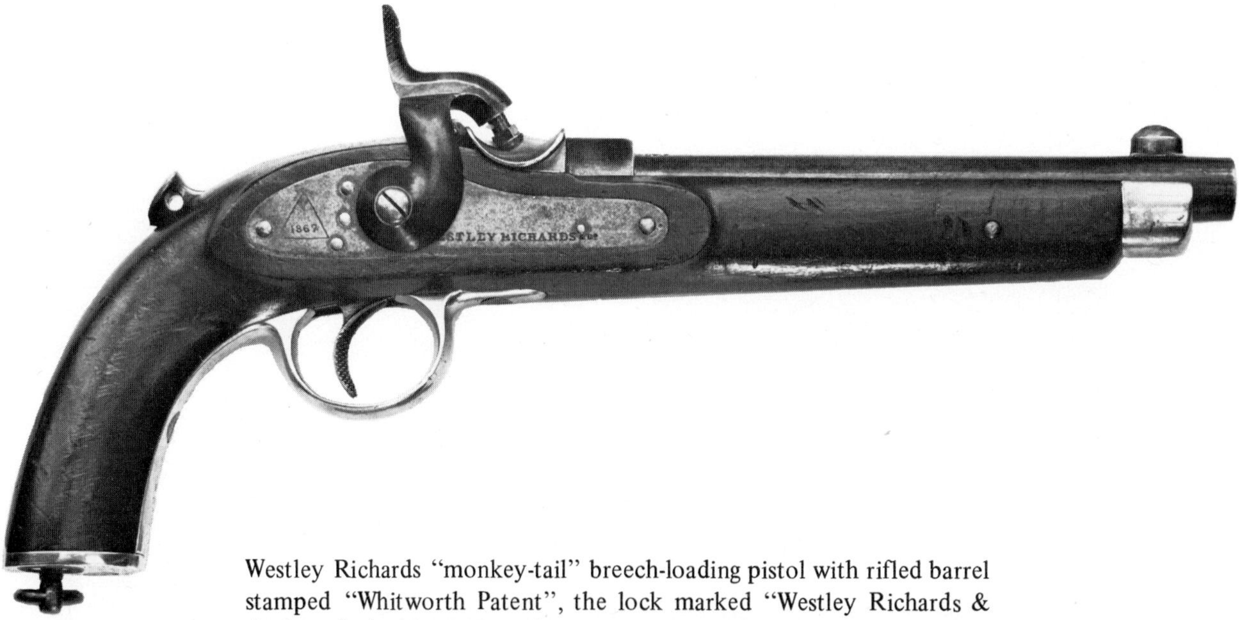

Westley Richards "monkey-tail" breech-loading pistol with rifled barrel stamped "Whitworth Patent", the lock marked "Westley Richards & Co." and dated 1867 within a triangle, with full stock and brass mounts. 9in. barrel. 14½in. overall. *Wallis & Wallis*

Over £200

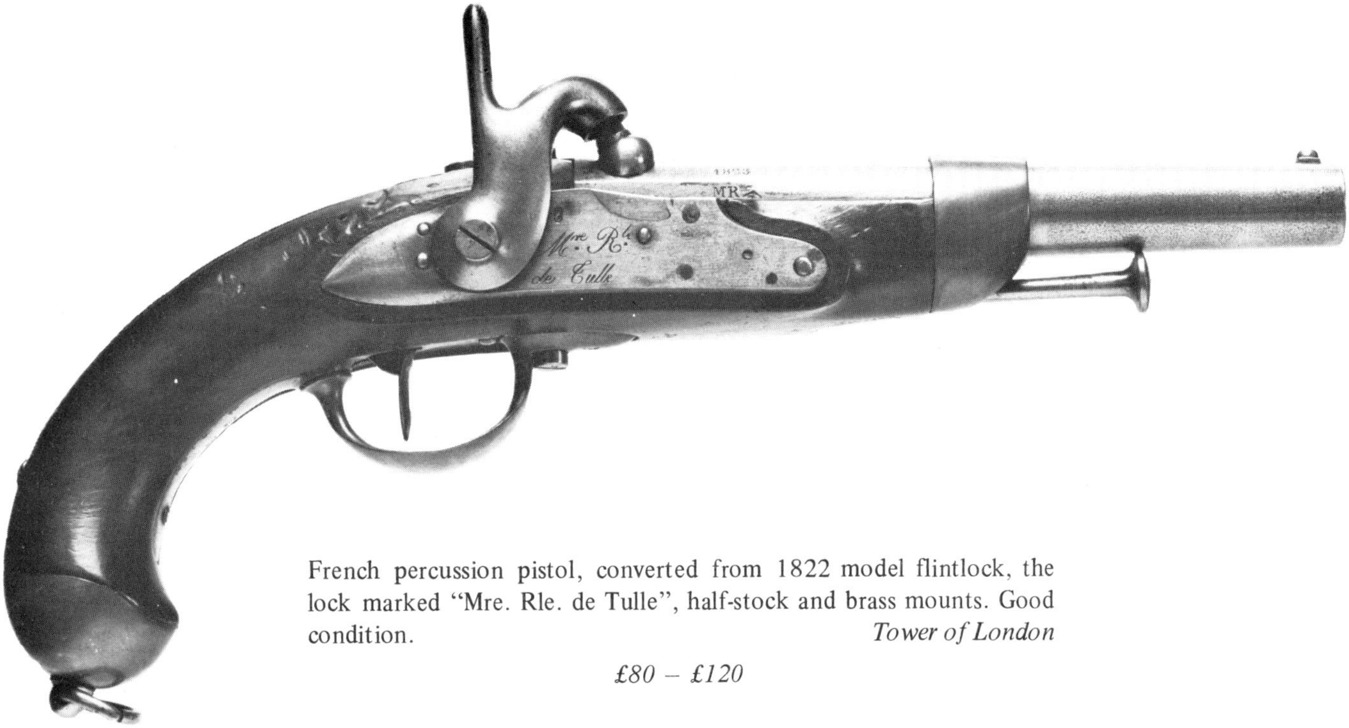

French percussion pistol, converted from 1822 model flintlock, the lock marked "Mre. Rle. de Tulle", half-stock and brass mounts. Good condition. *Tower of London*

£80 – £120

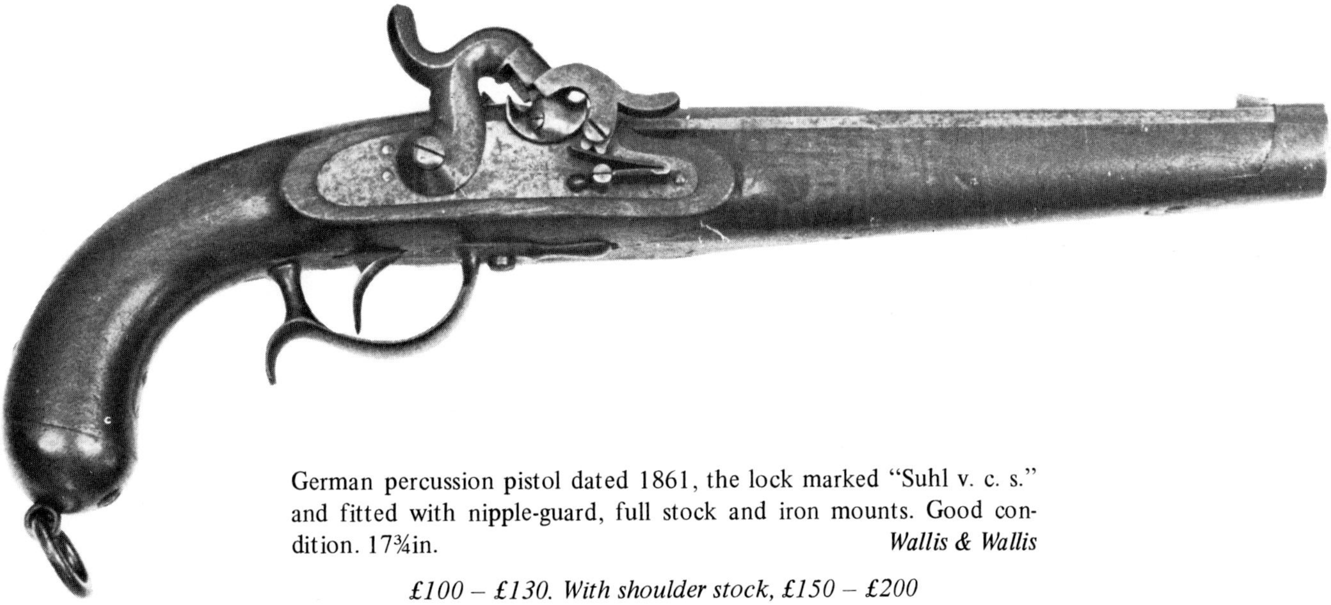

German percussion pistol dated 1861, the lock marked "Suhl v. c. s." and fitted with nipple-guard, full stock and iron mounts. Good condition. 17¾in. *Wallis & Wallis*

£100 – £130. With shoulder stock, £150 – £200

American Pistols

Flintlock duelling pistol in the English style, with octagonal barrel, gold-lined vent and pan, half-stock, chequered butt, set trigger and engraved silver furniture. Medium quality, fair condition. By B. & J. Cooper, New York, circa 1820. 15½in.
Christie's

£500 – £600

Although of inferior quality to English examples, the rarity of American flintlock duelling pistols accounts for the price.

One of a pair of percussion duelling pistols with half-stock and steel furniture. Poor quality, fair condition. By R. Constable, Philadelphia, circa 1840. 14¼in. *Christie's*

£400 – £500 the pair. Rarity value.

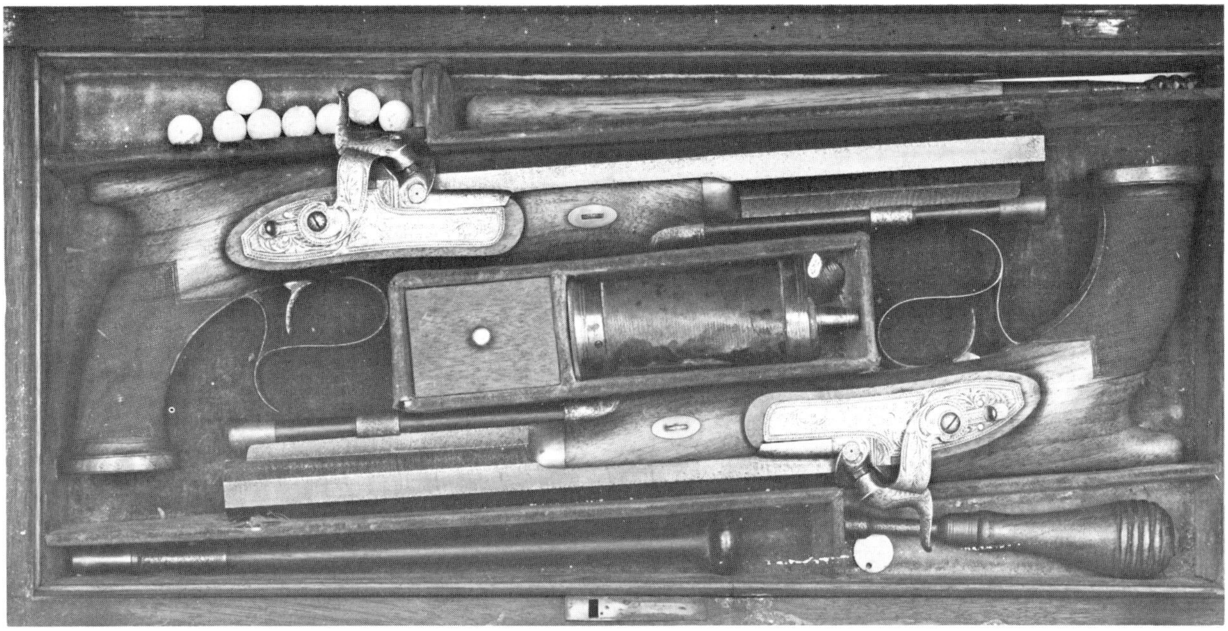

Cased pair of saw-handled percussion duelling pistols with half-stocks and engraved steel furniture, the barrels with gold lines at the breech. Original case with fittings. Moderate quality, rather clumsy, some pitting, some original finish. By R. Constable, Philadelphia, circa 1840. 15½in. *Sotheby's*

About £800

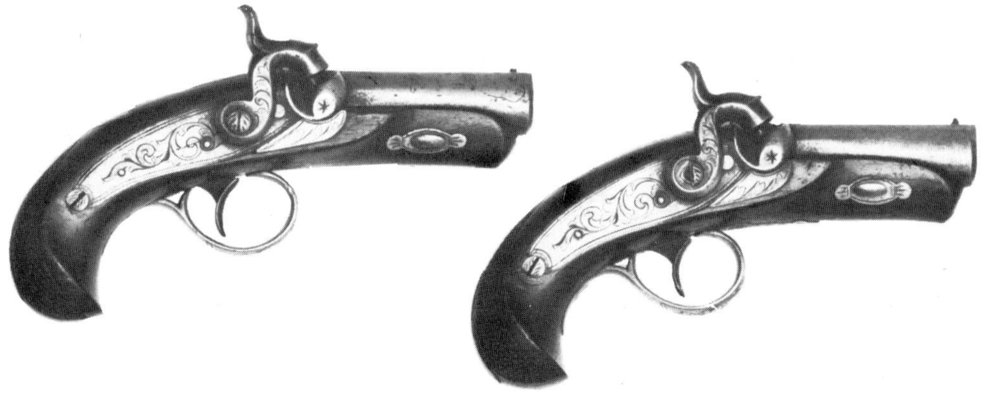

Pair of Deringer pistols, the rifled barrels with top flat, with engraved locks, full stocks, engraved nickel silver furniture. Moderate quality and condition. Unsigned, Circa 1850. 5½in. *Sotheby's*

About £400 the pair

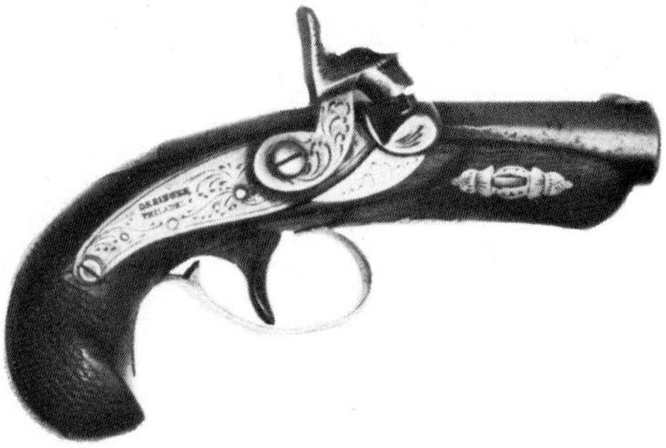

Deringer pistol with full stock and silvered mounts, the breech and lock stamped "Deringer Philadel", the barrel with the agent's name "N. Curry & Bros. San Franco Cala. Agents". Moderate quality, fair condition. Circa 1863-8. 5in. *Sotheby's*

About £250

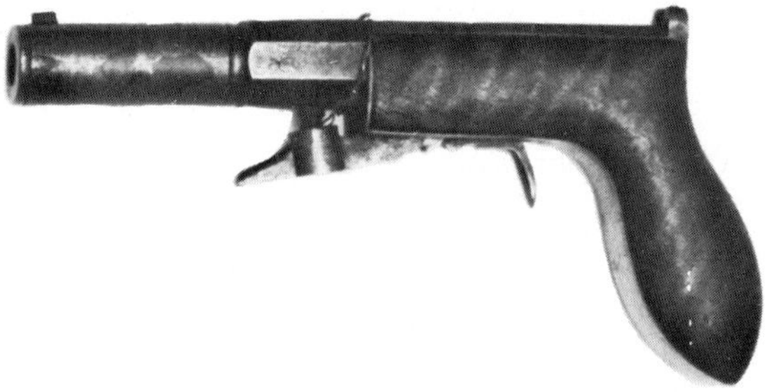

"Bootleg" pistol, the barrel with octagonal breech stamped "cast steel" the top strap engraved and signed "A. Ruggles, Stafford (Conn.)", brass backstrap wood grips. Poor quality, fair condition. Circa 1,840. 5¾in *Sotheby's*

£50 – £75

Cased Allen & Thurber pepperbox revolver, the cylinder stamped "Allen & Thurber, Worcester" and the bar hammer, "Allen's Patent 1845", original velvet-lined mahogany case with bullet mould. Poor quality, fine condition with most original finish. Circa 1847-56. 7¼in. *Sotheby's*

£150 – £200

Stocking & Co. pepperbox revolver, the cylinder stamped "Stocking & Co., Worcester Warranted, Cast Steel" and the long hammer "Patent Secured 1848". Crudely engraved action. Poor quality but good condition with much finish. Circa 1847-65. 8in. *Sotheby's*

£100 – £125

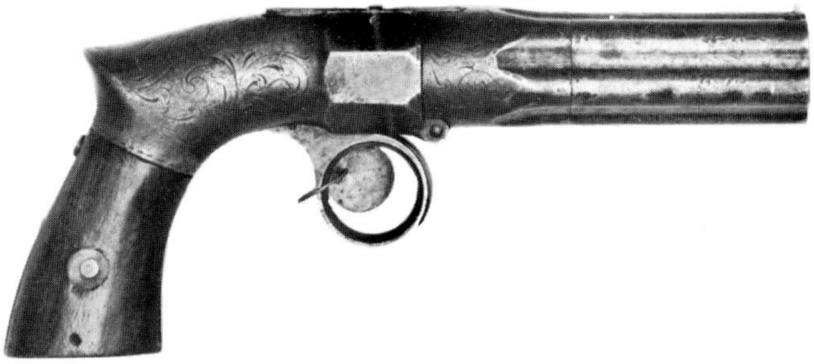

Robbins & Lawrence pepperbox revolver, the cylinder stamped "Robbins & Lawrence Co. Windsor, Patent 1845". Poor quality, fair condition. Circa 1851-2. 7¾in. *Sotheby's*

£60 – £90

Allen & Thurber pepperbox revolver, the cylinder stamped "Patented 1837" and the hammer "Allens Patent", with engraved nickel silver grips. Poor quality, fair condition. Circa 1837. 5¾in. *Sotheby's*

£100 – £140

Colt Revolvers

With Colt revolvers condition is all-important, for they were made and have survived in large numbers. Condition is less important only with the very rare types.

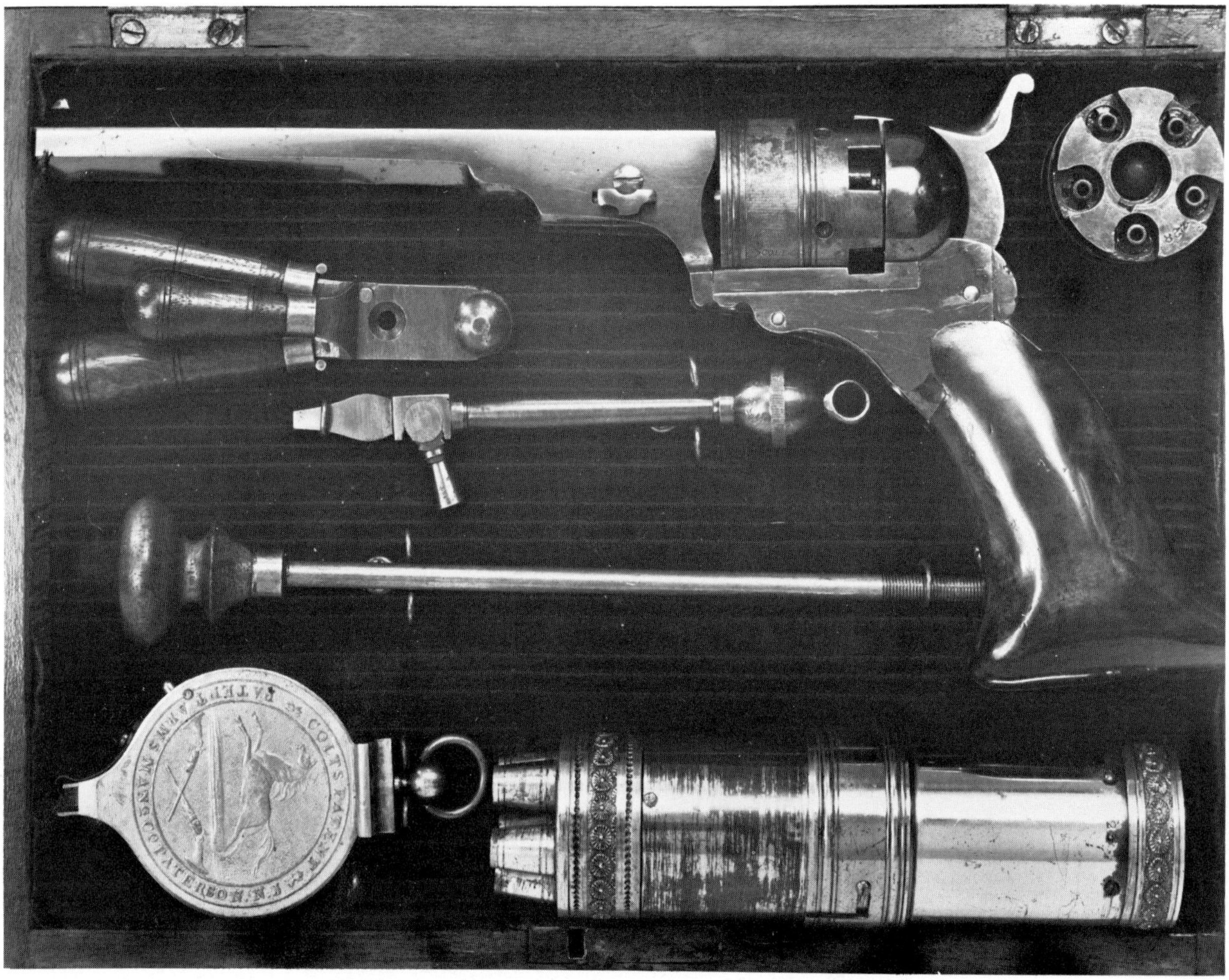

Cased Colt Paterson belt pistol, the barrel inscribed "Patent Arms M'g Co. Paterson, N-J Colt's Pt." the cylinder engraved with centaurs in combat. In original velvet-lined case with fittings. Excellent condition with nearly all original finish. 5½in. barrel. Circa 1839. *Sotheby's*

Over £6,000. Extremely rare

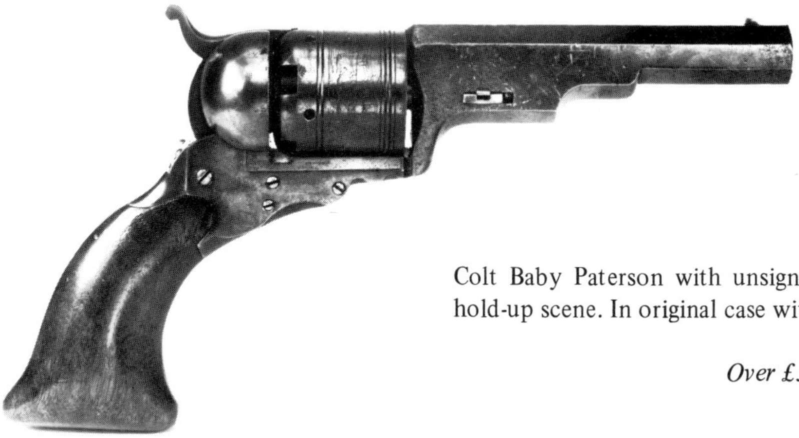

Colt Baby Paterson with unsigned blued 4½in. barrel, the cylinder with stage hold-up scene. In original case with fittings. Good to fine condition. 9¼in.

Sotheby's

Over £3,000. Extremely rare.

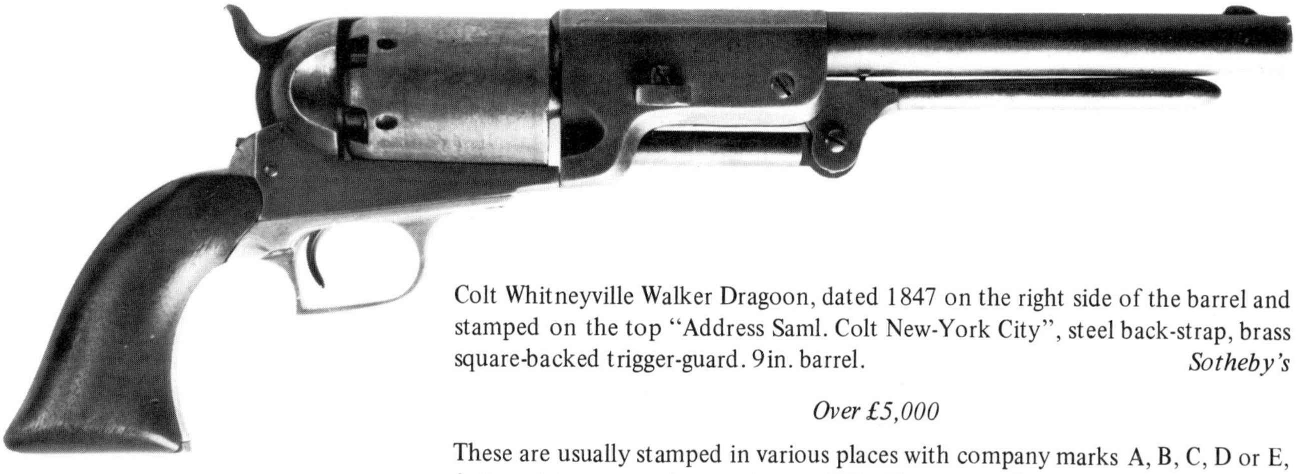

Colt Whitneyville Walker Dragoon, dated 1847 on the right side of the barrel and stamped on the top "Address Saml. Colt New-York City", steel back-strap, brass square-backed trigger-guard. 9in. barrel. *Sotheby's*

Over £5,000

These are usually stamped in various places with company marks A, B, C, D or E, followed by a number, not over 200. Most examples are in poor condition. Generally speaking those which are not must be suspect. Fakes abound, mainly of Italian manufacture. A genuine one weighs exactly four pounds.

Modern copy of a Whitneyville Walker Dragoon.

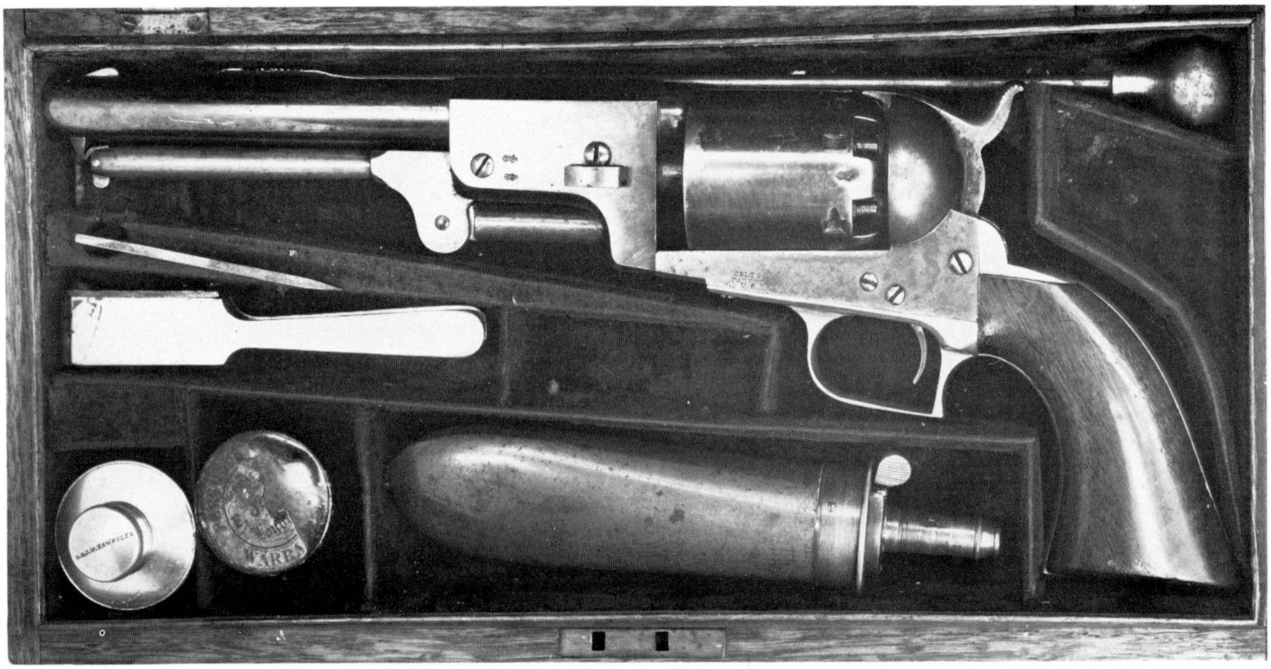

Cased Colt 2nd Model Hartford Dragoon, the barrel marked "Address Saml. Colt New York City", nickel-plated frame, square-backed trigger-guard, London proof marks. Fair condition with much finish, but the cylinder possibly from another pistol. Original case lined in crimson velvet with some fittings and instructions label. 7½in. barrel. *Sotheby's*

£1,000 – £1,250 Much more for a really clean one.

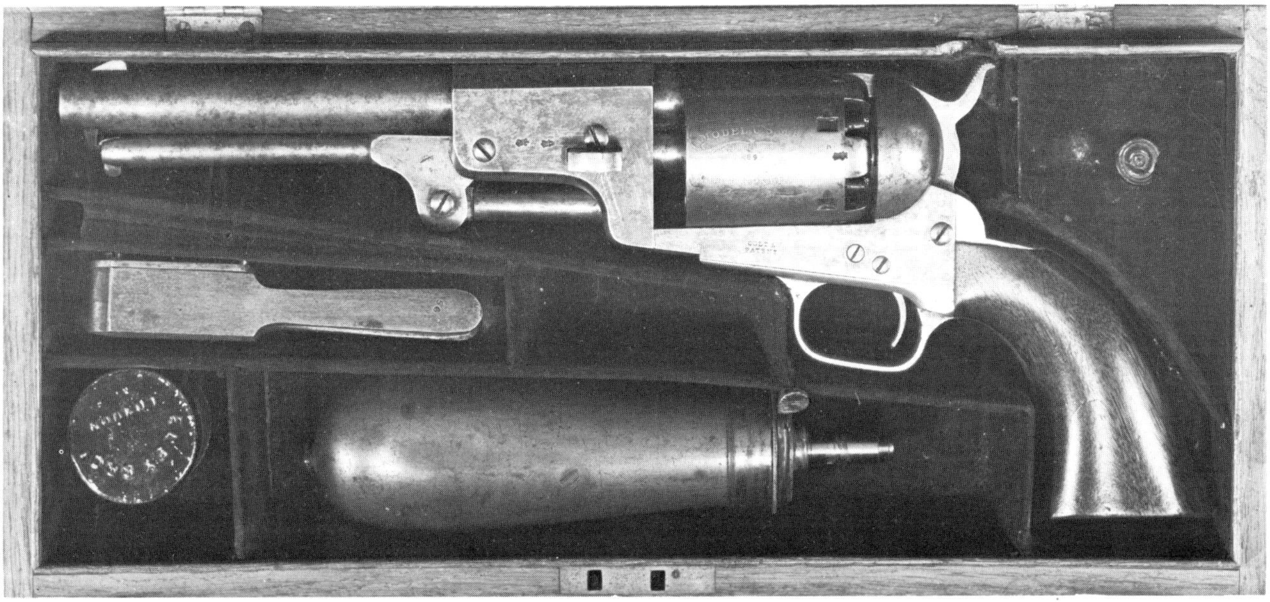

Two cased Hartford-English dragoons, one with New York City address and one with London address on the 7½in. barrel. Plated back-strap and round-backed trigger-guard, London proof marks and original London oak case with English flask. 14in. overall.
About seven hundred of these were made specially at Hartford for export to England. The serial numbers of the two are 123 and 89 respectively
The top pistol is in good working order but has no original finish. *Christie's*

About £1,200

The bottom pistol is almost mint.

Over £4,000

This ratio of price to condition is roughly standard to the rest of the Colt models.

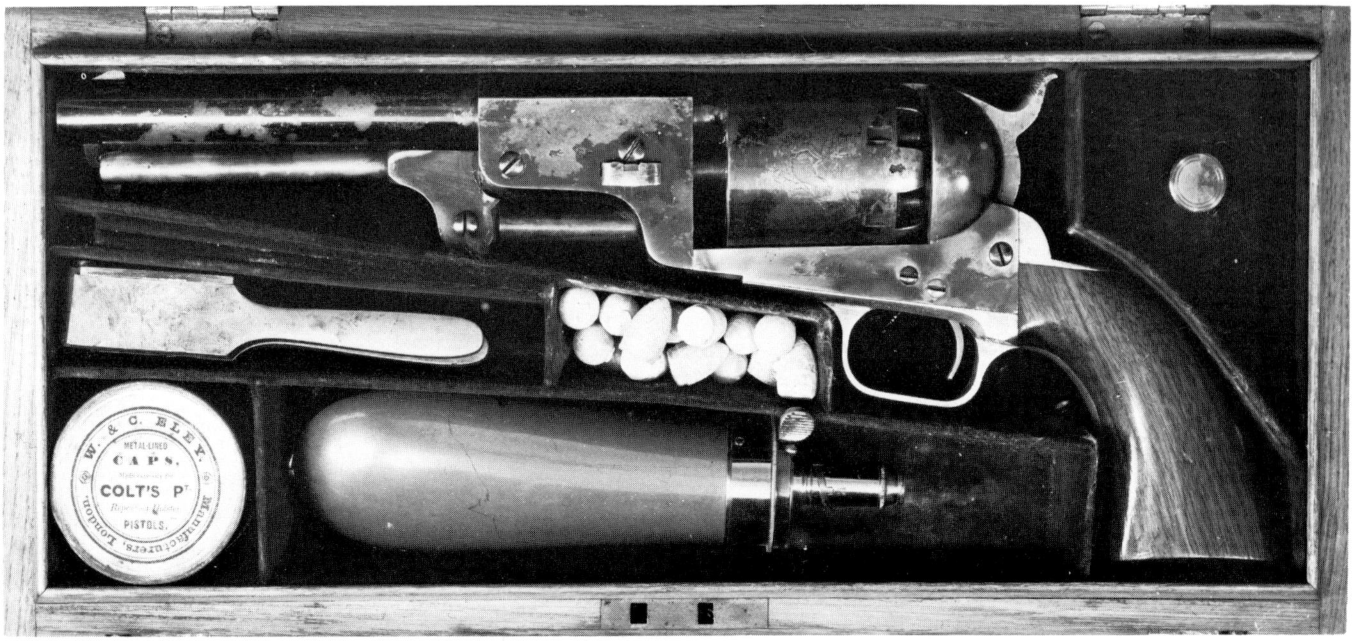

"Little Dragoon" with 5in. barrel stamped with New York City address, silvered back-strap and square-backed trigger-guard. Refinished, the cylinder serial number erased. 10¼in. The first 11,000 or so of these had no loading levers (as in illustration). *Sotheby's*

About £150 owing to condition.
Over £300 for a good one.

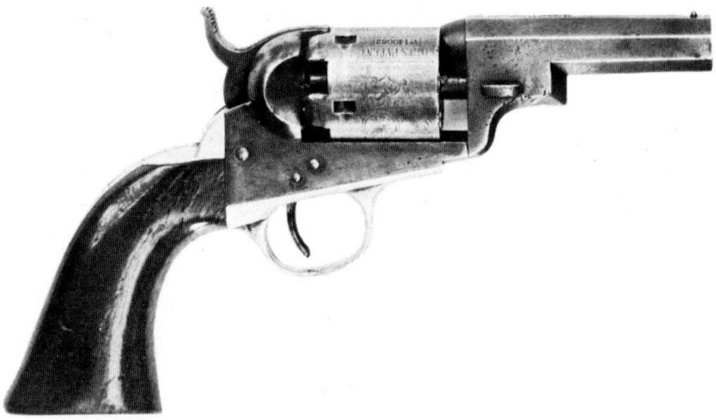

"Wells Fargo" model with 3in. barrel bearing New York City address and not provided with rammer, the cylinder with hold-up scene, plated trigger-guard and back-strap. Good condition, but little finish. 7½in. *Wallis & Wallis*

£250 – £300

Cased Pocket Model, the 5in. barrel (they were made with 3in., 4in., 5in., and 6in. barrels) with London address, the cylinder with stage hold-up scene, iron trigger-guard and back-strap. Original case line in brown velvet, with fittings. Clean condition with much original finish (cap tin missing). London proof marks. 10in. overall. *Christie's*

£300 – £400
Uncased £150 – £250

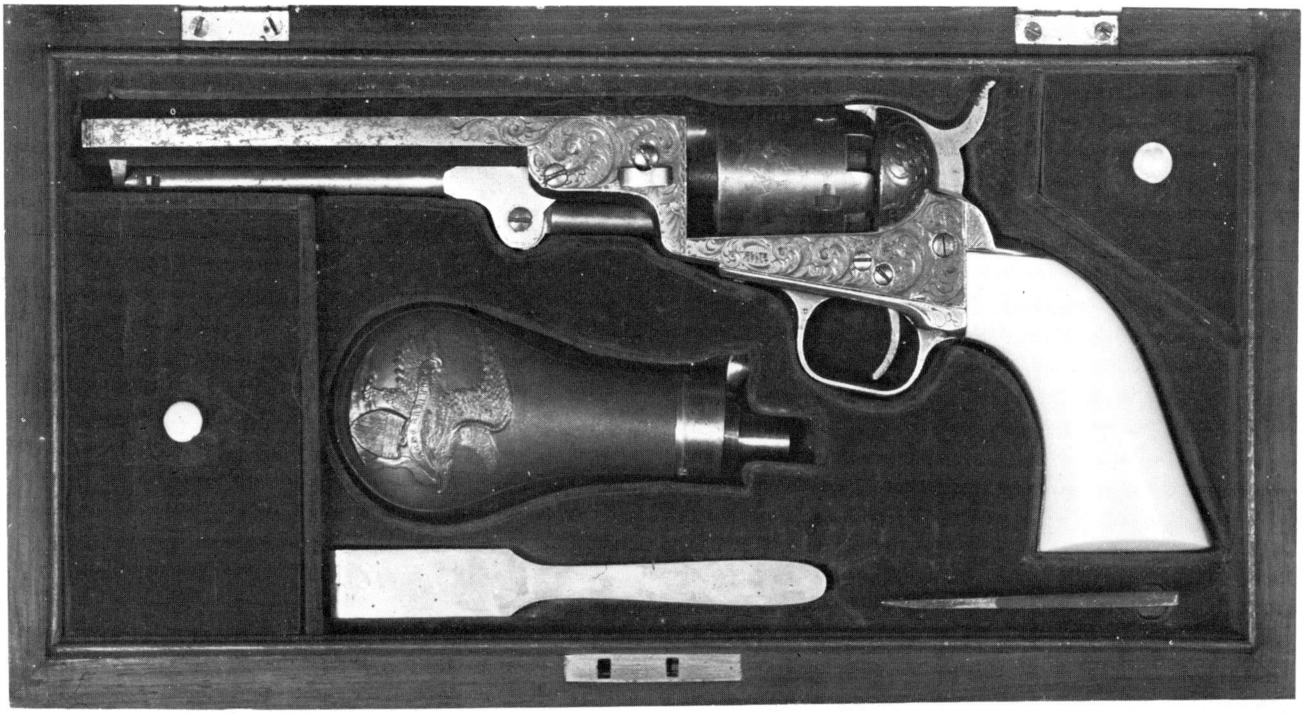

Cased Presentation Pocket Model, the 6in. barrel stamped with New York address, the cylinder with hold-up scene, plated back-strap and trigger-guard, these and the action engraved with scrolls of foliage, mother-of-pearl grips. Original rosewood so-called "French" casing, lined in maroon velvet, with accessories including embossed Eagle flask. Fine untouched condition. 11in. *Christie's*

Over £1,000
Uncased about £400

Navy or 1851 Model, of the second type, the 7½in. barrel with New York address, the cylinder with naval engagement scene, plated square-backed trigger-guard (this distinguishes it from the standard third type Navy model) and back-strap. Clean condition with some original finish. 13¼in. *Christie's*

£350 – £400

This second type is much rarer than the standard Navy with round-backed trigger-guard.

Standard Navy Model, this one with Hartford address on the barrel, plated back-strap and round-backed trigger-guard. Poor condition with pitting. 13¼in. *Sotheby's*

About £100 owing to condition. Up to £300 for a good one. £600–£1,000 for one in fine condition in its case complete with fittings.

Cased Presentation Navy Model, the barrel with London address and the cylinder with naval engagement scene, almost entirely covered with bold scrollwork engraving and with figured grips, plated trigger-guard and back-strap. Original case with some fittings. Fair condition, but no original finish. London proof marks.
Christie's

£500 – £700
Over £2,000 for a cased example in really fine condition.

Navy Model with London address on the barrel, London proof, iron trigger-guard and back-strap. Good condition, but no finish. 13¼in. *Christie's*

Cased with accessories £300–£450, in fine condition £600–£1,000.

This is the type supplied to British troops in the Crimean War. Should be marked with broad arrow and "WD". If so marked and with original finish, £250 – £300.

Cased Navy Model complete with shoulder stock, the barrel with Hartford address, the cylinder with naval engagement scene, plated back-strap and trigger-guard. Original case with most fittings. Fine condition with much finish.

Sotheby's

Over £3,000. Very rare with shoulder stock.

The rarest form of stock incorporates a canteen. These should be inspected with great care as imitations are more common than originals.

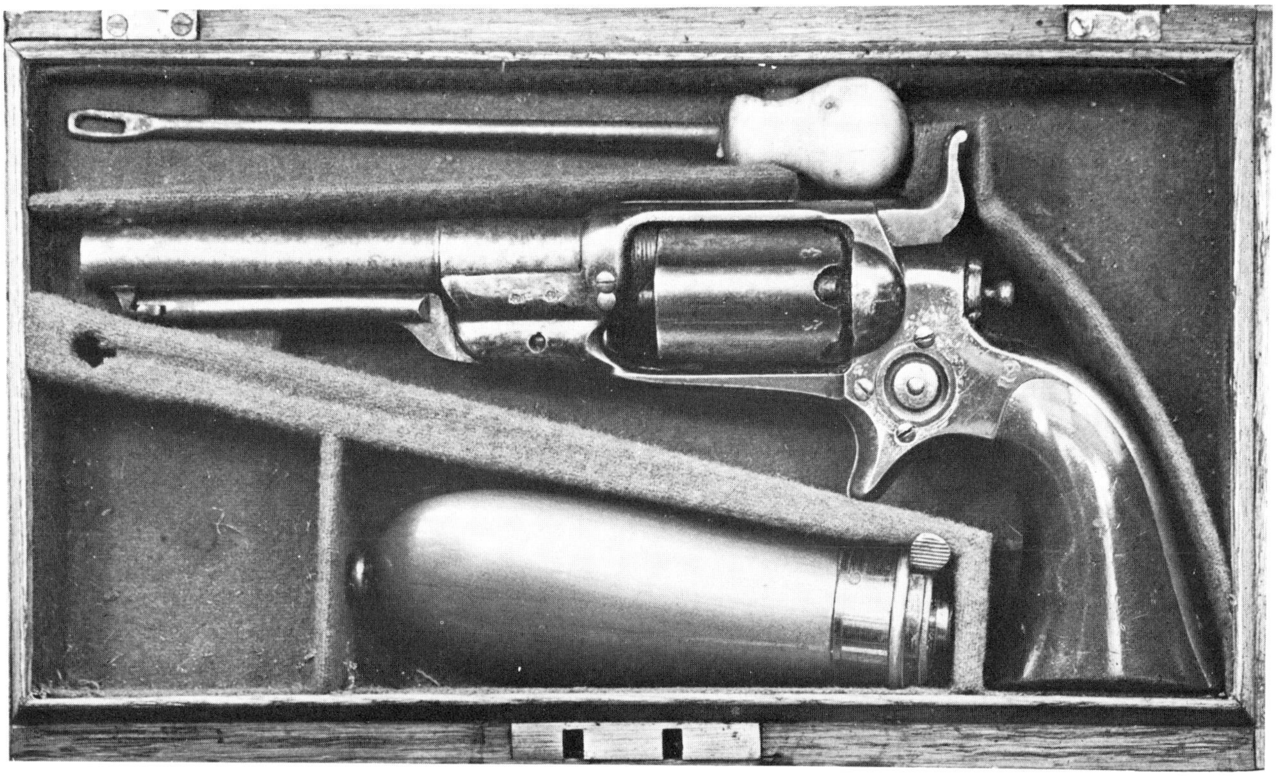

Cased Root model side-hammer with round 4½in. barrel marked with New York address, fluted cylinder, London proof marks. In lined and fitted oak case, with a flask (associated). Fair condition with some original finish. 8¾in.

Wallis & Wallis

£300 – £400

Uncased presentation version of the same pistol, scroll engraved and with ivory grips. Fine condition. *Sotheby's*

£400 – £500

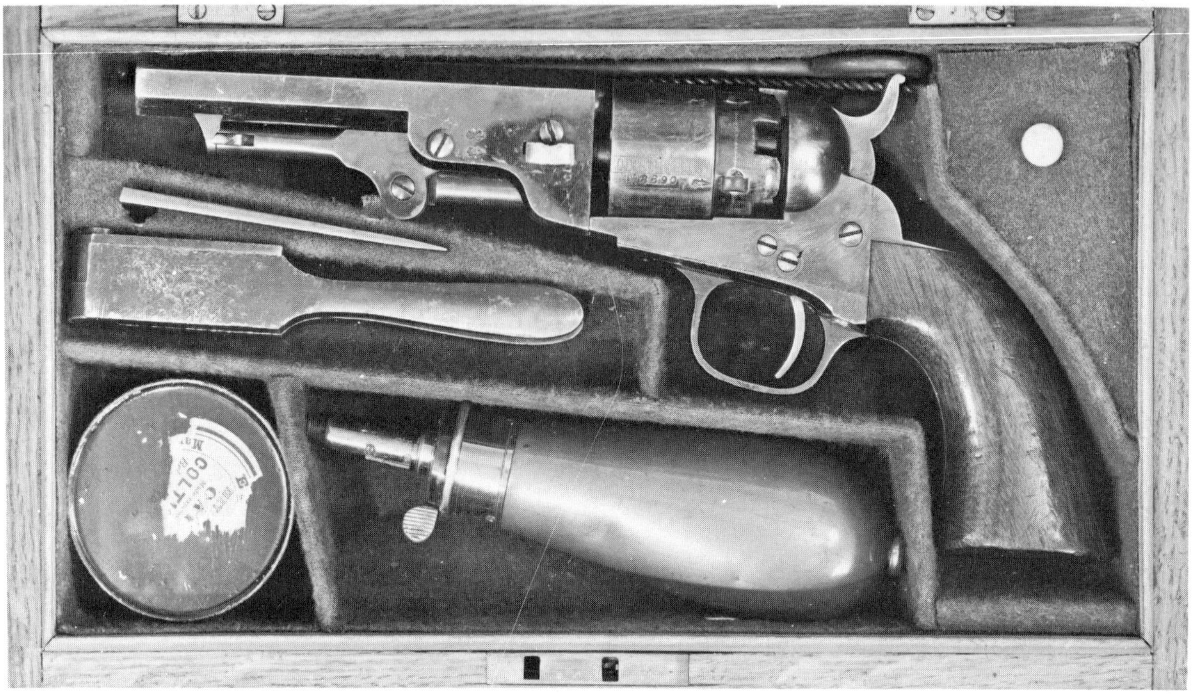

Cased pocket model of Navy (36) calibre (1853 model), the 4½in. barrel stamped with New York address, the rebated cylinder with hold-up scene, iron trigger-guard and back strap. Original London oak case with accessories. Fine condition with nearly all original finish. London proof marks. 9½in. *Christie's*

£600 – £750

This is a particularly good one, and the fact that the fittings are original and complete adds greatly to the value.

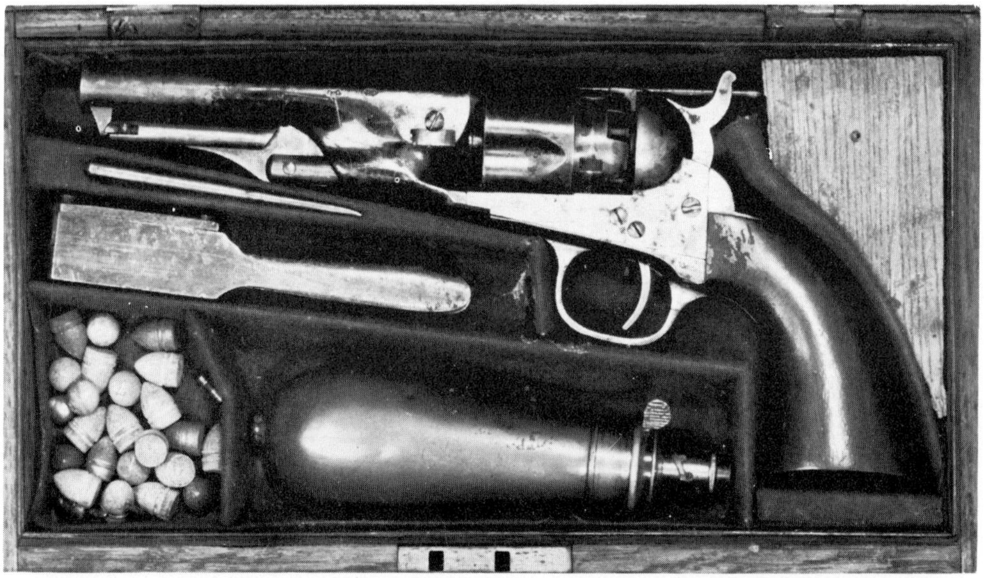

Police (1862) model with 4½in. barrel with "Saml. Colt" signature fluted cylinder, iron trigger-guard and back-strap. In original English oak case with fittings, the flask associated. Fair condition with some original finish. 9¾in.

Wallis & Wallis

£250 – £350

The Police model was made with 4½in., 5½in., and 6½in. barrel.

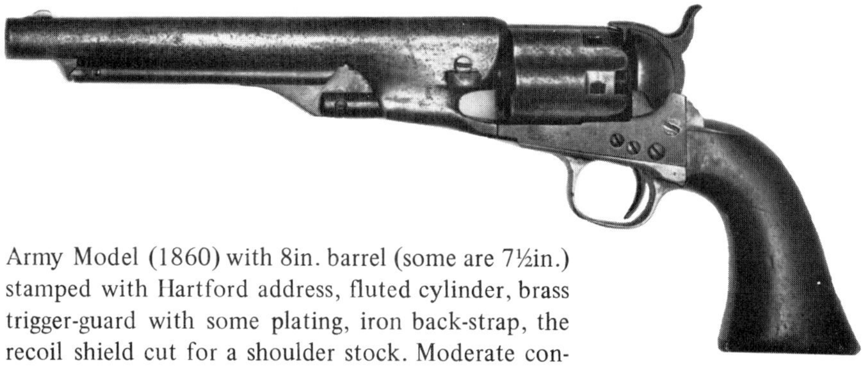

Army Model (1860) with 8in. barrel (some are 7½in.) stamped with Hartford address, fluted cylinder, brass trigger-guard with some plating, iron back-strap, the recoil shield cut for a shoulder stock. Moderate condition with no finish. 14½in. *Sotheby's*

About £180

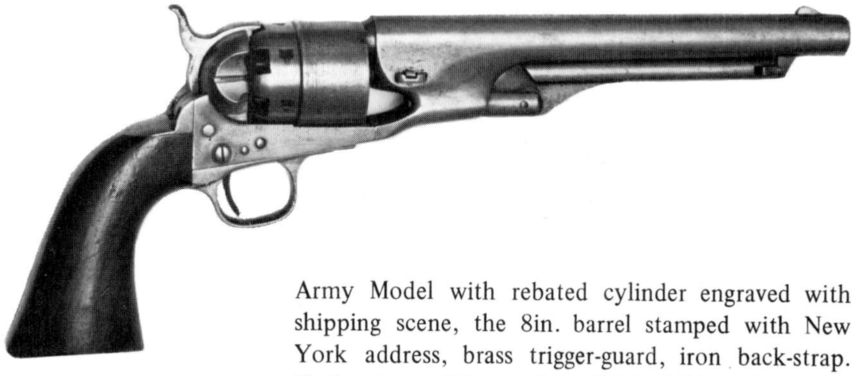

Army Model with rebated cylinder engraved with shipping scene, the 8in. barrel stamped with New York address, brass trigger-guard, iron back-strap. Moderate condition with no finish. 14½in. *Sotheby's*

About £140

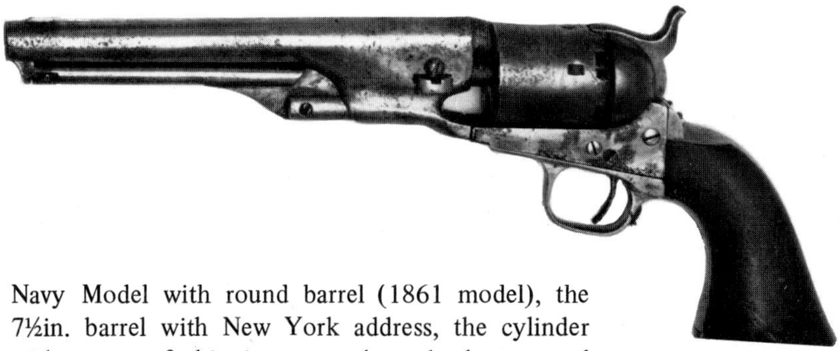

Navy Model with round barrel (1861 model), the 7½in. barrel with New York address, the cylinder with traces of shipping scene, brass back-strap and trigger-guard. Poor condition with pitting. 13½in. *Sotheby's*

About £100 owing to condition.

Prices for this model are slightly higher than for the Army model with rebated cylinder, as they seem to be more scarce.

Various American Revolvers

Starr's patent double-action Army revolver, the frame stamped "Starr's Patent Jan. 15 1856, Starr Arms Co. New York". Good condition with much original finish. 12in. *Sotheby's*

£100 – £120

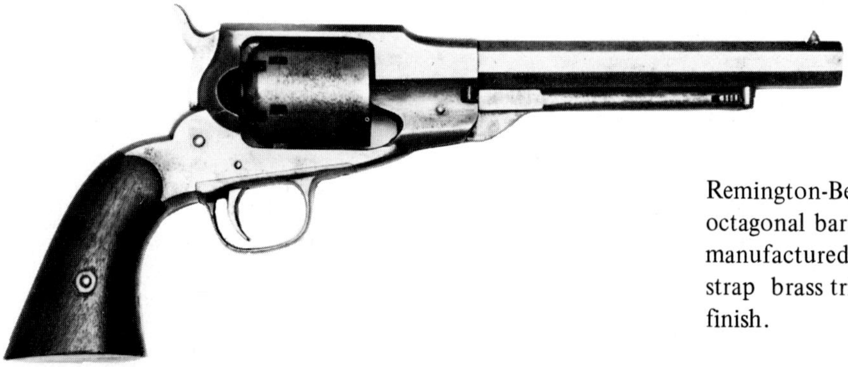

Remington-Beals patent Navy revolver with 7¼in. octagonal barrel stamped "Beals Patent Spt. 14 1859, manufactured by Remingtons, Ilion, N.Y." Iron back-strap brass trigger-guard. Moderate condition with no finish. *Sotheby's*

£100 – £150

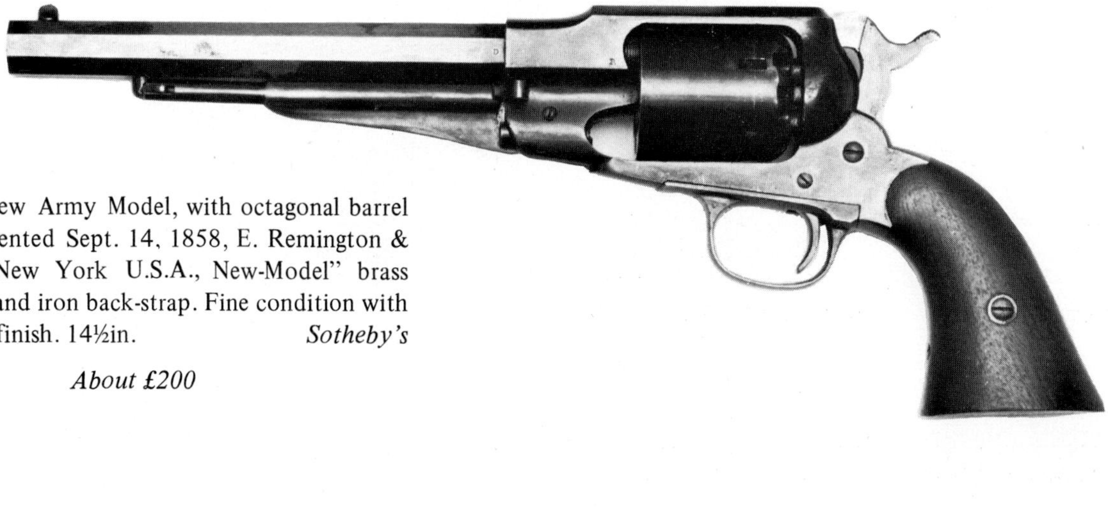

Remington New Army Model, with octagonal barrel stamped "Patented Sept. 14, 1858, E. Remington & Sons, Ilion New York U.S.A., New-Model" brass trigger-guard and iron back-strap. Fine condition with most original finish. 14½in. *Sotheby's*

About £200

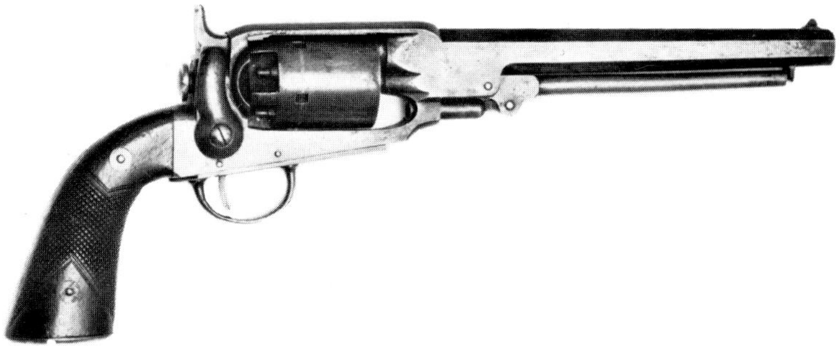

Joslyn Patent Army Model with octagonal barrel stamped "B.F. Joslyn Patd. May 4th 1858". Good condition with much original finish. 15in. *Sotheby's*

About £200

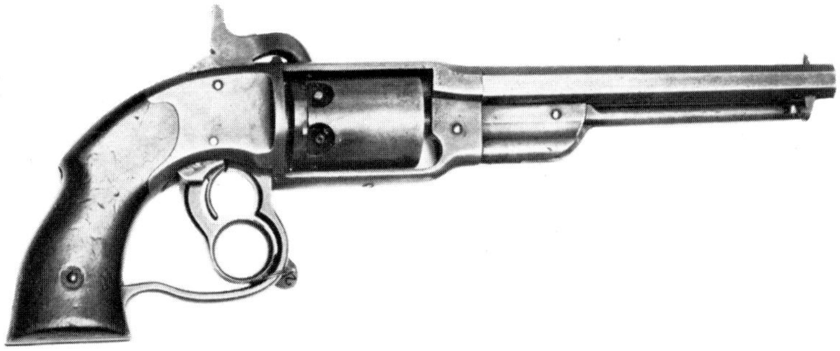

Savage Arms Co. Navy Model with octagonal barrel stamped "Savage R.F.A. Co. Middletown, Ct. H.S. North Patented June 17th 1856, January 18th 1859, May 15th 1860", with reciprocating cylinder, the butt cut for a shoulder stock. Fair condition. 14½in. *Sotheby's*

£100 – £150

Massachusetts Arms Co., revolver with hinged barrel, etched cylinder and engraved frame, the lock with Maynard tape primer engraved with American Eagle and Patent date Sept. 22 1845, silvered back-strap and trigger-guard. Refinished condition. 10½in. *Sotheby's*

£80 – £100

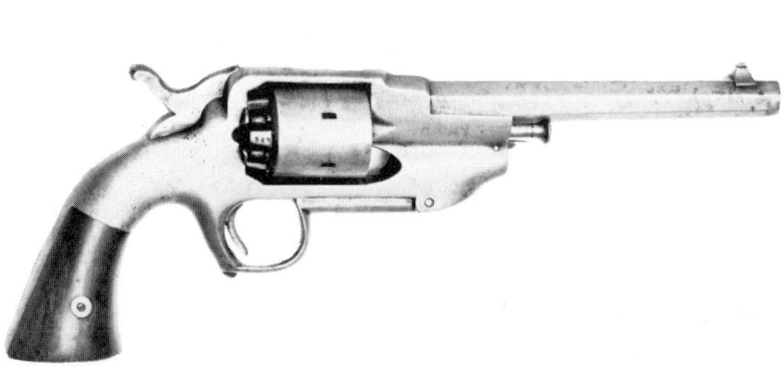

Allen & Wheelock Navy Model with octagonal barrel stamped "Allen & Wheelock, Worcester, Mass. U.S. Allen's Pt's Jan 19, Dec 15, 1857, Sept 7, 1858", with hinged trigger-guard which operates the creeping lever rammer. Moderate condition with no finish. 11½in. *Sotheby's*

£100 – £120

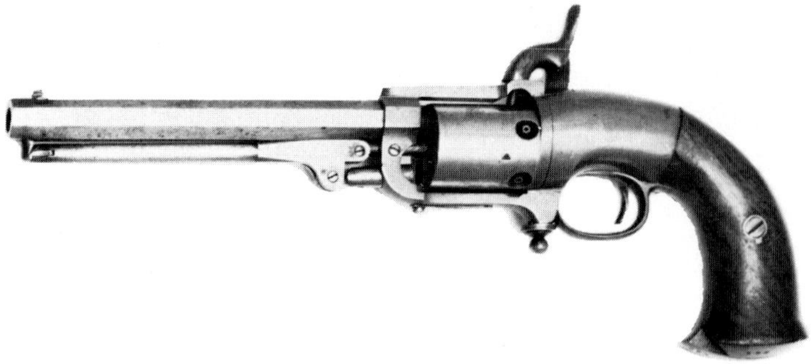

Butterfield's Patent revolver with octagonal barrel and bronze frame, the top strap stamped "Butterfield's Patent, Dec. 11, 1855, Philada." Moderate condition, right side of frame replaced. 14in. *Sotheby's*

About £300 rarity value (only about 2,000 were made between 1861 and 1862).

Pettengill's Patent Army revolver, stamped on the top strap "Pettengill's Patent 1856, Patented July 22, 1856 and July 27, 1858" and on the frame "Patented Nov 4, 1862". Moderate condition. 14½in. *Sotheby's*

£100 – £150

Ells Patent revolver with iron frame crudely engraved with leaves, the bar hammer stamped "Ells Patent Aug. 1 1854", iron back-strap. Poor condition. 9in. *Sotheby's*

£60 – £90

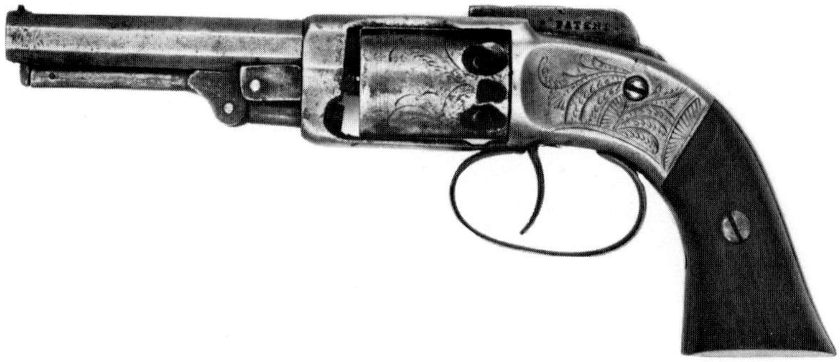

Walch patent ten-shot superimposed load revolver, with octagonal barrel stamped "Walch Firearms Co., New York, Pat'd Feb 8, 1859". Poor condition. 9in. *Sotheby's*

£100 – £150 in this condition.

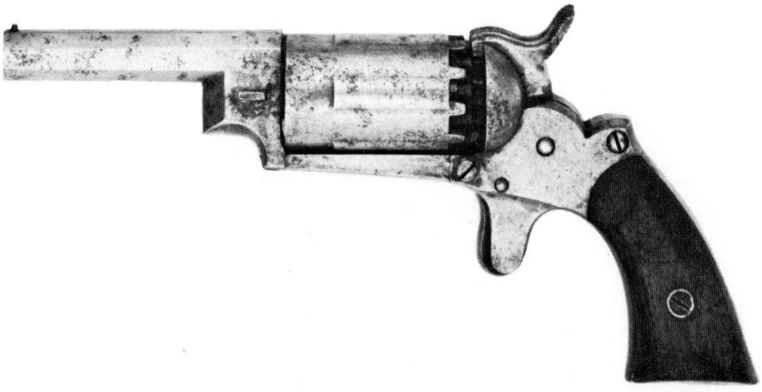

American Martial Pistols

Harpers Ferry 1805 Model, the lock stamped with Eagle, "US" and "Harpers Ferry" with the dated 1808, flat ring-neck cock, half-stock and brass mounts. 16½in.
About £300 for one in good condition, but beware of imitations, as with all U.S. martial pistols. The 1808 date is the commonest on this model; 1809 is rarer and 1806 the rarest of the three. *Christie's*

Prices range from £250 to £600 accordingly

Similar pistols with stirrup ramrods and "Richmond Virginia" marking, with date between 1802 and 1816 on the lock, can be worth up to £1,000.

Model 1807-1808, signed "J. Henry, Phila.", full stock, ring-neck cock and brass mounts. This is a good example with some original finish. 16in. *Sotheby's*

£400 – £500

This model was made under contracts in 1807 and 1808 and is found with the names of several gunmakers. The quality varies greatly. *Sotheby's*

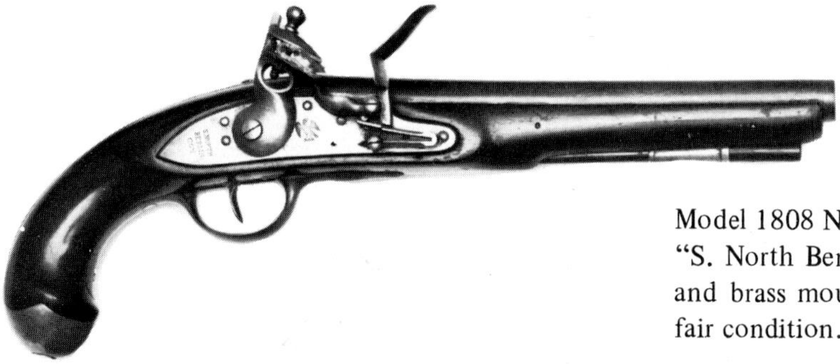

Model 1808 Navy, the lock marked with Eagle, "U. States" and "S. North Berlin Con.", full stock, ring-neck cock, brass pail, and brass mounts, iron back-strap and belt hook. This one in fair condition. 16¼in. 10in. barrel. *Sotheby's*

About £400

The 1811 model Army has the same markings on the lock and is of very similar appearance, but only 15in. long. It is worth approximately 30% more.

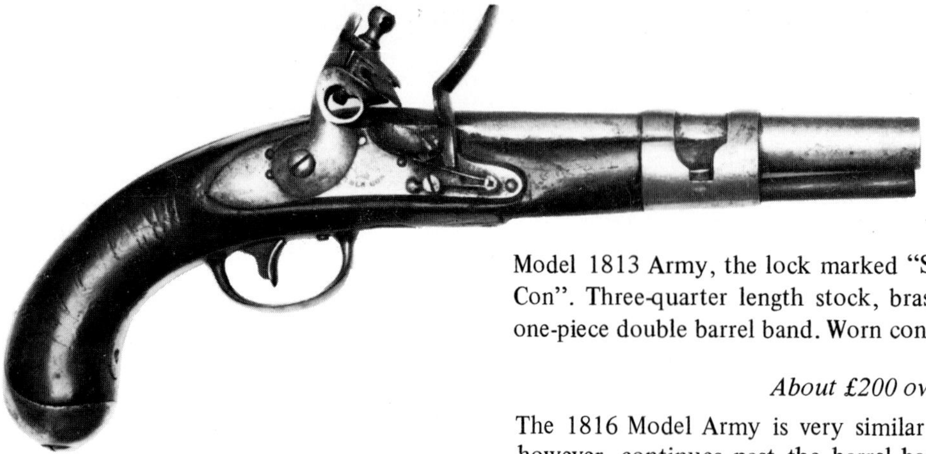

Model 1813 Army, the lock marked "S. North" with Eagle, "US" and "Midtn. Con". Three-quarter length stock, brass pan, ring-neck cock, iron mounts and one-piece double barrel band. Worn condition. 15¼in. 9in. barrel. *Sotheby's*

About £200 owing to condition

The 1816 Model Army is very similar and the same overall length. The stock however, continues past the barrel band. The 1816 model is less rare and proportionately less expensive.

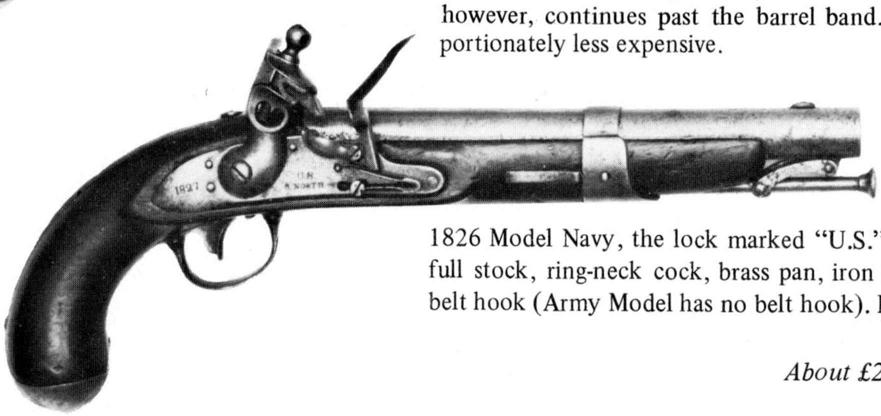

1826 Model Navy, the lock marked "U.S." and "S. North" with the date 1827, full stock, ring-neck cock, brass pan, iron mounts including stirrup ramrod and belt hook (Army Model has no belt hook). Fair condition. 13¼in. 8.6in. barrel. *Sotheby's*

About £200

Also found with the date 1828. The 1826 model Navy with lock marked "USN", "W. L. Evans" and "V. Forge" is worth about 25% more.

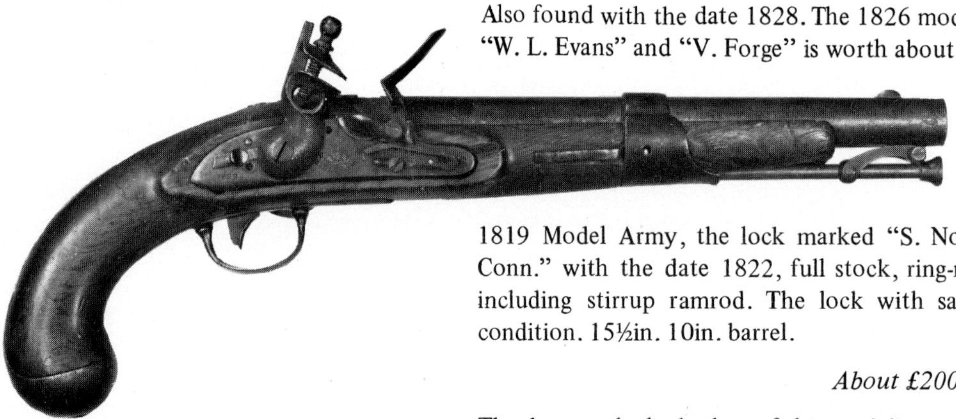

1819 Model Army, the lock marked "S. North", Eagle, "U.S." and "Midltn. Conn." with the date 1822, full stock, ring-neck cock, brass pan, iron mounts including stirrup ramrod. The lock with safety-catch behind the cock. Fair condition. 15½in. 10in. barrel.

About £200

The date on the lock-plate of this model may be 1820, 1821, 1822 or 1823.

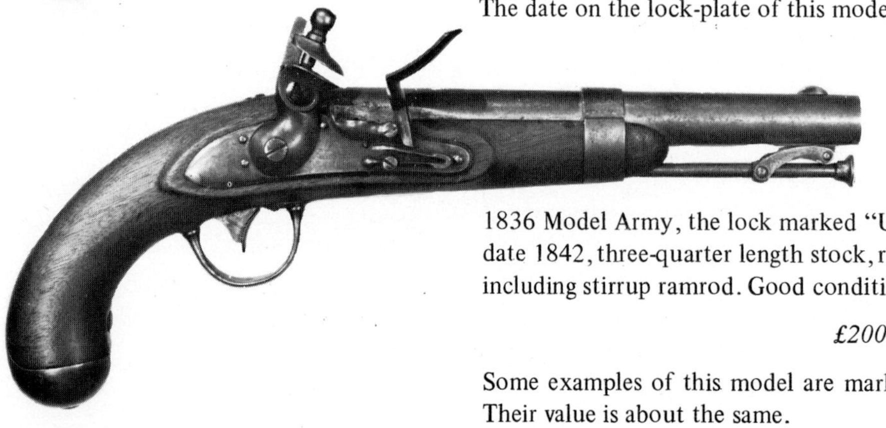

1836 Model Army, the lock marked "US", "R. Johnson, Middn. Conn" with the date 1842, three-quarter length stock, ring-neck cock, brass pan, and iron mounts including stirrup ramrod. Good condition. 14¼in. 8½in. barrel. *Christie's*

£200 – £250

Some examples of this model are marked "A. Waters, Milbury, Ms." with date. Their value is about the same.

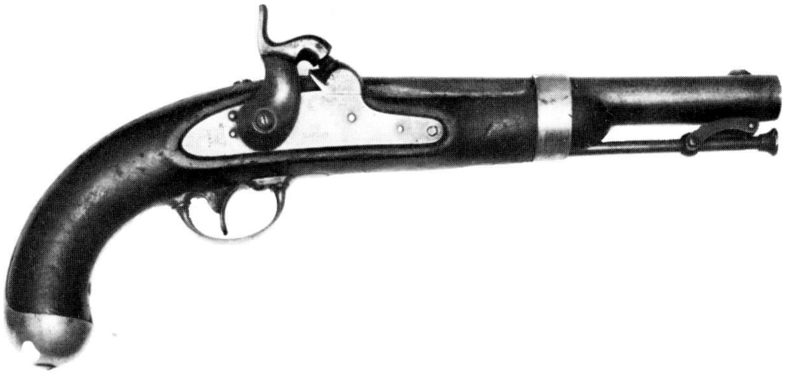

1842 Model Army, the lock marked "U.S. H. Aston, Middtn. Conn" and dated 1849, walnut half-stock with brass mounts and stirrup ramrod. Fair condition. 14ins. 8½in. barrel.

About £100

The same model is also found with "I.N. Johnson" marking on the lock. The value is about the same.

1842 Palmetto Armory Model, almost identical to the above, but with "Wm. Glaze & Co." and date 1853 on the barrel, and "Palmetto Armory SC", "Columbia SC" and palm tree on the lock with the date 1852, half-length walnut stock with brass mounts. Fair to good condition. 14in. 8½in. barrel.

£250 – £300

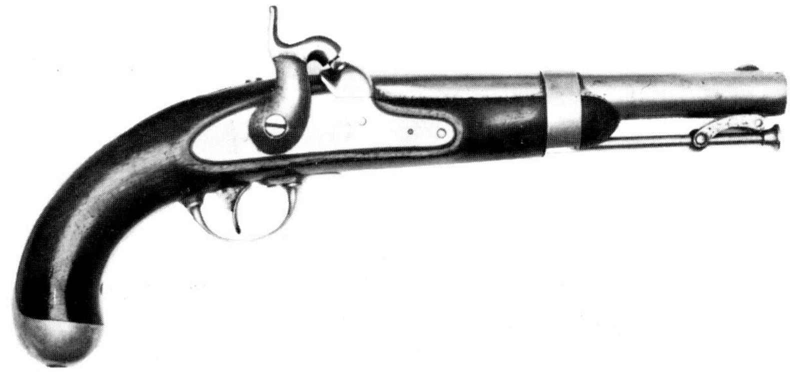

1843 Model Navy, the barrel marked "USN", "RP" and "P" with the date 1844, the lock marked "NP Ames Springfield Mass." and "USN" with the date 1843, the hammer inside the lock, full stock with brass mounts and stirrup ramrod. Fair condition. 11½in. 6in. barrel. *Sotheby's*

£100 – £140

The 1843 Model Army with "USMR" (United States Mounted Rifles) marking is worth slightly less. The 1843 Models Army and Navy with "US Deringer Philadela" marking on lock are worth almost double the 1843 Model Army.

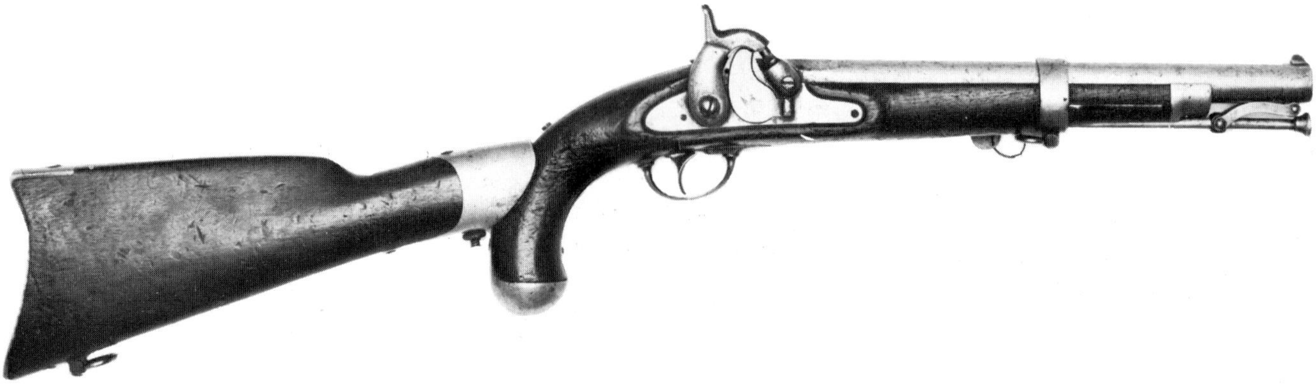

1855 Model pistol-carbine with rifled barrel, the lock marked "US Springfield" and dated 1855, the Maynard primer stamped with Spread Eagle, full stock with brass furniture and stirrup ramrod, complete with brass-mounted detachable shoulder stock. Good condition. 28¼in. assembled. 12in. barrel. *Sotheby's*

£300 – £400. Without stock about £200

The similar much rarer Harpers Ferry model is marked "Pistol Carbine", ' Harpers Ferry" and "US" on the lock. Value nearly double. *Sotheby's*

Elgin Patent Navy Cutlass pistol, the blade stamped "Elgin's Patent" and the action "C. B. Allen, Springfield, Mass. , serial No. 109, with plain trigger-guard and knuckle-guard, and walnut butt. Good condition. 17¼in. 11½ blade. circa 1837. *Sotheby's*

Over £1,000

Eastern Pistols

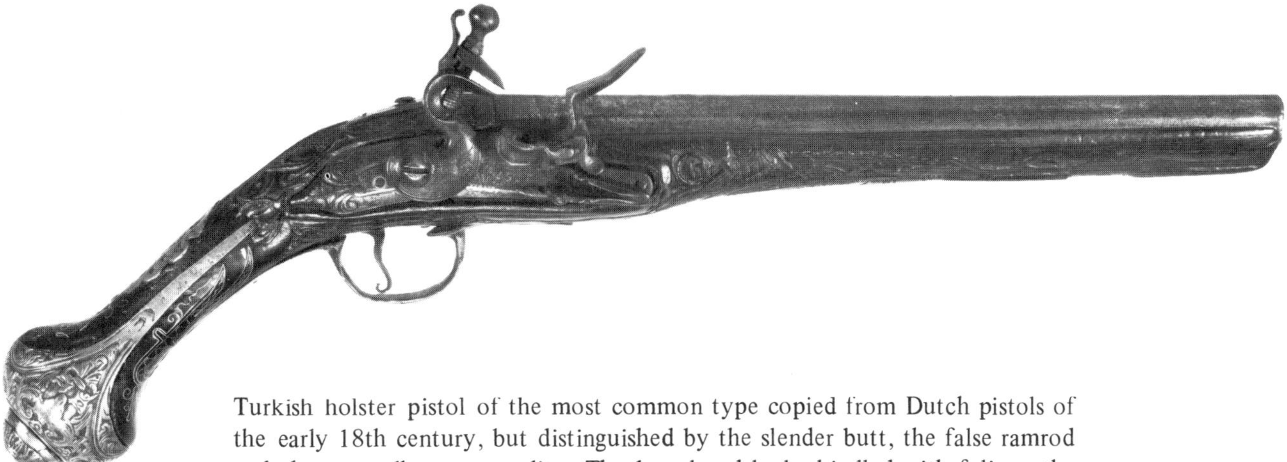

Turkish holster pistol of the most common type copied from Dutch pistols of the early 18th century, but distinguished by the slender butt, the false ramrod and the generally poor quality. The barrel and lock chiselled with foliage, the carved full stock with chiselled brass mounts. 19th century or later. 19¼in.

Christie's

£50 – £60

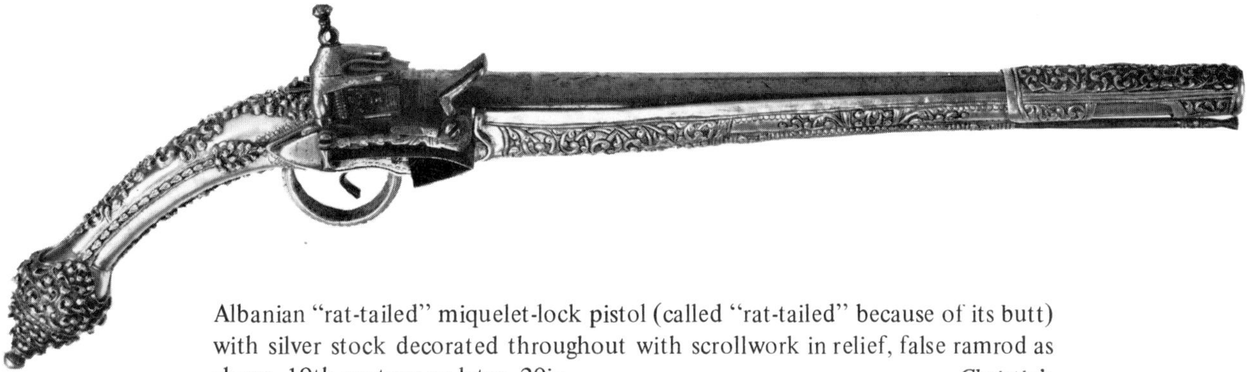

Albanian "rat-tailed" miquelet-lock pistol (called "rat-tailed" because of its butt) with silver stock decorated throughout with scrollwork in relief, false ramrod as above. 19th century or later. 20in. *Christie's*

About £150 as it has a silver stock (many are only silver-plated).

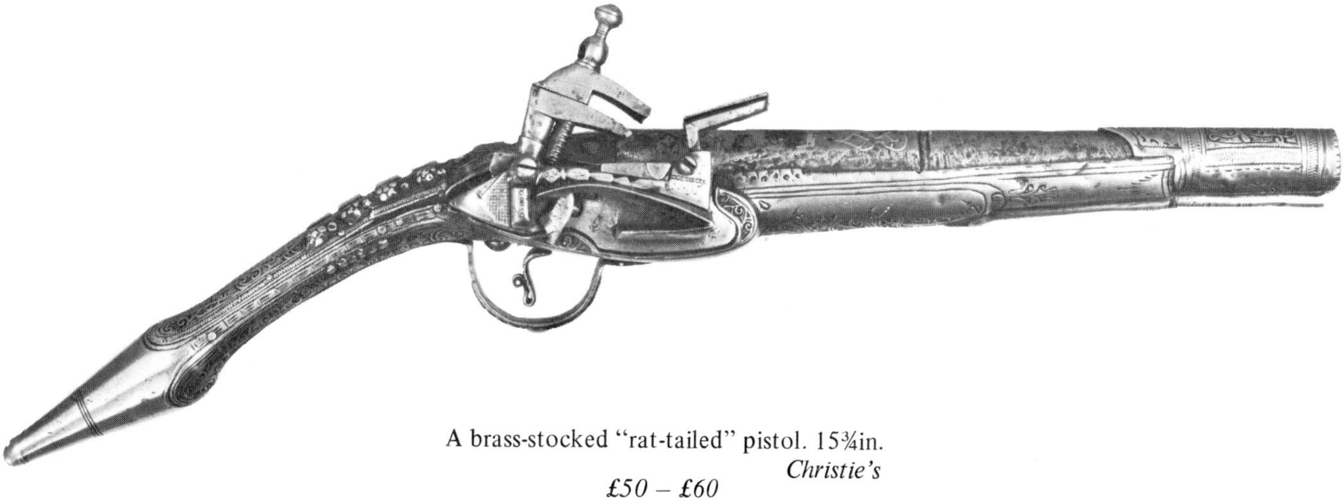

A brass-stocked "rat-tailed" pistol. 15¾in.

Christie's

£50 – £60

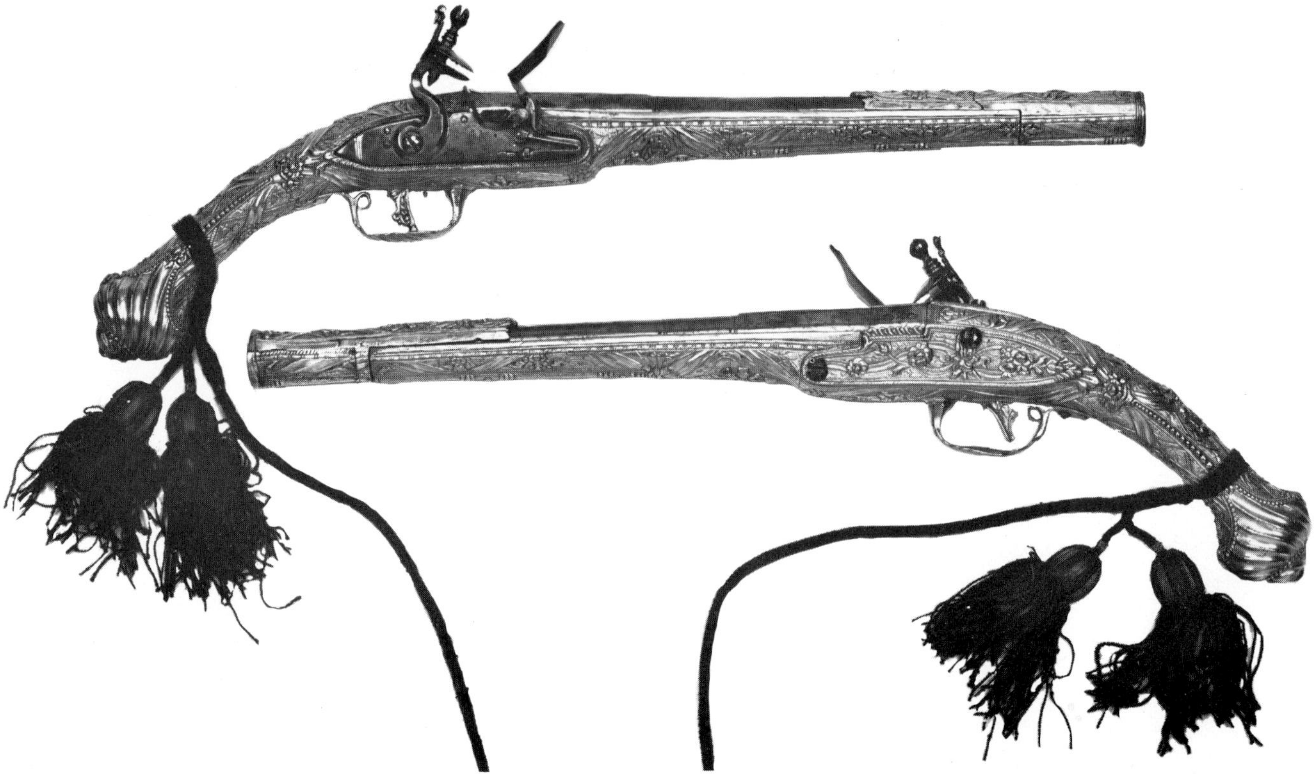

Pair of Turkish flintlock holster pistols with steel barrels and locks, the stocks of silver, parcel-gilt and decorated with flowers and foliage enclosing trophies of arms, with spirally fluted pommels and false ramrods. Fair quality and condition. 19th century. 20½in.

Knight, Frank & Rutley

£400 – £500 the pair

The locks on these are usually of very poor quality and the barrels often bear spurious proof marks.

Turkish flintlock holster pistol fitted with an English barrel and lock, each signed Grice, the stock of cast and chased silver decorated with flowers and foliage and enriched with niello, complete with ramrod en suite, the rod unscrewing to reveal a pair of tweezers. Good quality and condition. 18½in. Early 19th century. *Sotheby's*

About £400

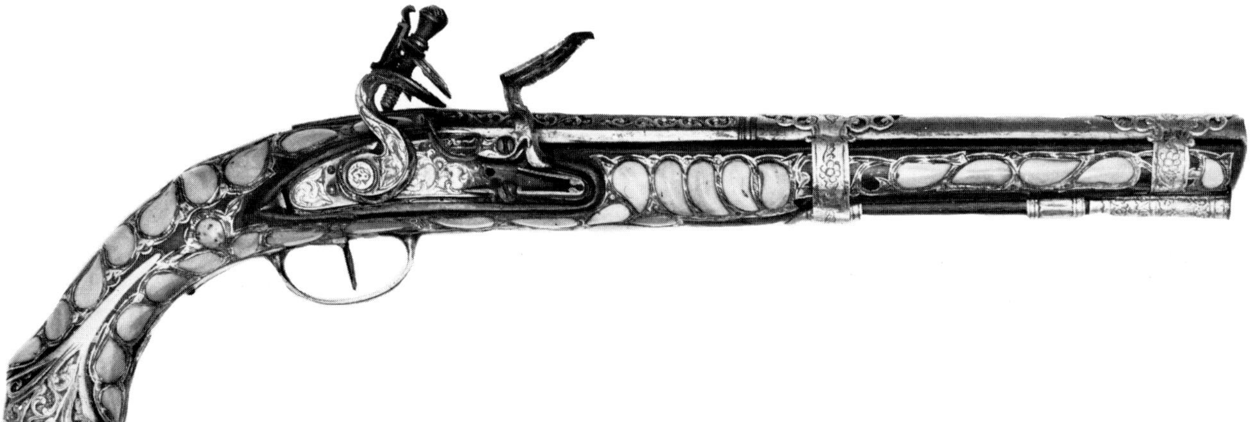

Turkish flintlock holster pistol, the barrel and lock set with panels of silver decorated with scrolling foliage, the cock en suite, the full stock with silver spurred pommel, barrel bands and trigger-guard and silver panels enclosing large corals, separate silver-tipped ramrod. Good quality and condition. 18in. Circa 1800. *Sotheby's*

£300 – £400

A pair of Algerian presentation pistols with French barrels and locks signed Piraube à Paris, the stocks inlaid with pierced silver panels and set with full silver furniture decorated with trophies of arms in high relief on a gilt ground, gilt spurred pommels and false ramrods. Moderate quality, fine condition. 19th century. 16in. *Christie's*

Over £800 the pair.

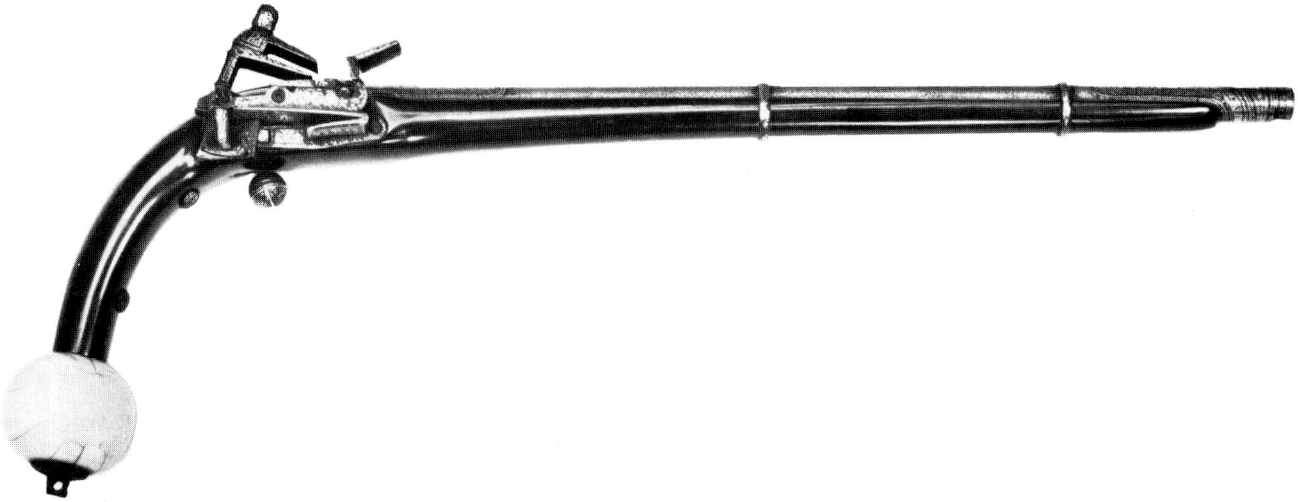

Russian miquelet-lock holster pistol with gold-damascened barrel and lock, the full stock of horn with ball trigger and ivory ball butt. Good quality and condition. Early 19th century. 16¾in. *Sotheby's*

£250 – £300

The stocks of these are often of wood covered with black leather.

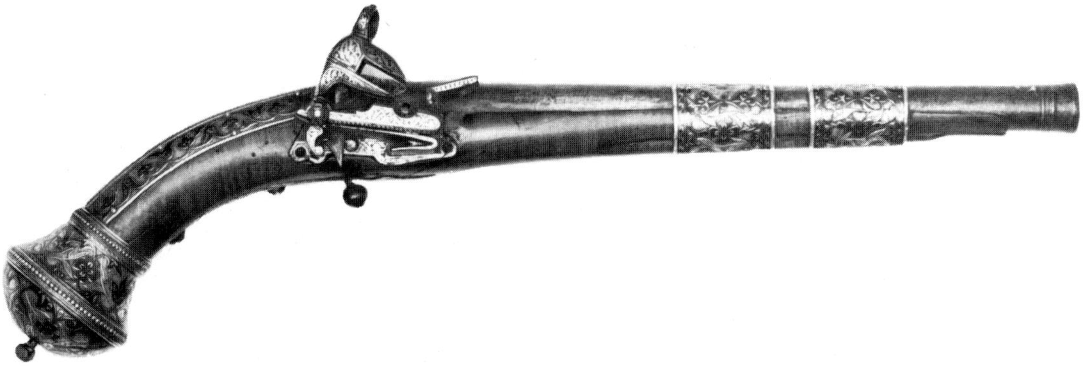

Another, with damascus barrel decorated with gold at the muzzle and breech, the lock damascened with gold scrollwork, walnut full stock, the back-strap, pommel and barrel bands decorated in nielloed silver with scrolls and flowerheads. Good quality, fair condition (stock cracked). Early 19th century. 17½in. *Sotheby's*

£250 – £350

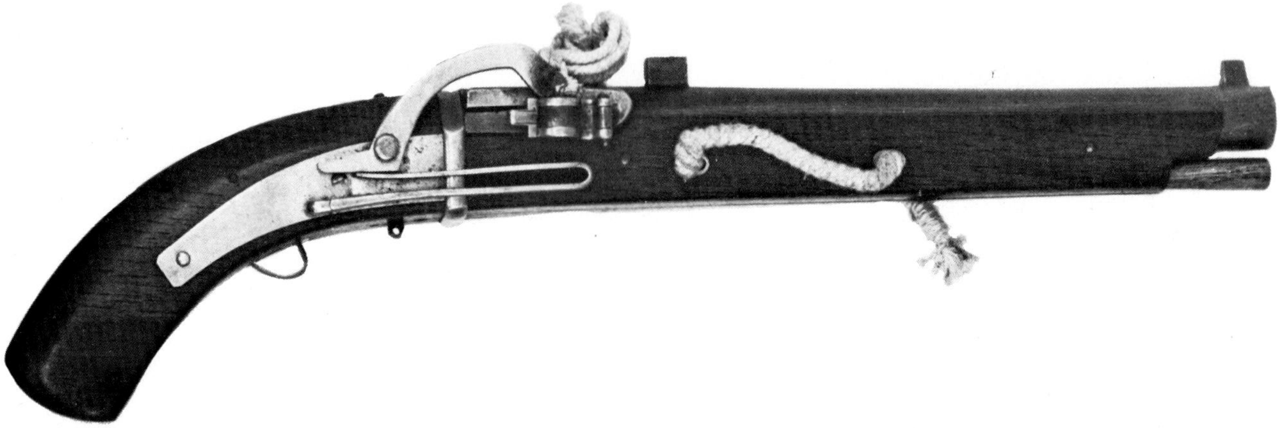

Japanese matchlock pistol with plain stock, brass lock and bronze barrel. Medium quality, good condition. 19th century.
Wallis & Wallis

About £200

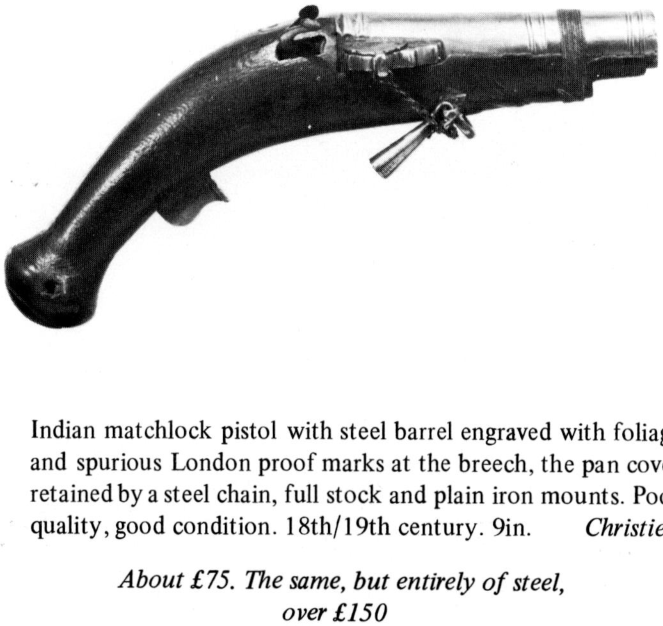

Indian matchlock pistol with steel barrel engraved with foliage and spurious London proof marks at the breech, the pan cover retained by a steel chain, full stock and plain iron mounts. Poor quality, good condition. 18th/19th century. 9in. *Christie's*

About £75. The same, but entirely of steel, over £150

Turkish over-and-under pistol with barrels damascened in gold and with silver bands, the lock en suite, the full stock with silver wire scrollwork and full silver furniture chased with military trophies, flowers and scrollwork. Moderate quality and condition. 19th century. 18in. *Christie's*

£300 – £400

Caucasian miquelet-lock blunderbuss-pistol with belled damascus barrel retained by nielloed silver bands, the figured full stock decorated with brass nails and mother-of-pearl inlays. Good quality and condition. 19th century. 16in.

About £200

Sets of more than two firearms

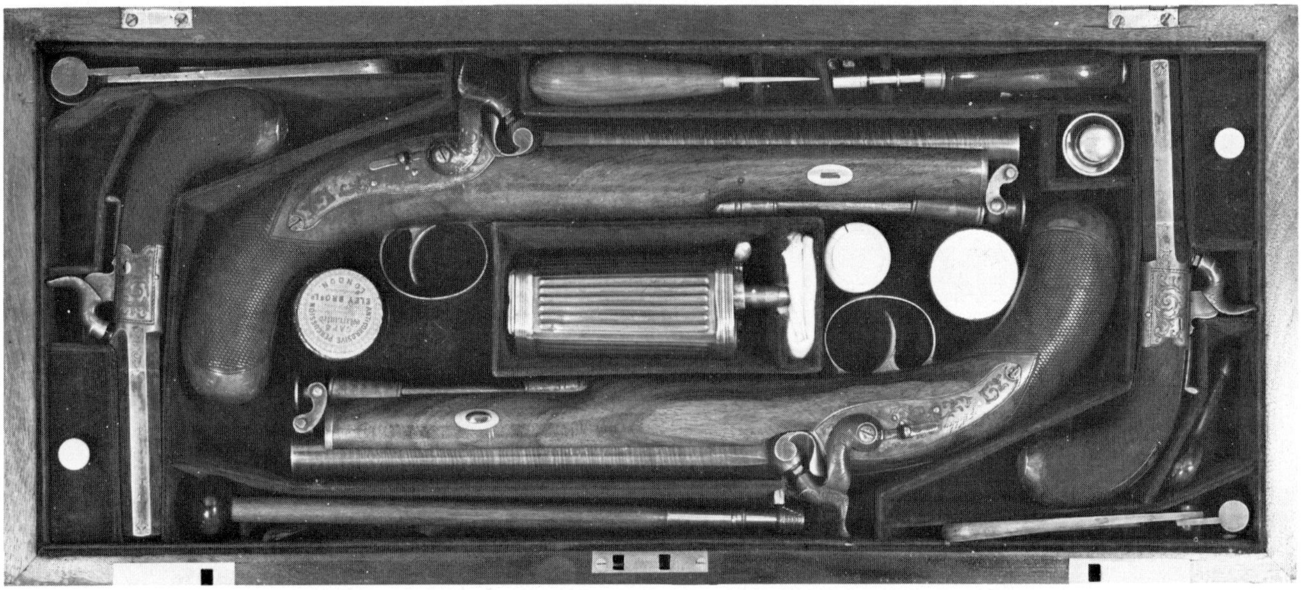

Cased set of four percussion pistols comprising a pair of back-action holster pistols with browned twist barrels, full stocks and engraved steel mounts, and a pair of box-lock pocket pistols en suite. In original fitted case lined in blue velvet, complete with accessories. Good quality but plain, very fine condition. By James Webley, circa 1840. The pistols 14½in. and 7½in. *Christie's*

Over £1,500 for the set

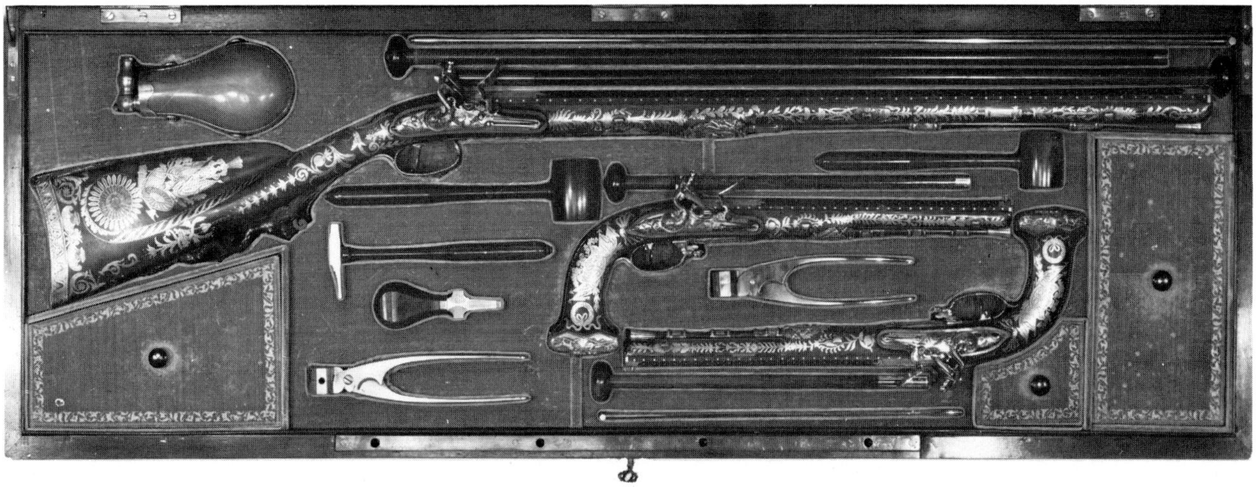

Magnificent presentation cased set of three flintlock firearms, comprising a rifle and a pair of pistols, the barrels inlaid with gold stars, the stocks with engraved silver and with elaborate silver mounts. In original velvet-lined case with full accessories including signed silver-mounted flask. Superb quality and condition. By Boutet, Versailles, circa 1805. This set made £43,050 in 1970.

Matchlock Long Guns

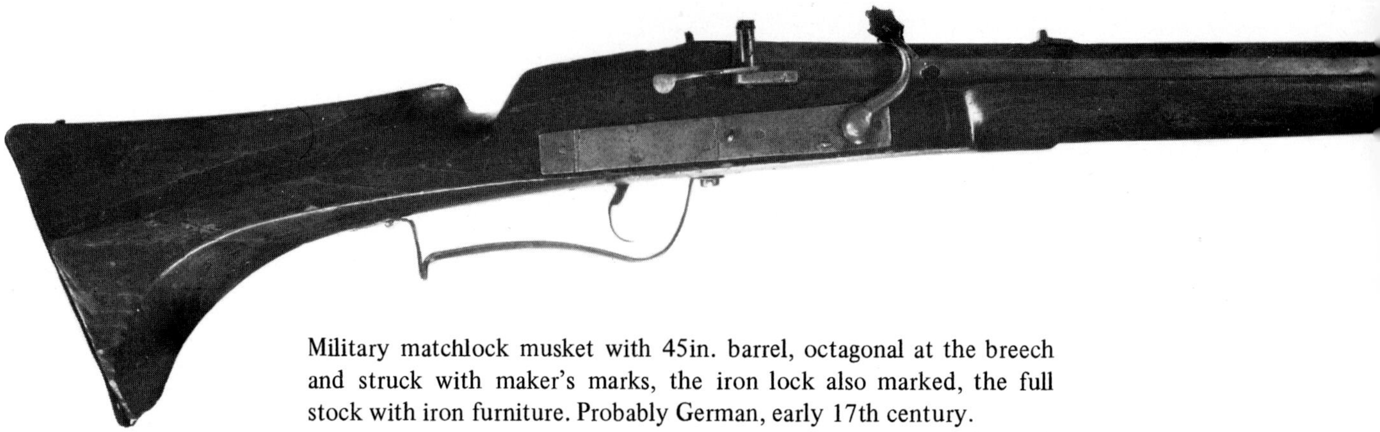

Military matchlock musket with 45in. barrel, octagonal at the breech and struck with maker's marks, the iron lock also marked, the full stock with iron furniture. Probably German, early 17th century.
Christie's

£300 – £500. More for an English one.
Genuine examples of these are rare, and even on these the stocks have often been replaced.

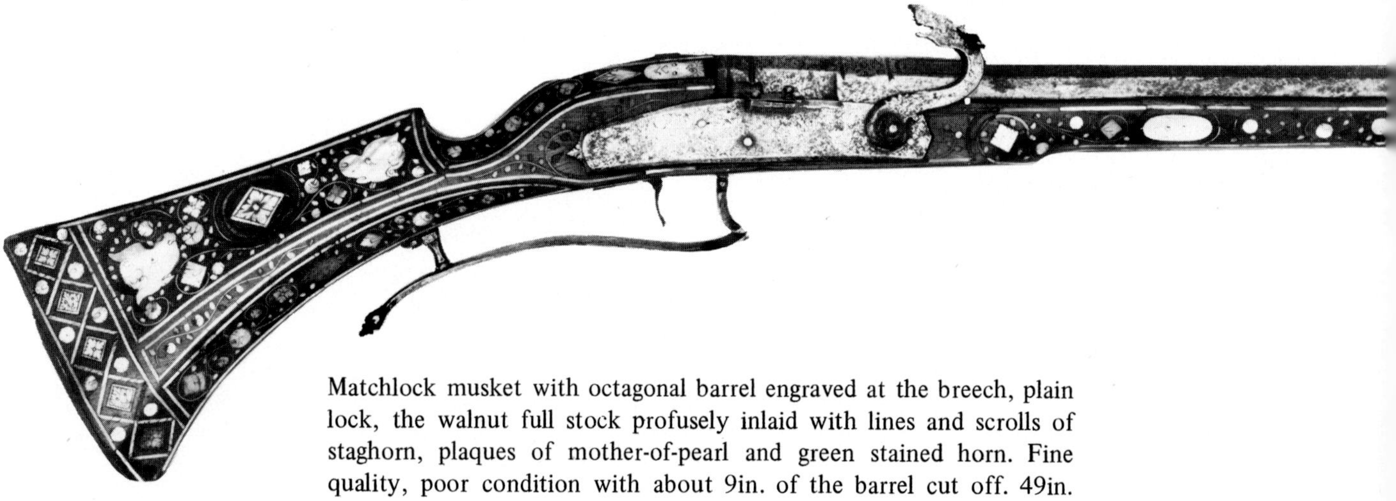

Matchlock musket with octagonal barrel engraved at the breech, plain lock, the walnut full stock profusely inlaid with lines and scrolls of staghorn, plaques of mother-of-pearl and green stained horn. Fine quality, poor condition with about 9in. of the barrel cut off. 49in. Early 17th century. Probably English. *Renwick Collection*

Over £1,000 even in this condition.
The value lies in its rarity as an English decorated piece.

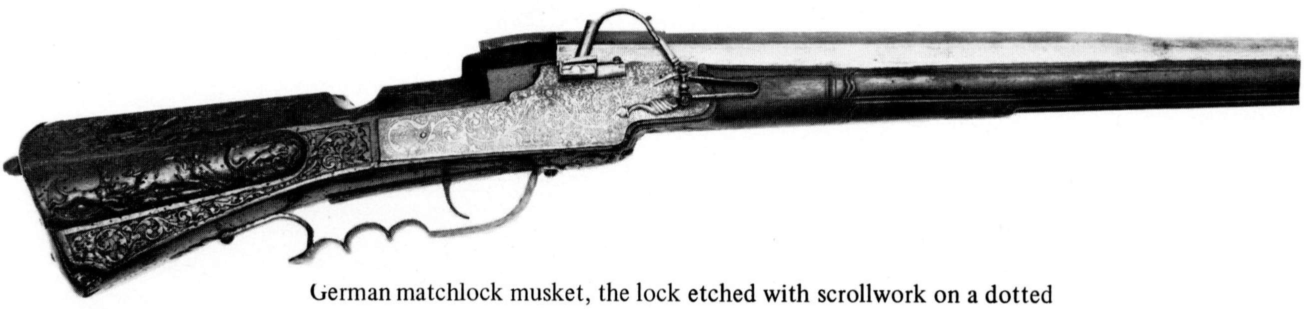

German matchlock musket, the lock etched with scrollwork on a dotted ground, the full stock carved on the butt with stags, hounds and scrollwork and with plain iron mounts. Moderate quality, poor condition with replacements. 55¼in. Mid-17th century. *Sotheby's*

About £500

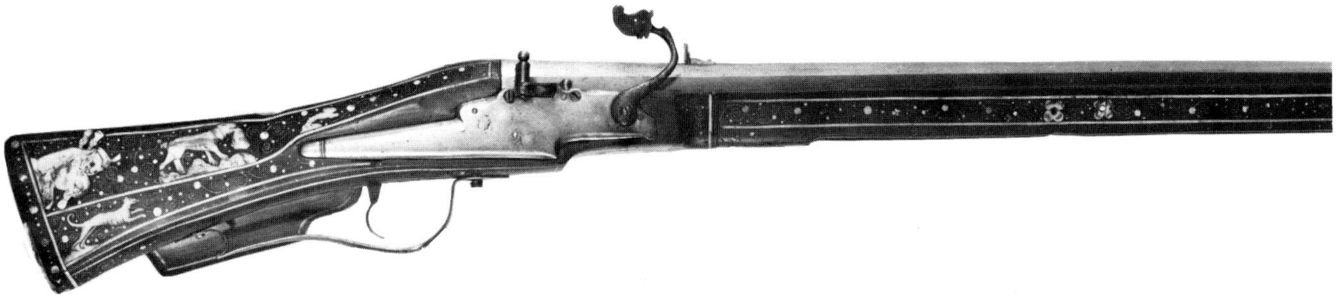

A finer and earlier example of the same type, the stock decorated throughout with ivory inlays including hounds, a boar, a unicorn, a lion and a monkey. Fair to good quality, fair condition with some restoration. 55in. barrel. Late 16th century. *Christie's*

Over £1,000

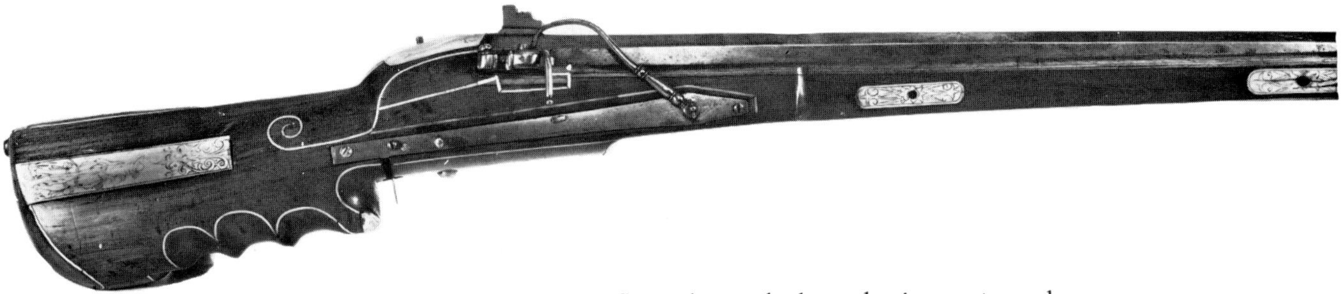

German matchlock target rifle with snap-lock mechanism, octagonal barrel and walnut full stock with rounded butt carved with notches for the hand, and decorated with engraved bone inlay. Good quality and condition. Dated 1625. *Sotheby's*

About £1,500

Rifles of this distinctive type rarely come on the market. One with elaborate inlays in worth several thousand pounds.

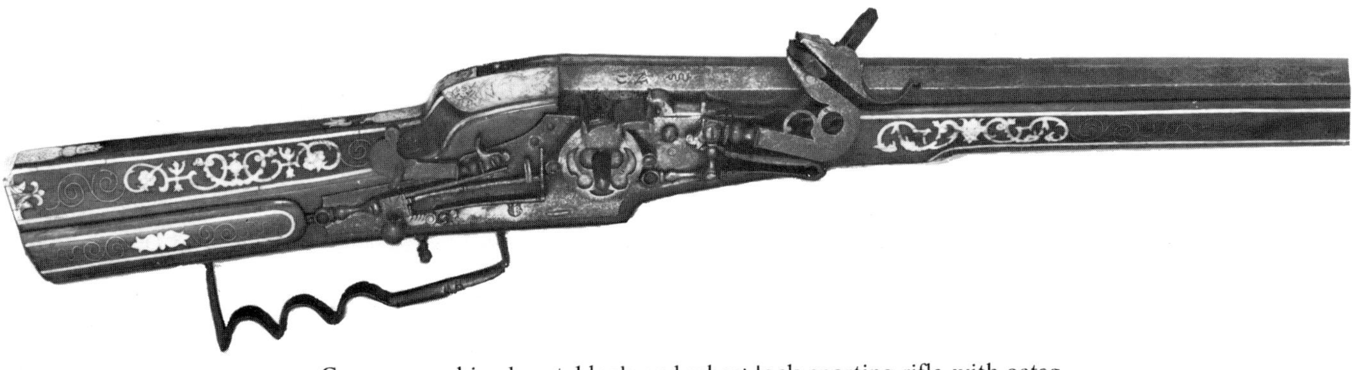

German combined matchlock and wheel-lock sporting rifle with octagonal barrel, the full stock with pierced ivory panels engraved with unicorns, masks and grotesque beasts within foliage. Fine quality and uncleaned condition. 50½in. The barrel stamped with the mark of Peter Danner of Nuremberg. Late 16th century. *Christie's*

Over £2,000

Wheel-Lock Long Guns

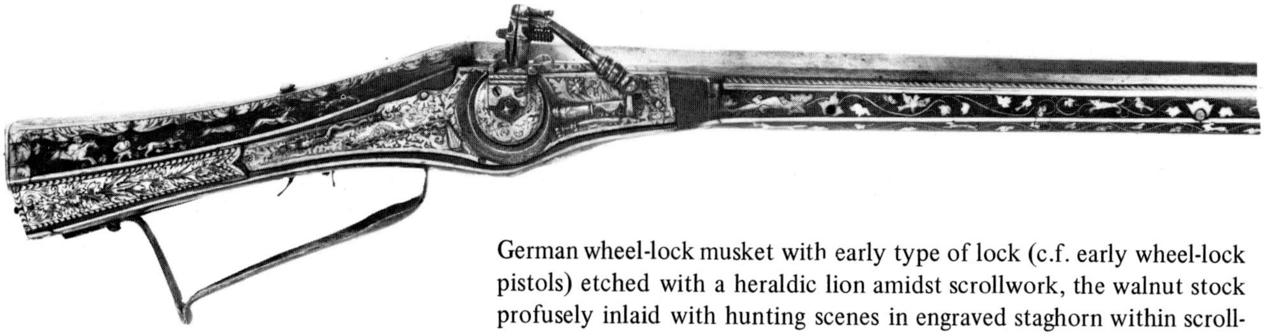

German wheel-lock musket with early type of lock (c.f. early wheel-lock pistols) etched with a heraldic lion amidst scrollwork, the walnut stock profusely inlaid with hunting scenes in engraved staghorn within scrollwork, the cheek-piece inlaid with the creation of Eve and the Temptation, and on the opposite side to the lock with a jousting scene. Fine quality, good condition. Circa 1560. 47in. *Sotheby's*

Over £5,000. Very rare.

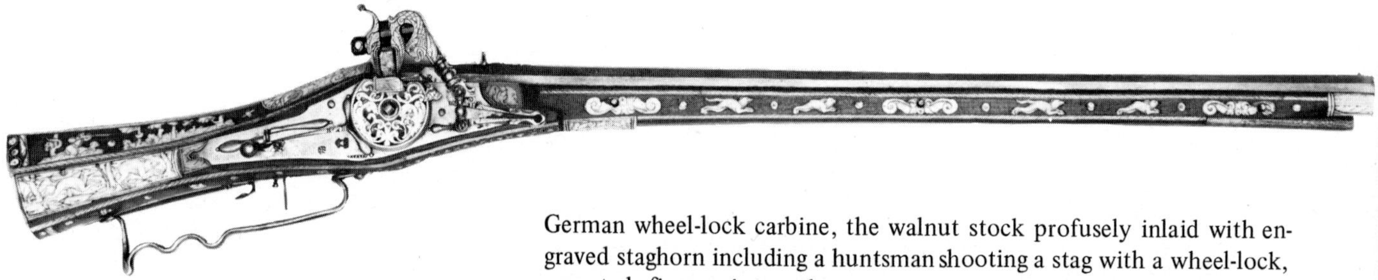

German wheel-lock carbine, the walnut stock profusely inlaid with engraved staghorn including a huntsman shooting a stag with a wheel-lock, mounted figures in combat, an amorous scene, etc., the lock with pierced brass wheel-cover. The barrel dated 1585 and stamped with the mark of Peter Danner, and the lock with the Nuremberg mark. Fine quality, good condition. 35½in. *Sotheby's*

Over £4,000

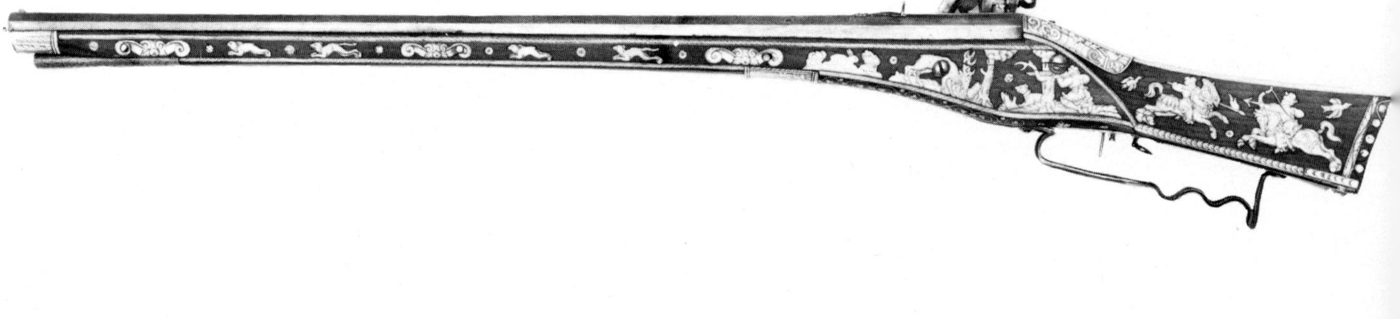

German wheel-lock hunting rifle, the barrel, lock and trigger-guard etched with scrollwork on a gilt ground, the stock profusely inlaid with pierced panels ot engraved horn and scrollwork incorporating masks, landscapes and portrait busts. Fine quality and condition. First quarter of the 17th century. 43in. barrel. *Christie's*

Over £3,000

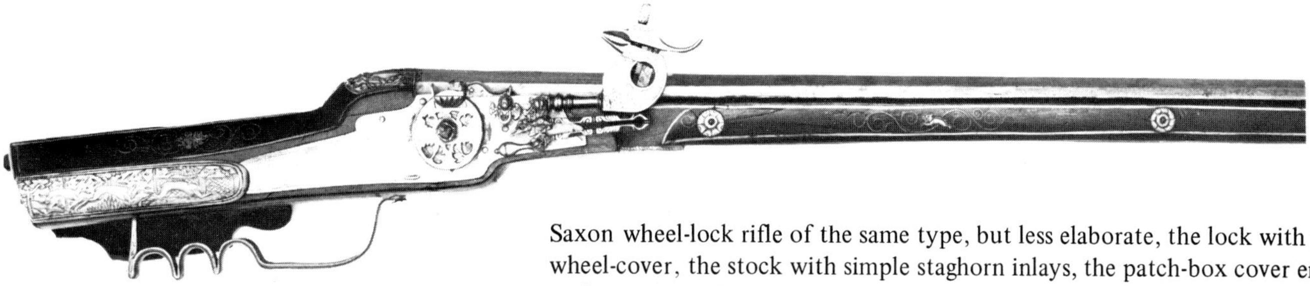

Saxon wheel-lock rifle of the same type, but less elaborate, the lock with pierced wheel-cover, the stock with simple staghorn inlays, the patch-box cover engraved with stags and hounds. Good quality and condition. 46in. First quarter of the 17th century. *Sotheby's*

Over £1,000

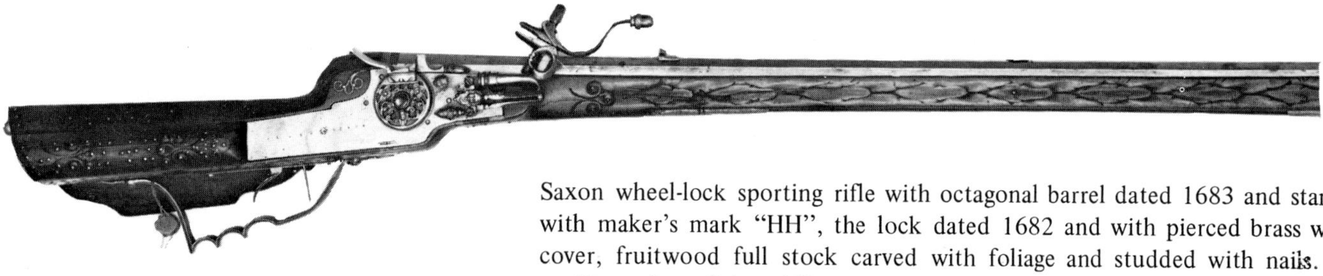

Saxon wheel-lock sporting rifle with octagonal barrel dated 1683 and stamped with maker's mark "HH", the lock dated 1682 and with pierced brass wheel-cover, fruitwood full stock carved with foliage and studded with nails. Fine quality and condition. 45in. *Sotheby's*

Over £1,500

From the Armoury of the Grand Dukes of Saxe-Weimar, Sililoss & Hersburg. Over £1,500 partly owing to the provenance.

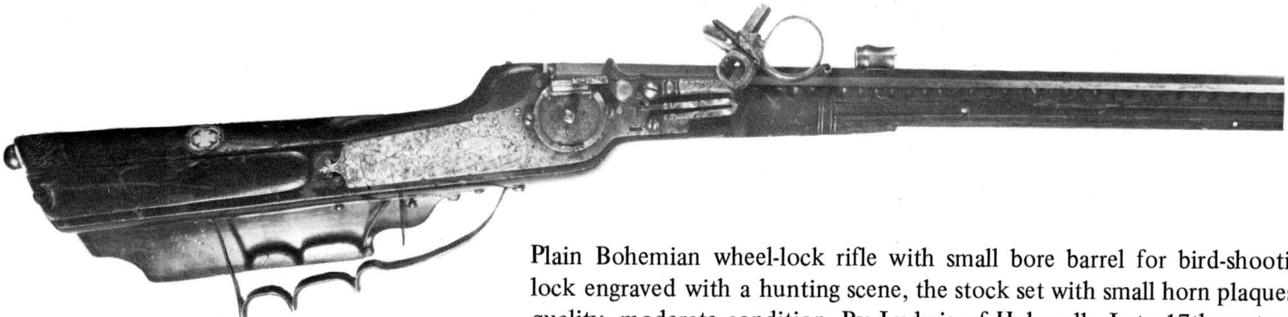

Plain Bohemian wheel-lock rifle with small bore barrel for bird-shooting, the lock engraved with a hunting scene, the stock set with small horn plaques. Good quality, moderate condition. By Ludwig of Hohenelb. Late 17th century. 33in. barrel. *Christie's*

£600 – £800

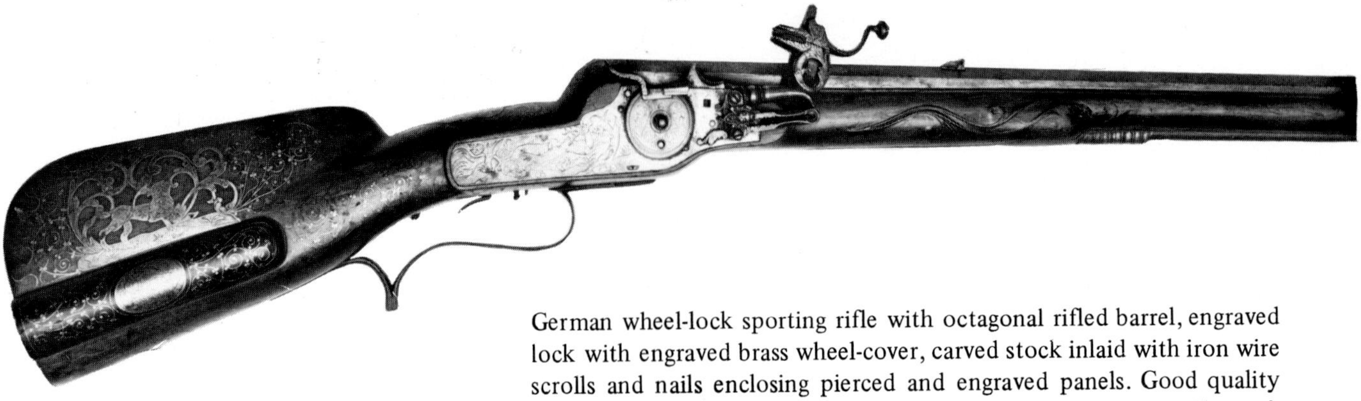

German wheel-lock sporting rifle with octagonal rifled barrel, engraved lock with engraved brass wheel-cover, carved stock inlaid with iron wire scrolls and nails enclosing pierced and engraved panels. Good quality and condition. Late 17th century. 33½in. barrel. *Christie's*

£750 – £1,000

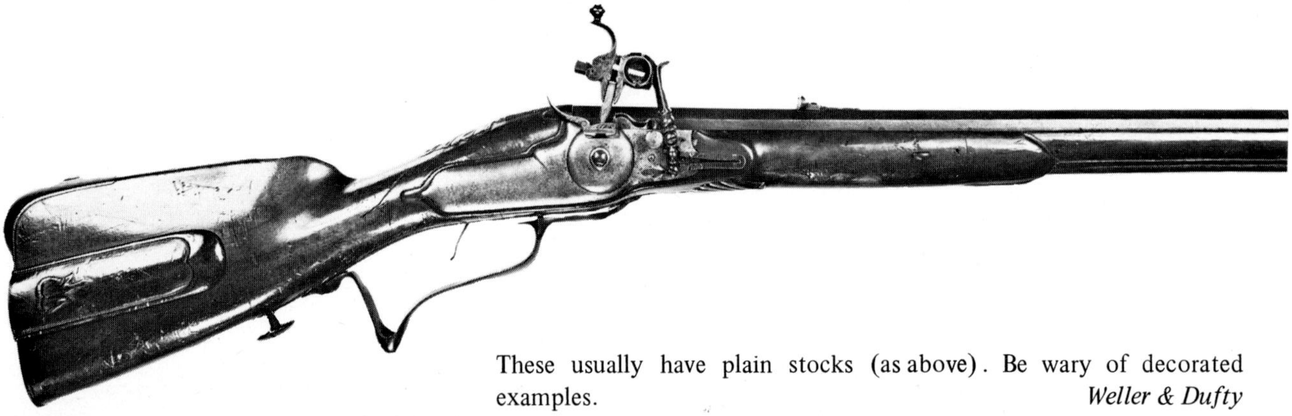

These usually have plain stocks (as above). Be wary of decorated examples. *Weller & Dufty*

About £500 for a plain one.

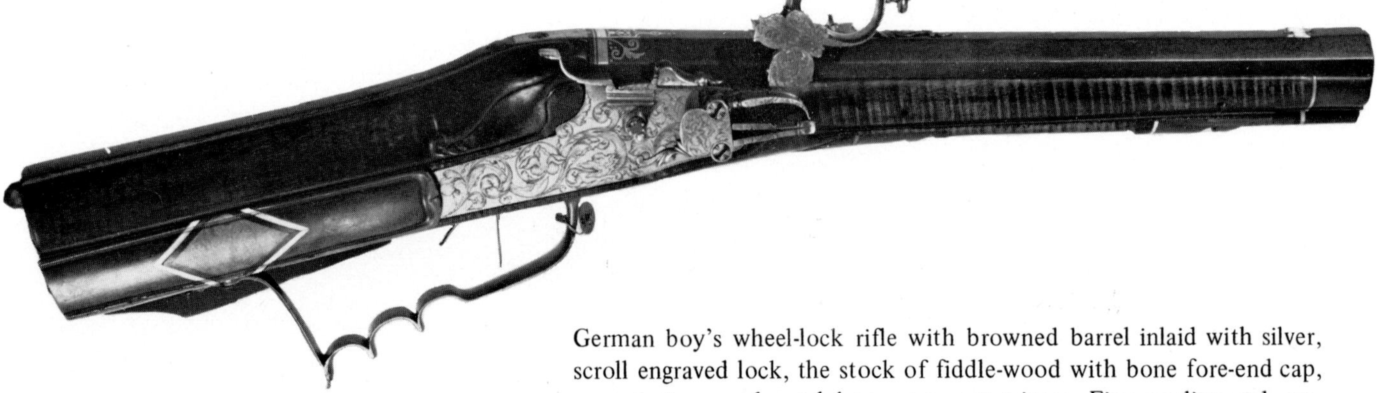

German boy's wheel-lock rifle with browned barrel inlaid with silver, scroll engraved lock, the stock of fiddle-wood with bone fore-end cap, ramrod-pipes and patch-box cover, set trigger. Fine quality and condition. Late 17th century. 21¾in. *Christie's*

Over £1.000. Rare.

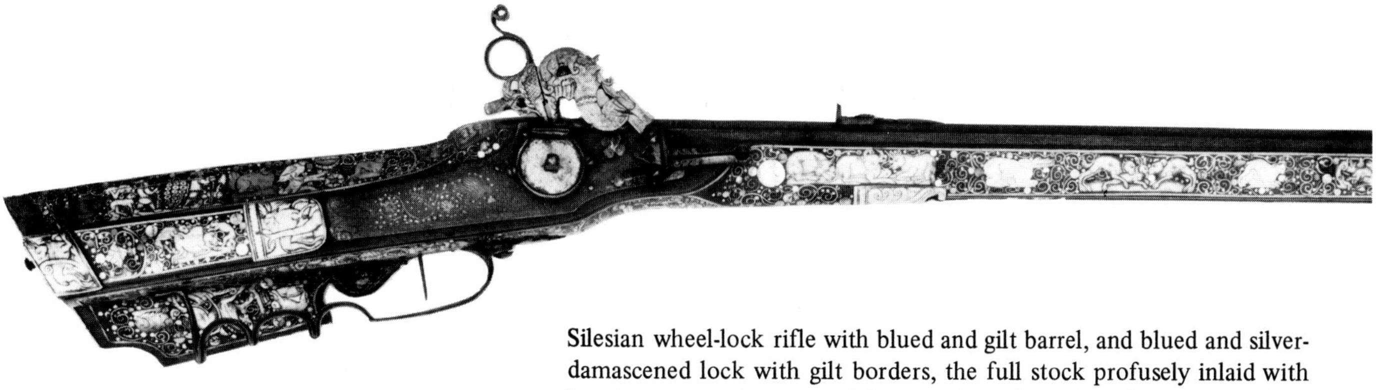

Silesian wheel-lock rifle with blued and gilt barrel, and blued and silver-damascened lock with gilt borders, the full stock profusely inlaid with hunting scenes in engraved horn and mother-of-pearl in the Teschian manner. Fine quality and condition, with original finish. Mid-17th century. 40¼in. *Sotheby's*

Over £4,000

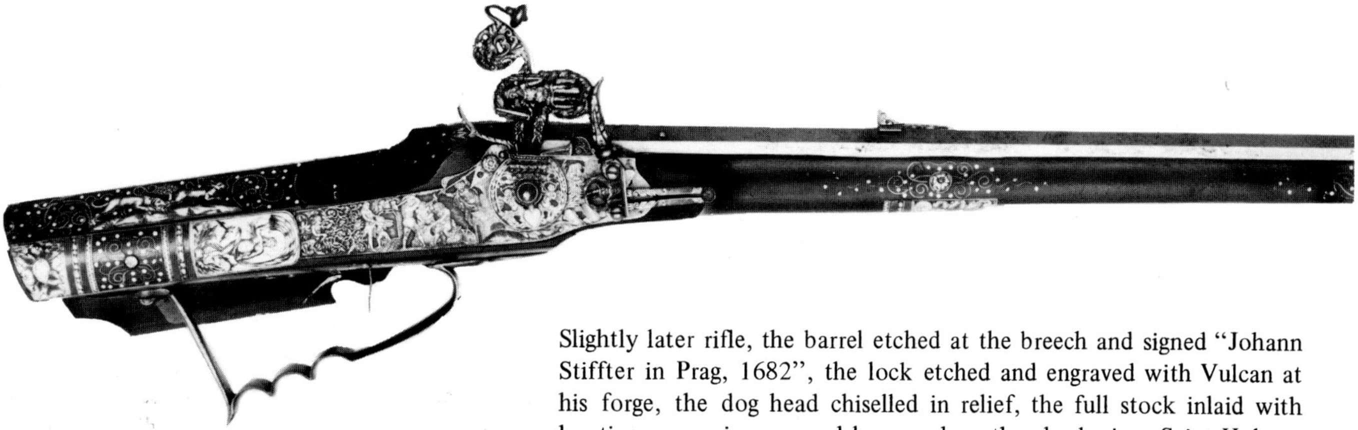

Slightly later rifle, the barrel etched at the breech and signed "Johann Stiffter in Prag, 1682", the lock etched and engraved with Vulcan at his forge, the dog head chiselled in relief, the full stock inlaid with hunting scenes in engraved horn and on the check-piece Saint Hubert. Fine quality and condition. Dated 1682. 43in. *Sotheby's*

Over £3,000

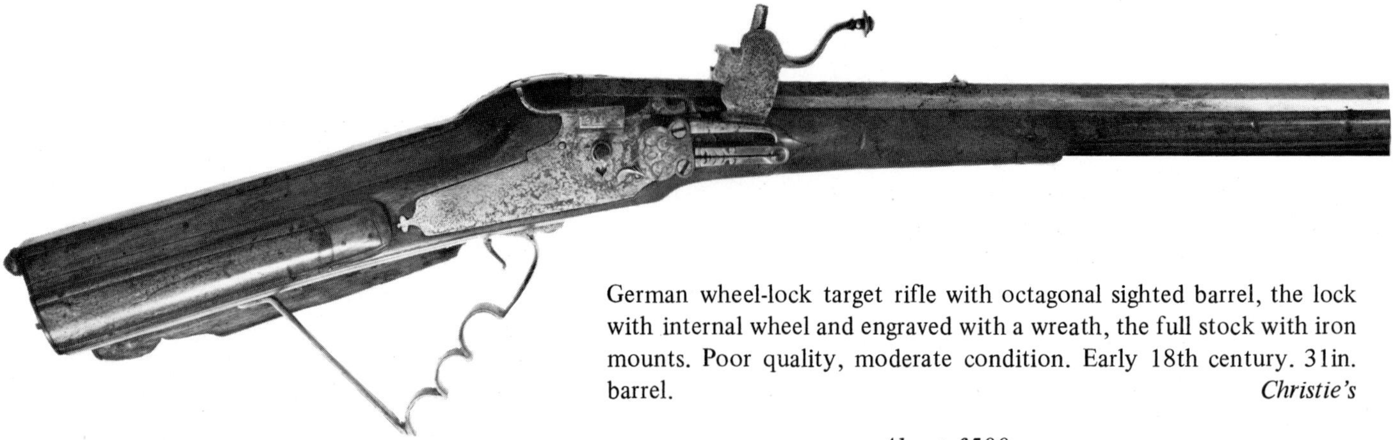

German wheel-lock target rifle with octagonal sighted barrel, the lock with internal wheel and engraved with a wreath, the full stock with iron mounts. Poor quality, moderate condition. Early 18th century. 31in. barrel. *Christie's*

About £500

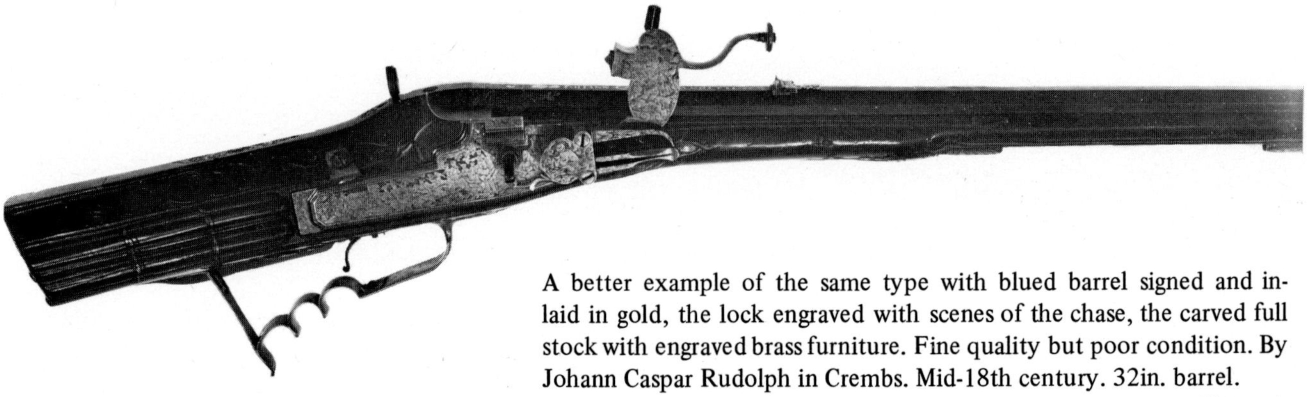

A better example of the same type with blued barrel signed and inlaid in gold, the lock engraved with scenes of the chase, the carved full stock with engraved brass furniture. Fine quality but poor condition. By Johann Caspar Rudolph in Crembs. Mid-18th century. 32in. barrel. *Christie's*

About £800 owing to condition.

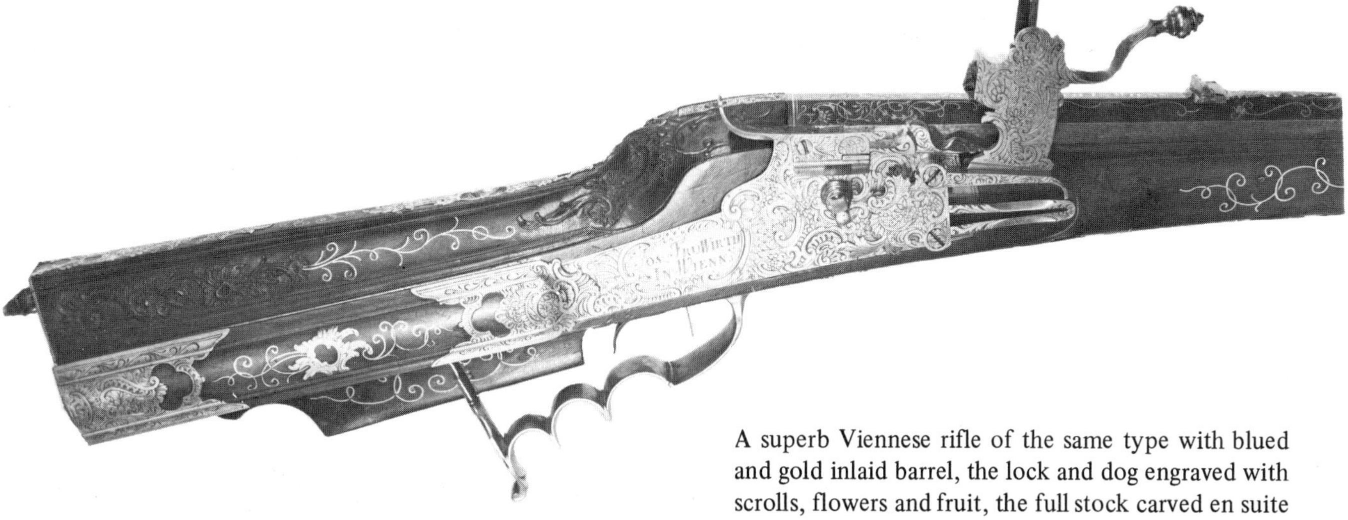

A superb Viennese rifle of the same type with blued and gold inlaid barrel, the lock and dog engraved with scrolls, flowers and fruit, the full stock carved en suite and mounted with gilt-brass furniture of exceptional quality and inlaid with silver wire. Exceptional condition. By Joseph Fruwith, circa 1740. 31in. barrel. *Christie's*

Over £3,000. Very few are anything like as good as this one.

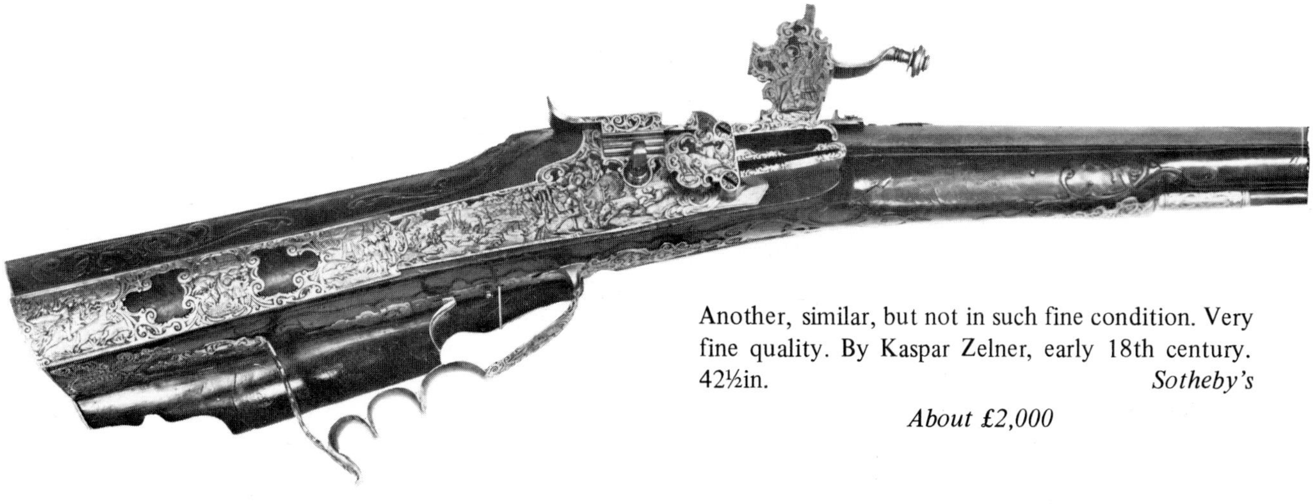

Another, similar, but not in such fine condition. Very fine quality. By Kaspar Zelner, early 18th century. 42½in. *Sotheby's*

About £2,000

Italian wheel-lock carbine (Tercerol) with octagonal barrel, the full stock with fluted fish-tail butt and plain iron furniture. Good quality, exceptional condition. Late 16th century. 24in. barrel.

Christie's

Over £1,500. Italian wheel-lock long arms are rare.

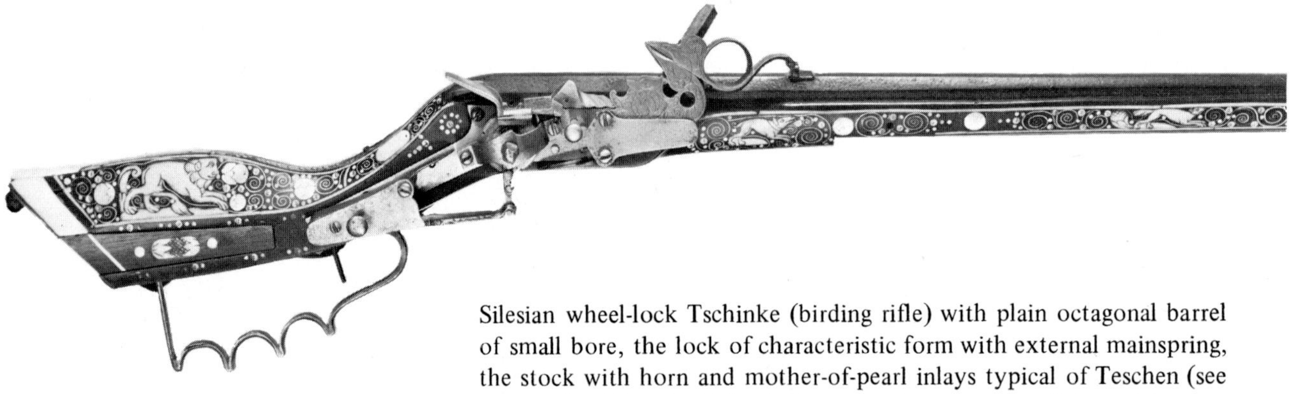

Silesian wheel-lock Tschinke (birding rifle) with plain octagonal barrel of small bore, the lock of characteristic form with external mainspring, the stock with horn and mother-of-pearl inlays typical of Teschen (see pages 37, 283 and 295). Moderate quality, poor condition with some restorations. First half of the 17th century. *Christie's*

£800 – £1,500

Tschinkes are unpredictable.

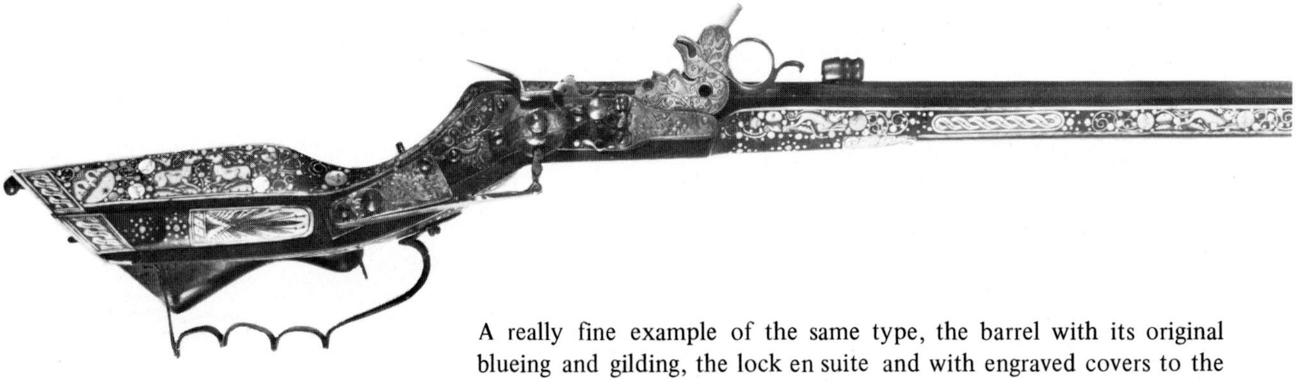

A really fine example of the same type, the barrel with its original blueing and gilding, the lock en suite and with engraved covers to the springs and lock, the stock finely inlaid. Very fine quality and excellent condition. First half of the 17th century. 34in. barrel. *Christie's*

Over £2,000

The very best have signed stocks.

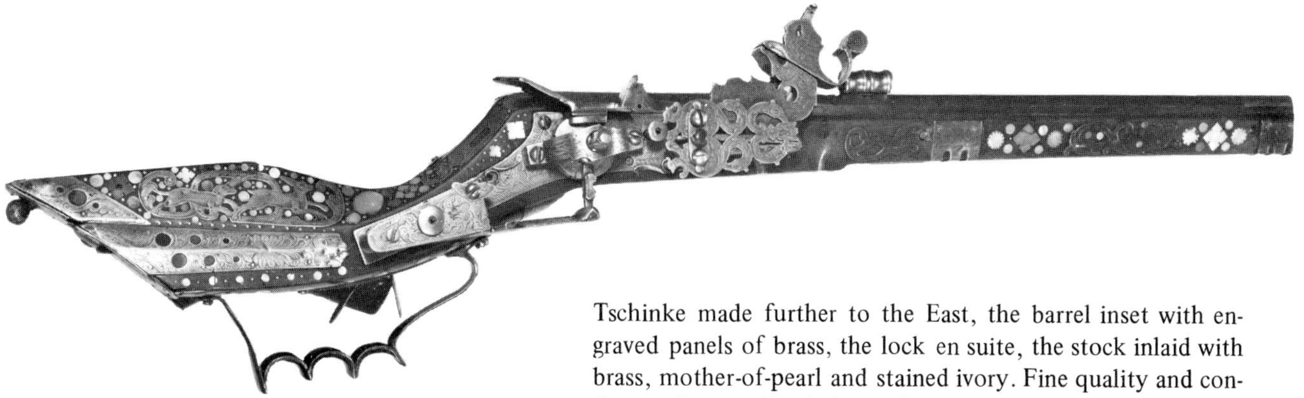

Tschinke made further to the East, the barrel inset with engraved panels of brass, the lock en suite, the stock inlaid with brass, mother-of-pearl and stained ivory. Fine quality and condition. First half of the 17th century. 36in. barrel engraved with the owner's name. *Christie's*

£1,000 – £1,500

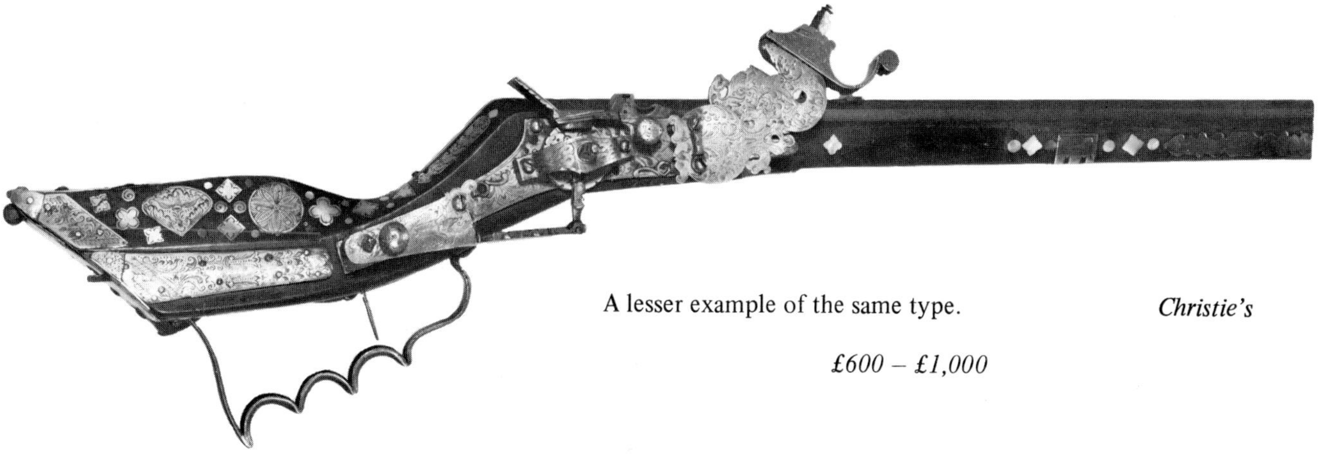

A lesser example of the same type. *Christie's*

£600 – £1,000

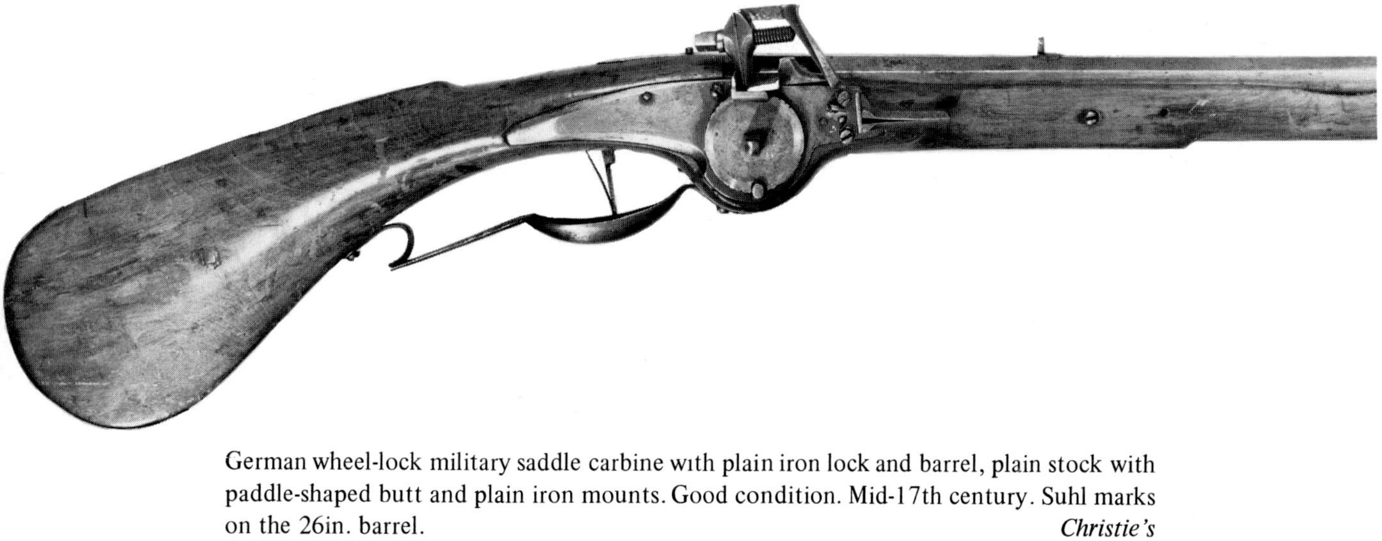

German wheel-lock military saddle carbine with plain iron lock and barrel, plain stock with paddle-shaped butt and plain iron mounts. Good condition. Mid-17th century. Suhl marks on the 26in. barrel. *Christie's*

£400 – £500

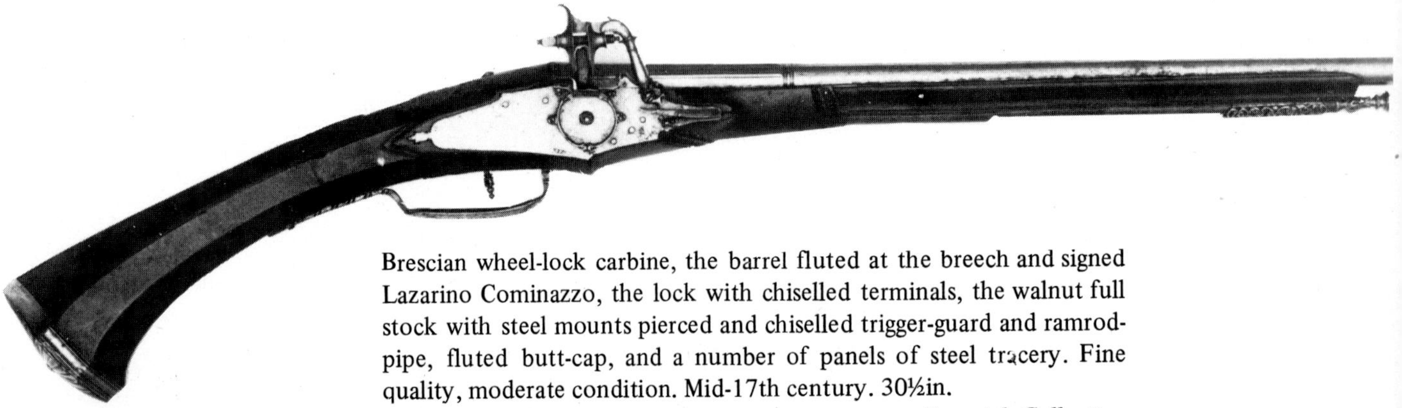

Brescian wheel-lock carbine, the barrel fluted at the breech and signed Lazarino Cominazzo, the lock with chiselled terminals, the walnut full stock with steel mounts pierced and chiselled trigger-guard and ramrod-pipe, fluted butt-cap, and a number of panels of steel tracery. Fine quality, moderate condition. Mid-17th century. 30½in.

Renwick Collection

Over £1,500

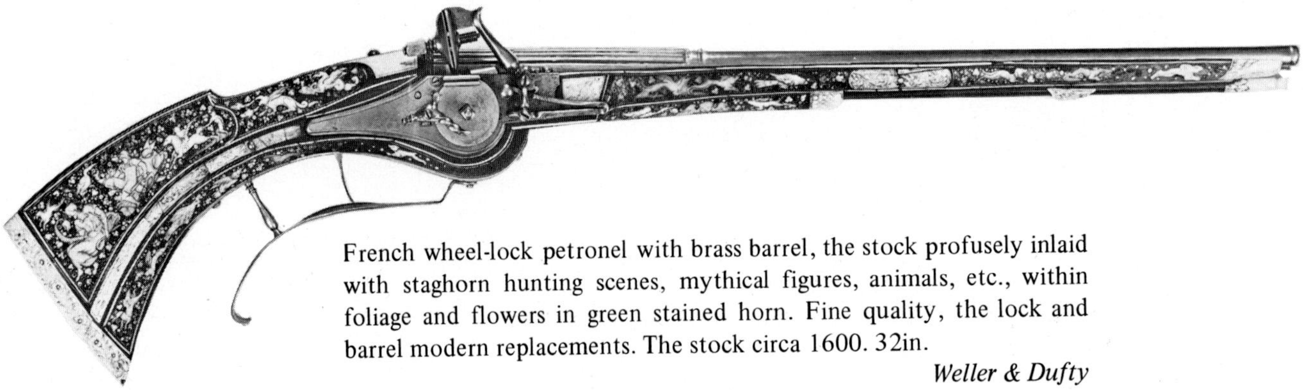

French wheel-lock petronel with brass barrel, the stock profusely inlaid with staghorn hunting scenes, mythical figures, animals, etc., within foliage and flowers in green stained horn. Fine quality, the lock and barrel modern replacements. The stock circa 1600. 32in.

Weller & Dufty

Over £1,000

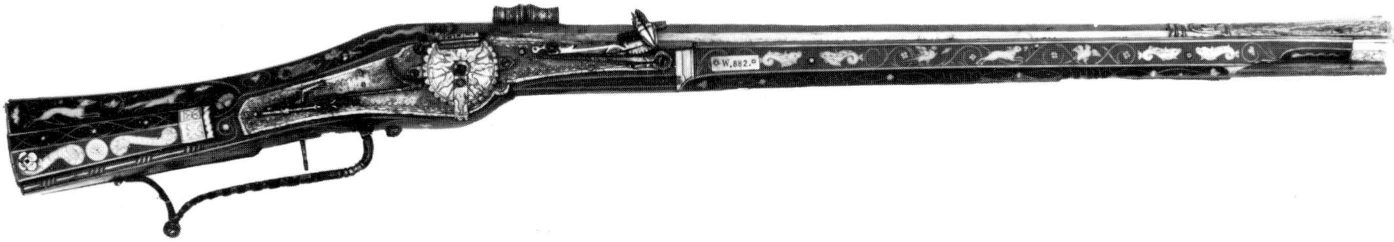

Two views of a superb early German wheel-lock carbine with octagonal barrel gilt at the breech and muzzle, the end swamped, the lock of early type with straight-armed cock, gilt wheel-cover and border, the walnut full stock inlaid with horn scrolls inhabited by birds and animals, and on the cheek-piece with Turks in combat with a pikeman. Fine condition. 36½in. Circa 1540/50. *Renwick Collection*

Over £10,000

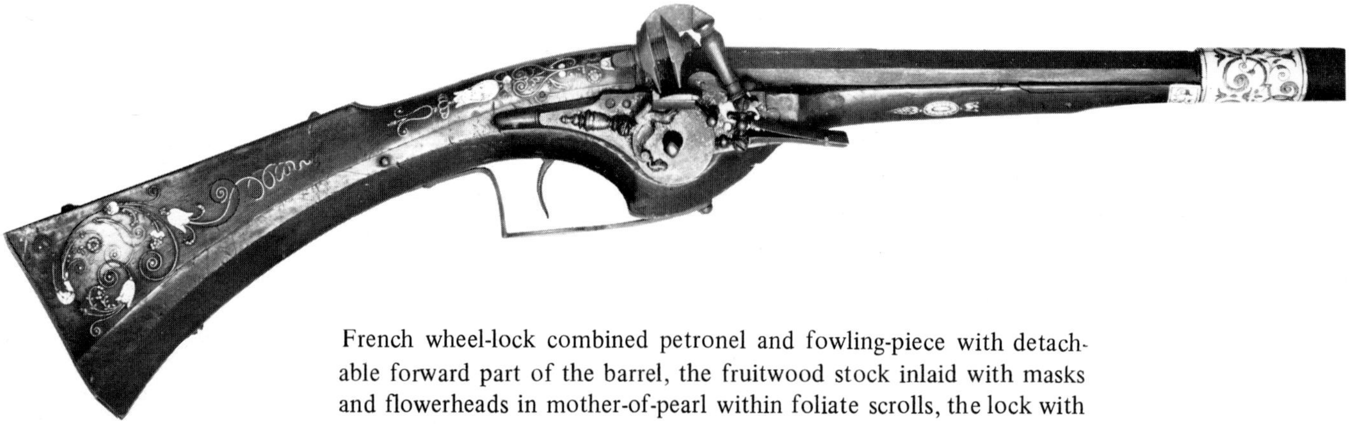

French wheel-lock combined petronel and fowling-piece with detachable forward part of the barrel, the fruitwood stock inlaid with masks and flowerheads in mother-of-pearl within foliate scrolls, the lock with dragon-shaped wheel-cover. Fine quality, good condition. By Pierre Le Bourgeoys of Lizieux, circa 1612. 3ft. 8in.
From the Cabinet d'Armes of Louis XIII. *Sotheby's*

Over £20,000

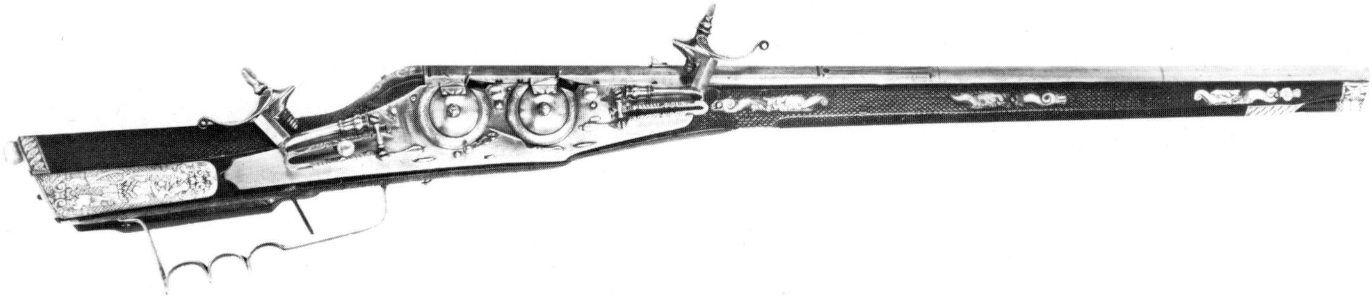

Wheel-lock superimposed load rifle, the barrel in three stages and dated 1600, the double lock with two wheels each with domed cover and engraved brass retaining ring, the stock stamped to simulate staghorn and with horn inlays. Fine quality and condition. 40in.

Extremely rare. This rifle made £7,000 in 1969.

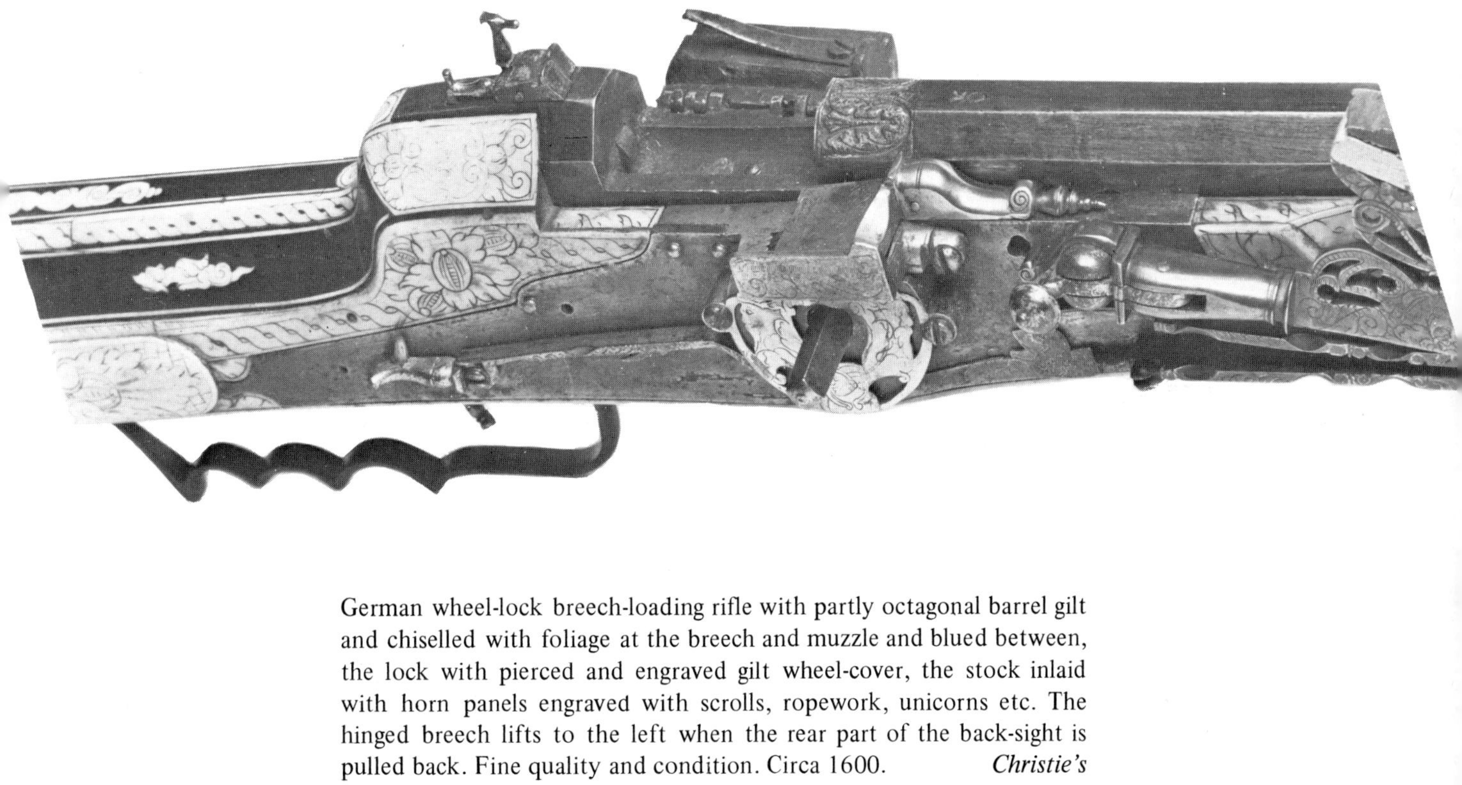

German wheel-lock breech-loading rifle with partly octagonal barrel gilt and chiselled with foliage at the breech and muzzle and blued between, the lock with pierced and engraved gilt wheel-cover, the stock inlaid with horn panels engraved with scrolls, ropework, unicorns etc. The hinged breech lifts to the left when the rear part of the back-sight is pulled back. Fine quality and condition. Circa 1600. *Christie's*

Over £4,000

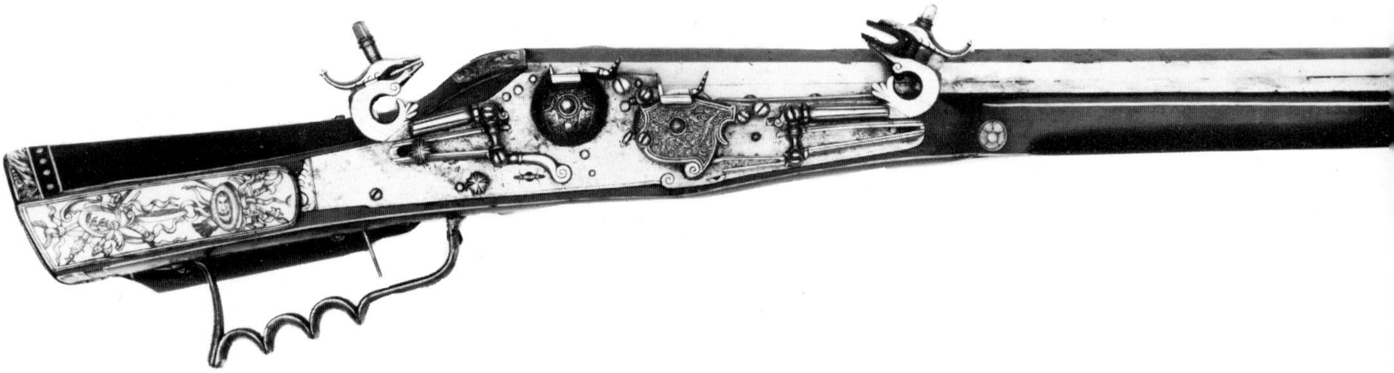

Saxon wheel-lock double-barrelled over-and-under arquebus, the upper barrel rifled, the lower smooth, the lock with two wheels, one with flat and one with domed cover, each etched with birds and foliage against a black ground, the palisander wood full stock inlaid with horn plaques finely engraved with monsters, snakes and fruit, the butt-trap cover etched inside and out, on the outside only with the arms of Saxony impaling the Archmarshalship of the Empire. Exceptional quality and condition. 44½in. Circa 1600. *Renwick Collection*

About £7,000

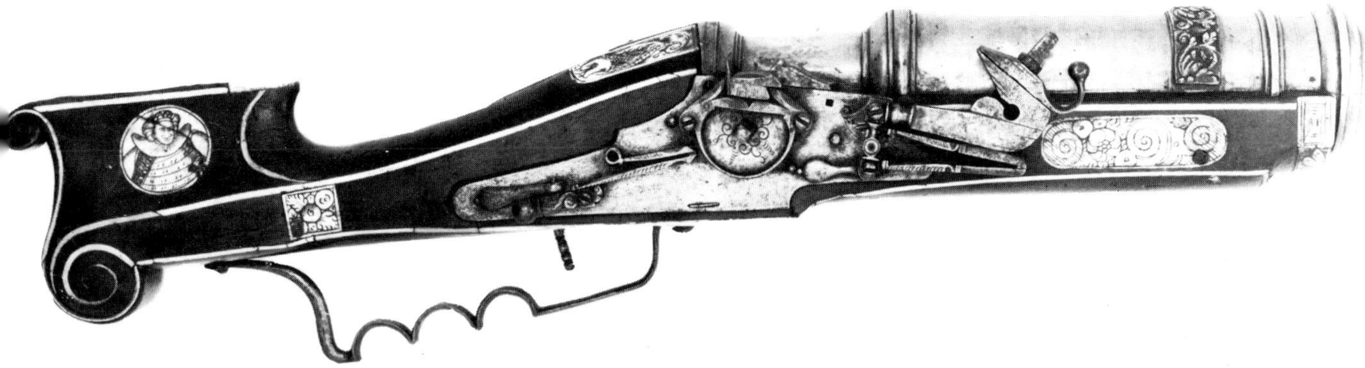

German wheel-lock grenade launcher with brass barrel decorated with mouldings and a band of foliage, the walnut full stock inlaid with stag-horn lines, engraved plaques and circular medallions engraved with portraits. Good quality and condition. Circa 1580. 25in.

Renwick Collection

Over £3,000. Very rare.

Snaphaunce, Miquelet-Lock and Baltic-Lock Guns

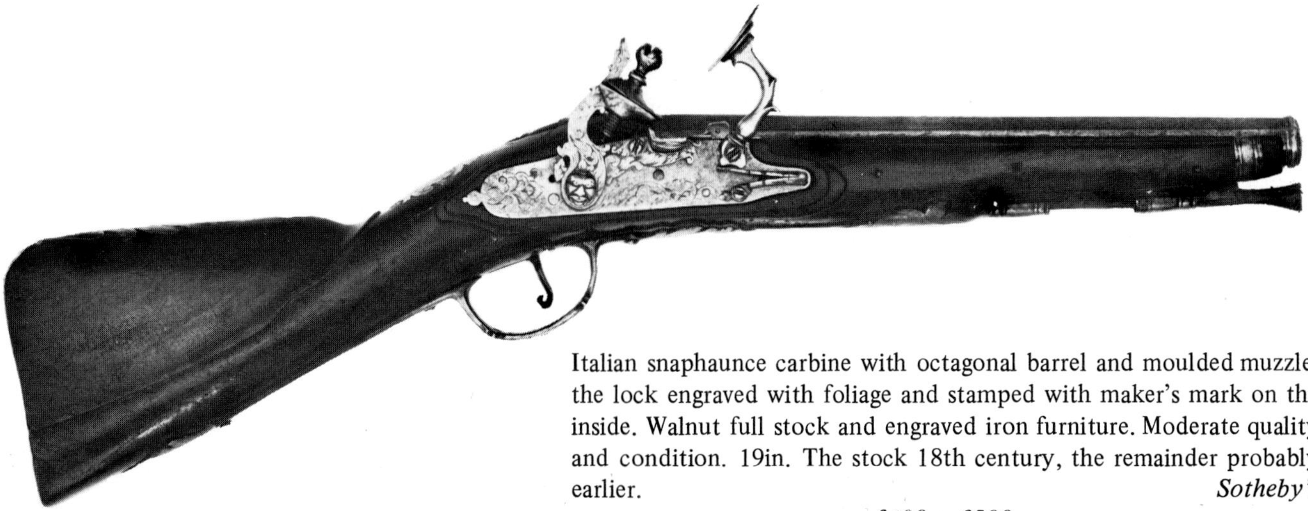

Italian snaphaunce carbine with octagonal barrel and moulded muzzle, the lock engraved with foliage and stamped with maker's mark on the inside. Walnut full stock and engraved iron furniture. Moderate quality and condition. 19in. The stock 18th century, the remainder probably earlier. *Sotheby's*

£400 – £500

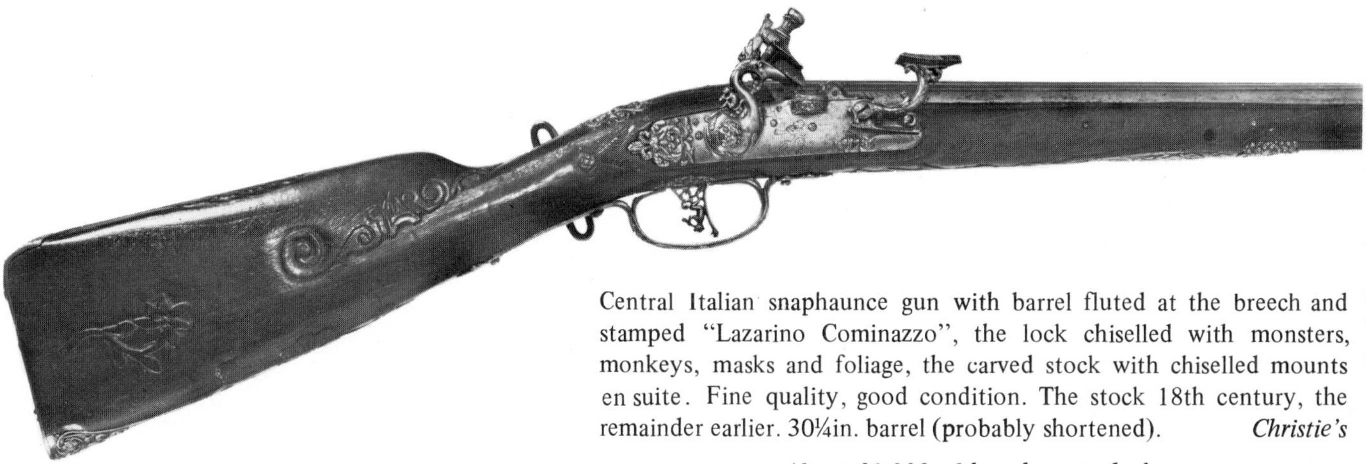

Central Italian snaphaunce gun with barrel fluted at the breech and stamped "Lazarino Cominazzo", the lock chiselled with monsters, monkeys, masks and foliage, the carved stock with chiselled mounts en suite. Fine quality, good condition. The stock 18th century, the remainder earlier. 30¼in. barrel (probably shortened). *Christie's*

About £1,000, although re-stocked.

Much more for a completely original example.

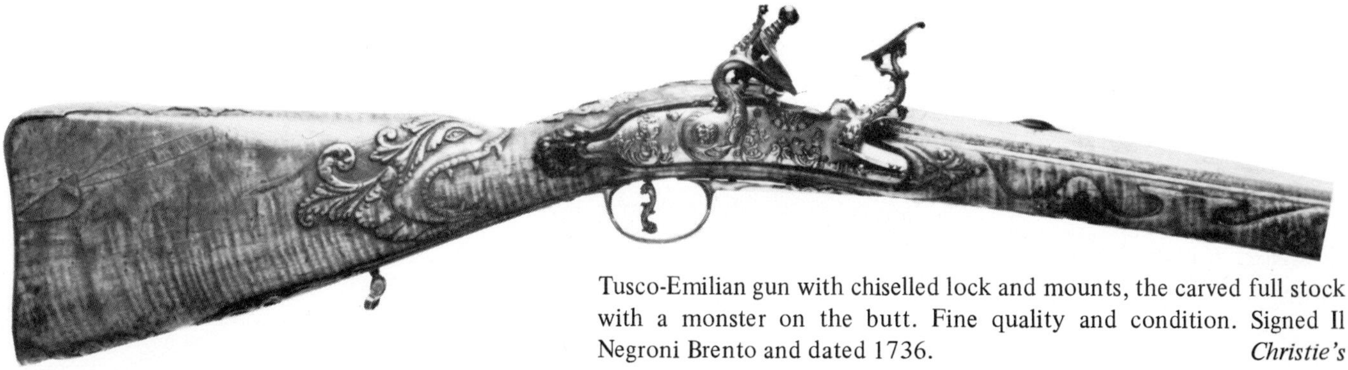

Tusco-Emilian gun with chiselled lock and mounts, the carved full stock with a monster on the butt. Fine quality and condition. Signed Il Negroni Brento and dated 1736. *Christie's*

Over £2,000

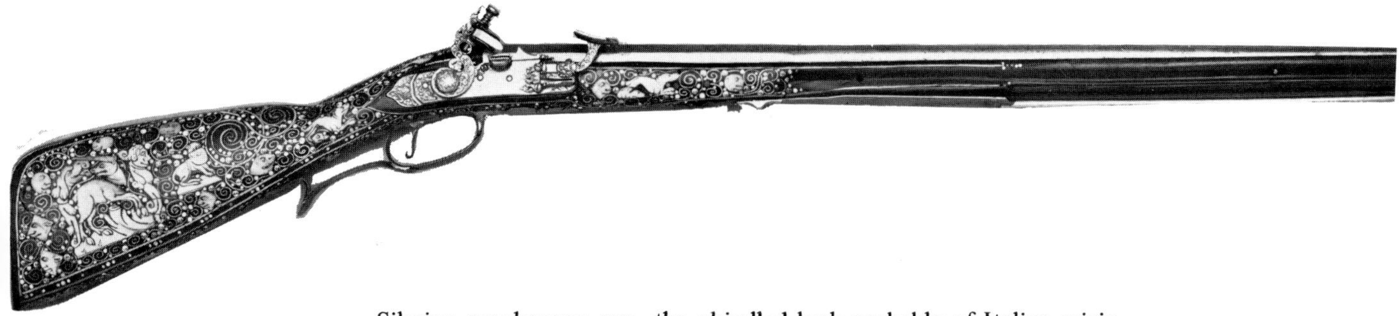

Silesian snaphaunce gun, the chiselled lock probably of Italian origin, the stock inlaid in the Teschian manner with bone scrolls and animals, fitted with a spear-headed spring bayonet. Fine quality, good condition, but with some restoration. 17th century. 36in. barrel. *Christie's*

Over £1,000

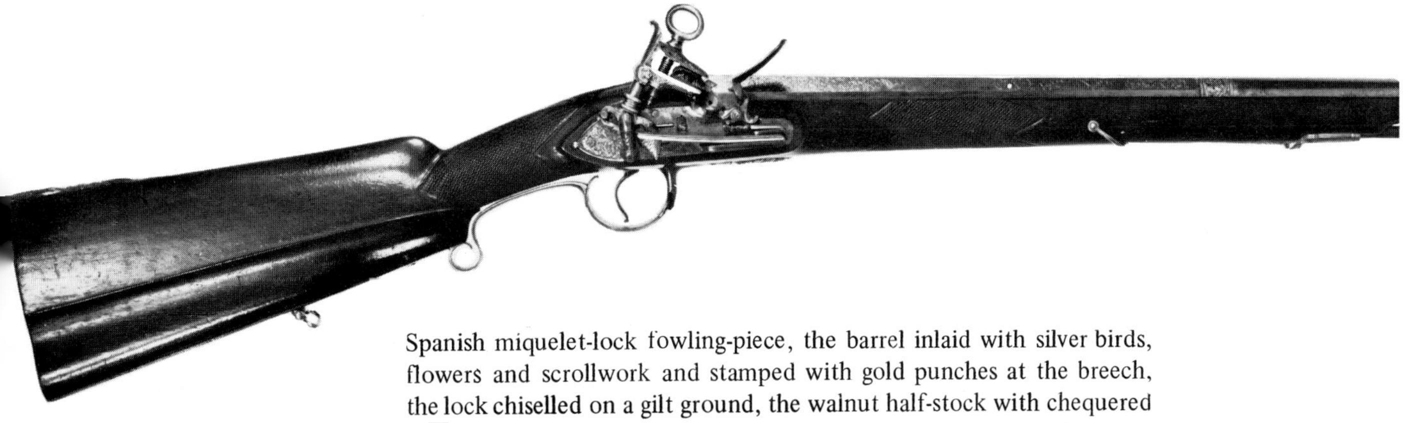

Spanish miquelet-lock fowling-piece, the barrel inlaid with silver birds, flowers and scrollwork and stamped with gold punches at the breech, the lock chiselled on a gilt ground, the walnut half-stock with chequered grip and fore-end, the mounts of chiselled steel. Fine quality but only fair condition. Eibar, early 19th century. 34½in. barrel. *Christie's*

£300 – £400

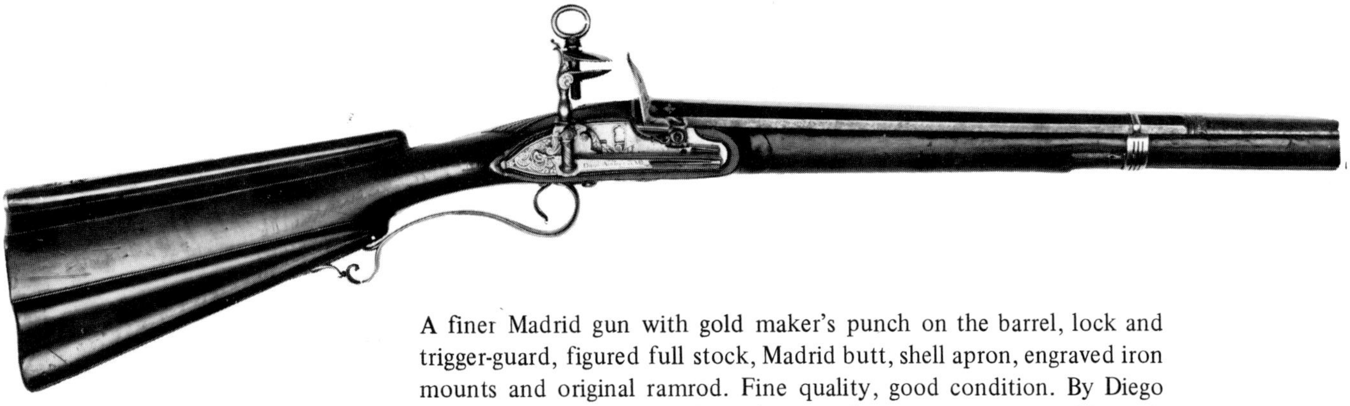

A finer Madrid gun with gold maker's punch on the barrel, lock and trigger-guard, figured full stock, Madrid butt, shell apron, engraved iron mounts and original ramrod. Fine quality, good condition. By Diego Alvarez, Madrid, circa 1780. 35½in. barrel. *Christie's*

£800 – £1,000

Italian miquelet-lock gun with barrel in two stages and gold vent, the lock engraved with foliage, the full stock with fluted butt and engraved silver furniture, the trigger-guard of wood with a silver strap. Fair quality and condition. The barrel by Geronimo Fernandez of Salamanca, early 18th century. 39¼in. barrel. *Christie's*

£400 – £500

Neapolitan snaphaunce fowling-piece with barrel of Spanish form and brass sights, lightly engraved flat lock, the half-stock decorated with panels of pierced brass and with brass trigger-guard and butt-plate. Moderate quality, fair condition. By Nicolo del Moro, mid-18th century. 45in. barrel. *Christie's*

£300 – £500

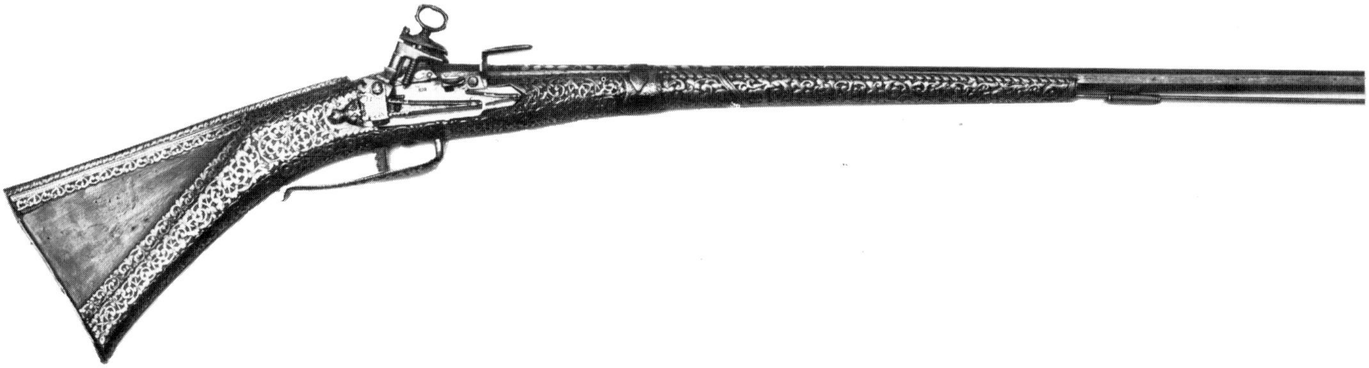

Sardinian miquelet-lock gun with octagonal barrel inlaid with silver at the breech, chiselled and engraved lock, the stock encased in pierced and chiselled steel cagework. Moderate quality and condition. Probably 18th century. 46in. barrel. *Christie's*

£125 – £200

Neapolitan miquelet-lock gun, the barrel stamped "Lazarino Cominazzo", the lock pierced and chiselled with figures and monsters in high relief, the stock with steel mounts en suite. Very fine quality and condition. Second half of the 17th century. 54in. *Sotheby's*

Over £3,000

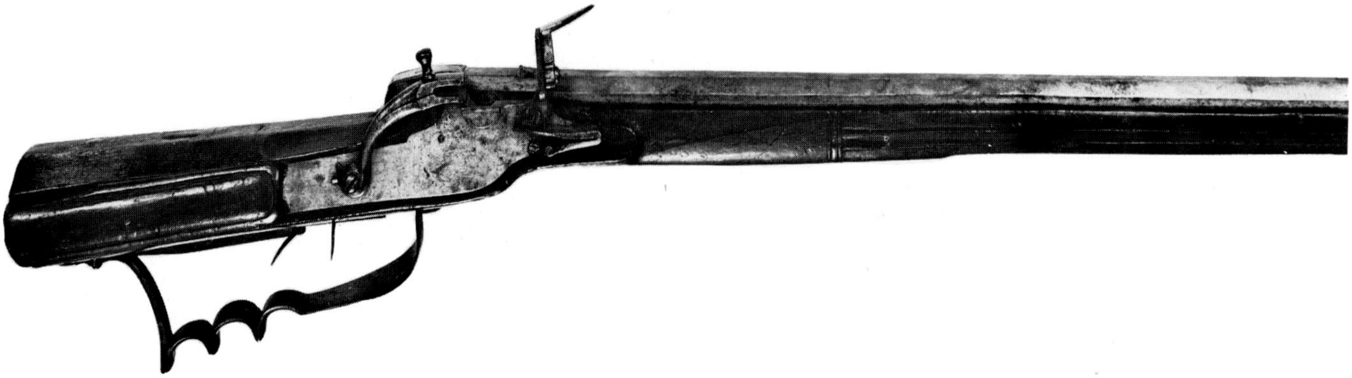

Plain Baltic-lock rifle with octagonal barrel, and full stock with iron mounts, patch-box and set trigger. Moderate quality and condition. 17th/18th century. 34in. *Weller & Dufty*

£200 – £250

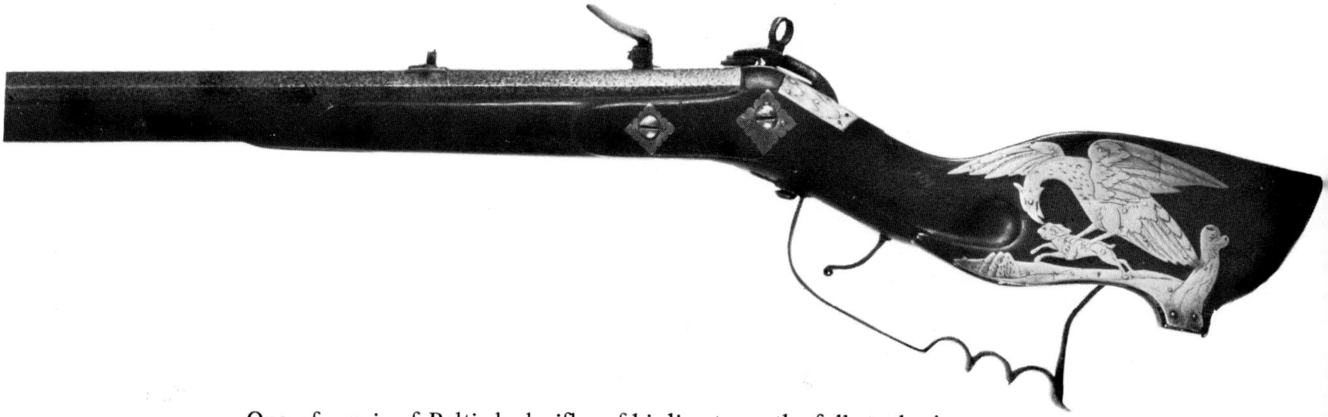

One of a pair of Baltic-lock rifles of birding type, the full stocks decorated with panels of brass engraved with animals and foliage, the cheek-pieces set with an eagle catching a hare. Good quality, moderate condition. 17th/18th century. 34½in. *Christie's*

£500 – £600

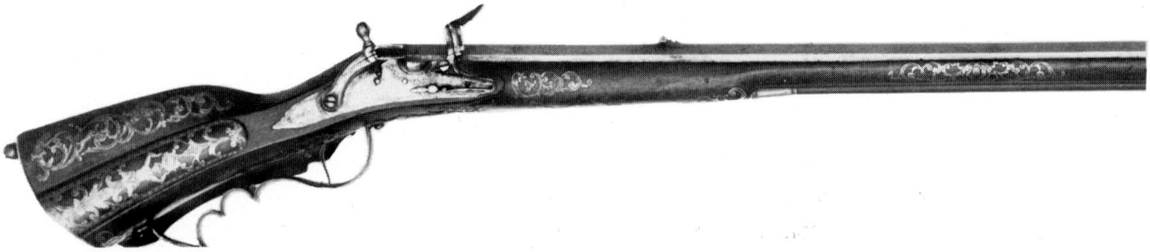

Very fine Swedish snap-lock sporting rifle with sighted octagonal barrel, the stock inlaid with numerous pierced brass plaques engraved with scrolls, animals and figures, the butt inlaid with a plate inscribed "Schertiger fecit 1722". Exceptional quality and condition, probably made for King Frederick I of Sweden. 46in. *Renwick Collection*

About £2,000

Flintlock Sporting Guns

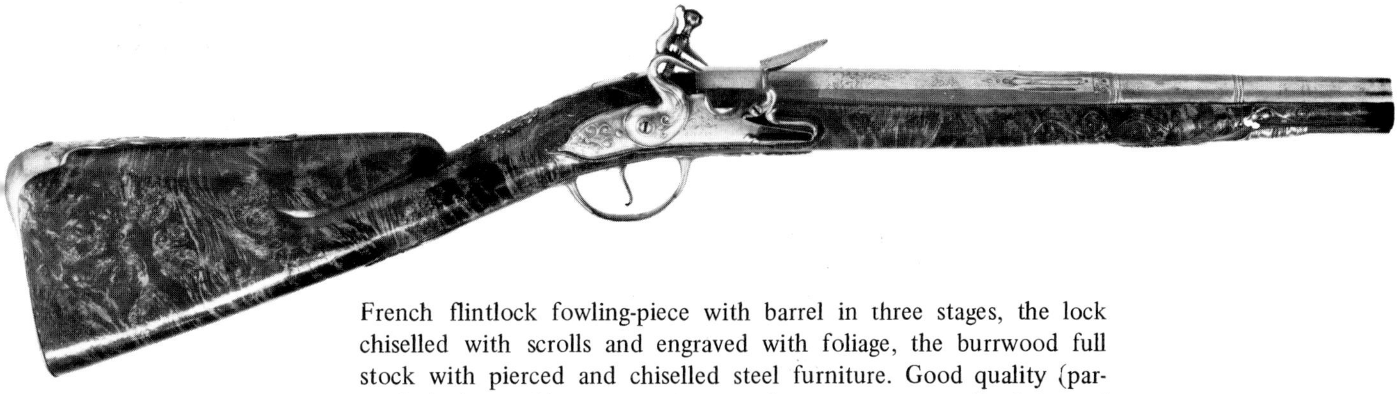

French flintlock fowling-piece with barrel in three stages, the lock chiselled with scrolls and engraved with foliage, the burrwood full stock with pierced and chiselled steel furniture. Good quality (particularly the stock), good condition with some restoration. By Soiron of Sedan, late 17th century. 48in. barrel. *Christie's*

Over £1,000

Many 17th century guns were brought up to date in the 18th century by reducing the length of the barrels. Where this has been done the value is greatly reduced. All 17th century flintlock guns are now very rare

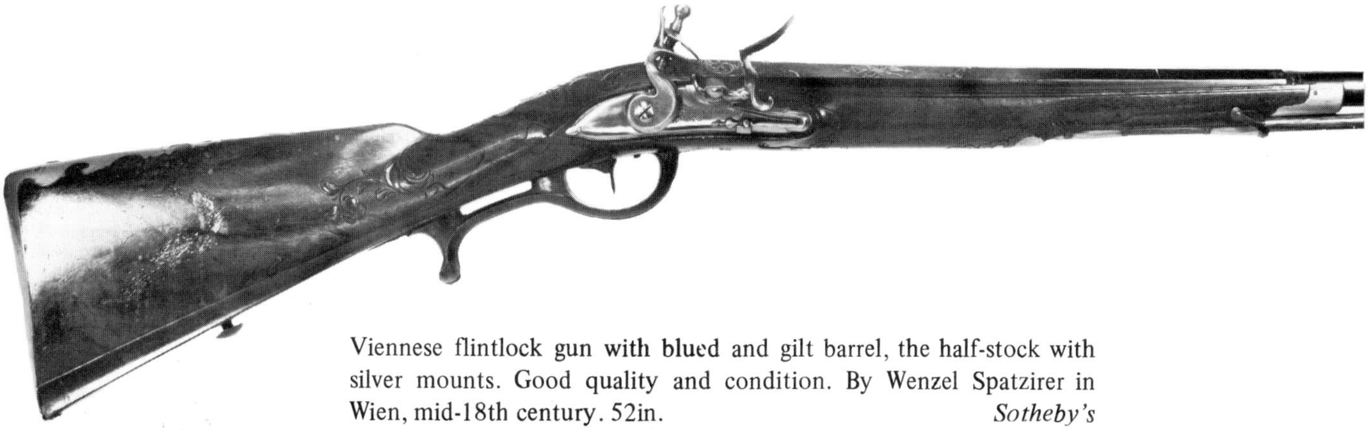

Viennese flintlock gun with blued and gilt barrel, the half-stock with silver mounts. Good quality and condition. By Wenzel Spatzirer in Wien, mid-18th century. 52in. *Sotheby's*

£300 – £450

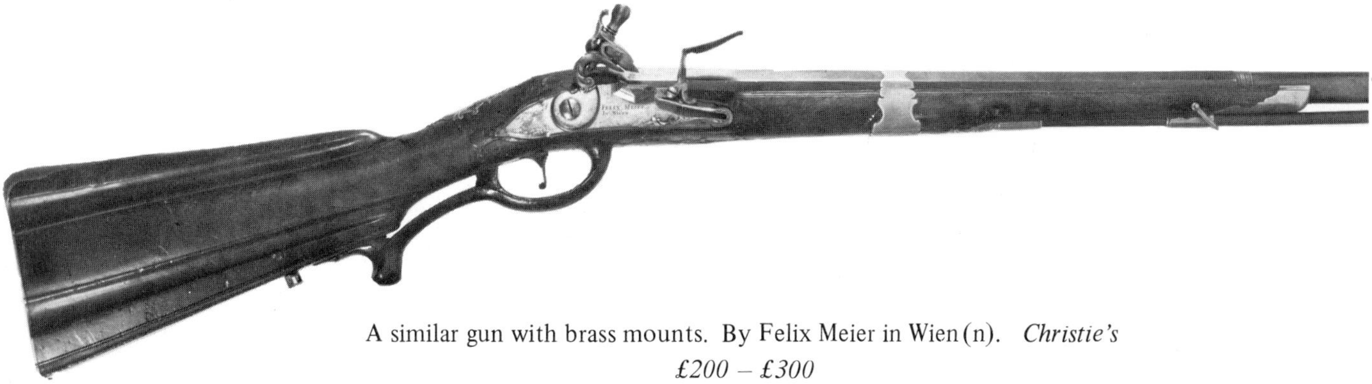

A similar gun with brass mounts. By Felix Meier in Wien(n). *Christie's*

£200 – £300

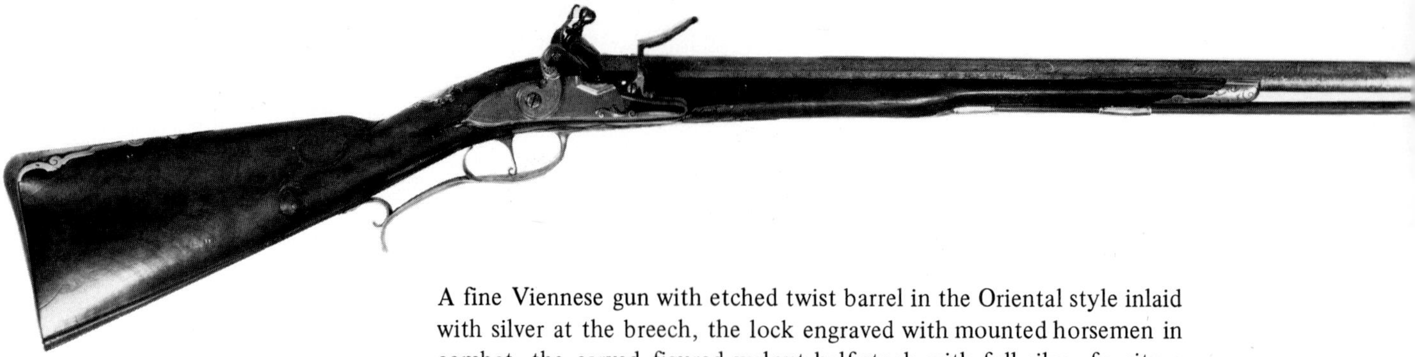

A fine Viennese gun with etched twist barrel in the Oriental style inlaid with silver at the breech, the lock engraved with mounted horsemen in combat, the carved figured walnut half-stock with full silver furniture including pierced side-plate. Fine quality, fair condition. By Felix Meier in Wien, circa 1730. 42in. barrel. *Christie's*

About £800

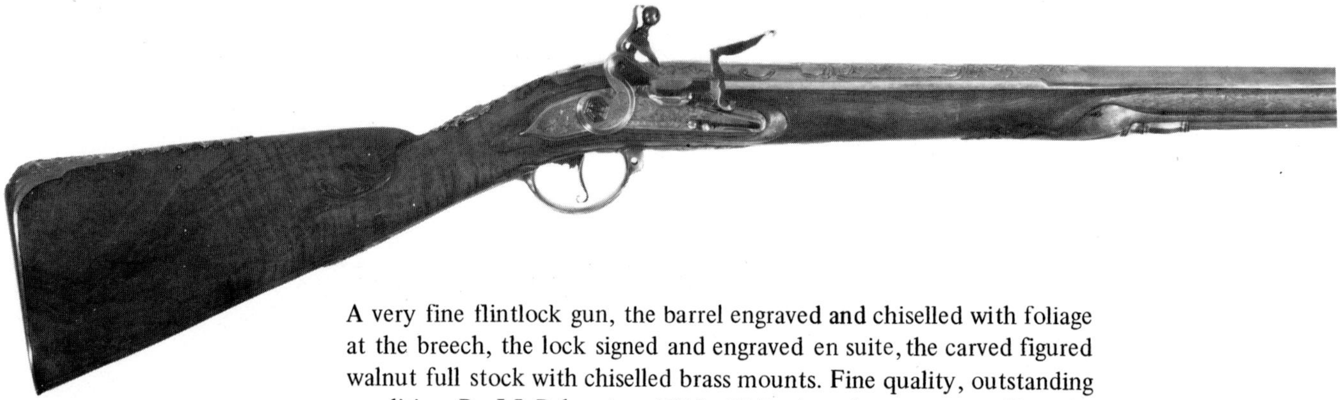

A very fine flintlock gun, the barrel engraved and chiselled with foliage at the breech, the lock signed and engraved en suite, the carved figured walnut full stock with chiselled brass mounts. Fine quality, outstanding condition. By J.J. Behr, circa 1725. 43½in. barrel. *Christie's*

Over £1,000

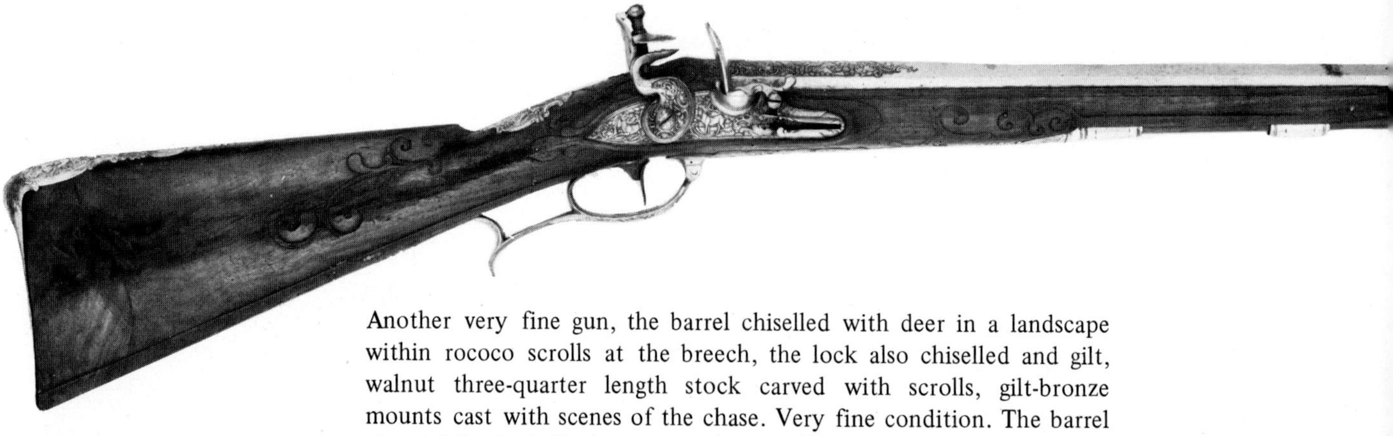

Another very fine gun, the barrel chiselled with deer in a landscape within rococo scrolls at the breech, the lock also chiselled and gilt, walnut three-quarter length stock carved with scrolls, gilt-bronze mounts cast with scenes of the chase. Very fine condition. The barrel signed Joh. And. Kuchenreuter, the chiselling by the Stockmar family of Heidersbach near Suhl. 52in. Third quarter of the 18th century.

Renwick Collection

Over £1,200

Extremely fine French flintlock gun, the barrel chiselled with figures of Mars and Diana, masks, satyrs, monsters, foliage and strapwork, the lock with a stag-hunting scene, the figured burrwood stock with chiselled steel mounts en suite and inlaid with silver wire. Exceptional quality, good condition but the stock with shortened fore-end. Early 18th century. *Christie's*

Over £15,000

Russian flintlock fowling-piece, the barrel signed in gold and dated 1790, chiselled at the breech and set with a medallion surmounted by a vase of silver and gold flowers, the carved full stock with silver wire inlay and steel mounts decorated with silver and gold, the escutcheon with the monogram of Czar Paul 1. Very fine quality, fine condition. *Christie's*

Over £3,000

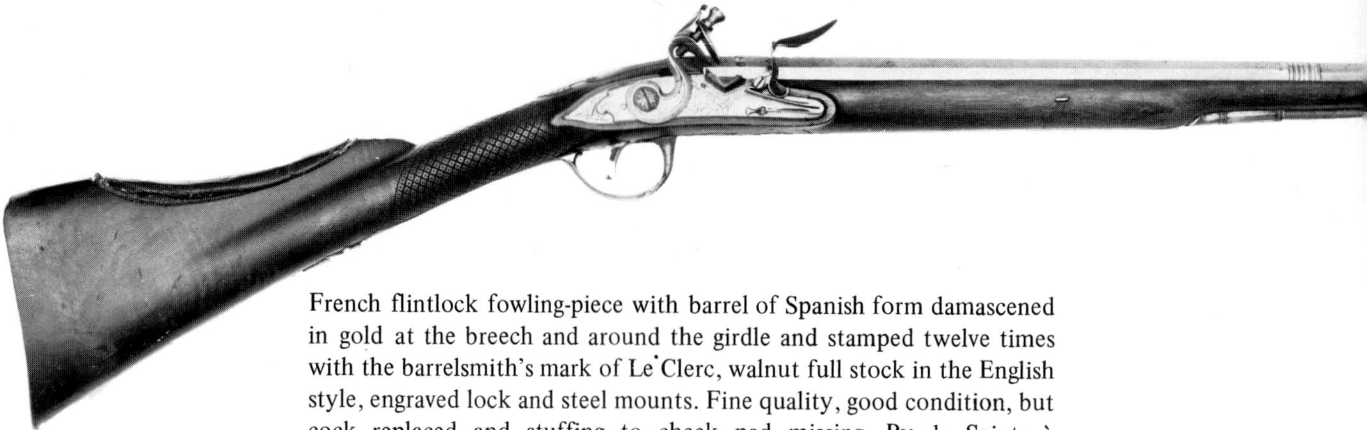

French flintlock fowling-piece with barrel of Spanish form damascened in gold at the breech and around the girdle and stamped twelve times with the barrelsmith's mark of Le Clerc, walnut full stock in the English style, engraved lock and steel mounts. Fine quality, good condition, but cock replaced and stuffing to cheek pad missing. By de Sainte à Versailles. 47½in. Circa 1780. *Sotheby's*

£300 – £500

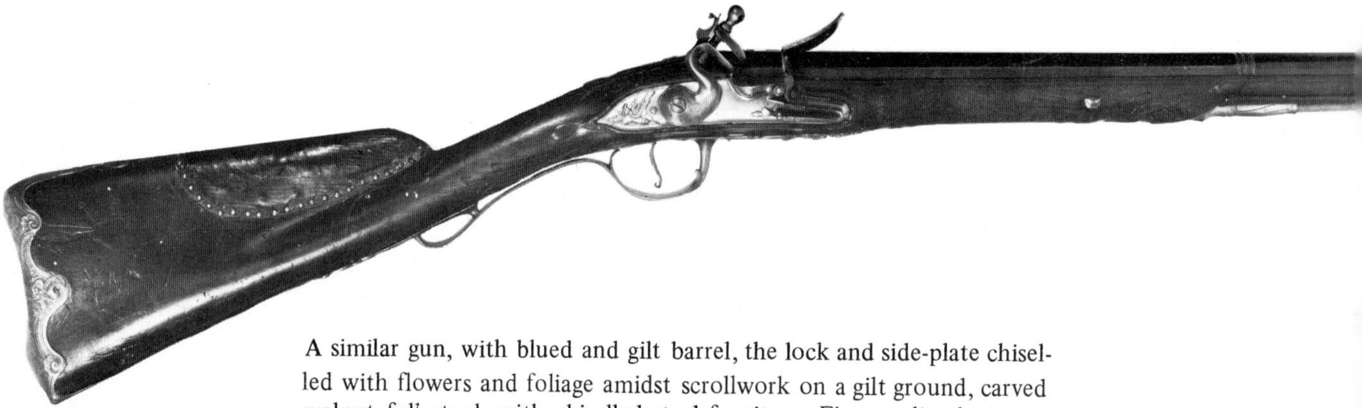

A similar gun, with blued and gilt barrel, the lock and side-plate chiselled with flowers and foliage amidst scrollwork on a gilt ground, carved walnut full stock with chiselled steel furniture. Fine quality but poor condition with restoration. By Le Page, Paris, circa 1780. 34in. barrel. *Christie's*

£300 – £400 owing to condition.

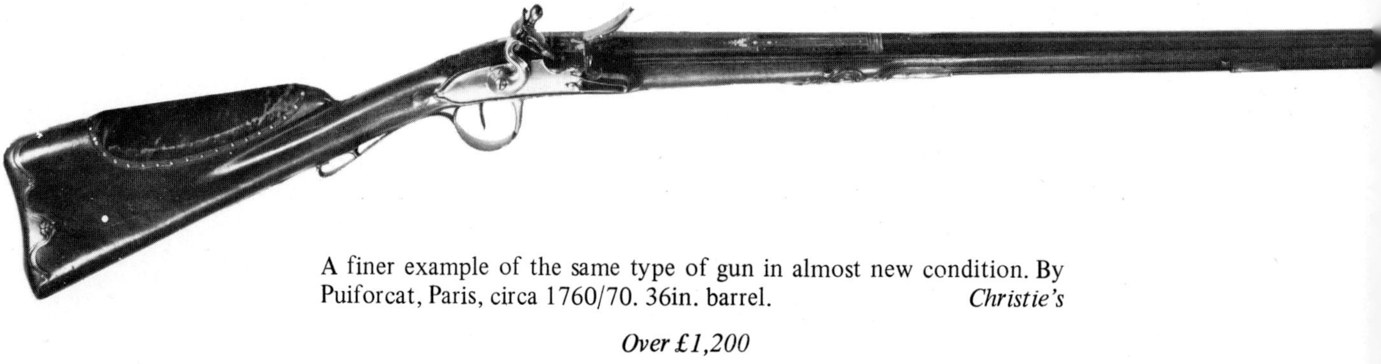

A finer example of the same type of gun in almost new condition. By Puiforcat, Paris, circa 1760/70. 36in. barrel. *Christie's*

Over £1,200

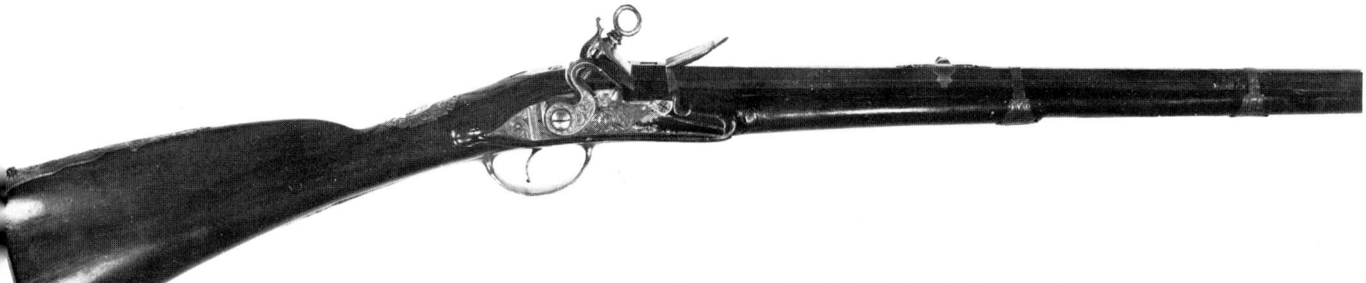

Spanish flintlock fowling-piece with engraved Madrid lock, the browned barrel in two stages inlaid with silver scrollwork and the date 1736 at the breech, the full stock with engraved brass furniture applied with silver medallions cast with classical busts, the butt-plate incorporating a butt-trap for a hunting bayonet (missing). Good quality and condition. By Manuel Cams of Barcelona, the lock signed Deop, dated 1736. 42in. barrel. *Christie's*

£500 – £800

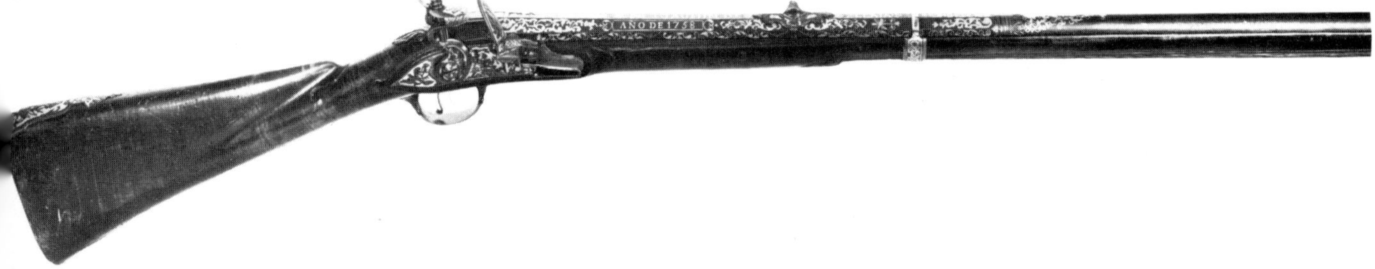

A very fine Madrid gun, the blued barrel profusely inlaid with gold, signed and dated in full and with gold maker's stamp, the Madrid lock, trigger-guard and butt-plate chiselled against a gilt ground with Diana, trophies, a warrior, etc. Fine condition. By Joachin de Zelaya, 1758. *Sotheby's*

Over £3,000

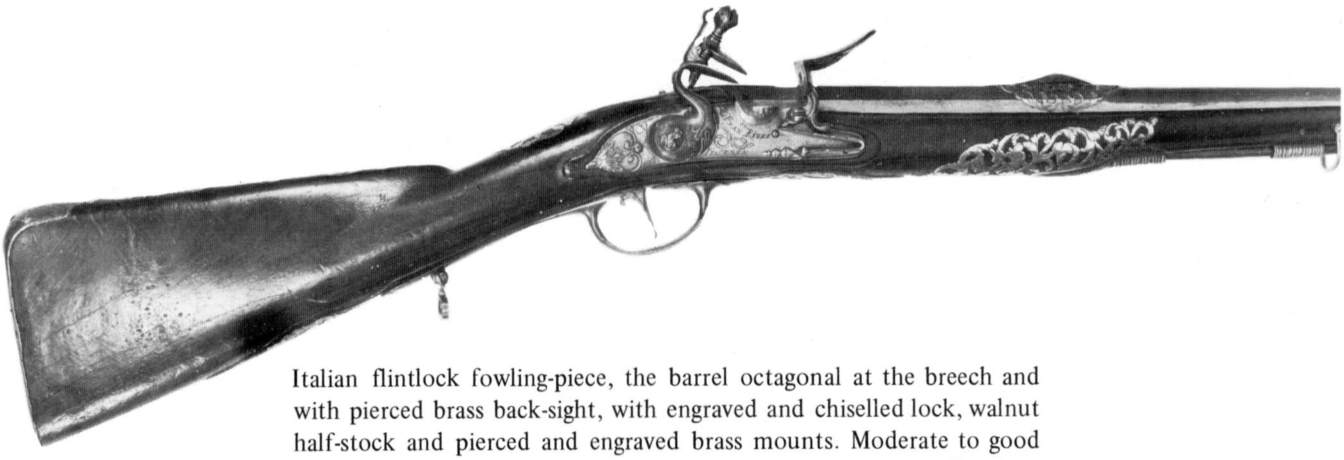

Italian flintlock fowling-piece, the barrel octagonal at the breech and with pierced brass back-sight, with engraved and chiselled lock, walnut half-stock and pierced and engraved brass mounts. Moderate to good quality, good condition. The barrel signed Giovanni Battista Guerino, the lock Francisco Rizzi, Piacenza, early 18th century. 43½in. barrel.

Christie's

£600 – £800

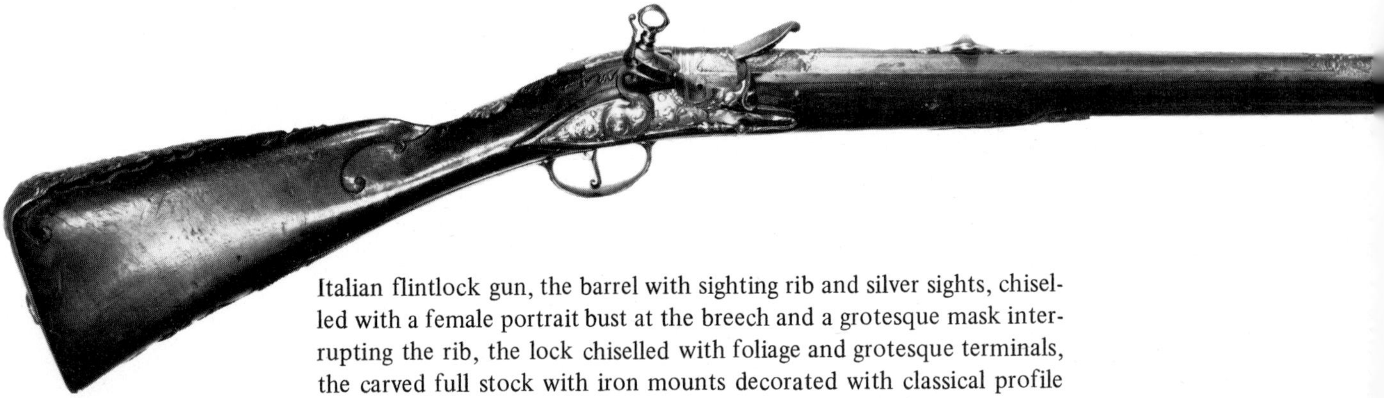

Italian flintlock gun, the barrel with sighting rib and silver sights, chiselled with a female portrait bust at the breech and a grotesque mask interrupting the rib, the lock chiselled with foliage and grotesque terminals, the carved full stock with iron mounts decorated with classical profile heads within scrollwork. Fine quality, good condition. Mid-18th century. 39½in. barrel. *Christie's*

About £800

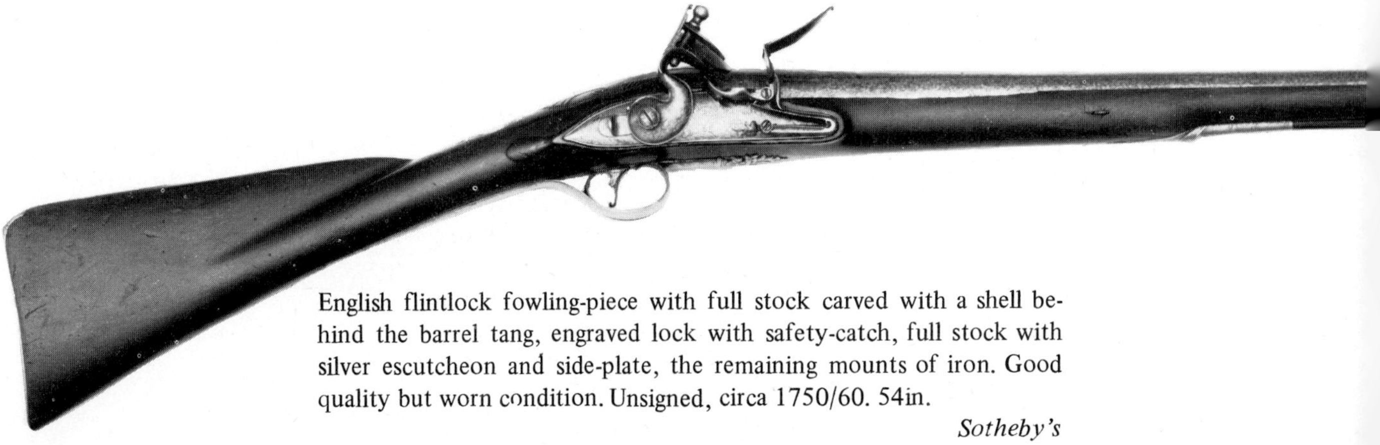

English flintlock fowling-piece with full stock carved with a shell behind the barrel tang, engraved lock with safety-catch, full stock with silver escutcheon and side-plate, the remaining mounts of iron. Good quality but worn condition. Unsigned, circa 1750/60. 54in.

Sotheby's

About £300

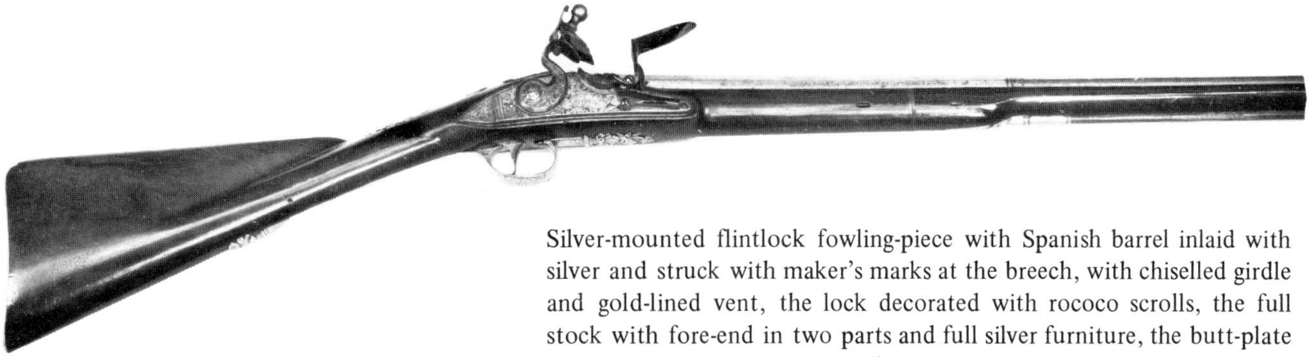

Silver-mounted flintlock fowling-piece with Spanish barrel inlaid with silver and struck with maker's marks at the breech, with chiselled girdle and gold-lined vent, the lock decorated with rococo scrolls, the full stock with fore-end in two parts and full silver furniture, the butt-plate with London silver hallmark for 1765, and maker's mark IK. Fine quality, fair condition with some restoration. By Griffin, London, the barrel by Bustindui. 56in. *Sotheby's*

This gun made £820 in 1970

This was a high price for a gun in this condition, but the Spanish barrel, the reputation of Griffin, and the rarity of English silver-mounted guns with unshortened barrels today makes it a very desirable piece. A really fine one is worth several thousand pounds and a shortened one £300 – £450.

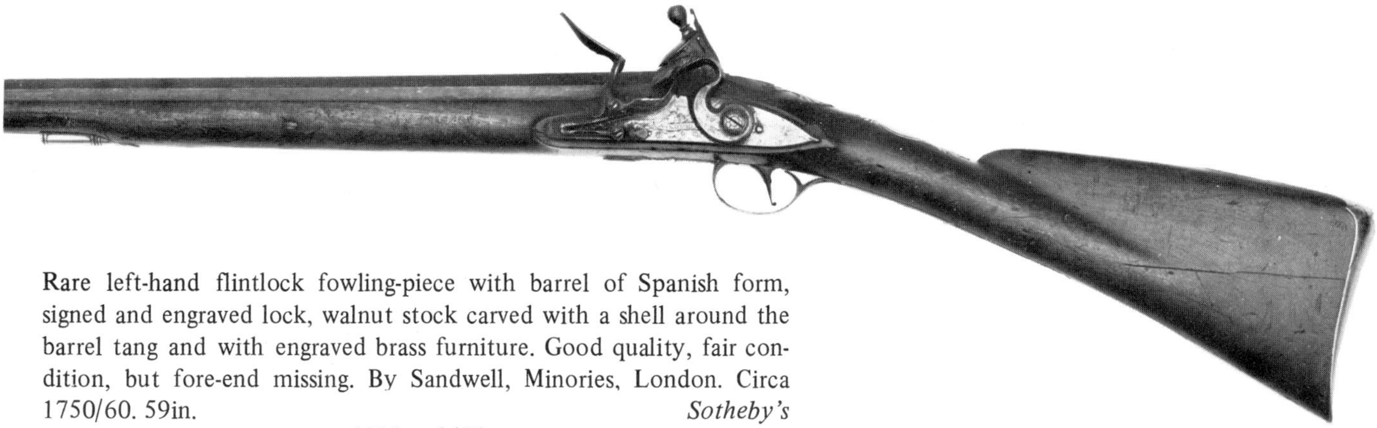

Rare left-hand flintlock fowling-piece with barrel of Spanish form, signed and engraved lock, walnut stock carved with a shell around the barrel tang and with engraved brass furniture. Good quality, fair condition, but fore-end missing. By Sandwell, Minories, London. Circa 1750/60. 59in. *Sotheby's*

£300 – £450

This is nearly double the price for a similar gun with normal right-hand lock.

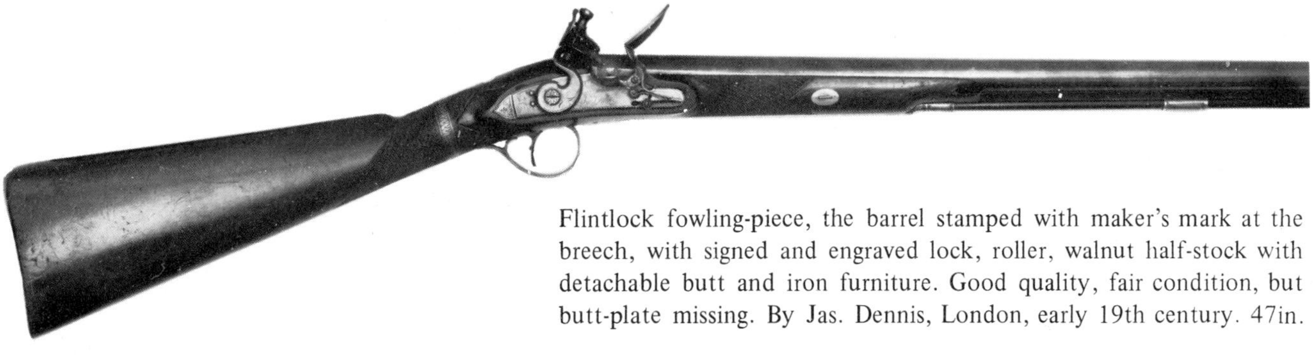

Flintlock fowling-piece, the barrel stamped with maker's mark at the breech, with signed and engraved lock, roller, walnut half-stock with detachable butt and iron furniture. Good quality, fair condition, but butt-plate missing. By Jas. Dennis, London, early 19th century. 47in.

£200 – £250

This is about the average price for early 19th century iron-mounted guns in fair condition. The rarity of the detachable butt makes up for the missing butt-plate.
In its case with accessories about £450.

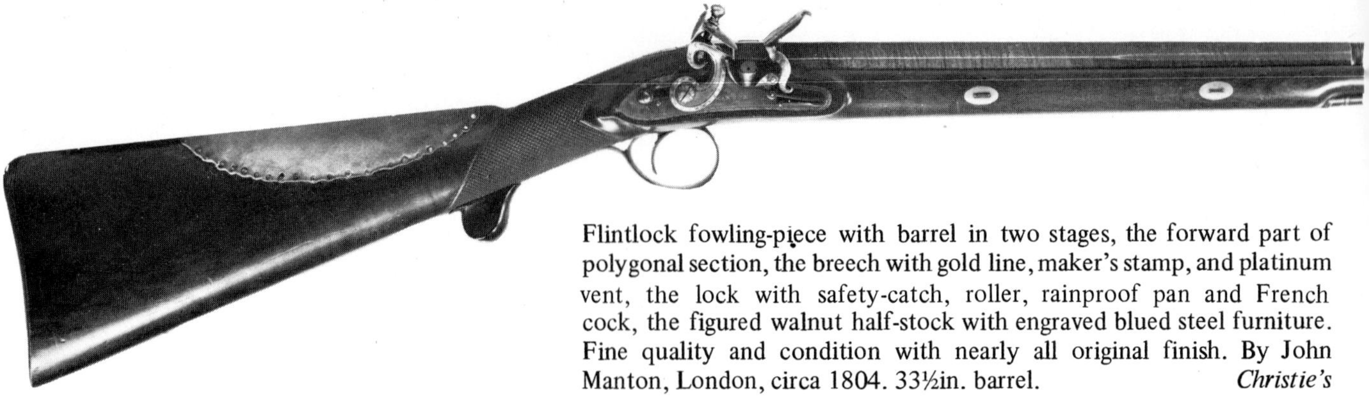

Flintlock fowling-piece with barrel in two stages, the forward part of polygonal section, the breech with gold line, maker's stamp, and platinum vent, the lock with safety-catch, roller, rainproof pan and French cock, the figured walnut half-stock with engraved blued steel furniture. Fine quality and condition with nearly all original finish. By John Manton, London, circa 1804. 33½in. barrel. *Christie's*

£500 – £600

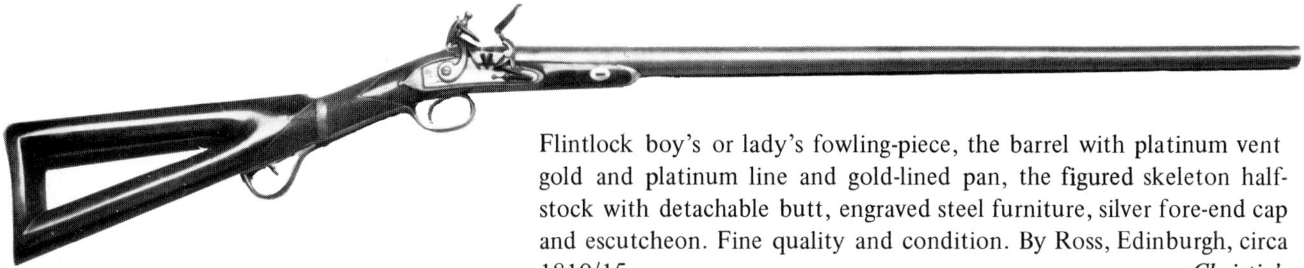

Flintlock boy's or lady's fowling-piece, the barrel with platinum vent gold and platinum line and gold-lined pan, the figured skeleton half-stock with detachable butt, engraved steel furniture, silver fore-end cap and escutcheon. Fine quality and condition. By Ross, Edinburgh, circa 1810/15. *Christie's*

About £600

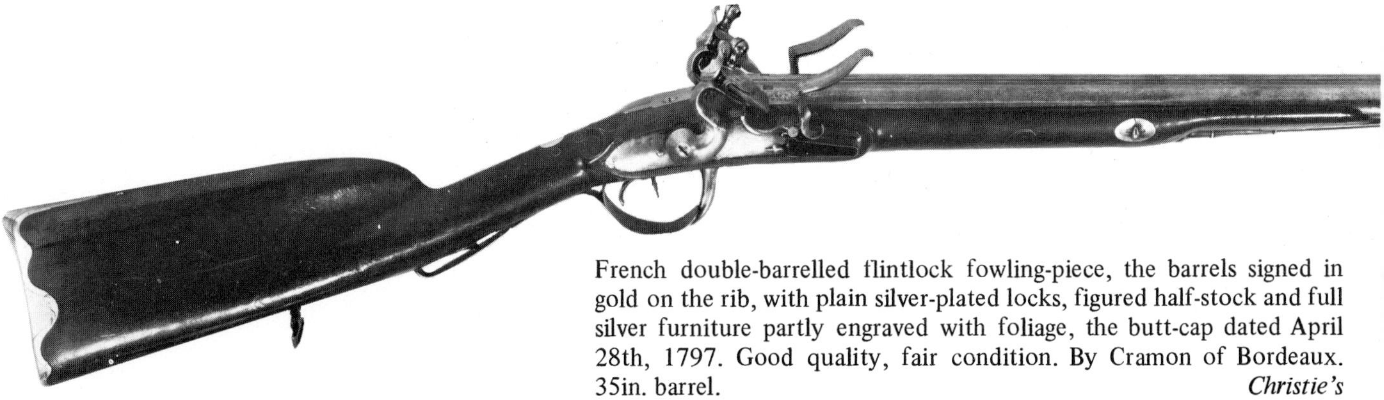

French double-barrelled flintlock fowling-piece, the barrels signed in gold on the rib, with plain silver-plated locks, figured half-stock and full silver furniture partly engraved with foliage, the butt-cap dated April 28th, 1797. Good quality, fair condition. By Cramon of Bordeaux. 35in. barrel. *Christie's*

£500 – £650

About half this figure for a steel-mounted example.

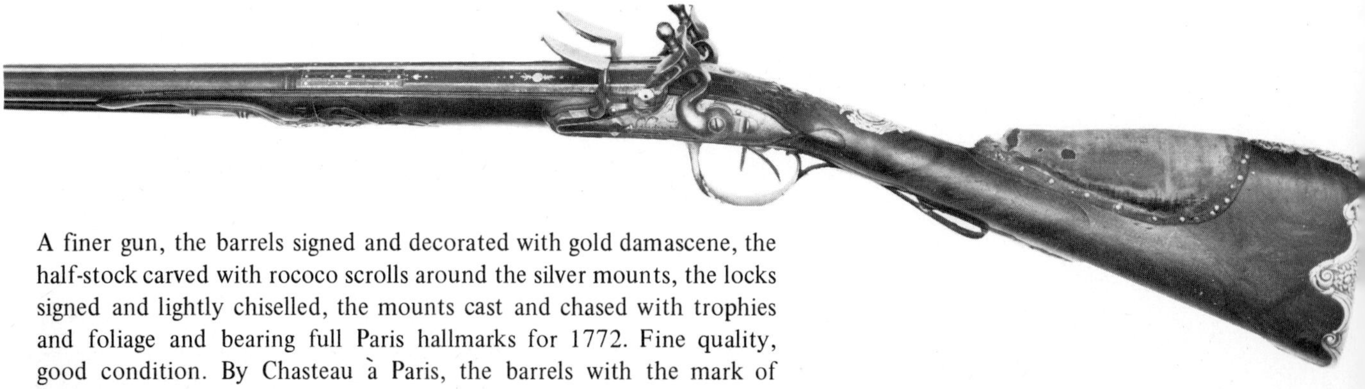

A finer gun, the barrels signed and decorated with gold damascene, the half-stock carved with rococo scrolls around the silver mounts, the locks signed and lightly chiselled, the mounts cast and chased with trophies and foliage and bearing full Paris hallmarks for 1772. Fine quality, good condition. By Chasteau à Paris, the barrels with the mark of Nicholas Le Clerc. 51in. *Sotheby's*

About £800

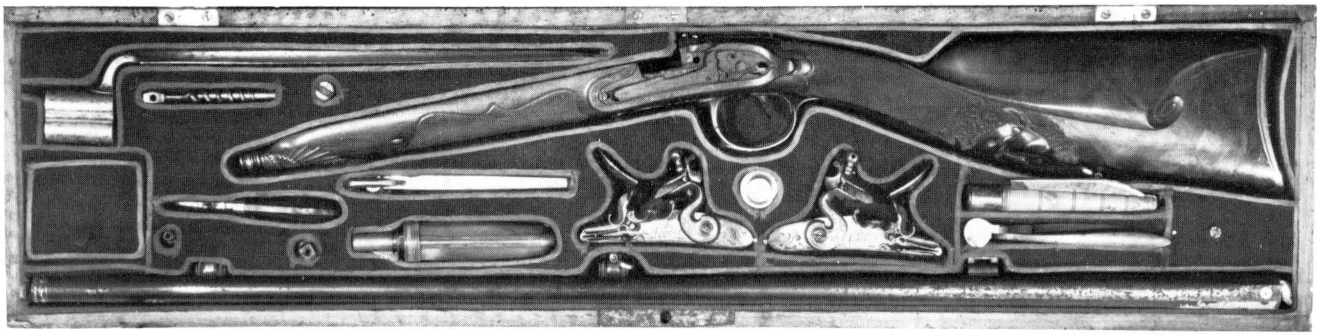

French cased double-barrelled flintlock gun with blued and gilt barrels, partly engraved locks, platinum-lined pans and vents, carved walnut half-stock and engraved silver furniture chiselled with shells, the butt carved with the mask of Pan behind the grip. In original lined and fitted case with full accessories including hunting bayonet. Good quality and condition, but one cock replaced and the case badly worm-eaten. By Aubron Jeune à Nantes, French provincial silver hallmarks. Circa 1815. 33in. barrels. *Christie's*

Over £1,000. Rare in case complete.

The gun by itself about £750.

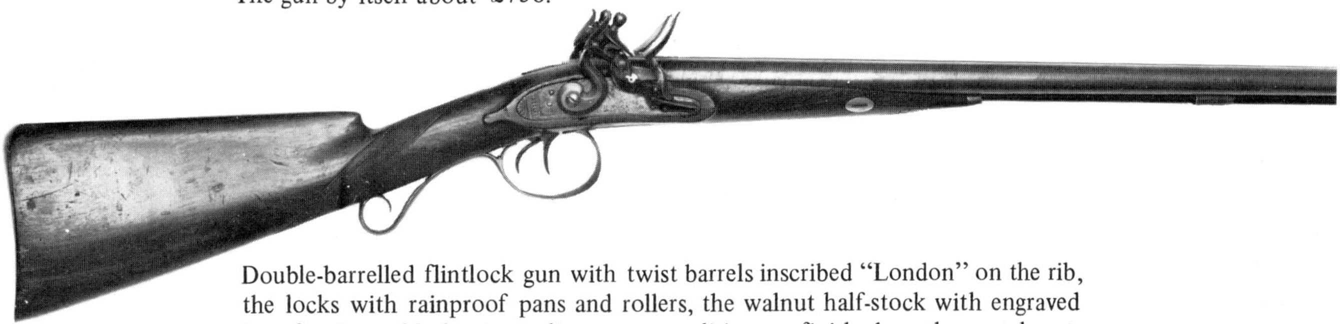

Double-barrelled flintlock gun with twist barrels inscribed "London" on the rib, the locks with rainproof pans and rollers, the walnut half-stock with engraved iron furniture. Moderate quality, poor condition, re-finished on the metal parts and both cocks replaced. The locks engraved "H. Nock". Early 19th century. 45in. *Sotheby's*

About £250

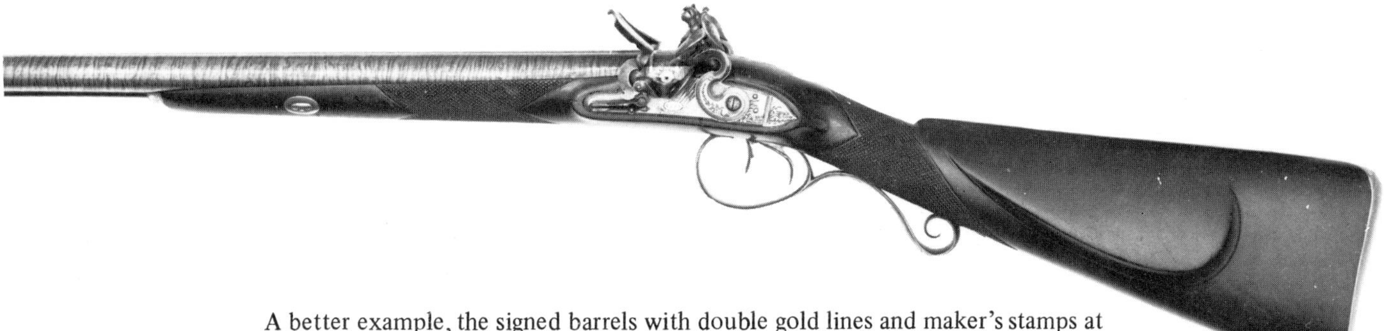

A better example, the signed barrels with double gold lines and maker's stamps at the breech, the engraved locks also with gold marks, rollers and rainproof pans, walnut half-stock with engraved iron mounts and silver rear ramrod-pipe. Fine quality, good condition. By Bass, London, circa 1790. 49½in. *Sotheby's*

£500 – £650

Double-barrelled flintlock fowling-piece with barrels signed and inlaid with a motto in gold, gold lines, platinum vents and gold-lined pans, half-stock and engraved steel furniture. Fine quality, good condition with some finish but one cock an old replacement. By Durs Egg, London, early 19th century. 29in. barrels. *Christie's*

About £1,000
In really fine condition over £1,500.

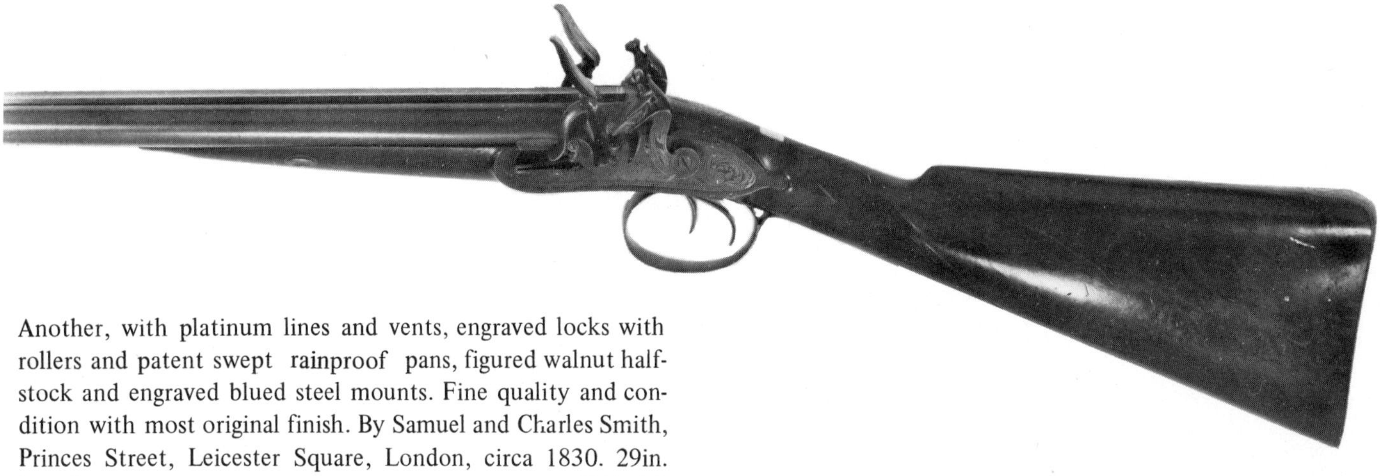

Another, with platinum lines and vents, engraved locks with rollers and patent swept rainproof pans, figured walnut half-stock and engraved blued steel mounts. Fine quality and condition with most original finish. By Samuel and Charles Smith, Princes Street, Leicester Square, London, circa 1830. 29in. barrels. *Christie's*

Over £1,200

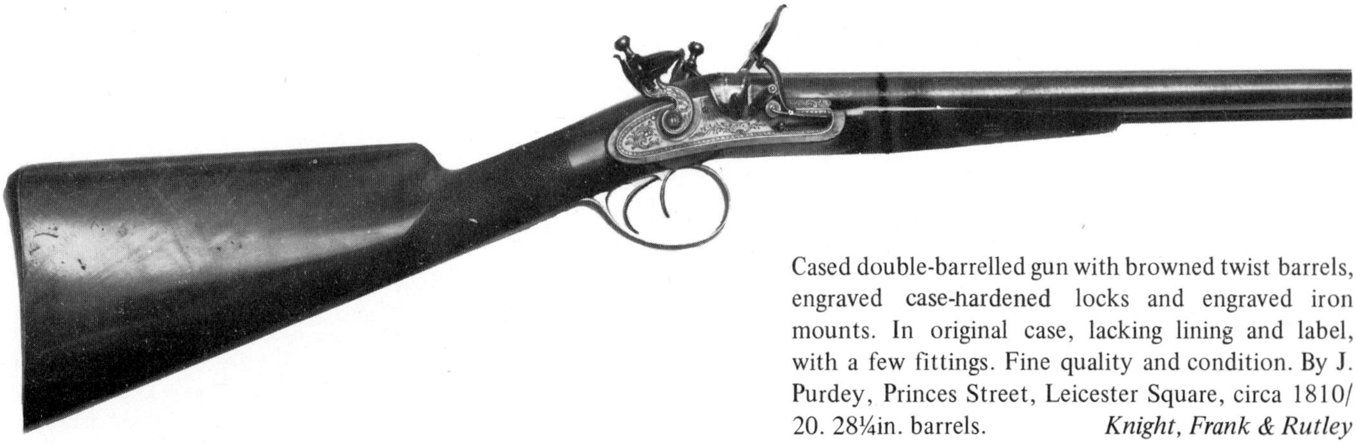

Cased double-barrelled gun with browned twist barrels, engraved case-hardened locks and engraved iron mounts. In original case, lacking lining and label, with a few fittings. Fine quality and condition. By J. Purdey, Princes Street, Leicester Square, circa 1810/20. 28¼in. barrels. *Knight, Frank & Rutley*

Over £2,000

Flintlock guns in their original case with fittings are now very rare.

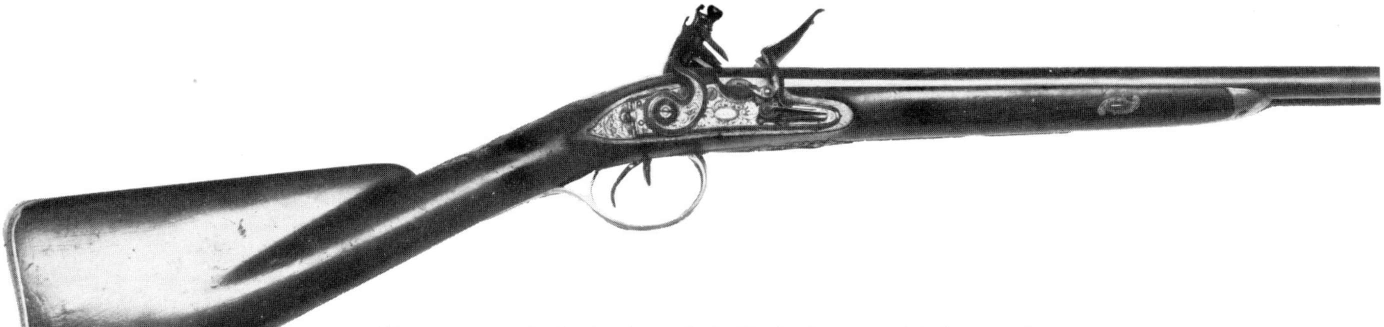

Silver-mounted double-barrelled flintlock gun with browned twist barrels inlaid with foliage and scrollwork in silver and gold enclosing the signature, gold-lined pans, engraved locks with gold signatures, walnut half-stock and full silver mounts chased in relief, bearing London silver hallmarks for 1776 and 1777 with maker's mark IK. Excellent quality, fine condition. By Bate, London. *Christie's*

Over £10,000

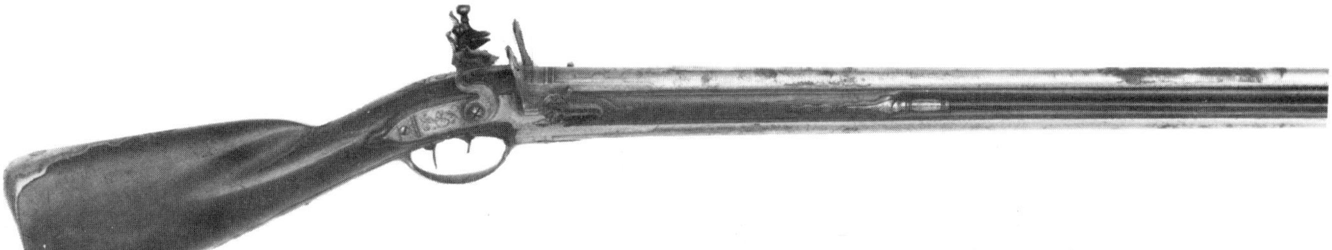

German over-and-under gun with fixed barrels and engraved locks set either side, the walnut stock with engraved iron mounts. Very fine quality and condition despite surface rust. By Armand Bongarde of Dusseldorf, early 18th century. 58in. *Renwick Collection*

Over £2,000

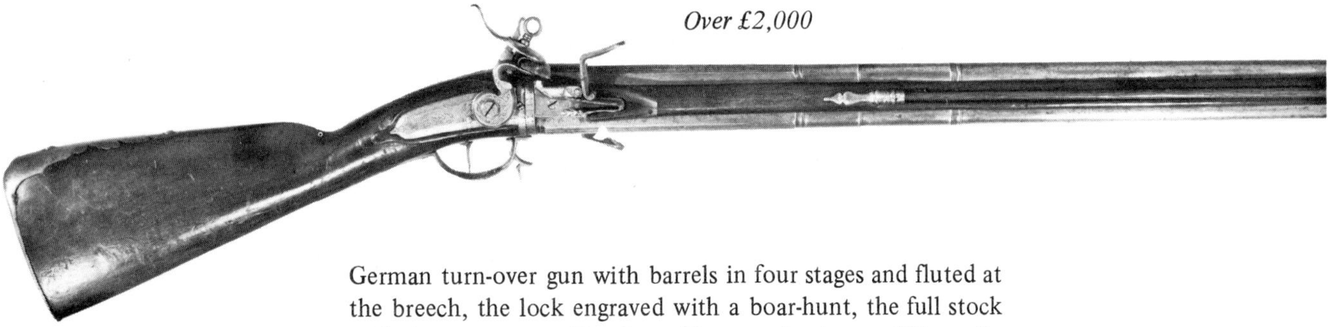

German turn-over gun with barrels in four stages and fluted at the breech, the lock engraved with a boar-hunt, the full stock with iron mounts. Good quality, moderate condition. By Christoph Gottfried Gros in Nimptsch, circa 1740. 42in. barrels. *Christie's*

£600 – £800

Flintlock Sporting Rifles

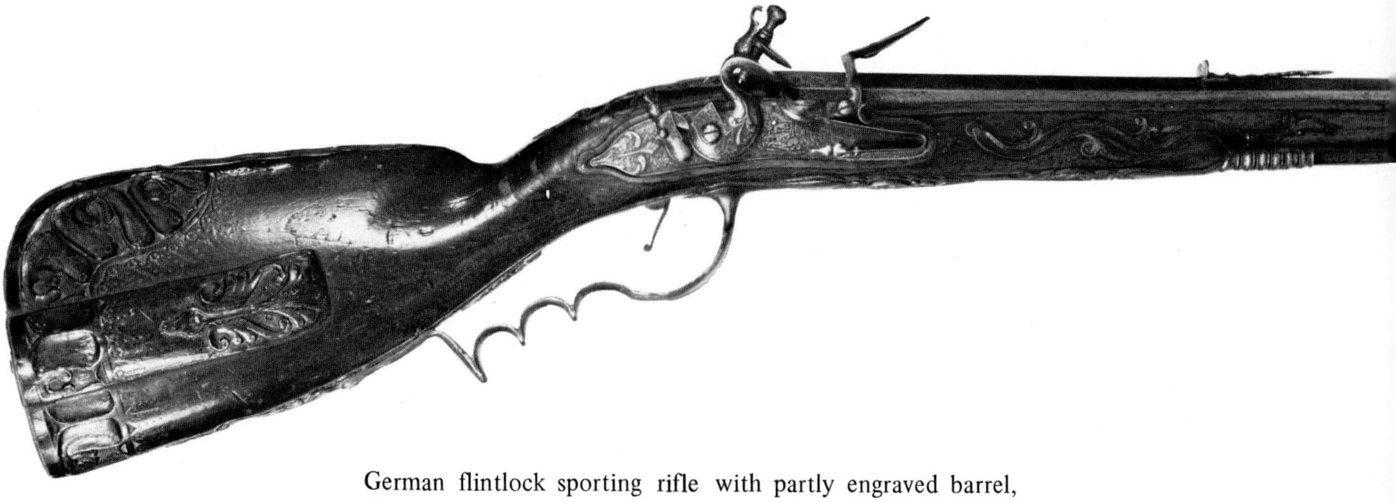

German flintlock sporting rifle with partly engraved barrel, the lock engraved with a boar hunt and fitted with dog catch behind the cock, carved walnut full stock, pierced and engraved steel furniture, pierced side-plate and carved patch-box cover. Good quality and condition. By Bernard Ortner, Stettin, late 17th century. 34in. barrel. *Christie's*

£750 – £900

A plainer rifle of the same type with foliate engraved lock, full stock and iron mounts engraved with foliage, the patch-box cover carved with foliage. Good quality and condition. By J. Bretge à Goslar, late 17th/early 18th century, 34in. barrel. *Christie's*

£300 – £450

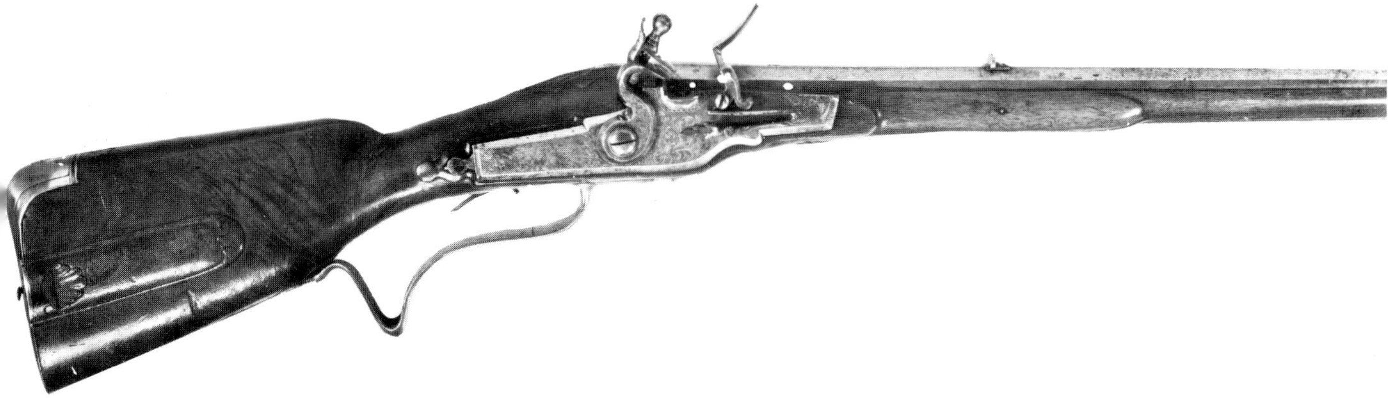

German flintlock light rifle with partly engraved lock of wheel-lock form, walnut full stock and brass furniture. Good quality and condition. Circa 1700. 29½in. barrel. *Christie's*

£350 – £500

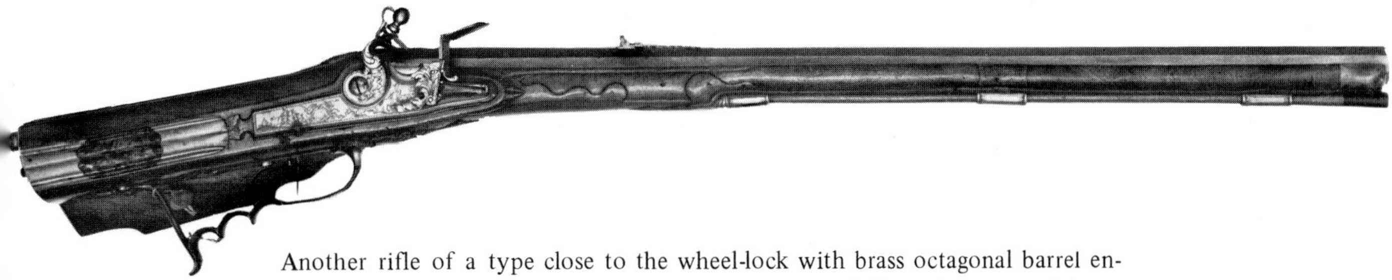

Another rifle of a type close to the wheel-lock with brass octagonal barrel engraved at the breech, engraved brass lock, walnut full stock, engraved brass furniture and horn patch-box cover. Good quality, excellent condition. Signed T.A. Maerckl à Carlsbaad, early 18th century. 39½in.

Over £1,000. Rare with a brass barrel.

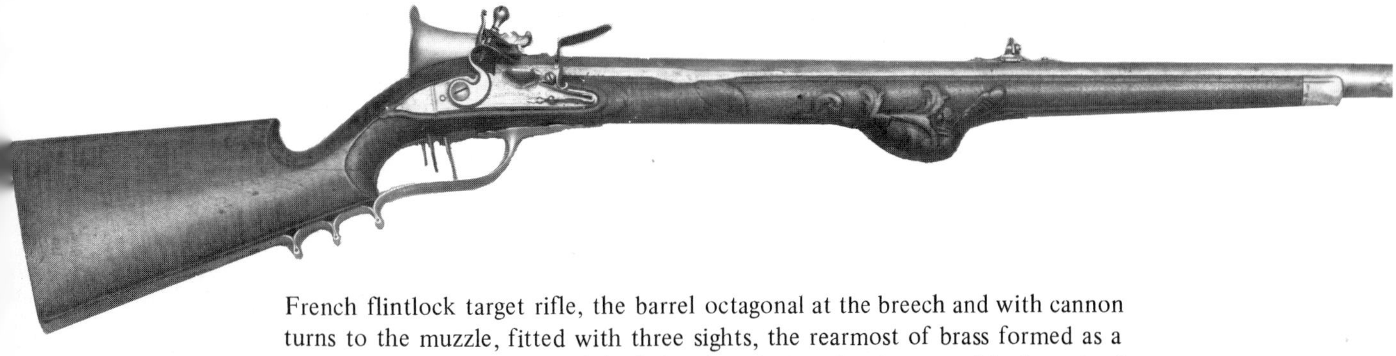

French flintlock target rifle, the barrel octagonal at the breech and with cannon turns to the muzzle, fitted with three sights, the rearmost of brass formed as a trumpet terminating in a dolphin's head, with signed and engraved lock retained by quick release screws, carved walnut full stock and engraved brass furniture. Good quality, worn condition. Signed Belon à Dole and dated 1724. 35in. barrel. *Christie's*

About £750. Very rare.

German flintlock sporting rifle with octagonal sighted barrel, the full stock carved with scrolls and with brass mounts of shaped outline. By Joseph Wirgler in Bruschsal. Good quality and condition. 37½in. barrel. Circa 1730/40. *Christie's*

£300 – £400

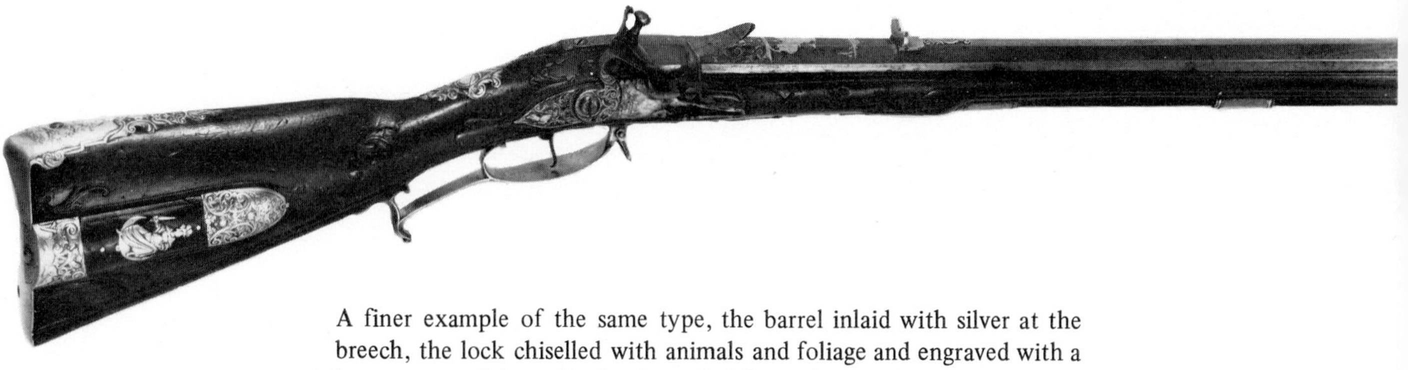

A finer example of the same type, the barrel inlaid with silver at the breech, the lock chiselled with animals and foliage and engraved with a huntsman and hounds, the figured full stock carved with interlacing scrolls and set with brass furniture decorated with scenes of the chase within foliage. Fine quality but moderate condition. Second quarter of the 18th century. 25in. barrel. *Christie's*

About £800
Over £1,500 for a similar rifle in fine condition.

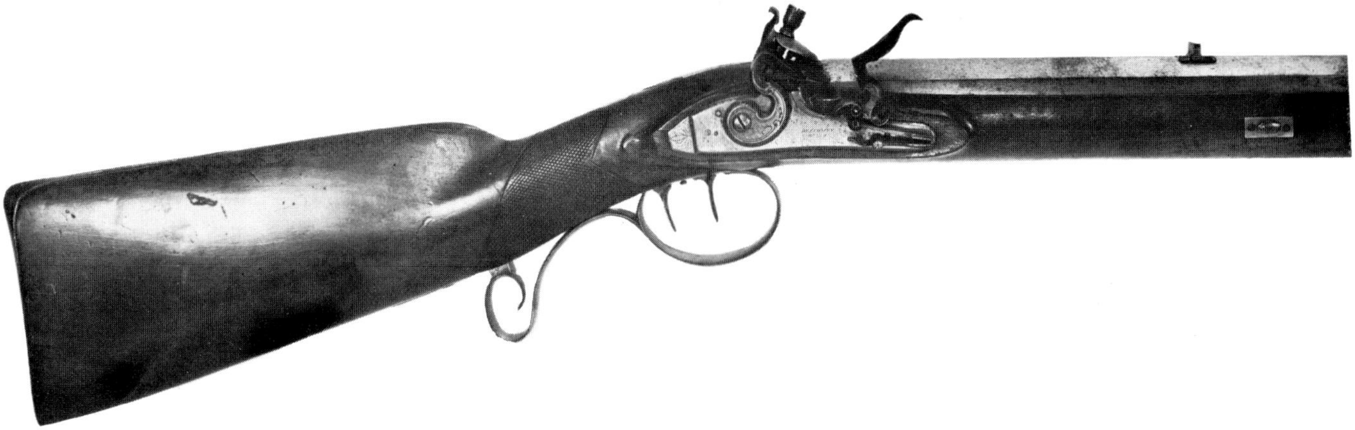

Danish sporting rifle with octagonal barrel, signed lock with roller and rainproof pan, walnut full stock, set trigger and engraved iron mounts. Moderate quality and condition. By Delcomyn, Copenhagen, early 19th century. 46½in. *Sotheby's*

£200 – £275

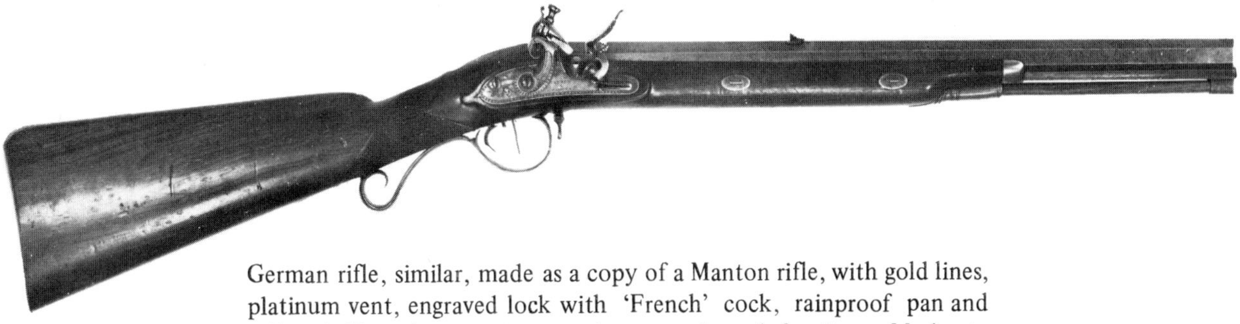

German rifle, similar, made as a copy of a Manton rifle, with gold lines, platinum vent, engraved lock with 'French' cock, rainproof pan and roller, half-stock, set trigger and engraved steel furniture. Moderate quality, good condition. By Tanner & Schultz, early 19th century. 30½in. barrel. *Christie's*

About £400. A genuine Manton rifle in equivalent condition over £600.

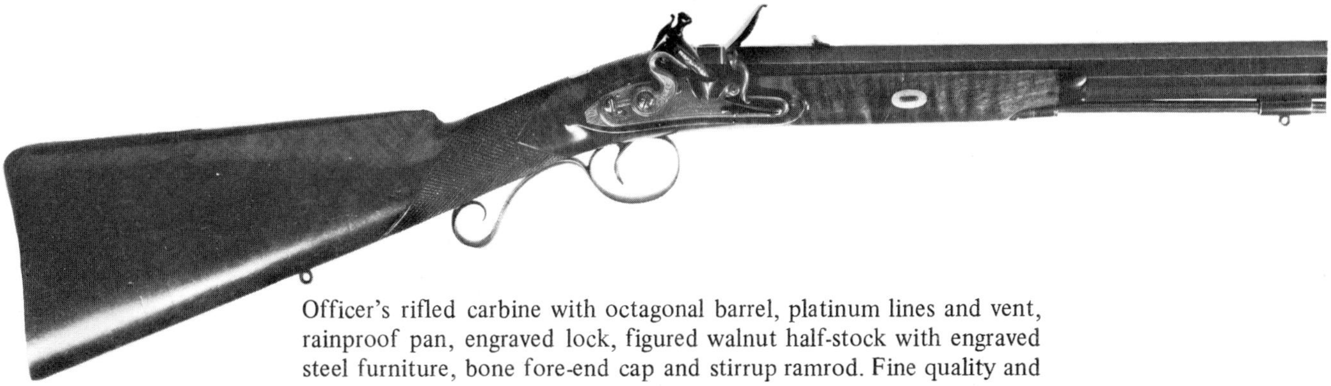

Officer's rifled carbine with octagonal barrel, platinum lines and vent, rainproof pan, engraved lock, figured walnut half-stock with engraved steel furniture, bone fore-end cap and stirrup ramrod. Fine quality and condition. By Staudenmayer, London, circa 1810. 17½in. barrel. *Christie's*

£500 – £650

Presentation rifle of the type given to Indian chiefs in Canada, with octagonal barrel, double platinum line and plaque decorated with the Royal Arms, platinum vent, engraved lock, full stock and engraved blued steel furniture, the patch-box cover decorated with trophies and a globe. Good quality and condition. By Tatham, London, early 19th century. *Sotheby's*

£400 – £500

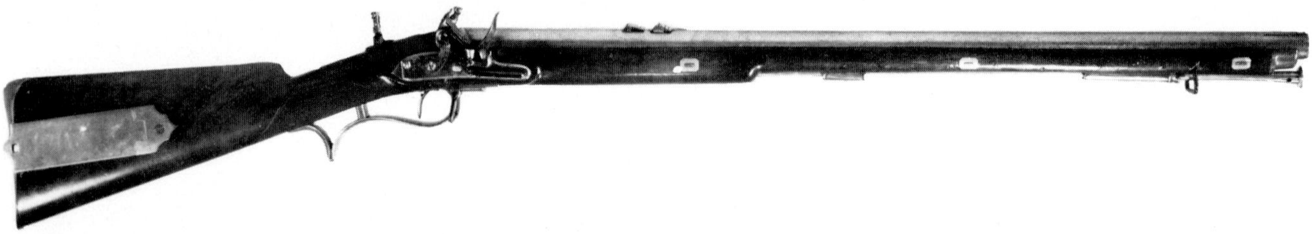

Baker pattern target rifle with sighted barrel cut with frictionless rifling and with gold touch-hole, the lock with special rainproof pan and roller directly beneath, full stock, chequered grip, brass mounts. Fine quality and condition. By William Moore, London, early 19th century. 30in. barrel. Made for Colonel Beaufoy, author of 'Schloppetaria' (1808).

£500 – £750

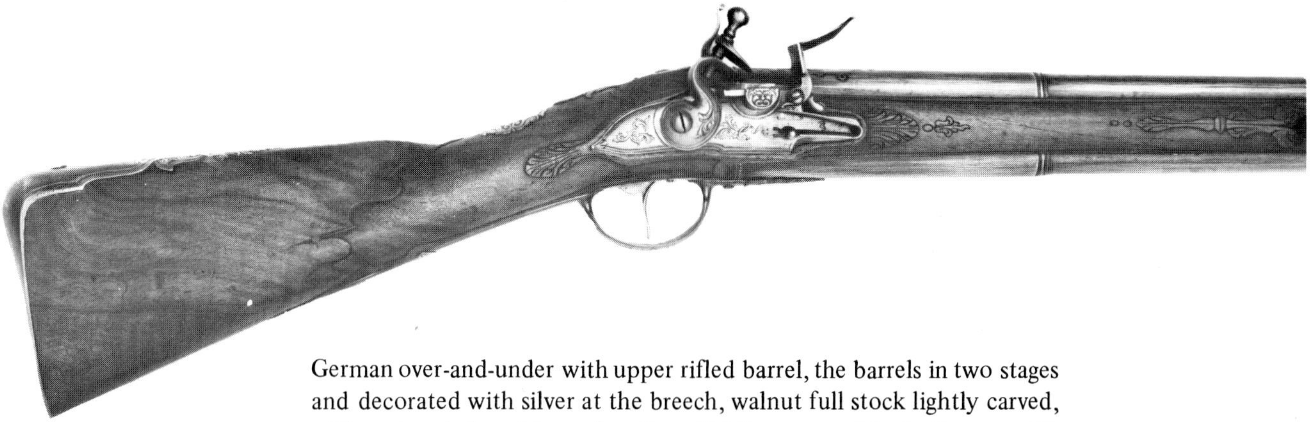

German over-and-under with upper rifled barrel, the barrels in two stages and decorated with silver at the breech, walnut full stock lightly carved, with cast and chased brass furniture, lightly engraved lock, the pan with two compartments and sliding cover. Good quality, fine condition with much original finish. Circa 1730. 49in. *Sotheby's*

Over £1,000

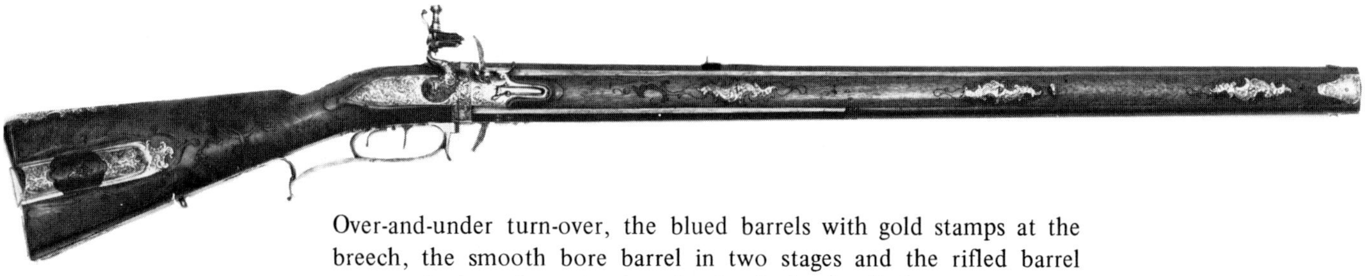

Over-and-under turn-over, the blued barrels with gold stamps at the breech, the smooth bore barrel in two stages and the rifled barrel octagonal throughout its length, the lock chiselled against a gold ground with deer and rococo scrolls, carved walnut full stock with steel furniture chiselled en suite with the lock on a gold ground. Very fine quality and condition. By Schirmer à Bamberg, mid-18th century. 46in. *Sotheby's*

Over £2,000. A plain example of this type, £500 – £800.

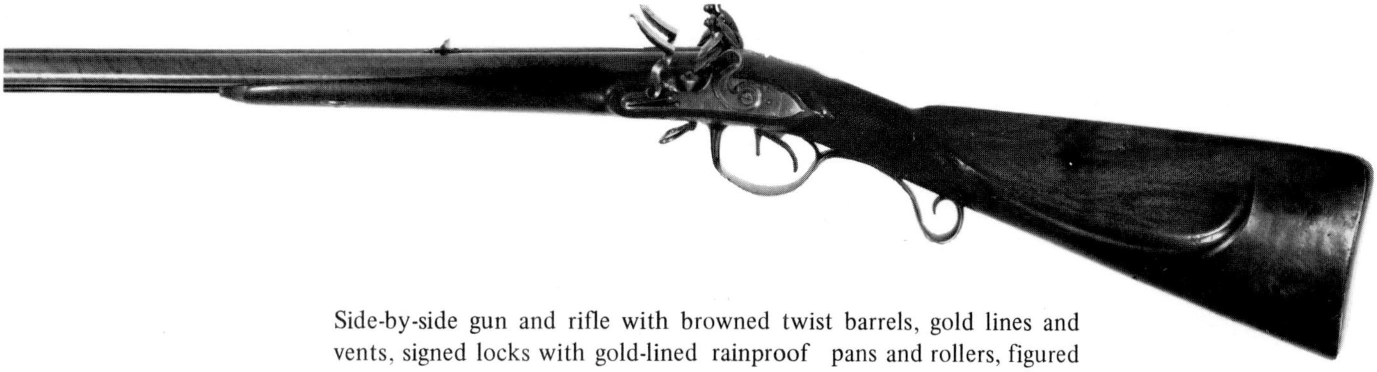

Side-by-side gun and rifle with browned twist barrels, gold lines and vents, signed locks with gold-lined rainproof pans and rollers, figured half-stock with engraved blued steel mounts and gold escutcheon. Very fine quality and condition. By Durs Egg, London, the barrels probably German. Early 19th century. 31½in. barrels. *Christie's*

Over £1,000

Flintlock Breech-Loading Rifles

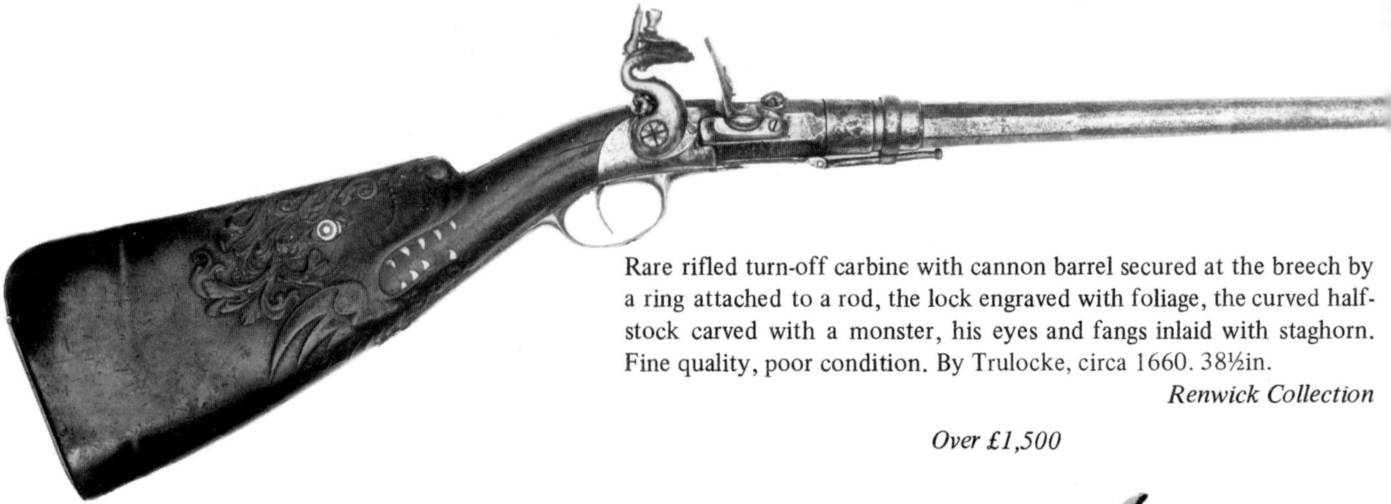

Rare rifled turn-off carbine with cannon barrel secured at the breech by a ring attached to a rod, the lock engraved with foliage, the curved half-stock carved with a monster, his eyes and fangs inlaid with staghorn. Fine quality, poor condition. By Trulocke, circa 1660. 38½in.

Renwick Collection

Over £1,500

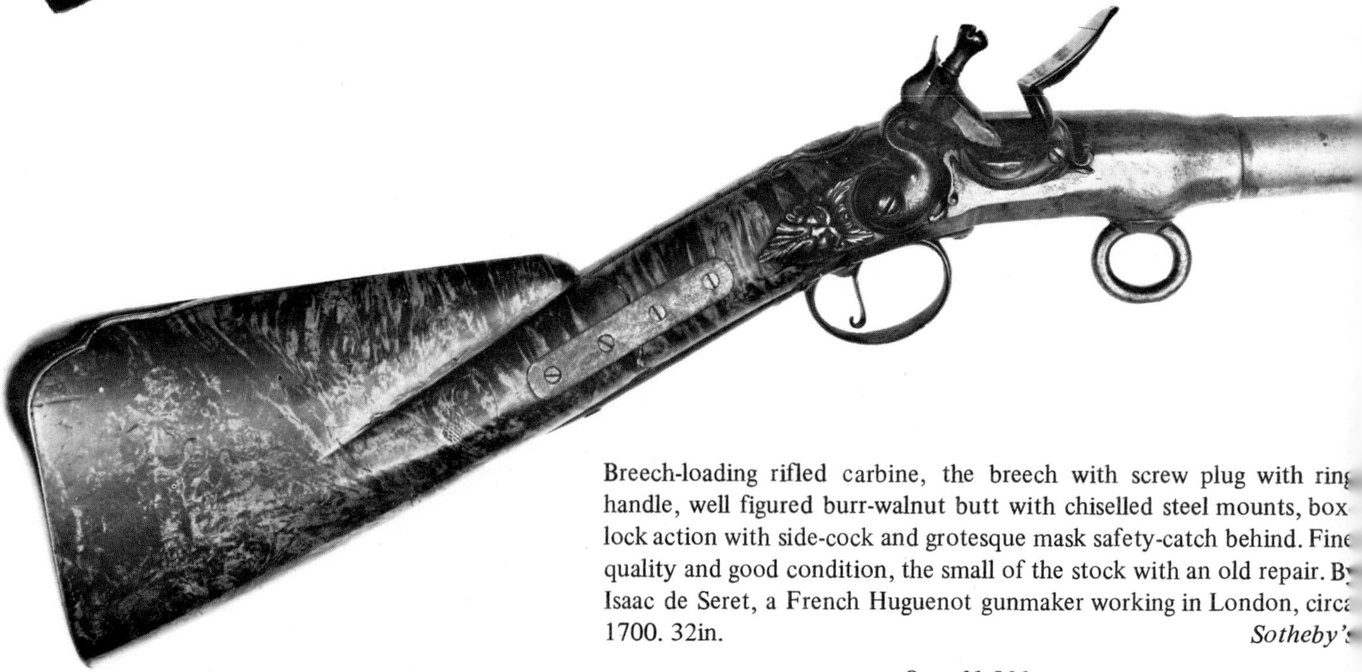

Breech-loading rifled carbine, the breech with screw plug with ring handle, well figured burr-walnut butt with chiselled steel mounts, box lock action with side-cock and grotesque mask safety-catch behind. Fine quality and good condition, the small of the stock with an old repair. By Isaac de Seret, a French Huguenot gunmaker working in London, circa 1700. 32in.

Sotheby's

Over £1,500

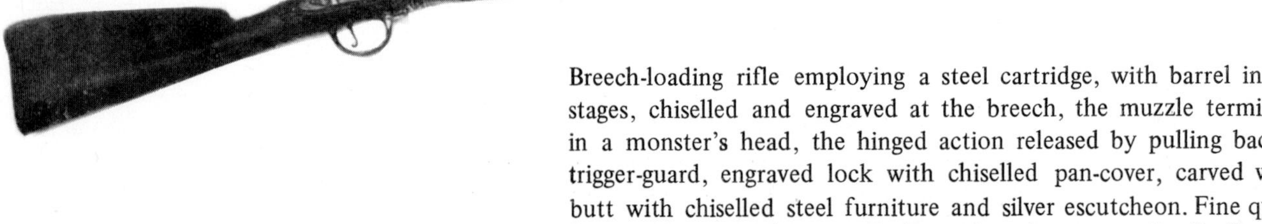

Breech-loading rifle employing a steel cartridge, with barrel in three stages, chiselled and engraved at the breech, the muzzle terminating in a monster's head, the hinged action released by pulling back the trigger-guard, engraved lock with chiselled pan-cover, carved walnut butt with chiselled steel furniture and silver escutcheon. Fine quality, fair condition, with some faults and replacements. By R. Rowland, London, early 18th century. 49in.

Sotheby's

Over £1,000

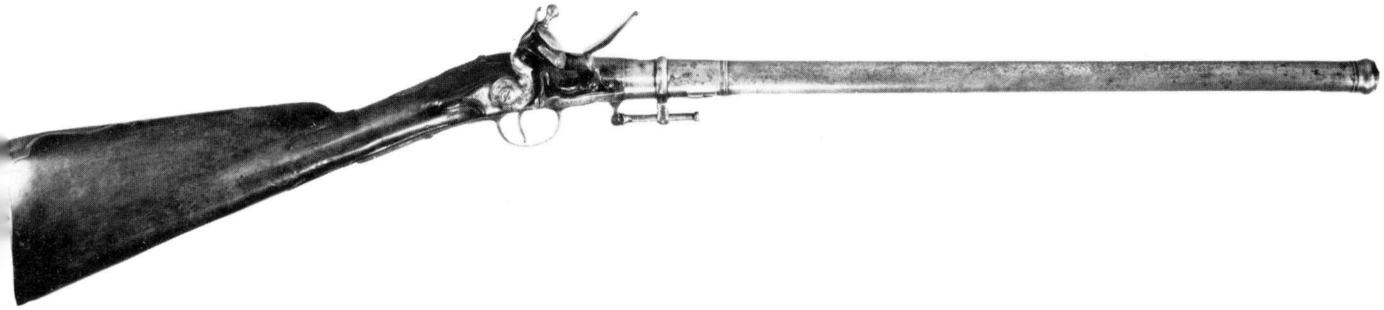

Turn-off carbine with rifled cannon barrel and retaining link at the breech, the action signed beneath the steel-spring, separate trigger-guard with foliate finial, and moulded walnut butt with iron escutcheon and butt-plate, the heel with long foliate tang. Fine quality and condition. By Henry Delany, a Huguenot working in London, circa 1720. 22½in. barrel. *Christie's*

Over £1,000

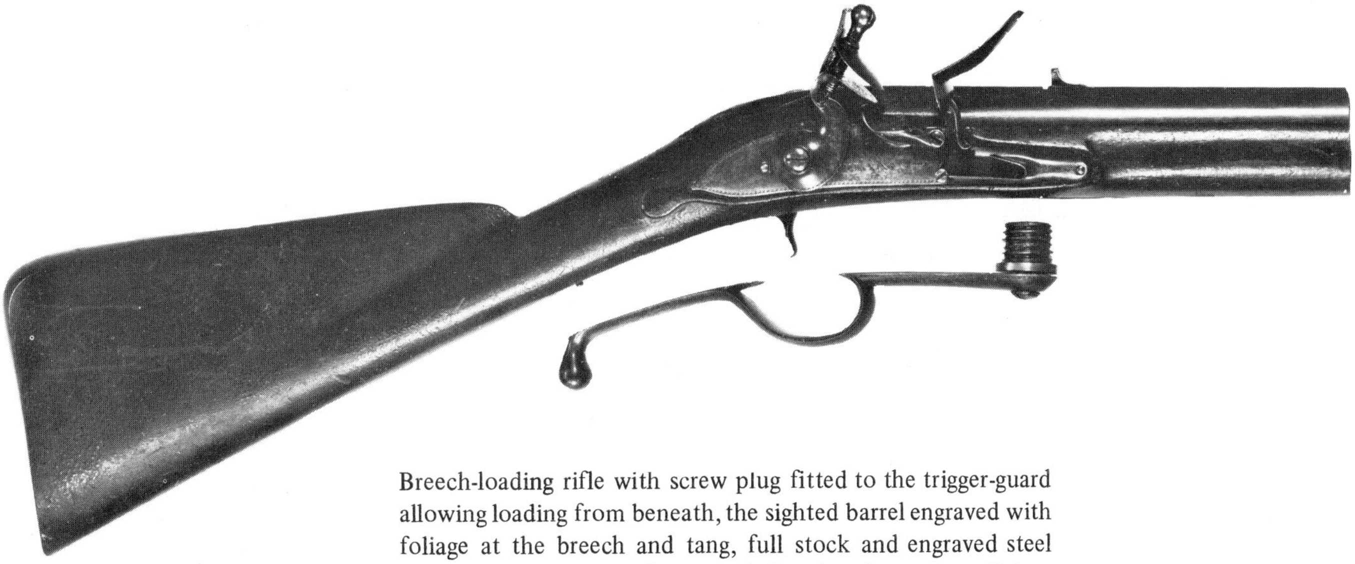

Breech-loading rifle with screw plug fitted to the trigger-guard allowing loading from beneath, the sighted barrel engraved with foliage at the breech and tang, full stock and engraved steel furniture. No provision for ramrod. Good quality and condition. By Richard King, London, first half of the 18th century. 27½in. *Christie's*

£500 – £700

Breech-loading carbine fitted with Henham's screwless lock signed D. Egg, London, the upward lifting breech block on the Egg system, with full stock, brass furniture and folding spear-type bayonet. Almost new condition. Circa 1787. *Sotheby's*

£700 – £1,000

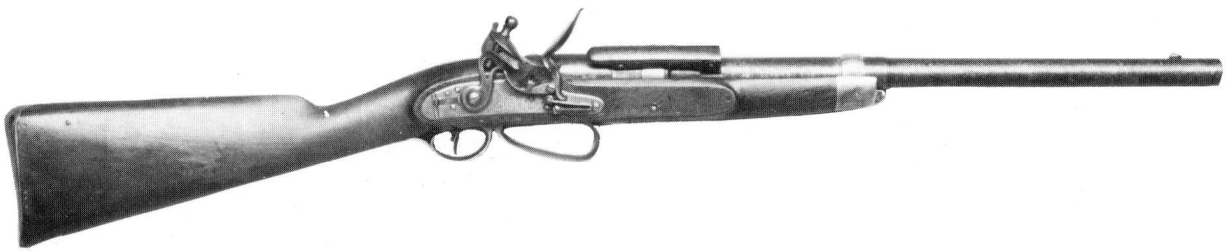

Breech-loading carbine on the Sartoris principle with tip-up breech released by turning and moving the barrel forward by means of a folding handle, the barrel held by two brass bands, walnut full stock and brass mounts including handle forward of the trigger-guard. Good condition. Early 19th century. *Christie's*

£400 – £600

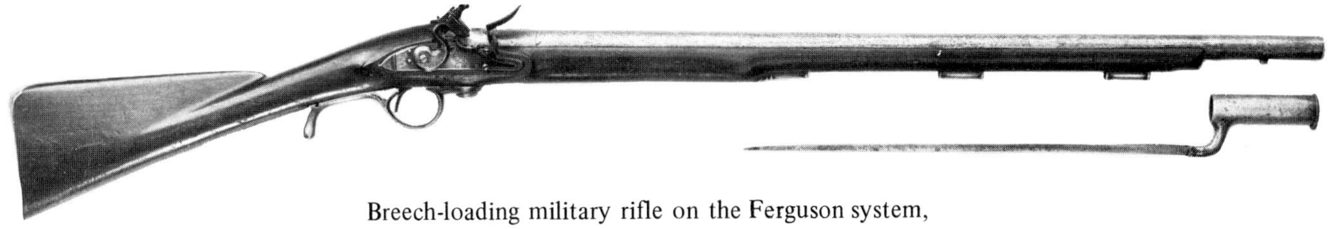

Breech-loading military rifle on the Ferguson system, the lock engraved with GR, crown and Hunt, the breech stamped Fergus, full stock and brass mounts with the exception of the steel trigger-guard, with a bayonet. Fair condition, trigger-guard loose, barrel and trigger-guard pitted. Circa 1770/80. 32in barrel with London proof marks. 48in. overall.

Wallis & Wallis

Over £2,000

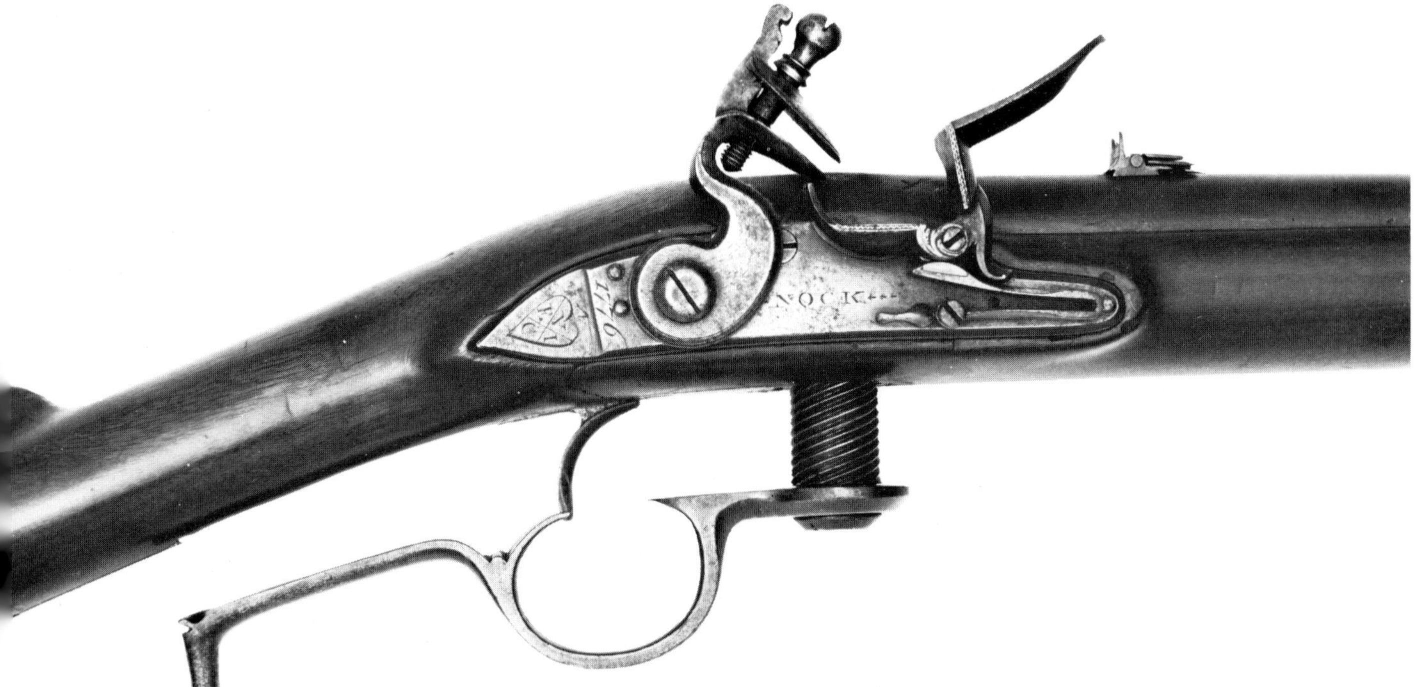

Detail of East India Company Ferguson carbine, the lock and barrel signed Nock and dated 1776, together with the company mark, with full stock and brass ramrod-pipes and butt-plate, iron trigger-guard and brass plug. Fair condition, stock slightly damaged, a part of it replaced behind the lock. 44½in.

This rifle reached £1,000 in 1970.

The East India Company association is not as popular as that of the American Civil War, these rifles having originally been designed for a body of British troops sent over to America under the inventor's command, seeing action in the attack on Brandywine Hill on September 11, 1777. *Sotheby's*

Detonator Guns

Cased Forsyth patent d. b. gun with roller or "scent bottle" primers, (c.f. page 145) the damascus barrels signed on the rib, the locks also signed and engraved with scrolling leaves terminating in peacocks, walnut half-stock and engraved iron furniture. In baize-lined mahogany case with trade label and some accessories. Fair quality and condition, not wholly original. Signed Forsyth & Co. Patent Gunmakers, London, circa 1816. 46½in. *Sotheby's*

Over £1,000. Very rare.
Much more for an original one.

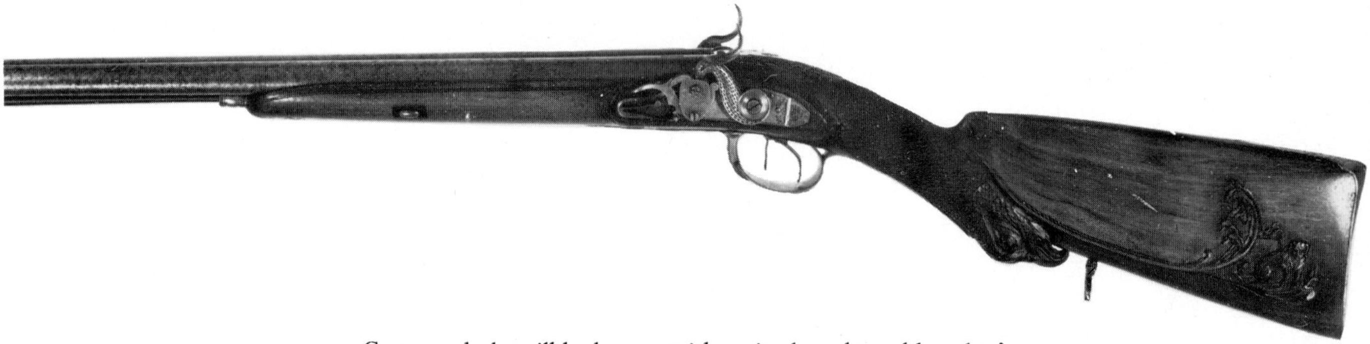

German d. b. pill-lock gun with twist barrels, gold maker's marks at the breech, partly engraved locks, the strikers formed as birds, carved walnut half-stock and engraved steel mounts. Moderate quality, fine condition. Signed Pfeuffer, Oberndorff, dated 1820. 33in. barrels. *Christie's*

About £500. Rare.

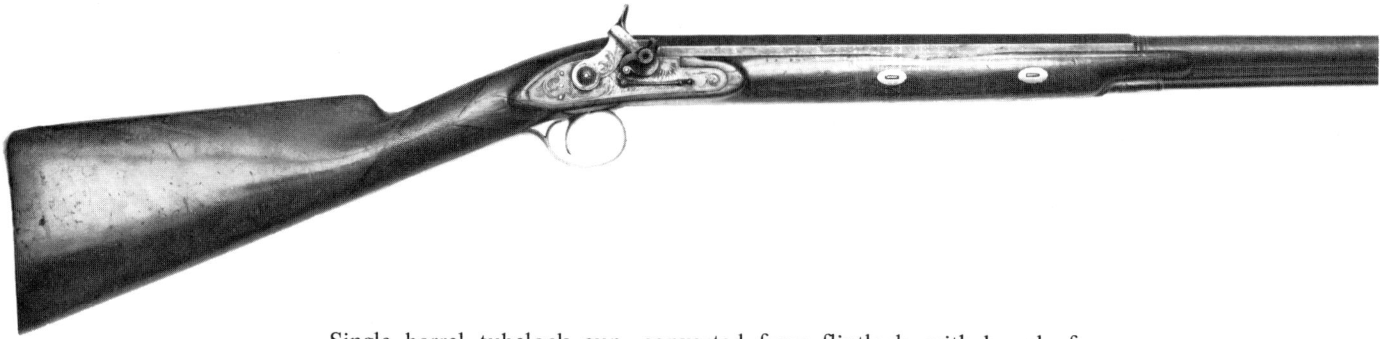

Single barrel tubelock gun, converted from flintlock, with barrel of Spanish form, the breech with platinum line and maker's stamp, signed and engraved lock, half-stock, engraved iron mounts and original ramrod. Good quality but moderate condition. By Joseph Manton, serial number for 1806-7. 48in. *Sotheby's*

about £200

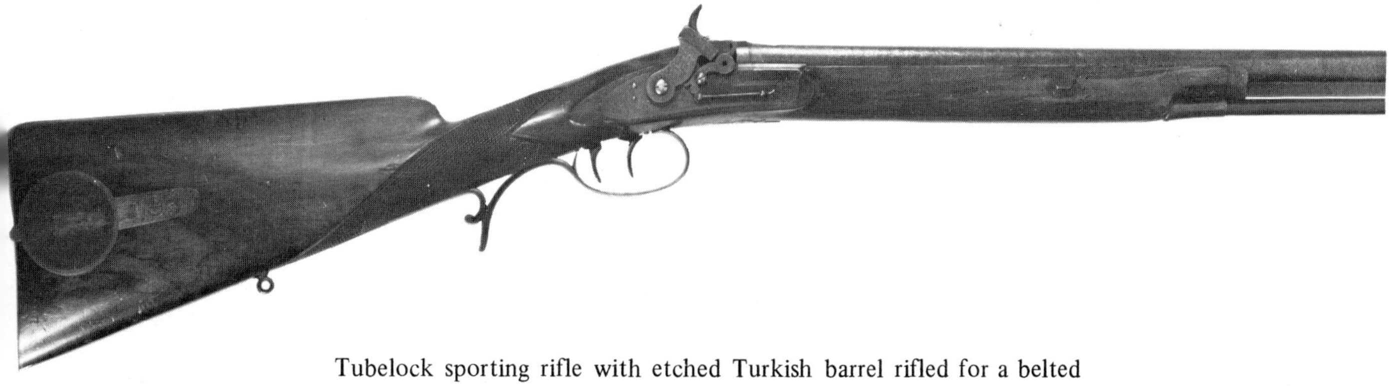

Tubelock sporting rifle with etched Turkish barrel rifled for a belted ball, the lock and hammer engraved with scrolling foliage, the breech with platinum vent, the figured walnut half-stock with finely engraved steel mounts, set trigger and engraved patch-box cover. Fine quality and condition. By Witton, 82 Old Broad Street, London, circa 1830. 40½in. barrel.

£400 – £500

Percussion Cap Sporting Guns

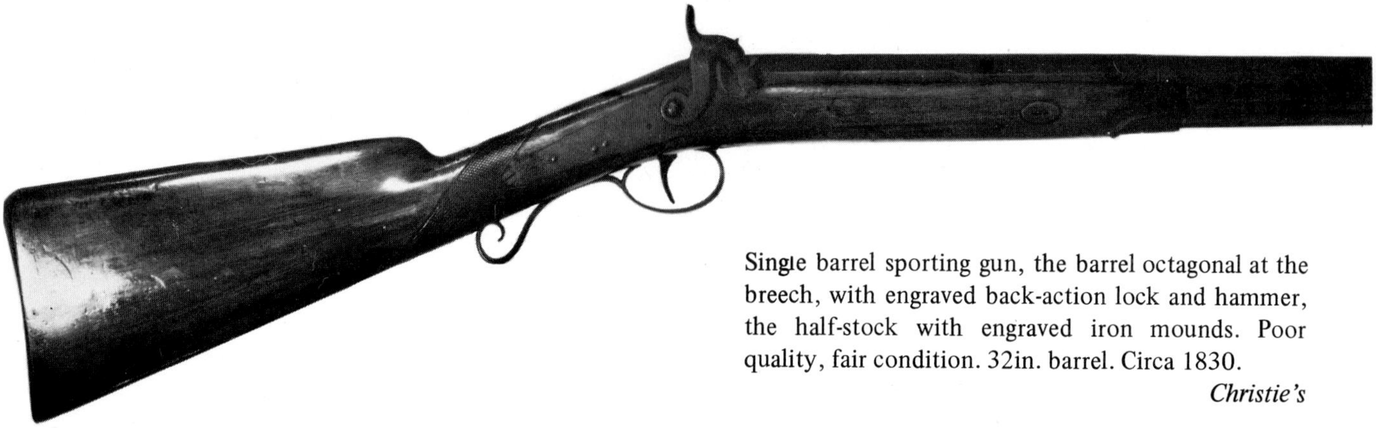

Single barrel sporting gun, the barrel octagonal at the breech, with engraved back-action lock and hammer, the half-stock with engraved iron mounds. Poor quality, fair condition. 32in. barrel. Circa 1830.

Christie's

£30 – £50

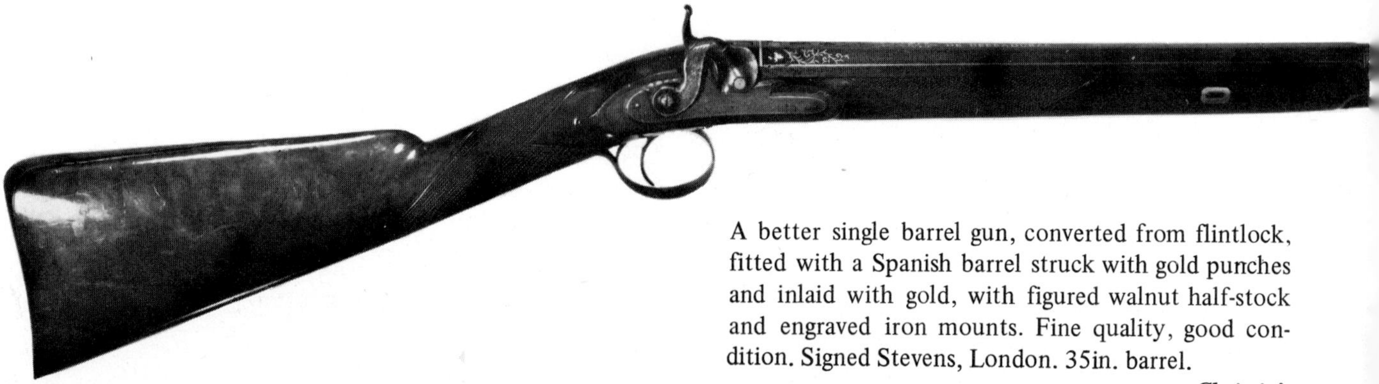

A better single barrel gun, converted from flintlock, fitted with a Spanish barrel struck with gold punches and inlaid with gold, with figured walnut half-stock and engraved iron mounts. Fine quality, good condition. Signed Stevens, London. 35in. barrel.

Christie's

£80 – £120

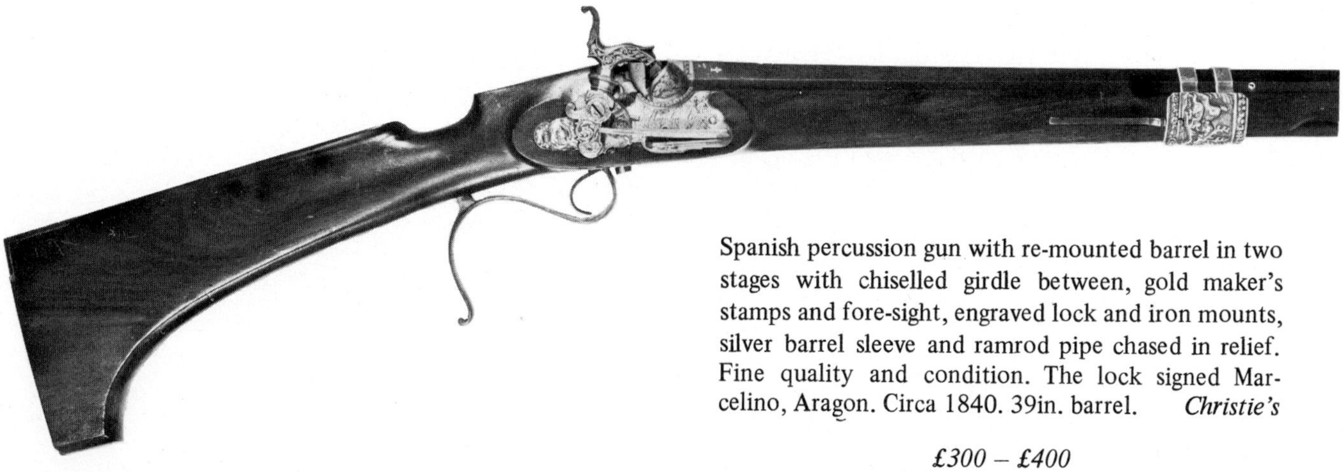

Spanish percussion gun with re-mounted barrel in two stages with chiselled girdle between, gold maker's stamps and fore-sight, engraved lock and iron mounts, silver barrel sleeve and ramrod pipe chased in relief. Fine quality and condition. The lock signed Marcelino, Aragon. Circa 1840. 39in. barrel. *Christie's*

£300 – £400

Most Spanish percussion guns are of far inferior quality.

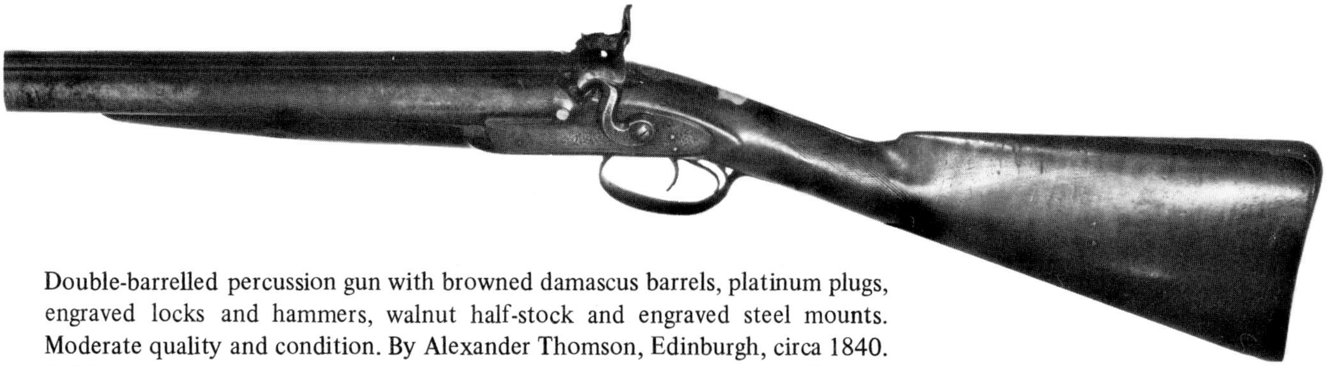

Double-barrelled percussion gun with browned damascus barrels, platinum plugs, engraved locks and hammers, walnut half-stock and engraved steel mounts. Moderate quality and condition. By Alexander Thomson, Edinburgh, circa 1840. 29¾in. barrels. *Christie's*

£50 – £100

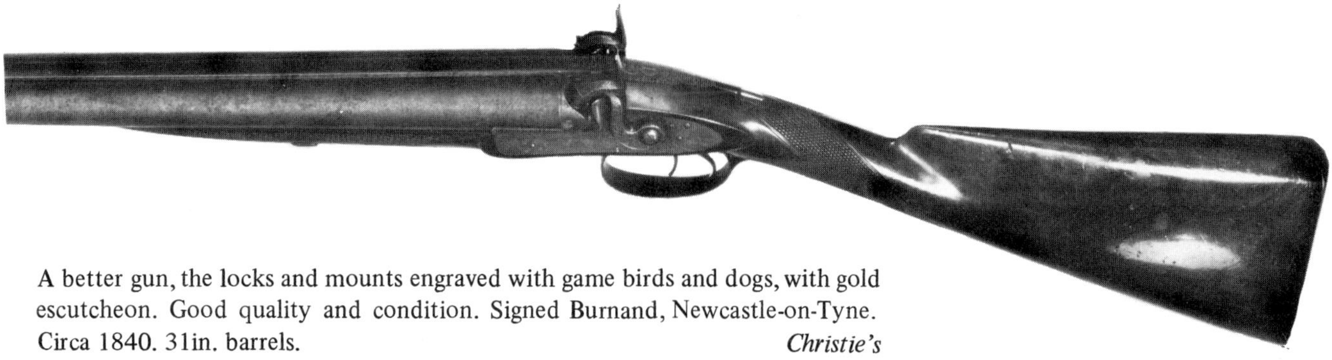

A better gun, the locks and mounts engraved with game birds and dogs, with gold escutcheon. Good quality and condition. Signed Burnand, Newcastle-on-Tyne. Circa 1840. 31in. barrels. *Christie's*

£175 – £225

This is about the average price for a good quality d. b. gun in shootable condition.

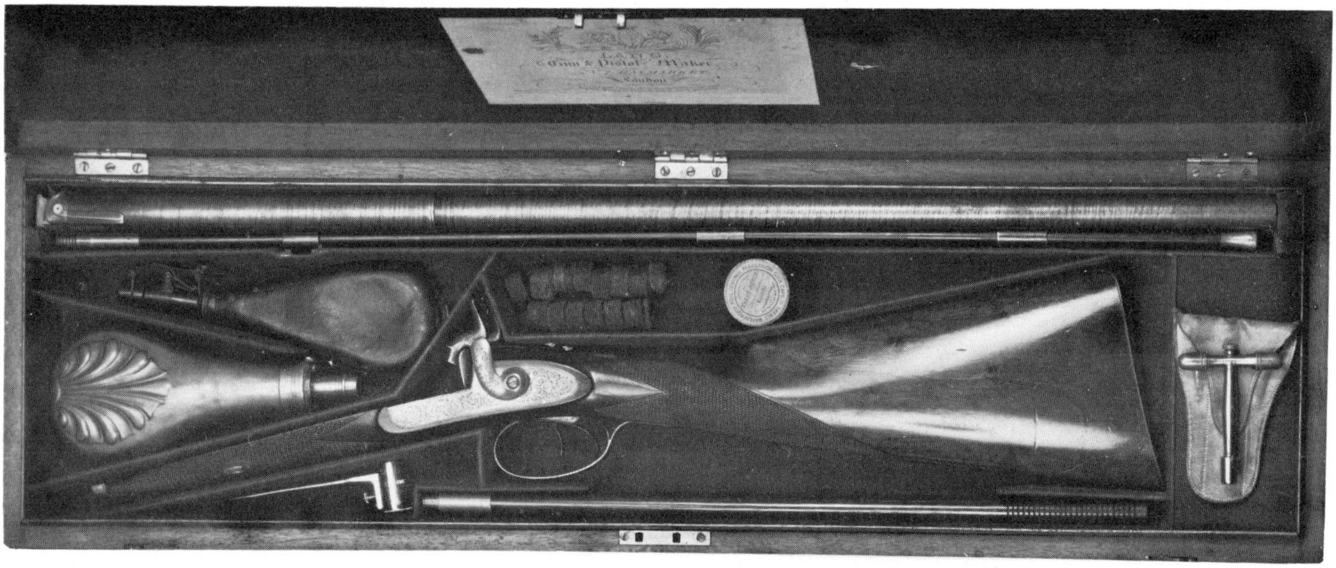

Cased d.b. gun with browned damascus barrels, platinum plugs, engraved locks, hammers and steel furniture, with silver escutcheon. In original lined and fitted mahogany case with some accessories and trade label. Good quality and condition. By Lang, 7 Haymarket, London, circa 1840. 30in. barrels.

Knight, Frank & Rutley

£300 – £400

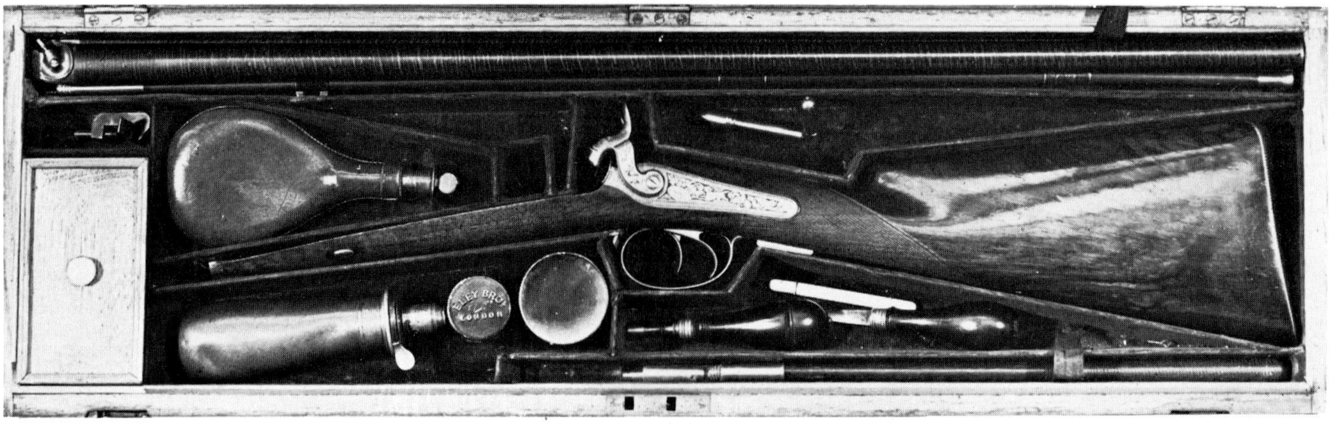

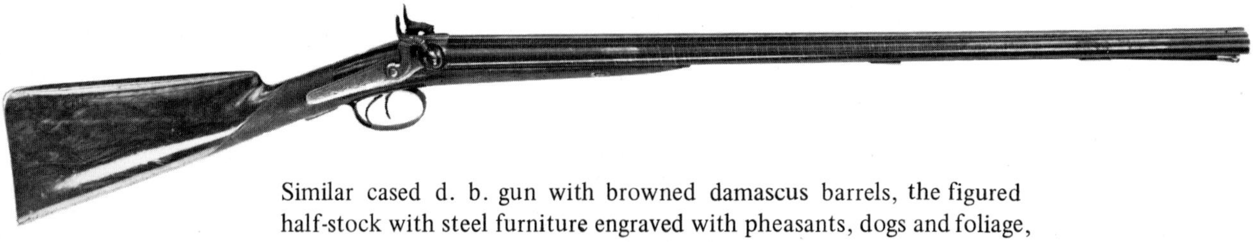

Similar cased d. b. gun with browned damascus barrels, the figured half-stock with steel furniture engraved with pheasants, dogs and foliage, with grip safety-catch. In original velvet-lined oak case with accessories and trade label. Fine quality and exceptional condition with nearly all original finish. By W. Mills, 120 High Holborn, London, circa 1840. 30in. barrels. *Wallis & Wallis*

£500 – £700

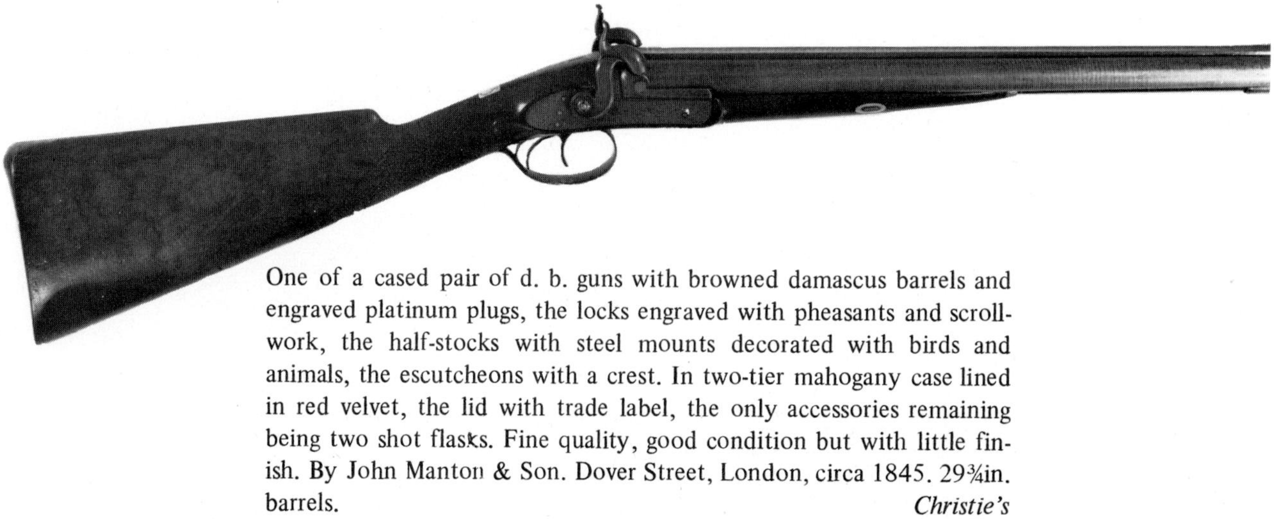

One of a cased pair of d. b. guns with browned damascus barrels and engraved platinum plugs, the locks engraved with pheasants and scroll-work, the half-stocks with steel mounts decorated with birds and animals, the escutcheons with a crest. In two-tier mahogany case lined in red velvet, the lid with trade label, the only accessories remaining being two shot flasks. Fine quality, good condition but with little finish. By John Manton & Son. Dover Street, London, circa 1845. 29¾in. barrels. *Christie's*

Over £1,000 the pair

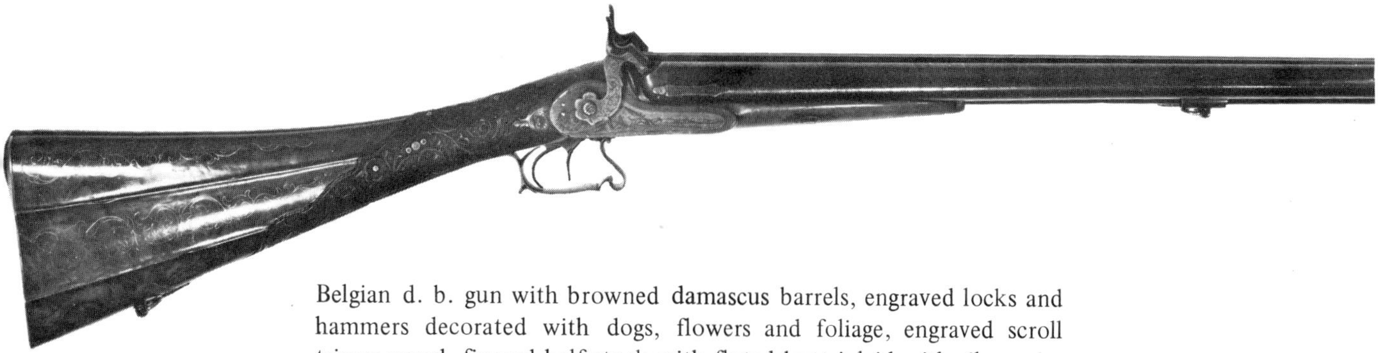

Belgian d. b. gun with browned damascus barrels, engraved locks and hammers decorated with dogs, flowers and foliage, engraved scroll trigger-guard, figured half-stock with fluted butt inlaid with silver wire and carved with foliage on the grip. Moderate quality but fine condition. Unsigned. Circa 1860. 30in. barrels. *Christie's*

£300 – £400

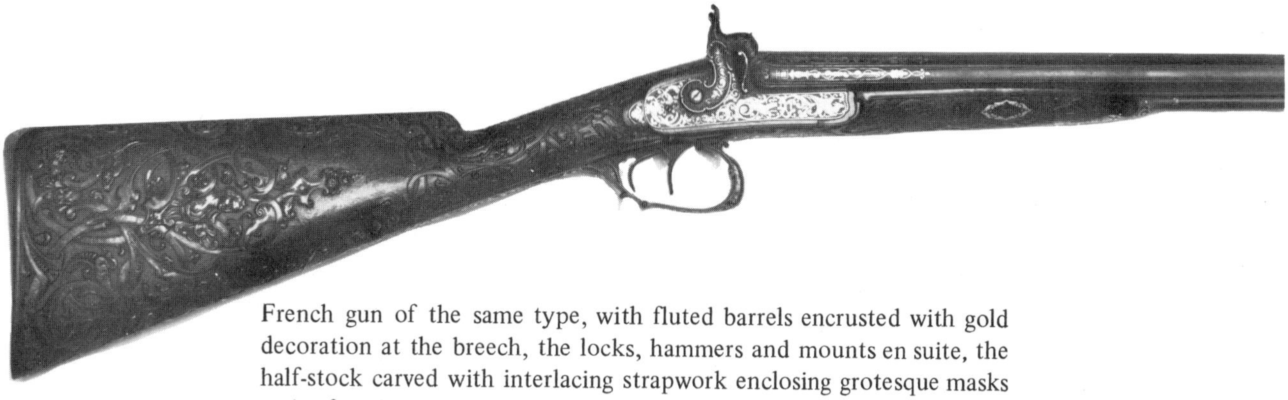

French gun of the same type, with fluted barrels encrusted with gold decoration at the breech, the locks, hammers and mounts en suite, the half-stock carved with interlacing strapwork enclosing grotesque masks and a female portrait bust on the butt. Very fine quality and fine condition. Circa 1860. 30in. barrels. *Christie's*

About £1,500
In case complete, over £2,000.

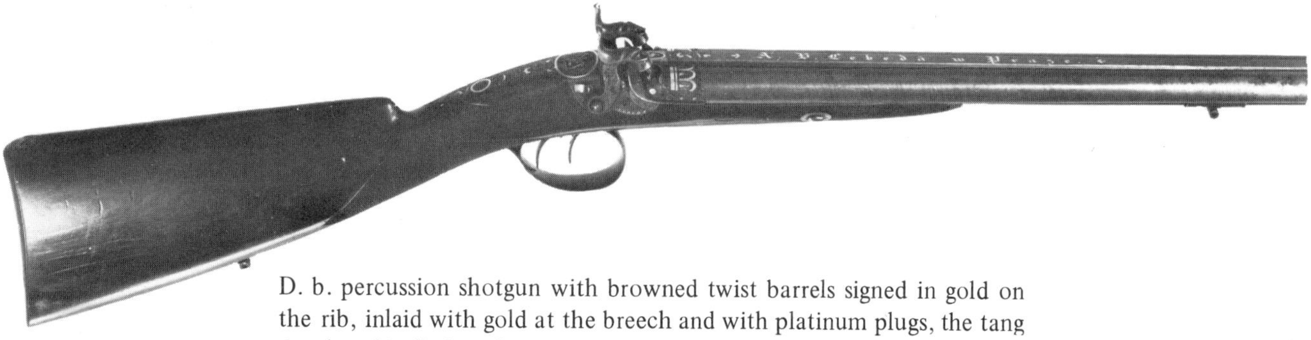

D. b. percussion shotgun with browned twist barrels signed in gold on the rib, inlaid with gold at the breech and with platinum plugs, the tang deeply chiselled and engraved, the locks with patent safety-catches engaging with the breast of the hammers, the stock with engraved and partly chiselled steel mounts. In fitted case for two guns. Fine quality and condition. By A.V. Lebeda of Prague, dated 1837. 27½in. barrels. *Christie's*

£700 – £800

Possibly made for Alfred Ernest, second son of Queen Victoria. Less without this Royal provenance.

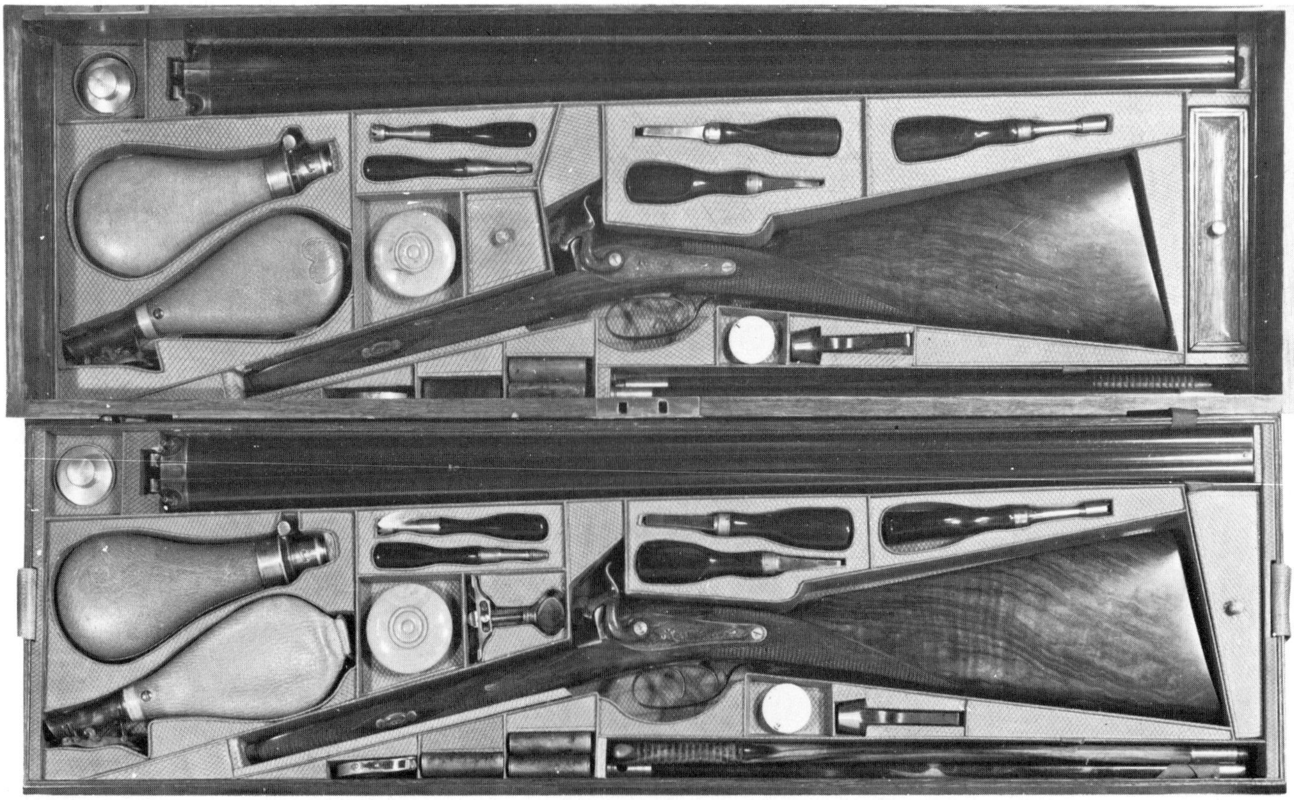

Exceptional cased pair of d. b. back-action percussion guns with browned damascus barrels and platinum plugs, the figured walnut half-stocks with blued close scroll engraved mounts, the locks and hammers en suite. In original fitted two-tier oak case lined in tooled pigskin, complete with full accessories and label. Fine quality, condition as new and probably unused since manufacture. By John Dickson & Son, 63 Princes Street, Edinburgh, late 19th century. 30in. barrels.

Christie's

About £2,000

These guns belong to a group (which also includes flintlocks) made by Dickson for Charles Gordon. Most of these are unused, and the cases are nearly always of oak, usually with pigskin lining. The Gordon guns were dispersed on his death in 1909.

Percussion Cap Sporting Rifles

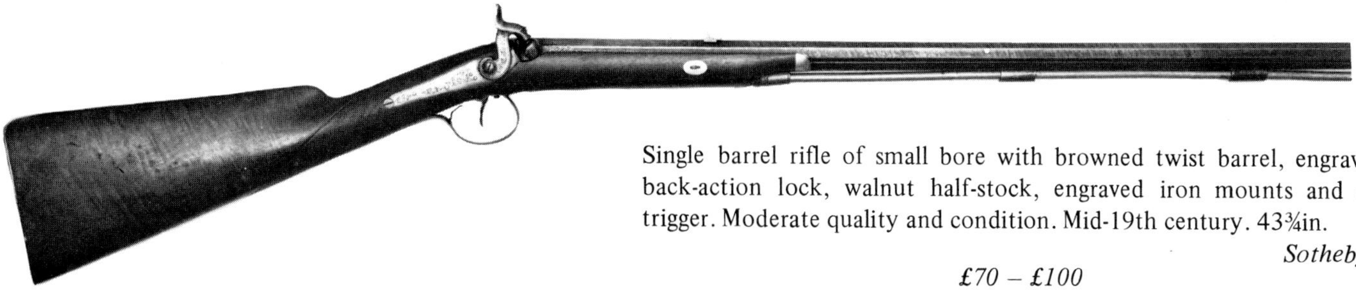

Single barrel rifle of small bore with browned twist barrel, engraved back-action lock, walnut half-stock, engraved iron mounts and set trigger. Moderate quality and condition. Mid-19th century. 43¾in. *Sotheby's*

£70 – £100

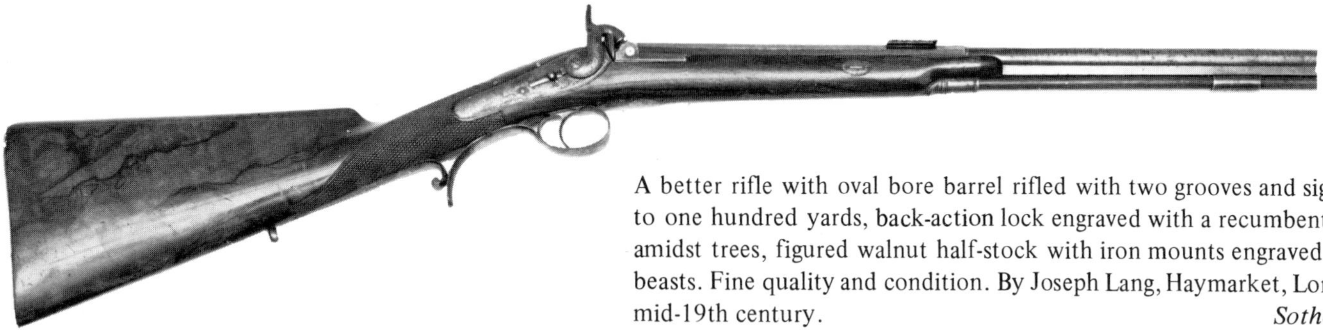

A better rifle with oval bore barrel rifled with two grooves and sighted to one hundred yards, back-action lock engraved with a recumbent stag amidst trees, figured walnut half-stock with iron mounts engraved with beasts. Fine quality and condition. By Joseph Lang, Haymarket, London, mid-19th century. *Sotheby's*

£250 – £300

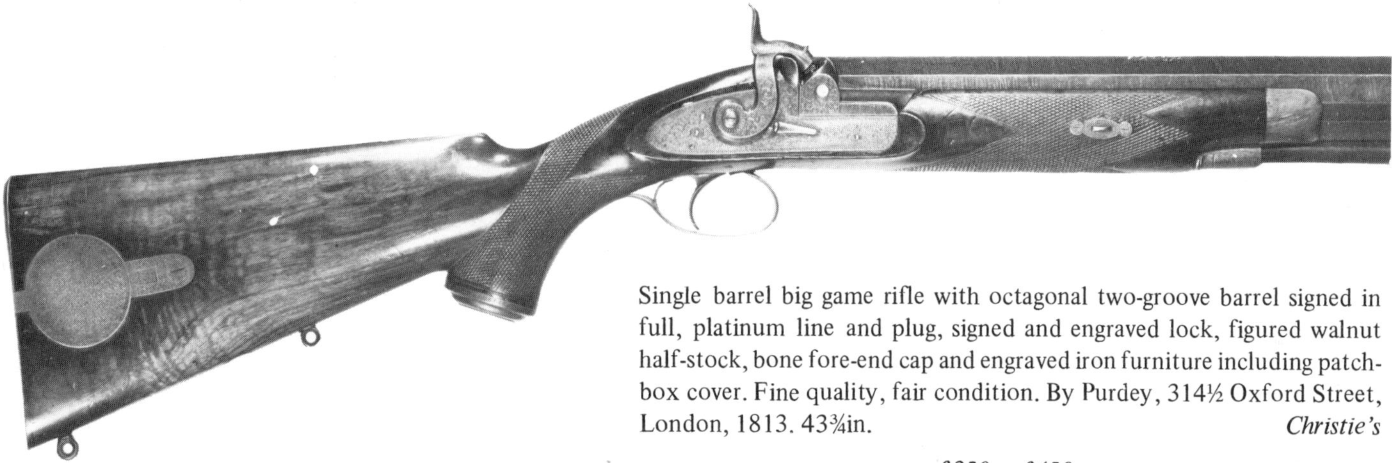

Single barrel big game rifle with octagonal two-groove barrel signed in full, platinum line and plug, signed and engraved lock, figured walnut half-stock, bone fore-end cap and engraved iron furniture including patch-box cover. Fine quality, fair condition. By Purdey, 314½ Oxford Street, London, 1813. 43¾in. *Christie's*

£350 – £450

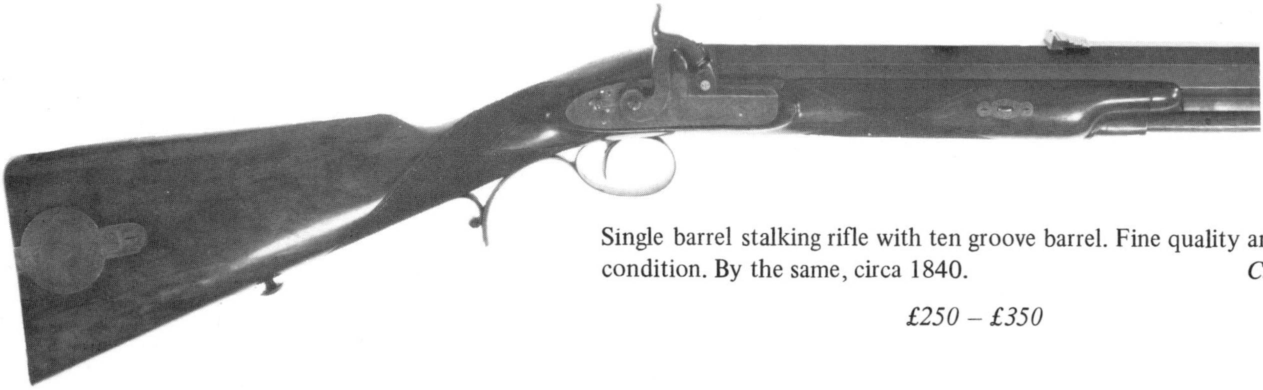

Single barrel stalking rifle with ten groove barrel. Fine quality and good condition. By the same, circa 1840. *Christie's*

£250 – £350

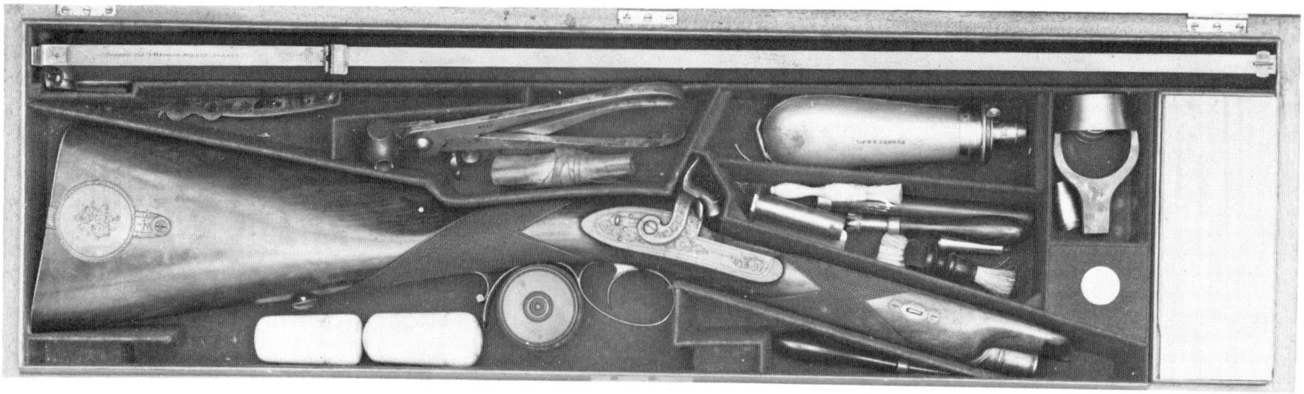

Cased single barrel sporting rifle similar to the last, in original case with complete fittings, including alternative set trigger mechanism and trade label. Fine quality, excellent condition. By Purdey, 314½ Oxford Street, London, 1838. Case 32½in. by 10in.
Sotheby's
About £1,000

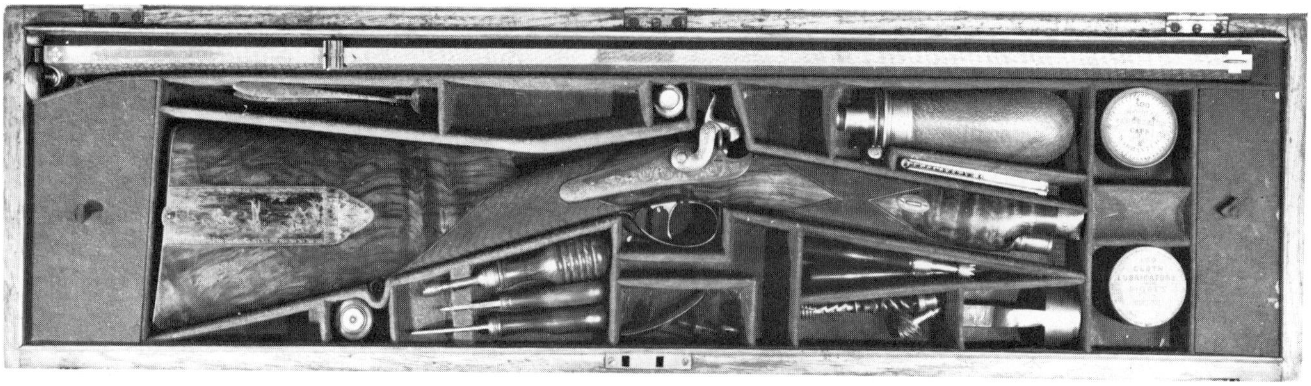

Similar cased sporting rifle with etched twist barrel signed in gold, signed boldly engraved back-action lock and iron mounts in typical Rigby style, figured walnut half-stock, the patch-box cover engraved with a sportsman being devoured by a lion. In original case with full accessories and trade label. Fine quality and condition with some finish. By Wm. & Jn. Rigby, Dublin, circa 1840. 34in. barrel.
Christie's
£700 – £900

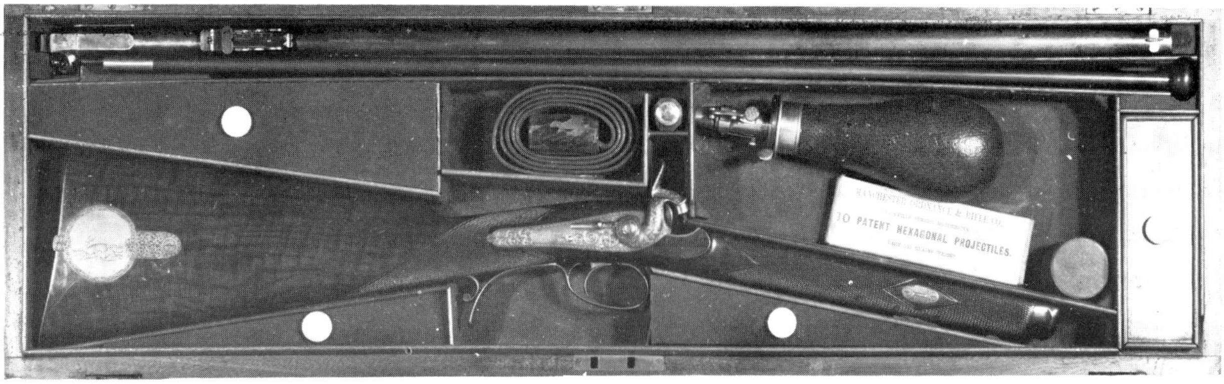

Cased Whitworth back-action sporting rifle with round barrel, the breech with platinum plug and engraved with a stag, the half-stock with chequered grip and fore-end, engraved lock and steel mounts. In original mahogany case with fittings and label. Fine quality and excellent condition. Circa 1860. 29¼in. barrel. *Christie's*

£700 – £850

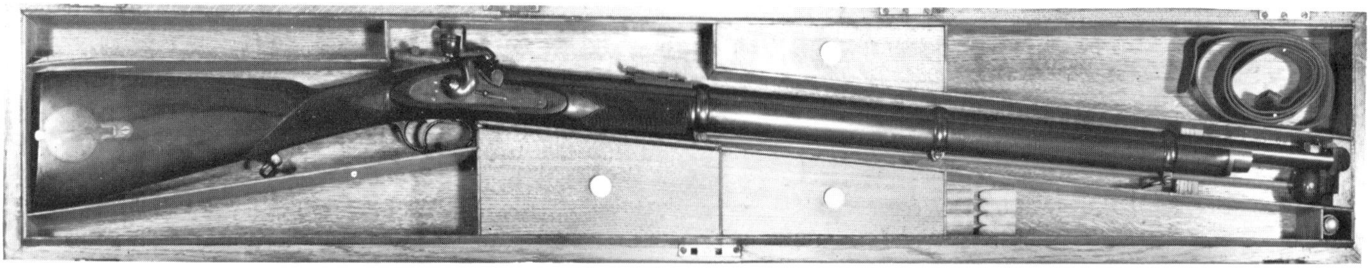

Cased Whitworth military target rifle, the full stock with chequered grip and fore-end and plain blued steel mounts. In original oak case with accessories and trade label, the lid with presentation inscription on a silver plaque. Good quality and excellent condition. Circa 1860. 32in. barrel. *Christie's*

£800 – £1,000

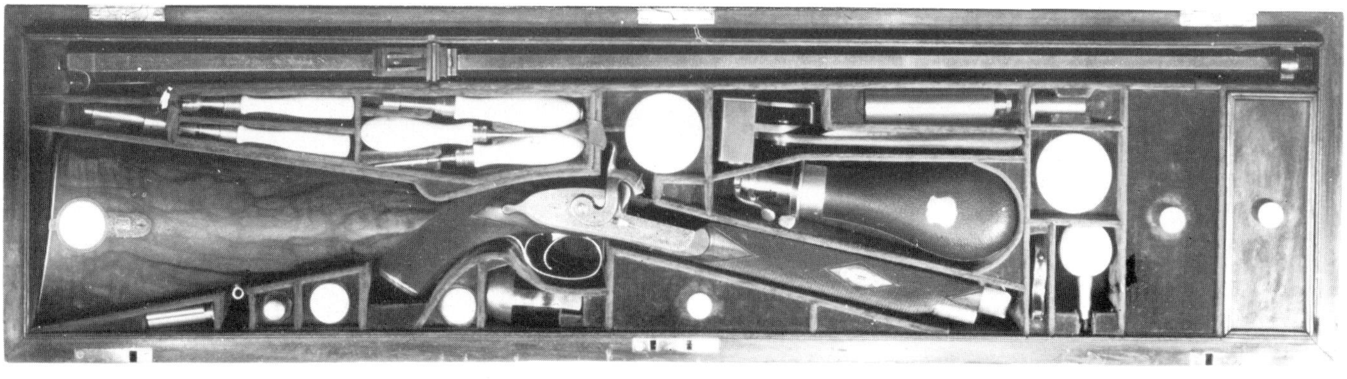

Exceptional cased presentation target rifle with scroll engraved lock and full engraved silver mounts. In rosewood case lined in red velvet with full accessories. Very fine quality, almost unfired condition. By Joseph Harkom, Edinburgh, Edinburgh silver hallmarks for 1861. 36in. barrel.

Presented to Edward Ross, son of Horatio Ross, for winning the Prize of Champion Shot of Great Britain at Wimbledon in 1860. *Christie's*

Over £3,000

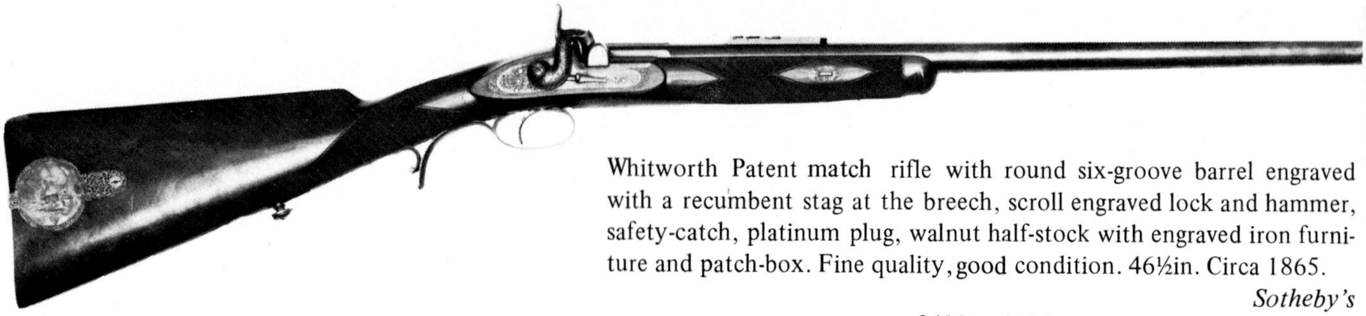

Whitworth Patent match rifle with round six-groove barrel engraved with a recumbent stag at the breech, scroll engraved lock and hammer, safety-catch, platinum plug, walnut half-stock with engraved iron furniture and patch-box. Fine quality, good condition. 46½in. Circa 1865.
Sotheby's

£400 – £500

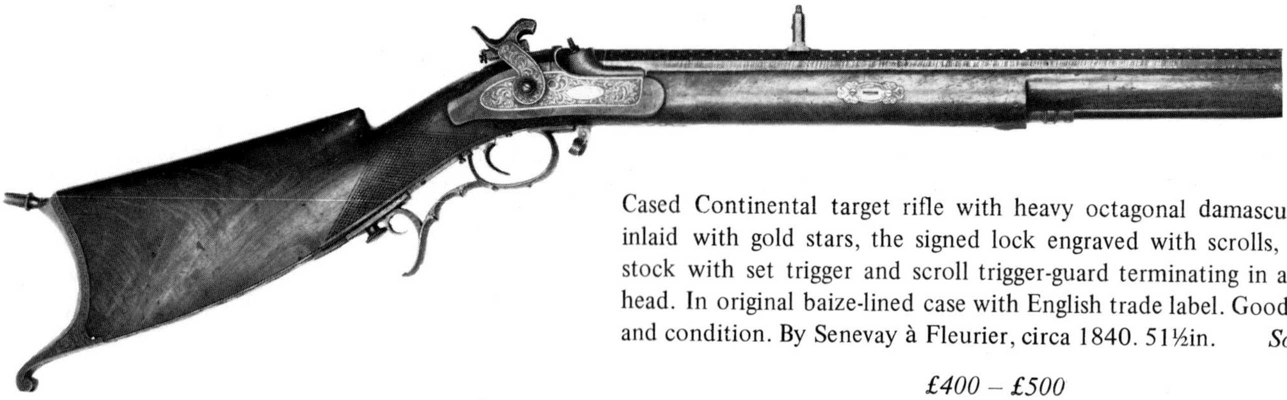

Cased Continental target rifle with heavy octagonal damascus barrel inlaid with gold stars, the signed lock engraved with scrolls, the full stock with set trigger and scroll trigger-guard terminating in a snake's head. In original baize-lined case with English trade label. Good quality and condition. By Senevay à Fleurier, circa 1840. 51½in. *Sotheby's*

£400 – £500

Uncased, about £300.

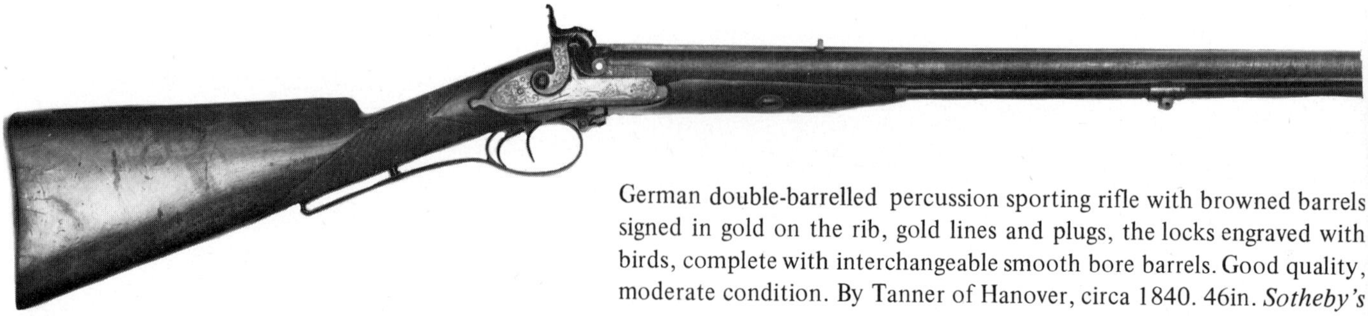

German double-barrelled percussion sporting rifle with browned barrels signed in gold on the rib, gold lines and plugs, the locks engraved with birds, complete with interchangeable smooth bore barrels. Good quality, moderate condition. By Tanner of Hanover, circa 1840. 46in. *Sotheby's*

£150 – £200

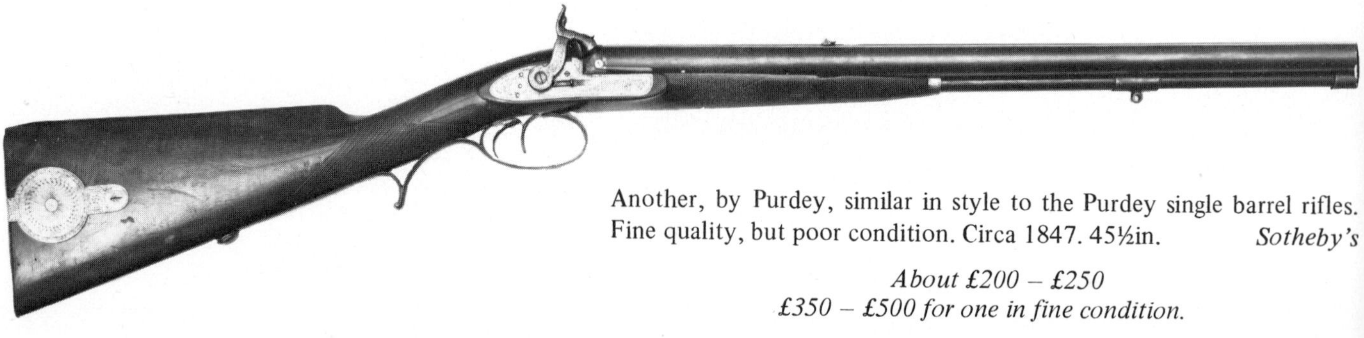

Another, by Purdey, similar in style to the Purdey single barrel rifles. Fine quality, but poor condition. Circa 1847. 45½in. *Sotheby's*

About £200 – £250
£350 – £500 for one in fine condition.

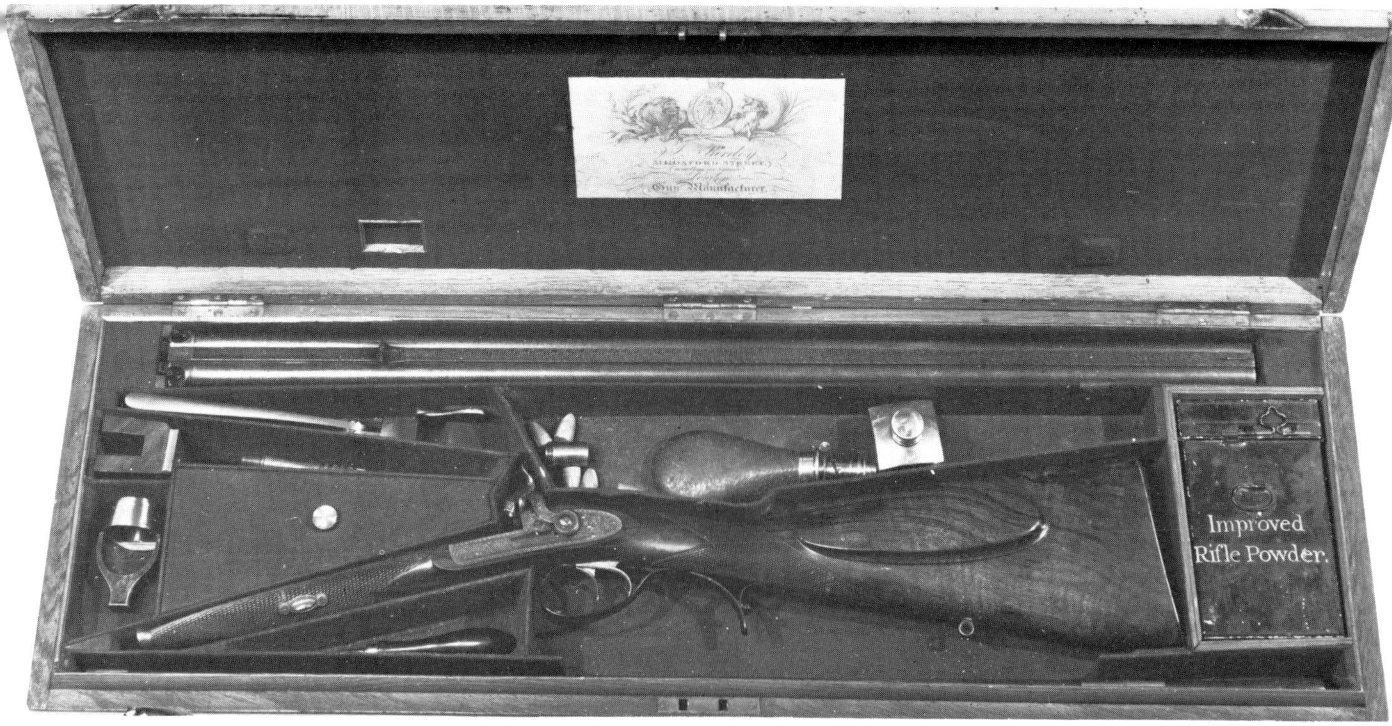

Cased Purdey double-barrelled rifle with two-groove barrels, engraved locks and iron mounts in typical Purdey style. Original oak case lined in red baize with label and some fittings. Fine quality and condition, with nearly all original finish. Circa 1858. 29in. barrels. *Knight, Frank & Rutley*

£600 – £850

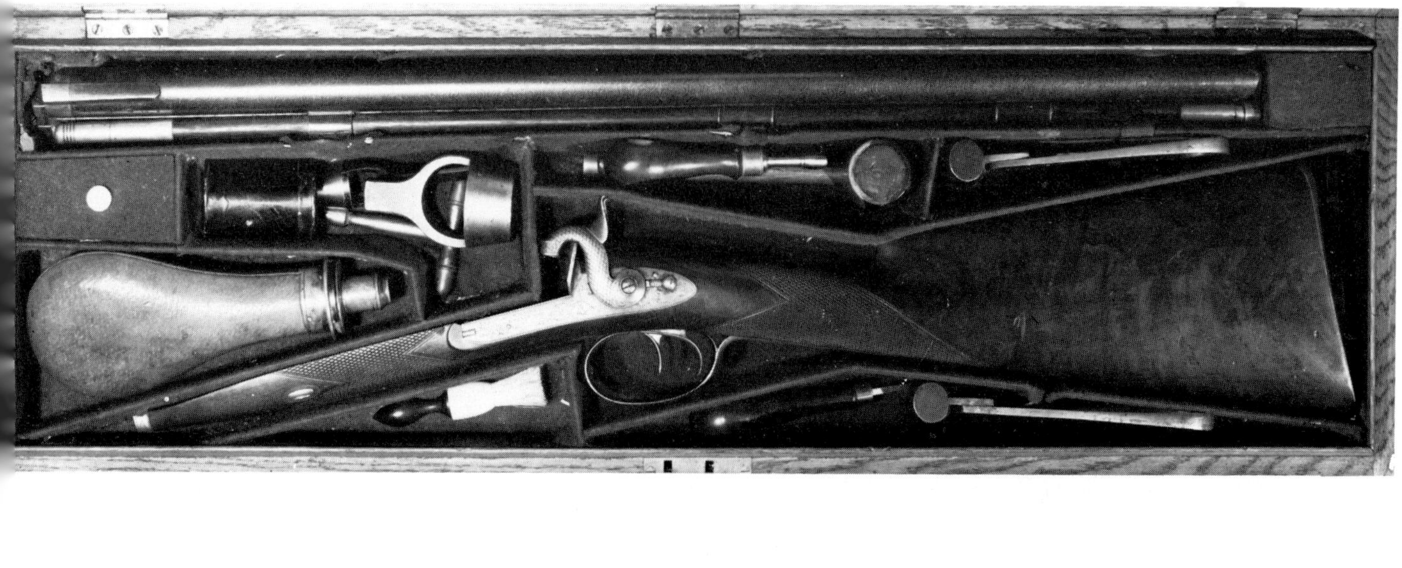

Cased double-barrelled rifle also with two-groove barrels, in original oak case with fittings and label. Fine quality and condition, with most original finish. By Charles and Samuel Smith, Princes Street, Leicester Square, London, circa 1830/40. 25½in. barrels. *Christie's*

£450 – £600

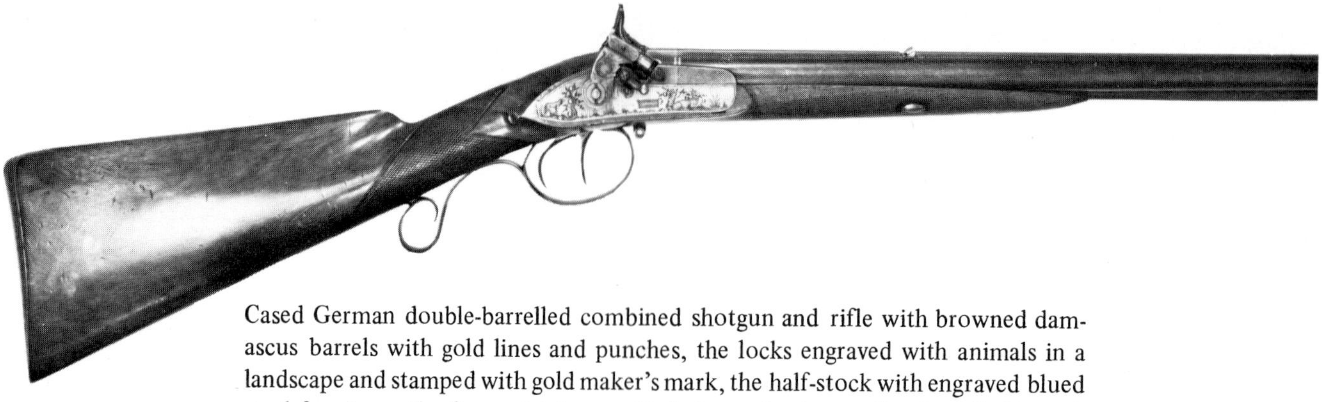

Cased German double-barrelled combined shotgun and rifle with browned damascus barrels with gold lines and punches, the locks engraved with animals in a landscape and stamped with gold maker's mark, the half-stock with engraved blued steel furniture, the forward trigger with hair mechanism to fire the rifled barrel. In original green velvet lined case, complete with a pair of interchangeable smooth bore barrels en suite. Fine quality and condition. By C.P. Crause, Hertzberg am Harz, circa 1830. 29½in. barrels. *Christie's*

£300 – £500

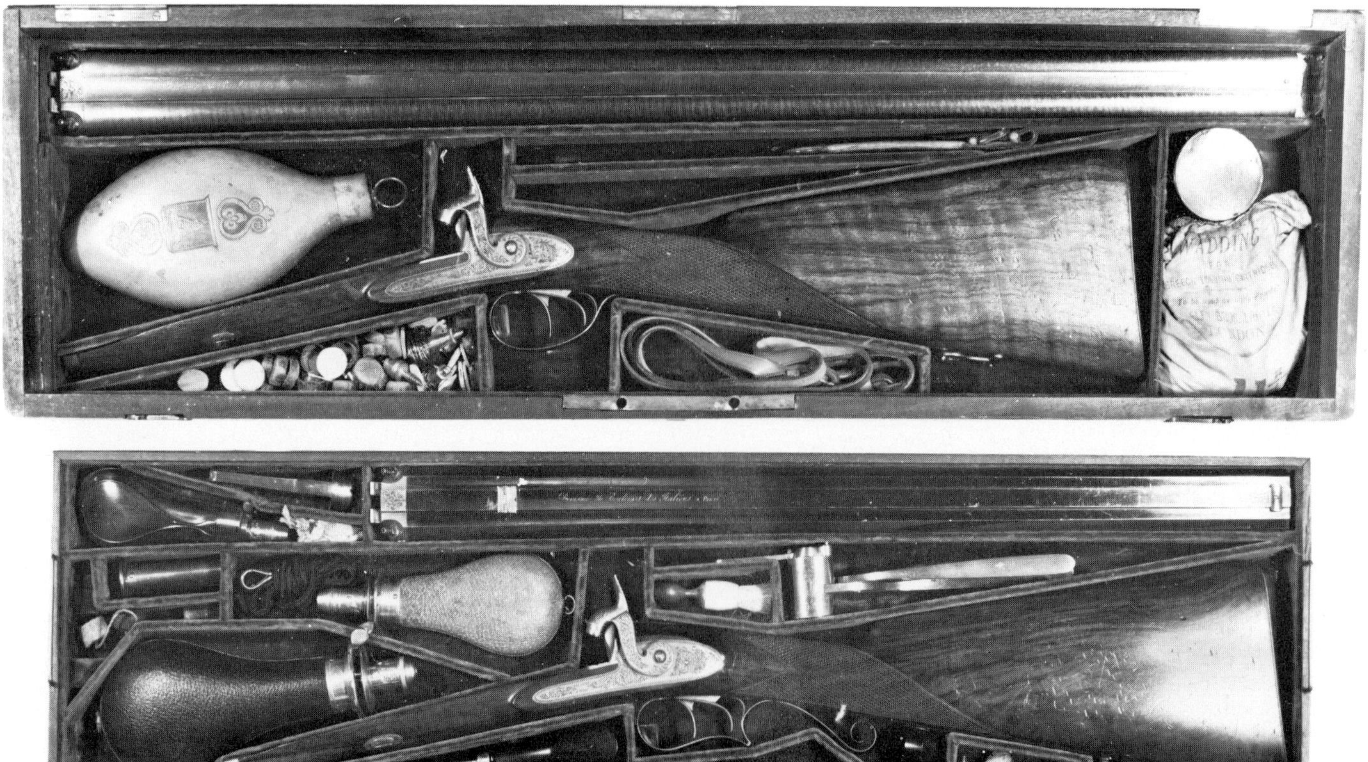

Cased double-barrelled shotgun and rifle set, the rifle with blued octagonal barrels and the shotgun with browned damascus barrels, each with half-stock and engraved steel mounts. In original two-tier mahogany case lined in red velvet and complete with full accessories, the lid signed in gilt letters. Fine quality and condition. By Devisme, Paris, dated 1850. 22in. and 30in. barrels. *Christie's*

About £1,000

Percussion Cap Breech-Loading Rifles

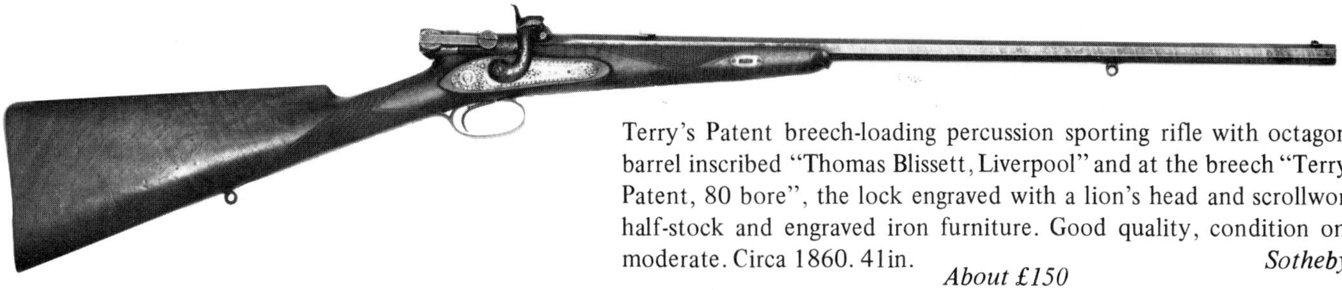

Terry's Patent breech-loading percussion sporting rifle with octagonal barrel inscribed "Thomas Blissett, Liverpool" and at the breech "Terry's Patent, 80 bore", the lock engraved with a lion's head and scrollwork. half-stock and engraved iron furniture. Good quality, condition only moderate. Circa 1860. 41in. *Sotheby's*

About £150

Slightly less for a military one in equivalent condition. More for a heavy bore example.

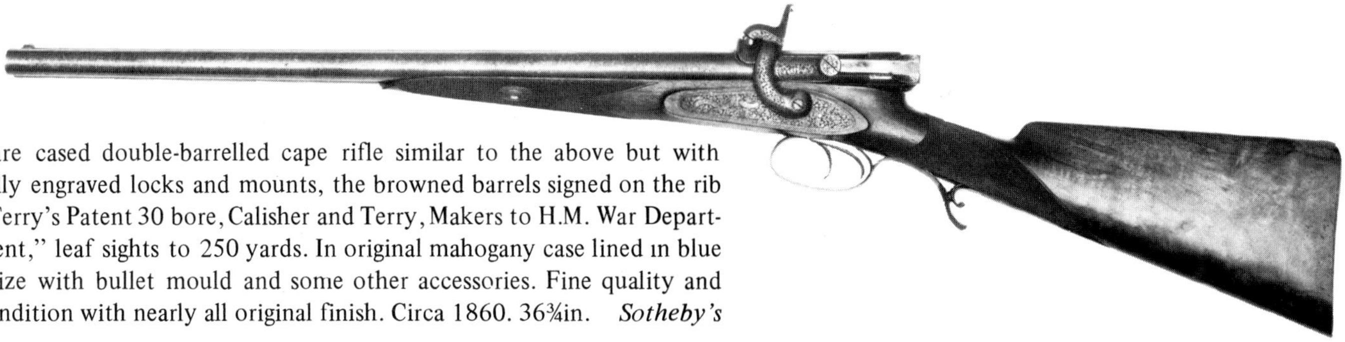

Rare cased double-barrelled cape rifle similar to the above but with fully engraved locks and mounts, the browned barrels signed on the rib "Terry's Patent 30 bore, Calisher and Terry, Makers to H.M. War Department," leaf sights to 250 yards. In original mahogany case lined in blue baize with bullet mould and some other accessories. Fine quality and condition with nearly all original finish. Circa 1860. 36¾in. *Sotheby's*

£500 – £750

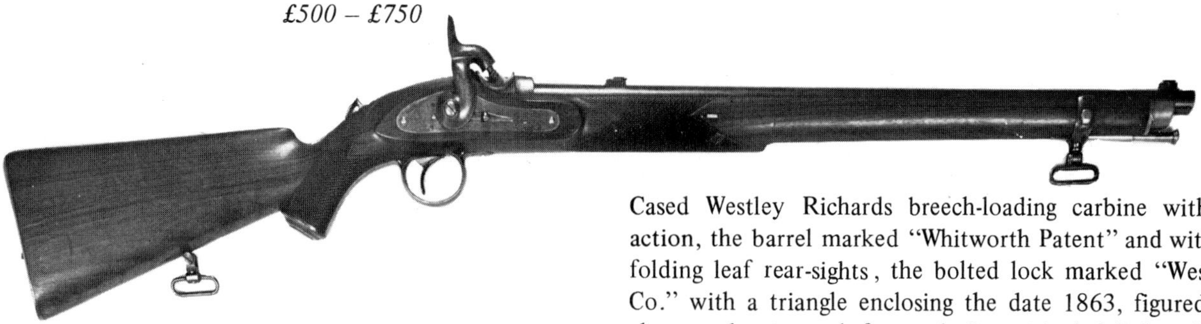

Cased Westley Richards breech-loading carbine with "monkey-tail" action, the barrel marked "Whitworth Patent" and with platinum-lined folding leaf rear-sights, the bolted lock marked "Westley Richards & Co." with a triangle enclosing the date 1863, figured full stock with chequered grip and fore-end. In original full length oak case with instructions label, partly re-lined. Fine condition with much finish. 25in. barrel. *Weller & Dufty*

£200 – £300

Without the case, £100 – £150.

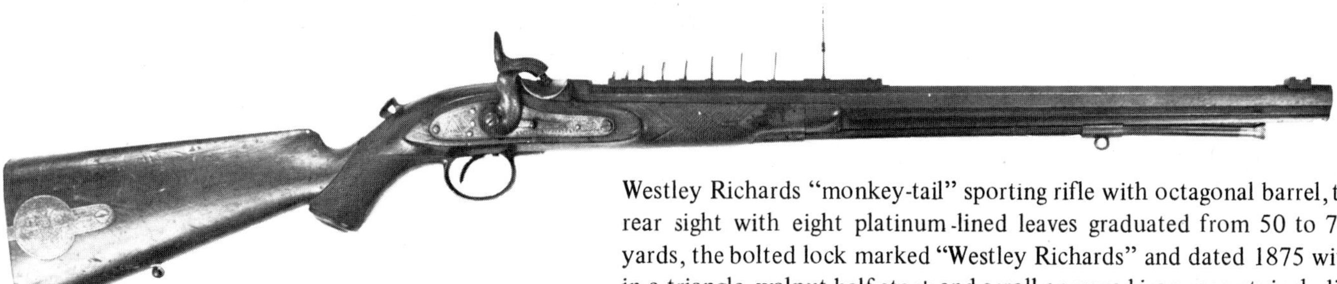

Westley Richards "monkey-tail" sporting rifle with octagonal barrel, the rear sight with eight platinum-lined leaves graduated from 50 to 700 yards, the bolted lock marked "Westley Richards" and dated 1875 within a triangle, walnut half-stock and scroll engraved iron mounts including patch-box. Fair condition. 25in. barrel. *Weller & Dufty*

£150 – £200

Multishot Guns and Rifles

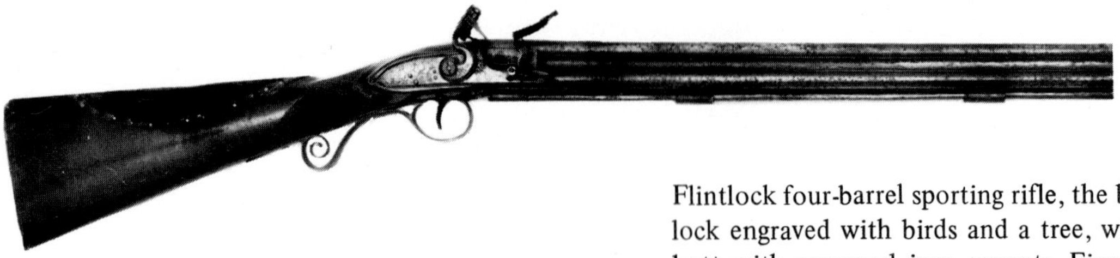

Flintlock four-barrel sporting rifle, the barrels with gold vent, the signed lock engraved with birds and a tree, with rainproof pan and roller, the butt with engraved iron mounts. Fine quality but poor condition. By Bate, London, circa 1800. 36in. *Sotheby's*

£600 – £800

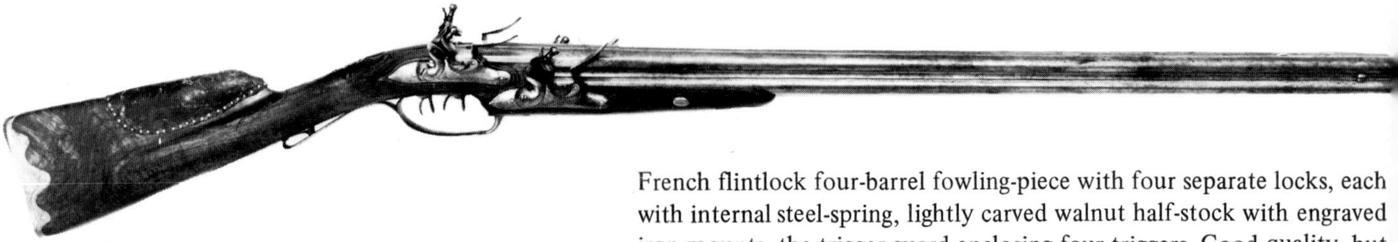

French flintlock four-barrel fowling-piece with four separate locks, each with internal steel-spring, lightly carved walnut half-stock with engraved iron mounts, the trigger-guard enclosing four triggers. Good quality, but poor condition with restoration and replacements. By Bouillet, Paris, circa 1780. 48in. *Sotheby's*

£800 – £1,000. Rare.

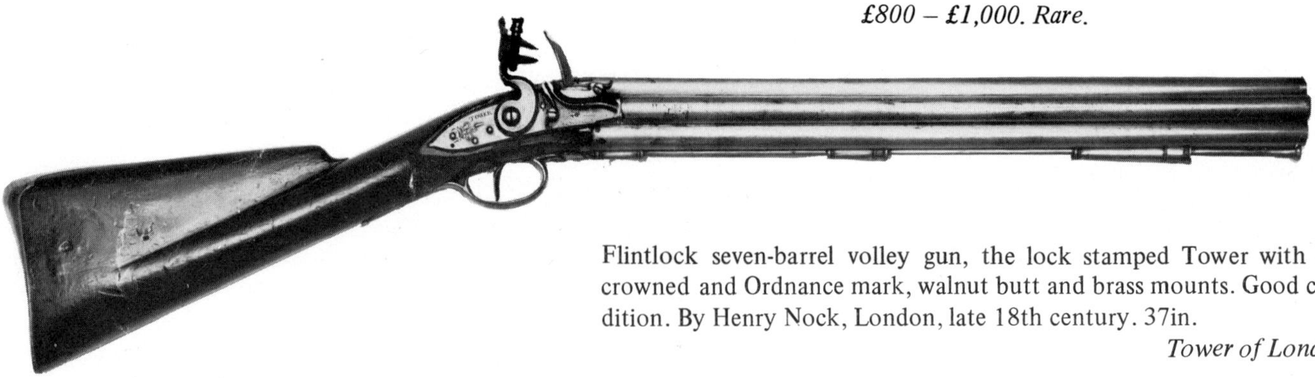

Flintlock seven-barrel volley gun, the lock stamped Tower with GR crowned and Ordnance mark, walnut butt and brass mounts. Good condition. By Henry Nock, London, late 18th century. 37in.

Tower of London

£800 – £1,000

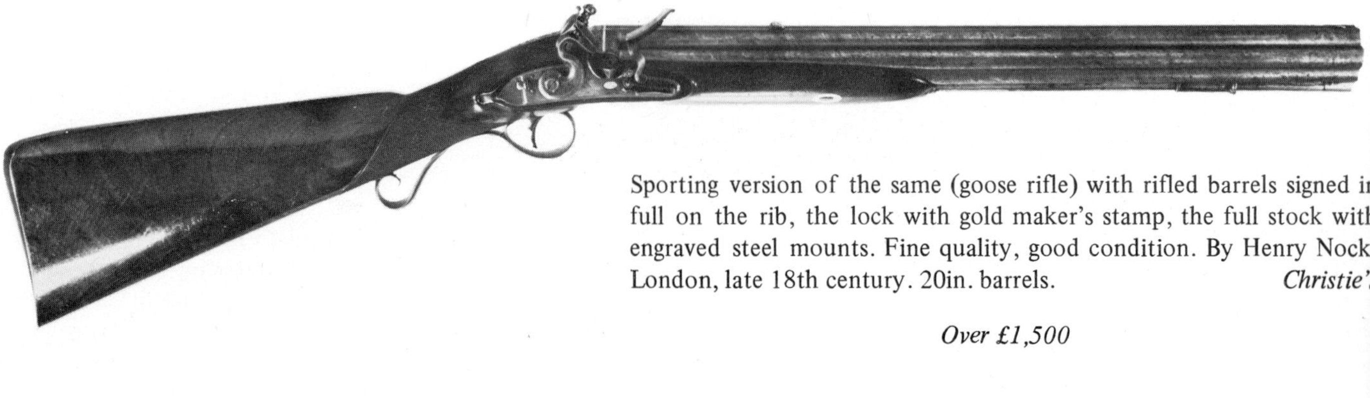

Sporting version of the same (goose rifle) with rifled barrels signed in full on the rib, the lock with gold maker's stamp, the full stock with engraved steel mounts. Fine quality, good condition. By Henry Nock, London, late 18th century. 20in. barrels. *Christie's*

Over £1,500

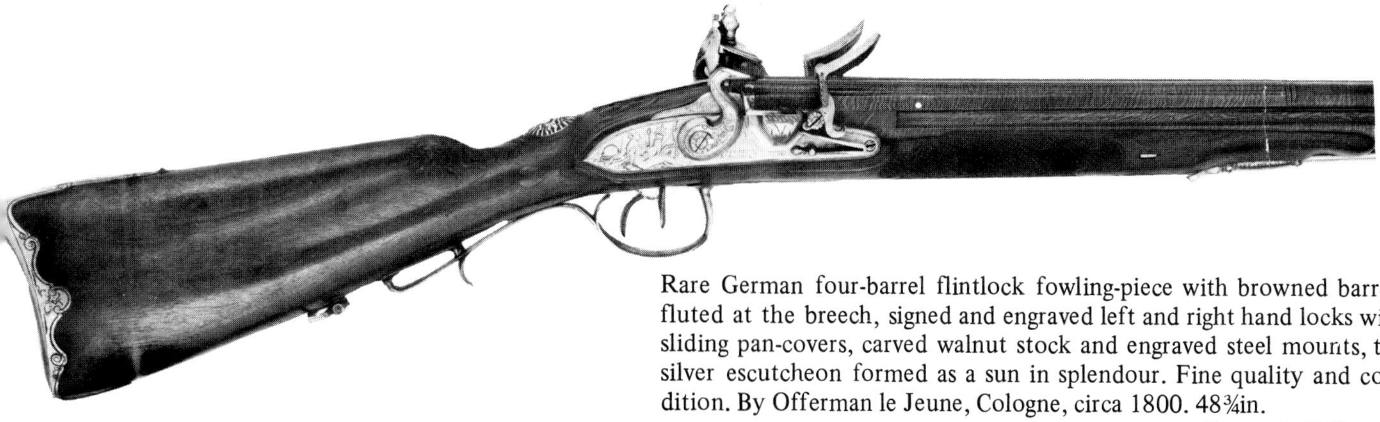

Rare German four-barrel flintlock fowling-piece with browned barrels fluted at the breech, signed and engraved left and right hand locks with sliding pan-covers, carved walnut stock and engraved steel mounts, the silver escutcheon formed as a sun in splendour. Fine quality and condition. By Offerman le Jeune, Cologne, circa 1800. 48¾in.

Renwick Collection

Over £1,000

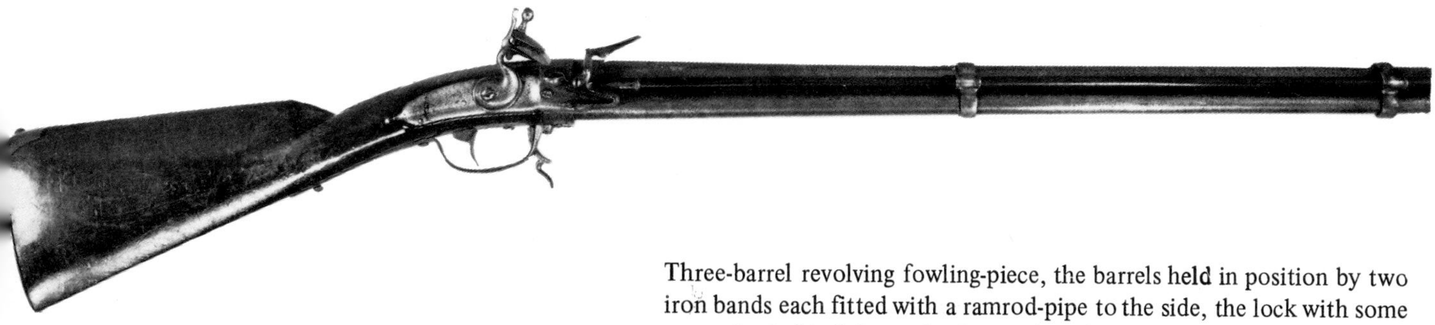

Three-barrel revolving fowling-piece, the barrels held in position by two iron bands each fitted with a ramrod-pipe to the side, the lock with some engraving behind the cock, the stock with iron mounts. Fair quality but condition only moderate. Unsigned, late 17th century. 34½in. barrels.

£700 – £900

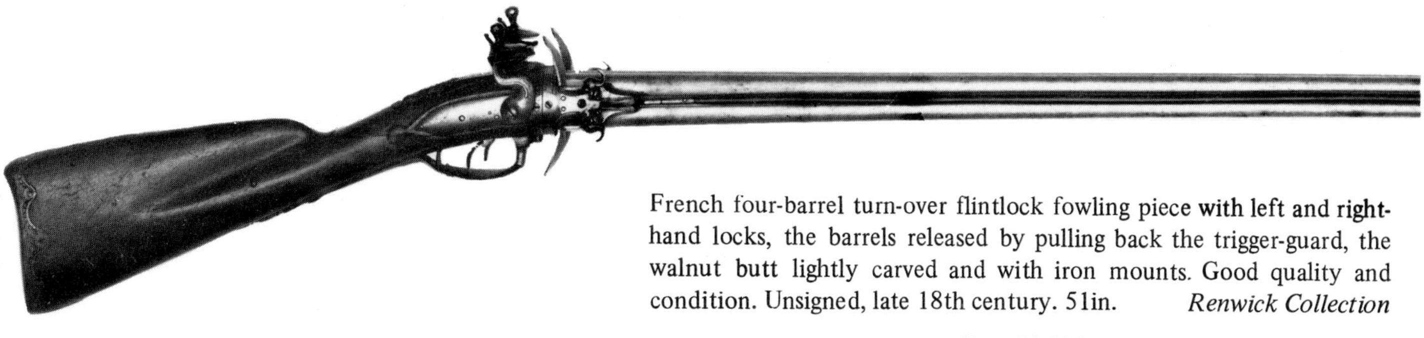

French four-barrel turn-over flintlock fowling piece with left and right-hand locks, the barrels released by pulling back the trigger-guard, the walnut butt lightly carved and with iron mounts. Good quality and condition. Unsigned, late 18th century. 51in. *Renwick Collection*

Over £1,500

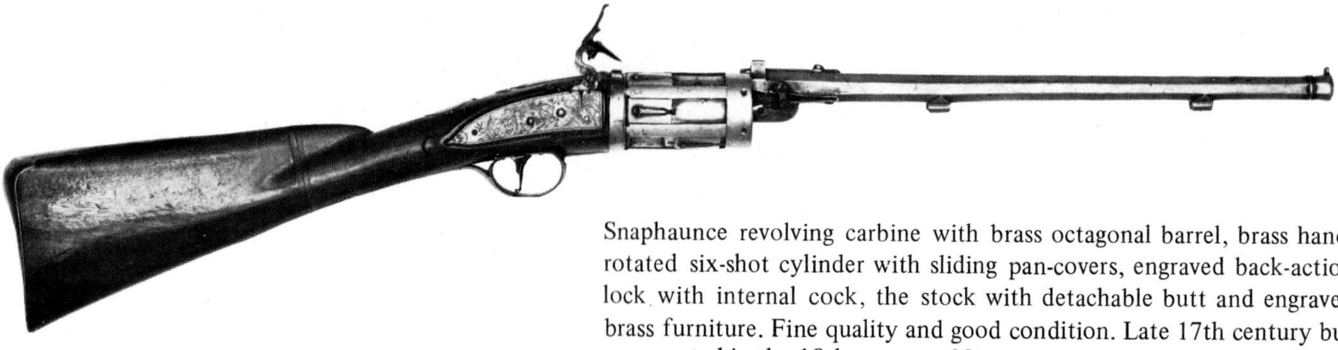

Snaphaunce revolving carbine with brass octagonal barrel, brass hand-rotated six-shot cylinder with sliding pan-covers, engraved back-action lock with internal cock, the stock with detachable butt and engraved brass furniture. Fine quality and good condition. Late 17th century but re-mounted in the 18th century. 33in. *Sotheby's*

About £2,000

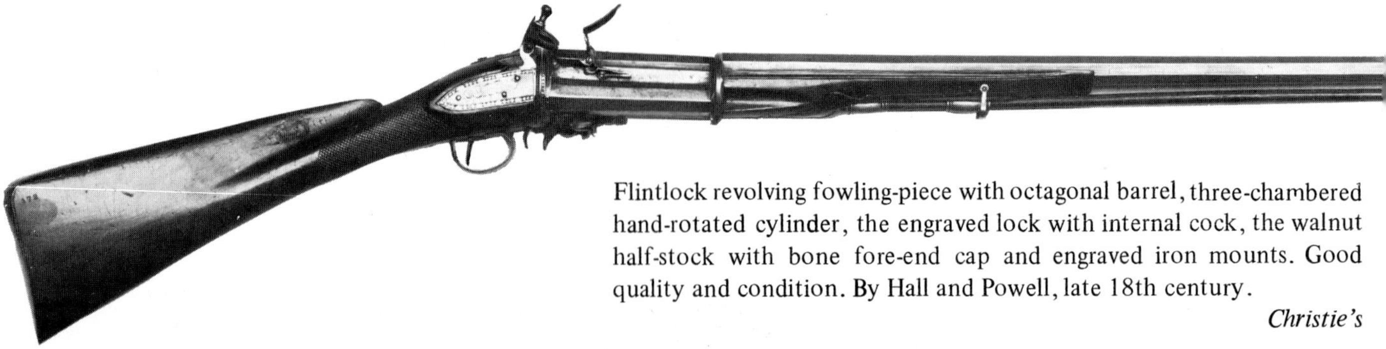

Flintlock revolving fowling-piece with octagonal barrel, three-chambered hand-rotated cylinder, the engraved lock with internal cock, the walnut half-stock with bone fore-end cap and engraved iron mounts. Good quality and condition. By Hall and Powell, late 18th century. *Christie's*

Over £1,000

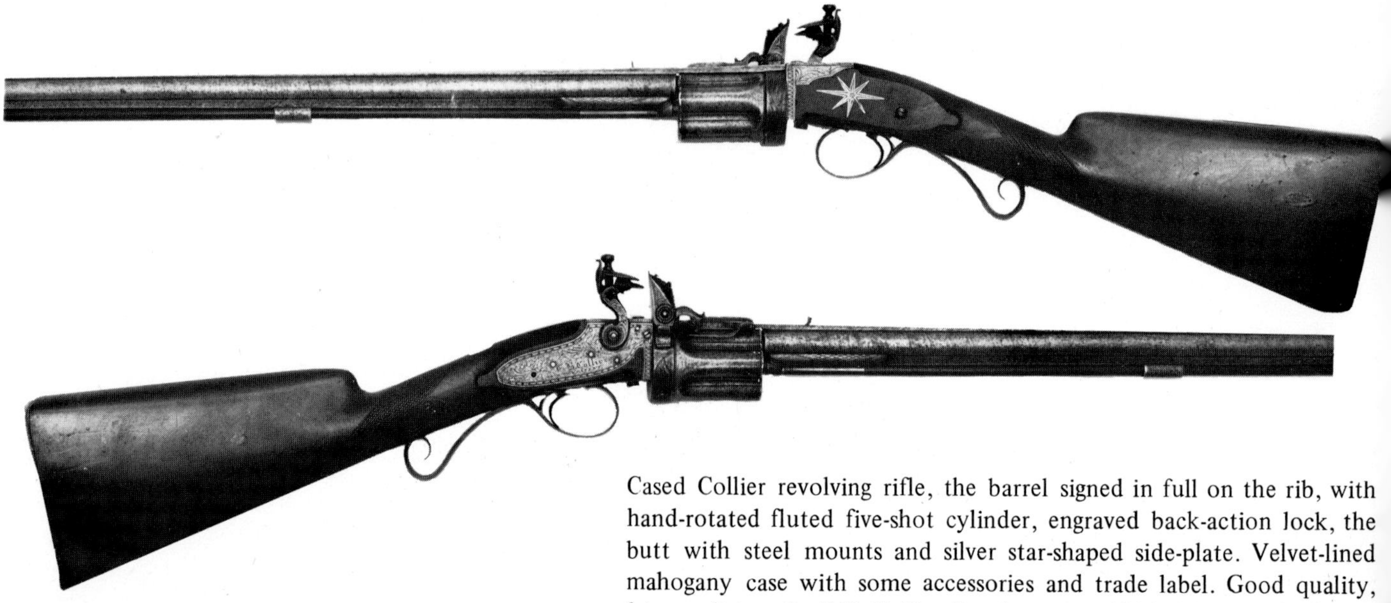

Cased Collier revolving rifle, the barrel signed in full on the rib, with hand-rotated fluted five-shot cylinder, engraved back-action lock, the butt with steel mounts and silver star-shaped side-plate. Velvet-lined mahogany case with some accessories and trade label. Good quality, fair condition. By E.H. Collier, London, circa 1820. 47in. *Sotheby's*

Over £2,000

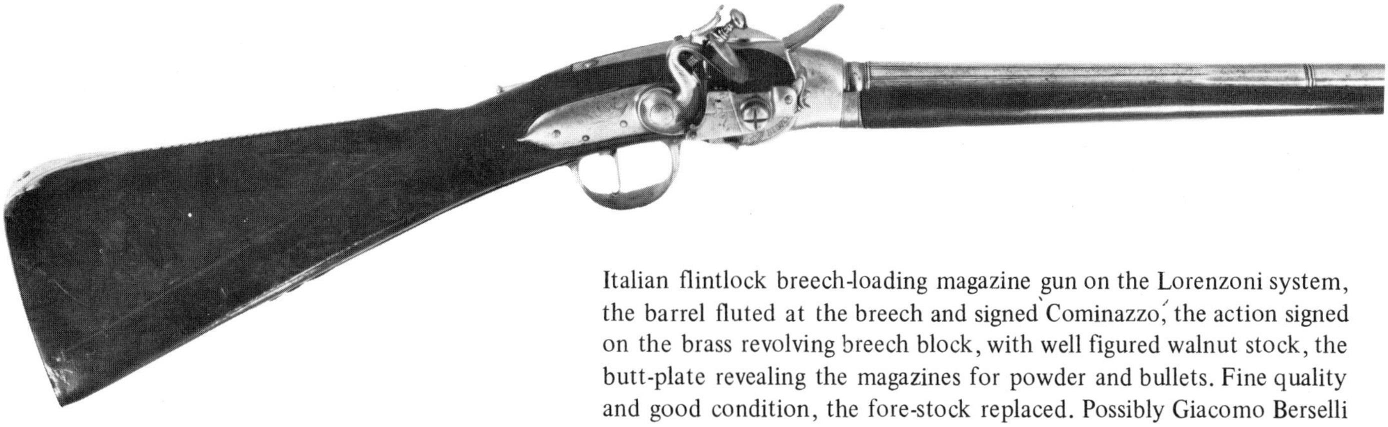

Italian flintlock breech-loading magazine gun on the Lorenzoni system, the barrel fluted at the breech and signed 'Cominazzo', the action signed on the brass revolving breech block, with well figured walnut stock, the butt-plate revealing the magazines for powder and bullets. Fine quality and good condition, the fore-stock replaced. Possibly Giacomo Berselli of Bologna, late 17th century. 33in. barrel. *Christie's*

About £2,000. Extremely rare.

Much more for a signed Lorenzoni magazine gun.

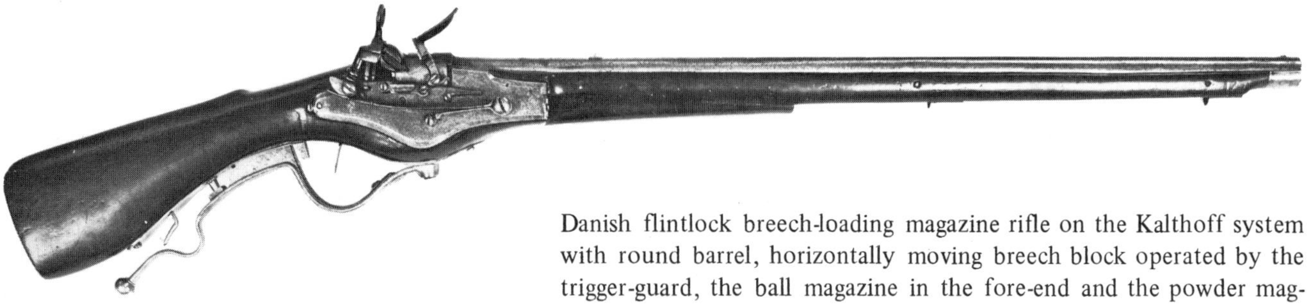

Danish flintlock breech-loading magazine rifle on the Kalthoff system with round barrel, horizontally moving breech block operated by the trigger-guard, the ball magazine in the fore-end and the powder magazine in the butt, plain full stock and iron mounts. Fair condition but some repairs to the stock. Mid-17th century. 27in. barrel. *Weller & Dufty*

£1,500 – £2,000

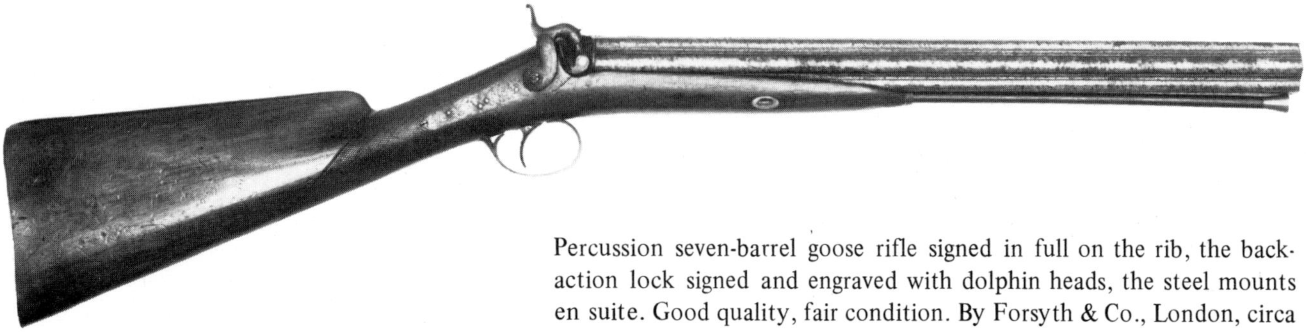

Percussion seven-barrel goose rifle signed in full on the rib, the back-action lock signed and engraved with dolphin heads, the steel mounts en suite. Good quality, fair condition. By Forsyth & Co., London, circa 1827. 36¾in. *Sotheby's*

£600 – £900

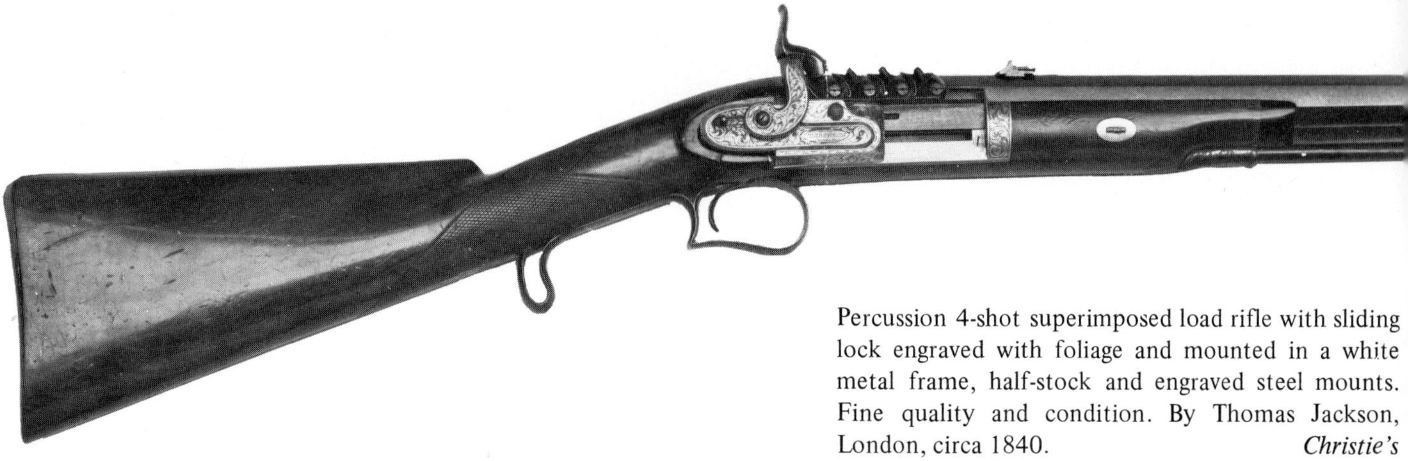

Percussion 4-shot superimposed load rifle with sliding lock engraved with foliage and mounted in a white metal frame, half-stock and engraved steel mounts. Fine quality and condition. By Thomas Jackson, London, circa 1840. *Christie's*

Over £1,000

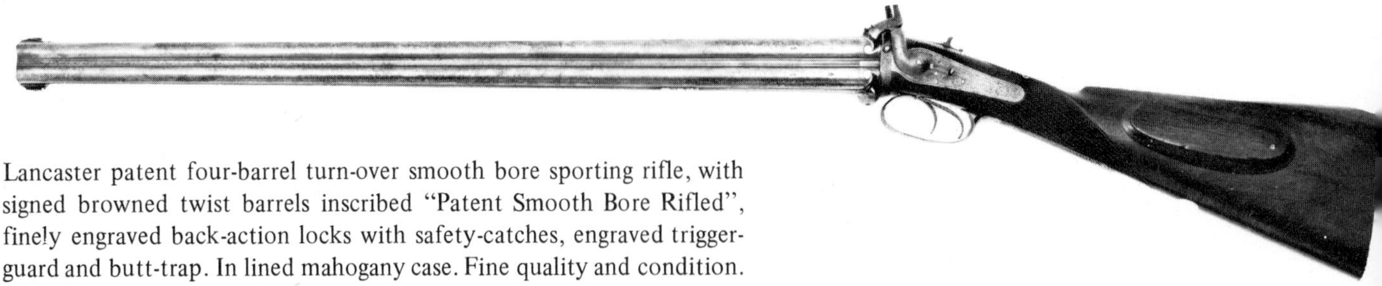

Lancaster patent four-barrel turn-over smooth bore sporting rifle, with signed browned twist barrels inscribed "Patent Smooth Bore Rifled", finely engraved back-action locks with safety-catches, engraved trigger-guard and butt-trap. In lined mahogany case. Fine quality and condition. By Charles Lancaster, 151 New Bond Street, London, circa 1850. 43$\frac{3}{8}$in. *Sotheby's*

£500 – £650

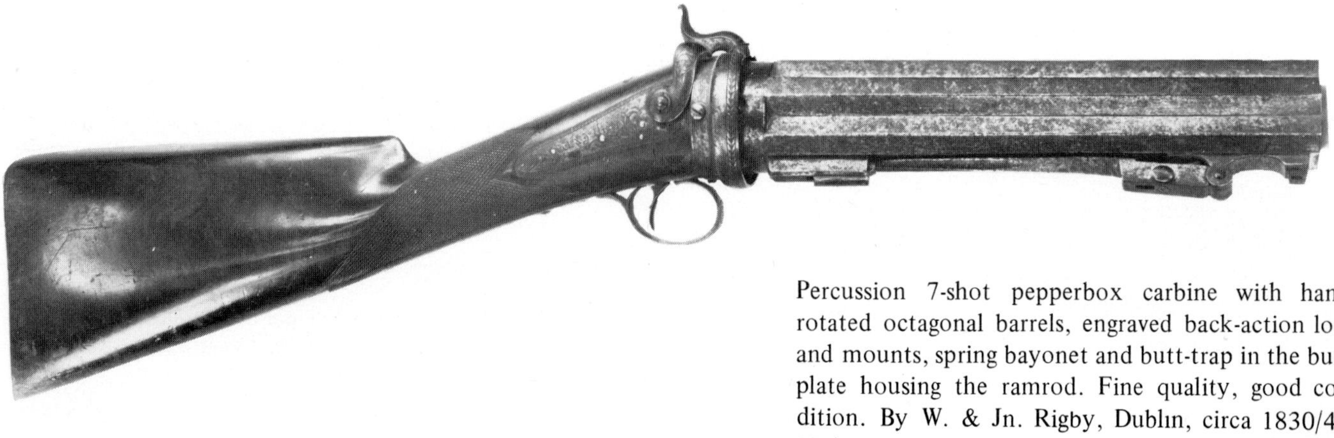

Percussion 7-shot pepperbox carbine with hand-rotated octagonal barrels, engraved back-action lock and mounts, spring bayonet and butt-trap in the butt-plate housing the ramrod. Fine quality, good condition. By W. & Jn. Rigby, Dublin, circa 1830/40. 27½in. *Christie's*

Over £1,000

Tranter carbine with double-trigger self-cocking action, and octagonal barrel, the top strap engraved "Walter Adams, King William St. City. London", the stock with chequered pistol grip and iron butt-cap. Fair condition, re-blued overall. 21in. barrel. *Weller & Dufty*

£250 – £300

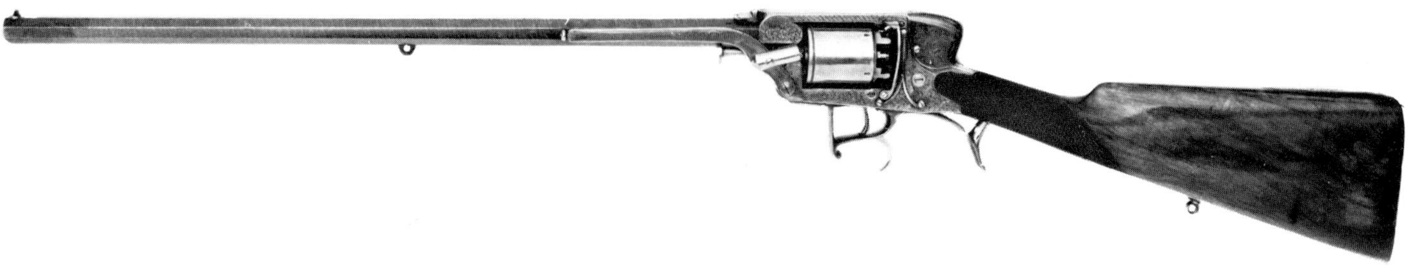

A finer example by Adams, the barrel engraved "C. Maybury, 15 St. Mary's Square, Birmingham", with patent rammer, engraved frame, walnut butt, chequered grip and engraved iron butt-cap. Fine condition with nearly all finish. In relined oak case. 41¼in. *Sotheby's*

£600 – £800

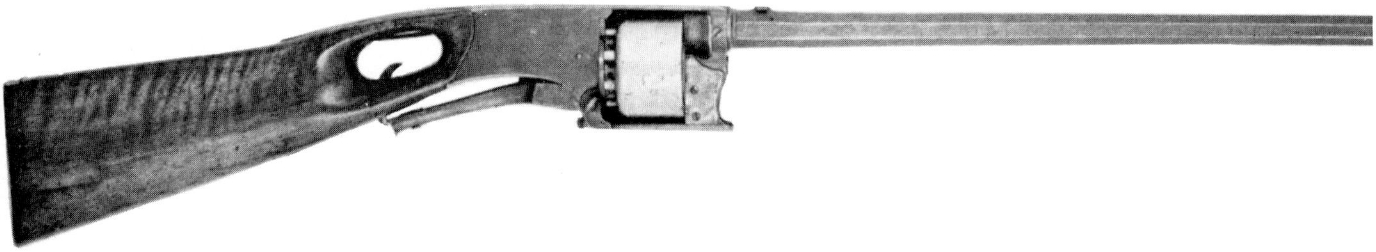

Danish Rasmussen revolving rifle with eight-shot brass cylinder, figured walnut butt and brass butt-plate, complete with spare cylinder stamped with matching serial number. Fair condition. 45¼in. *Sotheby's*

£500 – £600

Flintlock Military Long Guns

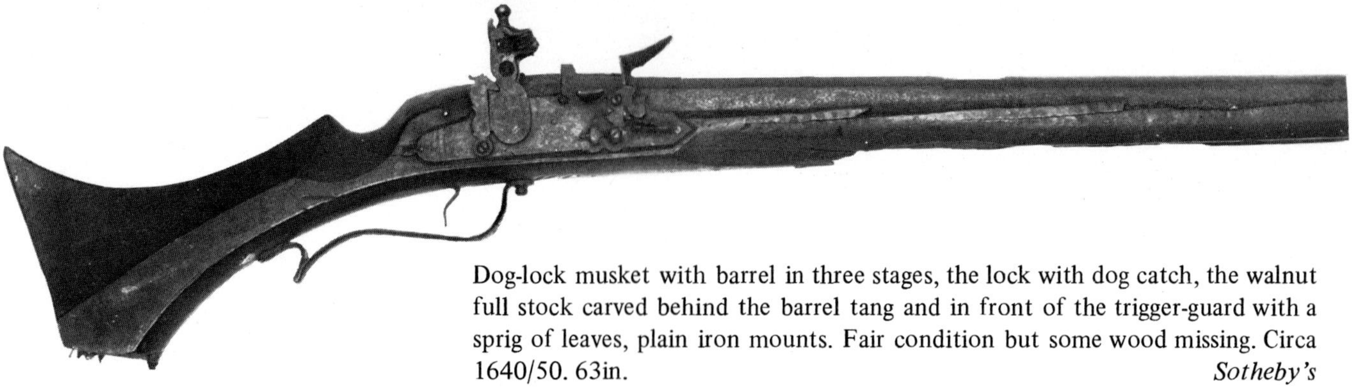

Dog-lock musket with barrel in three stages, the lock with dog catch, the walnut full stock carved behind the barrel tang and in front of the trigger-guard with a sprig of leaves, plain iron mounts. Fair condition but some wood missing. Circa 1640/50. 63in. *Sotheby's*

£400 – £600

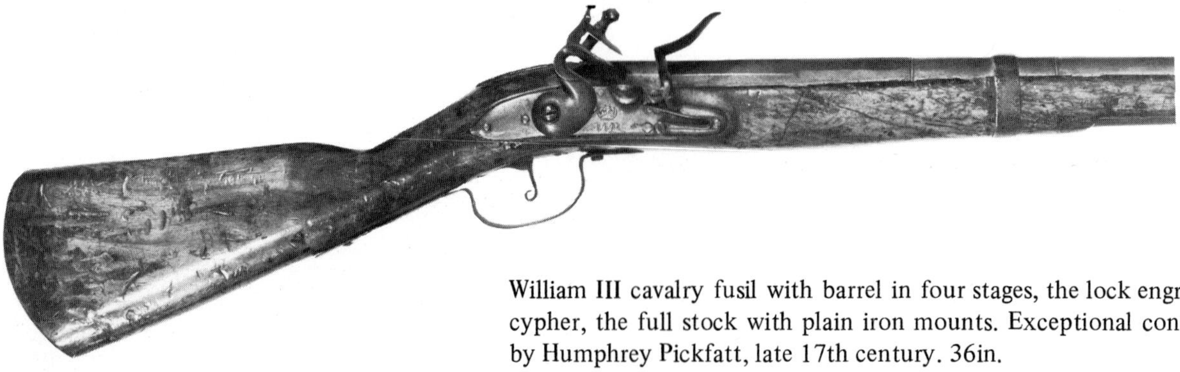

William III cavalry fusil with barrel in four stages, the lock engraved with Royal cypher, the full stock with plain iron mounts. Exceptional condition. Probably by Humphrey Pickfatt, late 17th century. 36in. *Christie's*

Over £1,000

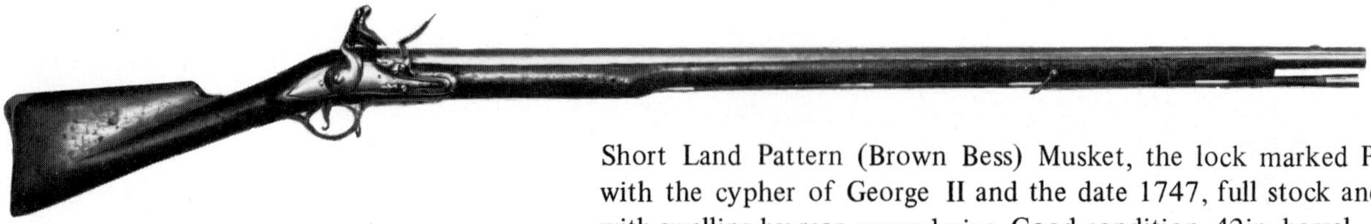

Short Land Pattern (Brown Bess) Musket, the lock marked Powell, together with the cypher of George II and the date 1747, full stock and brass mounts, with swelling by rear ramrod-pipe. Good condition. 42in. barrel. *Tower of London*

Over £500

Without the signature and date, £400 – £500. The earlier the date the higher the value.

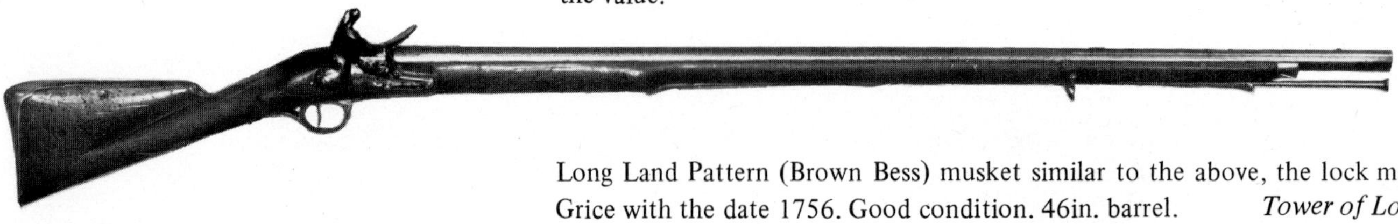

Long Land Pattern (Brown Bess) musket similar to the above, the lock marked Grice with the date 1756. Good condition. 46in. barrel. *Tower of London*

Over £600

Without the signature and date, £500 – £650. The earlier the date the higher the value.

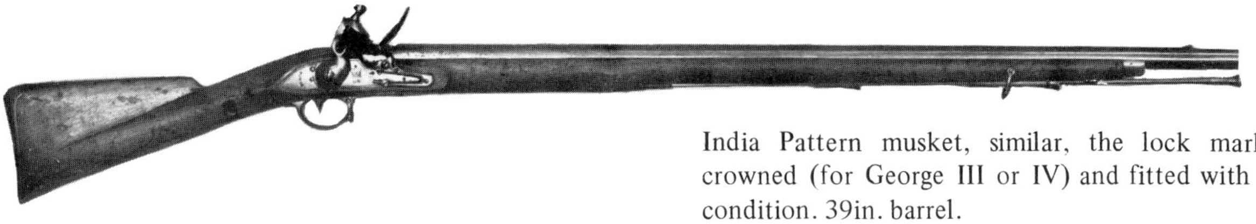

India Pattern musket, similar, the lock marked Tower with GR crowned (for George III or IV) and fitted with ring-neck cock. Good condition. 39in. barrel. *Tower of London*

£175 – £225

Note: Militia markings raise the value.

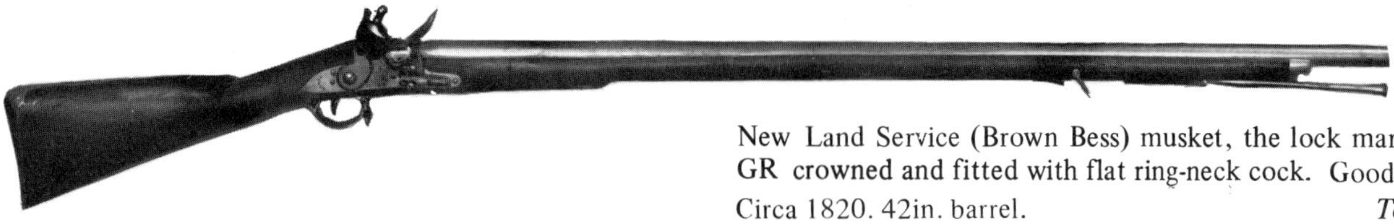

New Land Service (Brown Bess) musket, the lock marked Tower with GR crowned and fitted with flat ring-neck cock. Good condition Circa 1820. 42in. barrel. *Tower of London*

£150 – £200

Note: Militia markings raise the value.

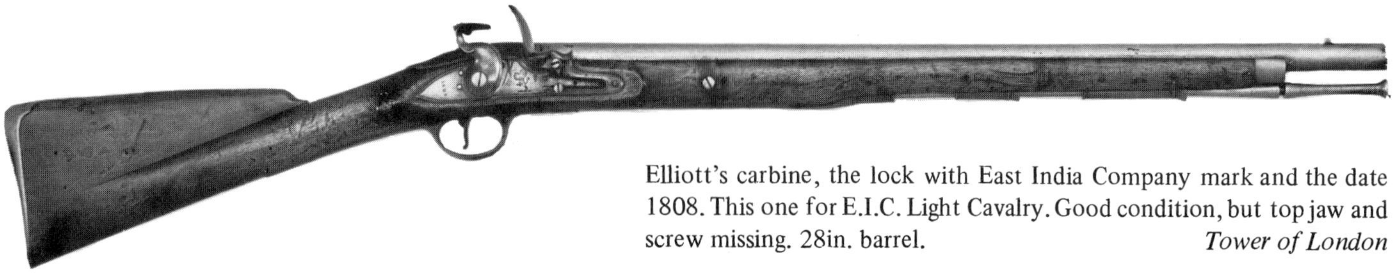

Elliott's carbine, the lock with East India Company mark and the date 1808. This one for E.I.C. Light Cavalry. Good condition, but top jaw and screw missing. 28in. barrel. *Tower of London*

£200 – £300

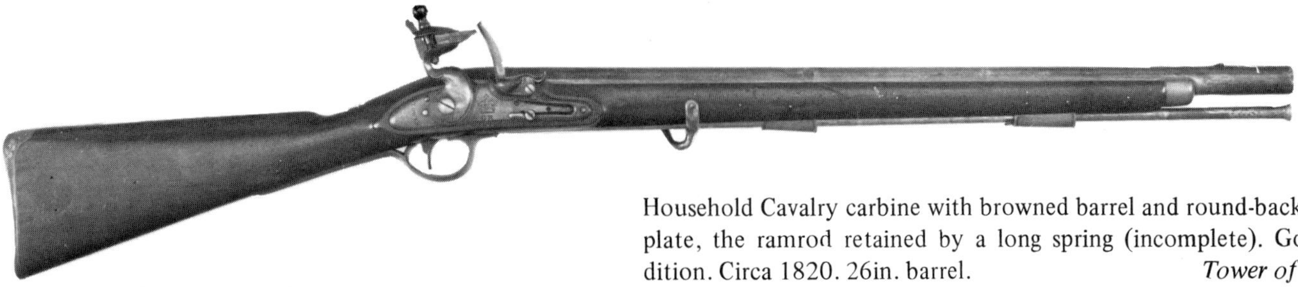

Household Cavalry carbine with browned barrel and round-backed lock-plate, the ramrod retained by a long spring (incomplete). Good condition. Circa 1820. 26in. barrel. *Tower of London*

£200 – £250

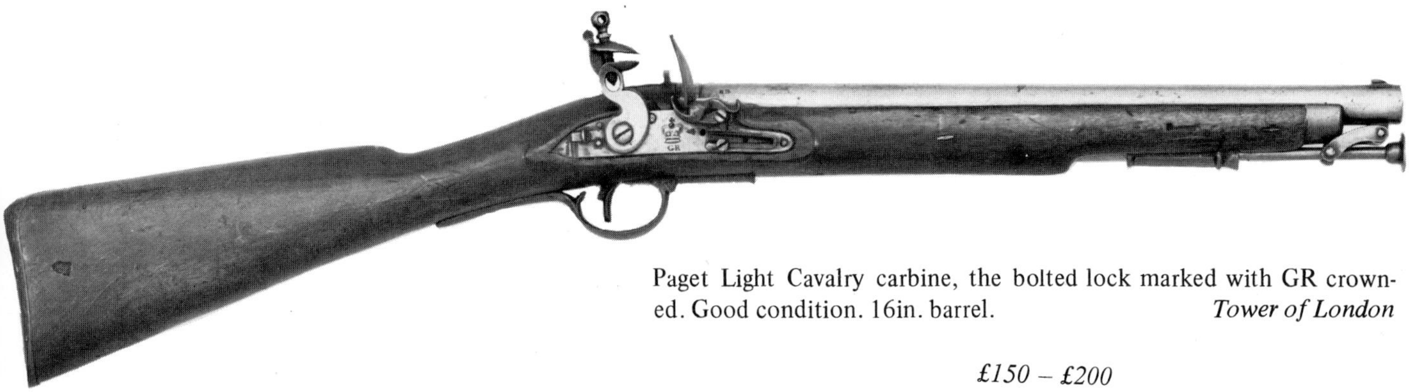

Paget Light Cavalry carbine, the bolted lock marked with GR crowned. Good condition. 16in. barrel. *Tower of London*

£150 – £200

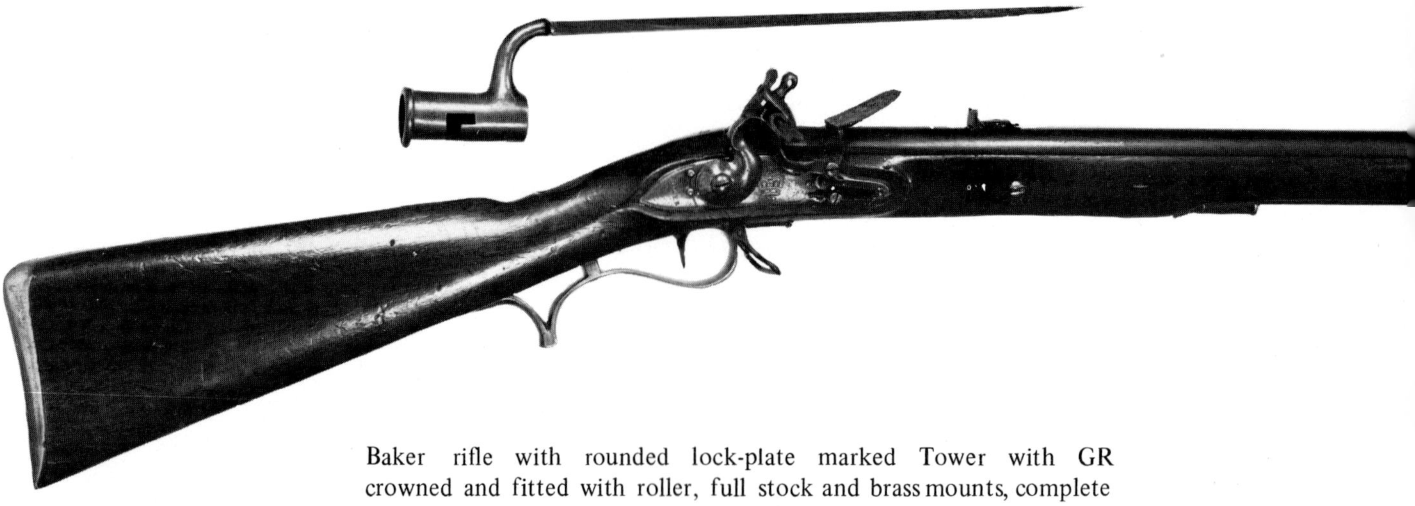

Baker rifle with rounded lock-plate marked Tower with GR crowned and fitted with roller, full stock and brass mounts, complete with bayonet. Good condition. 30in. barrel. *Christie's*

About £400

See also Baker pattern target rifle on page 314.

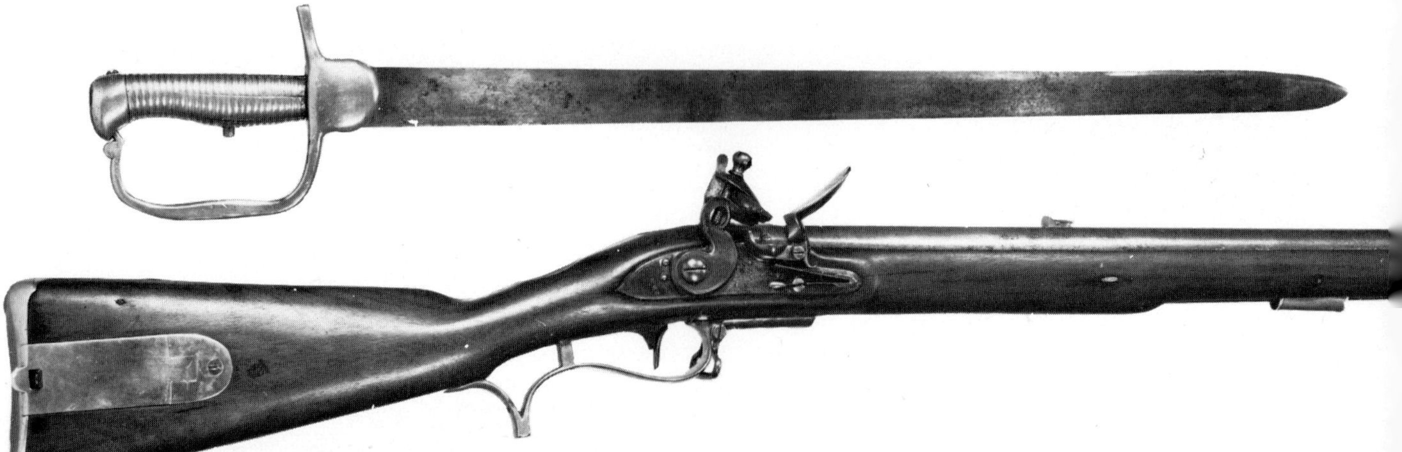

Later Baker rifle with flat lock engraved as above and fitted with flat ring-neck cock, the stock of split pattern, with rounded patch-box, complete with sword bayonet. Good condition. 30in. barrel. *Christie's*

About £400

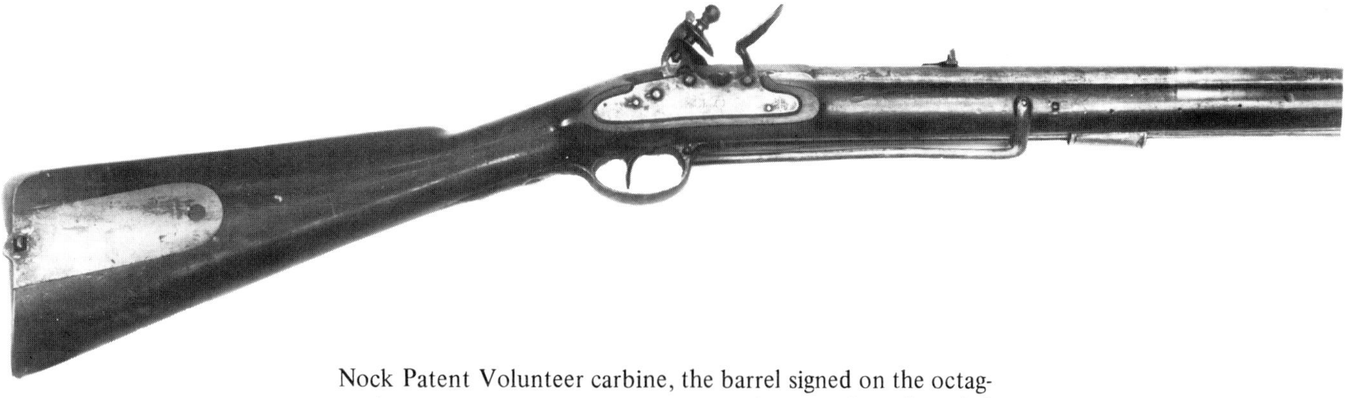

Nock Patent Volunteer carbine, the barrel signed on the octagonal breech H. Nock, with signed enclosed lock, walnut full stock and brass mounts. Good condition. 42½in. Circa 1796.
Sotheby's

£350 – £450

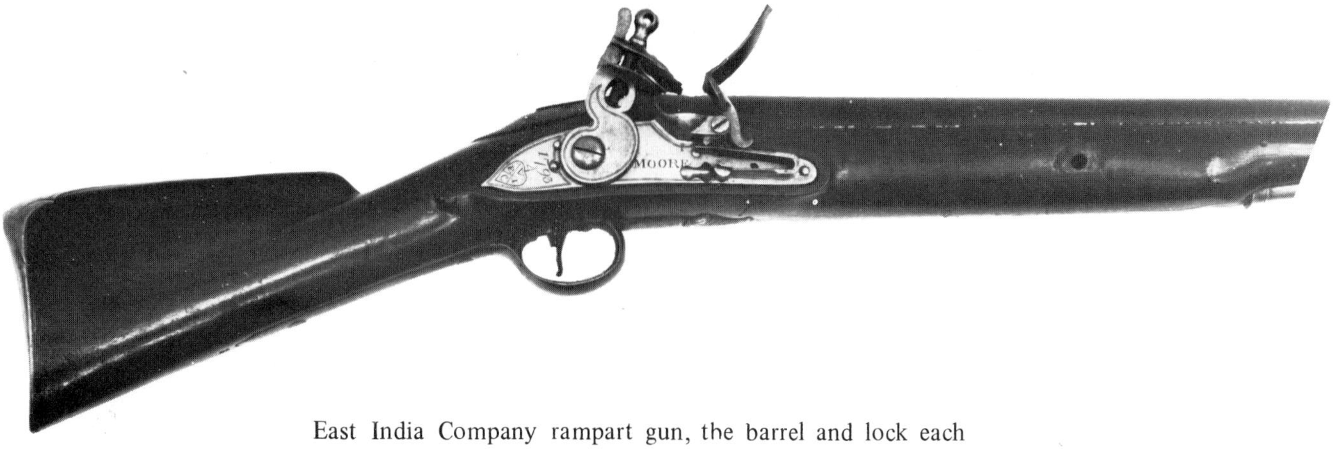

East India Company rampart gun, the barrel and lock each bearing the company mark, the maker's name and the date 1793, with full stock and brass mounts. Good condition. 54in. barrel.
Wallis & Wallis

£400 – £500

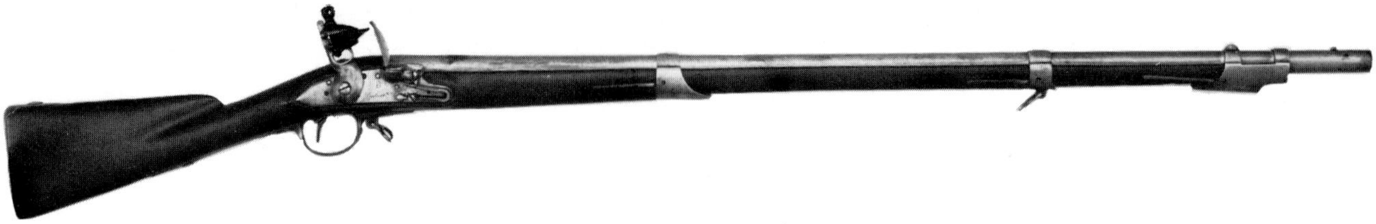

French 1774 model musket engraved M. 1774 on the breech strap and Charleville on the lock, the barrel retained by steel barrel bands. Good condition, but ramrod missing. 38½in. barrel. *Tower of London*

Over £200

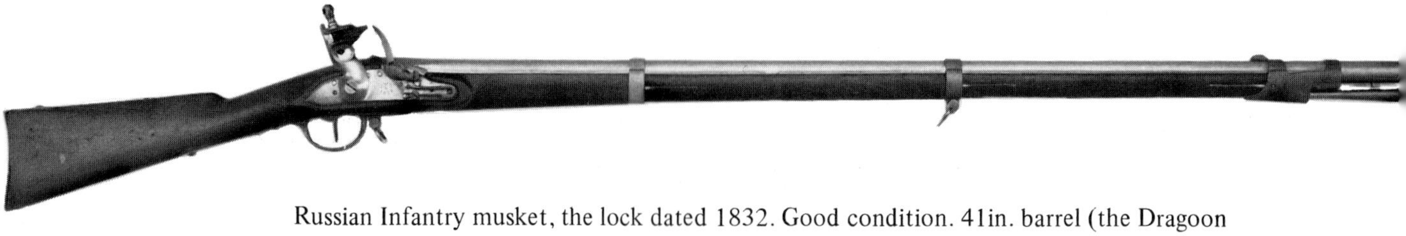

Russian Infantry musket, the lock dated 1832. Good condition. 41in. barrel (the Dragoon model has a 37in. barrel). *Tower of London*

Over £100

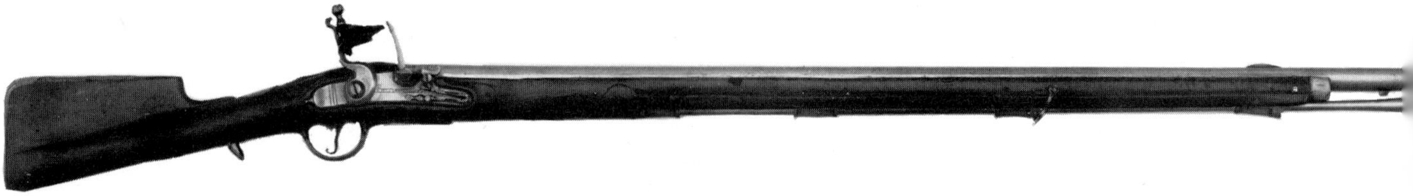

Prussian Infantry musket, the lock marked ´Potzdammagaz´ with full stock and brass mounts, the butt with high comb. Good condition. Late 18th century. 41in. barrel. *Tower of London*

About £100

French 1814 model Royal Body Guard musket, the blued and gilt barrel inscribed "Gardes du Corps du Roi" and with the French Royal Arms on the breech, the lock fitted with brass pan and revolving cover and signed "St. Etienne M. fre Royale", walnut full stock and brass mounts with fleur-de-lys finials. Fine quality, good condition. 40½in. barrel. *Christie's*

£700 – £1,000

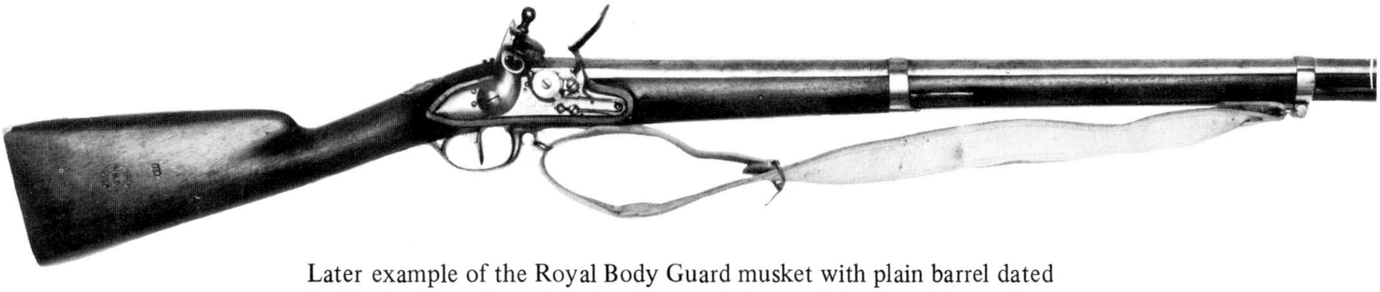

Later example of the Royal Body Guard musket with plain barrel dated 1817, the escutcheon bearing the inscription and the Royal Arms. Fine quality, good condition. 45½in. barrel. *Sotheby's*

£400 – £500

German flintlock grenade launcher, the bronze barrel with raised bands, one decorated with running foliage, the stock with bronze mounts including scrolling dragonesque side-plate. Good quality and condition. Circa 1740. 26in., 3in. calibre. *Christie's*

About £1,500

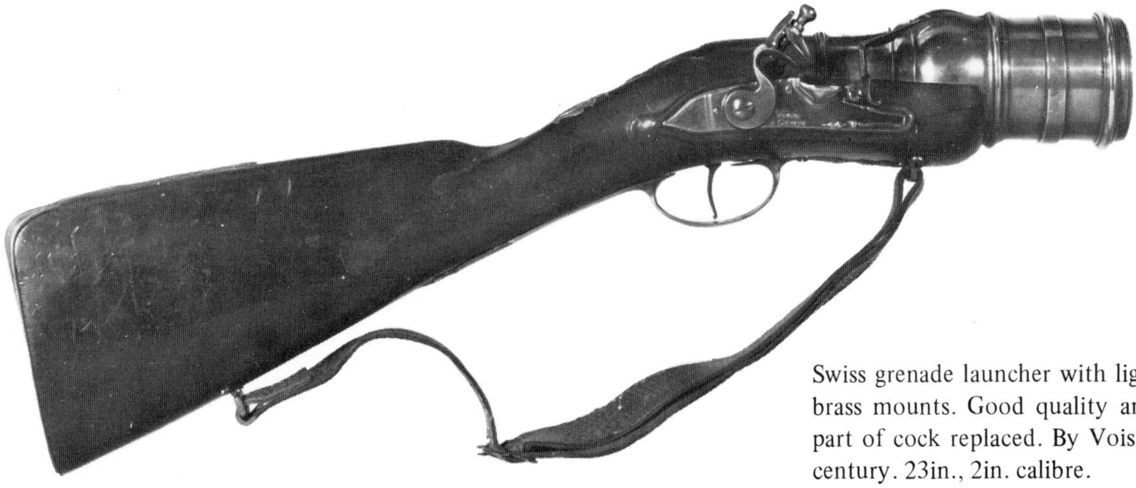

Swiss grenade launcher with lightly carved stock and brass mounts. Good quality and condition, but top part of cock replaced. By Voisin à Genève, mid-18th century. 23in., 2in. calibre. *Christie's*

About £1,000

Percussion Cap Military Long Guns

1851 Pattern or Minié rifle with side-action lock, full stock and brass mounts, the barrel with leaf sight, the lock marked Tower with VR crowned and date 1853. Good condition. 39in. barrel. *Tower of London*

£120 – £140

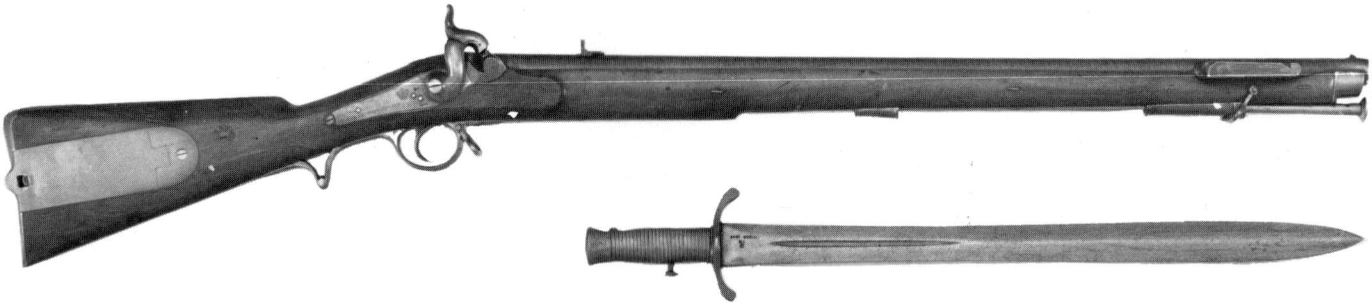

Brunswick back-action percussion rifle with browned twist barrel, full stock, brass mounts including large patch-box, steel ramrod and bayonet bar with slot, complete with bayonet. The lock with VR crowned, Enfield, and the date 1844. Good condition. 30in. barrel. *Tower of London*

£120 – £180

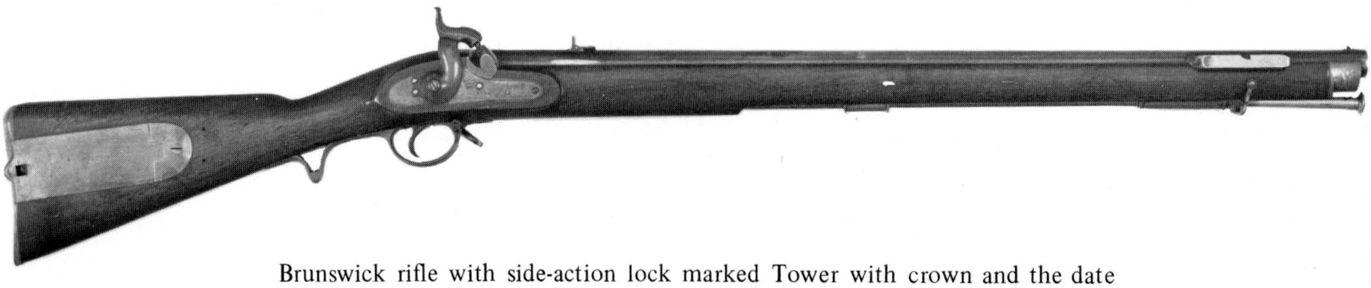

Brunswick rifle with side-action lock marked Tower with crown and the date 1847, the barrel with improved bayonet bar (notch half-way along the bar). Good condition. 30in. barrel. *Tower of London*

About £150

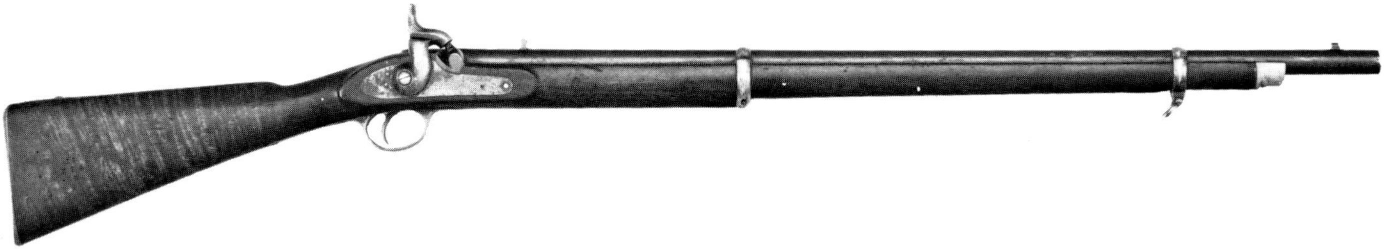

Enfield two-band musket (for Indian Artillery), the lock marked Enfield with crown and the date 1868. Good condition but the ramrod missing. 33in. barrel.
Tower of London

£80 – £100

Down to less than half this price for an Indian copy or an Indian assembled and re-stocked example.

Enfield three-band musket (for India), the lock marked as above with the date 1858. Good condition. 39in. barrel. *Tower of London*

£100 – £140

The same applies as above for Indian examples.

Snider 3-band rifle (probably Volunteer), the barrel with London proof marks, engraved lock. Fine condition. Circa 1865. 35½in. barrel. *Tower of London*

£50 – £80

Most Snider-action rifles and carbines are in moderate condition and therefore worth under £50.

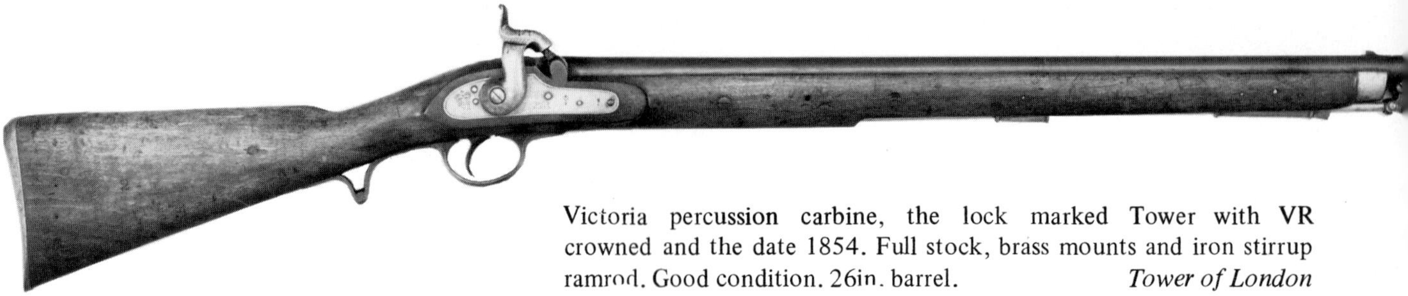

Victoria percussion carbine, the lock marked Tower with VR crowned and the date 1854. Full stock, brass mounts and iron stirrup ramrod. Good condition. 26in. barrel. *Tower of London*

£60 – £80

This one is the Heavy Cavalry 1842 model, distinguished by the pins (rather than bolts) which secure the barrel. Indian or Indianised examples half this figure.

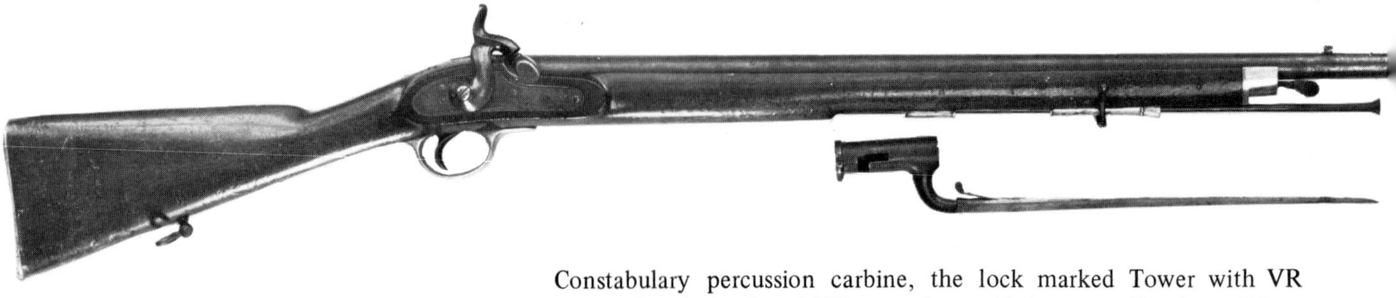

Constabulary percussion carbine, the lock marked Tower with VR crowned and the date 1855, complete with bayonet. Good condition. 26½in. barrel. *Wallis & Wallis*

Over £100

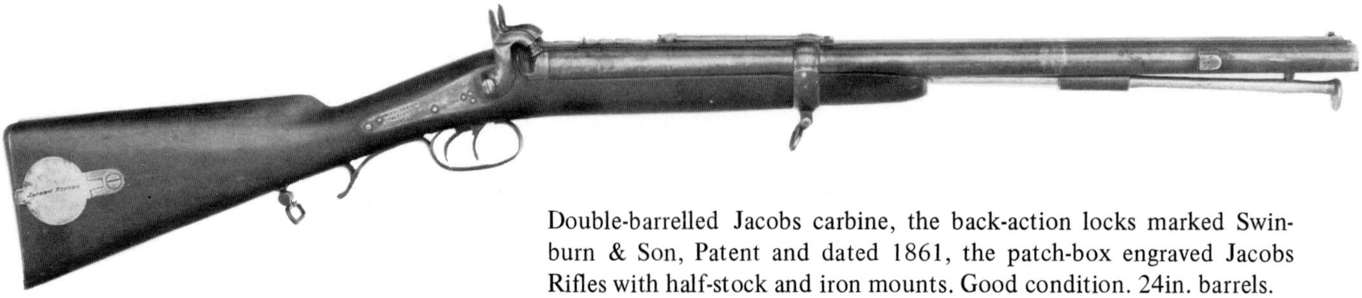

Double-barrelled Jacobs carbine, the back-action locks marked Swinburn & Son, Patent and dated 1861, the patch-box engraved Jacobs Rifles with half-stock and iron mounts. Good condition. 24in. barrels. *Tower of London*

£250 – £300

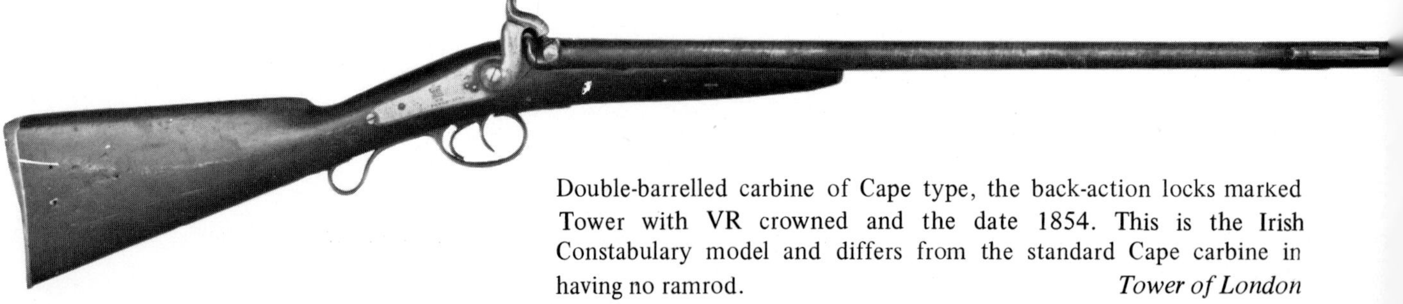

Double-barrelled carbine of Cape type, the back-action locks marked Tower with VR crowned and the date 1854. This is the Irish Constabulary model and differs from the standard Cape carbine in having no ramrod. *Tower of London*

£120 – £180

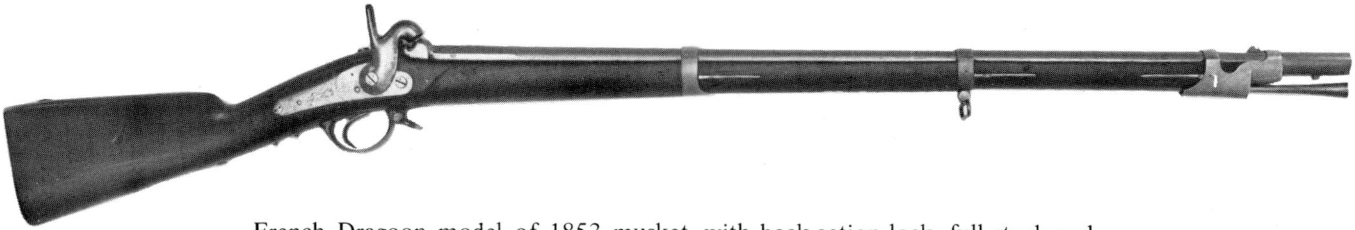

French Dragoon model of 1853 musket, with back-action lock, full stock and brass mounts. Good condition. 36in. barrel. *Tower of London*

£60 – £80

Russian Infantry musket, converted from flintlock, with full stock and brass mounts. Moderate condition. 41in. barrel. *Tower of London*

£30 – £50. For an original percussion example, £60 – £80.

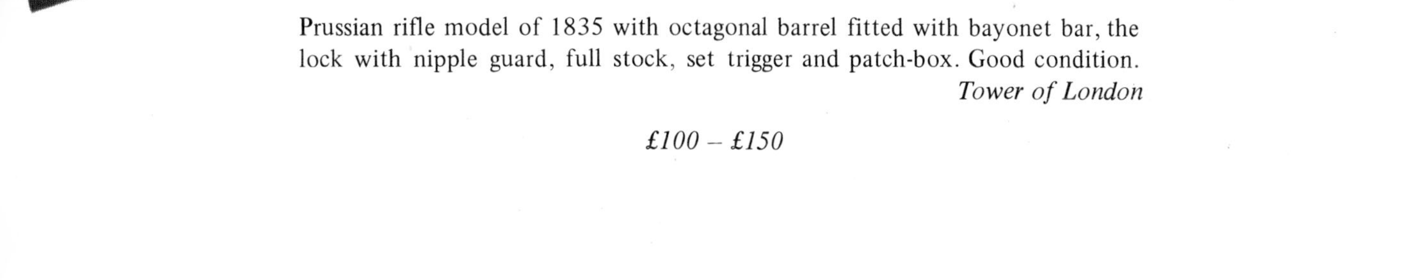

Prussian rifle model of 1835 with octagonal barrel fitted with bayonet bar, the lock with nipple guard, full stock, set trigger and patch-box. Good condition. *Tower of London*

£100 – £150

American Long Guns

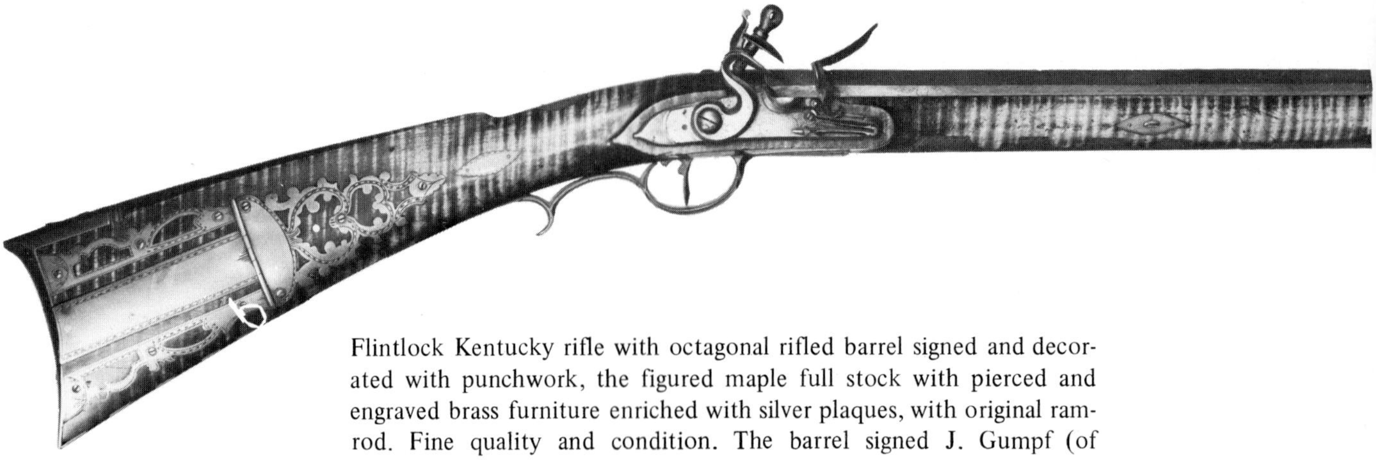

Flintlock Kentucky rifle with octagonal rifled barrel signed and decorated with punchwork, the figured maple full stock with pierced and engraved brass furniture enriched with silver plaques, with original ramrod. Fine quality and condition. The barrel signed J. Gumpf (of Lancaster, Pa.), early 19th century. 43in. barrel. *Christie's*

Over £1,000

More for a similar rifle with original browning on the barrel and a good number of silver inlays or carved patterns in the stock (15 to 20).

When pricing Kentucky rifles make sure that they have not been converted back from percussion. These rifles had hard use and many were converted around 1840. The lock mechanisms are rarely of fine quality. Many are moderate to poor English export mechanisms. Most Kentuckys are unsigned on either barrel or lock. Signatures add greatly to the value. Kentucky rifles are a highly specialised field.

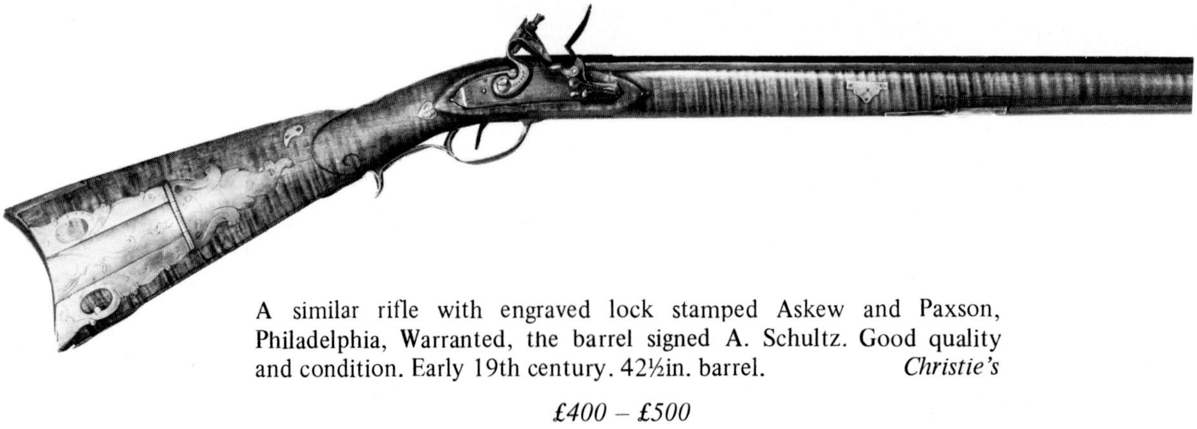

A similar rifle with engraved lock stamped Askew and Paxson, Philadelphia, Warranted, the barrel signed A. Schultz. Good quality and condition. Early 19th century. 42½in. barrel. *Christie's*

£400 – £500

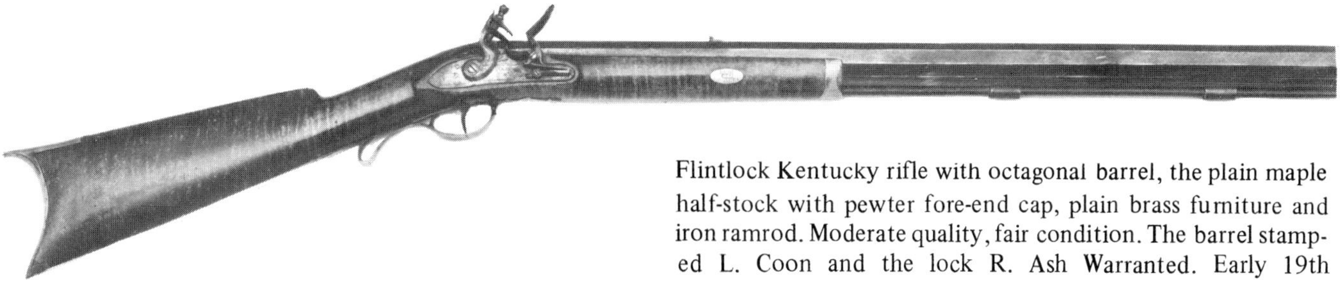

Flintlock Kentucky rifle with octagonal barrel, the plain maple half-stock with pewter fore-end cap, plain brass furniture and iron ramrod. Moderate quality, fair condition. The barrel stamped L. Coon and the lock R. Ash Warranted. Early 19th century. *Christie's*

About £250

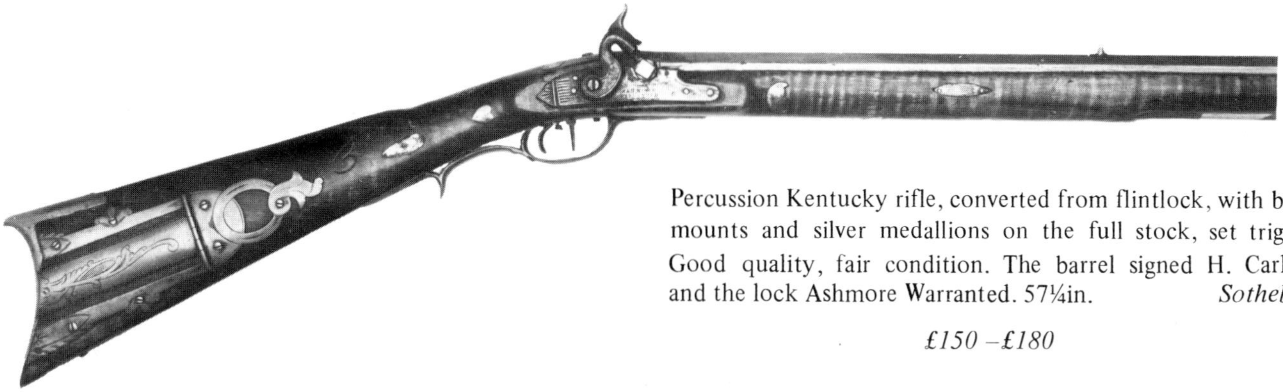

Percussion Kentucky rifle, converted from flintlock, with brass mounts and silver medallions on the full stock, set trigger. Good quality, fair condition. The barrel signed H. Carlisle and the lock Ashmore Warranted. 57¼in. *Sotheby's*

£150 – £180

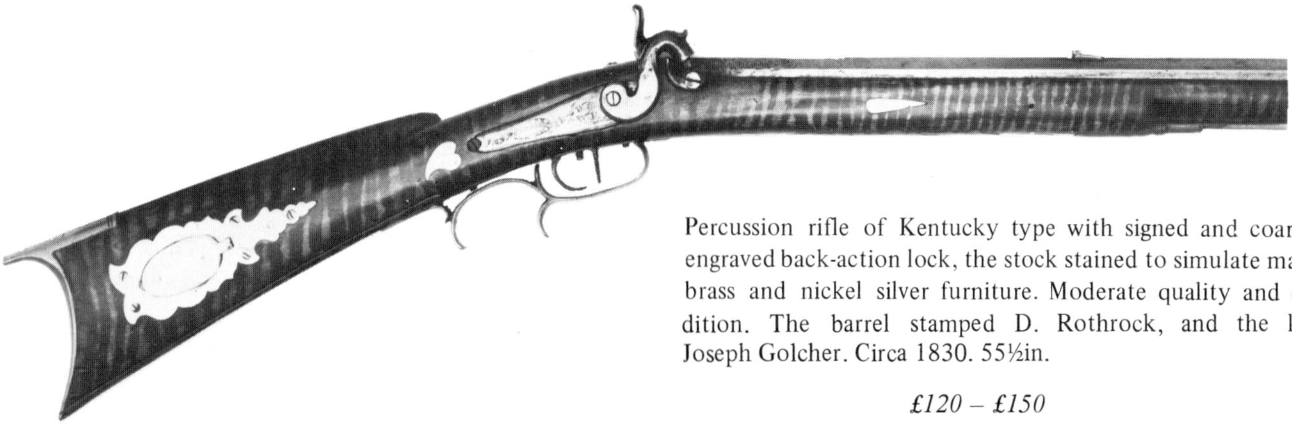

Percussion rifle of Kentucky type with signed and coarsely engraved back-action lock, the stock stained to simulate maple, brass and nickel silver furniture. Moderate quality and condition. The barrel stamped D. Rothrock, and the lock Joseph Golcher. Circa 1830. 55½in.

£120 – £150

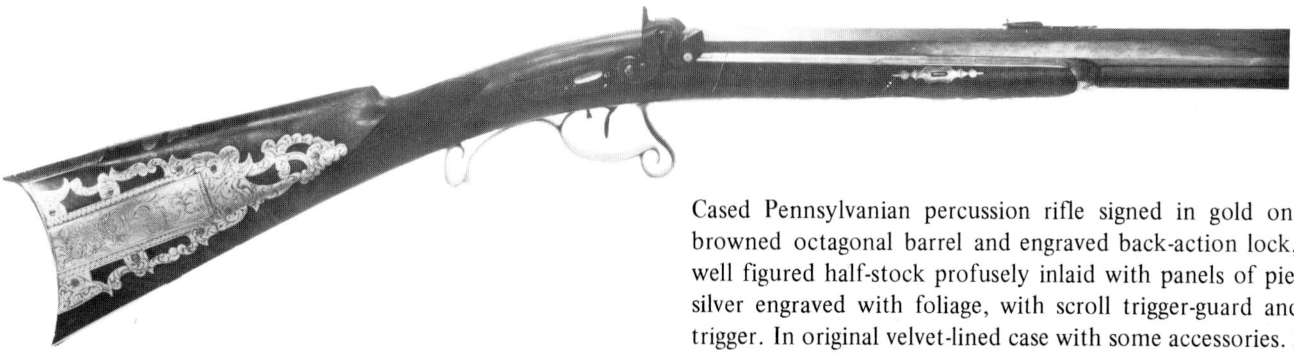

Cased Pennsylvanian percussion rifle signed in gold on the browned octagonal barrel and engraved back-action lock, the well figured half-stock profusely inlaid with panels of pierced silver engraved with foliage, with scroll trigger-guard and set trigger. In original velvet-lined case with some accessories. Fine quality and condition. By Tryon, Philadelphia, circa 1830/40. *Sotheby's*

Over £2,000

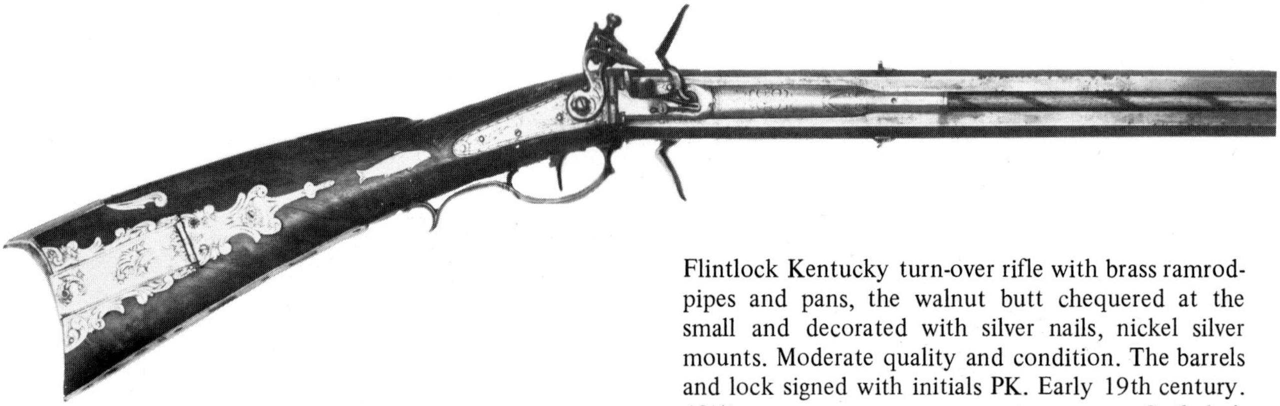

Flintlock Kentucky turn-over rifle with brass ramrod-pipes and pans, the walnut butt chequered at the small and decorated with silver nails, nickel silver mounts. Moderate quality and condition. The barrels and lock signed with initials PK. Early 19th century. 48½in. *Sotheby's*

£400 – £600

A really fine one is worth several thousand pounds.

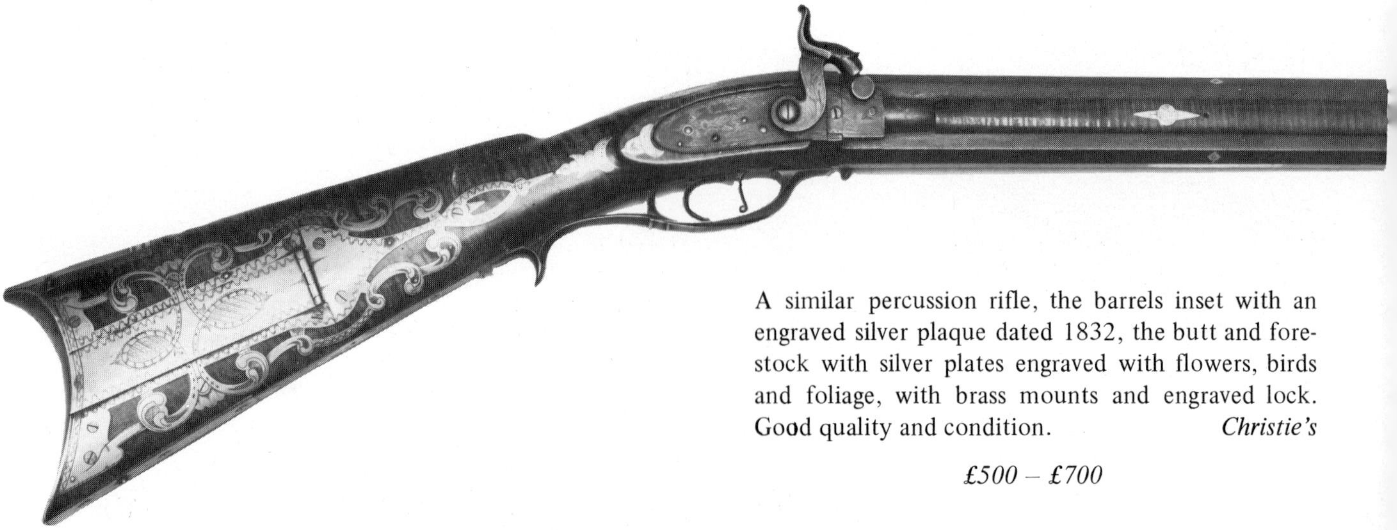

A similar percussion rifle, the barrels inset with an engraved silver plaque dated 1832, the butt and fore-stock with silver plates engraved with flowers, birds and foliage, with brass mounts and engraved lock. Good quality and condition. *Christie's*

£500 – £700

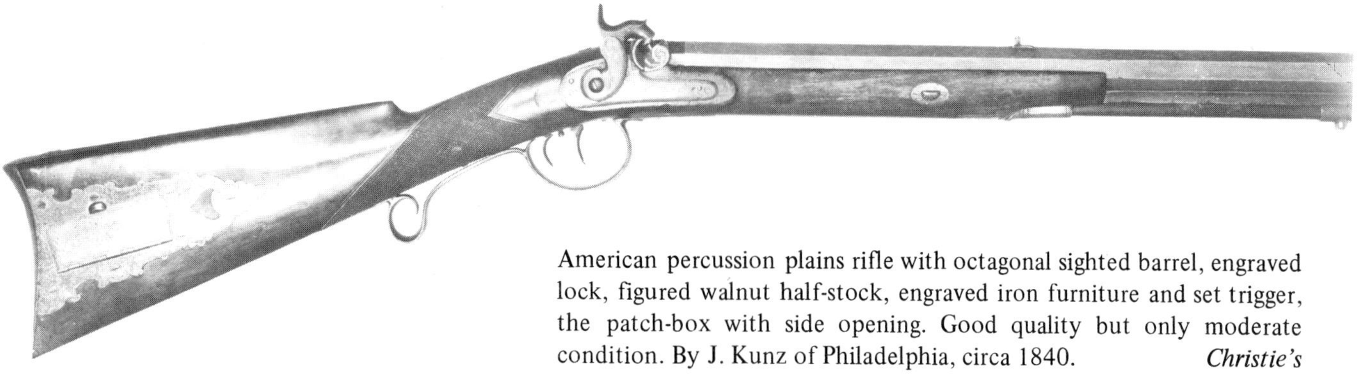

American percussion plains rifle with octagonal sighted barrel, engraved lock, figured walnut half-stock, engraved iron furniture and set trigger, the patch-box with side opening. Good quality but only moderate condition. By J. Kunz of Philadelphia, circa 1840. *Christie's*

£200 – £300

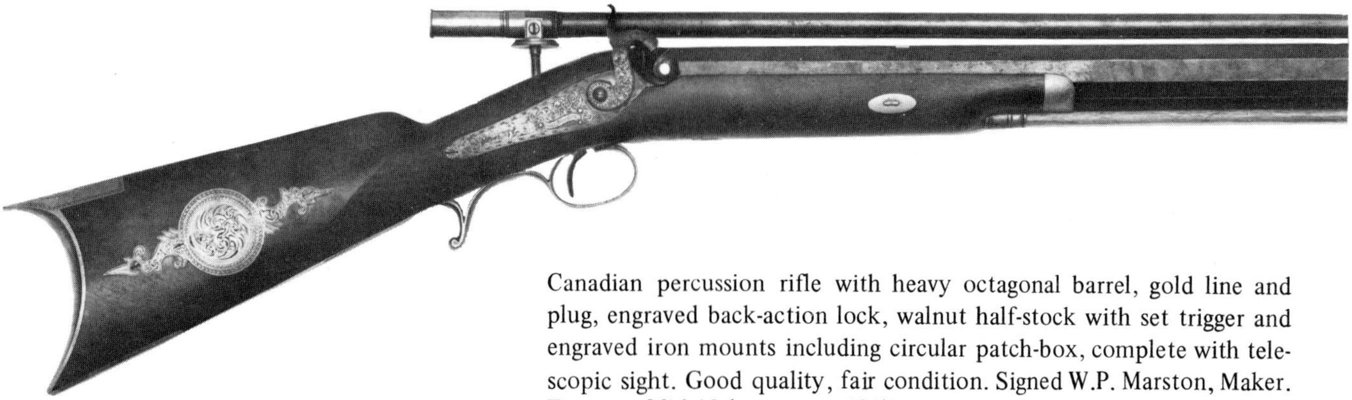

Canadian percussion rifle with heavy octagonal barrel, gold line and plug, engraved back-action lock, walnut half-stock with set trigger and engraved iron mounts including circular patch-box, complete with telescopic sight. Good quality, fair condition. Signed W.P. Marston, Maker. Toronto. Mid-19th century. 48½in. *Sotheby's*

£400 – £500

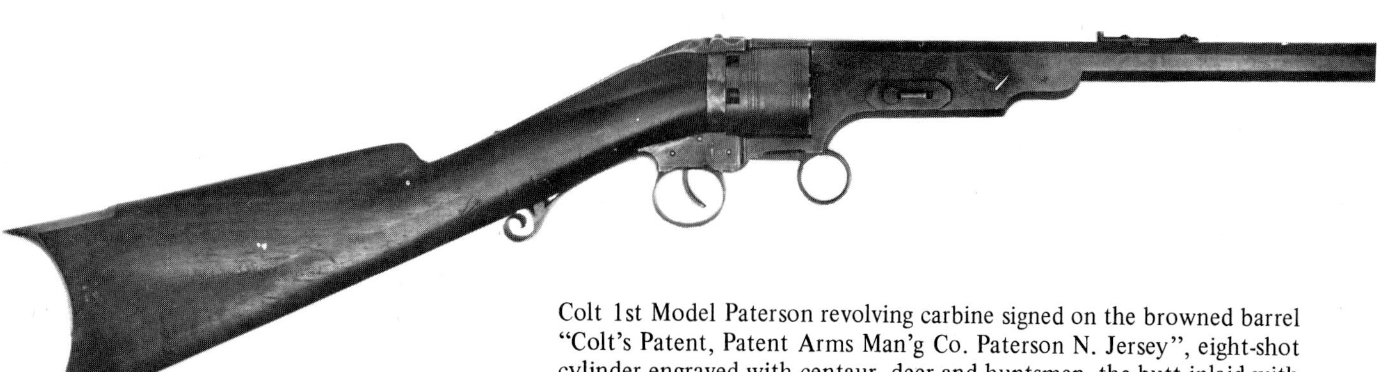

Colt 1st Model Paterson revolving carbine signed on the browned barrel "Colt's Patent, Patent Arms Man'g Co. Paterson N. Jersey", eight-shot cylinder engraved with centaur, deer and huntsmen, the butt inlaid with four horse-head emblems in silver. Excellent condition. *Sotheby's*

Over £2,000 owing to condition.

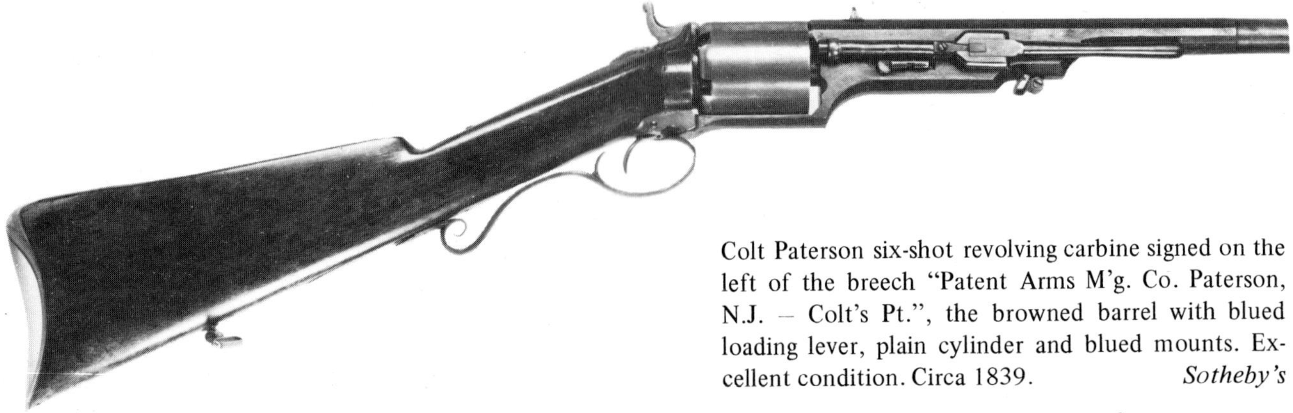

Colt Paterson six-shot revolving carbine signed on the left of the breech "Patent Arms M'g. Co. Paterson, N.J. – Colt's Pt.", the browned barrel with blued loading lever, plain cylinder and blued mounts. Excellent condition. Circa 1839. *Sotheby's*

Over £1,500 owing to condition.

The same without finish £400 – £500.

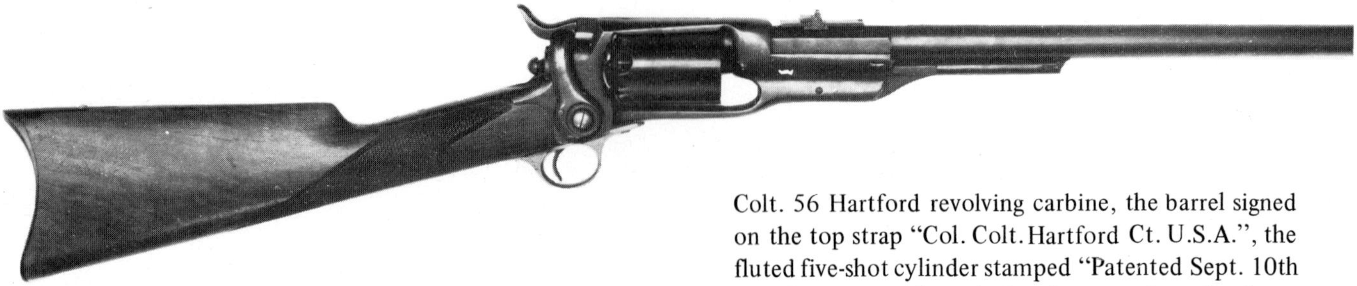

Colt. 56 Hartford revolving carbine, the barrel signed on the top strap "Col. Colt. Hartford Ct. U.S.A.", the fluted five-shot cylinder stamped "Patented Sept. 10th 1850" and struck with London proof marks, brass trigger-guard. Metal refinished, butt an old replacement. 21in. barrel. *Sotheby's*

£200 – £250

For one in fine condition. £400 – £500.

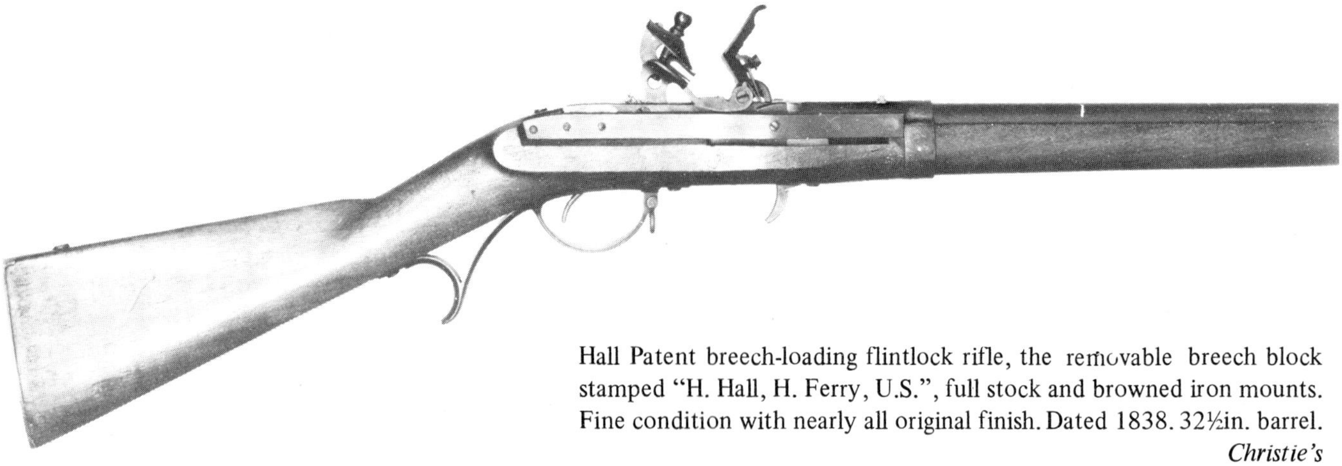

Hall Patent breech-loading flintlock rifle, the removable breech block stamped "H. Hall, H. Ferry, U.S.", full stock and browned iron mounts. Fine condition with nearly all original finish. Dated 1838. 32½in. barrel.
Christie's

£300 – £400

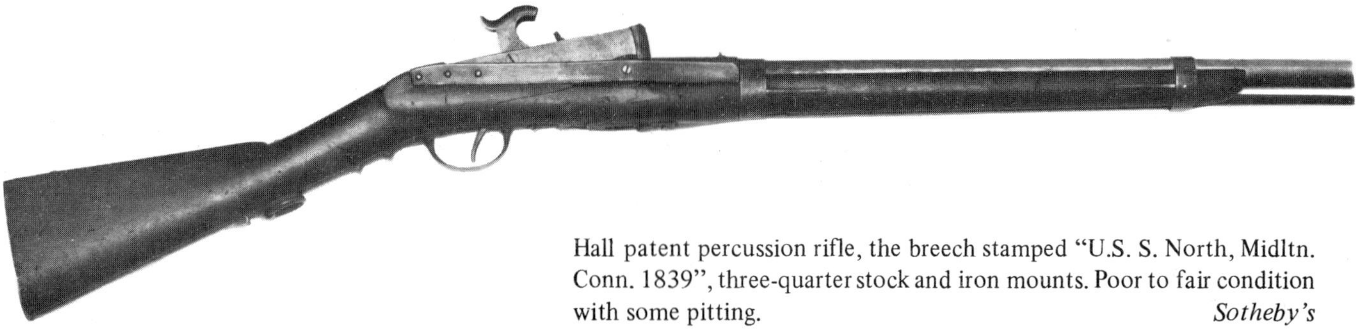

Hall patent percussion rifle, the breech stamped "U.S. S. North, Midltn. Conn. 1839", three-quarter stock and iron mounts. Poor to fair condition with some pitting.
Sotheby's

£100 – £150

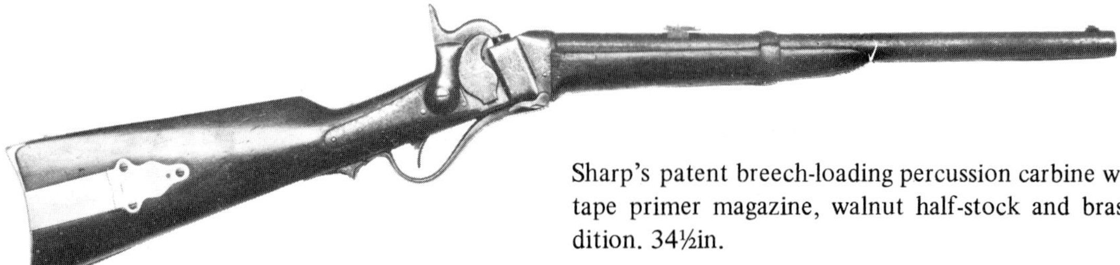

Sharp's patent breech-loading percussion carbine with Maynard's patent tape primer magazine, walnut half-stock and brass mounts. Fair condition. 34½in.
Christie's

About £150

Eastern Long Guns

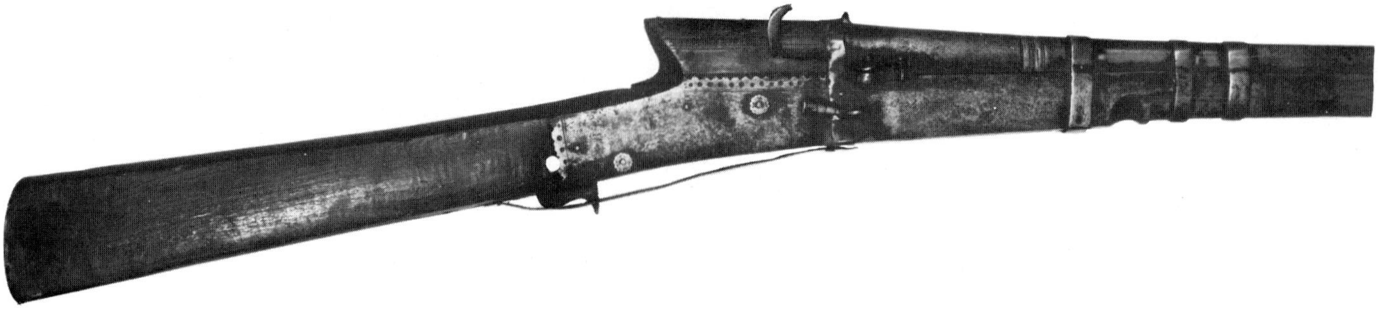

Plain Indian matchlock gun (Toradar) with full stock and iron mounts. Poor quality, fair condition. 19th century. 47in. barrel. *Christie's*

£15 – £20

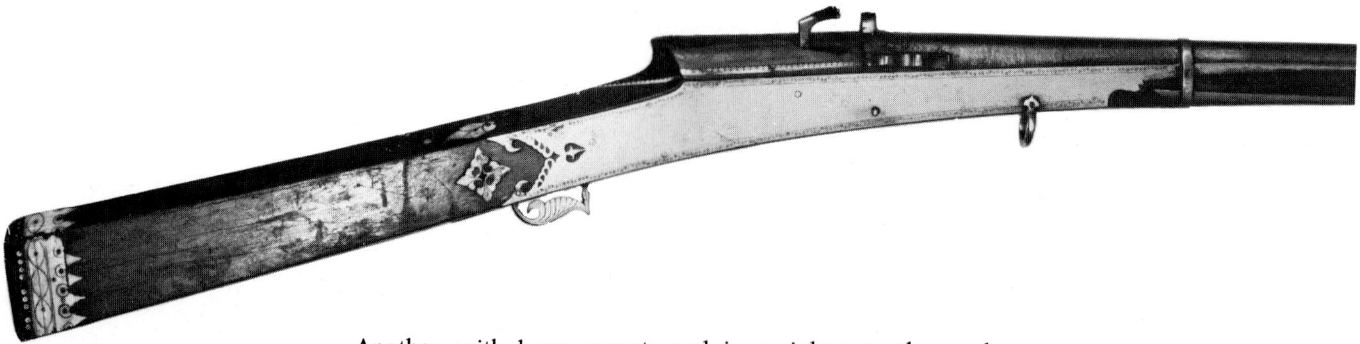

Another, with brass mounts and ivory inlays to the stock. Moderate quality and condition. 19th century. 47½in. barrel.

Christie's

£30 – £60

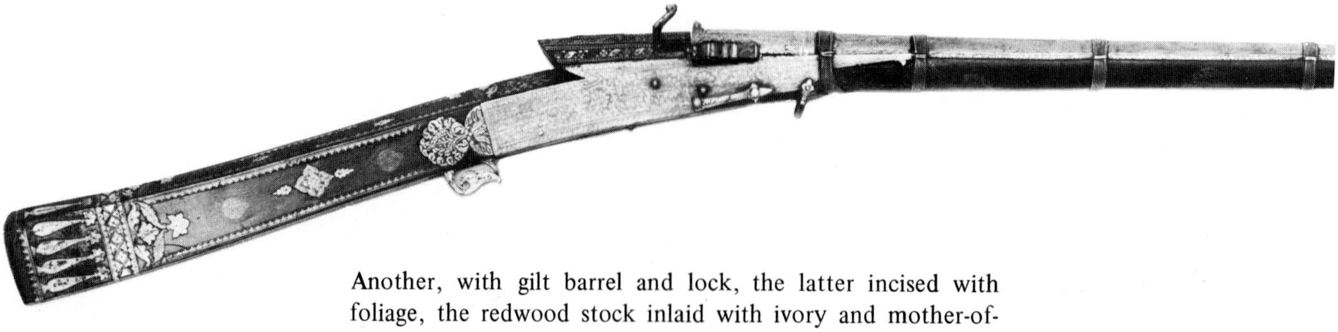

Another, with gilt barrel and lock, the latter incised with foliage, the redwood stock inlaid with ivory and mother-of-pearl, with pierced and gilt trigger, silver wire barrel bands. Good quality and condition. 48¼in. 18th/19th century.

Sotheby's

About £200

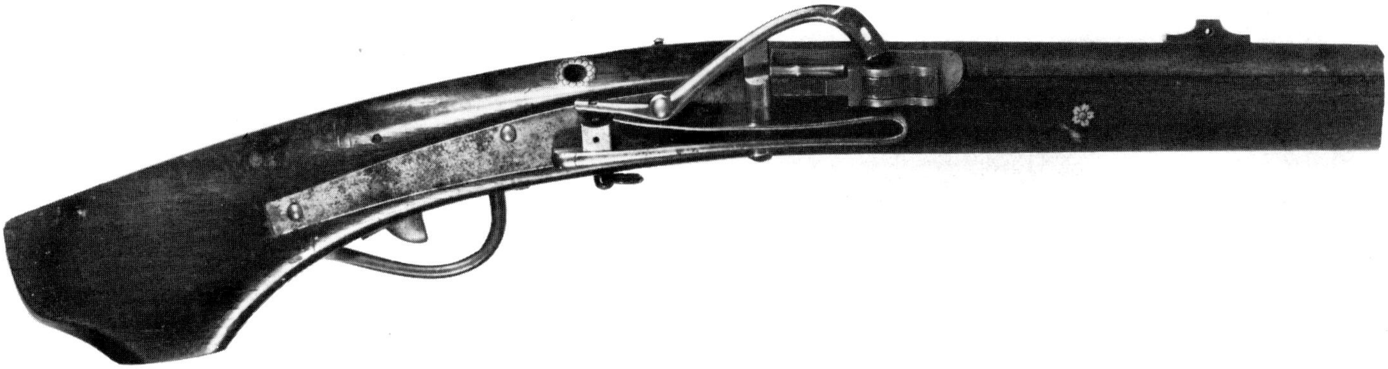

Japanese matchlock gun, the barrel with top flat and moulded octagonal muzzle, with plain lock and stock, brass mounts and rosette insets to the stock. Moderate quality, good condition. 19th century. 39½in. barrel. *Christie's*

About £150

This is a plain one of its type. Better examples have silver and gold decoration on the barrel and lacquered stocks. For these, over £300. The heavy version of this gun (Temple Gun) has a massive barrel quite out of proportion to the stock; these are worth about double.

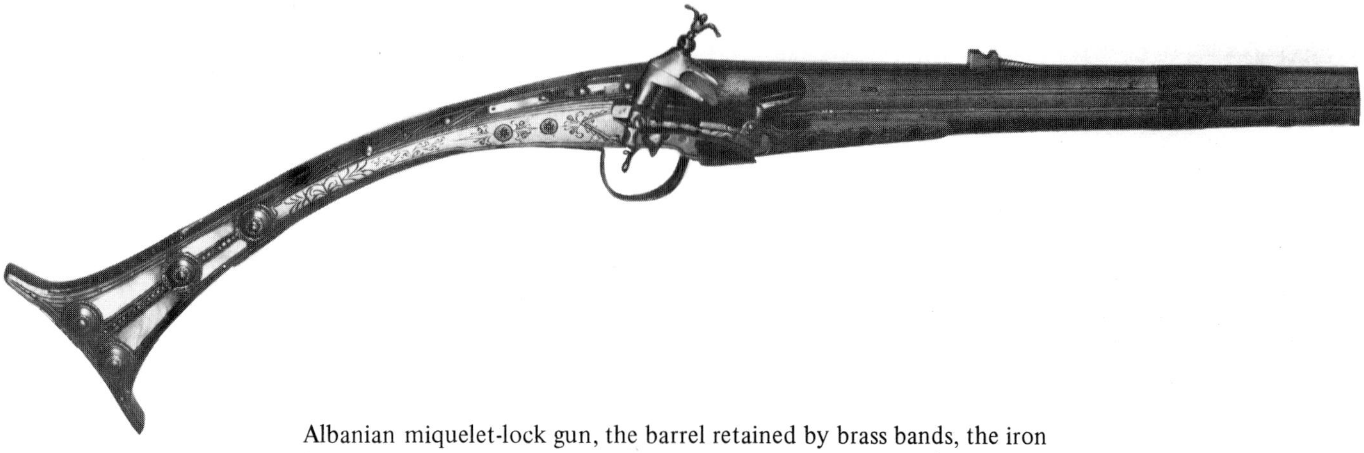

Albanian miquelet-lock gun, the barrel retained by brass bands, the iron full stock engraved with foliage and decorated with panels of brass and mother-of-pearl. Good condition. 19th century. 55in. barrel. This is an above average example. *Christie's*

Over £100

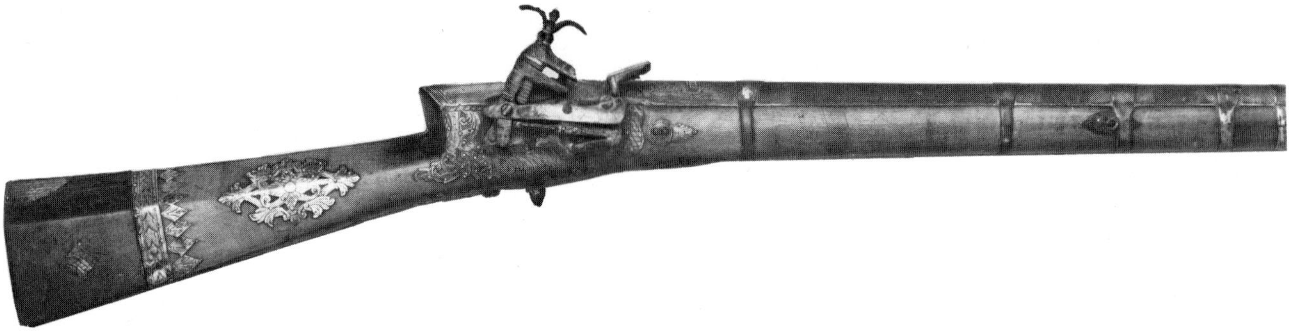

Turkish miquelet-lock rifle with octagonal barrel secured by silver bands, the stock with engraved silver insets. Moderate quality and condition. 19th century. 52in.

Knight, Frank & Rutley

£150 – £200

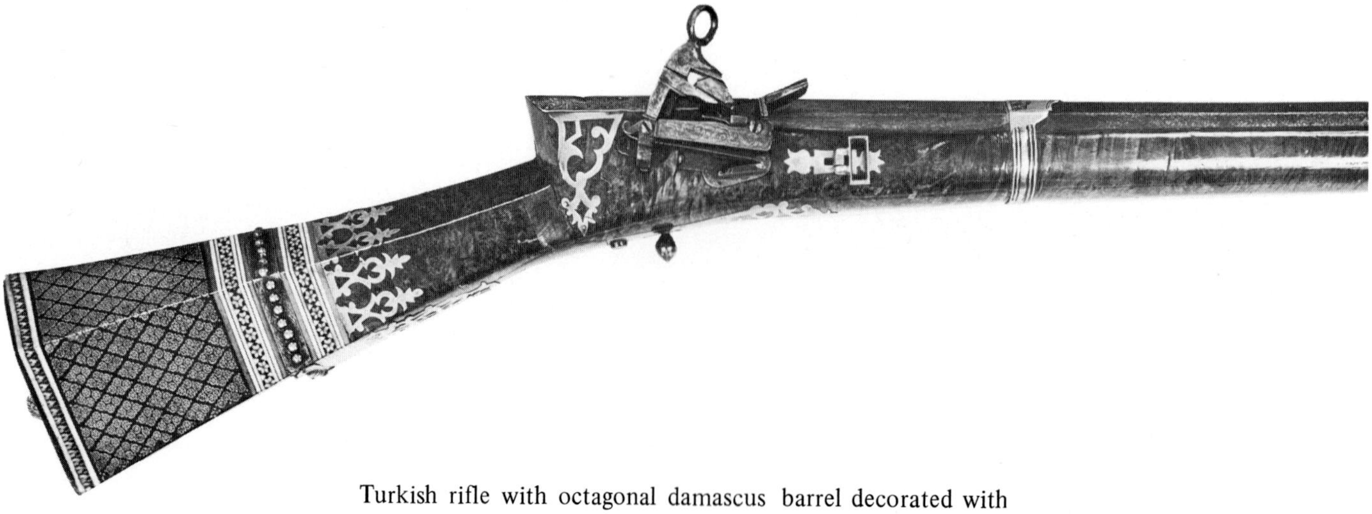

Turkish rifle with octagonal damascus barrel decorated with gilding at the muzzle and breech, the stock with green ivory fore-end tip and inlaid with black, green and white ivory bands and brass nail-heads on the butt. Good quality and condition. Early 19th century. 27in. barrel. *Weller & Dufty*

£200 – £300

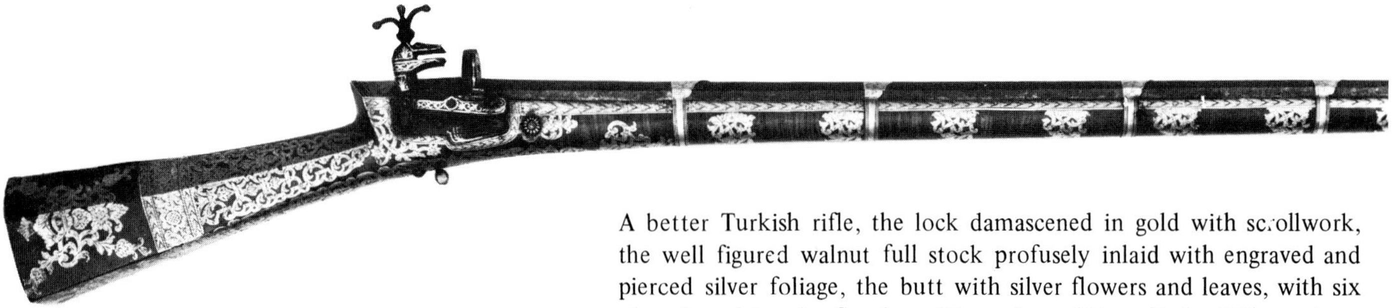

A better Turkish rifle, the lock damascened in gold with scrollwork, the well figured walnut full stock profusely inlaid with engraved and pierced silver foliage, the butt with silver flowers and leaves, with six silver barrel bands. Good quality and condition. Early 19th century. 58in. *Sotheby's*

£400 – £500

Rare Turkish wall gun with heavy octagonal damascus barrel encrusted with gold decoration at the muzzle and breech and with standing back-sight en suite, the lock also encrusted with gold, the full stock with silver insets and silver barrel bands. Fine quality, good condition. Maker's mark on the lock, stock and barrel. Late 18th century. 39½in. barrel. *Christie's*

Over £1,000

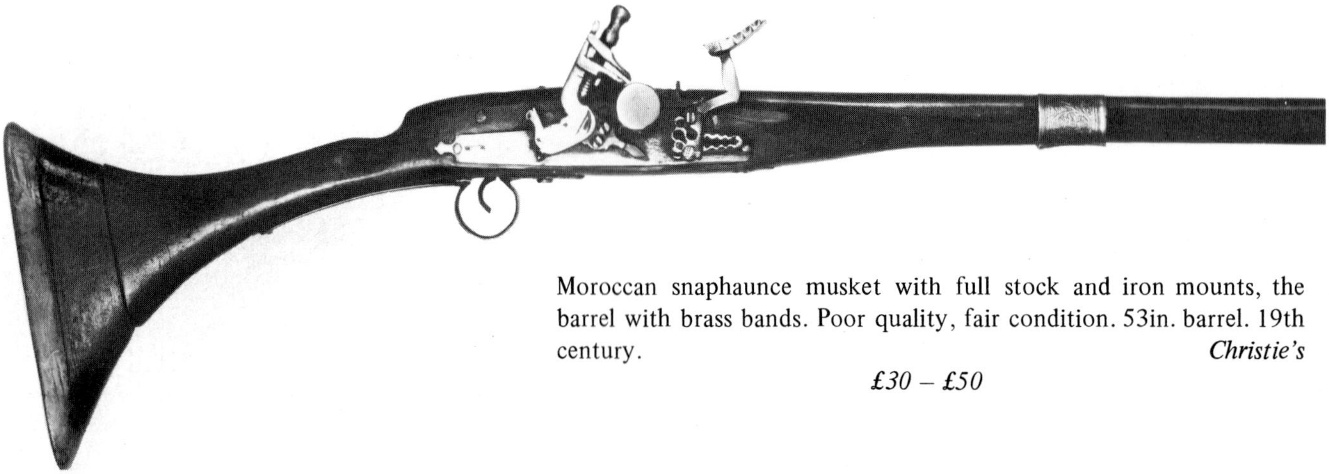

Moroccan snaphaunce musket with full stock and iron mounts, the barrel with brass bands. Poor quality, fair condition. 53in. barrel. 19th century. *Christie's*

£30 – £50

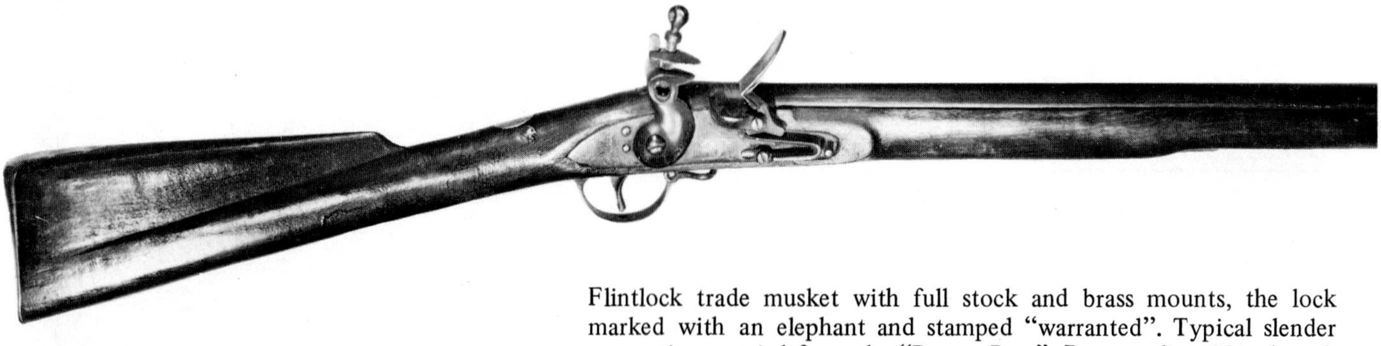

Flintlock trade musket with full stock and brass mounts, the lock marked with an elephant and stamped "warranted". Typical slender proportions copied from the "Brown Bess". Poor quality, 39in. barrel. *Christie's*

£40 – £50

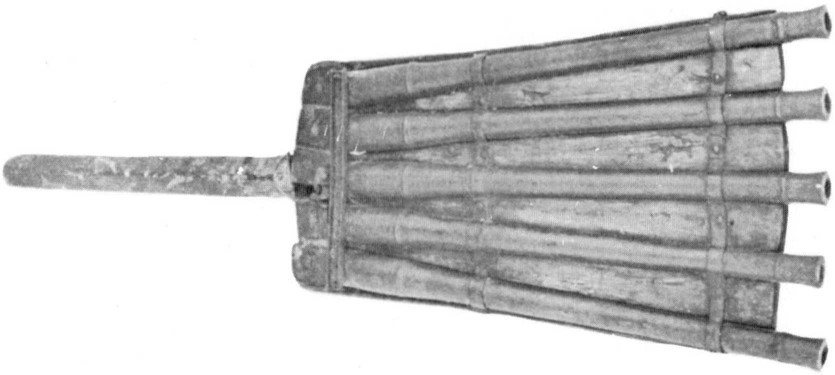

Indian five-barrelled matchlock gun, the horizontally set barrels with open ignition trail at the breech, with red painted stock. 18th century. 36in. *Sotheby's*

Over £300. Rare

Blunderbusses

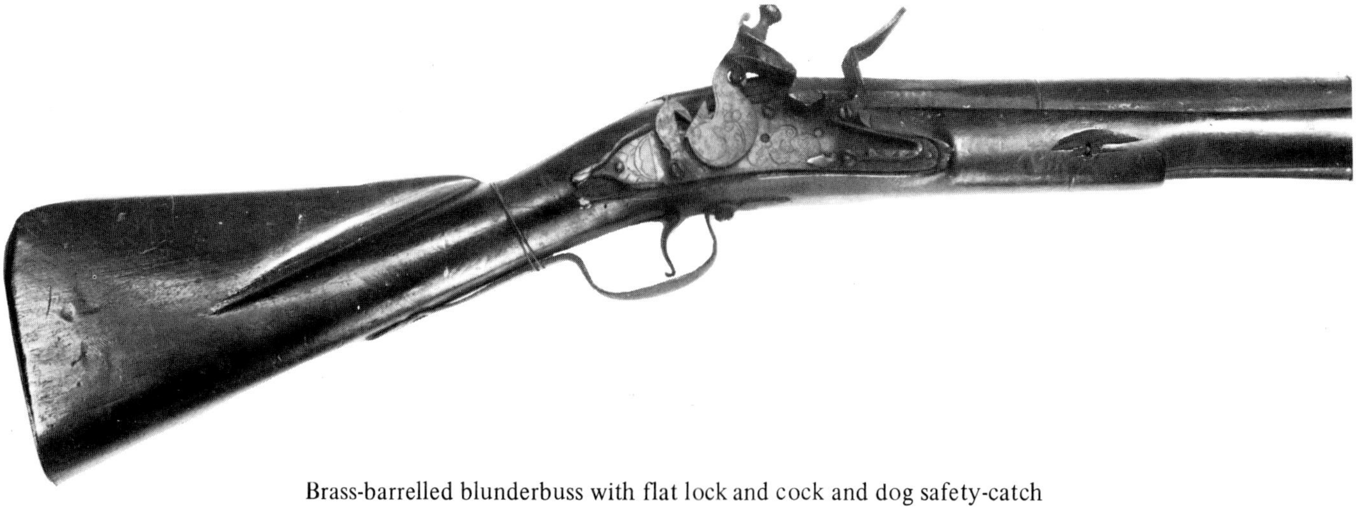

Brass-barrelled blunderbuss with flat lock and cock and dog safety-catch engaging with the back of the cock, the lock retained by three screws, the stock with brass furniture except for the iron trigger-guard. No ramrod tail pipe or side-plate. The barrel with raised flange at the breech cut with a sighting slot. Thin butt-plate secured by tacks. Finely engraved lock with scroll signature. Good quality and condition. By Robert Silke (Master of the London Gunmakers Company 1696-1697), circa 1660. 30½in. *Sotheby's*

£700 – £1,000

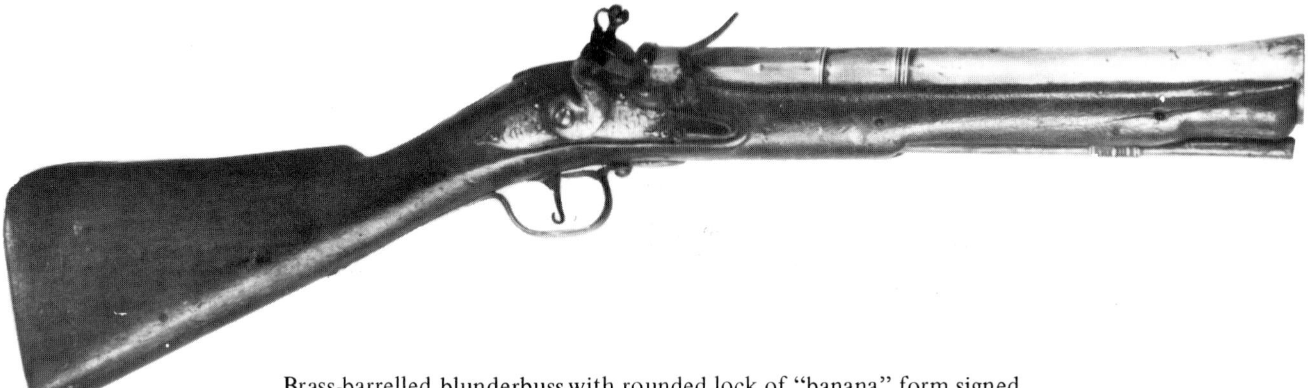

Brass-barrelled blunderbuss with rounded lock of "banana" form signed and engraved with strawberry leaves, beech wood stock with brass furniture including scroll side-plate. No ramrod tail pipe. Raised flange at the breech as above. Good quality and condition. By James Spencer, London proof, circa 1690/1700. *Christie's*

£600 – £700

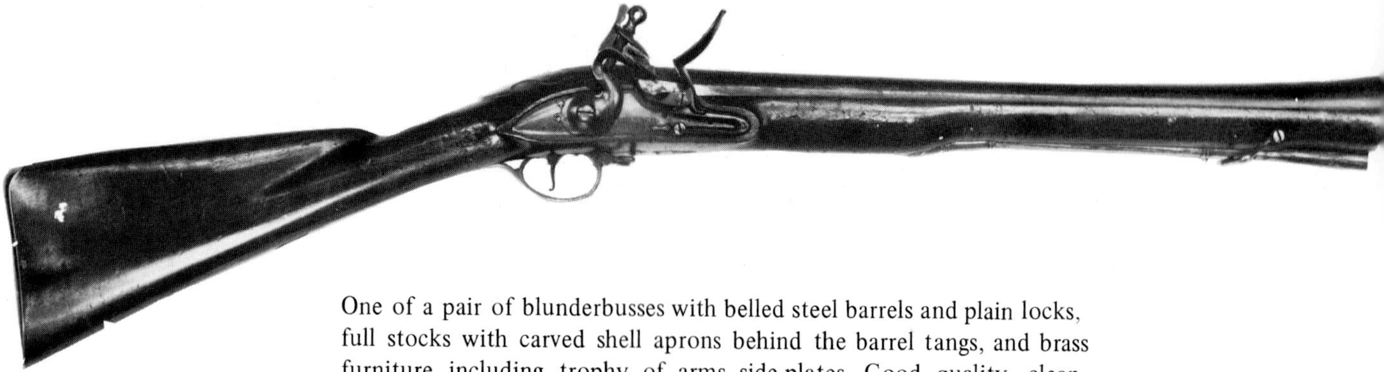

One of a pair of blunderbusses with belled steel barrels and plain locks, full stocks with carved shell aprons behind the barrel tangs, and brass furniture including trophy of arms side-plates. Good quality, clean condition. By Brander, London, circa 1760. 34½in. *Sotheby's*

About £1,000

Pairs of blunderbusses are rare.

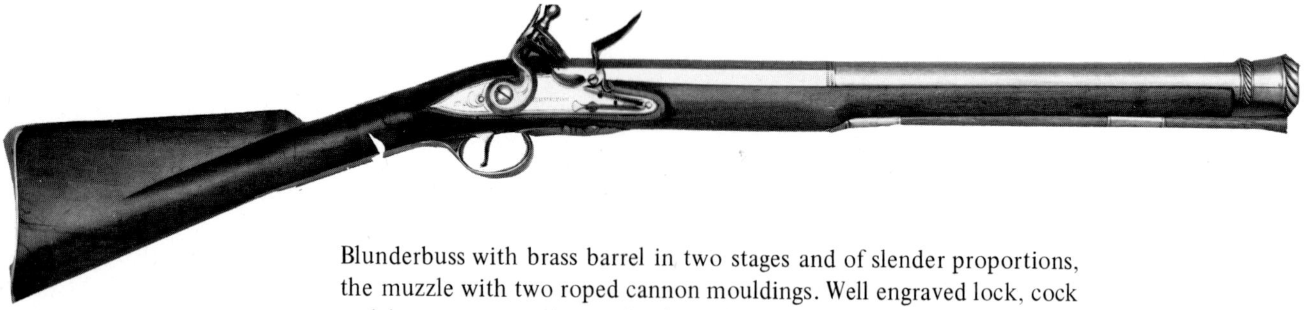

Blunderbuss with brass barrel in two stages and of slender proportions, the muzzle with two roped cannon mouldings. Well engraved lock, cock and brass mounts. Acorn finial to the trigger-guard. Fine quality and condition. By Brueton, London, circa 1780. 19½in. barrel. *Christie's*

£600 – £850

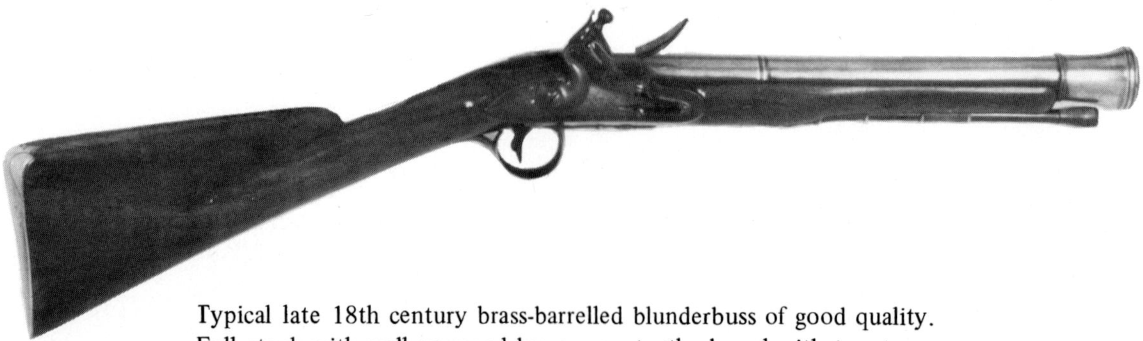

Typical late 18th century brass-barrelled blunderbuss of good quality. Full stock with well engraved brass mounts, the barrel with two turns at the muzzle. Fine condition. By one of the best makers, H.W. Mortimer, London, circa 1790. 29¾in. *Christie's*

£500 – £600

Down to £250 for a blunderbuss of this type by a lesser maker.

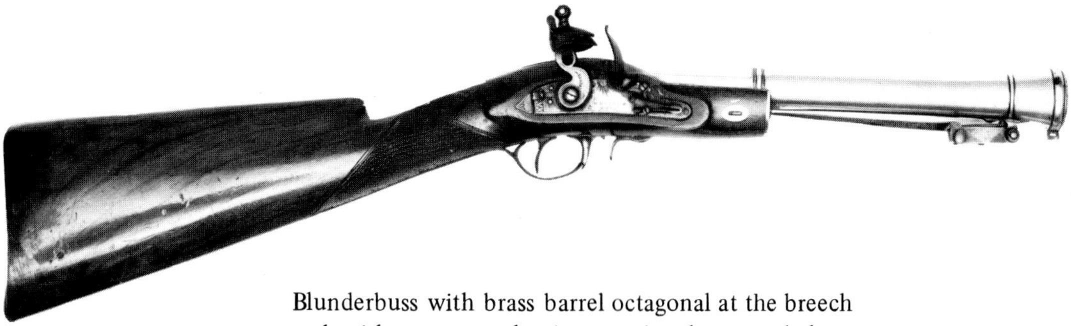

Blunderbuss with brass barrel octagonal at the breech and with two muzzle rings, spring bayonet below, released by a catch forward of the trigger-guard, walnut half-stock with brass mounts. Good quality and condition. Wheeler & Son, Birmingham, early 19th century. 14in. barrel. *Christie's*

£400 – £500

Durs Egg made very similar ones, over £600 in equivalent condition.

Iron-barrelled blunderbuss with lightly engraved blued steel mounts, spring bayonet. Moderate quality, good condition. Birmingham made, early 19th century. 27½in. *Christie's*

£200 – £275

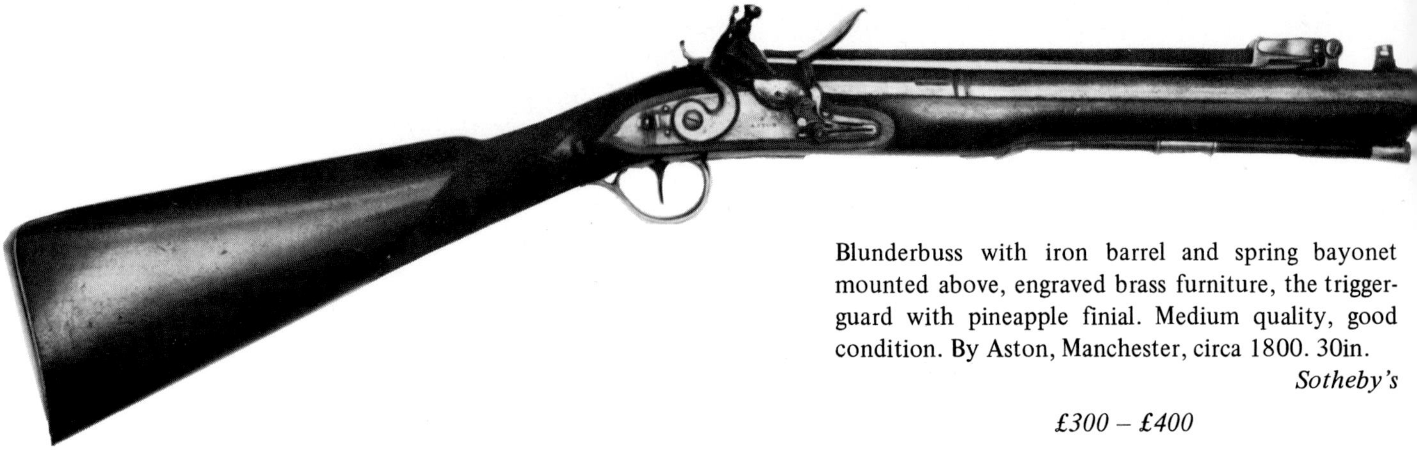

Blunderbuss with iron barrel and spring bayonet mounted above, engraved brass furniture, the trigger-guard with pineapple finial. Medium quality, good condition. By Aston, Manchester, circa 1800. 30in. *Sotheby's*

£300 – £400

For a brass-barrelled example, £400 – £500.

Similar blunderbuss, but engraved around the muzzle "Happy he that escapes me". Fine quality, medium condition, the cock replaced. By H.W. Mortimer, London, circa 1800. 29in. *Christie's*

£500 – £700

A particularly fine one of these recently sold for £1,000. Other inscriptions include "Fly or Die" and "For His Majesty's Mail Coach". These add considerable interest and value, but inscriptions are easily faked.

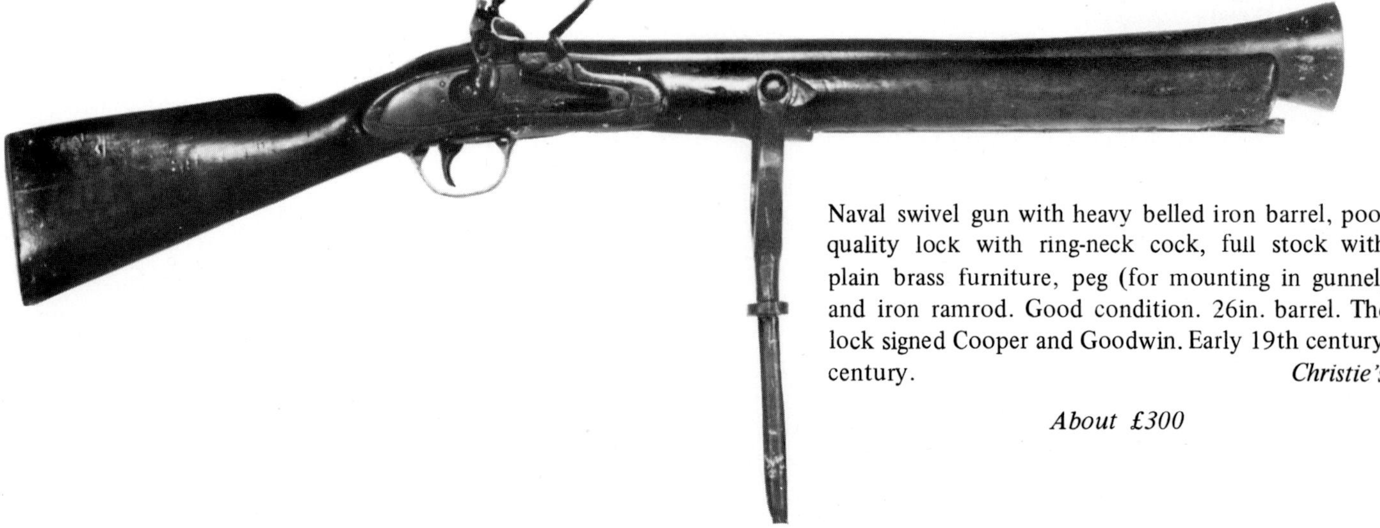

Naval swivel gun with heavy belled iron barrel, poor quality lock with ring-neck cock, full stock with plain brass furniture, peg (for mounting in gunnel) and iron ramrod. Good condition. 26in. barrel. The lock signed Cooper and Goodwin. Early 19th century. century. *Christie's*

About £300

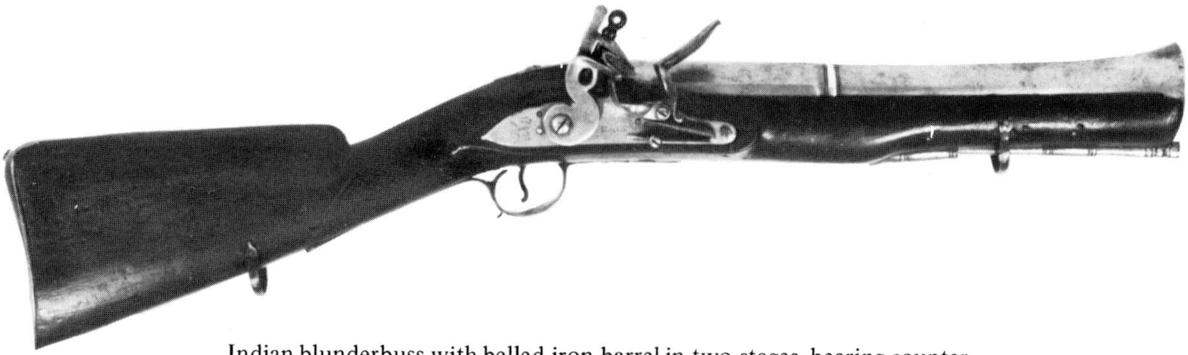

Indian blunderbuss with belled iron barrel in two stages, bearing counterfeit London proof marks, the lock engraved with a spurious signature, a retrospective date and an imitation of the East India Company mark, the stock of typical reddish wood with coarsely engraved brass mounts. Some have new stocks fitted to replace badly wormed ones. Poor quality, fair condition. Early 19th century or later. 25in. *Christie's*

£80 – £100

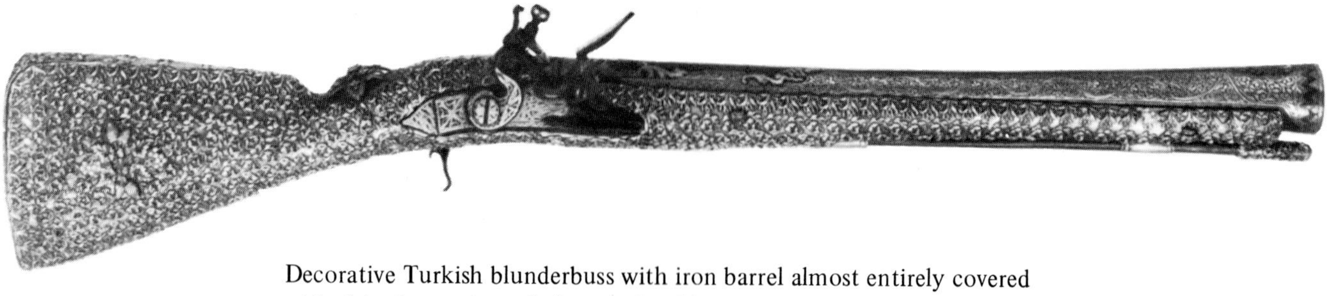

Decorative Turkish blunderbuss with iron barrel almost entirely covered with thin decoration of silver and gold damascene, the lock also decorated with gold, the stock entirely encased in silver, gilt and embellished with flowers and foliage in relief. A highly ornate piece (probably for presentation) but of no great quality. Good condition. Unsigned. Early 19th century or later. 28½in. *Christie's*

About £800

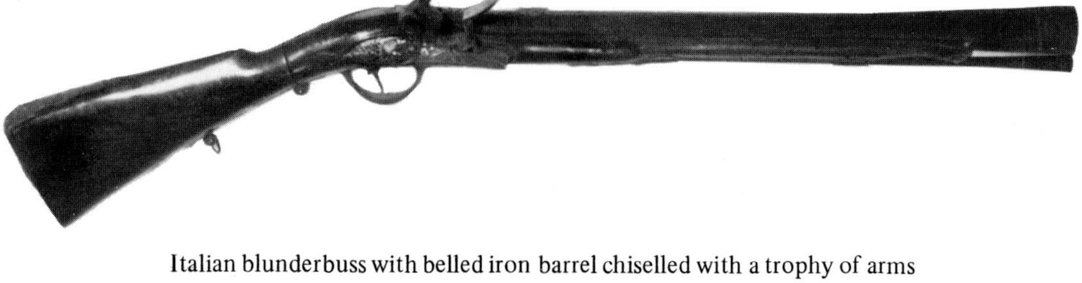

Italian blunderbuss with belled iron barrel chiselled with a trophy of arms at the breech, the lock chiselled with further trophies, the walnut full stock with folding butt and chiselled steel mounts and partly inlaid with silver scrollwork. Iron belt hook and ramrod. Good quality and good untouched condition. Signed P. Martinoni. Late 18th century. 34½in. *Christie's*

£500 – £800

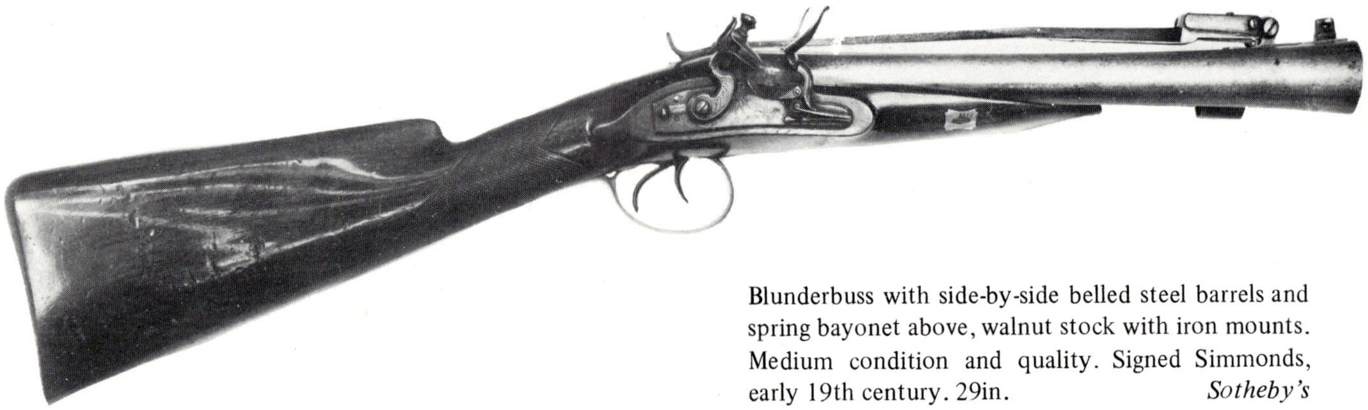

Blunderbuss with side-by-side belled steel barrels and spring bayonet above, walnut stock with iron mounts. Medium condition and quality. Signed Simmonds, early 19th century. 29in. *Sotheby's*

£700 – £900

Over £1,000 with brass barrels.

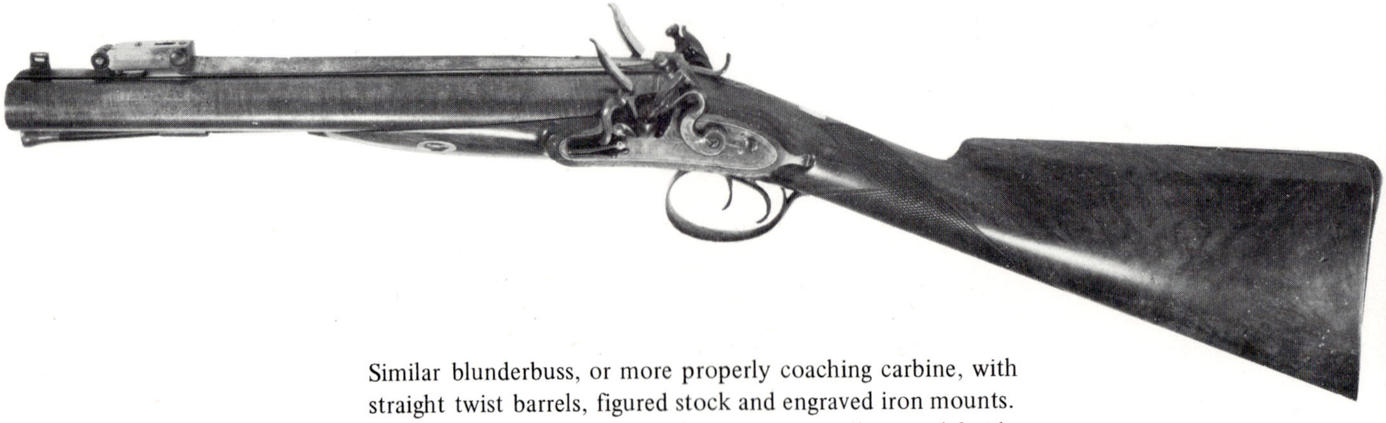

Similar blunderbuss, or more properly coaching carbine, with straight twist barrels, figured stock and engraved iron mounts. Fine quality, very clean condition and nearly all original finish. By Westley Richards, Birmingham, early 19th century. 14½in. barrels. *Christie's*

Over £1,000

Air Weapons

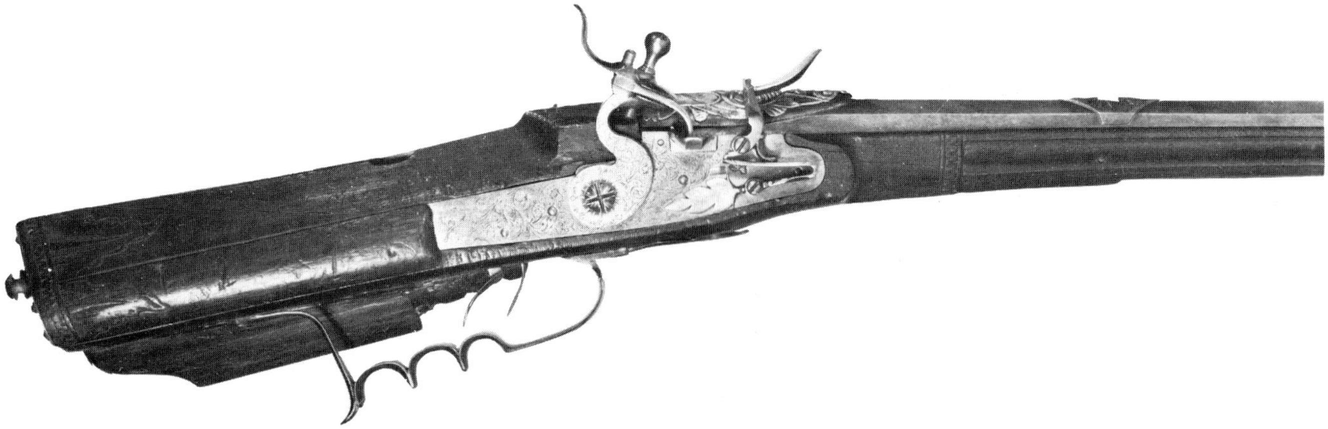

Early air gun with brass octagonal barrel set with an embossed silver plaque at the breech, the lock finely engraved with flowers and foliage, the full stock with brass side-plate and iron mounts, the butt with internal pump. Good quality and condition. German, second half of the 17th century. 36in. barrel. *Christie's*

£400 – £600. Extremely rare.

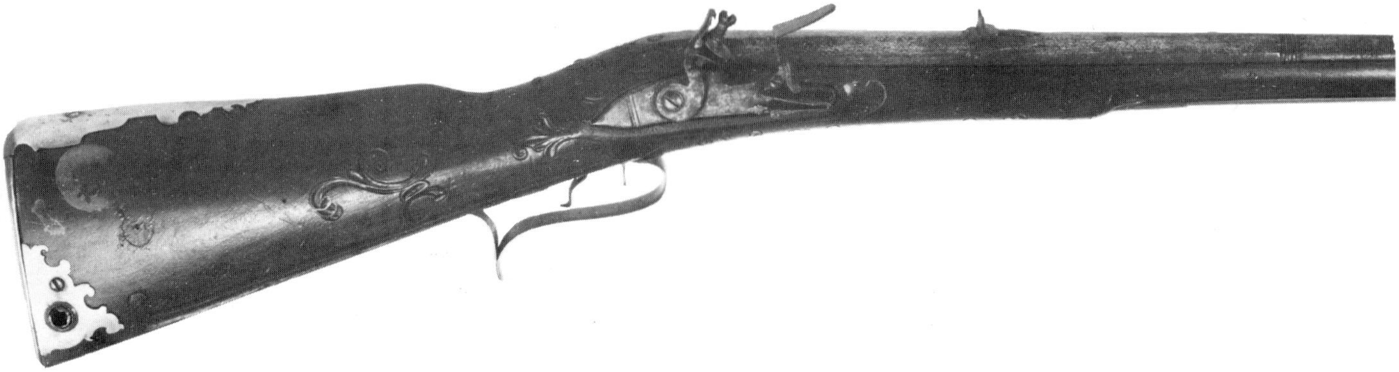

Austrian air gun and fowling-piece combined, with iron barrel of Spanish form, the air gun barrel disguised as a brass ramrod, the carved full stock with brass mounts, the butt fitted with a pair of bellows on the inside. Moderate quality, poor condition. Probably Viennese, mid-18th century. 33½in. barrel. *Christie's*

£200 – £250

Pair of air pistols with spherical reservoirs, the barrels and locks signed in gold, the full stocks with chequered butts, engraved steel mounts and set triggers. Fine quality, good condition with some pitting. Cocking levers not a pair. Late 18th century. 16in.

Wallis & Wallis

£800 – £1,000. Very rare.

Air gun with spherical reservoir and bar-lock mechanism. Walnut half-stock with engraved steel furniture and set trigger, the silver side-plate and escutcheon bearing Birmingham silver hallmarks for 1777 and maker's mark of Charles Freeth. Fair quality and condition. 32in. barrel. *Christie's*

About £200

Air gun, the barrel with three silver lines at the breech and signed within a silver band, with signed and engraved lock, full stock, skeleton butt and full silver furniture bearing London silver hallmarks for 1775. Fine quality, good condition but reservoir missing. By Bate, London, 33½in. barrel. *Christie's*

£250 – £350

Bate was one of the best air gun and air pistol makers.

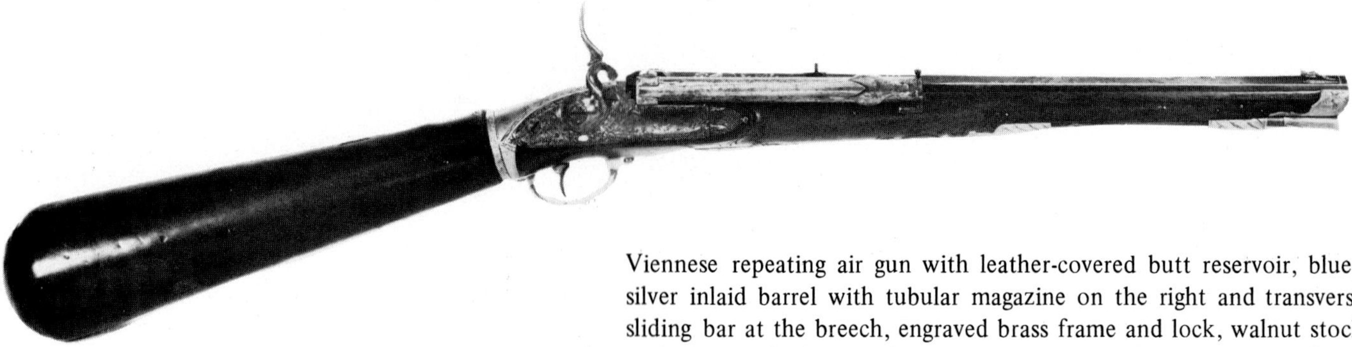

Viennese repeating air gun with leather-covered butt reservoir, blued silver inlaid barrel with tubular magazine on the right and transverse sliding bar at the breech, engraved brass frame and lock, walnut stock with engraved gilt-brass furniture, complete with a spare butt. Good quality and condition. Probably by Josef Contriner, late 18th century. 32½in. *Sotheby's*

£500 – £600

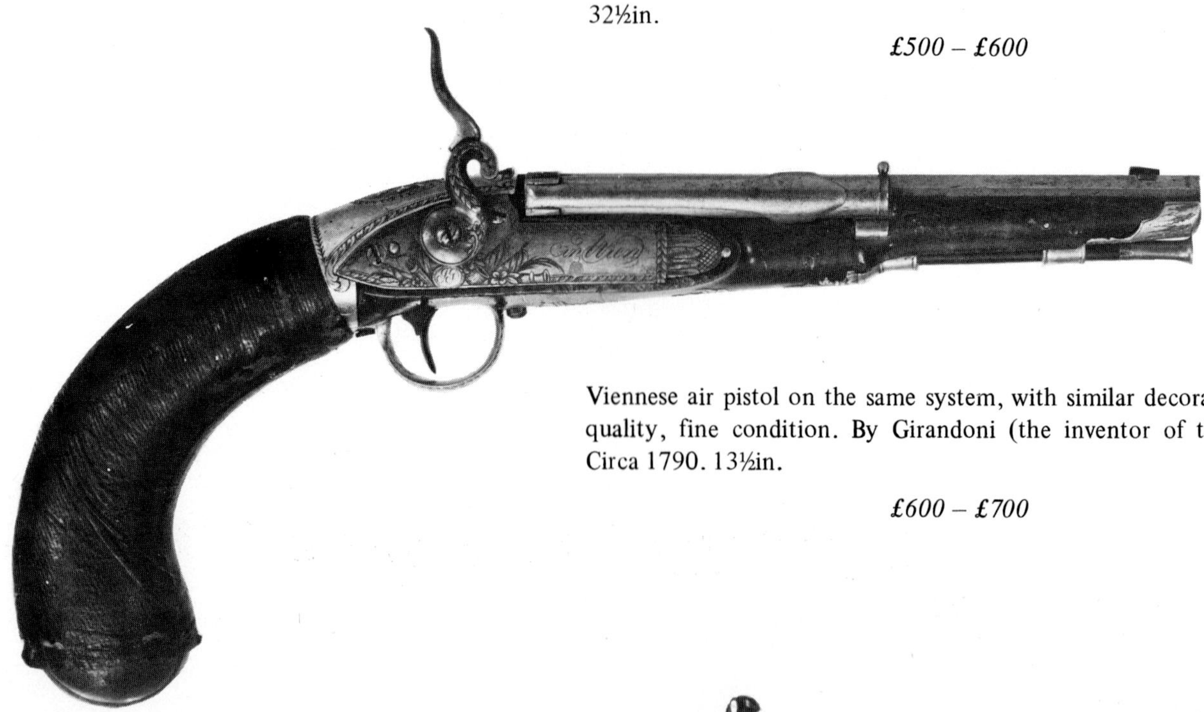

Viennese air pistol on the same system, with similar decoration. Good quality, fine condition. By Girandoni (the inventor of the system). Circa 1790. 13½in. *Christie's*

£600 – £700

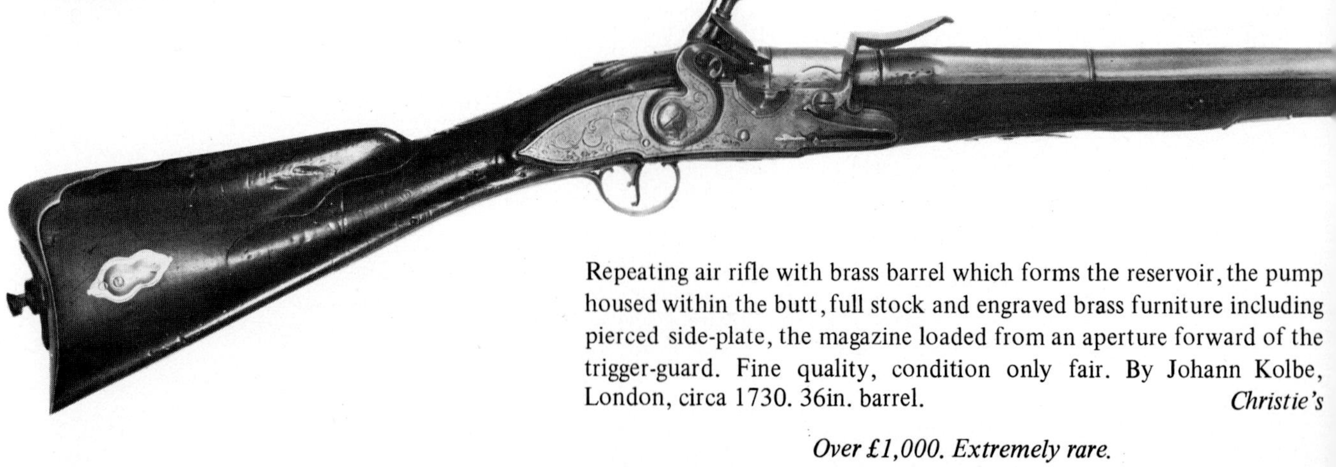

Repeating air rifle with brass barrel which forms the reservoir, the pump housed within the butt, full stock and engraved brass furniture including pierced side-plate, the magazine loaded from an aperture forward of the trigger-guard. Fine quality, condition only fair. By Johann Kolbe, London, circa 1730. 36in. barrel. *Christie's*

Over £1,000. Extremely rare.

Similar guns were made later by Bate.

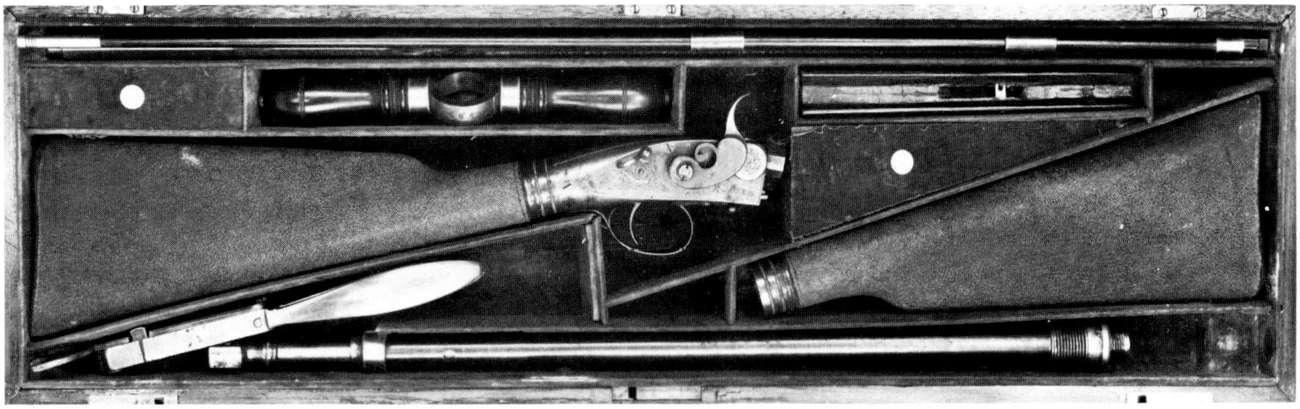

Cased air rifle with browned twist barrel, engraved action, shagreen-covered butt forming the reservoir, with a spare butt. In original case with fittings and trade label. Good quality, fine condition. By Spencer, Lynn, early 19th century. 32½in. case. *Sotheby's*

About £500

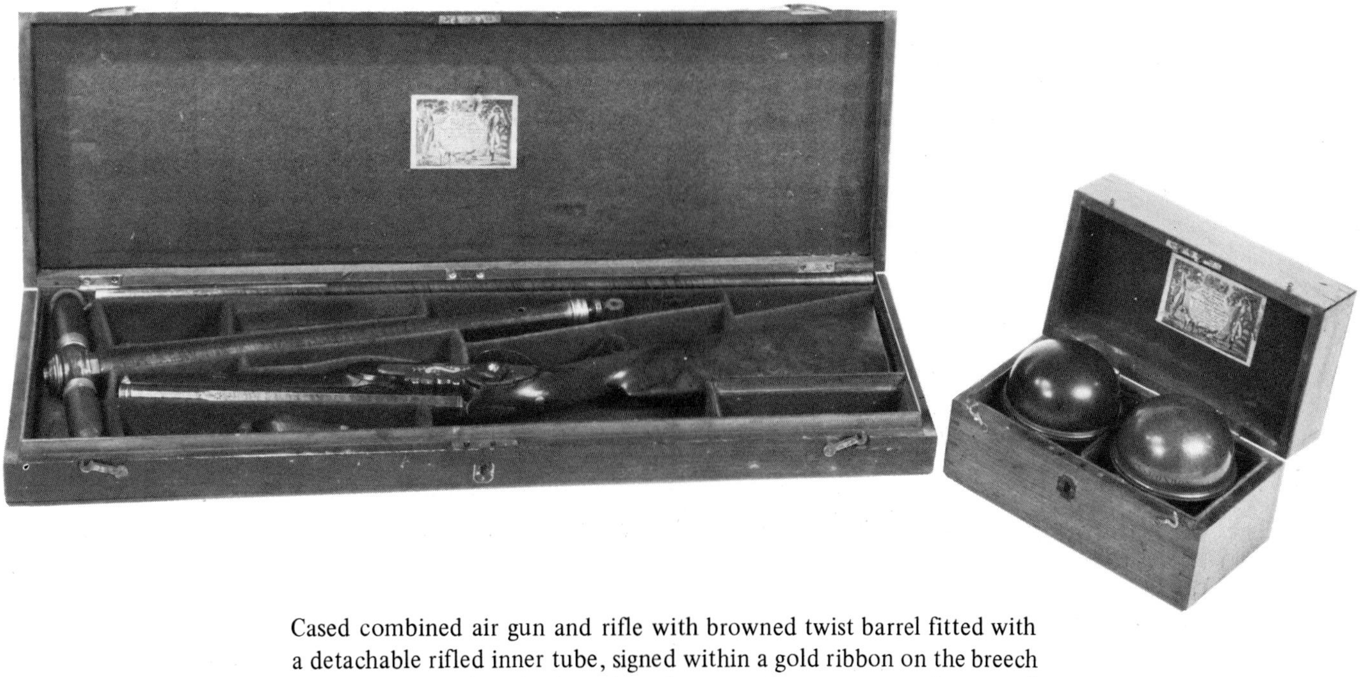

Cased combined air gun and rifle with browned twist barrel fitted with a detachable rifled inner tube, signed within a gold ribbon on the breech and lock, the walnut half-stock with engraved iron mounts. In original lined and fitted case with pump, and complete with two signed spherical copper reservoirs in a separate case, each case with trade label. Fine quality with some finish, but the fittings incomplete. By W. Parker, Holborn, London, early 19th century. 32in. barrel. *Christie's*

£600 – £700. Rare with separate cased reservoirs.

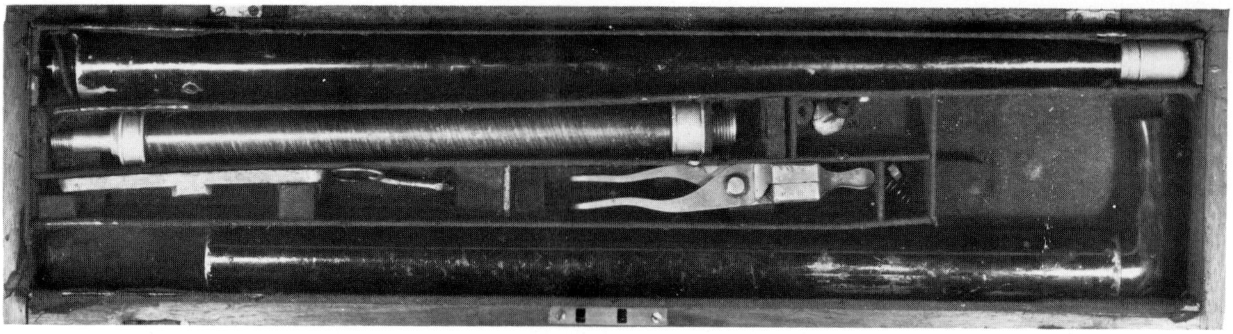

Cased walking-stick air gun in two parts connected by a screw joint and painted black overall. In original lined and fitted case with pump, cocking key and bullet mould. Poor to moderate quality, poor condition. Mid-19th century. The case 23in. x 6in. *Christie's*

About £100

Without the case and accessories, £30 – £40.

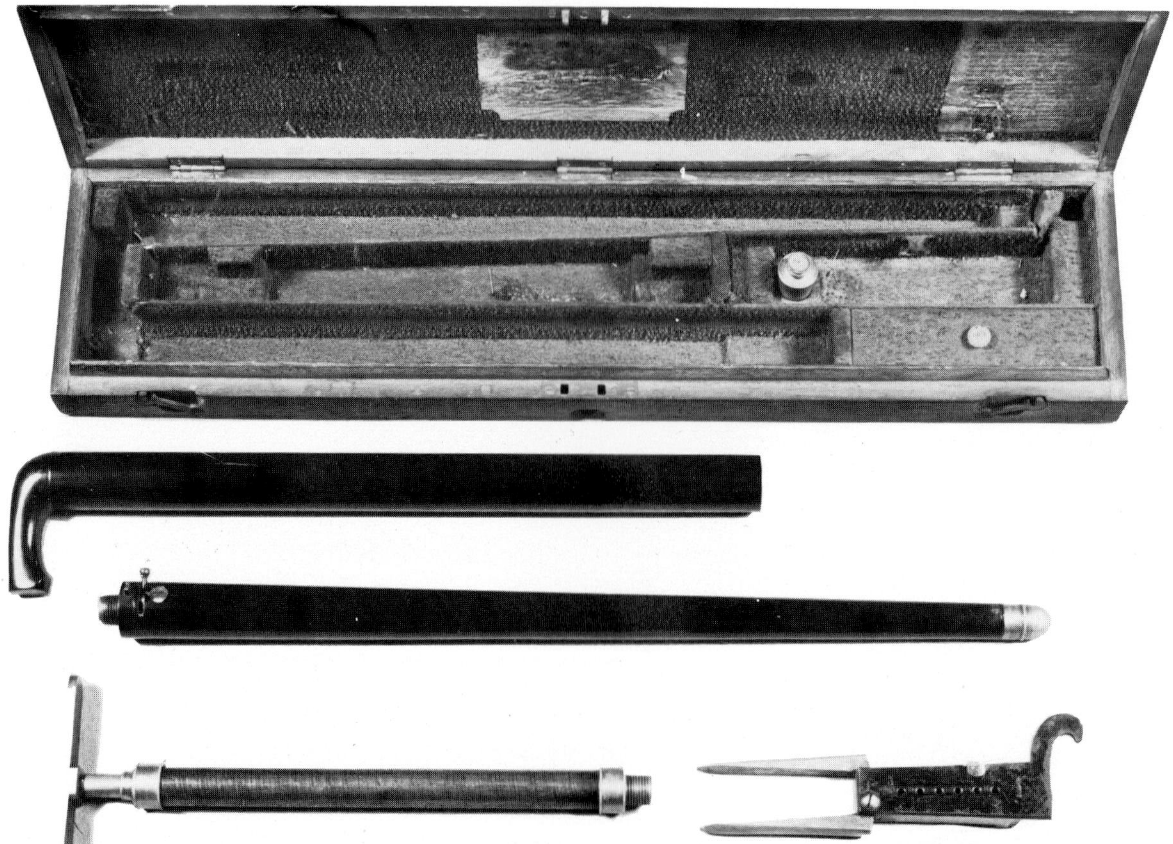

A much better set in fine condition, the lid with Edward London trade label. *Knight, Frank & Rutley.*

Over £200

Combination pistols, Powder Testers, Curiosa

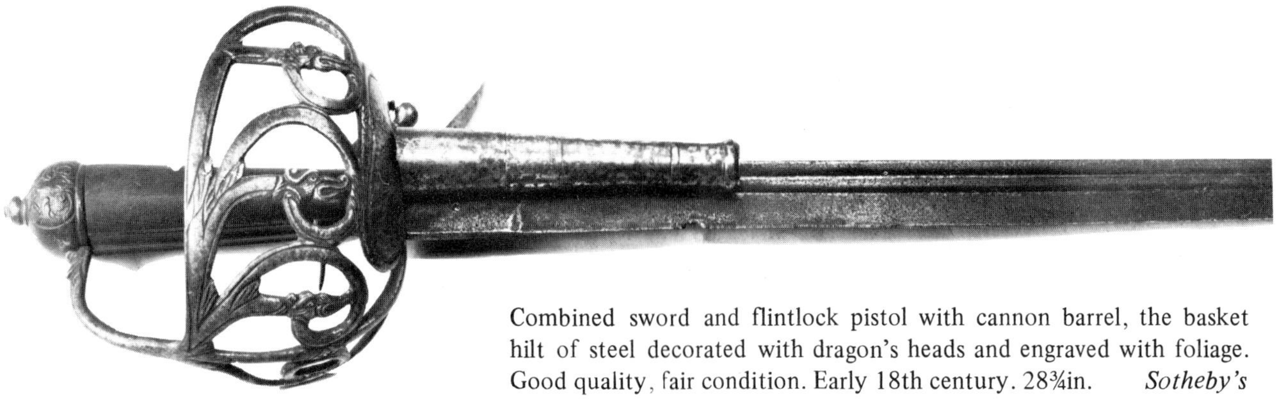

Combined sword and flintlock pistol with cannon barrel, the basket hilt of steel decorated with dragon's heads and engraved with foliage. Good quality, fair condition. Early 18th century. 28¾in. *Sotheby's*

£400 – £500

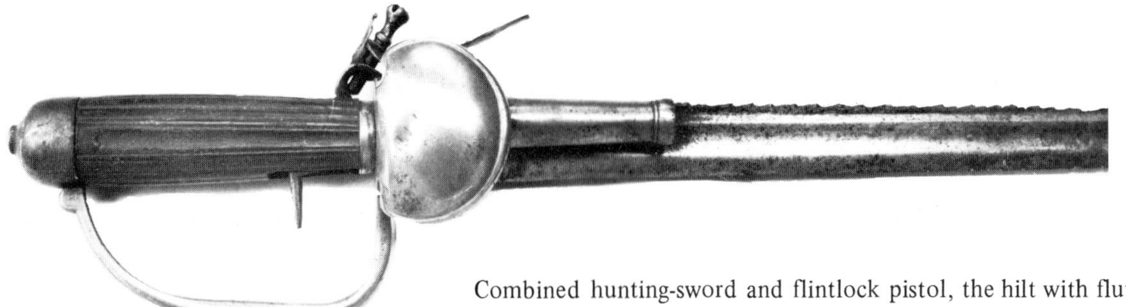

Combined hunting-sword and flintlock pistol, the hilt with fluted horn grip, steel pommel, silver guard and knuckle-bow, struck with maker's mark. Good quality, fair condition. Early 18th century. 24¼in.
Sotheby's

£300 – £400

A much finer example of the same type, with silver hilt and staghorn grip. Fine quality and condition. The action signed Vandebaize, London. Early 18th century, with indistinct London silver hallmarks. 27½in.
Christie's

Over £1,000

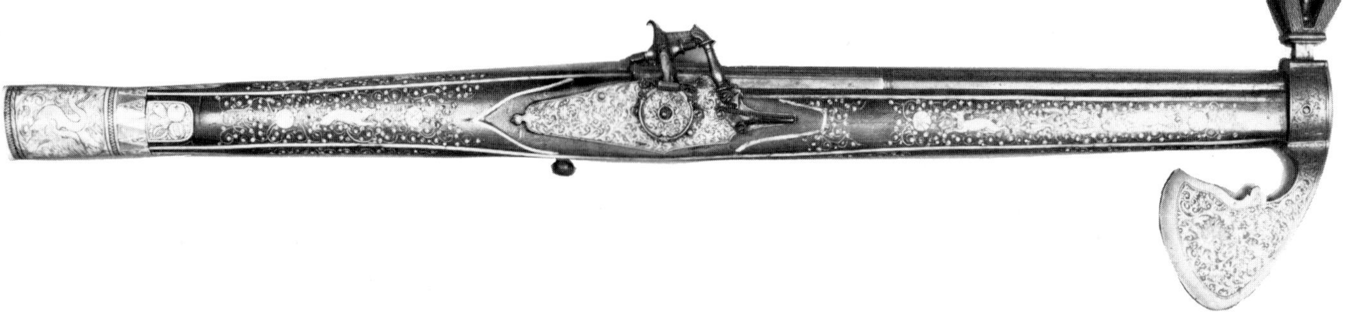

Composite wheel-lock combined axe and pistol with engraved blade and lock, the stock decorated with close-set horn inlays. Partly 17th and partly 19th century, like many of this type of weapon. Good condition. 30½in. *Knight, Frank & Rutley*

Up to £1,000

Combined flintlock axe and pistol with plain walnut shaft, the axe-head etched with two warriors holding shields, fighting a wolf on one side and a horseman on the other, the lock engraved with scrolls, brass furniture. Good quality, moderate condition. Second quarter of the 18th century. 37in. *Sotheby's*

£400 – £500

Italian combined hunting-sword and two flintlock pistols each with turn-off cannon barrel, the hilt with fluted ivory grips, retaining its original leather scabbard. Fine quality and condition. Signed Guiseppe Averan. Circa 1770. 28in. *Christie's*

Over £1,000

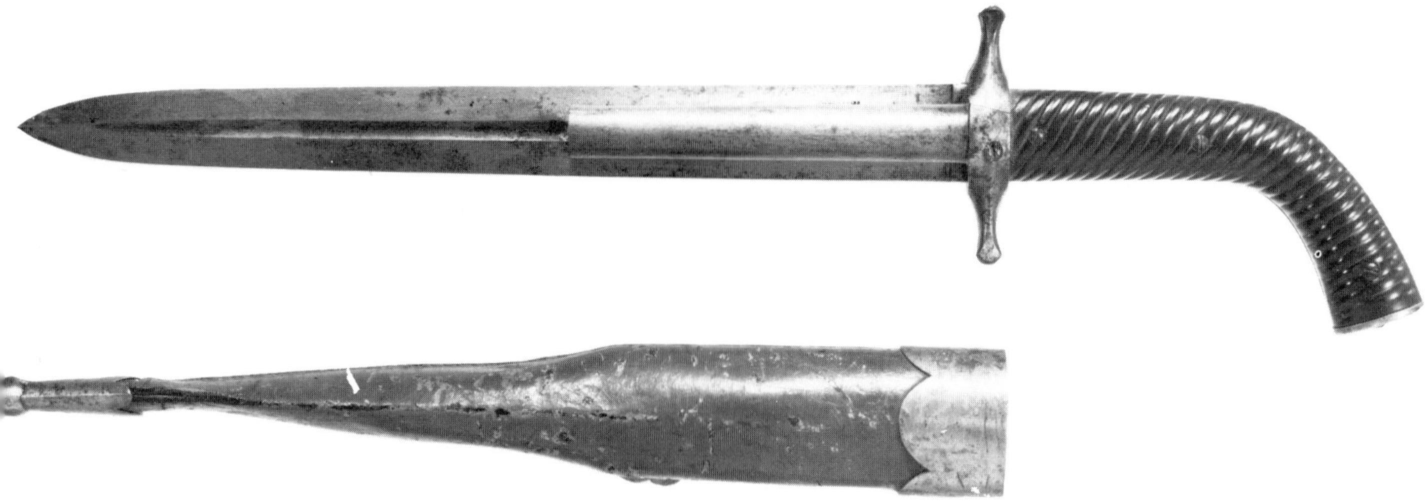

French combined dagger and two percussion pistols, the hammers formed as the quillons, complete with scabbard. Good condition. Circa 1850. 16½in. *Christie's*

£300 – £400

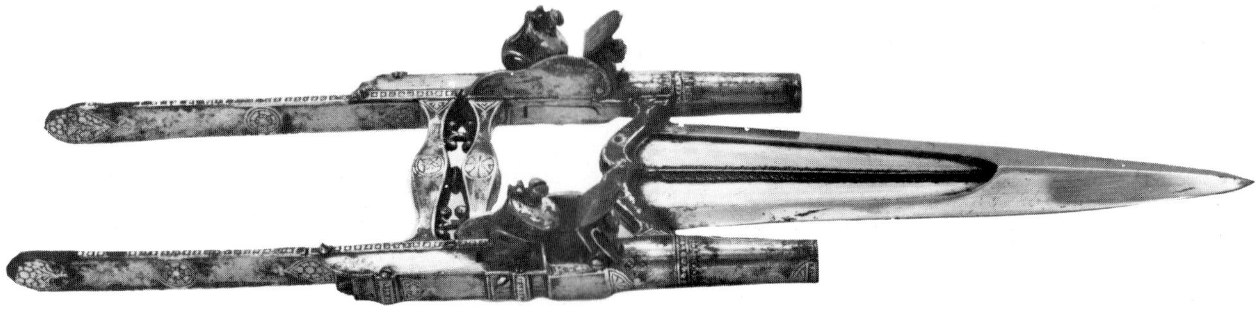

Indian katar with two flintlock pistols on the guard, folding triggers opening within the bars of the hilt, the locks and guard damascened with gold. Good quality and condition. Early 19th century. 16½in.

Sotheby's

About £500

A similar weapon with percussion pistols. Very poor quality. 19th century or later. 19in. *Sotheby's*

£100 – £150

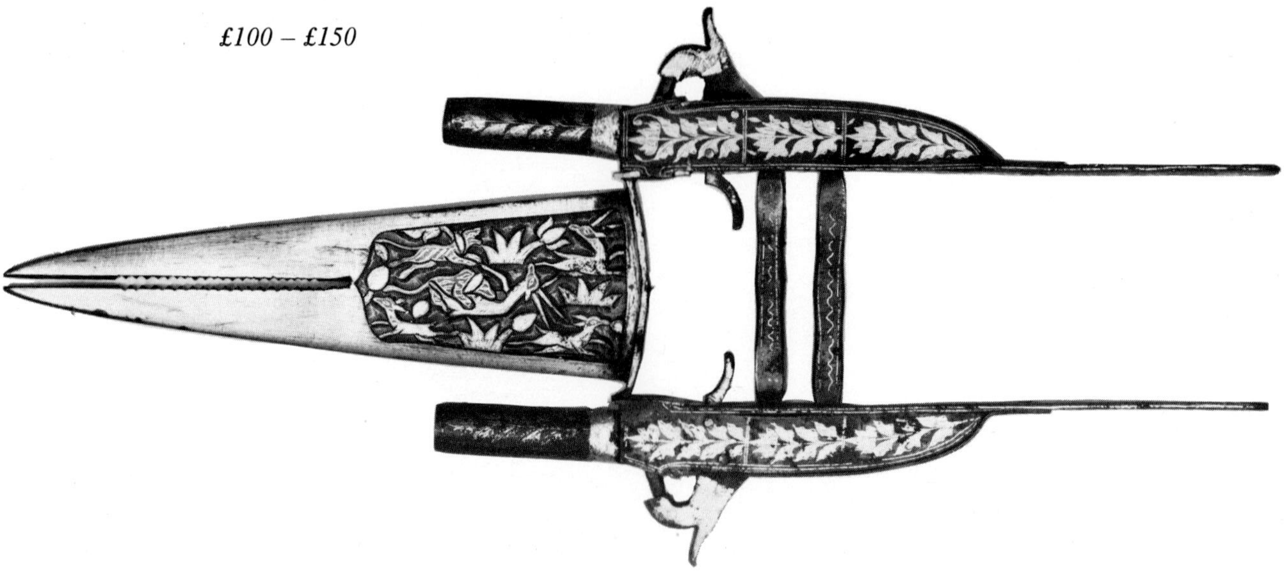

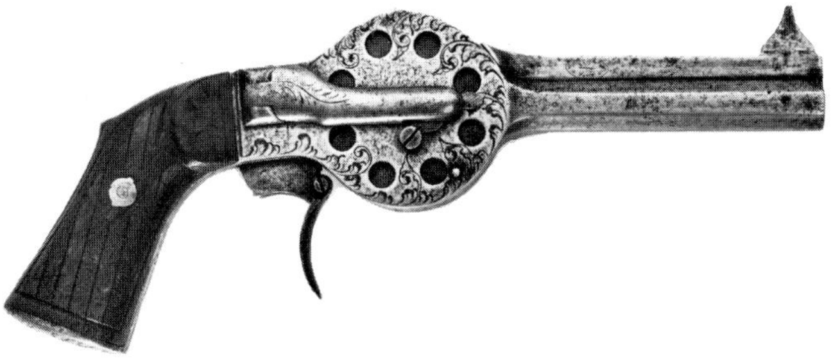

Ten-shot double-action turret pistol, the barrel stamped "Système A Noel Bte. Paris" the vertical cylinder employing pills to detonate the charges, this and other parts scroll engraved. Moderate condition. Circa 1865. 8¾in. *Wallis & Wallis*

About £200

Flintlock powder-tester with engraved brass box-lock action, calibrated iron wheel and plain walnut butt. Good quality and condition. Signed J.R. Evans, London, circa 1800. 6in. *Christie's*

£150 – £200

Simple powder-tester with open touch-hole, brass action and walnut butt. Early 18th century. 7in.

£50 – £60 *Christie's*

Danish flintlock powder-tester with vertical chamber, iron wheel with monster's head finial, walnut full stock, iron furniture, pierced dragonesque side-plate and flattened spurred pommel Good quality and condition. By Heinrich Kappel of Copenhagen, early 18th century. 13in. *Christie's*

About £300 partly on the reputation of the maker.

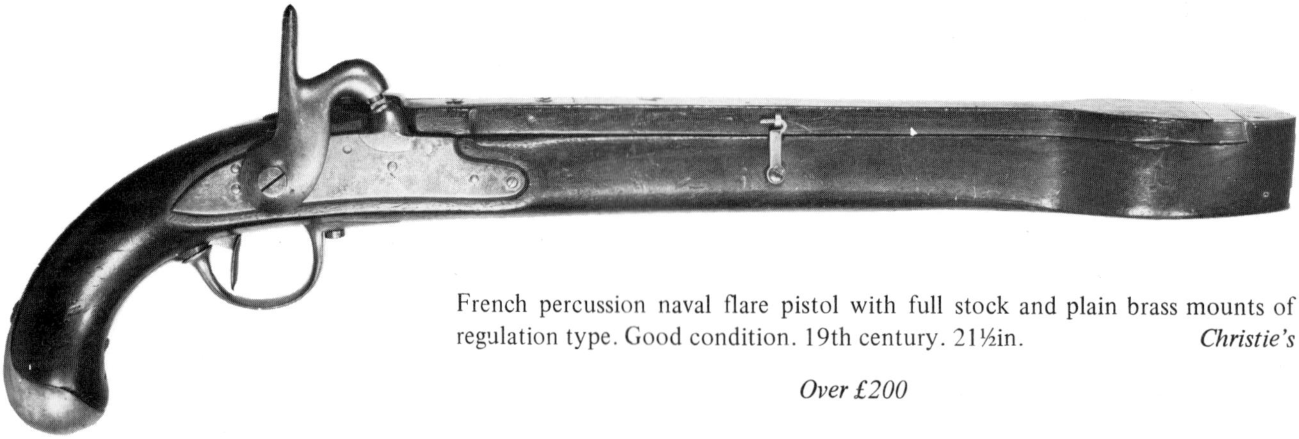

French percussion naval flare pistol with full stock and plain brass mounts of regulation type. Good condition. 19th century. 21½in. *Christie's*

Over £200

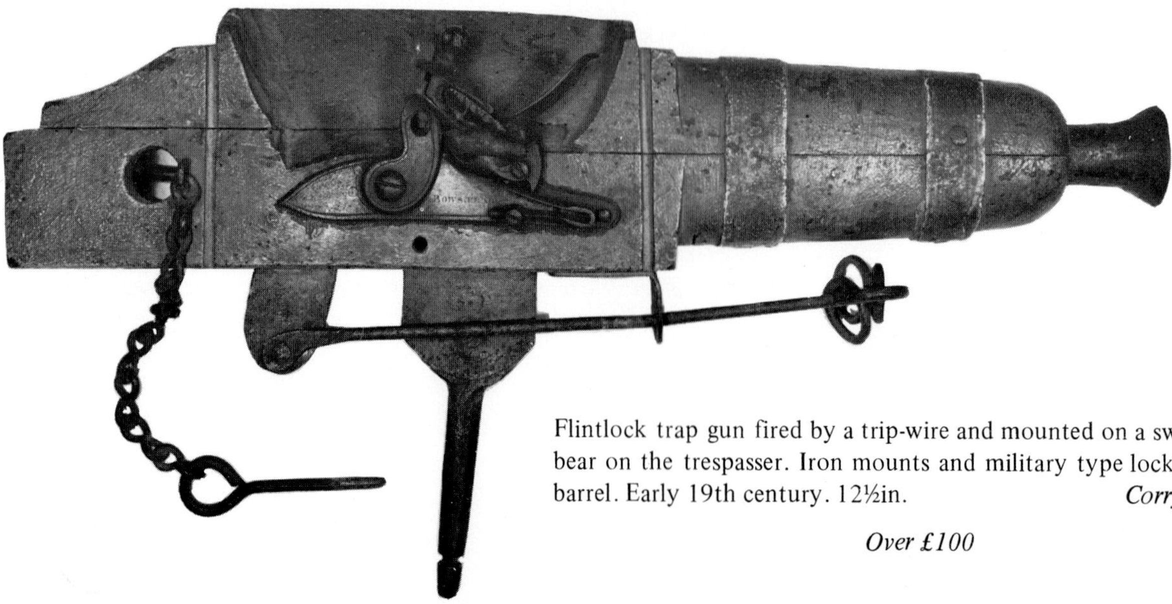

Flintlock trap gun fired by a trip-wire and mounted on a swivel so as to bear on the trespasser. Iron mounts and military type lock, belled iron barrel. Early 19th century. 12½in. *Corry Collection*

Over £100

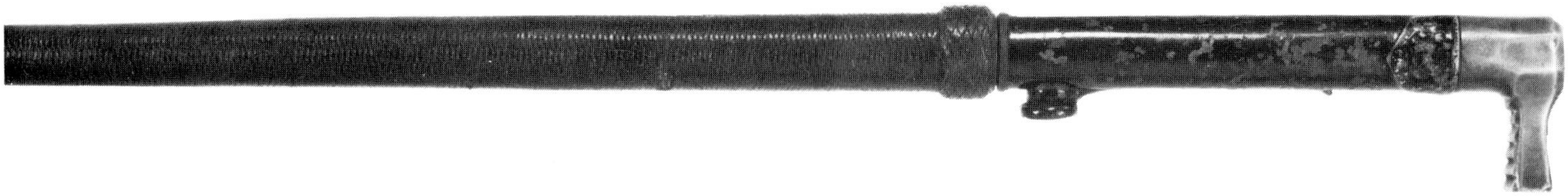

Day's patent under-hammer whip-pistol. Circa 1825. Good condition. The pistol 10in. *Christie's*

About £200

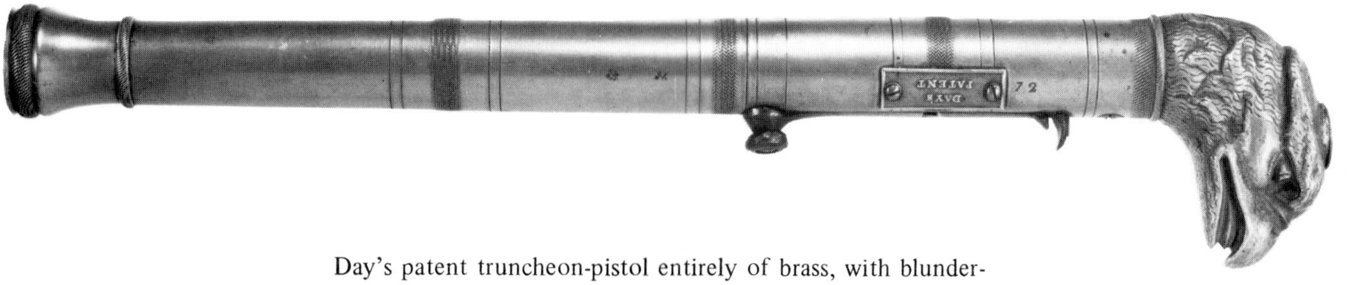

Day's patent truncheon-pistol entirely of brass, with blunderbuss barrel, under-hammer percussion action, and bird's head pommel. Circa 1823. 15½in. *Christie's*

About £300

Day's patent walking-stick pistol. Fair condition. Circa 1823. *Weller & Dufty*

£30 – £40

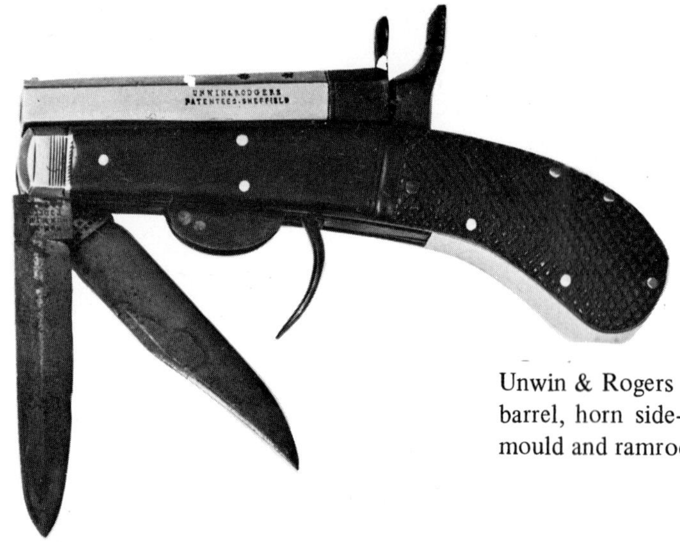

Unwin & Rogers knife pistol with 3½in. octagonal Birmingham proved barrel, horn side-plates and folding trigger, the butt containing bullet mould and ramrod. Fair condition. *Weller & Dufty*

£50 – £80

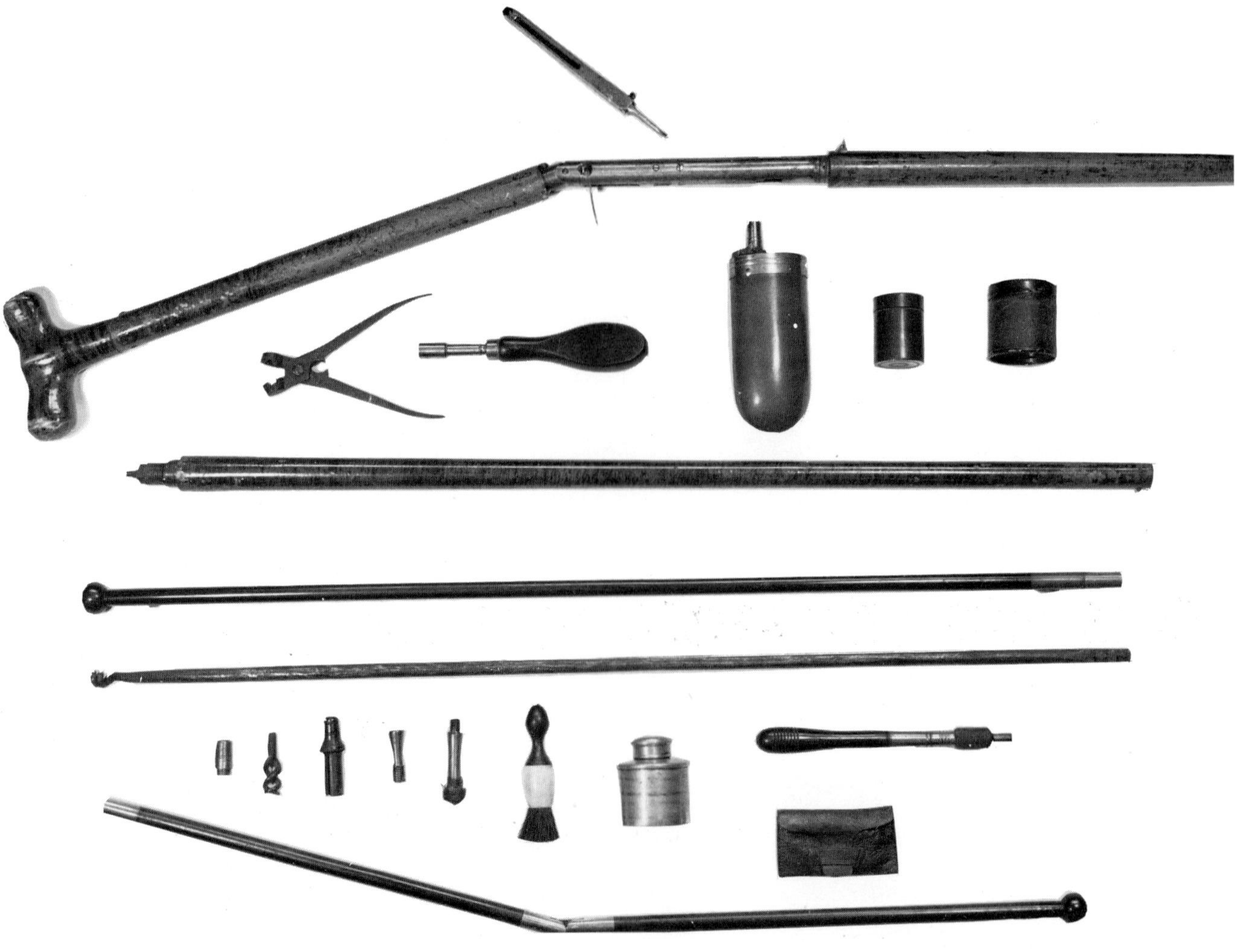

Cased J. Lang percussion walking-stick gun in two parts, painted to simulate wood, complete with spare barrel. In original case with fittings and label. Good condition. 43in. *Corry Collection*

About £200